Romantic Poetry

Romantic Poetry
RECENT REVISIONARY CRITICISM

Edited by Karl Kroeber
and Gene W. Ruoff

RUTGERS UNIVERSITY PRESS
New Brunswick, New Jersey

Library of Congress Cataloging-in-Publication Data

Romantic poetry : recent revisionary criticism / edited by Karl
  Kroeber and Gene W. Ruoff.
    p.   cm.
  Includes bibliographical references and index.
  ISBN 0-8135-2009-6 (cloth) — ISBN 0-8135-2010-X (paper)
  1. English poetry—19th century—History and criticism.
2. Romanticism—Great Britain. I. Kroeber, Karl, 1926–
II. Ruoff, Gene W.
PR590.R59   1993
821'.709—dc20   93-17229
                                    CIP

British Cataloging-in-Publication information available

Contents

Romantic Poetry

General Introduction

This collection of critical essays aims to define some fundamental directions pursued by contemporary romantic critics and to articulate the current tendencies—and tone—of romantic literary studies in the final decade of the twentieth century. We do not claim that these are the best of recent work or even that they perfectly represent fin de siècle romantic criticism. They are, rather, excellent indicators of how romantic literary criticism seems to be evolving and why earlier assumptions, methods, and purposes have given way to new directions.

One permanent change is writ large in the gender of the critics whose work we reprint. More than a third of our selections were written by women. The first edition of M. H. Abrams's *English Romantic Poets* (1960) contained no essays by women, and Harold Bloom's collection *Romanticism and Consciousness* (1970) included but one. Within another ten years an anthology like this may well be dominated by women critics. Growing incrementally rather than dramatically, feminism has been so successful in our field that we are likely to take it for granted. But such a sociological transformation must have profound critical effects. Extrapolation from current graduate enrollment trends suggests that within twenty-five years English literature will be taught primarily by female professors. In this respect our collection embodies a major transmutation in our profession, but one whose intellectual implications we are not yet able fully to discern. As Julie Ellison puts it in her fine book *Delicate Subjects: Romanticism, Gender, and the Ethics of Understanding* (1990), "The question of gender needs to be introduced into the history of criticism in order for the ethical stresses of the tradition to become more fully apparent" (13).

Making a collection that neither sums up nor memorializes but instead highlights the evolutionary process in literary scholarship has impressed us with the variety and ebullience of contemporary critics. Even with a generous allotment of space from our publisher, we have had to exclude consideration of romantic prose, excising both novelists and essayists, along with what are considered, perhaps unjustly, minor poets (concise biographies of some forty critics, intellectuals, and minor poets can be found in Marilyn Gaull's *English Romanticism: The Human Context* [1988]). Our discomfort with these constraints is the greater because we are both on record as calling for increased attention to what we here are forced to exclude.

The basis of the collection was a request we sent to some two dozen well-known scholars of romantic literature, asking each to provide us with what they thought were their own most significant contributions to romantic criticism during the past decade and to suggest what works by others, particularly by their juniors, they believed most valuable. Their splendidly cooperative responses, including often quite detailed discussions in very long letters, are the foundation for this collection. Yet in a majority of cases where we include work by these respondents, we have finally selected an essay or chapter different from that individual's choice. A major reason for this reveals the intellectual vigor of our field. Almost every respondent thought most valuable whatever he or she had been working on most recently. Few romanticists apparently like resting on their laurels—even to the point of minimizing their ground-breaking work of a few years back.

Other constraints emerged that prevented us from reprinting some essays. Since we treat all six of the canonical poets, the collection to be practically useful had to include commentaries on some of the famous and commonly taught poems. But criticism's move away from the genre of the new-critical essay has meant that much of its most interesting work has not centered on frequently taught poems. Yet our experience (confirmed by our respondents) tells us that classroom practice has rarely begun to mirror critical practice. Most limiting but most intriguing was our discovery of how various are the methods, scholarly and critical, currently being applied to English romantic poetry. Readers will find exemplified here plenty of critical "isms"—such as feminism, deconstructionism, more than one variety of new historicism, Marxism—along with essays making use of modern psychology (Freudian, Lacanian, Winnicottian), reader-response theory, "culture studies," as well as selections embodying the newest techniques and theories of textual editing, biography, and stylistic analysis. Even so, we have not concentrated on "pure" representations of these critical tendencies, for the impact of theoretical criticism on romantic studies has seemed to us most profound when it has assimilated longer-standing traditions of commentary.

We remain, however, like Wordsworth in *The Prelude,* distressed by how much has been omitted. Exemplary of our excisions (cited for diplomatic reasons, since it involves some of our own work) is the relation of literature to the visual arts. When less than twenty years ago Karl Kroeber published *Romantic Landscape Vision: Constable and Wordsworth* (1975), there was almost no significant inter-art criticism of the romantic era. This is today a flourishing, expanding subfield, but it, along with half-a-dozen equivalent areas of specialization, are here unrepresented. In partial compensation, we have in the headnotes tried to indicate where our selections are positioned within the larger development of romantic studies.

Broadly considered, the critical bias of the past few years has been against the formalism that dominated romantic studies in the sixties, usually associated with the "Yale school." The reaction, plainly enough, is in the direction of increased attention to historical aspects of literary performances. But the truly profound nature of that reaction has often been misunderstood by commentators who have failed to see the new historicism as only part of the reactive movement, and, as Paul Fry suggests in his essay in this collection, sometimes surprisingly limited in its "historicality." New historicism's most celebrated practitioners, such as Jerome McGann and Marjorie Levinson, are committed to methodologies derived from principles of Marxist analysis, and they quite deliberately focus on description of synchronic ideological structurings. But the "historical" bias of recent criticism appears at least as significantly in the works more oriented toward more biographical and "reader-response" methods. Paul Magnuson demonstrates that we misread "Frost at Midnight" as a "conversation" poem if we do not comprehend the play of political pressures to which Coleridge's lines so complexly respond. Contemporary criticism habitually interconnects intensified awareness of a poem's immediate social context with a sensitivity to textual details that are not merely "accurate" but also historically faithful to the poets' self-revisionary activities.

Equally interesting in the light of this historicizing is recent feminist criticism, illustrated by Karen Swann's explanation of the "hysterical" reception of Cole-

ridge's "Christabel" and Alicia Ostriker's explanation of the involuted transforma-
tions in Blake's attitudes toward women. These commentaries, the latter explicitly
and the former more implicitly, define psychosocial processes in a way that illumi-
nates how ever more subtle feminist perspectives may be developed by a conscien-
tiously historical criticism. This is but a specific examplification of how all our
selections self-reflexively advertise the history of their critical mode as determin-
ing the nature of their revelations about romantic literary history.

The selections in our "Backgrounds" segment describe the bases for the current
historicizing tendency, the simplest, but not for that reason the least important,
exemplification being Stuart Curran's demand that we recognize the full context
of romantic canonical texts as including a huge body of poetry by extraordinarily
popular women writers of the time. What we call the romantic age, he observes, is
distinguished by the emergence of an enduring professional status for women
writers. It is difficult to deny that such a sociological phenomenon must be at least
as important as changes in the political commitment of an individual poet.

The kind of approach employed by Curran, which is paralleled by the highly
detailed, densely concrete explorations into more traditional socioeconomic con-
texts by David Simpson and Alan Liu, could be perceived as "applications" of
Thomas McFarland's argument that critics must understand how their understand-
ing of constellations of aesthetic objects is determined by their preconceptions of
each constellation's *field*. Much recent criticism, in fact, primarily aims to expand
and deepen our ideas of the romantic field. Marilyn Butler, for instance, makes a
strong case for perceiving English romanticism not merely as being foretold but
actually beginning in the 1740s, and as determined in good measure by strong
nationalistic ambitions common to all European nations.

All these forms of historicizing derive from critics subscribing, more or less
consciously, to some version of Larry J. Swingle's view that the "heartland of
English romantic territory is to be found in the space that opens out between the
claims of competing systems of thought." The dynamics of this space of contestation
appears even in Tilottama Rajan's "revisionary deconstructionism," which finds in
Shelley's *Triumph of Life* means for reconstituting her earlier application of Paul de
Man's reading, thereby self-reflexively displaying how deconstructive approaches
may be enhanced by a sophisticated historical awareness.

It is worth noticing, finally, that precise contextual description is characteristic of
every one of our selections. The context may be the psychosocial circumstances of
Byron's life as portrayed by Jerome Christensen, or it may be the text of the poem
itself, as in Susan Wolfson's analysis of how diverse cross-dressings in *Don Juan*
modulate as the poem progresses. In such criticism, as with Donald Reiman's
portrait of Shelley's self-fashioning as a new kind of poet, or Kenneth Johnston's
demonstration that the politics of "Tintern Abbey" is discernible in the very ab-
sence of political comment, context established on the basis of concrete detail is
essential to the critic's persuasiveness. This style reflects two underlying assump-
tions common to all our selections: the acceptance of the basic premise of Freudian
psychology—that all manifest acts and thoughts conceal powerful latent impulses
(the significance the critic seeks will always already be concealed)—and the under-
standing of language as inherently misleading, unstable, even duplicitous, yet never-
theless constituting what is normally regarded as "reality."

These characteristics enable us to suggest something of the defining limits estab-
lished by the very success of recent romantic criticism, which is, as is widely

recognized, fundamentally reactive. Against earlier formalistic structuralizing, contemporary critics stress historical concreteness; against the Yale school's dismissal of politics, the role of political ideology; against concepts of a single definitive text, the genetic superimposition of revisions, and so on. But of course all criticism moves forward by reacting to (against) its immediate predecessors in a manner that nonetheless subtly assimilates some features of the preceding work. One may best define, therefore, the power of a particular criticism's accomplishment by looking ahead rather than behind, by identifying what its triumphs necessarily prevent it from doing.

A simple illustration for our critics is provided by Wordsworth's line from *The Prelude* addressing "Ye Presences of Nature." The plural noun is uncertain in meaning, that is, intellectually and emotionally dynamic, not because it conceals or displaces but because it articulates a linguistic inadequacy, a "sad incompetence" of received language to constitute and convey Wordsworth's experience and his valuation of that experience. Our criticism can scarcely address this innovative tendency of romantic poetry, which extends the frontiers of perception and the cultural sustaining of such perceptions, because our criticism's focus is elsewhere in the poet's psyche. "Presences" invokes spiritual or religious concerns, probes from a ground of enlightened skepticism into the possibility, and the possible significance of, belief. But on this topic recent criticism is voiceless.

It is necessarily as inarticulate on the singular noun in Wordsworth's line, "Nature." The reasons are most explicitly presented by new historicists, who programmatically treat references to natural phenomena as displacements of ideological anxieties. But virtually all present-day critics dismiss romantic "Nature," which they explain as a cultural construct—and to very good purpose. No achievement of recent romanticists is more impressive than their analyses of how representations of the natural are culturally fabricated. We are rightly situated to develop such insights. Comfortably housed, equipped with electronic word processors, and protected by antibiotics, it is easy for us to judge nature to be unimportant. The blindness of that insight appears, however, in the fact that Margaret, the protagonist of *The Ruined Cottage,* whose husband's career is wrecked by disease, dies of exposure, and that the teller of her story (whose brother drowned at sea) soon after was willing so surprisingly to propose a perhaps "vain belief" that "Nature never did betray / The heart that loved her," that the natural world is "full of blessings."

The best qualities of the criticism it has been our pleasure and reward to gather together here, then, may ultimately appear in the fashion by which its finest intellectual successes open the way for other commentators, bringing to our subject new, and sometimes antagonistic, aesthetic perspectives, critical foci, and moral engagements, the shadows of which futurity we hope our selections and notes may partially reveal.

Backgrounds

The essays in this section have not been especially "influential" in themselves, but they do define causes for the new directions taken in contemporary criticism of romantic poetry. Each finds its origin in the 1970s, whether through reaction against the limitations of then prevailing attitudes or methods, or through development of new conceptions then just beginning to emerge. Thus Marilyn Butler begins from a perception of oversimplifications in previous definitions of "English Romanticism," noticing, for example, that romanticism is not an expression of the French Revolution. Stuart Curran's piece reflects the influence of feminist studies. Our excerpt from Thomas McFarland's essay, literally the product of an evolution of some fifteen years of thought, dramatizes a personal response of mixed attraction to and repulsion from the Yale school's apocalyptic formalism. Larry J. Swingle's article represents the mature development of a view that when first expressed at the beginning of the seventies seemed very much against the grain, but is now widely accepted.

Romanticism in England

At first glance the following excerpt from Marilyn Butler's
"Romanticism in England" (1988) might seem part of a quite
traditional literary history. But through a careful critique of recent
new-historicist criticism Butler revalidates by reorienting an older
historical approach. She accomplishes this by revealing how the
romantics (and their immediate predecessors) understood the process
of literary history and its linkages to political history. Our selection
concentrates on Butler's depiction of the eighteenth-century
background of this figuring of historical forces because her analyses of
such clear expressions of nationalism as the "country movement" and
the popularity of James Macpherson and Thomas Chatterton dramatize
our current need for rehistoricizing the literary-intellectual milieu of
romantic poetry—a project being carried forward now by several
younger scholars, such as Jon Klancher, whose *The Making of English
Reading Audiences 1790–1832* (1987) provides background on the
nature of the society for whom the romantic poets wrote, and Karen
Swann, whose forthcoming *Transports of Delight* describes the role
gothic sensationalism played in how the romantic poets shaped a new
role for themselves in relation to a wholly new kind of literary
audience. Such works validate Butler's key observation that the
romantic poets remain today populist and accessible and to that extent
seem "modern," even though modernist art was neither populist nor
accessible.

Butler herself would situate her work as cultural history, or the
social history of literature and the other arts, or (more broadly) the
history of knowledge(s). The book in which it appears is an exercise in
comparative criticism, stressing both national differences within
romanticism as a cultural phenomenon and the relationship between
romanticism and the idea of nationalism. For further readings in these
areas, see Eric Hobsbawm and Terence Ranger's *Invention of Tradition*
(1983) and Butler's recent essay, "Literary London" (1992).

English Romanticism is impossible to define with historical precision because the
term itself is historically unsound. It is now applied to English writers of the first
quarter of the nineteenth century, who did not think of themselves as Romantics.
Instead they divided themselves by literary precept and by ideology into several
distinct groups, dubbed by their opponents 'Lakeists', 'Cockneys', 'Satanists',
Scotsmen. It was the middle of the nineteenth century before they were gathered

From *Romanticism in National Context,* ed. Ray Park and Mikulas Teich (Cambridge:
Cambridge University Press, 1988), pp. 37–48.

into one band as the English Romantics, and the present tendency of textbooks to insist upon the resemblance to one another of (especially) six major poets—Blake, Wordsworth, Coleridge, Byron, Shelley and Keats—dates only from about 1840. . . .[1]

English 'Romanticism', or whatever term we prefer for the era's cultural revolution, has to be dated from about 1740, when the new readership was felt to have emerged, to somewhere in the mid-1820s, when the conditions of publication underwent a further change. By lowering the price of books from 1825, publishers greatly enlarged the readership once more, and thus produced the conditions for Victorian middle-class literature. Within those dates, literature displays consistent characteristics, or rather it evolves through a number of phases which are sometimes antithetical rather than akin. The notional readership addressed will be literate but not perhaps well-educated: there is more emphasis on feeling and on life-experience (or a hunger for it) than on prior knowledge gained from reading. The great majority of new readers were necessarily excluded from direct political power, which remained in the hands of an oligarchy in the capital. Apparently the new poetry and fiction was less political than the court poetry of earlier periods, which circulated among a smaller elite; but latently the eighteenth-century mode had a political content, for it tended to oppose the central British state and its institutions. This underlying civic preoccupation was one of the features of English Romanticism which was most excitingly new.

The common impression in England of the politics of Romanticism has derived from English poetry, and is quite different from the German impression derived from German criticism and creative writing. The British, from the late eighteenth century on, have tended to associate the poetry we now call Romantic with social change and even revolution. This is because the English poems thought most typical visibly appeal to a democratised audience, either in taking up themes favourable to the lower orders or hostile to the powerful, or in employing diction, metres and (as we shall see) symbols with popular connotations. Blake's *Songs* and *The Lyrical Ballads* of Wordsworth and Coleridge retain their populism and accessibility even in the twentieth century. They are in this sense modern, but it is not a sense which embraces the literary term modernist, for modernist art was not populist and accessible. . . .

. . . The word 'country' in English puns on two quite different, even incompatible concepts: the countryside, a part or even a negation insofar as it is undeveloped, not-town; and the nation, which implies the whole rather than the part. Eighteenth-century poets beginning with James Thomson (1700–48), and going on through Thomas Gray (1716–71) to William Blake (1757–1827) and William Wordsworth (1775–1850), replace the 'court' or London or aristocratic discourse of Dryden, Pope, Swift and Gay with a symbolic language exalting provincialism. By keeping in view the term country in both its possible senses, they express, and further shape, attitudes which are representative of the attitudes of some of the gentry and much of the 'middling orders', especially of the commercial and entrepreneurial classes in eighteenth-century London and the provinces.

The term in use at the time for the sentiments I am describing, and for those who upheld them, was 'patriot'.[2] Both the sentiment and the word patriot as a descriptive term for it go back into the seventeenth century, especially the civil war period, when two of its strands were already visible: (1) a coherent sense of nationhood, and (2) a tendency to cite 'the nation' in selective contexts, e.g. when a Stuart monarch's right to levy taxes was being challenged. In other words, 'patriot' was often used in opposition to 'Crown' and the centralised bureaucracy at Westminster. Though early in the eighteenth century a Tory aristocrat such as Bolingbroke would deploy the term, as in his essay *The Idea of a Patriot King* (1740), it became much more commonly associated with liberal or radical thinking. This is why the Tory Dr Johnson opined that 'Patriotism is the last refuge of a scoundrel.' Patriot writing generally sounded chauvinistic, expansive and aggressive: France and Spain, Britain's chief trading rivals, were the favourite enemies, and the government was much criticised for its reluctance to go to war with them. . . .

The two most brilliant and imaginative mid-century poets, certainly the two who used history most creatively, are seldom now studied as serious writers. The simple reason for this is that their enemies, whose motives were often more political than literary, succeeded in pinning on them the charge of forgery. Read literally, Macpherson and Chatterton certainly were forgers, but their partisans urged that they should be read imaginatively, and posterity has lost the key to the most exciting strand of mid-eighteenth-century poetry by not following this advice.

James Macpherson (1736–96) grew up a Highlander in a Jacobite region of Scotland, and was ten when Bonnie Prince Charlie's rebellion was crushed at Culloden, a few miles from his home. The Scottish culture he encountered as a university student at Aberdeen, and later as a schoolmaster and minor poet, was not in rebellion against Scotland's political union with England of 1707. But articulate university men did resent the centralising of power and professional opportunities in London, the cultural snobbery of the English and the national insult to Scotland administered in 1756, whereby, during a new war with France, the pro-Hanoverian Scottish gentry were not permitted to arm. Encouraged by well-known Edinburgh professors like Adam Ferguson and Hugh Blair, Macpherson 'discovered' two Gaelic epics, *Fingal* (1761) and *Temora* (1763). By this 'find', he demonstrated the heroic and warlike character of Scotsmen, along with the legitimacy of their claim to the soil, and the age of their culture. The symbolic point was at once seized upon, for example, by enthusiastic Scottish patriots like Blair, and by incensed defenders of orthodoxy in London. James Boswell, a Scotsman in heated rebellion against an Edinburgh culture he associated with his enlightened, Whiggish, lawyer father, quickly identified Macpherson's subversive aims. He described him to Samuel Johnson, who soon became Macpherson's arch-enemy, as 'an impudent fellow from Scotland, who affected to be a savage, and railed at all established systems'.[3]

But it was precisely Macpherson's elemental reduction of provincial patriotism to cultural and historical first principles that made him re-usable elsewhere. Just as he became an inspiration to provincial and iconoclastic British poets in the next half-century so, perhaps more importantly, he became a force in revolutionary America and successively in different parts of Europe. His translation was retranslated into Italian (1763) and thereafter into German, French, Spanish, Danish, Dutch, Swedish, Russian, Czech and Polish. Macpherson made a very large contribution to the great upsurge of purchases of English books recorded in Germany in the early 1770s and again in the late 1780s and early 1790s.[4] Part of the appeal of English was that it was not French; the more resentfully French cultural hegemony was felt, the more popular another 'northern' literature was likely to be. But the source of Macpherson's charm was more specific than this. He was himself an articulate cultural nationalist on behalf of a small nation.

Fingal, a third-century Scottish tribal chief, goes to help defend his Gaelic kinsmen in Ireland, first in *Fingal* from an invasion of Norsemen, afterwards in *Temora* against the treachery of a southern Irish tribe. These plots support a series of contrasts between one people and another, and the notes and introductory material develop them further. The reader is prompted to read the poem comparatively and analytically, to see it as a model heroic poem, an expectation Macpherson satisfies with his brilliantly simplified settings and situations, and his use of a vocabulary, rhythm and imagery which appear to be literally rendered from ancient originals. Ultimately it is not the individual characters who hold the attention, Fingal and his son, the bard Ossian, but their people, who have been submerged by political destiny but never fully assimilated by their powerful neighbours. Eighteenth-century historians already tended to idealise the people of northern Europe for their symbolic resistances to southern empires—ancient Rome, and its successor, the Catholic Church. Macpherson's band of brothers, whose idealised society has no courtiers, no priests, no hierarchy of church or state, implicitly made a case on behalf of any marginalised group; not specifically against London, but equally well against Bourbon or Napoleonic France, Austria or Russia.

Macpherson's immediate notoriety in England is partly a tribute to the effectiveness as a spokesman for orthodoxy of Samuel Johnson (1709–84). Though a provincial himself, Johnson sturdily upheld mainstream metropolitan culture, its Latin roots and its link with the Church of England. The problem with nineteenth- and twentieth-century textbook accounts is that they exaggerate Johnson's typicality, and underplay the extent to which his values were contested by other able writers in his lifetime. The most drastic opposition offered to Johnson's London-centred literary values came from the Bristol poet who killed himself before his eighteenth birthday, Thomas Chatterton (1752–70), the author of an entire corpus of allegedly fifteenth-century poetry and prose. These manuscripts all appeared to have been written in and around Bristol, or to have Bristol connections. Significantly, a handful emanated from Wales or the Isle of Man, and were supposedly contemporaneous translations from the respective Celtic languages; others dated from about 1100, and related details about the Bristol region before the Norman Conquest. In this way Chatterton associates culture and the true civic spirit with everywhere that is not London, for Londoners, he insinuates, have been half-foreign and pro-foreign in all periods.

It is for the comprehensiveness of his civic claims, not merely on account of the pathos of his early death, that Chatterton remains a hero to three succeeding generations of poets, notably to Blake, Wordsworth, Keats and Browning. Chatterton no less than Macpherson had a clear theoretical understanding of the spirit of an incipient nationalism that would apply everywhere, not merely in the British provinces. Shortly before his death, he wrote three brilliant 'African Eclogues', the first of which, 'Heccar and Gaira', describes a tropical Eden, simple, sensuous and primary. The idyll of two lovers is interrupted by the arrival of European slavers, who carry off the woman, Cawma; it is both a personal and a tribal or national rape. In the last of the eclogues, 'The Death of Nicou', Chatterton brilliantly imagines a 'national' religion, similar in structure and incident to the

Hebraic. It includes a war in heaven and a fall, implying that these are universal myths, not peculiar to Hebraism. Again, however, the vividly colourful detail also particularises the world of the poem, along with its religion, as specifically African. Chatterton writes here as a sympathiser with cultural autonomy worldwide. Bristol was a slavetrading port: by moving his ground and his angle of vision to Africa, Chatterton suddenly represents his own whiteskinned people and their religious traditions as ugly and alien. This is a transference of the goals of provincial patriotism to another people which has parallels in the humanitarian literature of the late eighteenth century, and as we shall see recurs impressively in the early nineteenth century too, but nowhere with more respect for the otherness of the east and south than in Chatterton.

Macpherson and Chatterton were unorthodox members of a network of scholars engaged in the distinct history of peoples, and thus with characteristic localised traditions in poetry, in historiography, in religion and in language. It is a form of historicism we now associate more readily with Herder's Germany in the 1770s, but from the mid-1730s to the 1770s the cultural history of heroic-age societies such as Homer's Greece, republican Rome and Gaelic Scotland was a leading preoccupation of Scottish academics such as Thomas Blackwell (1701–57), Adam Ferguson (1723–1816) and Hugh Blair (1718–1800). By the era of the American Revolution, 1775–82, Scottish academic and professional opinion was more reconciled with the *status quo* and the many opportunities it offered to well-educated young Scotsmen in London and in the expanding possessions overseas. Even if the well-orchestrated English campaign against Macpherson as a forger had not done much to discredit Gaelic-based cultural nationalism, the Scottish professoriate now had more to gain from identifying with mainstream English interests, including the central literary tradition.

Even before the French Revolution, Scots professors like Blair, who (seventy years before the first English university) offered university-level courses in literature, were presiding over the formation of a more limited, confined, academicised and gentrified concept of Literature as, in a fairly full sense, a discipline. Blair was the first professor in Britain of 'belles lettres' or polite letters (1762), and his lectures, published in two volumes on his retirement in 1783, show that he taught the subject synoptically as a continuous world tradition incorporating the European (but not the Asiatic) ancients, and modern texts written in standard southern English rather than in regional dialects. At the same time the new sub-field of aesthetics was emerging, strengthened by Scottish medicine's empirical work in psychology. As for a literary syllabus, the poetry in English fittest for study was reissued in a convenient form by two Scottish anthologists who, as the latest editor of the *Oxford Book of Eighteenth Century Verse* has observed, have had a surprisingly strong influence on modern conceptions of what eighteenth-century English poetry is like.[5] Anderson and Chalmers, making their selections in the post-revolutionary years of 1795 and 1810, confined themselves to dead authors whose collected works had been published, which meant that they also chose men and not women, the established and not the occasional—those who found favour with publishers and with received opinion, both in the public and in the rapidly defining profession of letters.

By the same process of literary natural selection, certain late eighteenth-century notions of literature and literary history have had a better chance of survival than others. The views of the Johnson circle in London and of the Scottish professoriate have received ample attention in the late twentieth century.[6] Less visible now, but through journals a more familiar component of the literary scene at the time, were the 'popular antiquarians' who, by exchanging ideas, discoveries, manuscripts and books, between them opened up the field of folk or people's history and culture. Thomas Gray's network, involving the Wartons, Thomas Percy, Horace Walpole, Richard Hurd, is well-remembered; another of Gray's correspondents, the Welshman Evan Evans, who found a genuine sixth-century long heroic poem, the *Gododdin,* has had less notice. Equally, Percy's collection of ballads, *The Reliques of Ancient English Poetry* (1765), now outshines the collections made in the 1780s and 1790s by the tough and relatively rigorous Northumbrian, Joseph Ritson, who was not only more scrupulous in his editorial procedures, but far more accurate than Percy in locating the origins of ballads in an oral tradition emanating from the illiterate masses.[7]

Especially between 1760 and 1800, studies of popular language burgeoned. Dictionaries of English slang and provincialisms appeared to challenge Johnson's great dictionary of the *written* English language (1755).[8] Revisionist grammarians, who in the middle of the century were generally Dissenters addressing middle-class readers, but in the 1790s were sometimes radicals speaking for the half-lettered, challenged a tradition in writing English which insisted upon 'correctness' and upon a knowledge of Latin, for, in effect, such rules ensured that written discourse was controlled by the expensively educated.[9] Meanwhile the two greatest literary geniuses of the 'mainstream' tradition, Shakespeare and Milton, were reclaimed for the popular side. The Shakespearean scholars Francis Douce and George Steevans interpreted the comedies and histories, especially, as a product of Elizabethan popular culture, and the influence of this type of work is plainly seen in the paintings and engravings done in the 1790s for Boydell's exhibition-room in London, the Shakespeare Gallery.[10] In 1790 a similar project was begun for Milton, who as the 'great republican', a participator in England's own revolution, was an even more apt subject for canonisation in the stirring new times. Fuseli and Blake worked together on illustrations to Milton, and for Blake this meant a doubly significant apprenticeship, to a continental-trained, Michelangelesque painter and to the most exalted of English poets. But then it is hard to exaggerate the central signficance of Milton, the outspoken prophet-poet and religious iconoclast, as a prototype for every major English poet who passed through a liberal phase during the Romantic period. . . .

. . . Though it is common to think of Romanticism as an artistic expression of the French Revolution, this cannot be correct in any simple sense if, as the previous section argued, a symbolic language of liberty, equality and popular nationhood had been evolving in England over the previous half-century. The political effect of the French Revolution was to provoke counter-revolution in England, at least in the propertied classes, and thus to scale down and muffle the rhetoric of liberty and nationhood in a literate pursuit like poetry. Concepts such as Nature and national history had to be divested of much of their recently acquired meaning, or they would remain oppositional and socially divisive. One of the commoner responses to the political crisis of 1790–1800 was to make both concepts more detailed, literal and particularised, so that their uncomfortable associations with the populace were lost.

NOTES

1. Standard works on English Romanticism which have influenced perceptions of its important writers, its date of commencement and its place in the history of ideas include René Wellek, 'The concept of romanticism in literary history', *Comparative Literature*, 1 (1949), and *A History of Modern Criticism*, vol. 3 (London, 1957); M. H. Abrams, *The Mirror and the Lamp* (New York, 1953), *Natural Supernaturalism* (New York, 1971), and his selections for the period in the *Norton Anthology;* Northrop Frye, beginning with his book on Blake, *Fearful Symmetry* (New York, 1947); Harold Bloom, *A Visionary Company* (New York and London, 1962), and subsequent work. Among studies published in England are Basil Willey, *Nineteenth-Century Studies* (New York, 1949), Graham Hough, *The Romantic Poets* (London, 1967), and the broad survey, including England, by H. G. Schenk, *The Mind of the European Romantics* (London, 1966).

2. For recent work by historians on the eighteenth-century patriot movement, see Hugh Cunningham, "The Language of patriotism, 1750–1914', *History Workshop*, 12 (1981), 8–33; Linda Colley, 'Whose nation? Class and national consciousness in Britain, 1750–1830', *Past and Present*, 113 (1986), 96–117, and J. R. Dinwiddy, 'Patriotism and national sentiment in England, 1790–1805', paper delivered Paris, Nov. 1985.

3. James Boswell, *Life of Johnson*, ed. R. W. Chapman (Oxford, 1953), p. 302.

4. For Macpherson's reception in Germany, see especially Bernhard Fabian, 'English books and their German readers', in Paul J. Korshin (ed.), *The Widening Circle: Essays on the Circulation of Literature in Eighteenth-Century Europe* (Philadelphia, 1976), p. 127. His impact on Europe in general is surveyed in Paul van Tieghem, *Ossian en France*, 2 vols. (Paris, 1917), and 'Ossian et l'ossianisme dans la littérature européenne au XVIIIe siècle', in his *Le Preromantisme* (Paris, 1924), pp. 195–287. Macpherson's achievement and significance have been thoughtfully reassessed by Howard Gaskill, 'Ossian Macpherson: towards a rehabilitation', *Comparative Criticism*, 8 (1986), 113–46.

5. Robert Anderson (ed.), *Works of the British Poets*, 13 vols. (Edinburgh, 1792–5), and Alexander Chalmers (ed.), *Works of the English Poets*, 21 vols. (London, 1810). 'It need be no surprise that moderation, decorum, restraint and propriety were the criteria controlling admission . . . , the very qualities which have helped to impart an air of remoteness and insubstantiality to much eighteenth-century poetry. There could be no place for the eccentric, the vulgar, the extravagant, the disturbing, the subversive.' Roger Lonsdale, *The New Oxford Book of Eighteenth Century Verse* (Oxford, 1984), p. xxxvi.

6. See for example Abrams, *The Mirror and the Lamp*, and Lawrence Lipking, *The Ordering of the Arts in Eighteenth-Century England* (Princeton, 1970).

7. Ritson's most important single work was probably his *Select Collection of English Songs*, 3 vols. (London, 1783). Blake was one of a team of engravers who worked on the illustrations done for this book by Thomas Stothard: both the drawing and engraving styles aimed at reproducing the folk art effect of woodcut. Ritson prefaces the volume with his important 'Historical Essay on National Song', in which he censures Percy and Warton for carelessness and for a bias towards gentility. Even more popular and widely influential was his *Robin Hood: A Collection of All the Ancient Poems, Songs and Ballads, now Extant*, 2 vols. (London, 1795), in which he argues polemically and topically that the songs amount to the populace's own history of their experiences and attitudes, an element missing from official written history. See my *Burke, Paine, Godwin, and the Revolution Controversy* (Cambridge, 1984), pp. 203–5.

8. E.g., Francis Grose, *A Classical Dictionary of the Vulgar Tongue* (1785) and *A Provincial Glossary* (1787).

9. Both Ritson and Thomas Spence (1750–1814), a self-educated pamphleteer who preached an agrarian communism, also campaigned for a simplified spelling. But the most celebrated single effort to challenge orthodox grammar in the interests of the radicals was John Horne Tooke's *Diversions of Purley,* 2 vols. (1786, 1805). See M. Cohen, *Sensible Words: Linguistic Practice in England, 1640–1785* (Baltimore, 1977), J. Barrell, 'The language properly so called', in *English Literature in History, 1730–1780* (London, 1983), and Olivia Smith, *The Politics of Language* (Oxford, 1984).

10. Though the prestigious painters of the day such as Reynolds and West were offered tragic or serious historical subjects, Winifred Freidman points out in *Boydell's Shakespeare Gallery* (New York, 1975) that illustrations for the comedies by Henry Fuseli and Robert Smirke attracted quite as much notice, and were held to realise particularly well the distinct qualities of Shakespeare and of his characters. Smirke specialised in scenes of broad comedy set in low or middle life, for which he used a style of semi-caricature in the English tradition derived from Hogarth. Fuseli invoked a stronger, more grotesque and even horrific tradition of German folk art in order to realise the witches in *Macbeth* or the fairies in *A Midsummer Night's Dream.*

THOMAS McFARLAND

Field, Constellation, and Aesthetic Object

Because it is more personal and narrowly focused than Swingle's article, Thomas McFarland's essay, a reworking of ideas and writing going back to 1969, illuminatingly complements the fourth selection in this section by displaying the evolution of romantic criticism out of countermovements to dominant critical modes of the late sixties and early seventies. McFarland concludes by distinguishing his concept of literary-intellectual history from that of Harold Bloom and the Yale school by associating himself with Herder, whom the cultural historian Isaiah Berlin identifies as a central figure of the European "counter-enlightenment." In contrast to Bloom's "lurid apocalypse" of "mortal struggle and oedipal combat" between "strong poets and strong precursors," McFarland extends an older intellectual tradition to establish "minimal and almost imperceptible relationships" in all their historical complexity of detail.

Focus on "almost imperceptible relationships" is highly characteristic of contemporary critics talking about very diverse topics—political and social history, linguistics, readers' responses, editorial practices. The phenomenon may be clearest in works such as Magnuson's *Coleridge and Wordsworth: A Lyrical Dialogue* (1988) and Gene W. Ruoff's *Wordsworth and Coleridge: The Making of the Major Lyrics, 1802–1804* (1989), fine-grained accounts of poetic creation which extend the insights of McFarland's "Symbiosis of Coleridge and Wordsworth" (1972), but it also appears even in such background studies as Colin Campbell's *Romantic Ethic and the Spirit of Modern Consumerism* (1987) and Iain McCalman's investigation of romantic underground publishing in *The Radical Underworld: Prophets, Revolutionaries, and Pornographers in London, 1795–1840* (1988).

McFarland's special achievement is to highlight why we now believe that only through an understanding of the minute particulars of historical reality can we distinguish the originality in any era's poetic art. Originality has become for us today a delicate, infinitely complicated phenomenon; it appears a topic that cannot effectively be analyzed by methods modeled on patterns derived from the physical sciences. Natural objects like the star and the diamond McFarland finds only metaphorically useful because so much simpler than the phenomena of cultural study. Both the strength and the ease of the best contemporary criticism springs from critics' new assurance that

From *New Literary History* 13, no. 5 (Spring 1982): 421–447. This essay is a slightly revised version of the paper entitled "Patterns of Parataxis in Anglo-German Cultural Currents" delivered in Houston on February 26, 1981, to the conference on "English and German Romanticism: Cross-Currents and Controversies."

they need not justify their analyses by associating them with the supposed rigor of an abstract "scientific method"—or, swinging desperately to the opposite extreme, of reducing criticism to an "astrological" verbal playfulness.

The decade of the 1970s witnessed a revolution in the perception of the interrelation of literary events, and by extension the interrelation of cultural events in general. Before then the New Critical emphasis on the work of art as isolated object, inspected purely in its interior coherence somewhat as a fine blue-white diamond is reverently laid for viewing on a black velvet cloth, had tended to evict the older historical studies whereby *race, moment,* and *milieu,* or at all events biographical considerations and sources and influences, were the keys to elucidation. "The first law to be prescribed to criticism," said the New Critical standard-bearer, John Crowe Ransom, was "that it shall be objective, shall cite the nature of the object rather than its effect upon the subject."[1] Historical studies continued to be produced, of course, but they seemed musty and even wrongheaded compared to the exciting modernity of the cognitive object analysis espoused by Ransom and his circle, and by the even more theoretical W. K. Wimsatt.

The idea of influence in particular seemed rigid and mechanical, and even mistaken, suited only for doctoral dissertations and signifying nothing. As I wrote in 1969, " 'Influence', once the dominating theme of scholarship, is rapidly drying up as a meaningful line of approach: titles beginning 'Der Einfluss . . . ' today command only a small and restive audience."[2] My dismissal was no doubt conditioned not only by my training in New Critical procedures, but also by a residual effect of Romanticism, whereby the demand for uninfluenced originality outweighed the claims of neoclassical imitation, and where the creative imagination was at once free and unfathomable. "Who shall parcel out / His intellect by geometric rules," asks Wordsworth,

> Split like a province into round and square?
> Who knows the individual hour in which
> His habits were first sown, even as a seed?
> Who that shall point as with a wand and say
> "This portion of the river of my mind
> Came from yon fountain?"[3]

After asking these questions, Wordsworth hails Coleridge:

> No officious slave
> Art thou of that false secondary power
> By which we multiply distinctions, then
> Deem that our puny boundaries are things
> That we perceive, and not that we have made.
> To thee, unblinded by these formal arts,
> The unity of all hath been revealed. . . .
> Hard task, vain hope, to analyse the mind.[4]

Another formulator of the Romantic emphasis, Blake, for his part says that

I must Create a System or be enslav'd by another Mans
I will not Reason & Compare: my business is to Create[5]

and he says that "we do not want either Greek or Roman Models if we are but just
& true to our own Imaginations."[6]

Such denials of the pertinence of influence existed side by side with another way
of freeing the imagination: namely, simply to obliterate distinctions by saying that
all cultural formation is influence. Influence thus became, to use the words of
Hegel from another context, a night in which all cows are black. Goethe most
definitively urged this defense. He denounces as "ridiculous" the "doubting of this
or that famous man's originality and the seeking to trace his sources." One might

> just as well question a well-nourished man about the oxen, sheep and hogs that he
> ate and that gave him strength. We bring abilities with us, but we owe our develop-
> ment to a thousand workings of a great world upon us, and we appropriate from
> these what we can and what suits us. I owe much to the Greeks and the French; I am
> infinitely indebted to Shakespeare, Sterne and Goldsmith. But the sources of my
> culture are not thereby established; it would be an unending and also an unneces-
> sary task to do so. The main thing is that one have a soul that loves the truth and
> takes that truth where it finds it.[7]

The relation of influence to originality is thus paradoxical. I had realized this in
my work published in 1969, even as I had dismissed the concept of influence,
explaining there that "the paradox is not of my making, but is inherent in the very
existence of tradition in its relation to individual talent. 'It is not in Montaigne,
but in myself', said Pascal, 'that I find all that I see in him'."[8] By 1974, however, I
had elevated the principle of paradox to what I then called "an inescapable cul-
tural dilemma," revealed in twin phrases of Emerson now as the counsel to "insist
on yourself; never imitate," and now as the insight that "there never was an
original writer."[9]

My statements of 1969 and 1974 thus constitute a parataxis whose structure will
serve to introduce the larger body of cultural concerns I am addressing at this
juncture. On the one hand, the intensified statement of 1974 obviously arose from
the statement of 1969 and in a certain sense can be fully accounted for simply as a
broadening of a current of thought—as a widening of the river of my mind. On the
other hand, the intervening five years had seen the beginning of the revolution I
noted above. In particular, two books had appeared that were already changing
the critical scene and that generated lateral currents that flowed into my own, or
perhaps, to improve the metaphor, lateral winds that caused my own coals to glow
more brightly. The two books were Paul de Man's *Blindness and Insight: Essays in
the Rhetoric of Contemporary Criticism,* which appeared in 1971, and Harold
Bloom's *The Anxiety of Influence: A Theory of Poetry,* which appeared in 1973.
Though departing from different premises and points of view, together they laid
the foundation for what has since become known as the Yale school of criticism.

De Man's book was important in that it mediated to the American critical scene
the deconstructionist theory of Derrida, which in its turn was an outgrowth of
slightly earlier structuralist theories quarried out of Lévi-Strauss and Saussure,
out of Husserl, out of Marx and Freud. In structuralist conception the literary or
other cultural event, far from being an object of isolated purity, is merely a

pressure point on an entire network of cultural meanings and relationships. And if in structuralism the cultural object tends to disappear into the dynamics of cultural interrelationship, in Derrida even the author's intent is dismantled. Wimsatt had screened out intent as interfering with our contemplation of the purity of the diamond; Derrida deconstructed that intent to make its sublative structure even more important than the text.

But I am not so much interested on this occasion in the European foundations of the Yale school as in the contribution of Bloom, who seems to me both more important and more challenging than Derrida or other contemporary French theorists, all of whom I might somewhat dismissively characterize as being less important than their sources. Bloom, however, is another matter. He metabolizes a deep and idiosyncratic erudition into a powerful, detailed, and exceptionally dynamic reformation of the theory of influence. Just as staid figures like George Washington and King George the Third, with other worthies of the American Revolution, are invested in Blake's *America* with apocalyptic rhetorical dynamic—"Fiery the Angels rose, & as they rose deep thunder roll'd / Around their shores: indignant burning with the fires of Orc / And Bostons Angel cried aloud as they flew thro' the dark night"—just so do the inert alignments of historical influence become transformed in Bloom's work.

They become transformed both rhetorically and structurally. Indeed, one must understand how definitively Blakean Bloom's entire enterprise is. Bloom creates his own system so as not to be enslaved by Frye's. He elaborates it so tenaciously that one thinks not only of Blake but of Blake's prolix predecessor, Swedenborg. He encloses himself in the system; in it giant forms struggle in shadowy and portentous configuration. Where Blake constructs recurrent energic personifications called by such idiosyncratic names as Orc and Rintrah and Palamabron and Bromion and Theotormon, Bloom presents recurrent dynamisms called in his own private mythology Clinamen, Tessera, Kenosis, Daemonization, Askesis, and Apophrades. Where Blake projects his godlike Zoas, personified as Urthona, Luvah, Urizen, and Tharmas, Bloom elevates rhetorical tropes into his own version of Platonic first forms: irony, metonymy, metaphor, synecdoche; and over them all, like Blake's divine humanity, there broods metalepsis. Like Blake, too, Bloom's utterance can sometimes become overemphatic babble, most notoriously, perhaps, in the statement in *The Anxiety of Influence* that "the meaning of a poem can only be another poem,"[10] a hyperbole so absolute that Bloom returns to it a trifle nervously in *Kabbalah and Criticism,* where he says that "I recall venturing the apothegm that the meaning of a poem could only be another poem. Not, I point out, the *meaning* of another poem, but the other poem itself, indeed the *otherness* of the other poem."[11] This perhaps illuminates matters even less than does the earlier statement, but at least the hyperbole is reined in a bit.

To sum up, like Blake's system, Bloom's is apocalyptic, increasingly oblique as he continues to construct *midrash* on it, and like Blake's it chews up and digests public and external materials and recasts them into visionary forms dramatic. Like Blake's, too, it is uttered in prophetic tones.

I have been at some pains to characterize Bloom's mode of theoretical criticism because I shall, in my consideration of certain interrelations in German and English culture, be attempting to make theoretical points that define themselves by contrast to his arguments and yet can be taken as in some sense complementary to those arguments.

Specifically, where Bloom is interested above all in what he calls "strong" poets and "strong" precursors—with the relations between them cast into lurid apocalypse as mortal struggle and oedipal combat, with metaphors of warfare and other dynamics of power howling through the scene—I am interested in minimal and almost imperceptible relationships. My audience may recall that one of Leibniz's most telling points against Locke's description of the provenance and structure of the human mind was that Locke's clear and distinct data[12] entirely failed to take into account all kinds of twilight phenomena of consciousness that Leibniz called "minute perceptions" (*petites perceptions*)—such things as dreams and reverie and other indistinct perceivings.[13] We must not, said Leibniz, neglect "τὸ μικρόυ, the insensible progressions."[14] Leibniz's *perceptions insensibles,* indeed, when they were called to the attention of the intelligentsia by Raspe's publication of the *Nouveaux essais* in 1765, were a major formative influence leading to the advent of Romanticism. The distinctions I shall propose can hardly anticipate such high historical effect, and very probably Harold Bloom would not be unequivocally enthusiastic about being projected into the role of a Locke of criticism; I am myself, however, rather placidly content, if only for the moment, to step into the role of Leibniz.

For Bloom the writing of a strong poem involves a struggle to clear imaginative space, for it must always be a shifting of the weight of a prior strong poem from the poet's mind and therefore a "misprision" or "misreading" of that poem. "The father is met in combat, and fought to at least a stand-off, if not quite to a separate peace."[15] Even Bloom's sacred tropes are embattled: they "are defenses against other tropes" (*MM*, p. 74). The characteristic images of combat and embattlement in Bloom's discourse, however, are not mere idiosyncrasy; on the contrary, they serve to define his theory's full range. Paul Valéry, writing a half-century earlier, points out that "influence is clearly distinguishable from imitation," for *"what a man does* either repeats or rejects *what someone else has done*—repeats it in another tone, refines or amplifies or simplifies it, loads or overloads it with meaning, or else rebuts, overturns, destroys and denies it, but thereby assumes it and has invisibly used it."[16]

In testing his theory in terms of one poem, Browning's *Childe Roland,* Bloom relies wholly on the vocabulary of combat: "Shelley is the Hidden God of the universe created by *Childe Roland to the Dark Tower Came.* His is the presence that the poem labors to void, and his is the force that rouses the poem's force. Out of that struggle between forces rises the form of Browning's poem, which is effectively the *difference* between the rival strengths of poetic father and poetic son" (*MM*, p. 116).

Curiously enough, Bloom's performance on his own chosen ground is here one of his least impressive; he does not even really relate Browning's poem to Shelley's *Triumph of Life,* where the comparative materials are so persuasively rich. Indeed, this is a recurring feature of Bloom's actual critical practice: he frequently overlooks the richest illustrations for his own theory. He might have written an entire brief book on the compelling topic of *Childe Harold* as a misprision of *The Ancient Mariner*—we recall that Byron actually lifts phrases from the precursor poem—and of *Don Juan* as another misprision, this time with the double struggle to free itself from *Childe Harold* as well as *The Ancient Mariner* (from which it too openly borrows). But I do not know any place where he mentions these matters.

To criticize Bloom's trope of strong poets struggling in giant combat is, how-ever, not to dismiss it, and I have found my own understanding fecundated by Bloom's insistences even when I am not convinced by his rhetoric or by his examples. First of all, we might note that Bloom presupposes a field anterior to any particular works in it. He begins *The Anxiety of Influence,* for instance, by saying that he "offers a theory of poetry by way of a description of poetic influ-ence, or the story of intra-poetic relationships," and that "poetic history" is "in-distinguishable from poetic influence, since strong poets make that history by misreading one another, so as to clear imaginative space for themselves." Then he inserts the proviso that "my concern is only with strong poets, major figures with the persistence to wrestle with their strong precursors, even to the death" (*AI,* p. 5). But where does he find his strong poets? The answer is that they are given to him under the rubric of English literature. He rarely questions the canon, nor does he question the use of poetry as such, as Keats does in *The Fall of Hyperion.* Bloom's primary urge is to create his own system, and he sets about it posthaste, without wondering about his materials. Aside from such personally generous gestures by which he includes his own friends—John Ashbery, A. R. Ammons, Angus Fletcher, Paul de Man—in his listings of canonical figures, he is docile in accepting the valuations already given by literary history, as is strikingly apparent in his book called *The Visionary Company,* which is simply a résumé of the canon of English Romantic poetry.

But perhaps even more indicative of Bloom's acceptance of the priority of established field is a locus at the beginning of *Kabbalah and Criticism* where, after vatic musings on the theological origins—"When the Holy One entered the Gar-den, a herald called out," and so forth—he says that "the first chapter of this book offers an account of that primordial scheme" (that is, of the Kabbalah's view of the origin of all things), and "in the second chapter, the scheme is related in detail to a theory of reading poetry" (*KC,* pp. 11–12). In one step we have descended from the "primordial scheme" to "reading poetry": the mountain labors and brings forth the concerns of a graduate student of English.

Poetry has had many defenders and apologists, but only a radical withdrawal from primary realities can see it as among the most truly urgent of human activi-ties. Much of human culture, to say nothing of human life as such, has little to do with poetry, as do many of the finest spirits that that culture has produced. For Bloom, however, the realm of poetry constitutes an *epoche,* or a cessation, of the complexities of human awareness. Everything is translated into the concerns of poetry. "I find it curious," he says, "that many modern theorists actually talk about poems when they assert that they are talking about people" (*KC,* p. 108). Again: "I question the grand formula that Poetry is a man speaking to men. Poetry is poems speaking to a poem, and is also that poem answering back with its own defensive discourse" (*KC,* p. 108). Still again: "I knowingly urge critical theory to stop treating itself as a branch of philosophical discourse. . . . A theory of poetry must belong *to* poetry, must *be* poetry, before it can be of any use in interpreting poems" (*KC,* p. 109). The thought of the psychoanalyst Freud is reduced to poetry, as Bloom, following Lacan, transmogrifies the Freudian unconscious into merely a metaphorical ground for rhetorical figures. The thought of the philoso-pher Nietzsche is also reduced to poetry. "Nietzsche," explains Bloom, "speaks of ideas as if they were poems. In the following excerpt, I have changed only one word, substituting 'poem' for 'ideal' (*KC,* p. 112); and he then calmly appropriates Nietzsche's discourse for the Bloomian system. It is scant wonder, in this wholesale funneling into poetry, that the forms of tropes—metonymy, irony, synecdoche, and the rest—become the Thrones, Dominations, and Powers of a new angelology.

These evidences of Bloom's *epoche* all witness what I shall henceforth term the *anteriority of field*. So too do those conceptions called English Romanticism and German Romanticism. My knowledge is certain only with regard to myself, but I assume that my situation extends to us all, when I say that my command of the specific content of either English Romanticism or German Romanticism is radically incomplete; indeed, it would be difficult to say in which of the two cultural regions are more things missing from my awareness. Yet, fortified by the anteriority of field, I have no hesitation in speaking and writing in both realms.

It is the anteriority of field that allows us to see how vulnerable historically is the object analysis espoused by the New Criticism. I began this essay with the image of a blue-white diamond laid upon a black velvet cloth as illustrative of the critical stance of Wimsatt and other New Critical theorists. From their standpoint no inquiry is demanded as to who wove or dyed the cloth or who quarried and polished the diamond. Since such contexts are void, the trope of diamond and velvet can be transumed; in the resulting metalepsis we are not justified in saying that the velvet is cloth, or that the diamond is a diamond: we see only a bright object twinkling against a dark field. If we draw back a little, we see more such objects and then still more; but no matter how many bright objects we view, there is still the same dark field.

The sense of uniqueness in the original isolated object is therefore something like the result of a zoom closeup in photography, whereby the object is enhanced by eliminating the original dimension of the field. The field in its unmagnified perspective, on the other hand, is like Kant's starry heavens above. To look at cultural events is like looking at stars in the night sky.

We look up with unaided vision and see stars, more than we can count, and of varyinng brightness and no immediately discernible pattern. When we undergo cultural education, we as it were look at the sky through a telescope. We see more stars and we see them in more detail; but there are still more than we can count, and we infer that there are many more we do not see. When we look at the sky in different hemispheres, we seem to see the same thing, stars against a field. Only after study and reflection do we realize that the stars seen from the differing perspectives are not identical.

After more study, we begin to ascribe pattern to the seemingly random configuration of the stars. We begin to outline constellations, although only from the anteriority of field is this process possible. As Hume says, "There is no object, which implies the existence of any other if we consider these objects in themselves." "Objects have no discoverable connexion together; nor is it from any other principle but custom operating upon the imagination, that we can draw any inference from the appearance of one to the existence of another."[17] So from the unity supplied by the anteriority of field we begin to connect constellations of cultural patterns, by which, with deeper observation, we can locate whole galaxies: classical Greek culture, or German Romanticism, or English Romanticism. When the zoom effect of Wimsattian object analysis takes place, the constellational location of the object is denied; and yet the constellational location is necessary to isolate the object in the first place. Apart from his theories as to critical orientation, Wimsatt was the academic master of several cultural fields.

The rule derived thus seems invariable: first there is field, then constellation, and only as a third awareness is there object considered as focus of observation. Even when as children we ask our fathers to tell us a story, the objectification presumes the anteriority of field and the parataxis of constellation.

Furthermore, though our primary intuition of the stars is of number and brightness and scattering, and only our secondary view, enhanced by meditation and magnification, begins to find pattern and interrelationship, that enhanced secondary view reveals to us that starry events differ in more ways than mere brightness or proximity. When Bloom sees only strong poets wrestling for imaginative space, it is as though he would limit the starry heavens to double stars of the first magnitude. But there are stars of differing intensity and size, and there are planets and moons; and what looks like stars sometimes turns out to be whole galaxies, which again take different shapes: pinwheels, blobs, rings—there is even one identified as the "Sombrero" galaxy. There are, in addition, quasars and pulsars and black holes. In the same way, the actual content of cultural field in its constellational groupings is not limited to poetry and strong poets but reveals other cultural configurations as well.

The galactic shape of English Romanticism is significantly different from that of German Romanticism in that much of the German achievement came to realization in the form of philosophical systems, which are largely absent from English Romanticism. Indeed, philosophy and music are the true vehicles of German genius. Hegel and Beethoven are each assuredly of greater cultural magnitude than even Hölderlin. Again, a contour of German Romanticism only faintly apparent in English Romanticism is *Gelehrsamkeit*. Matthew Arnold criticized the English Romantics, with the exception of Coleridge, for not knowing enough. One would not dream of making such a charge against the Schlegel brothers or Schleiermacher, or even against Tieck or Goethe, not to speak of Hegel. There are no Hegels in English Romanticism, and Coleridge, who comes the closest in aim and interest, is more like the Crab Nebula, a remnant of a supernova, than a churning Hegelian star.

Whatever the constellational differences may be, however, the metalepsis of starry heavens holds good for all aspects of cultural comprehension. I earlier suggested that much of life has little to do with poetry; much indeed has little to do with any form of high culture. But from antiquity onward, cultural events have always been there, like the stars overhead, even though not everyone heeds them, and others attend to them only sporadically. Still, they are always there; they are seen by every man, whether reflected upon or not; and we all intuitively realize that in cultural constellations, as in the starry heavens, our ultimate possibilities of transcendence lie.

It is interesting to note that in cultural awareness there need be no specific quantity of objects; the starry heavens are still themselves whether we conjecture a thousand visible stars or ten thousand, or for that matter merely a hundred: all we need is field, plurality, and, as prerequisite for examination, constellation. Indeed, Bloom's whole thrust is a corrective to his teacher Wimsatt in that whereas the final magnification of Wimsattian object analysis negates the plurality that determines the field, Bloom restores to poetic objects their defining plurality. "We need to stop thinking of any poet as an autonomous ego," he says in *The*

Anxiety of Influence, "however solipsistic the strongest of poets may be. Every poet is a being caught up in a dialectical relationship . . . with another poet or poets" (p. 91). And he says in *A Map of Misreading* that he "studies poetic influence, by which I continue *not* to mean the passing-on of images and ideas from earlier to later poets. Influence, as I conceive it, means that there are *no* texts, but only relationships *between* texts" (p. 3).[18]

Yet, though I accord with Bloom's restoration of plurality as preceding the object, his actual assessment of pluralities seems to me to be locked into something rather closer to a critical astrology than a critical astronomy: "Antithetical criticism as a practical discipline of reading begins with an analysis of misprision or revisionism, through a description of revisionary ratios, conducted through examination of tropes, imagery or psychological defenses, depending upon the preferences of an individual reader. An application of literary history, though greatly desirable, is not strictly necessary for the study of misprision. But as soon as one attempts a deeper criticism, and asks what is the interpretation that a poem offers, one is involved with the precursor text or texts as well as with the belated poem itself" (*MM*, p. 116). The methodology seems cumbersome when confronted with the caveat of Virginia Woolf: "But let us always remember—influences are infinitely numerous; writers are infinitely sensitive; each writer has a different sensibility."[19] I shall attempt the rudiments of a description of influence study more consonant with the elements noted by Woolf.

To that end I begin by substituting the neutral word parataxis for influence. In my discussion of 1969, I had noted that originality is "an error-freighted and ill-defined concept," as is the label *influence:* "Such labels are crude and makeshift; they arise from no genuine understanding of the symbolic functions of literary activity, and history itself is not long content with any of them."[20] Bloom, too, is not entirely happy with the word *influence.* "My motive," he says at one point, "is to distinguish once for all what I call 'poetic influence' from traditional 'source study' " (*MM*, p. 116).[21] Elsewhere, he feels it necessary to define the term in a special way: "What I mean by 'influence' is the whole range of relationships between one poem and another, which means that my use of 'influence' is itself a highly conscious trope, indeed a complex sixfold trope that intends to subsume six major tropes: irony, synecdoche, metonymy, hyperbole, metaphor, and metalepsis, and in just that ordering" (*MM*, p. 70). Again, he says that "if we consider 'influence' as the trope of rhetorical irony that connects an earlier to a later poet . . . then influence is a relation that means one thing about the intra-poetic situation while saying another" (*MM*, p. 71). Still again, in *The Anxiety of Influence,* he says that "Influence is *Influenza*—an astral disease" (p. 95).

Bloom is here playing with the literal meaning of the word as an influx, which in its turn is linked metaleptically with the idea of current. What I have hitherto been saying reveals why I substitute *parataxis* for *influence* and *cultural* for *poetical,* but I retain *currents.* It is a trope, however, that has no legitimacy in terms of the parataxis of aesthetic objects. If we look up into the night sky, we do not see the drift of stars: we see stars in simple juxtaposition. Conceptions of current are derived from the anteriority of field, not from the parataxes themselves. The river, as Wordsworth says, is our own mind. I bridle at a certain fashion of music criticism that speaks of, say, Mozart's D-Minor Piano Concerto as looking forward to Beethoven. On the contrary, Mozart's concerto looks forward to nothing: it simply is. In our historical sense of field alone can it be related to subsequent compositions by Beethoven. The work as a work is aesthetically complete and would not change were all memory of Beethoven suddenly to be obliterated from our cultural consciousness.

Still, the trope of current does pertain to the chronological schematisms with which we demarcate the sense of field, as does Bloom's insistence upon the word *precursor.* In that sense, indeed, Bloom's own ideas are the downstream in a continuing current. Some of his basic arguments were adumbrated in Walter Jackson Bate's volume of 1970 called *The Burden of the Past and the English Poet.* Further upstream, in 1957, was the important prefiguration of Northrop Frye's *Anatomy of Criticism,* where it is pointed out that "poetry can only be made out of other poems; novels out of other novels,"[22] a statement that finds its echo everywhere in Bloom, as, for instance, in his formula that "poetry begins, always, when someone who is going to become a poet *reads a poem*" (*KC,* p. 107). But Frye, too, has precursors. As Virginia Woolf notes in 1940, "Books descend from books as families descend from families. Some descend from Jane Austen; others from Dickens. They resemble their parents, as human children resemble their parents; yet they differ as children differ, and revolt as children revolt."[23] The insistence is identical with those of Frye and Bloom, as is the metaphor of the struggle of children with parents. Frye even says that "the new poem, like the new baby, is born into an already existing order of words, and is typical of the structure of poetry to which it is attached. The new baby *is* his own society appearing once again as a unit of individuality, and the new poem has a similar relation to its poetic society."[24]

But the line of precursorship could be traced almost endlessly into the past. Indeed, even a doctrine so seemingly original as psychoanalysis is involved in indebtedness, belatedness, and influence of various kinds, as Joseph Breuer conceded in one of the earliest treatises in the psychoanalytical movement:

> No one who attempts to put forward today his views on hysteria and its psychical basis can avoid repeating a great quantity of other people's thoughts which are in the act of passing from personal into general possession. It is scarcely possible always to be certain who first gave them utterance, and there is always a danger of regarding as a product of one's own what has already been said by someone else. I hope, therefore, that I may be excused if few quotations are found in this discussion and if no strict distinction is made between what is my own and what originates elsewhere.[25]

What Breuer is here conceding is raised to general formulation in Valéry's observation that "we say that an author is *original* when we cannot trace the hidden transformations that others underwent in his mind; we mean to say that the dependence of *what he does* on *what others have done* is excessively complex and irregular."[26]

Breuer's concession and Valéry's formulation tend to subvert Bloom's conception of culture as the struggle of strong poets. For Breuer speaks of "a great quantity of other people's thoughts," an awareness that undermines the idea of a single strong precursor, and the dramatic wrestling with influence is further undermined by Breuer's statement about the "danger of regarding as a product of one's own what has already been said by someone else." It is, I think, the regarding as one's own what has already been said by someone else that leads, in successive layers and imperceptible repetitions, to the formation of that mysterious entity called a *Zeitgeist,* of which a choice example is that elusive essence we call Romanticism. A cultural breath such as Romanticism or, if one wishes, Victorianism, or the hippiedom of the 1960s, or Florentine culture of the Renaissance, or any other *Zeitgeist* is not formed by the struggles of ephebes with strong precursors, though they wrestle into eternity; it is formed rather by the minimal and dispersed influences Breuer invokes, and which I earlier suggested may be thought of as Leibniz's "τὸ μιϰϱόυ, the insensible progressions" that undermine Locke's building blocks of consciousness.

Perhaps a most trivial incident from my own experience can serve to illustrate these minimal influences. A few years ago I invented, or in my complacent conviction thought I had invented, the phrase "have a good day" that we all constantly hear. I would offer this benediction to taxi drivers in New York, and it only added to my complacency when I began to hear them intoning the same formula to me. Their own use of the words simply fortified my fantasy that I was enormously influential on others, although even I was impressed by the speed and thoroughness with which my influence had worked itself into the popular culture. It was not until I happened to fly out to Chicago and saw on a billboard the exhortation, in letters thirty feet high, to "have a good day" that my self-congratulation on my creative individuality gave way to an understanding of the true situation. As Karl Mannheim insists, "isolated discoveries" are for the sociologist "expressions of general social trends." He goes on to say that "it is not important for us whether the dynamic logic which was achieved at about the same time by Hegel, Schelling and Müller, was arrived at independently or under mutual influence. What is important is to find the sources in the social and intellectual life of the time from which arose the impulse to search for a dynamic logic."[27]

Mannheim, of course, has his own cultural axe to grind no less than does Bloom; what he says, however, presumes the importance of the minimal influences I have just invoked. It is these minimal influences or "insensible progressions" rather than the influence of strong precursors that build the coral reefs of a *Zeitgeist,* or to use Hazlitt's rubric, the spirit of an age. To revert to the starry heavens of our metaleptic field, therefore, closer observation reveals not only strong poems and their juxtaposition, but philosophical systems, novels, journals, and other cultural formations, as well as clouds and streams of astral debris: dispersed metaphorical clusters, emotional solar winds of almost imperceptible effect, cosmic rays of doctrine detectable only by special examination, and so forth (it would, for instance, be very difficult to show that even so important a precursorship for the Romantic poets as that of Milton was "stronger" than the influence of that political upheaval known as the French Revolution). The streamings of this variegated astral matter can doubtless exist in many forms, but in their eddying between German and English culture I wish to call attention here to only five.

Our first awareness, if we adjust our sights so as to locate German and English culture within the same field of view, is that the joint structure seems to be a kind of streaming in the shape of the figure H, with a detour of currents at the joining bar. That is to say, from about 1700 to the Romantic era cultivated Germans read and were profoundly influenced by things English (and in the context of languages used, we may include Scottish writers under the term), but the British did not read the Germans in return. It was Hume who woke Kant from his dogmatic slumber, but the only foreign culture Hume himself was interested in was French. After the advent of Romanticism, the stream of influence almost completely reversed its direction of flow. Except for a fascination with Byron (and of course with Scott), it is astonishing how little the German intelligentsia after 1800 were aware of any of the English Romantic writers. By this time, however, the cultivated English were virtually scrambling to imbibe German culture. Shelley embarked on a translation of Goethe's *Faust* even though he did not know German; Coleridge translated Schiller's *Wallenstein,* though he made mistakes and found the labor "soul-destroying." Carlyle built the greater part of his reputation as a mediator of German culture to the English, and his angry reaction to Coleridge was at least in part conditioned by his unwillingness to accept Coleridge as a competitor priest in the ministration of German sacraments:

> Coleridge sat on the brow of Highgate Hill [wrote Carlyle] . . . looking down on London and its smoke-tumult, like a sage escaped from the inanity of life's battle; attracting towards him the thoughts of innumerable brave souls still engaged there. His express contributions to poetry, philosophy, or any specific province of human literature or enlightenment, had been small and sadly intermittent; but he had, especially among young inquiring men, a higher than literary, a kind of prophetic or magician character. He was thought to hold, he alone in England, the key to German and other Transcendentalisms. . . . The practical intellects of the world did not much heed him, or carelessly reckoned him a metaphysical dreamer: but to the rising spirits of the young generation he had this dusky sublime character; and sat there as a kind of *Magus,* girt in mystery and enigma; his Dodona oak-grove (Mr. Gilman's house at Highgate) whispering strange things, uncertain whether oracles or jargon.[28]

The prestige that attached to Coleridge's knowledge of things German was envied by others than Carlyle; indeed, the pursuit of German culture rapidly became not so much a cultural adornment as a cultural necessity. By 1841, for instance, an article in *Blackwood's Magazine* said that "German, in particular, we *must* study; for, like Goethe's magical apprentice, having set the imp agog after waterbuckets, he threatens to swamp and drown us altogether, unless we get hold of the word which he will obey."[29] In the succeeding year, 1842, Carlyle's friend and Coleridge's former disciple, John Sterling, wrote: "Still more remarkably than in poetry, the philosophical speculations of all Europe are daily learning obedience to the example of Germany. . . . In that country, poor as Germany is compared with England and France,—there may now probably be found the greater part of the generous knowledge and earnest meditation extant on earth."[30] In short, though the cultivated Briton of the Elizabethan age looked to Italy to improve his mind, and the cultivated Briton of Dryden's time and the Enlightenment looked to France, by Romantic and Victorian times he looked almost slavishly to Germany.

We need to be in no doubt when the radical shift occurred. In the eighteenth century a genius like Handel markedly improved his position by moving from Germany to England. In the late 1750s Hamann could write that "it is pleasant and profitable to translate a page of Pope . . . but vanity and a curse to leaf through a part of [Diderot's] *Encyclopédie.*"[31] In the 1770s and 80s men like Herder and Lessing, Moritz and Lichtenberg looked eagerly to England as a kind of spiritual home. "At last I am in my beloved London," writes Lichtenberg in February 1775, "for which I have longed and schemed and pined"; and when it came time to return to Germany, he wrote: "I do not return willingly to Göttingen and scarce think that I shall ever be able to live there contentedly."[32] Elsewhere Lichtenberg produced a comparison of English and German schoolboys that dramatically highlights the German sense of England's superiority:

> To amuse myself I sometimes imagine one of our learned fifteen-year-old German boys in company with a fifteen-year old boy from Eton. The first in his wig, powdered, humble, and tensely anxious to let loose a mass of learning, in all his opinions nothing but an imitation of his papa or his preceptor, a mere reflection. . . . The English boy, his clean, curly hair hanging over his ears and forehead, his face glowing, his hands all scratched, with a cut on each knuckle; Horace, Homer and Virgil are always in his mind; he is definite and original in his opinions, makes a thousand mistakes, but always corrects himself.[33]

By the 1790s, however, the tide was streaming strongly the other way. As a single instance that also involves schoolboys, Coleridge, without even knowing German, proposed in 1796 to have "Robinson, the London bookseller" pay his way to and from

> Jena, a cheap German University where Schiller resides. . . . If I could realize this scheme, I should there study Chemistry & Anatomy, [and] bring over with me all the works of Semler & Michaelis, the German Theologians, & of Kant, the great german Metaphysician. On my return I would commence a School for 8 young men at 100 guineas each—proposing to *perfect* them in the following studies in order as follows———— I. Man as Animal: including the complete knowledge of Anatomy, Chemistry, Mechanics & Optics.—2. Man as an *Intellectual* Being: including the ancient Metaphysics, the systems of Lockey & Hartley,—of the Scotch Philosophers—& the new Kantian S[ystem—] 3. Man as a Religious Being: including an historic summary of all Religions & the arguments for and against Natural & Revealed Religion.[34]

Less apocalyptic than Coleridge's plan, with its proposed wrestling with Kant and other strong precursors, was a cross-cultural pattern whose special structure makes it the first of the five constellations to which I referred above. These five formations may be called, respectively, *epanados, diadromos, periodos, hyetos,* and *aphycton.* All take their figuration from the anteriority of field; all are parataxes; three of them can be discerned as influence relationships; two of them can be ascribed only to *Zeitgeist* progressions.

The first of these five patternings, *epanados,* is a parataxis whereby a typical but not great work exerts formative influence by repetition. Its effect need not be decisive for any given strong poem, but, itself a product of minimal influences, it contributes significantly to the spirit of the age. A choice illustration from the reversal of current in the 1790s is provided by Gottfried Bürger's *Lenore,* which was of unmistakable effect in the deepening of English Romantic colorations, and probably can be discerned in some of the emphases of *The Ancient Mariner,* in *Christabel,* and most specifically in the "woman wailing for her demon lover" of *Kubla Kahn.*[35] The ballad was, as a commentator observes, "the first real touch of the German romantic movement in England"; remarkably, the German tributary to English Romanticism "overflowed in five translations and seven versions . . . during the single year 1796."[36] Bürger's ballad of unholy love is not a "strong" poem as Bloom uses that term; neither were its first English translators and revisers, with a single exception, what Bloom calls "strong precursors" (they were J. T. Stanley, William Taylor, H. J. Pye, W. R. Spencer, and Walter Scott); but the ballad and its translations constitute an *epanados* that contributed significantly to characteristic motifs of English Romanticism.

A different though related kind of parataxis of current, *diadromos,* occurs when the effect of an important or "strong" author or body of work is deflected from its obvious channel and runs lastingly into that of another country. Perhaps the most immediately familiar example of this phenomenon is Poe's vastly greater prestige in French culture than in English-speaking culture. Fully as important, however, even if less well known, is the role of the Englishman Shaftesbury in the stream of German culture. When Shaftesbury's *Characteristics* was published in 1711, it was immediately taken up by German intellectuals, and just as Baudelaire's enthusiasm hurled Poe into the French mainstream, so did the enormous authority of Leibniz hurl Shaftesbury powerfully into the eighteenth-century currents that led to German Romanticism. "I thought I had penetrated deeply into the opinions of our illustrious author," writes Leibniz upon reading the *Characteristics,*

> until I came to the treatise which is unjustly called Rhapsody. Then I perceived that I had been in the forechamber only and was now entirely surprised to find myself in the . . . sanctuary of the most sublime philosophy. . . . The turn of the discourse, the style, the dialogue, the new-Platonism . . . but above all the grandeur and beauty of the ideas, their luminous enthusiasm, the apostrophe to divinity, ravished me and brought me into a state of ecstasy. At the end of the book I finally returned to myself and had leisure to think about it. . . . I found in it all of my Theodicy before it saw the light of day. The universe all of a piece, its beauty, its universal harmony, the disappearance of real evil. . . . It lacked only my pre-established harmony, my banishment of death, and my reduction of matter or the multitude to unities or simple substances.[37]

Impelled by this kind of rapturous assessment, the work of Shaftesbury assumed a central place in the minds of young German intellectuals, especially Herder and Goethe, and many monographs and specialized articles have detailed the broad course of the Shaftesburian current in eighteenth-century German thought. Indeed, as Eduard Spranger says at one point in his magisterial study, *Wilhelm von Humboldt und die Humanitätsidee,* "Here, as so often, all lines and threads lead back to Shaftesbury, who, without being a thinker in the strictest sense, sowed seeds on all sides that sprout up in the metaphysics, ethics, and aesthetics of the eighteenth century. In universality of effect he is like the very great: Socrates, Kant, or Leibniz."[38]

Such was not at all the case in English culture leading into Romanticism. One well-known scholar even says that Coleridge did not know Shaftesbury. The scholar is in error; but it is certainly true that Shaftesbury does not loom large in English Romanticism. He commanded little enthusiasm among his later English readers, and the blocking effect of such lack of enthusiasm can be experienced in Thomas Gray's words as quoted by Dr. Johnson:

You say you cannot conceive how Lord Shaftesbury came to be a philosopher in vogue; I will tell you: first, he was a lord; secondly, he was as vain as any of his readers; thirdly, men are very prone to believe what they do not understand; fourthly, they will believe any thing at all, provided they are under no obligation to believe it; fifthly, they love to take a new road, even when that road leads no where; sixthly, he was reckoned a fine writer, and seems always to mean more than he said. Would you have any more reasons? An interval of above forty years has pretty well destroyed the charm. A dead lord ranks with commoners: vanity is no longer interested in the matter; for a new road is become an old one.[39]

A third kind of paratactic figure is formed when the effect of a cultural stress is deflected into another culture and then returns to its original culture further downstream. This figure we may call *periodos,* and it is well illustrated by A. D. Lindsay's observation: "It is a most interesting episode in the international exchange of ideas—how the thought of Locke, that most English of all philosophers, with his supreme commonsense, his acceptance of facts, his toleration and his love of liberty, and along with all this his dislike of working out principles to their logical consequences, fructified in France in clear consistent systems, and came back in its French form to inspire Bentham and his successors."[40] Or, to take our illustration from English and German rather than English and French currents, *periodos* can be illustrated from Hume in Britain to Friedrich Jacobi in Germany, and then from Jacobi in Germany back to Coleridge in Britain. While writing *The Friend* and the *Biographica Literaria,* Coleridge had busied himself with Jacobi's philosophical writings, and at one point in a marginal notation he defends Jacobi's *Glaubensphilosophie* in these words: "This is not a fair Criticism on Jacobi. What was his Object? To prove, that FAITH, which the Philosophers of his Day, held in contempt, was sensuous Evidence . . . No! But to prove that the sensuous Evidence itself was a species of Faith and Revelation."[41] Coleridge correctly recognized in Jacobi an ally in his attempt to save Christian guarantees of soul from the assault of the Enlightenment, and especially of scoffers like Hume. But Jacobi's argument that faith was necessary to all perception whatever ("Das Element aller menschlichen Erkenntniß und Wirksamkeit ist Glaube")[42] was itself, in a notable *periodos,* almost certainly suggested by the analysis of belief in Hume's *Enquiry Concerning Human Understanding* and in his *Treatise of Human Nature.*

The near certainty is reinforced because Jacobi somewhat later, in 1787, wrote a treatise called *David Hume über den Glauben, oder Idealismus und Realismus,* where he defends his faith-philosophy by enlisting Hume on his side. One of the interlocutors in the dialogue says that he has been reading Hume's essays. The other says, "Against faith, therefore?" and the first one replies unexpectedly, "For faith," whereupon the second interlocutor challenges him to "make me acquainted with Hume as teacher of faith."[43] Hume had specifically been talking of belief, whereas Jacobi uses the ambiguity of *Glaube* in German to change the emphasis to faith, which emphasis was the one taken up by Coleridge. But we are further pointed to Hume as formative for Jacobi's faith-philosophy by a statement of his close friend Hamann to Kant, in 1759, which shows how carefully the German literati were heeding the writings of the British philosopher. "The Attic philosopher, Hume," says Hamann, "needs faith if he is to eat an egg and drink a glass of water."[44]

A fourth pattern of cross-cultural parataxis, which I term *hyetos,* occurs when a theme is widely dispersed in the *Zeitgeist* without necessarily being connected by overt influences. The Wandering Jew is a prime example. This mythic figure plods through the most diverse Romantic contexts, from M. G. Lewis's *The Monk* to Nikolaus Lenau's heartfelt *Ahasuer, Der ewige Jude.* Indeed, though we are not at all surprised to find the Wandering Jew in Shelley and Byron, we are perhaps startled to find that even the least exotic and most tied to daily life of all Romantic poets—I refer, of course, to Wordsworth—composed in 1800 a poem called "Song for the Wandering Jew," of which the seventh and last stanza runs:

Day and night my toils redouble,
Never nearer to the goal;
Night and day, I feel the trouble
Of the Wanderer in my soul.

But even more revelatory of the *Zeitgeist* than the *hyetos* of the Wandering Jew is the *hyetos* of Prometheus. Goethe, as we know, returned repeatedly to the myth, and no less a critic than Georg Brandes says of his earliest poem on the subject that "everything that Spinoza had taught . . . everything that Ludwig Feuerbach later proclaimed is assembled—or anticipated—in this youthful, beautiful, profound poem. A greater poem of rebellion has never been written. It is eternal. Each line is moulded for all time. Each line stands like so many letters of fire in the nocturnal sky of humankind. Few verses that have ever been written on this earth can be compared to it."[45] In a well-known passage in *Dichtung und Wahrheit,* Goethe talks of his near obsession with the Prometheus myth, and he compares the character of Prometheus with that of Milton's Satan.[46] Remarkably enough, Shelley too makes the same comparison in the preface to his own *Prometheus Unbound.* "The only imaginary being resembling in any degree Prometheus," says Shelley, "is Satan; and Prometheus is, in my judgment, a more poetical character than Satan, because, in addition to courage, and majesty, and firm and patient opposition to omnipotent force, he is susceptible of being described as exempt from the taints of ambition, envy, revenge, and a desire for personal aggrandisement, which in the Hero of Paradise Lost, interfere with the interest."[47] But where Shelley's sources were Aeschylus and Byron, Goethe's were Wieland and Hederich's *Mythologisches Lexikon.* The two great realizations of the Prometheus myth by major poets in German and English, though similar in structure and emphasis, had no discernible relationship of cause and effect upon one another.

The hyetic dispersal of the theme of the Wandering Jew has been documented by George Anderson,[48] and that of Prometheus still more fully by Raymond Trousson.[49] No such documentation exists for the fifth and concluding paratactic constellation that I call *aphycton. Aphycton* exists when the inner logic of an intellectual emphasis leads to a similar disposition of metaphorical materials even when no influence is present. It differs from *hyetos* in that the latter relates to characteristics of the *Zeitgeist* as such—the Wandering Jew to Romantic homelessness and alienation, Prometheus to Romantic rebellion—while *aphycton,* though dispersed in much the same way as *hyetos,* relates primarily not to a thematic coloring but to a logical operation. I shall take as a fairly extended example the metaphor of sand, and I shall begin with a notable collocation in a brief poem by Blake:

Mock on Mock on Voltaire Rousseau
Mock on Mock on 'tis all in vain
You throw the sand against the wind
And the wind blows it back again

And every sand becomes a Gem
Reflected in the beams divine
Blown back they blind the mocking Eye
But still in Israels paths they shine

The Atoms of Democritus
And Newtons Particles of Light
Are sands upon the Red sea shore
Where Israels tents do shine so bright[50]

The common experience of a common substance, sand, being blown back into the face of one who throws it, becomes in Blake's beautiful progression an experience of gems, and finally an experience of a sacred situation, "the sands upon the Red sea shore." The sacred sands are conversions of mechanical and lifeless particles, "The Atoms of Democritus / And Newtons Particles of Light," which Blake's visionary physics was concerned to refute as inimical to the imaginative life of man.

The wonderful transformation of sand from atoms and particles to gems and sacred ground arises directly from the logical collocation, for Blake, who uses sand frequently in his writings, does not always use it honorifically, as we see, for instance, in his statement that "abstinence sows sand all over," where sand metaphorically equals desication.[51] But where sand metaphorically equals irreducible particles or atoms, Blake gives it a vast charge of significance:

To see a World in a Grain of Sand
And a Heaven in a Wild Flower
Hold Infinity in the palm of your hand
And Eternity in an hour[52]

In those lines from *Auguries of Innocence,* Blake presents a complex logical operation as an intuitive poetical surface. His connecting the infinitely small with the infinitely large rests upon the logical fact that infinity cannot be assigned predicates and is therefore identical in all its aspects, and his "Heaven in a Wild Flower" not only sounds like Tennyson's flower in the crannied wall, but also builds on the same logical truth.

The necessity of this logic is aphyctically invoked by Coleridge when he says that "one thought includes all thought, in the sense that a grain of sand includes the universe."[53] Fichte aphyctically expands the same metaphor by the same logic: "In every moment of her duration nature is one connected whole; in every moment each individual part must be what it is, because all the others are what they are; and you could not remove a single grain of sand from its place, without thereby, although perhaps imperceptibly to you, changing something throughout all parts of the immeasurable whole." Fichte goes on to argue that "you cannot conceive even the position of a grain of sand other than it is at the present," and after discussion he concludes "that you might never have been at all and all that you have ever done, or ever hope to do, must have been obstructed in order that a grain of sand might lie in a different place."[54]

Fichte's argument about sand metaphorically transliterates an argument in Leibniz about atoms: the smallest body, urges Leibniz, "is affected by all other things in the entire world . . . an effect in the atom must result from all the impressions of the universe and, conversely, the entire state of the universe can be gathered from the atom."[55] And if Blake's connection of sand to world encloses an aphyctic inevitability, so too does the connection of sand to the infinitely small and thereby the infinite itself. When Leeuwenhoek reported to the Royal Society his discovery of protozoa, which he called "animalcula or living Atoms," he says that he judged "that if 100 of them lay by another, they would not equal the length of a grain of coarse sand; and according to this estimate, ten hundred thousand of them could not equal the dimensions of a grain of such coarse sand."[56] Hume finds the invocation of sand equally inevitable when talking of the infinitely small: " 'Tis therefore certain that the imagination reaches a minimum. . . . When you tell me of the thousandth and ten thousandth part of a grain of sand . . . the images, which I form in my mind to represent the things themselves, are nothing different from each other . . . the idea of a grain of sand is not distinguishable, nor separable into twenty, much less into a thousand, ten thousand, or an infinite number of different ideas."[57]

Finally, we may note that the sand topos is a true *aphycton* and not an influence, for Hegel, in the *Wissenschaft der Logik,* terms a world in a grain of sand a philosophical tautology, and we can see that the metaphorical usage arose aphyctically in his mind and not by way of influence by his using the idiosyncratic but synonymous "Stäubchen"—little piece of dust—rather than sand: "A determinate or finite being," says Hegel, "is such as refers itself to another; it is a content that stands in a relation of necessity with other content or with the whole world. In view of the mutually determinant connection of the whole, metaphysics could make the assertion (which is really a tautology) that if the least grain of dust were destroyed the whole universe must collapse."[58]

The parataxis of *aphycton,* which casts into relief the constant renewal of individual discovery within the stream of tradition, defines one kind of limit for Bloom's radical suppression of poetic individuality. Despite the acuteness of his insight and the plangency of his formulations, Bloom's system is, not metaphorically but literally, one of half-truths. Most advancements of our understanding occur incrementally, by holding on to what we already know and extending its perimeter. Bloom varies this procedure by mortgaging what we already know to lay claim to what we have not previously seen. The new insights are exciting, but they cannot join on to prior knowledge to form a whole, because prior knowledge has been denied in order to gain the insight. The resulting half-truths necessarily occur within a system, for they can be vitalized only by reference back to their role in that system, not by reference to our common experience. A single example should make the contention clear: "Influence, as I conceive it," says Bloom in one of the formulations that shower like sparks from his pen, "means that there are no *texts,* but only relationships *between* texts" (*MM,* p. 3). The statement is vulnerable to the same logic by which Marx destroyed Proudhon's "property is theft": the existence of *texts* (or property) must be granted prior to any possibility of relationships *between* texts (or the conception of theft). The new understandings about influence relationships that Bloom proffers us are all too often purchased at the cost of logic and ineluctable experience.

It is precisely this hypothecation of our common sense to this new insight that characterizes Bloom's devaluation of individual experience as the basis of poetry. His half-truth is that poems take shape as resonances from earlier poems, and that no one would become a poet were there not prior poets to serve as models. But the other half of the truth, which his system cannot accommodate, is that it is an individual's unique experience that makes him feel like a poet in the first place, and that it is his distillation of that experience that provides him the essence of his poetry. The entire course of Keats's development—poetic, intellectual, emotional—documents this truth, and indeed demonstrates that the uniqueness of individual awareness must always occur and be distilled before there can supervene the phenomena of intrapoetic relationships.[59]

Yet Bloom often speaks as though poems were generated solely from other poems rather than from personal, monadic experience.[60] On the contrary, though it may have been the reading of earlier poems that made Wordsworth write verses, it was his personal experience of the orange sky of evening that made him a great poet. Moreover, "every great poet," as John Stuart Mill insists, "has had his mind full of thoughts, derived not merely from passive sensibility, but from trains of reflection, from observation, analysis, and generalization."[61] This monadic full-ness, urges Mill, actually works against the flow of tradition. It makes no differ-ence, he says, that something was known by others before one is born: "The question is, how is *he* to know it. There is one way; and nobody has ever hit upon more than one—by *discovery*."[62] Monadic experience, even more than the influ-ence of strong precursors, generates the content of great poetry. "Each person's own reason must work upon the materials afforded by that same person's own experience," says Mill: "Knowledge comes only from within."[63]

So the full truth is a tension of opposites. There is tradition, and tradition is extraordinarily important; but there is also such a reality as individual talent. Even after all respect is paid to the power and ingenuity of Bloom's conception of poetry's genesis and development, a truer accounting of cultural process would seem to be that rendered by Herder, who observes that two principles underlie intellectual history: "They are *tradition* and *organic powers*. All education arises from imitation and exercise, by means of which the model passes into the copy. What better word is there for this transmission than tradition? But the imitator must have powers to receive and convert into his own nature what has been transmitted to him, just like the food he eats. Accordingly, what and how much he receives, where he derives it from, and how he applies it to his own use, are determined by his own receptive powers."[64] Herder's specification of personal "receptive powers" refers to an individual's placement in cultural history; Mill's specification of personal "discovery" refers to his unique selfhood. Their com-bined weight rests in the scales against Bloom. Eloquence, says Mill in a famous distinction, is designed to be heard; poetry, on the contrary, can only be "*over-heard*." "Poetry," he urges, "is feeling confessing itself to itself in moments of solitude." "All poetry is of the nature of soliloquy."[65] For the poet, in the lyric instant, is addressing neither us nor other poets; he is speaking to himself alone, in an utterance that participates in the structure of rumination. And what is lastingly valuable in that utterance arises from the depths of his own life and his awareness of the real world in which he lives, moves, and has his being.

NOTES

1. John Crowe Ransom, *The World's Body* (New York and London, 1938), p. 342.
2. Thomas McFarland, *Coleridge and the Pantheist Tradition* (Oxford, 1969). p. 45.
3. *The Prelude: A Parallel Text*, ed. J. C. Maxwell (Harmondsworth, 1971), pp. 82, 84 (1805 version, Bk. II, ll. 208–15).
4. *The Prelude*, p. 85 (1850 version, Bk. II, ll. 215–28).
5. *The Poetry and Prose of William Blake*, ed. David V. Erdman, commentary by Harold Bloom, rev. ed. (Garden City, N. Y., 1968), p. 151.
6. *Poetry and Prose of Blake*, p. 94.
7. *Johann Wolfgang Goethe: Gedenkausgabe der Werke, Briefe und Gespräche*, ed. Ernst Beutler (Zurich, 1948–71), XXIV, 300–301.
8. McFarland, *Coleridge and the Pantheist Tradition*, p. 44
9. Thomas McFarland, "The Originality Paradox," *New Literary History*, 5 (1974), 447–76.
10. Harold Bloom, *The Anxiety of Influence: A Theory of Poetry* (New York, 1973), p. 94; hereafter cited in text as *AI*.
11. Harold Bloom, *Kabbalah and Criticism* (New York, 1975), p. 108; hereafter cited in text as *KC*.
12. Or rather, "determinate data." Cf. Locke: "*Clear and distinct* Ideas are terms, which though familiar and frequent in Men's Mouths, I have reason to think every one, who uses, does not perfectly understand. . . . I have therefore in most places chose to put *determinate* or *determined*, instead of *clear* and *distinct*, as more likely to direct Men's thoughts to my meaning in this matter" (*An Essay concerning Human Understanding*, ed. Peter H. Nidditch [Oxford, 1975], pp. 12–13).
13. Leibniz's own favorite example of the existence of "minute perceptions" below or on the borderline of the conscious was that in walking beside the sea, he heard a single roar of waves made up of the sounds of many individual waves that were not discernible in their particularity (*Die philosophischen Schriften von Gottfried Wilhelm Leibniz*, ed. C. J. Gerhardt [Hildesheim, 1960 (facsimile rpt. of the 1875–90 edition)], V, 47; VI, 515). It is an interesting triple chapter in the history of ideas that (1) in order to give formal grounding to the doctrine of "minute perceptions" Leibniz distinguished *perceptions* from *apperceptions* and thereby instituted the division between the unconscious and the conscious mind (e.g., "il y a mille marques qui font juger qu'il y a à tout moment une infinité de *perceptions* en nous, mais sans apperception et sans réflexion, c'est à dire des changements dans l'ame même dont nous ne nous apperçevons pas, parce que les impressions sont ou trop petites et en trop grand nombre ou trop unies" [V, 46]), a distinction that, transmitted through Schelling and Romanticism to Schopenhauer and Eduard von Hartmann, eventuated in Freud's psychoanalytical doctrine that now has penetrated all interstices of modern assumption; (2) that it specifically was criticism of the doctrine of "clear and distinct ideas" that led to the division of the conscious and the unconscious; and (3) that inasmuch as the requirement of "clear and distinct ideas" as components in a theory of knowledge was initiated by Descartes (*Quicquid clare distincteque percipio, verum est*), Leibniz developed the distinction of conscious and unconscious in opposition to the Cartesian tradition before he employed it in opposition to Locke, e.g.: "Ainsi il est bon de faire distinction entre la *Perception* qui est l'état interieur de la Monade representant les chose externes, et l'*Apperception* qui est la *Conscience*, ou la connoissance reflexive de cet état interieur, laquelle n'est point donnée à toutes les Ames, ny tousjours à la même Ame. Et c'est faute de cette distinction, que les Cartesiens ont manqué, en comptant pour rien les perceptions dont on ne s'apperçoit pas" (VI, 600).

14. Leibniz, *Die philosophischen Schriften*, V, 50.

15. Harold Bloom, *A Map of Misreading* (New York, 1975), p. 80; hereafter cited in text as *MM*.

16. *The Collected Works of Paul Valéry*, ed. Jackson Mathews et al. (Princeton, 1956–75), VIII, 241.

17. *A Treatise of Human Nature*, ed. L. A. Selby-Bigge, 2nd ed., rev. P. H. Nidditch (Oxford, 1978), pp 86, 103.

18. As to why "poetic influence" would *not* mean "the passing-on of images and ideas from earlier to later poets," Valéry supplies the enlightening illustration of Baudelaire: "He reached manhood at a time when . . . a dazzling generation had appropriated the empire of Letters. Lamartine, Hugo, Musset, Vigny were the masters of the moment. Let us put ourselves in the place of a young man who is about to begin writing in 1840. He has been brought up on artists whom an imperious instinct commands him to blot out. His literary vocation has been awakened and nourished by them, inspired by their glory, shaped by their works, yet his survival necessarily calls for the denial, overthrow, and replacement of the same men who appear to him to occupy the whole expanse of fame" (*Collected Works of Valéry*, VIII, 195).

19. Virginia Woolf, "The Leaning Tower," *Collected Essays*, II (London, 1966), 163.

20. McFarland, *Coleridge and the Pantheist Tradition*, p. 45.

21. Again: "Poetic influence, in the sense I give it, has almost nothing to do with the verbal resemblances between one poet and another" (p. 19). Still again: "Only weak poems, or the weaker elements in strong poems, immediately echo precursor poems, or directly allude to them. The fundamental phenomena of poetic influence have little to do with the borrowing of images or ideas, with sound-patterns, or with other verbal reminders of one poem by another. A poem is a deep misprision of a previous poem when we recognize the later poem as being absent rather than present on the surface of the earlier poem, and yet still being *in* the earlier poem, implicit or hidden *in* it, not yet manifest, and yet *there*" (*KC*, pp. 66–67).

22. Northrop Frye, *Anatomy of Criticism* (Princeton, 1957), p. 97.

23. Woolf, *Collected Essays*, II, 163.

24. Frye, p. 97.

25. *The Standard Edition of the Complete Psychological Works of Sigmund Freud*, tr. and ed. James Strachey, Anna Freud et al. (London, 1966–74), II, 185–86.

26. *Collected Works of Valéry*, VIII, 241.

27. *From Karl Mannheim*, ed. Kurt H. Wolff (New York, 1971), p. 209, n. 1.

28. *The Works of Thomas Carlyle in Thirty Volumes*, ed. H. D. Traill, Centenary Edition (London, 1896–99), XI, 53.

29. "Traits and Tendencies of German Literature," *Blackwood's Edinburgh Magazine*, 50 (1841), 160. The statement continues: "Nor is it from Germany only by external importation that the deluge floods in; we have a sort of indwelling Germanism at home, which is very powerful, and has many names. Undeniably, Coleridge was a German. . . . A German of the Germans was Percy Bysshe Shelley; a German in his pure incorporeal idealism; German in his pantheizing poetry and poetical pantheism; British only in his pride" (p. 160).

30. *Essays and Tales*, ed. J. C. Hare (London, 1848), I, 385, 404.

31. *Kant's gesammelte Schriften*, ed. Royal Prussian Academy of Sciences (Berlin, 1902–), X, 8.

32. *Lichtenberg's Visits to England*, tr. Margaret L. More and W. H. Quarrell (Oxford, 1938), pp. 79, 109.

33. *Georg Christoph Lichtenberg's Aphorismen,* ed. Albert Leitzmann (Berlin, 1902–8), III, 146.

34. *Collected Letters of Samuel Taylor Coleridge,* ed. Earl Leslie Griggs (Oxford, 1956–71), I, 209.

35. See Oliver Farrar Emerson, *The Earliest English Translations of Bürger's "Lenore": A Study in English and German Romanticism* (Cleveland, 1915). See further Evelyn B. Jolles, *G. A. Bürgers Ballade "Lenore" in England* (Regensburg, 1974).

36. Emerson, pp. 9, 60.

37. Leibniz, *Die philosophischen Schriften,* III, 429–30.

38. Eduard Spranger, *Wilhelm von Humboldt und die Humanitätsidee* (Berlin, 1909), p. 156.

39. Samuel Johnson, *Lives of the English Poets,* ed. George Birkbeck Hill (Oxford, 1905), III, 432.

40. Preface to Elie Halévy, *The Growth of Philosophic Radicalism,* tr. Mary Morris (New York, 1926).

41. W. Schrickx, "Coleridge and Friedrich Heinrich Jacobi," *Revue belge de philosophie et d'histoire,* 36, pt. 3 (1958), 815–16.

42. *Friedrich Heinrich Jacobi's Werke,* ed. Friedrich Roth and Friedrich Köppen (Leipzig, 1812–25), Vol. IV, pt. 1, p. 223.

43. *Jacobi's Werke,* II, 128–29.

44. *Kant's gesammelte Schriften,* X, 15.

45. *Wolfgang Goethe,* tr. Allen W. Porterfield (New York, 1936), I, 152–53.

46. Goethe, *Gedenkausgabe,* X, 699–700.

47. *The Complete Works of Percy Bysshe Shelley,* ed. Roger Ingpen and Walter E. Peck (New York, 1965), II, 171–72.

48. George Anderson, *The Legend of the Wandering Jew* (Providence, 1965).

49. Raymond Trousson, *Le thème de Prométhée dans la littérature européenne,* 2 vols. (Geneva, 1976).

50. *Poetry and Prose of Blake,* pp. 468–69.

51. *Poetry and Prose of Blake,* p. 464.

52. *Poetry and Prose of Blake,* p. 484.

53. *The Table Talk and Omniana of Samuel Taylor Coleridge,* ed. T. Ashe (London, 1888), p. 315.

54. *Johann Gottlieb Fichte's sämmtliche Werke,* ed. J. H. Fichte (Berlin, 1845–46), II, 178–79.

55. *Opuscules et fragments inédits de Leibniz,* ed. Louis Couturat (Hildesheim, 1961 [1903]), p. 522.

56. *Philosophical Transactions,* XII (London, 1677), 821.

57. Hume, *Treatise,* p. 27.

58. *G.W.F. Hegel: Werke in zwanzig Bänden, Theorie-Werkausgabe,* ed. Eva Moldenhauer and Karl Markus Michel (Frankfort, 1967–71), V, 87.

59. It was not prior poems, but intensity of experience, that generated the poetic genius of Keats: "Keats was in his glory in the fields!" testifies Haydon. "The humming of the bee, the sight of a flower, the glitter of the sun, seemed to make his nature tremble! his eyes glistened! his cheek flushed! his mouth positively quivered & clentched!" (*The Diary of Benjamin Robert Haydon,* ed. Willard Bissell Pope [Cambridge, Mass., 1960–63], II, 316). The unity and intensity of experience that precede and give meaning to the discursive techniques of poetry are signalized by Leibniz, who of all philosophers most unequivocally asserts the fullness and priority of individual knowledge. Even before Locke's essay appeared, Leibniz asseverated almost mystically that "it is a bad habit we have of thinking as if our souls received certain forms as

messengers and as if it had doors and windows. We have all these forms in our own minds, and even from all time, because the mind always expresses all its future thoughts and already thinks confusedly of everything of which it will ever think distinctly. Nothing can be taught us the idea of which is not already in our minds, as the matter out of which this thought is formed. This Plato has excellently recognized when he puts forward his doctrine of reminiscence. . . . Aristotle preferred to compare our souls to tablets that are still blank but upon which there is a place for writing and maintained that there is nothing in our understanding that does not come from the senses. This conforms more with popular notions, as Aristotle usually does, while Plato goes deeper" (Leibniz, *Die philosophischen Schriften,* IV, 451–52.

60. E.g., "Every poem we know begins as an encounter *between poems"* (*MM,* p. 70). "Poetry is poems speaking to a poem, and is also that poem answering back with its own defensive discourse" (*KC,* p. 108).

61. *Collected Works of John Stuart Mill,* ed. J. M. Robson et al. (Toronto, 1963–), I, 413.

62. Mill, *Collected Works,* I, 330.

63. Mill, *Collected Works,* I, 332.

64. Johann Gottfried von Herder, *Ideen zur Philosophie der Geschichte der Menschheit* (Berlin and Weimar, 1965), I, 337.

65. Mill, *Collected Works,* I, 348, 349.

The I Altered

Many of the selections in this collection reflect their author's
engagement, either contesting or admiring, with specific critical
attitudes and positions held by earlier critics. But some tendencies in
recent romantic criticism spring from ideas and concerns that played
almost no role in the writings of scholars who came to maturity during
or shortly after World War II. The most obvious of these "new" forces
is the rise of feminism in the 1970s, which only now, although rather
slowly, as Stuart Curran points out, is seriously deepening and
broadening our conceptions of romanticism.

That the most impressive romantic poets are all male (unlike the
most impressive romantic novelists) has perhaps retarded feminist
criticism in our field. As Julie Ellison points out, "Feminist theory has
exhibited a sustained dislike for the romantic" (*Delicate Subjects:
Romanticism, Gender, and the Ethics of Understanding*, p. 11). A
cogent examination of this question, appropriately titled "Why Women
Didn't Like Romanticism: The Views of Jane Austen and Mary
Shelley," is provided by Anne K. Mellor in Gene W. Ruoff's
Romantics and Us (1990). Yet it may be that these disinclinations have
allowed for an unusually complex and subtle *because* gradual
development of "feminist" approaches, above all in giving room for
consideration to the play of forces more intricate than those of simple
gender oppositions. Much of the recent criticism of the "bi-sexual"
Byron, for example, benefits from this complexity, and a growing
number of critics have begun to articulate intricacies of romantic
sexuality, among whom Marlon Ross, author of *The Contours of
Masculine Desire: Romanticism and the Rise of Women's Poetry* (1989),
merits special mention.

One should not overlook the impact on romantic poetic criticism of
such feminist works as Sandra Gilbert and Susan Gubar's *Madwoman
in the Attic* (1979) and Mary Poovey's *Proper Lady and the Woman
Writer: Ideology as Style in the Works of Mary Wollstonecraft, Mary
Shelley, and Jane Austen* (1984), which center on women prose writers.
Other important recent books include Mary Jacobus's *Reading Woman:
Essays in Feminist Criticism* (1986) and Anne Mellor's excellent
collection from which Curran's essay is taken, *Romanticism and
Feminism* (1988).

From *Romanticism and Feminism*, ed. Anne K. Mellor (Bloomington: Indiana University
Press, 1988), pp. 185–189, 206.

Let us suppose they all died young: not just Keats at twenty-five, Shelley at twenty-nine, and Byron at thirty-six, but Coleridge in 1802, Wordsworth in 1807, and Southey on the day in 1813 he became poet laureate. Let us suppose too of the other candidates for fame in verse that Blake was mad, that Campbell and Hunt were journalists, Moore a songster, Rogers a bonvivant, Scott a novelist, and the rest vicars of the church. Let us then suppose a retrospect on British Romanticism just after the death of Byron in the inimitable tones of *Blackwood's,* celebrating this "Age of Genius, only second to that of Elizabeth" and attempting to identify its particular source, "the strong influence in operating the change that has taken place in our poetic literature." It might run along these lines:

> We [are] delighted with the opportunity afforded us of offering our tribute of admira-
> tion to one, who, in point of genius, is inferior to no individual on the rolls of
> modern celebrity—whose labours have given a tone and character to the poetic
> literature of our nation—whose works were the manuals of our earliest years, and
> were carried by us, in our school-boy days, to shady nooks, and unfrequented paths,
> and our most favourite solitudes—whose touching portraitures of the workings of
> the human soul awakened in us an enthusiasm, to the full as ardent as that which is
> only inspired in our present youth by the effeminizing sensuality of Moore, or the
> gloomy and bewildering fascinations of Lord Byron—whose deep and affecting
> morals, illustrated by the moving examples of her scenes, touched the heart and
> mind, and improved the understanding by the delightful means of an excited
> imagination—and whose pages we have never returned to, in our days of more
> matured judgment, without reviving the fading tints of admiration, and justifying
> our early estimate of her high intellectual superiority.[1]

Without the pointed pronouns, a modern reader would surely anticipate from this description a contemporary estimate of the greatness of Wordsworth. But, instead, the subject is Joanna Baillie, who, two years before Wordsworth's celebrated preface, had published her own seventy-two-page argument for naturalness of language and situation across all the literary genres. Today, if she appears in modern literary histories, Joanna Baillie is fortunate to be able to duck into a footnote, usually derogatory. And yet, aside from the authority of its preface, her three-volume *Series of Plays: in which it is attempted to delineate the stronger passions of the mind* (1798–1812) was hailed in comparison to Shakespeare and, of all contemporary influences, exerted the most direct practical and theoretical force on serious drama written in the Romantic period. That with the exception of Shelley's *Cenci* we do not read this corpus and almost none of it is revived in the theater is apt testimony to the caprices of history with fame. The caprices of historians with history are quite another matter. Manifest distortions of the record have accrued, and these are the subject of this essay.

If we revert a generation from *Blackwood's* assessment of the contemporary scene, we might focus our perspective at a point midway between Baillie's and Wordsworth's prefaces, which is to say, before Baillie's impact on her culture had taken place. This is how Mary Robinson, a major literary voice of the 1790s, characterized its landscape:

> The best novels that have been written, since those of Smollet, Richardson, and
> Fielding, have been produced by women: and their pages have not only been embel-
> lished with the interesting events of domestic life, portrayed with all the refinement

of sentiment, but with forcible and eloquent, political, theological, and philosophical reasoning. To the genius and labours of some enlightened British women posterity will also be indebted for the purest and best translations from the French and German languages. I need not mention Mrs. Dobson, Mrs. Inchbald, Miss Plumptree &c. &c. Of the more profound researches in the dead languages, we have many female classicks of the first celebrity: Mrs. Carter, Mrs. Thomas, (late Miss Parkhurst;), Mrs. Francis, the Hon. Mrs. Damer, &c. &c.

Of the Drama, the wreath of fame has crowned the brows of Mrs. Cowley, Mrs. Inchbald, Miss Lee, Miss Hannah More, and others of less celebrity. Of Biography, Mrs. Dobson, Mrs. Thickness, Mrs. Piozzi, Mrs. Montagu, Miss Helen Williams, have given specimens highly honourable to their talents. Poetry has unquestionably risen high in British literature from the productions of female pens; for many English women have produced such original and beautiful compositions, that the first critics and scholars of the age have wondered, while they applauded.[2]

Robinson's landscape is then further delineated with a list of thirty-nine exemplary women scholars, artists, and writers, many of whom the modern reader could not have identified before the publication of Janet Todd's *Dictionary*. These thirty-nine articles of faith, as it were, were universally known among the literate of the 1790s and, indeed, could be multiplied several times over. Although our concern is with poetry, the breadth of the list should remind us from the start that by the 1790s in Great Britain there were many more women than men novelists and that the theater was actually dominated by women, all the more so as Joanna Baillie's fame and influence spread.[3] In the arena of poetry, which in the modern world we have privileged as no other in this age, the place of women was likewise, at least for a time, predominant, and it is here that the distortions of our received history are most glaring. Its chronology has been written wholly, and arbitrarily, along a masculine gender line.

That such distortions started early can be perceived in the midst of *Blackwood's* extolling of Joanna Baillie. For the reviewer, identified as William Harness, implicitly sets Baillie within a nationalistic Scottish milieu dominated before her entrance by James Beattie, whereas clearly the major poetic voice in England in the ten years between 1785 and 1795 was that of William Cowper. But the curious centering of Beattie, who staked his exaggerated claims on one unfinished poem, should alert us to how difficult it is for the customary history to center any poet writing in Britain in the last third of the eighteenth century. After the death of the mercurial and self-destructive Charles Churchill in 1764, there occurs (according to the standard account) a remarkable trough in English poetry, which cannot be filled in by two honored poems each from Oliver Goldsmith and Samuel Johnson, nor by the inventions of the brilliant Chatterton, an adolescent suicide, nor by those two antithetical voices of the Scottish Enlightenment, alike inventors of a spurious past, Macpherson and Beattie. And yet there was a rush to fill that trough by an entire school of poets—women poets—who came to maturity in the 1770s out of the intellectual energy of the bluestocking circle of Elizabeth Carter and Elizabeth Montagu. They were well aware of one another, sometimes conceiving themselves as rivals of one another, and found an audience that followed their careers and bought their books. That they constituted a coterie, however far-flung from its London origins, is absolutely true, with all the disadvantages we might associate with it, but with the energy, determination, and staying power to enforce a transformation in the history of British letters. Aside from intellectual encouragement, it is important to note, this coterie in its broadest manifestation furnished the economic base on which women writers depended for material support. Thus, while Goldsmith was writing his two poems and Beattie his one, a succession of women poets came to prominence: Anna Barbauld with five editions of her poems between 1773 and 1777; Hannah More with six sizable volumes of verse between 1773 and 1786; Anna Seward, the Swan of Lichfield, whose *Monody on the Death of Major Andre* of 1781 went through successive editions and was followed in 1784 by her influential amalgamation of genres, *Louisa, a Poetical Novel,* making her a literary force to be reckoned with until her death a quarter-century later; Charlotte Smith, whose *Elegiac Sonnets* of 1784 went through ten expanding editions in fifteen years; Helen Maria Williams, who capitalized on the fame of her first two books of poetry by publishing a collected *Poems, in Two Volumes* in 1786, when she was yet twenty-four; and Mary Robinson, whose first poetic volume was published in 1775, and who the year before her death in 1800 could survey a literary landscape and see it dominated by women intellectuals.

These six poets, however ignored today or misconceived in their own time, along with Cowper impel the history of poetry in the last quarter of Britain's eighteenth century. They are, as it were, the missing link, all the more missing since, deluged with reprints as the literary academy is today, only Seward's works have shared in that effort; indeed, only two of these six, Anna Barbauld and Hannah More, found their way into Victorian editions. As literary figures, these women poets are by no means isolated; there are dozens of other women of lesser ambition or simply less prominence who emulated them and thereby swelled their ranks into a literary phenomenon without parallel in earlier history. The six had their veritable differences in temperament and ideology—Anna Seward disparaged the propriety of Charlotte Smith's sonnets, for instance, and it is unlikely that Hannah More would have acknowledged the acquaintance of Mary Robinson, though a former student at the Misses More's Bristol academy, once she became celebrated as "Perdita," Mistress of the Prince of Wales—but even so, they could not help being linked in the public mind. They, and their emulators, are the unacknowledged subtext to Mary Wollstonecraft's *Vindication of the Rights of Woman* (1792), their achieved and independent excellence intimating a radical reordering of existing social institutions.

The dates of the six poets are instructive, for only one of them—Mary Robinson—died relatively young; Anna Barbauld lived until 1825, Helen Maria Williams until 1827, and Hannah More until 1833. And they were followed by a second generation of women poets who likewise confound our normative assumptions about the chronology of Romanticism. These are the dates of a handful of the most prominent: Joanna Baillie (1762–1851); Mary Betham (1776–1852); Margaret Hodson (1778–1852)—truly of a second generation, she dedicated her historical epic, *Margaret of Anjou,* in 1816 to her mother Margaret Holford, whose *Gresford Vale* was published in 1798; Mary Russell Mitford (1787–1855); Amelia Opie (1769–1853); Sydney Owenson, afterward Lady Morgan (1783–1859); Caroline Bowles Southey (1786–1854); Jane West (1758–1852). These are not only long-lived women, but for the most part they published far into the Victorian period and it would appear more productively and influentially than any male Romantic contemporary, with the exception of Leigh Hunt. Here, too, were it to be pursued, is a second missing link, only less important than the first because the terms were by this point so firmly set and the energy was so self-fulfilling. Still, in the writings of the two most famous women poets of this generation, Felicia Hemans and Letitia Landon, who died respectively in 1835 and 1838, we can discern what is otherwise almost strikingly absent in the male Romantic universe, an actual transition into the characteristic preoccupations of Victorian verse. Since, moreover, Hemans and Landon were the first women to earn a sizable income from writing only poetry, being accorded recognition in the public mind as professional poets, their success, whatever value we place on it today, testifies to a major transformation in the world of British letters. In fifty years women had come from the margins of that world to an assured, professional place at its center.

Hemans and Landon, to be sure, paid a price for their celebrity, at once fulfilling and defining a literary niche that, however important historically, may explain, if not exactly justify, their later neglect. For the bourgeois public of the 1820s and 1830s their names were synonymous with the notion of a poetess, celebrating hearth and home, God and country in mellifluous verse that relished the sentimental and seldom teased anyone into thought. There are other and darker strains in their voluminous production—a focus on exile and failure, a celebration of female genius frustrated, a haunting omnipresence of death—that seem to subvert the role they claimed and invite a sophisticated reconsideration of their work against the complex background of the transition between Romantic and Victorian poetic modes. But such an analysis must itself depend on our understanding of their principal inheritance, which is not that of the British Romanticism that died young but rather of a half-century of women writers who determinedly invaded a male fiefdom and reconceived its polity. On the surface the interests of these poets seem little different from the dominant poetic genres and modes of thought we associate with their time. They wrote satires as well as sonnets, tragedies along with *vers de société;* a few even wrote epics.[4] But to look with attention and historical discrimination is to realize that some of the genres we associate most closely with British Romanticism, notably the revival of the sonnet and the creation of the metrical tale, were themselves strongly impelled by women poets; that some of the distinctive preoccupations of women poets eventually color the landscape we think of as Romantic; and that others are so decidedly different as to suggest a terra incognita beneath our very feet.

NOTES

The research and writing of this essay were made possible by a fellowship, sponsored by the National Endowment for the Humanities, from the Henry E. Huntington Library, San Marino, California.

1. [William Harness], *Blackwood's,* 16 (1824); 162.

2. *Thoughts on the Condition of Women, and on the Injustice of Mental Subordination,* 2nd ed. (London: Longman's 1799), pp. 95–96. The first edition of this work was published under the pseudonymn Anne Frances Randall: although conclusive proof of Mary Robinson's authorship has not been advanced, the attribution is venerable. For the identities of the writers cited, consult *A Dictionary of British and American Women Writers: 1660–1800,* ed. Janet Todd (Totowa, N.J.: Rowman and Allenheld, 1985).

3. On the novelists, see Katherine M. Rogers, *Feminism in Eighteenth-Century England* (Urbana: University of Illinois Press, 1982), pp. 22ff. After the withdrawal of

Sheridan, the backbone of the London theater was supplied by such women as Frances Brooke, Hannah Parkhurst Cowley, Elizabeth Inchbald, and Hannah More, not to ignore the signal contribution of Sarah Siddons in giving professional and social respectability to a theatrical career.

4. Although this list is probably incomplete, the following ten poets, ranging from the mid-1780s to the mid-1820s, were authors of poems of epic ambition: Elizabeth Barrett, Sophia Burrell, Hannah Cowley, Charlotte Elizabeth Dixon, Elizabeth Hands, Margaret Hodson, Mary Linwood, Eleanor Ann Porden, Elizabeth Smith (of Birmingham), and Helen Maria Williams.

L. J. SWINGLE

The Romantic Emergence: Multiplication of Alternatives and the Problem of Systematic Entrapment

Philosophic critics, aware of the extraordinary complexity of the European eighteenth-century civilization out of which romanticism emerged, were among the first to react against the Yale school's formalistic apocalypticism—which of course took distinctly different forms in the work of Harold Bloom, Geoffrey Hartman, and Paul De Man. L. J. Swingle's landmark essay, "On Reading Romantic Poetry" (1971), has often been cited and several times reprinted. In it he proposed what was then a radical rethinking of the presuppositions underlying the romantic intellectual sensibility. By establishing how and why romantic poems were concerned more with "data" than with "dogma," Swingle started a new direction of romantic criticism that moved steadily away from the deconstructive misreadings of Paul de Man, the structuralist diagrams of Northrop Frye, and the "traditional" literary-historical analyses of M. H. Abrams and Earl Wasserman. Swingle's own analyses, however, were congruent with some of the most important cultural studies of scholars concerned with Europe as a whole, not just Britain. Most notable among these commentators, perhaps, were Morse Peckham, whose position is decisively articulated in *Beyond the Tragic Vision* (1962), and Isaiah Berlin, whose diverse cultural studies are well-represented in the collections *Against the Current* (1980) and *The Crooked Timber of Humanity* (1990). Recent studies of romantic culture compatible with Swingle's position include Alan Bewell's *Wordsworth and the Enlightenment* (1989) and Theresa M. Kelley's *Wordsworth's Revisionary Aesthetics* (1988).

The present essay was published in *Modern Language Quarterly* in 1978 and incorporated into Swingle's book, *The Obstinate Questionings of English Romanticism* (1987). Swingle's work suggests why so much recent commentary on romantic poetry resists summary. Most critics now regularly begin from premises akin to what Swingle describes as the romantic situation: writers faced not the disappearance of a system, but the burgeoning of a plethora of attractively competing systems. Critics must, therefore, occupy themselves with density of detail (as illustrated by most of the essays in this collection) and display a self-awareness adequate to the poets' exploratory efforts to "deliver the mind from its manacles by recalling. . . . the possibility of

From *Modern Language Quarterly* 39, no. 3 (September 1978): 264–283. Copyright © 1978 by the University of Washington. Reprinted by permission of the publisher.

alternatives . . . that one *can* think differently" (50). One may note, for example, how Rajan in her essay on Shelley's "Triumph of Life," which we have included in this collection, radically revises de Man's approach through her awareness of what Swingle would see as Shelley's characteristically romantic fear of self-enthrallment.

Indeed, most of the essays in this collection recognize in one fashion or another that for both romantic poet and romantic reader the central quest is, as Swingle puts it, "to gain control over the products of the mind's ordering impulse by rediscovering access to the activities of that impulse itself" (53). It is this perspective which is largely responsible for current focus on psychological analysis as a means of illuminating historical circumstances, a focus to which Jonathan Arac calls attention in his essay in our Wordsworth section, and which is almost paradigmatically illustrated by Andrew Cooper's psychohistorical description of the Shelleys' and Byron's first interactions in "Chains, Pains, and Tentative Gains: The Byronic Prometheus in the Summer of 1816," *Studies in Romanticism* 27, no. 4 (1988), 529–550.

Hypotheses about fundamental characteristics of the eighteenth century commonly exert strong influence on theories of Romanticism. Our older "attributional construction of Romantic theory," as Morse Peckham has termed it,[1] was given to building up theories of Romanticism on the basis of supposed antithetical relations between eighteenth-century and Romantic thought. Comparative analysis would reduce the rich complexity of eighteenth-century intellectual phenomena to some simple system of "essential" attributes; and then Romanticism would emerge as the embodiment of some equally simple but contrasting system of attributes. Thus association of the eighteenth century with such attributes as Reason, Restraint, and Society would generate a Romanticism associated with such contrasting attributes as Imagination, Freedom, and Individualism. When Romantic scholars were in control of the associational deal, Romanticism of course tended to be dealt the better hand. One recalls the old joke about defining Romanticism as a warm, mammalian profundity bursting forth winsomely from the reptilian coils of eighteenth-century neoclassicism.

Increasing recognition of the usual crudity of this attributional deal has prompted, in more recent years, a movement to change the theoretical game. Surveying the state of Romantic theory in 1970, for example, Peckham insisted that "the older attempts to build up a theory of Romanticism by discovering and listing sets of attributes must necessarily fail" because "what the Romantics had in common was a problem," not some fixed set of dogmas or propensities. According to this view, then, the "problem of understanding Romanticism is the problem of locating with accuracy its problem" (p. 217). This problematic orientation to Romantic theory seems to me fruitful; and I wish to pursue it in the following essay.

Like the older attributional theory, the problematic theory of the Romantic emergence is grounded in notions about things going on in eighteenth-century thought. Our most influential movements in the direction of problematic theory have gravitated toward the common notion of associating the eighteenth century with some process of disintegration—whereby Romanticism is then understood to inherit some problem in reintegration. One recalls the catch phrase popularized some years back by R. A. Foakes: "Order out of Chaos: The Task of the Romantic Poet."[2] Hypotheses have varied concerning the nature of this eighteenth-century "chaos" and Romantic impulse to "order"; but the fundamental chaos/order syndrome remains a most conspicuous element in problematic Romantic theory. Peckham, for example, has associated the eighteenth century with exhaustion of "logical possibilities of identifying Nature with order and value," from which follows the Romantic problem of "reconstituting value."[3] Earl R. Wasserman has argued for the phenomenon of a gradual breakdown of traditional "cosmic syntax" during the eighteenth century, from which follows the Romantic problem of developing a "subtler language."[4] One thinks too of Wasserman's subsequent essay, "The English Romantics: The Grounds of Knowledge," which posits the "impotence of later eighteenth-century poetic epistemology," from which follows the Romantic problem of discovering a "significant relationship between the subjective and objective worlds."[5] This manner of thinking continues to exert significant influence upon more recent Romantic criticism. Thus in Michael G. Cooke's recent study of *The Romantic Will*, one encounters the following idea: in neoclassicism "No man is an island; and it is therefore necessary to look at the self in the light of the system (in the romantic period, I might interject, the self is seen rather in search of a system."[6] Underlying this sentence, of course, is the notion that "system" somehow breaks down during the eighteenth century, and that the Romantics thus inherit the problem of building up system again from the ashes of that presumed eighteenth-century disintegration.

I think there are several reasons for being cautious about enthusiastically entertaining views of Romanticism built up from such theories of problematic grounds. First of all, I am made uneasy by the fact that this particular orientation to problematic theory seems to commit almost as much violence upon the body of eighteenth-century complexity as did the older attributional theories. If in the older theories the eighteenth century tended to suffer reptilian debasements for the sake of Romantic apotheosis, in the newer theories the eighteenth century is made to play dying animal for the sake of Romantic problematics. Much scholarly effort has been devoted recently to combating the old notion of the eighteenth-century progress as manifesting simply the decline of an aged neoclassical system. Instead of viewing the mid-eighteenth century as merely a sort of low and uncertain ebb between the two rising tides of neoclassicism and Romanticism, we have been encouraged rather persuasively to consider the period an age that possesses its own distinctive potency and aggressive character.[7] To begin thinking again of the eighteenth-century progress in terms of "impotence" and "exhaustion" suggests a return to some very dubious notions about eighteenth-century complexities. One has to wonder, therefore, whether a sufficiently just and accurate approach to Romantic phenomena can be built up from such questionable axioms about problematic origins.

Still more significant, however, is the fact that this association of the eighteenth-century progress with processes of exhaustion and impotence gives rise to puzzling questions. First, by what mysterious process does the Romantic phoenix rise up from eighteenth-century ashes? For the sake of argument let us grant that "eighteenth-century poetry hedged on" the epistemological problem: "the problem of the transaction between the perceiving mind and the perceived world was either evaded or left uneasily indecisive in descriptive verse."[8] But then just what occurs to generate a Romantic reaction against such hedging? Perhaps one might appeal to some vision of "natural law" here, positing that a hedge can flourish only so long before a "natural" reaction sets in. But the mind hesitates to give up critical analysis to natural ghosts like this (it is a bit like eighteenth-century appeals to something called phlogiston). A second question has to do with where we place revolutionary phenomena in this problematic conception of Romanticism's emergence out of the eighteenth century. If we associate the eighteenth century with those processes of enervation that generate problems of recovery, and if we then associate Romanticism with activities of wrestling with those problems and seeking some means of solving them, then what do we do with the outbursts of energy, confidence, and unhesitating insistence that Answers Are at Hand which characterize the revolutionary "spirit of the age" in later decades of the eighteenth century? M. H. Abrams, among others, has forcefully reminded us that the "formative age of Romantic poetry was clearly one of apocalyptic expectations, or at least apocalyptic imaginings."[9] For critics like Abrams, in other words, Romanticism emerges out of an energetic bang, not out of a whimper of exhaustion and perplexity. The puzzle is how to reconcile this vision of explosive energy with the vision of decay and groping rebirth that tends to characterize problematic theories of Romanticism.

Difficulties of this sort suggest there is something amiss in the orientation of problematic theory. I think we need to change this orientation by inverting our way of thinking about what the eighteenth-century progess bequeaths to the Romantics. Instead of conceiving of the eighteenth century as passing on some sort of intellectual desolation to the Romantics, a landscape of mental ruins upon which the Romantics were forced to build new systems of thought and value, we need to consider the possibility that the Romantics really inherit a state of intellectual overabundance. The eighteenth century burdens the Romantics not with too little, but rather with too much. Instead of impotence, exhaustion, the disintegration of system, Romanticism involves confrontation with the embarrassments of an overproductive mental potency. Romanticism's problem is an eighteenth-century proliferation of systems and, following from that, a multiplication of seemingly viable but conflicting alternatives.

Instead of associating the eighteenth century with some process of enervation and decay, we do better to associate it with contrary processes of multiple development. The eighteenth century offers a hospitable environment for the growth of diverse systems of thought and value: old systems continue to command allegiance; but at the same time new systems (or new variations of still older systems) emerge and find space in which to flourish. It is, after all, that age in which both a Rousseau and a Voltaire could cultivate their considerable gardens; and yet it is also that age in which the gardens of Versailles could maintain a considerable body of cultivators as well. During the course of the eighteenth century, many of the knavish or foolish systems that the company of Pope and Swift consigned fondly to realms of darkness manage either to find their own spots in the sun, or, still more cleverly, to render darkness a desirable habitation. The man of feeling as well as the man of reason, good sense and sensibility, the call of the wild and conversation in the coffee house—all manage to gain or to maintain their eager or decorous followings during the century. The plain dealer might receive satisfaction from

The School for Scandal, where investigation of surfaces results in the triumph of Charles over his sentiment-strewing brother, Joseph. But the flowers of sentimental rhetoric find more sympathetic soil in Sterne's *Sentimental Journey.* The devotee of imagination might find Johnson's warning against the dangerous prevalence of imagination in *Rasselas* heavy reading; but he could take consolation from Johnson's awareness of that prevalence, and he could close his Johnson and open his Mark Akenside or William Collins. The admirer of Pope might lament the fortunes of the heroic couplet while skimming through Edward Young or Percy's *Reliques;* but he could recover some degree of faith in the right order of things by turning to the verse of Johnson or that of Crabbe. It is with such multiplication of alternatives that we should associate the eighteenth-century background of the Romantic emergence.

If, taking a very broad view, we observe that the eighteenth century begins in satire and ends in revolution, we may of course consider that this progress implies a disintegration of order. But closer thought suggests that this argument betrays a limited, party viewpoint. A more objective view would observe in that progress a proliferation of seriously competing systems of order. For an Alexander Pope, the pen can be mightier than the sword because those Tibbalds who know not their own point are piddling. A revolutionary "spirit of the age" develops when the Tibbalds have managed to consolidate sufficient influence *and* when the Popes have managed to retain sufficient influence for a state of highly charged indeterminacy to develop. Revolutions do not emerge simply out of the decay of some predominant system and an atmosphere of disintegration. Quite the reverse: revolutionary atmospheres develop in a cauldron of multiple-party expansion and maturation, wherein it has become increasingly uncertain which party is the piddler. Revolutionary atmospheres are characterized by energetic expressions of confidence, belief, and exertions in behalf of order—but when different parties have developed conflicting yet seemingly equally potent conceptions of what that order is. That the eighteenth century evolves into such a revolutionary atmosphere should serve to remind us that the period is more sensibly to be associated with processes of proliferation than with disintegration.

This proliferation of competing orders exerts significant pressures upon the mind; and it is with the nature of these pressures that we must particularly concern ourselves in thinking about the emergence of Romanticism. From such dogmatic formulas as "One truth is clear, 'Whatever is, is right,' " eighteenth-century thought evolves in the direction of such revolutionary formulas as "We hold these truths to be self-evident." What has shifted here is the mind's awareness of the possibility that alternative *systems* of truth might be seriously entertained by thought. In Pope's intellectual environment, the only matter at issue is a distinction between "clear" thinking and muddled thinking: clear thinking leads to "one" truth, muddled thinking to error; and what "we hold" (or they hold) is no factor in intellectual calculation, because intellectually viable alternative systems are not granted the possibility of existence. But in the revolutionary formula, such alternative systems are acknowledged (just as, toward the close of the eighteenth century, it began to appear that non-Euclidean as well as Euclidean geometries might need to be acknowledged). Thus, while "we hold" *these* truths to be self-evident, there is by implication some "they" out there busily holding some other system of truths equally self-evident. And the fact that both "we" and "they" are holding *different* truths to be self-evident means that mere clarity of thought alone is no longer the basis upon which commitment to one system or another may be determined. Both "we" and "they" may think with apparent clarity without ever reconciling our systems or exposing the error of the one and validity of the other, because our thoughts are operating within the confines of different geometries, or different languages. Our argument now is over fundamental axioms, the postulates we *hold* true, prior to the generation of our differing systems of theorems or sentences.

Now this mental situation is really quite different from seemingly like situations that occurred in earlier periods of intellectual upheaval. One thinks, most obviously, of those Renaissance proliferations of thought that underlie the intense strain of intellectual contrariety in Shakespearean drama and prompt the mental urgencies of such poems as Donne's *Satire III*. Shakespeare can set an Antony off against a Brutus, for example, disturbing our minds with the generation of seemingly cogent arguments defending the course of action adopted by each of those warring protagonists. But when Shakespeare has Portia appear before Brutus, asking, "Is Brutus sick? . . . No, my Brutus; / You have some sick offence within your mind, / Which, by the right and virtue of my place, / I ought to know of" (*Julius Caesar* II.i.261–70), he gives us to understand that Brutus's direction of thought is in some fundamental respect diseased. Similarly, Donne can unsettle our minds with the exhibition of a confusing array of conflicting theological options in his *Satire III;* but his injunction, nonetheless, is to "Seeke true religion" (43), and he holds out the prospect of the courageous soul's ability to fight its way through these conflicting options, arriving ultimately at the top of that "huge hill, / Cragged, and steep," whereon "Truth stands" (79–80). In both cases the crucial assumption is that somewhere beyond or above the confusions of competing systems which one *might* hold, there remains the one, overriding truth of a single system that the tenacious and healthy mind can attain and *should* hold. This is quite different from the situation developing toward the close of the eighteenth century, wherein the one truth has commenced division and multiplication into systems of "these truths" which "we hold" and those other systems of truths held by some opposing party or parties. In this situation, we find ourselves beginning to stumble down the darkling intellectual path toward Alice and the Cheshire Cat: "Would you tell me, please, which way I ought to go from here?" asks Alice. " 'That depends a good deal on where you want to get to,' said the Cat." Where the mind ought to go depends, first, on where the mind *wants* to get to. The system one follows depends, first on the system one chooses to adopt. The priority of obligation (one recalls Pope's "Our *proper* bliss depends on what we blame" [*An Essay on Man*, 1.282; my italics]) dissolves into the priority of choice. By the late eighteenth century, competing systems are beginning to offer the mind serious options for choice.

The heartland of English Romantic territory, it seems to me, is to be found within the space that opens out between the claims of competing systems. On the one side stands a "we" holding these truths to be self-evident, and on the other side stands a "they" holding alternative truths to be equally self-evident. Out of the middle, then, or the border territory (cf. Wordsworth's *Borderers* and Scott's obsessions with border country) emerges the potentially Romantic mind, somewhat like Everyman in the old play, puzzled to determine what truths, if any, are to be held when the pressure of contrary claims appears equal. What renders the potentially Romantic mind actively Romantic is the persistence of indetermination. Many of those artists we think of as "romantic" indulge in momentary flirtation with commitment to some revolutionary system. One recalls the young Wordsworth composing (but then not publishing) his letter to the Bishop of Llandaff; Shelley advocating the necessity of atheism, and flinging pamphlets down upon the people from his balcony; Blake toying with devotion to the flames of Orc. But these flirtations are not Romanticism; or, alternatively, it is the fact that these journeyings forth from the middle ground amount *only* to flirtation that renders them associable with Romanticism. Romanticism proper is the state of being in the middle, surrounded not by the vacancy of exhaustion but rather by the potent and even strident claims of multiple and competing systems of order, each seemingly valid within itself—were one willing to hold its fundamental postulates to be self-evident.

To extend our earlier mathematical analogy, the Romantic is like a geometrician of traditional inclination whose original impulse is to do geometry, *the* geometry, but who finds himself confronted with two geometries, Euclidean and non-Euclidean, and with the apparent fact that he might work with equal validity within each. A mind oriented to the notion that truth should be a function of the "nature of things," and that systems are thus true or false in relation to that nature of things, confronts an intellectual situation wherein it appears that truth may refer only to coherence within a given system of thinking, and thus that contrary systems might seem to be equally "true." The mind, so it appears, can think coherently in radically opposed ways about the nature of things; and that nature of things, rather than revealing the distinction between the validity of one of those ways and the invalidity of the others, bends itself, plasticlike, into conformity with different systems imposed upon it.

The eighteenth century bequeaths to Romanticism this awareness of perplexities associated with experience of opposed systems of thought; and the so-called failure of the French Revolution, among other things, underscores Romantic suspicion that what data the mind seems able to gather concerning the nature of things may prove insufficient for distinguishing the true system from its false competitors. Writing in 1789, Edmund Burke likened the outbreak of the Revolution to a wild gas that had broken loose; and he opted for suspension of judgment upon whether that outbreak constituted a blessing or a curse "until the first effervescence is a little subsided, till the liquor is cleared, and until we see something deeper than the agitation of a troubled and frothy surface."[10] But the course of the Revolution did not settle arguments between contrary systems of thought. Minds committed to the notion that traditional hierarchical constructions of society are good and proper could discover in the revolutionary bloodbath confirmation of their view that mankind set free is a beast unleashed. But minds committed to the contrary notion that such hierarhcical constructions wrench the essential goodness of mankind into bestial transformations could also discover in that bloodbath confirmation of their view that man had been rendered bestial by generations of tyranny under god, priest, and king. Those reflecting upon the revolutionary period with a firm mental grasp on the self-evidence of this or that system of truths could persist in their different dogmatisms. Those whose grasp was less firm, however, or those who had yet to determine what system to grasp tended to be driven into those realms of more brooding and skeptical reflection that characterize the operation of Romantic thought.

In the remainder of this essay, I will seek to ground the above generalizations in discussion of particular characteristics of Romantic literary art.

Romantic thought is preoccupied, first of all, with competing systems. If we encounter a voice proclaiming *alpha* on Romantic ground, we are most likely to encounter close by some contrary voice defending *omega*. Romantic intellectual life reflects pressure from the antipathies of a late eighteenth-century world of thought: it involves confrontation with a world that has too many answers in it. Romantic life is a tale told by more than one idiot, and the sound and fury signify too much rather than too little. Thus the cottage girl of Wordsworth's "We Are Seven" has her own vision of things, and this vision refuses to accommodate itself to the contrary vision of her adult inquisitor. Keats's Apollonius insists upon seeing Lamia's metamorphosis as accident rather than a change of essence, and so he persists in pronouncing her a serpent; but for Lycius and for the dramatic voice narrating the poem, Lamia's appearance is her essence: "Ha, the serpent! certes, she / Was none" (*Lamia*, 2.80–81). In "The Nightingale," Coleridge invites us to recall the Miltonic vision of that creature: "And hark! the Nightingale begins its song, / 'Most musical, most melancholy' bird!" (12–13). But evocation of this Miltonic vision serves only to evoke in turn a contrary vision, the "different lore" that the poet and his party proclaim: " 'Tis the merry Nightingale" (41–43). Romantic poetry is almost obsessively concerned with "different lore" and, consequently, with stubborn party oppositions. The idealistic naïveté of a Don Juan is set off against the world-weary sophistication of a Byronic narrator; Proverbs of Hell are opposed to the commandments of Heaven; the party of Prometheus is organized in opposition to the party of Jupiter.

Novels of the Romantic period exhibit a similar preoccupation with opposed systems. In William Godwin's *Caleb Williams,* the aristocratic Mr. Falkland plays Heaven to the plebeian Caleb's Hell: "Why do you trifle with me? You little suspect the extent of my power. . . . You might as well think of escaping from the power of the omnipresent God, as from mine!" (Vol. 2, chap. 7). In the *Frankenstein* of Godwin's daughter Mary, Frankenstein and his monster take turns playing Heaven to the other's Hell. Still more significant, to my mind, is the fact that seemingly more conservative novelists of the Romantic period like Sir Walter Scott and Jane Austen exhibit the same sort of structural preoccupations. In Scott's fiction, Mary Shelley's Heaven and Hell metamorphose into such contraries as Whig and Tory, the party of the King and that of the Pretender, supporters of new political accommodations and defenders of the Covenant; and Scott's man in the middle—Henry Morton, for example, in *Old Mortality*—is torn by the same dilemma of conflicting claims of justice and proper allegiance as that which confronts a Walton in the climactic pages of *Frankenstein*. In Austen, of course, such strains are embodied in shapes of less epic or mythic proportion. But Austen is weaving like dilemmas into her seemingly more private, domestic tapestries. In *Emma,* for example, when we find the heroine responding to Mr. Knightley's objections to Frank Churchill with the reminder, "You have not an idea of what is requisite in situations directly opposite to your own" (Vol. 1, chap. 18), we may well call to mind the structuring of "situations directly opposite" that militates against sharing of axioms in Scott's Claverhouse and Burley, in Mary Shelley's Frankenstein and Monster, in, for that matter, a Blakean Angel and Devil. Like other literary artists of her period, Austen is preoccupied with problems that evolve from consolidations of thought into systems of fundamental opposition. Thus in another passage from *Emma,* when Mr. Woodhouse expresses bewilderment over what seems to him the chaotic atmosphere of his son-in-law's household, Emma responds with the significant observation: "That is the case with us all, papa. One half of the world cannot understand the pleasures of the other" (Vol. 1, chap. 9). The world gets divided into halves, and each becomes an order, The Order, unto itself.[11]

Austen touches on the heart of the Romantic matter in the passages quoted above. Romanticism is hardly alone of course in cleaving experience into different parties—Heaven/Hell, Spirit/Body, King/People, Reason/Imagination. But what is peculiarly Romantic, I would argue, is the inclination to think of these parties as differing so fundamentally at the axiomatic level that each becomes a viable system unto itself and a mystery to systems beyond itself. When antipathy between parties is no longer viewed simply as a struggle between righteousness and perversity or between clear and erroneous thought or action, when antipathy is viewed, instead, as a function of each party's radical inability to understand the other—"You have not an idea of what is requisite in situations directly opposite your own"—then we begin moving into the intellectual atmosphere of Romantic thought. In Romanticism, the voice of Hell does not oppose the voice of Heaven with the slogan, "Evil, be thou my Good." To the contrary, both Heaven and Hell are righteously defending Good against the onslaughts of Evil. Their dispute traces to disjunction among axioms, the one party holding certain 'truths' to be self-evident which render it incapable of entertaining the contrary "truths" of the opposition party. Thus in Scott's *Old Mortality,* for example, lines of opposition are drawn between the forces of Claverhouse, representing the King's party, and the forces of Burley, representing the Covenanters. Both Claverhouse and Burley think of themselves as champions of Good; their antipathy traces to axiomatic differences in defining this Good. Claverhouse himself admits that he and Burley are "both fanatics." But, he goes on, "there is some distinction between the fanaticism of honour and that of dark and sullen superstition" (chap. 35). In Burley's vocabulary of thought, however, the "honour" of a Claverhouse translates into idolatrous devotion to Mammon, and "dark and sullen superstition" translates into heroic devotion to the inward light. The one party's light is the other party's dark; but each party is, according to its own light, seeking to prevail over darkness.

This uneasy awareness that any one party's light may be some other party's darkness cultivates in Romantic thought suspicions about the sufficiency of any given system of thought. Thus we encounter a kind of paradox: generalized Romantic awareness of the existence of multiple possibilities of thought tends to engender fear in particular situations that the mind may not be recognizing some alternative, and hence that it is drifting into a trap of blind fanaticism. After all, if thought begins to proceed in any given direction, does this not mean that it has turned away from, blinded itself to, the cogent claims of some other direction? Any act of mental assertion, then, may seem to be entangling the mind within boundaries of some particular vocabulary of thought which thereby render it incapable of understanding that "one half of the world" lying beyond those boundaries.

Among Romantic poets, it is Blake who is most sensitive to the fundamental dynamics of this problem. In *The First Book of Urizen,* the primal Fall is precipitated by the emergence of a voice:

I have sought for a joy without pain,
For a solid without fluctuation.
Why will you die, O Eternals?
Why live in unquenchable burnings?
                    (54–57)

This Urizenic voice casts a "shadow of horror" in Eternity (1–2), not because it promulgates the particular system it does, but because it promulgates system as such. Prior to Urizen's emergence,

Earth was not, nor globes of attraction.
The will of the Immortal expanded
Or contracted his all-flexible senses;
Death was not, but eternal life sprung.
                    (36–39)

Urizen seeks to give a *meaning* to this eternal activity, proposing value distinctions and a goal to be gained. But in so doing, he gives rise to "globes of attraction": creation of a quest generates also a quantity or context distinguished from and negated by that quest, as the isolation of *A* involves generation of *Not-A*. The Urizenic globe of attraction—a system of thought whereby expansion means ill rather than good, "all-flexible" means "fluctuation" and "death" rather than desirable fertility—produces, first, an act of isolation, and then a contrary globe of attraction whereby Urizenic ill becomes Orcean good. Thus of course the original expansion and contraction of the Immortal will persist (like Pope's earlier Great Chain, it cannot be fundamentally disrupted); but now the activity of will divides along lines of contrary party allegiances, the one party gathering under the banner of contraction and the other under the banner of expansion. Each party is sincerely devoted to the cause of truth and righteousness; but each party speaks a different language, and neither can understand the other.

Since the publication of Robert Langbaum's influential study of *The Poetry of Experience* in 1957, it has been popular to pursue the notion that Romanticism invokes tests of experience as a means of resolving such confusions of mind. But actually, the appeal to experience is much more a mid-eighteenth-century phenomenon than a Romantic one. Experience may be invoked to persuade us that cultivation of one's garden yields more pistachio nuts than does argument over whether this be the best or worst of possible worlds; and experience may serve to reveal that Tom Jones is a better fellow than his rival Blifil. But experience does not demonstrate that Frankenstein's monster, for example, is either the good-natured creature he claims to be or the foul fiend Frankenstein claims him to be.[12] The problem is Romanticism's suspicion that the basic premises of thought mold understanding of experience, rather than the other way around. Thus the important line with which Blake marks our introduction to the world of his *Songs of Innocence and of Experience:* "And I stained the water clear" ("Introduction" to *Songs of Innocence,* 18). However one reads this line—whether one takes it to mean that clear water is stained dark or that dark water is stained clear—the fundamental point Blake makes here is that the very act of composition, voicing an awareness—*any* awareness—of experience, involves coloring (or bleaching) a precompositional nature of things.

The song the mind sings constructs the "reality" it perceives; and the mind's singing of its particular song tends to inhibit thought from entertaining other understandings of the world. Thus Blake's *Songs:* in the language of Innocence, for example, the act of "guarding" someone is perceived as protecting him from harm; but in the language of Experience that same act implies confinement, as in a prison. For Innocence, "white as snow" means purity; but for Experience it implies lack of life-giving warmth, absence of color, barren sterility. Instead of appearing the humble handmaiden mediating between the mind and experience, then, the vocabulary of thought begins to look like the master. This very mastery, of course, may be understood in contrary ways, depending upon whether thought sings in the language of Innocence or in that of Experience. For the mind operating within an Innocent vocabulary of thought, "a tender voice, / Making all the vales rejoice" ("The Lamb," 7–8), is a lovely expression of the proper and desirable impulse to order, the power of the word gathering up life's divisions into a union of celebration. But for a mind tuned to the vocabulary of Experience, sensitive to the biting chords of "mind-forged manacles" ("London," 8), that word "Making" in "The Lamb" sounds like the clenching of a kid-gloved fist, and "tender" has a nasty, ironic ring to it.

Romantic concern with competition among alternative systems of thought leads, then, to meditation upon the extent to which a given vocabulary of thought exerts dominion over the mind. And this leads literary Romanticism, in turn, toward meditations on both the weakness and the power of language. The weakness of language seems to reveal itself in contexts wherein conspicuous absence of a controlling voice encourages multiple systems to compete for expression of the same object. One thinks of Shelley's lament in his "Hymn to Intellectual Beauty":

No voice from some sublimer world hath ever
    To sage or poet these responses given—
    Therefore the names of Demon, Ghost, and Heaven,
Remain the records of their vain endeavor,
Frail spells. . . .

(25–29)

We may recall, too, the discouraging product of the inconclusive debate in Wordsworth's "We Are Seven": " 'Twas throwing words away," the adult inquisitor finally mutters in exasperation (67). The potency of language may appear to exhaust itself in competition. Words begin to seem mere incantation of "Frail spells"—ignorant armies of names that clash by night. Hence the "Darkness" of Keats's sonnet "Why Did I Laugh?": "O Darkness! Darkness! ever must I moan, / To question Heaven and Hell and Heart in vain" (7–8). Once the mind stands back from the contention of contrary voices, contemplating the confusion of dogmas among parties which claim sanctions of Hell and Heart as well as Heaven, then it runs the danger of falling into total disenchantment. Just as new Presbyter can begin looking like old Priest writ large, so Heaven, Hell, and Heart can come to seem aspirants (or, better, only aspirates) of the same dubious value. This sense of linguistic frailty may help to account for the romantic poet's interest in nonlinguistic arts: perhaps music or painting or the plastic arts can express a tale more sweetly than rhyme. It may also help to account for the still more fundamental inclination of the Romantic poet to associate art with expression of a *tale,* particularly. When the adequacy of language becomes suspect, then the mind's impulse may be to fall back in the direction of the most primitive form of attempted communication, "acting things out." Romantic inclination toward narrative art reflects an inclination of literary thought in this direction.

On the other hand, however, Romantic literary thought cannot of course completely free itself from the bonds of language. When Wordsworth writes, "Imagination—here the Power so called / Through sad incompetence of human speech" (1850 *Prelude,* 6.592–93), he expresses a Romantic literary predicament: our speech may be sadly incompetent, but some word must be employed to address that power which rises from the mind's abyss. Faced, therefore, with the unavoidable necessity of operating within linguistic confines, literary Romanticism confronts the dangerous potency inherent in that language which the mind cannot help employing. Names may be frail spells; but to the mind perforce engaged in naming things, those spells threaten to become extremely strong. A fundamental problem attendant upon Romanticism, then, is how to weave the spells of language without becoming helplessly enchanted by them, how to work competently with the sad incompetence of human speech. Wordsworth notes in his third *Essay upon Epitaphs* that "Words are too awful an instrument for good and evil to be trifled with: they hold above all other external powers a dominion over thoughts."[13] The problem, if that dominion be inescapable, is to find means of breaking free from tyrannical despotism and of turning the potency of language to advantage.

In the penultimate line of Blake's "The Sick Rose," a lamenting singer refers with bitter irony to the "dark secret *love*" (my italics) through which the invading worm works to "destroy" the life of the rose. However, the singer's irony here calls attention to a way of thinking about the relations between worm and rose that differs considerably from that which the singer himself entertains. What the lamenting gardener (or perhaps father, or worshiper, or even would-be lover) sees as devastation of his beloved object's purity might be viewed, alternatively, as an act of fulfillment, quite literally as an act of love, between male and female elements of a natural process wherein destruction is actually perpetuation of ongoing life. In Keats's *La Belle Dame sans Merci,* the knight-at-arms says of the faery's child he has encountered in the meads, "She look'd at me *as* she did love, / And made sweet *moan*" (19–20; my italics), and then later, "And *sure in language strange* she said— / 'I love thee true' " (26–27; my italics). As in the Blake lyric, Keats's employment of these phrases serves to alert the mind to a manner of thinking that is at odds with the one being expressed by the dramatic voice addressing us in the poem. Could this faery child's "language strange" be understood, we are encouraged to muse, then it might convey to us a much less amiable vision of her encounter with our forceful and single-minded knight.

As Austen's heroine puts it, one half of the world cannot understand the pleasures of the other: what looks like joy to the world's knights may look like rapine to the world's faery children; and what looks like rapine to the world's gardeners may look like love to the worms and roses of the world. The specter of enthrallment to such single-minded perception haunts Romantic literary art, and it generates Romantic concern for cultivating awareness that there either are or may be significant alternatives to any given manner of thinking about a given issue or phenomenon. Hence Romantic determination to seek out and give due attention to some "language strange" that might wrench the mind free from blind submission to the limits of whatever familiar language it is tempted to employ and to trust without question. "With what strange utterance did the loud dry wind / Blow through my ear!" exclaims Wordsworth in *The Prelude* (1.337–38). The Romantic mind strives to tune the ear to strange utterance. It listens to the confessions of opium eaters and justified sinners. It tries to hear the "ghostly language of the ancient earth" (*Prelude,* 2.309); and it entertains speculations about learning "the language of another world" (*Manfred,* III.iv.7). It attends to the voice of the Idiot Boy: "The cocks did crow to-whoo, to-whoo, / And the sun did shine so cold" (450–51). It teases the mind out of human thought and into confrontation with the tautological utterance of a Grecian Urn.

The purpose of such Romantic strains is not, as some older criticism believed, to lead the mind into uncommon Revelation; it is, instead to deliver the mind from its manacles by recalling thought to the prima facie possibility of alternatives. Thus, for example, in his much-misunderstood *Excursion,* Wordsworth weaves an extremely complex drama out of confrontation between the "bitter language of the heart" (3.462) and the consolatory language of a reasoning and distanced intellectual perspective. As more recent Romantic criticism has begun to recognize, the conflict in the poem does not resolve itself so readily as was once supposed into distinctions between error and right reason.[14] Instead, *The Excursion* is a dramatic meditation on the persistence of irresolution; it exhibits closer relations with a Johnsonian "Conclusion, In Which Nothing Is Concluded" than with a Popean "One truth is clear." The bitter language of the heart is not silenced in *The Excursion,* nor is the voice of consolation delivered over to despondency. It is our observing mind rather than the minds of the Solitary and the Wanderer which experiences significant modification; and this modification has to do with heightened sensitivity to the fact that argument proves incapable of mediating between the radically different ways in which the mind can view the same object. In a significant passage from Book 3, we find the Solitary responding to one of the Wanderer's consolatory effusions:

> "Forgive me, if I say
> That an appearance which hath raised your minds
> To an exalted pitch (the self-same cause
> Different effect producing) is for me
> Fraught rather with depression than delight."
>   (152–156)

As the passage suggests, Wordsworth's Solitary and Wanderer are a variant of the recurring Romantic drama: like Blake's voice of Innocence and voice of Experience, Scott's Claverhouse and Burley, Shelley's Prometheus and Jupiter, they are manifestations of the mind's tendency to become enthralled within boundaries of some given fanaticism (color the world light or color it dark, proclaim it fire or proclaim it ice) from which it is not readily moved.

We are the ones being moved by these dramas of contrary immobility and irresolution. The reader and the Romantic artist behind the literary manipulation are delivered into a moment's free mental space beyond enthrallment by virtue of simultaneous experience of competing enthrallments. When the tyranny of words is pitted against itself, in that space wherein both Innocence and Experience (for example) are played off against each other before the mind's eye, consciousness carves out some room for itself in which it can evade blind submission. The Romantic question then becomes, however, what further is to be done—what more, if anything, can be achieved—with this hard-won and fragile free space?

With this question we move into the realm of what are most profitably thought of as Romantic*isms*. One obvious possibility is to try to make for oneself within this free space a permanent home of indeterminacy. Thus we find Keats toying with his famous notion of *"Negative Capability, that is when man is capable of being in uncertainties, Mysteries, doubts, without any irritable reaching after fact & reason."*[15] Another obvious possibility is, as it were, to beat the problem at its own game and to create for oneself within the middle space so potent a system that it wards off all other systems that might pretend to encroach upon it. Thus we find Blake, through his projection Los, asserting, "I must create a system, or be enslaved by another man's" (*Jerusalem,* pl. 10:20). Different Romantics, and individual Romantics at different times, toy with widely varying responses to the question. One thinks of Coleridge's wandering pursuit of "that eternal language, which thy God / Utters" ("Frost at Midnight," 60–61), or of Wordsworth's musings upon the "humour of the game" ("To the Same Flower," 15), or of Byron's flirtation with the possibility of radical self-control in *Manfred,* then of radical accident in *Don Juan:* "I never know the word which will come next" (9.328). Romanticism divides, in other words, into a serpentine network of different movements—complex responses to an anxious intellectual situation wherein the mind is inclined to view any given movement as suspect.

Up to a point, however, it is profitable to speak of some singular pattern of mental tendencies which can be called Romanticism. This Romanticism is not, to be sure, the "Movement" that our college course catalogues still like to term it, which verbal banner conjures up visions of hordes of true believers storming the heretical neoclassical fortress. Nor is it to be so readily associated with problems of reconstituting order, discovering a philosophy, establishing a system of value, as some tendencies in recent Romantic scholarship are wont to posit. Romanticism is associable, first of all, with considerable distrust of orders, philosophies, systems as such—distrust of them in principle, because they look suspiciously like mental entrapments to a Romantic consciousness. Much of the energy of Romanticism is channeled into tactical exercises designed to keep such entrapments at arm's (or mind's) length.

All this has significant implications, it seems to me, for determining how one should approach works of Romantic literature. We need to be much less anxious to discover conceptual conclusions or propositional endpoints in a Romantic work ("He prayeth best, who loveth best," for example, or "Beauty is truth, truth beauty"), and we need, instead, to focus much more attention upon the play of language that surrounds, qualifies, casts into question the mind's inclination to accept these conclusions. Instead of thinking of the Romantic artist as a discoverer of conceptual havens for the mind, we might more fruitfully think of him as an explorer of the spaces that exist between the claims of opposing conceptual havens. The Romantic artist is more given to the manipulation than to the inculcation of systems of thought and value; he employs systems to set up perimeters to, rather than goals for, the mind's activity. And it is the mind's activity within these perimeters that becomes the proper focus of attention.

As a sort of corollary to this proposition, it follows that we should be much less easy in our minds about recognizing supposedly stable points of reference in Romantic literature. The history of Romantic scholarship is marked by the gradual increase of awareness that Blake's Los, Coleridge's Mariner, Keats's Porphyro are not so unambiguously normative as one might at first take them to be, that Wordsworth's "love of Nature" may not be so pure as earlier critics thought, that Shelley's Prometheus may not be so unbound as he seems at the conclusion of *Prometheus Unbound*. Most of us are only beginning to recognize that Jane Austen's reference points are a little less stable than we once thought: Mr. Knightley, for example, may have more night in him than at first appears. Some day, whenever the perennially announced Scott revival comes to pass, good critical minds will begin looking more carefully into Scott's dialectics of Past and Present, and discovering there more tension than is now generally recognized. We could hasten this rather slow and haphazard development of recognitions if, at the outset, we approach the complexity of Romantic literature with less distorting presuppositions.

When Keats bids adieu to his Nightingale, the reaction is one not of loss but of gain. Like Angel or Devil, Solitary or Wanderer, Lamia or Apollonius, the Nightingale represents an apparent refuge for thought to which the mind is tempted to commit itself. But this refuge is a temptation, urging the mind on toward conviction; and convictions are what prison sentences are made of. When Keats draws back with the words, "Forlorn! the very word is like a bell / To toll me back from thee to my sole self," there is a significant verbal pun on the word "sole." The analogue is Faust, whose soul is drawn back from the cup of poison by the sound of bells and choirs, and a chorus of angels singing, "Christ is arisen!" The inclination of Romanticism is to rise beyond enticing solutions and to occupy spaces wherein the persistence of alternatives seems to offer promise of the soul's freedom.

NOTES

1. "On Romanticism: Introduction," *SIR*, 9 (1970), 218.
2. The title of the third chapter of Foakes's study, *The Romantic Assertion* (New Haven: Yale University Press, 1958).
3. "Toward a Theory of Romanticism: II. Reconsiderations," *SIR*, 1 (1961), 4–5; see also Peckham's *Triumph of Romanticism* (Columbia: University of South Carolina Press, 1970), pp. 132–33 *et passim*.
4. *The Subtler Language* (Baltimore: Johns Hopkins Press, 1959), chap. 1.
5. *SIR*, 4 (1964), 20, 33.
6. New Haven: Yale University Press, 1976, p. 58.
7. See, for example, Northrop Frye's influential essay, "Towards Defining an Age of Sensibility," *ELH*, 23 (1956), 144–52.
8. Wasserman, "The English Romantics," p. 18.
9. "English Romanticism: The Spirit of the Age," in *Romanticism Reconsidered*, ed. Northrop Frye (New York: Columbia University Press, 1963), p. 37.
10. *Reflections on the Revolution in France*, ed. Thomas H. D. Mahoney, Library of Liberal Arts (Indianapolis: Bobbs-Merrill, 1955), p. 9.
11. Some colleagues may want to question me about whether Austen and Scott are actually "Romantic" enough, in the view of that term I am proposing, to be given the weight I allow them here. I think they are, although I admit we are only beginning to glimpse just how far awry may be those conventional notions that characterize Austen and Scott as intellectual conservatives who somehow managed to avoid falling into the

Romantic mainstream of their age. Scott's affinities with at least some aspects of Romanticism are of course obvious. Readers predisposed to doubt the existence of affinities between Austen and Romanticism should look into *The Wordsworth Circle*'s special issue on that subject (Autumn 1976).

12. For evidences underlying this understanding of *Frankenstein,* see my essay, "Frankenstein's Monster and Its Romantic Relatives: Problems of Knowledge in English Romanticism," *TSLL,* 15 (1973), 51–65.

13. *The Prose Works of William Wordsworth,* ed. W. J. B. Owen and J. W. Smyser (Oxford: Clarendon Press, 1974), II, 84.

14. See, for example, A. H. Gomme, "Some Wordsworthian Transparencies," *MLR,* 68 (1973), 507–20, esp. 519–20.

15. Keats to George and Tom Keats, December 21–27, 1817, in *The Letters of John Keats, 1814–1821,* ed. H. E. Rollins (Cambridge, Mass.: Harvard University Press, 1958), I, 193.

William Blake

The most radical transformations in the criticism of romantic poets during the past decade took place in the treatment of the poetry of Lord Byron and William Blake. Critical esteem for Blake skyrocketed in the 1960s and 1970s—for reasons succinctly articulated by Alicia Ostriker in the selection printed below. This led to his inclusion for the first time in *The Romantic Poets: A Review of Research* (in the fourth edition, 1985). Subsequently, however, there has been a reassessment of earlier, often freewheeling, commentaries. This stabilizing process has gone hand-in-hand with revisionary revelations about Blake's actual methods and purposes of publication, principally through the research of Robert Essick, *William Blake: Printmaker* (1980), and Joseph Viscomi.

We illustrate these findings with Viscomi's essay, derived from two chapters of his recent book. The new comprehension of Blake's practices seems certain to determine the contours of Blake studies for the remainder of this century, as is perhaps suggested by Heather Glen's thoughtfully comprehensive analysis of "London" and by such recent essays as Andrew Cooper's "Blake and Madness: The World Turned Inside Out" (1990). Cooper brilliantly applies modern psychological concepts to elucidate how Blake uses (both graphically and verbally) his age's interest in and understanding of madness to articulate his own sociopolitical fears and aspirations.

William Blake, Illuminated Books, and the Concept of Difference

This selection is derived from Joseph Viscomi's monumental *Blake and the Idea of the Book* (1993). Although Viscomi's work reflects a general trend among romanticists to attend closely to the relations between literary and graphic arts, it is simultaneously part of our increasing desire both to establish solid texts and to define more precisely the historical processes through which texts and their social contexts interact. This desire, the subject of Jerome J. McGann's influential study, *A Critique of Modern Textual Criticism* (1983), is reflected elsewhere in such heroic editorial projects as McGann's poetry of Byron, the Cornell Wordsworth edition, and the Bollingen Coleridge edition.

Blake, of course, is a special case, the one romantic poet who was also a distinguished graphic artist. The combination has strained the capabilities of literary scholarship, and it has led recently to sharply detailed attempts to comprehend historically Blake's practice as an artist. Study of Blake's printmaking technology underlies Essick's *William Blake: Printmaker,* as well as Morris Eaves's *William Blake's Theory of Art* (1982). Attempts to capture Blake's linguistic practice include Nelson Hilton's *Literal Imagination: Blake's Vision of Words* (1983) and Essick's *William Blake and the Language of Adam* (1989). Interest in the theoretical as well as practical difficulties presented by Blake's texts is reflected in the excellent collection of essays edited by Nelson Hilton and Thomas A. Vogler, *Unnam'd Forms: Blake and Textuality* (1986).

It is a sobering thought that such fine scholars and critics as David Erdman and Northrop Frye did not correctly understand how Blake created his illuminated works. It is even more sobering to realize how many elaborate analyses of Blake's graphic art produced in the 1960s and 1970s (and some, one must add, still appearing today) are vitiated by erroneous assumptions about his printing techniques and publishing purposes.

Viscomi's fundamental argument is that critical judgments ought to be founded in a careful study of historical facts. In Blake's case these facts demonstrate that current cherished assumptions—that he was determined that every print should be unique and that his methods prove his utter hostility to the printing traditions of his time—are insupportable. Viscomi discovers a far more complex, and interesting,

From *Blake and the Idea of the Book* (Princeton: Princeton University Press, 1993), Chaps. 4 and 18, pp. 32–44 and 163–176.

relation between Blake and his society. He shows that Blake printed his books in editions, and that his illuminated prints in fact may represent Blake at his most fashionable. Viscomi's persuasiveness at upsetting ideological prejudices of our day derives in good measure from his sensitivity to the generative force of artistic activity in itself. The evidence suggests that Blake's unusual combining of words and pictures was suggested by his illuminating technique, rather than the technique's having been invented to render a prior conception. Viscomi understands, for example, that for a practising artist the use of a particular technique is not synonymous with rejection of another—precisely the reason why one must carefully tease out the unique historical evolution of the artist's work, not explain it by fitting it to a ready-made ideological template. Viscomi demonstrates, then, that the fascinating unusualness of Blake's illuminated poetry resides in its pictorial display of how intricate artistic intentions, with all their various psychological, social, and political componenets, come into being through the process of composition. For Blake, it is in the *act* of drawing that he finds both idea and image.

Copies of Blake's illuminated books differ one from the other. Inferred from this fact are a set of mistaken assumptions about production, editing, and intention. Illuminated books appear to have been produced "one by one" (Grant 281) "as [Blake] got commissions" (Davids and Petrillo 154), or "with a particular customer in mind" (Erdman, *Complete Poetry and Prose* 786; henceforth referred to as E), and "over many years, beginning . . . in the late 1780s and not ending until the last years of his life" (Essick "William Blake, William Hamilton, and the Materials of Graphic Meaning" 857; henceforward referred to as "Materials").[1] Moreover, revision seems continuous and deliberate, making each copy of a book seem like "a new edition" (Johnson 126), which in turn seems to express Blake's contempt for and rejection of conventional modes of graphic and book production. Hence, "every copy of every book" not only appears to have been produced uniquely, but also Blake appears to have "certainly intended [illuminated books] to be different" (Plowman 11). These positions are neatly summarized by Jerome McGann, who states that Blake intended that "each of his works *be* unique" and that "these differences" among copies were not "merely accidental [or] unimportant for the 'meaning' of Blake's work. Certainly to Blake they seemed immensely consequential; indeed—and he was quite right—they seemed definitive of the difference between one sort of art (free, creative) and another (commonplace, generalized)" ("Text" 275, 276). And yet, while designs as initially drawn on plates do differ from the designs as printed, and prints do differ one from the other, such variations do not signify a rejection of uniformity and all it supposedly represents, nor do they determine the print's meaning. The first kind of difference was inherent to a mode of production in which finishing was conceived as part of the inventive process, and the second kind—for example, the varying width of a river in a particular image—requires comparisons that Blake could not have expected or intended his readers to make. Before assuming ideological causes, one needs to examine the technical and material grounds for difference and to understand the history of the works being compared.

First, much of the coloring and recoloring of books, especially of early copies, was done by Mrs. Blake, who appears to have worked independently of Blake on some books and with him on others. Thus, the marks and colors distinquishing one impression from another may not reflect Blake's hand or intention at all. Second, illuminated books were not printed and colored uniquely, one at a time over a number of years, but, with Mrs. Blake's help, in small editions.[2] Copies of an illuminated book produced in the same printing session, and thus in the same printing and coloring styles, are technically, materially, and stylistically far more *alike* than copies from different printing sessions, which could be and frequently were more than twenty years apart. And third, copies of books produced at different times are different because they were produced in different styles and according to different ideas of the Book. Indeed, *Songs of Innocence* copy B and *Songs of Innocence and of Experience* copy Z, which have been reproduced by Dover Publications and are routinely compared in classrooms to prove that each copy of an illuminated book is unique, were produced in 1789 and 1825 respectively, the former when illuminated prints were produced as pages in a book of poems and the latter when the prints were produced as miniature paintings (Viscomi, *Art* 18). If you were to compare the former with *Innocence* copy E, with which it was produced (but which, like most copies, has never been reproduced to provide such a comparison), and the latter with copy AA (reproduced only on microfilm), with which it was produced, you would see immediately how alike edition copies are (see *Book*, plates I, III). You would not only see how ahistorical such comparisons and the claims of intentional uniqueness are, but also how suspect are readings based on such differences. For example, the river in "The Little Black Boy" in *Songs of Innocence and of Experience* copy Z is wider than that of *Songs of Innocence* copy B, which for Myra Glazer indicates that "the child has had a longer, more arduous journey to endure" than in the first impression (235). Robert Essick, recognizing that "absences become present only through comparison," asks, "To whom could [Blake] be communicating the message?" ("Materials" 855, 858).[3] The river is wider in the copy Z impression because the plate borders were printed, which necessarily extended the bottom line of the river. But the presence of the border was due to the printing style used at that time for all illuminated books and not to Blake's desire to widen this particular river, let alone the river in this particular impression. Indeed, the features characteristic of late copies of illuminated books, such as single-sided printing, plate borders, frame lines, washed texts, translucent colors, and outlined figures, all of which alter the reader's experience and movement through a book's text, do not represent a rethinking of any particular image, poem, or book. They are matters of production style that show up in *all* copies of all illuminated books reprinted at that time, *Songs*, as well as *Visions*, *America*, *Europe*, *Urizen*, *Marriage*, and *Milton*.

The overt similarities among impressions printed and colored in editions challenge Steven Carr's assertion that the "variability . . . embedded in the material processes of producing illuminated prints" was "radical" (182) and require the qualification of another assertion, that "Blake's habitual 'touching up' of prints with ink or scratchwork and, most especially, his ever-changing manner of illuminating a page further differentiate every version of a design, producing not only large-scale iconographic variants but also a subtler alterity in background details, figures' lineaments and expressions, and the visual relationships linking together pictorial elements" (185).[4] Like most critics and scholars, Carr expresses an ahistorical idea of Blake's style in that he compares works regardless of when and how they were produced. Relatively speaking, few copies of illuminated books (e.g., none of the eleven recto/verso copies of *Visions* produced in 1793) were outlined in pen and ink, a feature characteristic of late copies and of early copies that had been recolored and/or salvaged (see *Book*, chaps. 15 and 33). Carr's claim that Blake's "manner" was "ever-changing" seems based on bibliographical descriptions of illuminated prints and not examination of an edition's impressions. For example, in G. E. Bentley's *Blake Books*, *Visions* plate 7 is described as follows:

COLOURING: The MAN'S ROBE is Blue (A, B, G, J, O), Green (C), Purple (D, I), Pink (E), Black (E), reddish-Brown (H), pale Brown (K, Tate pull), Yellow (L), Green (M), or Grey (BMPR pull). The WOMAN, usually nude-Pink, is sometimes yellowish-Green (G) or Green (I). The SKY is bright with Purple (A–C, E, K–M), Pink (B, P), Yellow (D, G, M, O, P), Red or Orange (E–G, I, K, M, O, P, BMPR and Tate pulls) or Mustard (J). The SUN, usually Yellow or Orange, is Red (A, G) or pale Green (D). VARIANTS: There is no sun in copies B, C, H, and the Tate pull. In B, C, E, L, there are Grey or Purple clouds from the wave to the right margin. Ordinarily the sun is a semicircle, but in E, F, I, M only one quarter of the sun is visible, and in O, P one eighth is visible, while in L we see the whole sun. In F, a thin, leafless Brown tree is added in ink in the bottom right margin. Copy B is incribed "Solitary Coast." (471)

Such detail, a requisite of descriptive bibliography, helps one to visualize individual impressions. But because plate 7 and the other plates in *Visions* are grouped by repeated motifs and colors and not by technique and style, no two plates from *Visions* share the same groups. Consequently production patterns for the book are impossible to discern, chronology and sequence are impossible to determine, and variation among copies is impossible to dismiss as anything but intentional and extensive. Statements about illuminated books based on such bibliographical descriptions will be misleading, while those based on the examination of actual copies will be puzzling when infused with the idea of continuous variation. For example, David Erdman states that Blake "loathed . . . monotony . . . and when we consider how much variety he introduced into the printing and painting of his works, how distinctive each copy is in coloring and in the finishing of details, it is surprisingly how few truly variant details are to be found" (*Illuminated Blake* 15; henceforth referred to as *IB*). Erdman's summary of work produced between 1789 and 1827 combines characteristics of edition printing ("few truly variant details") and characteristics of various production styles (distinct copies). When impressions from different editions are compared, variety does indeed seem to have been deliberately introduced into the printing itself, since formats and even tactile surfaces varied with each printing session. But impressions from the same printing session were *printed* the same. The inks, paper, pressure, size, wiping, even accidentals, and so on were repeated exactly and "monotonously."[5]

Given the potential for change, the absence of pronounced differences among copies within an edition is quite surprising and the differences themselves seem minor, the inevitable result of a mode of production involving two people printing and coloring numerous impressions by hand and before collation and without prototypes. Differences within an edition were due also to the parameters of what was visually acceptable being very large—which is a kind way of saying that Blake kept many impressions that printmakers then as now would deem poorly printed, illegible, misaligned, etc., features that prompted William Muir, a professional lithographer and Blake's main nineteenth-century facsimilist, to declare that illuminated prints were produced with "a *skilful carelessness.*"[6] These parameters may reflect paper costs, but they may also reflect an awareness that absolute control over relief etching was not possible. As we shall see, Blake's idea of uniformity permitted variation; if variations were technically inevitable and aesthetically acceptable, then they could also be deliberately *allowed* to occur. Such variations among copies of the same edition, then, do not represent a rethinking of the poem or page but a sensitivity to the generative powers of execution, to the logic of the tools, materials, and processes—and to the original contributions of an assistant. They no more signify *deliberate* revision or alteration of models or earlier copies than the repetition of colors, technique, and plate order in the last copies of *Songs* signifies "servile copying" of models. As is evinced by commercially produced engravings and colored prints, variation among illuminated prints is not extraordinary or unprecedented. Even the overt variations within an edition, like different ink colors or hand-drawn compositions, appear motivated by the desire to diversify stock, comparable to a publisher's practice of issuing a book in various formats, and not by anger at or desire to reject conventions or modes of production that Blake *chose* not to employ. Apparently the Blakes were not graphic purists; they were not interested in making an edition's copies *exactly* the same, but neither were they interested in making them completely different. The latter objective was technically realizable and the former almost so, but both would have required far more time and labor than was actually expended.

Edition printing means that copies of illuminated books can be grouped according to printing sessions, which in turn can be dated to reveal the history of a particular book and the pattern of illuminated print production in general. Such information refutes the idea that illuminated books cannot be edited, and supports the idea that they can be edited historically. By identifying variants and calculating their significance, the editor can define, date, and sequence the various versions of a book. Theoretically, all and *every* variation alters the relation among the signs that constitute the verbal-visual system of an illuminated poem (Carr, 182), but in practice it appears that the variations in production styles create distinct versions of a poem while coloring and even compositional variations within an edition usually do not. Variations in the style of production, because they are different in kind (e.g., facing pages vs recto-only leaves, or lightly washed images vs. images painted, outlined, and framed), alter the reading experience, whereas the latter type of variant, different in degree, usually do not—or, if they do, then how must be shown concretely and in detail and not simply asserted theoretically. Indeed, part of the critical and editorial process is to distinguish one kind of difference from the other, to determine whether a variant generates a new reading, and to ascertain whether that new reading was intended. Otherwise, as Essick has warned, the "interpreters . . . are in danger of using Blake's graphics as little more than a foundation for their own mythologies" ("Materials" 859).[7]

As this brief summary suggests, theories about Blake's mode of book production and about how the books should be edited are grounded in the misinterpretation of a bibliographical fact and, as the remainder of this essay will argue, of Blake's intentions. The questions we need to ask ourselves are, How did Blake perceive these differences? Were they "immensely consequential"?

The assumption that variants were intended or perceived by Blake as meaningful, produced deliberately to destabilize the text and to make every copy of a book a separate version, is based partly on a misunderstanding of Blake's mode of production and partly on Blake's statement that "not a line is drawn without intention & that most discriminate & particular as Poetry admits not a Letter that is Insignificant so Painting admits not a Grain of Sand of a Blade of Grass Insignificant much less and Insignificant Blur or Mark" (E 560). Blake wrote this in *A Vision of the Last Judgment,* an important twenty-page elucidation in the *Notebook* of his aesthetics in general and, in particular, of an exceedingly detailed painting of the same title now presumed lost (Butlin 2:648).[8] The passage actually expresses one of Blake's primary aesthetic theories, that line was the foundation of art and that colors and washes were secondary. The entire passage reads:

> General Knowledge is Remote Knowledge it is in Particulars that Wisdom consists & Happiness too. Both in Art & in Life General Masses are as Much Art as a Pasteboard Man is Human Every Man has Eyes Nose & Mouth this Every Idiot knows but he who enters into & discriminates most minutely the Manners & Intentions the Characters in all their branches is the alone Wise or Sensible Man & on this discrimination All Art is founded. I intreat then that the Spectator will attend to the Hands & Feet to the Lineaments of the Countenances they are all descriptive of Character & not a line is drawn without intention & that most discriminate & particular as Poetry admits not a Letter that is Insignificant so Painting admits not a Grain of Sand or a Blade of Grass Insignificant much less an Insignificant Blur or Mark (E 560).

In practice, however, not all lines are equal. As revealed by Blake's sketches, drawings, and the pentimenti of the watercolors, the line that discriminates and particularizes is the line that finds and fixes form in the initially chaotic sketch of lines, marks, and blurs. Such a line, whether made in pencil or, as in finished watercolors, in pen, is necessarily made intentionally, with a "firm and decided hand" (E 576). In this two-part drawing process it is not the blank white paper that is minutely organized but the initial marks made on it, which requires a mind open to chance and a decisive hand. Described as "Making out the Parts,"[9] Blake's drawing style united invention and execution, a point Blake makes explicit in other descriptions of his drawing process: "an Original Invention [cannot] Exist without Execution Organized & minutely Delineated & Articulated Either by God or Man," and, to differentiate his linear technique from the tonal techniques of the Flemish and Venetian artists, "Their art is to lose form, [Mr. B's] art is to find form, and to keep it" (E 576, 538). "Organization," sometimes used as an appositive to execution (E 637), implies having something to organize, and is thus a stage within the execution process. Because execution incorporates organization and involves decisions, it is also inseparable from intellect and invention: "A Facility in Composing is the Greatest Power of Art & Belongs to None but the Greatest Artists i.e. the Most Minutely Discriminating & Determinate" (E 643). Execution so defined means that "The unorganized Blots & Blurs of Rubens & Titian are not Art nor can their Method ever express ideas or Imaginations any more than Popes Metaphysical Jargon of Rhyming" (E 576). In effect, material execution is to the artist as chaos is to God; it must be organized, which requires drawing out decisively its every beauty and firmly delineating them so invention can speak clearly. Indeed, Blake makes the analogy explicit in *A Descriptive Catalogue:* "Leave out this line and you leave out life itself; all is chaos again, and the line of the almighty must be drawn out upon it before man or beast can exist" (E 550). By these acts invention is articulated, is clear and intelligible utterance; without them, "Without Minute Neatness of Execution[,] The Sublime cannot Exist." For Blake, firm outlines signified decisiveness; conversely, indetermined form reflected indecision and fuzzy thinking. The connection between mental perspicacity and material form was variously expressed: "All Sublimity is founded on Minute Discrimination," "Singular & Particular Detail is the Foundation of the Sublime," and the "Grandeur of Idea is founded on Precision of Ideas," (E 643, 647, 646).[10]

Drawing is also the foundation of the sublime in the sense of being the place of origin, the place where grand ideas and images are *found.* By drawing—and making the initial marks constituting the drawing—the artist invents, in the sense of the word's root, "invenire," to find. Henry Fuseli defines invention much the same way in his seventh lecture (1801): "to invent is to find: to find something presupposes its existence somewhere, implicitly or explicitly, scattered or in a mass" (Knowles 1:136–137). Artistic form and meaning are found in the material world and by extension the medium itself, which Blake seems explicitly to acknowledge. Blake's comments about "finding form and keeping it," about "organizing execution" and "making out the parts" reflect an awareness that form and meaning were not fully preexistent, or as Essick has carefully shown that "intentionality" did not fully exist "prior to and outside the artist's medium" (*William Blake and the Language of Adam* 190). The point is that in drawing as Blake practiced it not all lines and marks were intended and intention itself evolved through the medium. Blake's comments and practice challenge the theory that his was an eidetic imagination, or, at any rate, that his art was a faithful copying of fully formed, preexistent mental images.[11] Rather, form and meaning evolve from the continual interactive relation between mind and language/medium, between invention and execution, as marks and erasures suggest other marks, directions, images, and ideas.

Blake expressed the idea that form was defined by line and not by colors many times over: "In a work of Art it is not fine tints that are required but Fine Forms, Fine Tints without, are loathsome. Fine Tints without Fine Forms are always the Subterfuge of the Blockhead" (E 571), and, more troubling, "there is no difference between Rafael's Cartoons and his Frescos, or Pictures, except that the Frescos, or Pictures, are more finished" (E 549). Apparently Raphael's "fine tints" were true to his "fine forms," his coloring or finishing extending instead of distorting the work's foundation. Nevertheless, Blake's comments about finishing having no substantial effect on foundation contradict the idea that every line or mark was intended and significant, and they reinforce the idea that the most decisive stage in painting was not coloring but deciding what to admit to the work's final form—which, paradoxically, was synonymous with building the work's foundation. Blake's comments about finishing and foundation raise these questions: Were plate image and illuminated print analogous to cartoon and fresco, with the print's meaning dependent on its foundation (that is, the image as delineated on the plate) instead of its coloring and finishing, on its beginning rather than its end? Does Blake's subordination of finishing to line, in other words, imply that illuminated books had ideal forms impervious to the changes that occurred through production?

Blake's 1793 prospectus intimates the role coloring played in the conception of illuminated books. He defines illuminated printing as a "method of Printing both Letter-press and Engraving in a style more *ornamental, uniform,* and *grand,* than any before discovered" (E 692, my emphasis). The ultimate source for Blake's description appears to be Joshua Reynolds's well-known response to William Gilpin's theory of the picturesque, which was published in 1792 in Gilpin's *Three Essays on Picturesque Beauty* (35). Blake quoted Reynolds approvingly years later in an 1802 letter to Thomas Butts: " 'You are certainly right in saying that Variety of Tints & Forms is Picturesque: but it must be rememberd on the other hand; that the reverse of this (*uniformity of Colour & a long continuation of lines*) produces Grandeur' " (E 718–719). Blake underlined Reynolds's parenthetical statement apparently to validate his own painting style, which consisted of flat, minimally modeled washes over pencil lines strengthened and unified in pen and ink. Blake, however, disagreed with Reynolds's definition of "ornament." Reynolds associated "ornament" with the Venetian style of coloring, in contrast to the "grand" style of the Florentine's. He believed that "the union of the two may make a sort of composite style" (71), an idea Blake thoroughly dismissed: "There is No Such Thing as A Composite Style" (E 652). For Blake, "ornamental" depended "altogether . . . on Distinctness of Form. The Venetian ought not to be calld the Ornamental Style" (E 651). Blake associated "ornament" with the grand and uniform style, a link that Blake appears to have made as early as 1793.[12]

Illuminated prints, then, are "ornamental" in that their coloring is part of the print's original form and meaning and not mere "decoration" or something *added* to principles. They are "grand" in the sense that the long printed line dominates the design. They are "uniform" in the double sense of being printed from metal plates and covered in unbroken and evenly laid-in washes.[13] When Blake wrote his prospectus, he had printed over sixty copies of *Innocence, Thel, Marriage, Visions,* and *America;* he would have known that what remained uniform, in addition to the unchanging printed line, was the *style* of coloring and not the individual placement of colors or ornamental flourishes.[14] A concept of uniformity that permits variation suggests that coloring was itself an integral part of conception but that variants of the kind we have been discussing were of little consequence, or at least they were not intended to make each copy of an edition a new version of the book or each impression an independent drawing.

While visual differences among copies are believed to signify unique production and revision, *difference* (that is, the idea of difference) is believed to be ideologically significant. As noted, Erdman states that it reveals a "loth[ing]" of "monotony" (*IB* 15); McGann claims that it was "part of Blake's artistic project" to make "each of his works *be* unique" ("Text" 275). Essick argues that it signifies "Blake consciously violat[ing]" the "mechanization, efficiency, and uniformity" or "conventional tastes and methods of production," "a revolt against empire, against the hegemony of machine over man" ("Preludium" 6). Although Essick's opinion has changed, his initial assessment was deeply influential.[15] Illuminated printing came to be interpreted as an "artistic practice significantly in opposition to historically dominant modes of artistic production" (Carr 183), a practice that was "partly designed as an artistic escape from . . . narrow commercial anxieties (Eaves, "Machine" 63) and "in deliberate defiance of [Blake's] period's normal avenues of publication" (McGann, *Critique* 44). Indeed, the idea that "Blake's methods of engraving and copperplate printing purposefully set themselves apart from industrially-determined print technologies" is now, as the Santa Cruz Blake Study Group recognized, "commonly believed." From this "fact," the study group infers that Blake's "practice may even have constituted an active critique or subversion of what Walter Benjamin has called the age of mechanical reproduction, anticipating Brecht's combined aesthetic and ideological insistence on exhibiting—rather than hiding—the means of producing the artistic effect" ("Type" 323). It is in this light that Stewart Crehan can define illuminated printing as a "rebellion against the artistic dominance of the aristocracy and commercial bourgeoisie," its production motivated primarily by "the historical need to transform the conditions within which art was produced," and illuminated books as a socio-aesthetic as well as manifesting the political "struggle to transform the relation of artistic production in favour of the creative artisan" (241).[16]

But to what exactly are illuminated prints and books being compared? What were the "historically dominant modes of artistic production," the "industrially-determined print technologies," and the "normal avenues of publication"? They seem little other than the graphic *ideal,* whether in the form of letterpress printing or commercial line engraving, in which images are repeated exactly and labor is divided among various hands. Indeed, according to Carr, "the logic of mechanical reproduction is one of identity: it leads to a multiplication of the same, to a mass publication of what are taken to be identical copies" (182). At first the contrast between illuminated printing and conventional modes of production seems justified, given that Blake likened William Woollett's engravings to machines: "A Machine is not a Man nor a Work of Art[;] it is Destructive of Humanity & of Art" (E 575). With the competition so defined, illuminated prints do indeed stand out and seem heroically alone. But the contrast breaks down when examined closely. First, variation—in the form of states, proofs, prints before letters, size and type of paper, and so on—was inherent to the aesthetics and economics of conventional print production. As Essick has demonstrated with Blake's own engraving of William Hogarth's *Beggar's Opera, Act III,* the "history of a reproductive engraving reveals the same differential pattern as the multilayered production of variation in Blake's unconventional etchings. The differences are in emphasis and detail, not in the nature of the phenomenon, and in our tendency to consider its presence in copy engravings as a matter of 'mere connoisseurship' (to use Carr's phrase) while granting great consequence to the same processes in Blake's work" ("How Blake's Body Means," 201). Second, Blake himself did not contrast illuminated printing with engraving. In the prospectus he announces that "two large highly finished engravings" were also available and that two more were in progress, which suggests that he believed that engraving was like illuminated printing in that it too provided the means to "propagate such works as have wholly absorbed the Man of Genius," in this particular sense "the Labours of the Artist" (E 692). While illuminated printing incorporated the work of the painter and poet with that of the printmaker or engraver, it was not engraving's contrary. Each was appropriate for the job asked of it. Third, Blake did not criticize engraving per se, but the idea that engravings were reproductive only, a self-fulfilling and self-limiting perception that rendered him a mere craftsman. With engraving and painting both grounded in drawing, hierarchical structuring of the two arts made no sense. The inherently artistic value of engraving, however, did not mean reproductions were unnecessary (Blake himself treasured the reproductions after Raphael and Michaelangelo), but that they too, like original engravings, should display the "firmness of a Masters Touch," like that of James Basire, his teacher and a master reproductive engraver, and not the "undecided bungling" that marks the mechanical labor of a journeyman (E 575). It is the latter style of engraving, represented by Woollett, that Blake attacks.

But what exactly was Woollett's crime? He produced engravings in the best tonal manner of the day, in the style of the Rubens and LeBrun gallery prints that George Michael Moser showed Blake, and in opposition to the "Hard Stiff & Dry Unfinished Works of Art" of Blake's heroes, Dürer and Raimondi. Blake told Moser: "These things that you call Finishd are not Even Begun how can they then, be Finishd? The Man who does not know The Beginning, never can know the End of Art" (E 639).[17] The "beginning," as in foundation, was line, which was also its "end" in that line was not obscured by color or tone. "End" also referred to purpose, and the purpose of art was to articulate effectively and clearly the artist's imagination. For Blake, the imagination was manifest in outline and not brushwork, for the latter appealed to the sensual at the expense of the intellectual eye. The absence, then, of firmly decided line was a sign of bungling, indolence, or indecision, was the formulaic labor of a craftsman and not the execution of a master.

This connection between Woollett's engraving style and the Dutch and Venetian painting styles is problematic, for while the latter painting styles cause "every thing in Art [to] become a Machine" (E 547), they in fact show far more of the artist's hand; that is, they exhibit more of "the means of producing the artistic effect" than Blake's own painting style or the Florentine style he emulated. This overt exhibition of the means of production is why Reynolds ranked the Venetian below the Florentine: it addressed primarily the senses rather than the intellect. According to Reynolds, "the great end of [painting] is to strike the imagination. The Painter is therefore to make no ostentation of the means by which this is done; the spectator is only to feel the result in his bosom. An inferior artist is unwilling that any part of his industry should be lost upon the spectator. He takes as much pains to discover, as the greater artist does to conceal, the marks of his subordinate assiduity" (59). More concisely still he writes: "Tintoret, Paul Veronese, and others of the Venetian school, seem to have painted with no other purpose than to be admired for their skill and expertness in the mechanism of painting, and to make a parade of that art, which as I before observed, the higher stile requires its followers to conceal" (63). It was an observation Reynolds made many times over: "Young minds are indeed too apt to be captivated by this splendour of stile; and that of the Venetians is particularly pleasing" because it gives "pleasure to the eye or sense" (64).[18]

Reynolds equates an overt style of execution with execution itself, which is partly why he safeguards the intellectual integrity of invention by separating it from execution. Blake, on the other hand, while agreeing with Reynolds's devaluation of indistinct form and his idea of painting's primary purpose, believed that associating execution with the Venetian and Dutch painting styles was to "prostitute" the concept (E 652). For Blake, true execution was inseparable from invention, hence it needed to be differentiated from mere labor. Dutch and Venetian paintings were essentially sketches, mere "blots & blurs" overlabored in colors and finished with loaded brushes, which necessarily rendered form indistinct and showed more of the artist's hand or means of production than did the "grand style" (E 576). Blake derides the loaded brush, asserting that those who equate painting with the "Pant Brush" live in "the house of Rembrant" (E 515). "Pant," which Blake repeats three times, suggests labored breath and exhaustion as opposed to inspiration and decisiveness.[19] It follows that Blake should deride the engraving style that attempts to imitate these features, the style of Woollett and Robert Strange: "The Labourd Works of Journeymen employed by Correggio. Titian Veronese & all the Ventians ought not to be shewn to the Young Artist as the Works of original Conception any more than the Engravings of Strange Bartollozzi [and] Woollett . . . [they] are Works of Manual Labour" (E 644).[20] By equating these graphic and pictorial styles, Blake implies that the paintings are no more original than reproductive engravings; both styles are formulaic and could be executed by anyone trained in that style, "by What all can do Equally well" (E 573). These kinds of engravings and paintings, which represent "high finishd Ignorance" and "Mental Weakness," as well as "endless labour"—labor without end, or purpose, and continued beyond what was necessary (E 573, 548)—are poor examples for art students precisely because they are labored; that is, they show too readily the hand of the artist, either literally in the form of brush work or metaphorically in the virtuoso handling of a complex and illusionistic line system (Landseer 138).[21]

We cannot use Blake's criticism of labor and mechanical form to support the position that Blake abhorred the mechanical and favored exhibiting the means of production since by "mechanical" he is referring to works that call attention to themselves, that overtly show the "means of producing artistic effects." As revealed by his firm belief in inspiration and the primacy of an artist's first thoughts, Blake advocated the aesthetic of the sketch, but his attacks on "blots and blurs" reveal that he abhorred the indistinctness of its various forms, believing that art engaged the imagination through subject and theme and not through handling.[22] It is not that Blake failed to show his hand in illuminated printing: books color printed, through the impasto-like effects of the ink and paint, are reminiscent of *alla prima* painting, and white-line etching, woodcut-on-pewter, and the Virgil wood engravings were executed with tools clearly reflecting the body's motion and thereby calling attention to the medium. While color prints are in effect imitations of paintings, the experimental graphics are neither imitations nor translations but images unique to their medium. To have made them so is essentially to have put into practice Landseer's argument for elevating the status of engraving: engraving is aesthetically valuable because its language is unique, a truth hidden by its own film of familiarity (138ff). In these more experimental graphics Blake seems intent on confronting the viewer, on defamiliarizing the print. But all of these startling visual effects were created after 1788, and thus they do not reflect Blake's intentions for inventing illuminated printing or his early use of it, nor do these effects signal a change in Blake's intentions or signify a desire to overthrow graphic convention, since the world of graphic art was far more inclusive and eclectic than the simple contrast between Woollett's style of engraving and illuminated printing suggests. Indeed, as Landseer's survey of the age's new (and presumably "industrially-determined") print technologies demonstrates, graphic art was anything but monolithic and conventions were everywhere breaking down.

The abiding taste was not for things mechanical, efficient, and uniform, but for proofs, facsimiles of drawings, and color and colored prints. According to *The Artist's Repository,* etchings "executed by painters are seldom anything further advanced than by aqua-fortis; and herein [we] discover the master's hand and facility of design, which is their merit" (2:18–19). Hand-colored etchings, like Thomas Rowlandson's caricature prints, which Blake noted in 1799 ought not to be as popular as they were (E 704, 702), along with aquatints and the "soft blending and infantile indefinity" of stipple and chalk engraving, had become the "rage" (Landseer 126). These techniques were stimulated by the taste for drawings and sketches, including the "rough sketches" that had become "the prevailing tide of fashion" by 1793 (Craig 5–6). Aquatint, which Gilpin used to reproduce his "rough sketches," had become "the principle process employed in book illustrations" between 1790 and 1830 (Hardie 87; see also Prideaux).[23] From a purist aesthetic, unfinished etching and color and colored prints were abominations as offensive as aquatint's and stipple's obliteration of firm outlines (Landseer 180; *Book,* chaps. 13 and 14).[24] In effect, to applaud illuminated printing as "an active critique or subversion of what Walter Benjamin has called the age of mechanical reproduction" (Santa Cruz 323), or a "rebellion against the artistic dominance of the aristocracy and commercial bourgeoisie" (Crehan 241), is essentially to applaud Blake for not being a graphic purist at a time when few purists were left.

Illuminated printing appears politically significant partly because *innovation* per se is defined as a deliberate break with established practice. When Blake's innovations are defined technically and placed historically, however, illuminated printing can be seen to share many of the aesthetic aims of techniques that were then becoming established precisely because they were meeting the demands of a commercial bourgeoisie. In other words, Blake was joining an argument—and endorsing, reinterpreting, and rejecting the various ideological positions underlying that argument—rather than starting one, joining a growing print market that included the "legitimate artist" and the many "empirical pretenders" (Landseer 138), line engravings as well as monochrome, colored, and color chalk engravings, stipples, aquatints, etchings, mezzotints, and now "a method of Printing both Letter-press and Engraving in a style more ornamental, uniform, and grand, than any before discovered" (E 692). His designs were drawn in firm outline with pens and brushes, and the plates were printed in colors and/or the impressions were hand colored with an assistant. Illuminated prints are exactly as J. T. Smith described them: impressions "printed in any tint" so that Blake "or Mrs. Blake [could] colour the marginal figures up by hand in imitation of drawings" (Bentley, *Blake Records* 460). The difference between illuminated printing and other techniques that sought to imitate drawings is that the brush and pen marks in the former were actually created by pens and brushes and not, as in the latter, imitated with metal instruments and indirect processes (e.g., aquatint).[25] And even then the differences were not absolute. Creating dark areas directly as positive pen and brush marks was possible in a variation of aquatint called sugar-lift aquatint, the method used by Thomas Gainsborough in the early 1780s to reproduce a few of his pen-and-ink drawings and by Alexander Cozens to reproduce "blots" in *New Method of Assisting the Invention in Drawing Original Compositions of Landscapes* (1784). The image is drawn on the plate with pens and brushes using an ink mixed with sugar. The design is covered with a thin ground and immersed in water, which causes the sugar in the ink to swell and break through the ground, thereby leaving the autographic gestures of ben and brush as positive shapes. The method is perfectly analogous to illuminated printing, except that the design is given an aquatint ground and is etched in intaglio. Its similarity to illuminated printing suggests that Blake and Gainsborough were responding to the same aesthetic and possibly commercial forces (as was Alois Senefelder when he invented lithography, then known as "polyautography"), and not necessarily that Blake knew of the earlier method.[26]

"Artistic effect," like difference, appears to be a "radical" aspect of illuminated printing when examined outside its historical and technical context. Other kinds of prints, however, particularly colored and color prints, were also "radical" in the sense that they varied one from the other and showed the "master's hand and facility of design." Instead of perceiving illuminated printing as a *reaction against*—or an effort to *reject*—"conventional taste" or the "commercial bourgeoisie," we need to see in it Blake's desire to tap into a market created by the status quo's demand for drawings, a market actively supplied by commercial and original printmakers. Illuminated prints exhibit "the means of producing the artistic effect" because they were printed and colored by hand in an age that placed great value on color prints and autographic gestures. Like etchings and facsimiles of sketches, they move toward the simple and spontaneous, toward drawing, and away from the overtly skillful performance characteristic of reproductive engraving. But this move away from the reproductive ideal does not make them "subversive," except to purists like John Landseer; indeed, to collectors of the day, illuminated prints may have represented Blake at his most fashionable.[27]

While the combination of word and image is the most obvious feature of illuminated printing, it appears to have been suggested by the possibilities of the technique and not the impetus for the technique's invention. Relief etching appears to have been invented to reproduce drawings, or, at any rate, the *Approach of Doom,* a pen-and-ink-wash drawing executed by Blake's brother Robert, appears to have been the first work executed in the new technique (see *Book,* chap. 20). This production, which presumably answered Blake's desire to publish original images in general and to imitate wash drawings in particular, revealed through the association of pen and ink with writing the potential of relief etching to reproduce words—at which time the idea for illuminated printing and poetry was born. While the full technical and aesthetic origin of relief etching and illuminated printing cannot be examined here, suffice it to say that illuminated printing evolved out of a preexistent technique and was not invented to realize a preexistent form, the illuminated book, or a political agenda, the overthrowing of conventional modes of book production. The idea for illuminated books, in other words, did not determine the technique; assuming that it did is yet another example of assuming that invention precedes execution. That Blake invented and used a graphic technique modeled on drawing, in process and in appearance, and that he chose to use it to publish poetry is no doubt ideologically significant, both to him, in that it appears to have supplied the grounds for an aesthetic theory advocating the unity of invention and execution, and to us, in that it illuminates the contemporaneity and context of his experiments. Nevertheless, defining exactly what those ideological positions were and how they were manifested is difficult. The use of a technique (as opposed to a style) is not necessarily synonymous with the rejection of another technique, at least not from an artist's point of view, though it may indeed become that (e.g., Blake's early use of water-based paint did not express a hatred of oil paint). Its use depends more on its appropriateness to the project at hand than on an aversion to alternatives, on reasons that are more practical, economic, and aesthetic than overtly political. Moreover, we must be careful about ascribing undue significance to Blake's undertaking all stages of illuminated printing. First, Blake's control over production was not as complete as imagined, given the nature of the technique and Mrs. Blake's assistance is printing and coloring impressions. Second, even if it were, it would not necessarily be politically significant or signify a desire to escape the division of labor characteristic of commercial graphics or letterpress printing. This is because an artist (as opposed to a writer) accustomed to controlling all stages of labor in the production of original prints—whether the prints are engravings like *Job* or etchings like *Albion rose*—is not really varying his practice or controlling more of his labor by using a new technique or by producing prints with words. It only seems so when the process is approached from the perspective of book publishing instead of printmaking and drawing. This is not to say that Blake failed to perceive and discuss illuminated printing symbolically, but only to point out that the technique was not invented to realize a desire to control his own labor or all aspects of an artwork, let alone to provide analogies, symbols, and metaphors for later poems.

The facts that Blake owned his own press, produced original images in various graphic techniques, controlled images from beginning to end, and perceived graphic art as being equal to painting and drawing, that is, as sharing in the same "end" or purpose of "Art," are ideologically significant precisely because they reflect an idea of printmaking not widely shared. But if the signature in the first state of *Albion rose* is "WB inv 1780," as it is in the second state, then Blake's radical approach to and perception of graphic art was probably already in place when he invented relief etching in 1788, even if it was not much practiced.[28] That he, a professional engraver, exhibited watercolors at the Royal Academy in 1784 and 1785 indicates that he perceived himself as both artist and printmaker, the necessary prerequisite for producing original prints. Blake's eyes were already open to the possibilities of using graphic art creatively; that is to say, Blake's idea of graphic art in general, and not of illuminated printing in particular, was the "dramatic break" with "the engraving and printing conventions of his time" (Essick, *Printmaker* 255). Essick has argued that "in the early 1780s, Blake attempted to fulfill his expectations as an artist and poet through the normal channels of publication. Failure in this endeavor" led to this break and to "the invention of relief etching" (255). Given Blake's ambitions after leaving Basire's shop, this seems like a fair assessment of events, even though there is no documentary evidence to prove that Blake tried to publish poetry through normal channels at this time.[29] I am suggesting that illuminated poetry evolved out of relief etching, which was itself generated by Blake's desire to produce original prints in imitation of drawings—or rather to produce original drawings in metal—as well as to supplement his income. The technique broke less dramatically from graphic conventions than it first appears because it was an extension of an idea of printmaking that was already in effect and because it joined other techniques that shared some of its practical, if not also theoretical, objectives.

We must also be careful before interpreting self-publication as evidence that Blake "was plainly aspiring to become a literary institution unto himself" (Mc-

Gann, *Critique* 47), or to "make him[self] independent of publishers as well as of patrons, so that he could achieve personal independence as both poet and painter at a single blow" (Frye 120), or that "Blake clearly had high hopes that 'Illuminated printing' would make his fortune" (Mitchell *Composite* 42). First, one cannot assume that this was Blake's intention when one also assumes that he printed illuminated books one at a time, since the latter assumption means that productions costs for books like *Innocence,* which was advertised for five shillings in 1793, could not be recouped for many years. Second, such interpretations are suspect because they merely echo Alexander Gilchrist's romanticized notions of artist and production. Blake lists in the prospectus six illuminated books, priced between 3s. and 10s.6d. apiece, along with two engravings and two "small book[s] of Engravings" (E 693). Gilchrist apparently believed that the prospectus signaled a financial turning point. He assumed that the illuminated books provided Blake with the "principle means of support through his future life" (1:69). Bentley corrects this assumption, noting that Blake may have "earned L600 with them, not counting expenses—perhaps six years' income for thirty-eight years' work" (*Blake Records* 33 n. 1). But even this sum is far too generous, since approximately 75 percent of Blake's stock, or 125 illuminated books (counting copies of *Innocence* and *Experience* that were initially produced or issued separately) of 168 extant or known copies of illuminated books (discounting the broadsheets of *On Homers Poetry* and the *Ghost of Abel*), were produced between 1789 and 1795 and probably sold at the prices nearer those listed in the prospectus of 1793 than in the letter to Dawson Turner in 1818 (see *Book,* chaps. 31, 33, and the appendix).[30] By the time of the prospectus, Blake had produced twenty-two copies of *Innocence* (see *Book,* chap. 24). At five shillings a copy, *Innocence* would secure a larger audience and reputation than income. The total income that Blake could have realized from *Innocence* in 1793 was L5.10s., minus the approximately L1.11s the book probably cost to produce.[31] The income from the forty or so copies of the other five books advertised in the prospectus would have realized under seventeen pounds. The total value of his stock of books in 1793, in other words, was the equivalent of about forty impressions of the *Job* and *Edward and Elinor* engravings (at 12s. and 10s.6d. respectively), or the labor required to engrave just one medium-size separate plate for the publishers—which was the equivalent of about three month's income.[32] Blake also notes in the prospectus that his technique produced books at one-fourth the cost of conventional modes of publication, which was probably true, but not because it was more efficient than letterpress. Blake did not pay for labor, manuscripts, or designs. No doubt his boast was made to encourage sales, indicating that *Innocence,* for example, was actually worth one pound, a sign that this hand-printed and hand-colored octavo-size book of poems, with only "25 designs," was indeed both deluxe and rare and a real steal at the price.

Mitchell has suggested that "Blake was never able to mass-produce his books as he hoped, partly because the new method was not so easy as he supposed, and partly because 'republican art' was in the 1790s a dangerous commodity" (*Composite* 43). But did Blake ever hope or expect to make his fortune by mass-producing his books? In 1793 Blake knew the strengths and weaknesses of his method, he knew the size of his stock, and he knew how to add. While he no doubt hoped to earn some money as well as reputation, he must also have realized that illuminated printing, no matter how large and varied the stock, even after the costs of copper plates were recouped, could never have provided a dependable source of income at the prices he was charging, that its profits would always be supplemental to income derived from painting, designing, and engraving. If Blake truly believed that illuminated printing would "deliver [him] from his perennial poverty and obscurity," then, ironically, as Paul Mann concludes, Blake's "private technologies" appear to have hindered rather than helped, in that his failure to secure a large audience resulted from the limited capability of the technologies, from his working outside the "social machinery of production," and ultimately from "his project's own inexorable aesthetic and economic self-absorption" ("Apocalypse" 8–9, 22). But how large was Blake's envisioned audience? The "numerous great works now in hand" (E 693) and which had been produced by that date amounted to as many as seventy-four copies of seven titles (including eight copies of *Experience,* which was advertised but not yet printed). This is not many books from the perspective of conventional publishing, but it is a goodly number for a cottage industry and especially from the perspective of a painter. Blake appears to have advertised primarily to connoisseurs, collectors, and other artists, all of whom, like Flaxman, Romney, Humphrey, and Blake himself, collected books, paintings, and prints. Basically, this is the same audience he sought for his watercolors, which by nature were usually unique and stored in portfolios or hung in parlors of private homes. From the perspective of the watercolorist, then, edition printing ensured that a set of particular works would have a larger-than-usual audience, "sufficient," he told Turner in 1818, to have gained a "reputation as an Artist which was the chief thing Intended" (E 771).[33]

Even if Blake had somehow grossly deceived himself regarding the financial benefits of his new mode of printing, it is still mistaken to imply that he somehow "sold out" later on, when he began charging higher prices. To interpret Blake's burgeoning awareness through William Hayley that "The Profits arising from Publications are immense" and Blake's hope "to commence publication with many very formidable works" (E 726) as a rejection of or a "swerv[ing] from his early radical project," and thus somehow a capitulation to the very "commercial system of his own day . . . from which [he] early sought to gain his independence" (McGann, *Critique* 45, 44), is to ignore a crucial fact of edition printing. The production of numerous copies of the same illuminated book was motivated not by numerous single commissions but by a desire to build stock and hence by the very practical reasons of realizing "profits" (even if they were supplemental) and of securing an audience, however limited in size.[34] When Blake returned to printing illuminated books in 1818, printing ten copies of six titles, he produced fewer works per printing session, but the books were priced as series of colored prints or paintings and had the potential to add substantially to Blake's declining income (see *Book,* chap. 33). Even so, these late printing sessions seem to have been motivated by at least one commission, apparently used to finance the production of other titles. In other words, inferring Blakes's motivation for early production sessions from that for late ones is as fallacious as inferring his early practice from his late practice and statements. At the time of the prospectus and for the next two years, Blake used the technique of illuminated printing not because he hoped or expected to make his fortune but because it was appropriate to his temperament and vision, and, as Smith states, it enabled him to avoid the "expense of letterpress" (Bentley, *Blake Records* 460). Moreover, because Blake's initial investment per book was minimal, he did not require a large audience to make a profit unlike the far more expensive self-publication projects of the 1790s (see Bentley, "Great Illustrated-Book" 61–62). On the other hand, this profit was so small that the early editions of illuminated books appear to have been financed by Blake's earnings as a commercial engraver.

If illuminated impressions were grouped according to editions or printing sessions, then one would see that changes of printing ink indicate issues of an edition and that colors, despite being placed differently, were the same and applied in the same manner. Instead of being *exactly* repeatable, such impressions are slight variants of one another, forcing us to ask: Is a raw sienna copy of *Visions* heavier than a yellow ochre copy? Is a pink Theotorman in *Visions* plate 7 warmer than a green one? Is a blue one sadder or more contrite than a yellow one? Was the change in robe color motivated by something other than Blake thinking he already had enough pink and green Theotormons? Was it even Blake's decision? Indeed, had the same colors always been placed exactly the same, the job of coloring would have been tedious for the Blakes and would have taken longer to finish than coloring freely or even in loose imitation of a model supplied by Blake. Jonathan Richardson's comment about how true artists copy models, whether other drawings or nature, is relevant: "Every man will naturally and unavoidably mix something of himself in all he does if he copies with any degree of liberty: If he attempts to follow his original servilely and exactly, that cannot but have a stiffness which will easily distinguish what is so done from what is performed naturally, easily, and without restraint" (Richardson 230; also quoted in Rogers 1:72).[35] In other words, variations among and edition's copies cannot be read as revisions, for they are technically, aesthetically, and psychologically inevitable among an edition of impressions colored by artists, rather than by colorists hired to wash prints systematically and strictly according to the artist's prototype—and even there variations are inevitable.[36]

While Blake knew that his process produced variations necessarily, the abstract object of "variation" was not in itself Blake's primary intention. His intention when printing and reprinting was, as he told Turner, to "take care that [the books] shall be done at least as well as any I have yet Produced" (E 771). As noted, the Blakes were not graphic purists; they were not interested in making an edition's copies look exactly the same, but neither were they interested in making them look completely different. The technical evidence demonstrates that Blake was far more catholic than a purist like Landseer and far more practical and efficient in his printmaking than has been heretofore imagined. He may not have been a very good businessman, professional in the manner of Boydell, Bartolozzi, or Woollett, but then neither is the average professional in any field.

NOTES

1. Lily Zimmermann, describing *Songs of Innocence and of Experience* copy BB for *Christie's Newsletter* (November 1988), summarizes these assumptions concisely: "Because Blake made the engravings and printed the copies of *Songs* himself, it was an expensive and time-consuming project. He could not afford to produce these illuminated books except upon individual order for his private customers" (4).

2. For a detailed analysis of edition printing and coloring and Mrs. Blake's role in these processes, see my *Blake and the Idea of the Book*, chaps. 12, 14, and 16,

forthcoming from Princeton University Press and referred to as *Book* throughout this article.

3. For similar comparisons, see Myra Glazer and Gerda Norvig's essay, "Blake's Book of Changes: On Viewing Three Copies of the *Songs of Innocence and of Experience*," which Carr thinks is "the best reading of the subtle changes in illumination from version to version" (185 n. 9).

Although he approached the issue with slightly different assumptions about production, Essick reached similar conclusions regarding the meaning of differences among illuminated prints and books, that they do not necessarily reflect revision but are the inevitable result of Blake's mode of production. His articles on the subject ought to be read by any one interested in reading Blake's illuminated books. See "Materials," "Teaching the Variations in *Songs*," and "How Blake's Body Means." This last article is a penetrating response to Carr's "Illuminated Printing: Toward a Logic of Difference." Both works are in Hilton and Vogler's *Unnam'd Forms*.

4. Carr associates difference in illuminated books with Derrida's *differànce* and believes that "variations . . . help to define the conditions of representation within illuminated printing. They point to an ongoing, open-ended production of meanings rather than a re-presentation of an original meaning" (Carr 190). For a discussion about whether Derrida's concept has been adequately understood by Carr and other critics, see Dan Miller's review of *Unnam'd Forms*.

5. The idea that Blake "loathed monotony" cannot be inferred from variations among illuminated prints. It could be argued that Blake agreed with Reynolds that monotony was a feature of the grand style. Reynolds stated that "grandeur of effect" can be produced "by making the colours very distinct and forcible, such as we see in those of Rome and Florence," where the absence of chiaroscuro or modulation of colors makes "simplicity . . . the presiding principle. . . . Certainly, nothing can be more simple than monotony; and the distinct blue, red, and yellow . . . have that effect of grandeur which was intended" (61). Blake responded, "These are Fine & Just Notions" (E 650).

6. From a letter of 31 March 1922 to Bernard Quaritch, the bookdealer, shown to me by G. E. Bentley, Jr. The printability of an adequately etched relief plate depended on ink being properly made, on the plate being properly inked, and on the dabber being handled skillfully. As ink splatters in illuminated impressions evince, even shallows relatively deep will be blemished if the surface is poorly inked. By conventional standards then or now, such impressions would be considered poor. In fact, impressions were said to be "either good or bad, according to the truth with which they represent the work on the plate: if they are too faint, or too full, they are equally bad; the first being deficient in force, the latter in clearness; which two qualities ought to unite in a perfect impression" (*Artist's Repository* 4:102). Yet in illuminated printing poorly inked impressions, which are by no means rare, do not signify an unskilled hand, the work of Mrs. Blake, or a failure of the inking tool. They signify at the least that Blake was less fastidious than his contemporaries and at most was willing to redefine the acceptable in graphic art.

7. While Carr and I may disagree about what constitutes a significant variant, I believe we are both trying, as Carr notes, "to direct attention to graphic qualities of illuminated pages too often ignored or dismissed" and that to do this necessarily means our having "to rethink and redefine our critical and editorial procedures" (191 n. 12).

Despite his claim that the subtlest changes in the verbal-visual sign system are "radical," significant, and deliberated (182), Carr's main example of a significant variation is *representational* and not at all dependent on comparisons with other copies of itself or on its difference from the plate image. he correctly notes that the adult figure in "The Little Boy found" appears female in some copies and male in others and that such difference is not explained by Blake's supposed preference for an androgynous Christ (194). At issue, as Carr notes, is the validity of critical systems of interpretation that predetermine meaning and refuse to acknowledge variations or versions in favor of an ideal text. He is right that different gender (like race in "The Little Black Boy") could make for different versions of the poem, since in the one the figure functions naturalistically and in the other symbolically. Knowing the modes and dates of production, the editor can ask: were impressions with the male and female features printed in the same session? Were they colored by Blake and/or Mrs. Blake?

8. Blake worked on versions of the *Last Judgment* from 1806 to the end of his life. A watercolor version commissioned by the countess of Egremont in 1807 was the subject of a letter to Ozias Humphry, of which three drafts are extant (Keynes, *Letters* 131–135). Another watercolor version (ca. 1809) corresponds to most but not all the details of the *Notebook* account, which raises the possibility that the description is of the untraced "fresco" (i.e., distempera) version that Blake was working on at the time of his death, and that he apparently had been working on for many years (see Butlin 2:639–648).

9. "Working up Effect is more an operation of Indolence than the Making out of the Parts . . . I speak here of Rembrandts & Rubens & Reynolds's Effect.—For Real Effect. is Making out the Parts & it is Nothing Else but That" (E 639). For a discussion of Blake's drawing style, its relation to sketching, and his views of sketches and "first thoughts," see *Book* chap. 4.

10. The idea that Art involves the conscious and deliberate organization of imprecise markings is suggested as early as *The Marriage of Heaven and Hell* (1790), by Reason's building or ideas supplied by Desire and by its being the circumference of energy (plates 6, 4).

11. Mellor, for example, argues that Blake chose his linear style because it was the most appropriate for communicating mental images to others (237). That line was always philosophically important to Blake, and especially so after 1800 (see Paley), is not in question; that its meaning or use was predicated on the nature of his mental images, rather than vice versa, is questionable.

12. In the prospectus Blake also states that his technique "exceeds in elegance all former methods" (E 692). According to Reynolds, "The Venetian is indeed the most splendid of the schools of elegance" (67), to which Blake responded: "Vulgarity & not Elegance—The Word Elegance ought to be applied to Forms. not to Colours" (E 652).

13. According to Reynolds, "to give a general air of grandeur at first view, all trifling or artful play of little lights, or an attention to a variety of tints is to be avoided; a quietness and simplicity must reign over the whole work; to which a breadth of uniform, and simple colour, will very much contribute" (61). Essick has defined "uniform" as signifying the work of a single mind (*William Blake, Printmaker*, 119). In light of Mrs. Blake's participation in the production process, this sense of the word is probably inaccurate.

14. If extant work represents the complete printing runs, then by the time of the prospectus Blake had produced eleven copies of *America*, thirteen copies of *Thel*, twenty-two copies of *Innocence*, four copies of *Marriage*, five copies of *Gates of Paradise*, and eleven copies of *Visions*, and he was about to print eight copies of *Experience* (See *Book*, chaps. 24–28).

15. More recently, Essick argues that variation is not a "conscious violation" of the norm but the inevitable result of Blake's mode of production ("Materials" 859), a result intentionally not suppressed but rather encouraged and taken creative advantage of (*William Blake and the Language of Adam* 190). As noted, Blake was not so

obsessed with clean copy to be much bothered with "Spots & Blemishes[,] which are beauties and not faults" (E 576).

16. See also Phillips, who defines illuminated printing as a "rebellion against conventional printing and publishing" ("Manuscript Draft" 35–36 and again in "*Songs*" 220–221); Easson, who believes illuminated printing was motivated by Blake's desire to escape the "divisions . . . between author, illustrator, engraver, printer, and publisher" characteristic of conventional book production (35); and Essick, who had argued that the "rugged lineation in the illuminated books" was "one result of Blake's reaction to reproductive engravings" ("Traditions" 66). From a postmodernist view, graphic difference could be thought even to represent the cultural or psychic diversity reason seeks to repress in its desire for order and uniformity (see McGowan 6, 207). For the view that Blake was "a small-scale entrepreneur," an artist who "incarnates the marriage of neoclassicism and the nascent Industrial Revolution" in positive and creative ways and whose "notion of a graphic cutting edge was identified in his mind with craft and industry," see chapter 4 of Boime's fine historically grounded analysis.

17. George Michael Moser was the Keeper of the Royal Academy, and apparently one of "The Modern Chalcographic Connoisseurs & Amateurs [who] admire only the work of the journeyman Picking out of whites & blacks in what is calld Tints[;] they despise drawing which despises them in return. They see only whether every thing is coverd down but one spot of light" (E 577).

18. Reynolds characterizes the Venetian manner as "a mere struggle without effect; *a tale told by an ideot, full of sound and fury, signifying nothing,*" and as having "debauch[ed] the young and unexperienced," and "turn[ed] off the attention of the connoisseur and of the patron of art, as well as that of the painter, from those higher excellencies of which the art is capable" (64, 67).

19. Blake responds with a firm "Nonsense" to Reynolds's claim "that the [paint brush] is the instrument by which . . . to obtain eminence" (E 646). Blake's opinion of flashy brush work is revealed most clearly in his attacks on Rosa: "Handling is Labour & Trick [,] Salvator Rosa employd Journeymen" (E 655), and "Salvator Rosa was precisely what he Pretended Not to be. his Pictures. are high Labourd pretensions to Expeditious Workmanship. He was the Quack Doctor of Painting His Roughnessess & Smoothnesses. are the Production of Labour & Trick. As to Imagination he was totally without Any" (E 654).

For Blake, Rosa's style of painting was analogous to the blot and blur drawing technique of Gilpin and Cozens, what Gilpin referred to as the "*bold and free manner*" (*Three Essays* 17): "free" refers to a stroke that has "no appearance of constraint. It is *bold*, when a part is given for the whole, which it cannot fail of suggesting. This is the laconism of genius. But sometimes it may be free, and yet suggest only how easily a line, which means nothing, may be executed. Such a stroke is not *bold*, but *impudent*" (17). This last statement appears to have been a nod to Reynolds, who warned students to avoid the seduction of execution or mechanical felicity.

20. Blake associated Woollett's practice with the Venetian and his own with the Florentine, although in fact Blake's style was far closer to Woollett's than to that of Italian Renaissance engravers like Raimondi or Ghisi (see Essick, *William Blake, Printmaker* 199ff). It was only late in his life, through the influence of Linnell, that Blake began to rethink his own graphic training and effect a style corresponding to his earlier theories. Dennis Read reminds us that Woollett and Strange were attacked in part because of their association with Cromek, who Blake believed had lied to him about engraving the *Grave* designs and stole his idea for the engraving of *Chaucers Canterbury Pilgrims* (69ff). As Blake himself stated: "Resentment for Personal Injuries has had some share in this Public Address" (E 574).

21. All prints, including line engravings, show the means of production, either the artist's through imitation (or facsimiles), the colorist's, or the printmaker's through translation. Indeed, the primary reason Landseer hated facsimiles was that they required the complete erasure of the graphic—or mechanical—code and thus the hand of the engraver. He abhorred color prints (impressions printed in colors) and colored prints (impressions colored by hand) most of all and for the same reason.

22. Advocating the aesthetic of the sketch but not its form raises theoretical and technical problems for an artist committed to line, a stylistic feature associated with last thoughts and reason. Aesthetically, Blake needed to reground neoclassical form on romantic concepts of imagination and vision, a theoretical regrounding thoroughly investigated by Eaves in *William Blake's Theory of Art.* It is manifest in Blake's assertion that invention and execution were inseparable, and in drawing style in which firm outlines are extensions of and not departures from first thoughts. For a discussion of these problems, see *Book,* chap. 4.

23. Aquatint had become the medium of choice for the very popular books of picturesque and topographical views, starting with Sandby's *12 Views in Aquatinta from Drawings taken on the spot in South Wales* (1775). It was also used extensively in books of facsimiles, such as Rowlandson's *Imitations of Modern Drawings after Gainsborough, Sawrey Gilpin, and Others* (1784–1788).

24. Landseer engraved in the style of Woollett, which he held as the paradigm. From Blake's perspective, this style seemed to subordinate line to tone and to dominate the print market. From Lanseer's perspective, it was an overtly linear art losing the market to authentic tonal processes like stipple and aquatint.

25. The dark shapes in aquatint are created by their being bitten longer in acid than the areas around them, which are "stopped out" with an acid-resistant varnish to prevent them from being etched. Thus, dark shapes are formed indirectly, whereas light shapes actually show the shape of the brush used to stop out.

26. In addition to Blake and Gainsborough, Stubbs, Barry, Rowlandson, Mortimer, Crome, Cotman, and Sandby all produced original prints in small editions and with variations. In addition to Gainsborough and Cozens, John Hassell also used sugar lift. In fact, Hassell appears to have independently invented the technique in 1791, though he did not publish until 1811 his *Calcographia: or, the Art of Multiplying, with Perfection, Drawings, after the Manner of Chalk, Black lead Pencil, and Pen and Ink.* On the title page Hassell reported having been "honoured with a Medal and Thirty Guineas by The Society of Arts etc. etc. etc." "Calcographia" was a technique that Hassell believed provided amateurs with the means of producing "fac similes" of their own works (27) and would induce "many of our first rate artists to give to posterity their sketches" (title page). The engraver C. N. Cochin responded similarly to chalk engraving, which was invented in 1740 to reproduce chalk drawings: "At last it was possible for an amateur of a student, living in the remotest parts of the country, to copy drawings by the great Masters!" (quoted in Gross 152).

27. Wordsworth's experiments in prosody reflect a similar move toward the simple and autographic. As Robert Mayo has argued, Wordsworth put to original and brilliant use material that had already become conventional. More significantly, Wordsworth was the first important poet to claim that these simple forms were *serious art,* an idea "subversive" and "radical" to those holding what he dismissed as preconceived notions of poetry, but an idea that obviously had an audience. Like most dialectics, like Lanseer's, Blake's, and our own, the one presented by Wordsworth in the Preface does not readily admit to grays.

28. Only color-printed impressions of the first state are extant, and the signature is presumably obscured by the color printing (see Essick, *Separate Plates* 24–29).

29. Blake's *Poetical Sketches* was published in 1783, but it appears to have been a project orchestrated by Blake's friends and not by Blake himself. But whether Blake enouraged or submitted to the project, it is important to note that twelve of the twenty-two extant copies seem to have been in Blake's possession, uncut and unstitched, at the time of his death, suggesting that "he did not show much interest" in the book (Bentley, *Blake Books* 346, 345). There is no documentary evidence that Blake sought out bookdealers to distribute or sell *Poetical Sketches,* or that he approached publishers with the new lyrical poems that were to become *Songs of Innocence,* at least three of which were included in *An Island in the Moon* (ca. 1784).

30. The huge increase in the 1818 and 1827 prices relative to those of 1793 reflect a change in the idea of the book, from a book of poems to a book of painted prints. For example, the L3.3s. for *Innocence* in 1818 translates as approximately 2s.5d. per print, which was the average price for an octavo-sized hand-colored print according to print catalogues of Boydell, Macklin and other print dealers. We do not know when Blake began charging the higher prices; the earliest known example is 1806, when he sold *Songs* copy E to Thomas Butts for L6.6s. (Bentley, *Blake Books* 414).

31. In *Blake and the Idea of the Book,* I estimate Blake's production costs per book by focusing primarily on the amount of paper and metal used per edition and their costs. What emerged was a pricing formula that was roughly the same as that used by conventional publishers: retail price about five times the cost of production (Gaskell 179; see *Book,* chap. 24).

32. Blake received eighty pounds from Macklin to engrave *The Fall of Rosamond* after Stothard in 1783 (Bentley, *Blake Records* 569). In 1799 Blake told Trusler that his rate for engravings was thirty guineas (E 703). The idea that twenty-two pounds was equal to about three months' income is based on *The Book of Trades* of 1804, which notes that a copperplate printer earned forty shillings a week (116). An engraver's income would fluctuate more than a printer's, compositor's, or most others in the trade because the work was commissioned free-lance. It seems, though, that the Blakes would have required an average income of two pounds a week and that they averaged that from 1800 through 1810 (*Blake Records* 606).

33. Actually, Blake says that "the few I have Printed & Sold are suufficient to have gained me great reputation," and he describes illuminated books as "unprofitable enough" to him but "Expensive to the Buyer" (E 771). As *Book* chapter 16 points out, these statements, made twenty-five years after the prospectus and when Blake was just beginning to show interest in reprinting his early books—and when his financial situation had changed dramatically (see also chapter 33)—must be read carefully. The number of books produced and sold by 1818 was greater than implied (approximately 139 and 125 respectively), though that is not something Blake was likely to remember, and his reputation was probably smaller. Blake seems intent on convincing Turner, a Yorkshire banker and well-known collector, that the works that he inquired about were rare, beautiful, and fairly priced.

34. One would not accuse Fuseli of such capitulation when he complained that he was tired of "contributing to make the public drop their gold into purses not my own" and planned "to lay, hatch, and crack an egg for myself too" (Knowles 1:174–175), an egg that became the Milton Gallery. Indeed, it would have been surprising had Blake remained impervious to such ambition when so many of his friends were planning commercial projects and the illustrated book was in its golden period (see Boime, chap. 4; Bentley, "Great Illustrated-Book").

35. Sir George Beaumont says much the same: "The servile imitator seems to me to mistake the *body* for the *soul;* and will never touch the heart" (quoted in Gilpin, *Two Essays* 26).

36. Coloring prints by hand will always produce variations unless stencils are used. The Manchester Etching Workshop's facsimiles of *Songs* copy B were handcolored, intentionally like their model, yet no two impressions are exactly alike since no two washes can be laid in exactly the same (see my "Recreating Blake"). The commercially colored copies of Blake's *Night Thoughts* demonstrate this as well. At least fourteen copies (colored ca. 1797) appear to be modeled after the same copy colored by Blake, but they show far greater variation among copies than the Manchester facsimiles. In other words, far greater artistic license was "exercised by the commercial colorists" (Grant 303 n. 3; see also Lange 134–136; Bentley, *Blake Books* 645–646, 956, and "Great Illustrated-Book" 82–88). Taking liberties with the model may reflect the confidence of good colorists, but it may also reflect financial considerations. The more closely one adheres to a model, the more slowly one works.

WORKS CITED

The Artist's Repository and Drawing Magazine. 4 vols. London, 1784–1786.

Bentley, G. E., Jr. *Blake Books: Annotated Catalogues of William Blake's Writings in Illuminated Printing.* Oxford: Clarendon Press, 1977.

———. *Blake Records.* Oxford: Clarendon Press, 1969.

———. "The Great Illustrated-Book Publishers of the 1790's and William Blake." In *Editing Illustrated Books,* ed. William Blissett, 57–96. New York: Garland, 1980.

Boime, Albert. *Art in an Age of Revolution. 1750–;1800.* Chicago: University of Chicago Press, 1987.

Butlin, Martin. *The Paintings and Drawings of William Blake.* 2 vols. New Haven: Yale University Press, 1981.

Carr, Steven Leo. "Illuminated Printing: Toward a Logic of Difference." In *Unnam'd Forms: Blake and Textuality,* ed. Nelson Hilton and Thomas A. Vogler, 177–196. Berkeley and Los Angeles: University of California Press, 1986.

Craig, William, Marshall. *An Essay on the Study of Nature in Drawing Landscapes.* London, 1793.

Crehan, Stewart. *Blake in Context.* Dublin: Gill & Macmillam, 1984.

Davids, Betsy, and Jim Petrillo: "The Artist as Book Printer: Four Short Courses." In *Artists' Books: A Critical Anthology and Sourcebook,* ed. Joan Lyons. New York: Gibbs M. Smith, in association with Visual Studies Workshop Press, 1985.

Easson, Kay Parkhurst. "Blake and the Art of the Book." In *Blake in His Time,* ed. Robert N. Essick and Donald Pearce, 35–52. Bloomington: Indiana University Press, 1980.

Eaves, Morris. "Blake and the Artistic Machine: An Essay in Decorum and Technology." *PMLA* 92 (1977): 903–927.

———. *William Blake's Theory of Art.* Princeton: Princeton University Press, 1982.

Erdman, David, V. *Complete Poetry and Prose of William Blake.* Newly Revised Edition. Ed. David V. Erdman, with commentary by Harold Bloom. New York: Doubleday, 1988.

———. *The Illuminated Blake.* Garden City, N.Y.: Anchor Press, 1974.

Essick, Robert N. "Blake and the Traditions of Reproductive Engraving." *Blake Studies* 5 (Autumn 1972): 59–103.

———. "How Blake's Body Means." In *Unnam'd Forms: Blake and Textuality,* ed. Nelson Hilton and Thomas Vogler, 197–217. Berkeley and Los Angeles: University of California Press, 1986.

———. "Preludium: Meditations on a Fiery Pegasus." In *Blake in His Time,* ed.

Robert N. Essick and Donald Pearce, 1–10. Bloomington: Indiana University Press, 1980.

———. *The Separate Plates of William Blake: A Catalogue.* Princeton: Princeton University Press, 1983.

———. "Teaching the Variations in *Songs.*" In *Approaches to Teaching Blake's Songs of Innocence and Experience,* ed. Robert Gleckner and Mark L. Greenberg, 93–98. New York: Modern Language Association, 1989.

———. "Variation, Accident, and Intention in William Blake's *The Book of Urizen.*" *Studies in Bibliography* 39 (1986): 230–234.

———. *William Blake and the Language of Adam.* Oxford: Clarendon Press, 1989.

———. *William Blake, Printmaker.* Princeton: Princeton University Press, 1980.

———. "William Blake, William Hamilton, and the Materials of Graphic Meaning." *English Language History* 52 (Winter 1985): 833–872.

Frye, Northrop. "Poetry and Design in William Blake." In *Blake, A Collection of Critical Essays,* ed. Northrop Frye, 119–126. Englewood Cliffs, N.J.: Prentice Hall, 1966.

Gaskell, Phillip. *A New Introduction to Bibliography.* New York: Oxford University Press, 1972.

Gilchrist, Alexander. *Life of William Blake.* 2 vols. London: Macmillan, 1863.

Gilpin, William. *Three Essays on Picturesque Beauty.* London, 1972.

———. *Two Essays.* London, 1804.

Glazer, Myra. "Blake's Little Black Boys: On the Dynamics of Blake's Composite Art." *Colby Library Quarterly* 16 (Winter 1980): 220–236.

Glazer, Myra, and Gerda Norvig. "Blake's Book of Changes: On Viewing Three Copies of the *Songs of Innocence and Experience.*" *Blake Studies* 9 (1980): 100–121.

Grant, John. "Review Article: Who Shall Bind the Infinite and Arrange It in Libraries? *William Blake's Writings* and *Blake Books.*" *Philosophical Quarterly* 61 (Summer 1982): 277–304.

Gross, Anthony. *Etching, Engraving, and Intaglio Printing.* London: Oxford University Press, 1970.

Hardie, Martin. *English Colored Books.* London: Methuen, 1906.

Johnson, Mary Lynn. "William Blake." In *The English Romantic Poets: A Review of Research and Criticism,* 4th ed., ed. Frank Jordan, New York: Modern Language Association, 1985.

Keynes, Geoffrey, ed. *The Letters of William Blake.* 3d ed. Oxford: Clarendon Press, 1980.

Knowles, John, ed. *The Life and Writings of Henry Fuseli.* 3 vols. London: H. Colburn, 1831.

Landseer, John. *Lectures on the Art of Engraving.* London, 1807.

Lange, Thomas V. "A Rediscoverd Copy of Young's *Night Thoughts.*" *Blake/An Illustrated Quarterly* 15 (Winter 1981–1982): 134–136.

McGann, Jerome, J. *A Critique of Modern Textual Criticism.* Chicago: University of Chicago Press, 1983.

———. "The Text, the Poem, and the Problem of Historical Method." *New Literary History* 12 (1981): 269–288.

McGowan, John. *Postmodernmism and its Critics.* Ithaca: Cornell University Press, 1991.

Mann, Paul. "Apocalypse and Recuperation: Blake and the Maw of Commerce." *English Language History* 52 (Spring 1985): 1–32.

Mayo, Robert. "The Comtemporaneity of the *Lyrical Ballads.*" *PMLA* 69 (1954): 486–522.

Mellor, Anne Kostelanetz. *Blake's Human Form Divine*. Berkeley and Los Angeles: University of California Press, 1974.

Miller, Dan. Review of *Unnam'd Forms: Blake and Textuality,* ed. Nelson Hilton and Thomas A. Vogler. *Blake/An Illustrated Quarterly* 21 (Winter 1987–1988): 116–124.

Mitchell, W.J.T. *Blake's Composite Art*. Princeton: Princeton University Press, 1978.

Paley, Morton. "The Truchessian Gallery Revisited." *Studies in Romanticism* 16 (Spring 1977): 165–176.

Phillips, Michael. "Printing Blake's *Songs:* 1789–94." *The Library* 18 (September, 1991): 205–229.

———. "William Blake's *Songs of Innocence* and *Songs of Experience* from Manuscript Draft to Illuminated Plate." *The Book Collector* (Spring 1979): 17–59.

Plowman, Dorothy, ed. *The Book of Urizen* [copy A.]. London: J. M. Dent and Sons, 1929.

Prideaux, S. T. *Aquatint Engraving*. London: Duckworth, 1909.

Read, Dennis. "The Context of Blake's "Public Address": Cromek and the Chalcographic Society." *Philological Quarterly* 60 (1981): 69–86.

Reynolds, Sir Joshua. *Disclosures on Art*. Ed. Robert R. Wark. New Haven: Yale University Press, 1975.

Richardson, Jonathan. *Works*. London, 1773. Rpt. Hildesheim: G. Olms, 1969.

Rogers, Charles. *A Collection of Prints in Imitation of Drawings*. 2 vols. London, 1778.

Santa Cruz Blake Study Group. Review of *The Complete Poetry and Prose of William Blake,* ed. David V. Erdman. *Blake/An Illustrated Quarterly* 18 (Summer 1984): 4–30.

———. "What Type of Blake?" In *Essential Articles for the Study of William Blake, 1970–1984,* ed. Nelson Hilton, 301–33. Hamden: Archon Books, 1986.

Viscomi, Joseph. *The Art of William Blake's Illuminated Prints*. Manchester: Manchester Etching Workshop, 1983.

———. *Blake and the Idea of the Book*. Princeton: Princeton University Press, 1993.

———. "Recreating Blake: The M. E. W. Blake Facsimiles." *Blake/An Illustrated Quarterly* 19 (Summer 1985): 4–23.

Blake's "London"

This excerpt from Heather Glen's *Vision and Disenchantment: Blake's "Songs" and Wordsworth's "Lyrical Ballads"* (1983) splendidly consolidates previous criticism into a new comprehension of one of Blake's most celebrated poems. This thoughtful reworking of a critical tradition is peculiarly interesting because Glen's approach is fundamentally Marxist. But the conscientiousness of her scholarship in drawing attention to how Blake explored socioeconomic conditions more subtly than contemporary radical essayists and political commentators, for instance, enables her to enhance basic Marxist assumptions rather than to be imprisoned by them. Thus she arrives at the convincing judgment not just of "London" but of all the songs of Innocence and Experience, that they "offer a vision reaching beyond [the] antinomian theology . . . [and] political radicalism" that were the matrices of Blake's thinking.

Glen's study bears some relation to American new historicism, although she places it closer to British cultural materialism. For other recent historical, social and ideological contextualizations of Blake's work, see Stuart Crehan, *Blake in Context* (1984); Jon Mee, *Dangerous Enthusiasm: William Blake and the Culture of Radicalism in the 1790s* (1992); and Iain McCalman, *Radical Underworld.* Any student of "London," of course, should also consult E. P. Thompson's essay by that title in Michael Phillips's *Interpreting Blake: Essays* (1978). A new book by Thompson, *Witness against the Beast: William Blake's Antinomianism,* is forthcoming from Cambridge University Press.

. . . Unlike 'The human Image' or 'The Human Abstract', 'London' identifies its speaker as a lonely wanderer, who passes through the streets of a particular city, and sees it from a lamenting distance:

> I wander thro' each charter'd street,
> Near where the charter'd Thames does flow
> And mark in every face I meet
> Marks of weakness, marks of woe.
>
> In every cry of every Man,
> In every Infants cry of fear,
> In every voice; in every ban,
> The mind-forg'd manacles I hear.

From *Vision and Disenchantment: Blake's "Songs" and Wordsworth's "Lyrical Ballads"* (Cambridge: Cambridge University Press, 1983), pp. 208–221.

In choosing to present his vision of social disaster thus, Blake was engaging with a familiar literary mode. The assumption of a stance of 'observation', freely passing judgment on that which is before it, is common to much eighteenth-century literature: 'There mark what ills the scholar's life assail.'[1] But nowhere is it more prominent than in that which attempts to describe London, a place of bewildering diversity, changing and growing rapidly, in which a new kind of anonymity and alienation was becoming a remarked-upon fact of life.[2] Indeed, it seems that in the literature of London the implications of this state were beginning to become an explicit preoccupation. Thus, Ben Sedgly in 1751:

> No man can take survey of this opulent city, without meeting in his way, many melancholy instances resulting from this consumption of spirituous liquors: poverty, diseases, misery and wickedness, are the daily observations to be made in every part of the great metropolis: whoever passes along the streets, may find numbers of abandoned wretches stretched upon the cold pavement, motionless and insensible, removed only by the charity of passengers from the danger of being crushed by carriages, trampled by horses, or strangled with filth in the common sewers.[3]

'Take survey of', 'meeting in his way', 'observations to be made', 'whoever passes along the streets may find'—the sense throughout is of an anonymous and freely observing stranger, rather than a member of a society who sees himself as shaped by it and interacting with others within it. Perhaps such a perspective is natural in a documentary work such as Sedgly's. But this sense of the self in the city is central, too, to much of the most powerful imaginative literature of the century, literature which is after all not merely a description of or meditation upon the world, but the recreation of a certain mode of being within it. It is a sense that informs the novels of Defoe: the figures of Roxana and Colonel Jack and Moll Flanders move through the streets from adventure to adventure with a freedom from social constraint which is only possible because of the nature of London life.[4] It is to be found in Gay's *Trivia* and *The Beggar's Opera;* in Boswell's *Journal;* in Johnson's *London,* and even in those of his essays which seem to have nothing to do with London at all:

> He that considers how little he dwells upon the condition of others, will learn how little the attention of others is attracted by himself. While we see multitudes passing before us, of whom perhaps not one appears to deserve our notice, or excites our sympathy, we should remember, that we likewise are lost in the same throng, that eye which happens to glance upon us is turned in a moment on him that follows us, and that the utmost which we can reasonably hope or fear is to fill a vacant hour with prattle, and be forgotten.[5]

Here, the tone is one of judicious moralizing. But the imagery is that of the confusing eighteenth-century London street, in which relations with one's fellow beings involve attracting attention, deserving notice, glancing and turning, even *exciting* sympathy: in which the other is the object of observation rather than one with whom one interacts. And the supposedly free individual who sees those who pass before him as a mighty spectacle is himself 'lost in the same throng'.

The eighteenth-century London street was not, then, merely a place where suffering and distress could be seen on a hitherto unprecedented scale: it was also a place where that sense of the other as object—often as feeble and wretched object—which Blake exposes in 'The Human Abstract' ('we . . . make somebody Poor') was the dominant mode of relationship. And it is a sense which is an ironic point of reference in 'London'. For this poem begins with a speaker who seems to be a detached observer, who wanders 'thro'' the streets of the city and 'marks' the sights before him. Yet his is not the lively and distinctive London of Defoe or Gay or Johnson: what he records is not variety, but sameness. To him, both streets and river are simply 'charter'd': the different faces which pass all bear the same message, 'Marks of weakness, marks of woe'. And the tight quatrain with its present indicative tense conveys not flexible responsiveness to constantly changing possibilities, but entrapment. What this speaker sees is fatally linked to the way in which he sees it. In the notebook draft, the second word of the third line was 'see': Blake's alteration limits any incipient sense of freedom. The triple beat of 'mark'—an active verb materializing into two plural nouns—registers a new consciousness of this 'I's implication in the world 'thro' which he wanders. What he observes is the objectification of his own activity.

'Mark' is not the only change which Blake made in this stanza. In the notebook draft, the first two lines read:

> I wander thro' each dirty street,
> Near where the dirty Thames does flow.
> (K170)

The substitution, in the engraved version, of 'charter'd', signals a complex process of poetic thought. For 'charter'd' in 1793 was a word at the centre of political debate: a word whose accepted meaning of 'granted privileges or rights' had been challenged by Paine a year earlier, in a book whose sales had by now reached 200,000:

> It is a perversion of terms to say, that a charter gives rights. It operates by a contrary effect, that of taking rights away. Rights are inherently in all the inhabitants; but charters, by annulling those rights in the majority, leave the right by exclusion in the hands of a few . . . all charters have no other than an indirect negative operation. They do not give rights to A, but they make a difference in favour of A by taking away the right of B, and consequently are instruments of injustice.[6]

No contemporary of Blake's could have read the two altered opening lines of his poem as an objective description of the trading organization of the city. Their repetition of 'charter'd' forces into prominence the newly, ironically recognized sense that the very language of 'objective' description may be riddled with ideological significance: that beneath the assurance of polite usage may lurk another, 'cheating' meaning.[7] And this sense informs the stanza in a peculiar way. It is as though beneath the polite surface—the observer in London wandering the streets of a city whose 'charter'd' organization he notes, as the guidebooks noted its commercial organization, and whose manifestations of distress and depravity he, like hundreds of other eighteenth-century writers, remarks—there is another set of meanings, which are the *reverse* of those such description could customarily bear. They are not meanings private to Blake: and they are meanings which focus in those sound-linked and repeated words, 'mark' and 'charter'd'.

The ambiguities of 'charter'd' had been explicitly debated: those of 'mark' are perhaps less obvious. Yet Blake, altering the poem in his notebook, has done an extraordinary thing. He has chosen a term commonly found in polite descriptions of London, to indicate the expected attitude of detached interest, and used it in such a way as to evoke a whole cluster of powerful, far from detached and far from polite resonances—resonances which question the value and perhaps even the possibility of such detachment. For 'mark' was not simply used by polite gentlemen to indicate the different sights of London to one another: it was, in the late eighteenth century, a word used on the streets of London by those who were by no means gentlemen, those artisan classes whose newly articulate radical politics were still intertwined with, and sometimes framed in the language of, prophetic millenarianism. Such men did not causally wander through the city marking the sights: with desperate intensity they turned from the Bible to the world around them to read the signs of the coming millenium. The 'marks' which they saw were the 'marks' of God's promise, or—more often—those of damnation, the signs of a rotten society:

> And he causeth all, both small and great, rich and poor, free and bond, to receive a mark in their right hand, or in their foreheads:
> And that no man might buy or sell, save he that hath the mark of the beast.
>
> (Revelation 13:16–17)

In this, their 'marking' was akin to that of the prophet or the judge:

> And the LORD said unto him, Go through the midst of the city, through the midst of Jerusalem, and set a mark upon the foreheads of the men that sigh and that cry for all the abominations that be done in the midst thereof.
>
> (Ezekiel 9:4)

(This latter 'marker' is 'a man clothed in linen, with a writer's inkhorn by his side' [verse 3].)[8] And a mark on the face (in part, surely, a reference to the very real marks on the faces of the London crowd)[9] would to them suggest Cain, the 'man of blood' (K176) marked by God, the builder of the first city (referred to in *Poetical Sketches* as 'Cain's city built with murder', K41). Cain's was a city built in 'the Land of Nod', which in the Hebrew was the land of wandering. These Biblical allusions, abstruse though they may seem to the modern reader, would have been felt very immediately by anyone familiar with the language of London streets in the 1790s: felt not as pointing to a particular interpretation—the 'marker' as Ezekiel, or the 'marks' as marks of sin ('weakness') or pity ('woe')—but as signalling a stance towards the city at once very different from that of conventional polite observation, and posing a radical challenge to it.[10]

The feeling of this opening stanza is, then, most unlike that of other eighteenth-century accounts of London—a feeling not of detachment, but of involvement, not of emancipation, but of constriction. And it is a feeling which by the second stanza has become dominant:

> In every cry of every Man,
> In every Infants cry of fear,
> In every voice; in every ban,
> The mind-forg'd manacles I hear.

The illusory freedom of 'wandering' and 'marking', the visible 'marks of weakness, marks of woe' have given way to sounds, sounds which by their nature are less controllable than visual images.[11] The syntactic structure, with main verb and subject postponed until the last two words, is exact in its effect: this speaker is dominated by what he hears, trapped within the world on which he is trying to comment. And the repeated 'every', 'every', 'every', with the monotonously regular rhythym, conveys an impression of sameness even in difference. Almost overwhelmed by that which surrounds him, this thinly present 'I' reduces all to the same miserable message. The world of London debate and dissent, of real controversy and real suffering, of real passing people on the streets, which is in some sense there in the first stanza—at a remove, but felt, in those charged words 'marks' and 'charter'd', and in the images of streets and Thames and of faces meeting and moving on—has here been further abstracted, even, paradoxically, as it threatens to engulf him.

And this sense of entrapment within a world in which no possibility of change can be seen is taken up and confronted in the final line of the stanza. Like 'charter'd', the image of 'mind-forg'd manacles' evokes a contemporary political debate—a debate which concerns precisely this paradox. On the one hand, radical thinkers claimed that crime and suffering ('weakness' and 'woe') were the result of social oppression and official mystification: Godwin in 1793 was to affirm: 'In reality the chains fall off of themselves when the magic of opinion is dissolved.'[12] On the other, conservatives argued that 'human nature' made social control absolutely necessary:

> Society cannot exist, unless a controlling power upon will and appetite be placed somewhere; and the less of it there is within, the more there must be without. It is ordained in the eternal constitution of things, that men of intemperate minds cannot be free. Their passions forge their fetters.[13]

On the one hand, the ills of society are traced to the 'objective' manacles of repression, on the other to the 'subjective' failings of human nature. And Blake's use of the image seems an ironic commentary on both sides of the debate. The other-denying mechanisms of repression which are visible and audible all around his speaker are intimately present in the 'mind' which seeks to distance and to judge: the one cannot be said to cause the other, for both are interlocked. The facts which have been presented as alien and unalterable are the manifestations of an activity: that distancing of the other, that inability to realize transforming human *potentia* ('these flowers of London town') which has been implicit in his speaker's stance toward the world no less than in the abstracting (and constricting) legal process of chartering, and the 'bans' which seek licence and prohibit human freedoms. These 'manacles', binding the hands that might help one another, are 'forg'd' *both* for *and* by 'the mind'. There is, significantly, no direction as to whose mind is meant, for this is a condition from which no member of the society, including he who judges it, is exempt. 'Mind-forg'd manacles' expresses both dismay at what the speaker 'hears' and a defeated self-reflexiveness: there can be no position of detachment in this world, and any compassion within it is impotent.

The recognition implicit in this image is analogous to that at the end of 'The Human Abstract': 'There grows one in the Human Brain.' Yet this poem does not, like that, end here. What follows is at once integrally related to and yet startlingly different from what has preceded it:

How the Chimney-sweepers cry,
Every blackning Church appalls,
And the hapless Soldiers sigh
Runs in blood down Palace walls

But most thro' midnight streets I hear
How the youthful Harlots curse
Blasts the new-born Infants tear
And blights with plagues the Marriage hearse.

Instead of a monotonous, stereotyped picture of passive misery there are vivid images of violent activity: instead of the abstracted 'marking' of a solitary 'I' there is a sharply realized, surrealistic vision of a whole network of social relationships. The syntactic structure in which the 'I' is nominally in control becomes confused: the rhythm changes from iambic regularity to heavy trochees. Blake is alluding to real sights here, as his readers would have recognized: to the smog which covered late eighteenth-century London like a pall, and whose blackening effect on the buildings was frequently noted;[14] to the anti-war slogans that were beginning to be daubed with paint on the walls of public buildings.[15] But these familiar sights here become signs of the inner logic of the society: they constitute a concrete realization of that which has been implicit in the poem from the beginning. The essential mode of relationship with this city—between its institutions and its people—is here portrayed as one of *marking*—blackening, daubing with blood, blighting with plague. The violence of these two stanzas—of the Sweep and Soldier, outside of and marking church and palace, of the harlot, excluded from the society yet infecting it—is the mirror-image of that detached observation, isolated and alienated yet imprinting all with its own damning stamp, dramatized in the opening stanza.

Yet if it is a mirror-image, it is one which is realized in a way in which the image of London in the first two stanzas is not—more definite, more active, more complex. It is not simply that where there were 'faces' there are now actual people, the Chimney Sweeper, the Soldier, the Harlot: the social interconnections which in the first two stanzas were obscured by abstraction have become manifest. The 'marking' of a series of passing impressions has given way to a much more immediate vision of London as a city composed of human beings, not passing and separate, but in relationship. It is a distorted relationship, and felt more directly as such: that reversal of norms which was obliquely registered in the ironic use of 'charter'd' focusses finally in the concrete image of the 'Marriage hearse'. And the previously almost undifferentiated cries are not simply clearer and more distinctive: they have a force of a kind unperceived before. No longer are they the passive signs of a generalized 'weakness' and 'woe': they have taken on a startling—and by the last stanza actively destructive—materiality. The cries have become marks.

The first two stanzas of 'London', then, offer an alienated, observer's account of the city through which, oddly, reversed meanings seem to run: at the third stanza, with startling suddenness, those meanings leap into life. The hidden exclusiveness of 'charter'd' ('charters . . . leave the right by exclusion in the hands of a few')[16] becomes objectified in the Palace walls deaf to the 'sigh' which marks them, and in the excluding wall which provides no answer to the Chimney

Sweeper's cry. And in the final stanza observation turns to revelation, as the 'impolite' Biblical meanings of mark become prominent, with the image of the Harlot and of a plague from which none is spared.[17] The effect is extraordinary. And it brings to mind a third, and not irrelevant, meaning of 'mark'.

'London' seems much closer to Blake's own voice than do many others of the *Songs of Experience:* most obviously, this is because of the way in which it pushes beyond exposure of its speaker's limitations (such as find in 'Holy Thursday' or 'A Poison Tree') into a more apocalyptic mode. But there is another sense in which it seems to come from Blake, rather than an anonymous speaker—from 'The Author & Printer W Blake'. For the poem is a relief engraving, made by a process of deliberate and corrosive 'marking'. And the materialization of the Chimney Sweeper's, Soldier's, Harlot's cries recalls, by analogy, this other process in which words become marks—the process of engraving and printing in which Blake was more intimately involved than any other English poet. 'London', like the other Songs, was produced in two stages. The first was the preparation of the stereotype plate. Blake traced his text and design in gum arabic—which is resistant to acid—upon paper: he then applied the paper to the surface of a copper plate. When the plate was exposed to acid, those surfaces not covered with gum arabic were eaten away, and the upraised lines of the design and the words appeared, as in mirror-writing, reversed.[18] This is the 'method' which he described in *The Marriage of Heaven and Hell:* 'printing in the infernal method, by corrosives, which in Hell are salutary and medicinal, melting apparent surfaces away, and displaying the infinite which was hid' (K154). Once this first stage was carried out, the page was then printed from the stereotype and coloured.

The production of protruding stereotype 'marks' within which a reversed meaning was contained and the printing of the real design of which these were but a mirror-image, was thus a familiar process to Blake—and one which he seems to have seen as intrinsically linked to the vision he sought to present.[19] And it is a process which has a curious parallel in the progression of this poem. For the marks which Blake made would appear in relief when corroded by acid, when that which surrounded them was eaten away—just as the 'marking' of the speaker in the first two stanzas traces a single message which becomes more and more prominent as the surrounding world becomes less and less realized. The 'marks' on the plate were the reverse of what was ultimately to appear as the design. And the startling reversal in 'London', from a 'marking' speaker to the visible, actual, violent 'marks' of the two final stanzas—'marks' which mirror back his own 'marking', not as a reflection but as a realization of the hidden interconnections of a society in which any position of control is illusory—bears an extraordinary resemblance to that moment of reversal with which Blake would have been most familiar: the moment when the relief outline suddenly takes on an existence seemingly independent of the engraver, as the printed result appears. There is even an analogue to the colouring of the page in the colours which appear for the first time in the third stanza, the 'blackning Church' and the blood of the Soldier, the submerged pun of 'appalls'. And the fire which is portrayed halfway down the page recalls the Devil's activity in *The Marriage of Heaven and Hell:* 'with corroding fires he wrote the following sentence now perceived by the minds of men, & read by them on earth' (K150).

To read the poem with this in mind is, I think, to come closer to its essential feeling than it is to see it as a statement either of moral outrage or despair. It is more like the voice of a 'marking' prophet—'If you go on So, the result is So' (K392); a prophet whose 'marking' is also that of the artist, disclosing the hidden logic of a whole society in a way which transcends rational analysis, creating something which becomes independent of—and capable of questioning—his own activity, as the work of art achieves a revelatory life, beyond anything its creator may consciously have intended.[20] The first half of the poem, with its alienated, abstracting speaker, both dramatizes that mode of relationship which 'makes somebody Poor', and exposes the nature of a society in which it is dominant. In the London depicted here, there is no sense of human potentiality, and no creative change: this world simply *is*. Reciprocal human relationships in which otherness is acknowledged and the needs of all harmonized do not exist: the only relationships—as the recurrent imagery of licensing and prohibition, of buying and selling, of human passivity and misery suggests—are instrumental ones. People have become objects. And the intrinsic import of this is made strikingly manifest in the two final stanzas. 'If you go on So'— in the mode presented in *Songs of Experience*—the linear mode of control and domination, in which there is no realization of the uniqueness of others, no respect for difference or attempt to meet human needs—'the result is So': a destructive 'blighting' of the whole society. And it is a 'result' which is not projected into the future, but which, the relentless present tense insists, is implicit in what is.

Yet the effect is not one of defeat: these two final stanzas have none of the flattened immobility of 'There souls of men are bought and sold'. Partly, this is because of their 'revolutionary' suggestiveness: those who in the other fragment are passive victims here have a terrible force. There are certainly seditious reso-nances here, in the familiar subversive figure of the Chimney Sweeper, the possi-ble allusion to anti-war protests in 'Runs in blood down palace walls', even in the dramatic rendering of the voices of the oppressed (in 1795 *Pigott's Political Dictio-nary* was to define *Groan* simply as 'Sedition'). But Blake's vision is far from simply revolutionary, as a comparison with a modern, anti-colonialist vindication of violence reveals:

> when it is their turn to be broken in, when they are taught what shame and hunger and pain are, all that is stirred up in them is a volcanic fury whose force is equal to that of the pressure put upon them . . . first, the only violence is the settler's; but soon they will make it their own; that is to say, the same violence is thrown back upon us as when our own reflection comes forward to meet us when we go towards a mirror.[21]

The violence which erupts in the closing stanzas of 'London' *is* the mirror-image of that denied and suppressed violence implicit in 'charter'd' and 'mark'. Yet if Blake shows this, he also shows that such mirror-imaging provides no escape: for his poem remains locked within the present indicative tense. His images of violence are also images of impotence: the Soldier's sigh 'runs down' the outside of the palace; the Chimney Sweeper and the church remain paralysingly locked together ('to appall' is to dismay into inactivity, rather than to stir into action); the Harlot's curse, effective though it may be, offers no release. The 'revolutionary' import of these images does not, it seems, point toward potential change: and it is not centrally from this that the feeling of excitement in these stanzas comes. Rather, it comes from that surrealistic sharpness of realization, in which meanings hidden from conventional vision are suddenly made manifest: the vividness with which that which in the first two stanzas was distanced and abstracted leaps into life before us, as the work of art leaps into life before the artist.

It is not, however, a realization which is also a transformation, like the growing vision of the children as angels in the Innocent 'Holy Thursday'. The satisfaction here is of a wholly different kind: one which has led one critic to say of the poem that it 'shuts like a box'.[22] If we begin with an isolated observer 'marking' the faces he passes we end with an isolated Harlot and the suggestion of faces blighted with plague: if we begin with a city licensed out to trade we end with love as a financial transaction. That which in the opening stanzas was abstracted by convention is here simply exposed in its human reality. And by the final stanza the speaker merely registers what is around him: the compassion perhaps implicit in his recognition of 'weakness' and 'woe', of the 'haplessness' of the Soldier, has been reduced to passivity by the force of the two doubly emphasized final verbs.[23]

Yet embedded within the stanza is a haunting poetic sense of that which is missing; a sense which Fredric Jameson has declared to be the only way in which 'the concept of freedom' can arise in 'a stagnant time':

> an ontological impatience in which the constraining situation itself is for the first time perceived in the very moment in which it is refused . . . a sudden perception of an intolerable present which is at the same time, but implicitly and however dimly articulated, the glimpse of another state in the name of which the first is judged.[24]

The closing lines of 'London' contain just such a negative articulation of alternative possibility. For through their images of the babe and of tears, and that forceful final verb 'Blasts', plays a disquietingly counterpointing allusion:

> And pity, like a naked new-born babe,
> Striding the blast, or heaven's cherubin, hors'd
> Upon the sightless couriers of the air,
> Shall blow the horrid deed in every eye,
> That tears shall drown the wind . . .
>
> (*Macbeth*, ACT I, SC. 7)

These lines seem to have fascinated Blake: one of his large colour prints of 1795 was an illustration of them. And that sense of the enormous power of the apparently helpless, of the radical nature of the claim that is made by trust, the transcendent force of 'Pity', which is at their centre, is also central in *Songs of Innocence:* 'Then like a mighty wind they raise to heaven the voice of song', 'Then cherish pity; lest you drive an angel from your door.' Here, at the end of 'London', their evocation underlines, even amidst the images of violence, the absence of any such potency. 'Blasts' has become a verb, cancelling out those drowning tears; this babe has none of the paradoxical 'striding' energy of Shakespeare's—he is 're-duced to misery'. And that 'pity' which in the earlier passage rides out and vanquishes the storm of evil is here nowhere to be found. Unlike the Innocent 'Holy Thursday', this poem does not urge towards action, suggesting the disturbing possibility of a revalued 'Pity': rather, the allusions to *Macbeth* all point towards its paralysing obliteration:

But most thro' midnight streets I hear
How the youthful Harlots curse
Blasts the new-born infants tear
And blights with plagues the Marriage hearse.

Blake makes it very clear that the disaster portrayed here is not inevitable. It has not been imposed by an unchangeable social order, nor is it the product of 'the ancient curse', the inborn evil of mankind. In 'London' it is shown to be the inevitable result of particular, chosen modes of relating to others, here manifested throughout a whole society. And this realization in one sense does imply its opposite: what has been humanly chosen and created can be humanly reversed. As the 'ancient Proverb' of the 1792 notebook affirms:

Remove away that black'ning church,
Remove away that marriage hearse,
Remove away that—of blood,
You'll quite remove the ancient curse.
                    (K176)

Yet the difference between the final stanza of 'London' and the achieved vision of *Songs of Innocence* points very sharply to Blake's sense of the limitation of that implicit, negative 'concept of freedom' which might arise out of 'impatience' with and 'refusal' of 'an intolerable present', rather than out of the active realization of potentiality.[25] Against the Pity-less deadlock of 'London' we might place the freely emerging, forward-pointing interplay of 'The Ecchoing Green', that portrait of society organized in ways characteristic of *Innocence*. The difference is not simply one between a small, known community and a large bewildering city—although the characteristic polite stance of 'marking' the sights of the city provided Blake with a familiar example of that mode of relationship whose logic he wished to explore: it is a more fundamental difference, evident from the very first word of the Song of *Experience*. 'London' begins with an isolated 'I', wandering randomly, and reducing all the phenomena he notes to a common pattern: in 'The Ecchoing Green' the speaking voice is a plural one, which does not attempt to control. There is no 'I' trapped by, yet judging all, but a 'we' which is framed by a living landscape, and makes space to play within it. Where the Experienced speaker registers sameness yet division, the Innocent Song celebrates mutuality in diversity; each of the crescendo of sounds in the opening stanza, each of the activities of the succeeding generations, of dawn and of dusk, is realized separately and clearly, and each harmonizes with the others. But in 'London', this 'ecchoing' interplay of different perspectives is replaced by the unresponsiveness of dividing walls, and the impotent violence of isolated sighs and cries.

And the inherent logic of each of the societies thus produced is revealed in the very different endings of the two poems. 'The Ecchoing Green' as it approaches its close begins to take on the completed shape of a circle: a shape which plays against its other shape of linear progression and its images of cessation and nightfall. There is no such delicate tension in 'London': here, the final stanza is marked with irreversible concreteness. And if it has the excited energy of imaginative definition, it has none of the subtler satisfaction to be found in the Innocent Song: the satisfaction of confirmation in change—a confirmation which forms, against those images of ending, a configuration of continuing possiblity, of a 'sport' which will continue unseen. The protagonists there are not, as in 'London', locked up in a terrible *stasis*. For the engagement with actuality and its changing potentialities which this poem presents is diametrically opposed to that Experienced detachment and 'marking', that attempt to distance and to control, which is manifested so inescapably not merely in the rigidified, divisive institutions of the society, but in the answering 'marking' of its victims. There, where there is neither creative acceptance of nor interaction with difference, there can be no movement beyond what is. The contrast between these two poems is the essential contrast between the two 'states' which *Songs of Innocence* and *Songs of Experience* explore, here writ large as an absolute opposition between two modes of social organization.

Taken together, *Songs of Innocence* and *Songs of Experience* present a view of morality and its place in human affairs that is extraordinary in its difference from that of any other literature of their time. Their radical questioning of 'Ideas of Good & Evil'[26] seems in some ways very close to that of the antinomianism which remained an intimate part of Blake's mental universe to the end of his life.[27] These poems reveal much about the reasons for the continuing potency of that antinomianism in his thinking: for here its implications are realized and explored in terms of the acutal society in which he lived. Here, its rejection of the Moral Law is charged with the newly confident ironic energy of Paine-ite demystification: official moral absolutes are challenged by a sharp realization of the social strategies which they justify and perpetuate. Yet Blake's minutely articulate vision of the interconnections between the dominant modes of relationship of a society and the creative or destructive force of the 'virtues' to which it appeals is far more incisive and more subtly exploratory than anything to be found in the writings either of the radicals or of the sectaries. The tree of death and mystery which takes shape within and materializes at the end of 'A Poison Tree' and 'The Human Abstract' might be seen as an ironic version of that 'Mysterious Tree / Of Good & Evil & Mystery' (K759) which Blake was to attack in his most straightforwardly antinomian poem, 'The Everlasting Gospel'. But the way in which these Songs trace the manner of that tree's growth and its relation to human action, its compulsive power and its devastating psychological and social results, has no parallel in antinomian theology. Similarly, the antinomian belief in a coming millennium, the destruction of Babylon, becomes in the *Songs* not a vision of impending divine vengeance, but of a retribution actually immanent within present social relationships. The implicit warnings with which the Innocent 'Holy Thursday' and 'The Chimney Sweeper' end point not towards God's judgment, nor even (as the Paine-ite radicals might) toward the coming revenge of one exploited group upon those who have oppressed them: the disasters they threaten are seen as inescapable in a society whose structures fail to actualize the 'virtues' in which its real creative *potentia* consists. Even the evocative closing image of the Harlot in 'London' seems less the Whore of Babylon of millenarian prophecy than an actual 'youthful' victim, whose 'curse' brings not revolution but death: less a harbinger of future doom than the manifest symbol of a society which is even now being destroyed by its own internal logic.

And most importantly, that sense of the divine within the human central to antinomian thinking in all its forms becomes in these poems something more than a theological affirmation of individual human value—and something far more than a demand for the 'rights of man'.[28] For the Songs of *Innocence* trace the manifestations of the 'Divine Image' not in individuals, but in particular, active relationships, relationships which are shown to exist even in the midst of an all-too-familiar world of exploitation and division. In portraying the imaginative love of an anonymous little sweep, the transcendent beauty of the charity-children's ceremony, the world of confidence and security which may be created between mother and child, the 'third joyous kingdom of play',[29] the hope and trust that find their expression and vindication in prayer and its answering, the instinct of sympathy with 'anothers woe', Blake is affirming the fundamental importance of real experiences which the radical protest of his day tended to ignore: experiences which—both collections suggest—must be central to any creative human community, experiences of a mode of relationship quite different from the sterile opposition of privileged and unprivileged, oppressor and oppressed, in terms of which so much of late eighteenth-century English society was structured. Blake does not ignore those dominant exploitative structures or the human defamation and distress they caused: the Songs of *Innocence* are neither sentimental nor escapist. But neither is he guilty of the reverse sentimentalism of despair: one after another the Songs of *Experience* expose the destructive deadlock which results from even well-intentioned ('moral') failure to recognize and actualize that existing *potentia* which the earlier collection celebrated. The demystificatory ironies of these poems may derive some of their energy from that political rejection of official pieties which by 1792 was beginning to be widely articulated in the London which Blake knew: their more radical questioning of any morality, their presentation of the heavens and hells men create for themselves and one another within this world, seems to owe something to the antinomian tradition of which he was the heir. But inheritance is not necessarily a passive thing. And in their precise and sophisticated exploration of the interplay between social being and social consciousness, their articulation of the ways in which a transforming human *potentia* might be realized, *Songs of Innocence* and *Songs of Experience* offer a vision which reaches far beyond that of the antinomian theology or the political radicalism within whose matrix much of Blake's thinking seems to have been formed: a vision finely worked out in the deceptively simple language of song.

NOTES

1. Citations of Blake are to *The Complete Writings of William Blake with Variant Readings*, ed. Sir Geoffrey Keynes (London, 1972). Hereafter cited parenthetically as K.

2. See George Rudé, *Hanoverian London* (London, 1973), ch. 1; Raymond Williams, *The Country and the City* (London, 1973), pp. 142–52; Max Byrd, *London Transformed: Images of the City in the Eighteenth Century* (New Haven and London, 1978).

3. Ben Sedgly, *Observations on Mr. Fielding's Enquiry* (London, 1751), pp. 22–3, quoted in Byrd, *London Transformed,* p. 23.

4. See Byrd, *London Transformed,* esp. pp. 26–8, for an excellent discussion of this. Cf. also Richard Sennett, *The Fall of Public Man* (New York, 1976), pp. 28–122, on the more general issue of 'role-playing' within the eighteenth-century city.

5. Samuel Johnson, *The Rambler* 159.

6. Paine, *Rights of Man,* ed. Henry Collins (London, 1969), pp. 242–3. On the sale of the volume, see Henry Collins' Introduction to this edition, p. 36, and Richard

Altick, *The English Common Reader: A Social History of the Mass Reading Public, 1800–1900* (Chicago, 1957), p. 70.

For a fuller discussion of the debate over 'charters', see David Erdman, *Blake: Prophet Against Empire: A Poet's Interpretation of the History of His Own Times* (Princeton, 1969), pp.276–7 and E. P. Thompson, 'London', in *Interpreting Blake*, ed. Michael Phillips, pp. 6–10. An interesting footnote is provided by Burke himself, who seems to have drawn attention to this ambiguity in the word as early as 1784: 'The charters, which we call by distinction *great*, are public instruments of this nature; I mean the charters of King John and King Henry the Third. The things secured by these instruments may, without any deceitful ambiguity, be very fitly called the *chartered rights of men.*

These Charters have made the very name of a Charter dear to the heart of every Englishman. But, Sir, there may be, and there *are* Charters, not only different in nature, but formed on principles the *very reverse* of those of the great Charter. Of this kind is the Charter of the East-India Company. *Magna Charta* is a Charter to restrain power, and to destroy monopoly: the East India Charter is a Charter to establish monopoly, and to create power. Political power and commercial monopoly are *not* the rights of men; and the rights to them derived from Charters, it is fallacious and sophisticated to call "the Chartered Rights of men". These Chartered Rights . . . do at least suspend the natural rights of mankind at large; and in their very frame and constitution are liable to fall into a direct violation of them.' (Taken from 'a short Abstract from Mr. Burke's celebrated speech upon the East India Bill, in which the line of distinction between the different sorts of Charters is drawn with great truth and great precision', *Chartered Rights* (1784).

   7. Cf. Blake's notebook entry of these years:

Why should I care for the men of thames,
Or the cheating waves of charter'd streams? (K166)

   8. These 'marks' are marks of salvation. Harold Bloom, *Poetry and Repression* (New Haven, 1976) argues that this is 'the precursor-text' of the poem. This seems rather literal-minded, and at odds with the pervasive sense that the 'marks', like the marks of the Beast, might be marks of damnation. Michael Ferber, ' "London" and its Politics', *ELH,* 48 (1981), pp. 310–38, prefers (similarly rather literally) to trace them to Revelation: but argues that it is 'best to dwell little on either of them, lest you wander entirely out of the poem (p. 320)'. I would point less to a specific allusion—a key to the 'message' of the poem—than to a whole cluster of Biblical resonances, whose importance consists in their evocation of a quite different—and much more engaged—contemporary usage of 'mark' than that of polite convention.

   9. Sennett, *The Fall of Public Man*, p. 70. The notion of reading character from the face would have been familiar to Blake from Lavater's *Essays on Physiognomy,* for the first volume of which (1789) he had engraved three plates.

   10. For further discussion of the suggestiveness of 'mark' see E. P. Thompson, 'London', pp. 10–14; Heather Glen, 'The Poet in Society: Blake and Wordsworth on London', *Literature and History,* 3 (Spring, 1976); Stan Smith, 'Some Responses to Heather Glen's "The Poet in Society" ', *Literature and History,* 4 (Autumn, 1976).

   11. This point is well made by Thompson, 'London', pp. 18–19.

   12. William Godwin, *Enquiry Concerning Political Justice and Its Influence on Morals and Happiness* (Toronto, 1946), p. 149. See Thompson, 'London'; p. 15, and Ferber, ' "London" and its Politics', pp. 321ff., on Blake's change in the draft from 'german' (signifying, as Ferber notes, 'a kind of German yoke theory aimed at the

House of Hanover') to 'mind-forg'd': a change which—like his use of 'charter'd'—does not simply place him on the radical side of a contemporary debate, but offers a rather more complex perspective on it.

13. Edmund Burke, *Letter to a Member of the National Assembly* (1791), *Writings and Speeches* (London, Beaconsfield edn, n.d.), vol. IV, pp. 51–2.

14. E.g. Priscilla Wakefield, *Perambulations in London* (1809), p. 146. Ferber, ' "London" and its Politics', p. 325, discusses the different possible meanings of 'appals' and concludes: 'I think it makes the line more coherent to entertain the paradox of the church paling at the chimney sweeper's cry while blackening on its own, than to imagine the cry doubling that blackening by casting a pall.'
Cf. a suggestive Swedenborgian image for that Moral Virtue which is uninformed by a sense of spiritual potentiality, in Emanuel Swedenborg, *The True Christian Religion* (Philadelphia, 1885), p. 503: 'We have also separated charity from all relation to what is spiritual, and have made it a merely moral virtue; and so we have done likewise with the decalogue. . . . On this supposition . . . would not the church be like the black face of a chimney-sweeper, the only white spots about which are in his eyes?'

15. John Brewer, *Party Ideology and Popular Politics at the Accession of George III* (Cambridge, 1976), p. 153.

16. Paine, *Rights of Man;* see note 6 above and the text to which it pertains.

17. See Thompson, 'London', p. 23, for a discussion of the image of the Harlot in English radical Dissent in the eighteenth century.

18. David Bindman, *Blake as an artist* (Oxford, 1977), p. 43, offers a clear account of this process.

19. See Robert N. Essick, 'Blake and the Traditions of Reproductive Engraving', *Blake Studies,* 5 (Autumn, 1972).

20. For suggestive discussions of the work of art as a discovery see 'Joanna Field' (Marion Milner), *On Not Being Able to Paint* (London, 1950) and Anton Ehrenzweig, *The Hidden Order of Art* (London, 1967).

21. Jean-Paul Sartre, Preface to Frantz Fanon, *The Wretched of the Earth* (Harmondsworth, 1967), p. 15.

22. Thompson, 'London', p. 23.

23. Both words are strongly sound-linked: each stands at the beginning of a line.

24. Fredric Jameson, *Marxism and Form: Twentieth-Century Dialectical Theories of Literature* (Princeton, 1972), pp. 84–5.

25. Jameson, *Marxism and Form,* from the quotation cited at note 24.

26. A phrase scrawled by Blake on the fourth page of the notebook in which the poems of *Songs of Experience* were drafted (K889, n. 161).

27. Blake's sectarian background has never been satisfactorily explored. A. L. Morton, *The Everlasting Gospel* (London, 1958) points to similarities between his ideas and those of the antinomian sects: certainly, his intimacy with those ideas is evident throughout his lifetime's work. But—as I argue—his relation to that tradition was not a passive one. And his attitude towards actual membership of a sectarian group is indicated not merely by his revulsion from the New Church, but also in his annotations to Lavater (1788), where he underlies aphorism 339 ('he who adheres to a sect has something of its cant', K74) and comments on aphorism 416 ('He, who to obtain much will suffer little or nothing, can never be called great; and none ever little, who, to obtain one great object, will suffer much'): 'The man who does this is a Sectary: therefore not great' (K77).

28. See Christopher Hill, *Milton and the English Revolution* (London, 1977), pp. 302ff.

29. Friedrich Schiller, *On the Aesthetic Education of Man, In a Series of Letters* (New York, 1965), p. 144.

ALICIA OSTRIKER

Desire Gratified and Ungratified: William Blake and Sexuality

Alicia Ostriker's essay originally appeared in *Blake/An Illustrated Quarterly,* in an issue that also included essays by Anne Mellor, Nelson Hilton, and Michael Ackland addressing the question of Blake and sexuality. For further work on this topic, consult Diana Hume George, *Blake and Freud* (1980); Jean H. Hagstrum, *The Romantic Body: Love and Sexuality in Keats, Wordsworth, and Blake* (1985); and Ostriker's own autobiographical essay, "My William Blake," in *The Romantics and Us* (1990), edited by Gene W. Ruoff.

As well as displaying feminist criticism at its best, generous, but unsparingly clear-sighted, Ostriker's essay exemplifies the reassessments of which we spoke in the heading to this section, another instance of which is Nancy Moore Goslee's "Slavery and Sexual Character: Questioning the Master Trope in Blake's *Visions of the Daughters of Albion*" (1990). Ostriker's discrimination of the four sequential Blakean attitudes toward sex and gender provides a wonderful key to the history of Blake criticism. The first Blake, for example, was preeminent in the sixties, whereas the fallen misogynist dominated the late seventies. Not only does Ostriker judiciously trace the intertwined continuities and inconsistencies in Blake's career, but she finally brings us to appreciate Blake's awareness of even a prophet's inability to escape his own time—as is concretely demonstrated by Heather Glen in our previous selection. Ostriker enables us to grasp the full significance of Blake's idea that an artist gives "Body to Error," for, like the other romantic poets, he understood imagination as a transfiguring, not a transcendent, power. The same observation might be applied to Ostriker's understanding of the historicity of criticism. Like Viscomi and Glen, she not only refuses to let contemporary conceptions blind her to the realities of another time and place, but she is equally willing to reassess the presuppositions that have guided her earlier endeavors at historical reconstruction.

From *Blake/An Illustrated Quarterly* 16 (Winter 1982–83): 156–165. Reprinted by permission of *Blake/An Illustrated Quarterly,* University of Rochester.

To examine Blake on sexuality is to deal with a many-layered thing. Although we like to suppose that everything in the canon "not only belongs in a unified scheme but is in accord with a permanent structure of ideas,"[1] some of Blake's ideas clearly change during the course of his career, and some others may constitute internal inconsistencies powerfully at work in, and not resolved by, the poet and his poetry. What I will sketch here is four sets of Blakean attitudes toward sexual experience and gender relations, each of them coherent and persuasive if not ultimately "systematic;" for convenience, and in emulation of the poet's own method of personifying ideas and feelings, I will call them four Blakes. First the Blake who celebrates sexuality and attacks repression, whom we may associate with Freud and even more with Reich. Second, a corollary Blake whom we may associate with Jung, whose idea of the emanation—the feminine element within man—parallels Jung's concept of the anima, and who depicts sexual life as a complex web of gender complementarities and interdependencies. Third, a Blake apparently inconsistent with Blake number one, who sees sexuality as a tender trap rather than a force of liberation. Fourth, and corollary to that, the Blake to whom it was necessary, as it was to his patriarchal precursor Milton, to see the female principle as subordinate to the male.

Blake number one is perhaps the most familiar to the common reader, although professional Blakeans have paid little attention to him lately. He is the vigorous, self-confident, exuberant advocate of gratified desire, writing in his early and middle thirties (that is, between the fall of the Bastille and the execution of Louis and the declaration of war between England and France) the early *Notebook* poems, the *Songs*, *The Marriage of Heaven and Hell* and the *Visions of the Daughters of Albion*. A few texts will refresh the memory. Among the *Notebook* epigrams we are told that

> Love to faults is always blind
> Always is to joy inclind
> Lawless wingd and unconfind
> And breaks all chains from every mind
> (E 463)[2]

> Abstinence sows sand all over
> The ruddy limbs & flaming hair
> But Desire Gratified
> Plants fruits of life & beauty there
> (E 465)

> What is it men in women do require?
> The lineaments of Gratified Desire
> What is it Women do in men require?
> The lineaments of Gratified Desire
> (E 466)

It was probably these lines that converted me to Blake when I was twenty. They seemed obviously true, splendidly symmetrical, charmingly cheeky—and nothing else I had read approached them, although I thought Yeats must have picked up a brave tone or two here. Only later did I notice that the epigrams were tiny manifestoes announcing an identity of interest between sexuality and the human imagination.

During these years Blake wrote numerous minidramas illustrating how possessiveness and jealousy, prudery and hypocrisy poison the lives of lovers. He pities the chaste ("The Sunflower") and depicts the pathos of chastity relinquished too late ("The Angel"), looks forward to a "future Age" when "Love! sweet Love!" will no longer be thought a crime, while protesting its repression by Church and State in his own time. One of his two major statements about sexual repression in *Songs of Experience* is the deceptively simple "The Garden of Love," in which the speaker discovers a Chapel built where he "used to play on the green." The garden has a long scriptural and literary ancestry. "A garden shut up, a fountain sealed, is my sister, my bride," in *The Song of Solomon*. It is the site of the *Roman de la Rose*. It is where Dante meets Beatrice, it is Spenser's garden of Adonis and Milton's Paradise—"In narrow room, Nature's whole wealth." The garden is, in brief, at once the earthly paradise and the body of a woman. Probably Blake saw it so. Later he would draw the nude torso of a woman with a cathedral where her genitals should be. The briars at the poem's close half-suggest that the speaker is being crowned with something like thorns, somewhere about the anatomy, and it anticipates Blake's outraged demand, near the close of his life, in the *Everlasting Gospel:* "Was Jesus chaste? or did he / Give any lessons of chastity?" Since the design for "The Garden of Love" depicts a priest and two children kneeling at an open grave beside a church, the forbidden love may be a parent as well as a peer, and the speaker might be of either sex: all repression is one. It is important that the tone here is neither angry nor self-righteous, but pathetic and passive— indeed, pathetically passive, for after the opening "I went," the governing verb is "saw." That the speaker only "saw . . . my joys and desires" being bound with briars and did not "feel" anything, should shock us into realizing that this speaker, at least by the poem's last line, has been effectively self-alienated. Repression has worked not merely from without, but from within."[3]

The other major statement is "London," where Blake hears the clanking of the mind-forg'd manacles (chains such as "Love . . . breaks from every mind") he will later associate with Urizen. Economic exploitation sanctioned by blackening churches and political exploitation sanctioned by bleeding palace walls are grievous, but "most" grievous is sexual exploitation, perhaps because it is a denial of humanity's greatest virtue, charity, as sweep's cry and soldier's sigh are denials of faith and hope; or perhaps because, to Blake, sexual malaise precedes and produces all other ills:

> But most thro' midnight streets I hear
> How the youthful Harlots curse
> Blasts the newborn Infants tear
> And blights with plagues the Marriage hearse
>   (E 27)

That final stanza is Blake's most condensed indictment of the gender arrangements in a society where Love is ruled by Law and consequently dies; where virtuous females are pure, modest, and programmed for frigidity, so that healthy males require whores; where whores have ample cause to curse; and where their curses have the practical effect of infecting young families with venereal disease as well as with the more metaphoric plague of unacknowledged guilt.[4] Through his hissing, spitting and explosive alliteration Blake creates an ejaculatory harlot who is (and there are analogues to her in Spenser, Shakespeare, Milton) not the garden but the snake. That a syntactic ambivalence common in Blake makes her one who is cursed by others as well as one who curses, does not diminish the point.

The point recurs polemically in *The Marriage of Heaven and Hell,* where, according to Auden, "the whole of Freud's teachings may be found."[5] Here "Prisons are built with stones of Law, brothels with bricks of Religion," "Prudence is a rich ugly old maid courted by Incapacity," and we are exhorted: "Sooner murder an infant in its cradle than nurse unacted desires" (E 36–37). Here too is the famous pre-Freudian précis of Freud's theories on suppression: "Those who restrain desire, do so because theirs is weak enough to be restrained; and the restrainer or reason usurps its place and governs the unwilling. And being restrained it by degrees becomes passive till it is only the shadow of desire" (E 34). For Freud, this process was always in some degree necessary and irreversible, as *Civilization and its Discontents* and "Analysis Terminable and Interminable" ultimately confess. But Blake—and this is what makes him more Reichian than Freudian—joyfully foresees the end of discontent and civilization too: "For the cherub with his flaming brand is hereby commanded to leave his guard at tree of life, and when he does, the whole creation will be consumed, and appear infinite. and holy where it now appears finite & corrupt. This will come to pass by an improvement of sensual enjoyment" (E 38).[6]

In all such texts Blake is not only attacking the powers of repression, particularly institutional religion, which in the name of reason and holiness attempt to subdue desire. He is also asserting that gratified desire *does* what religion *pretends* to do: gives access to vision, the discovery of the infinite. Moreover—and this is a point to which I will return—Blake in these texts does not stress the distinction between male and female, or assign conspicuously different roles to the two sexes. Youth and virgin suffer alike under chastity, man and woman have identical desires, and the "ruddy limbs and flaming hair" of which an ardent imagination makes a garden, and an abstinent imagination makes a desert, may belong interchangeably to a lover or a beloved, a male or a female.

The poem in which Blake most extensively elaborates his celebration of love and his critique of repression is *Visions of the Daughters of Albion,* printed in 1793. *Visions* is also the poem most clearly delineating male sexual aggressiveness as a component of Urizenic patriarchy, and illustrating the kinds of damage it does to both males and females. First of all, Bromion is a number of things which to Blake are one thing. He is the slaveowner who converts humans into private property and confirms his possession by impregnating the females, the racist who rationalizes racism by insisting that the subordinate race is sexually promiscuous, the rapist who honestly believes that his victim was asking for it; and, withal, he does not actually experience "sensual enjoyment." But if Bromion represents the social and psychological pathology of sexual violence, Theotormon, represents its pitiable underside, sexual impotence. "Oerflowd with woe," asking unanswerable questions, weeping incessantly, Theotormon does not respond to Bromion's insult to his masculinity ("Now thou maist marry Bromions harlot," (pl. 2.1). Playing the hesitant Hamlet to Bromion's rough Claudius, intimidated slave to coarse slave-master, Theotormon has been victimized by an ideology that glorifies male aggressiveness, as much as by that ideology's requirement of feminine purity.

Dejected and self-flagellant (design, pl. 6), he cannot look Oothoon in her intellectual and erotic eye as she maintains her spiritual virginity and offers him her love, not only because she is damaged goods but because she is taking sexual initiative instead of being "modest." Only with incredulity and grief does Oothoon realize this (pl. 6.4–20).

Most of *Visions* is Oothoon's opera. Raped, enslaved, imprisoned, rejected, the heroine's agonized rhapsody of self-offering rushes from insight to insight. Though she begins by focusing on her individual condition, her vision rapidly expands outward. She analyzes the enchainment of loveless marriage and the unhappy children it must produce, she praises the value of infant sexuality and attacks the ethos which brands joy whoredom and sublimates its sexuality in twisted religiosity. She also bewails other ramifications of the tyranny of reason over desire, such as the abuse of peasant by landlord, of worker by factory owner, of the faithful by their churches. For Oothoon life means being "open to joy and to delight where ever beauty appears," and the perception of any beauty is an erotic activity in which eye and object join "in happy copulation." Made desperate by her lover's unresponsiveness, she cries out for "Love! Love! Love! happy happy Love! free as the mountain wind! / Can that be Love, that drinks another as a sponge drinks water?" Though remaining herself "bound" to Bromion, she nevertheless concludes with a vision of the vitality of all free things:

> Arise you little glancing wings, and sing your infant joy!
> Arise and drink your bliss, for everything that lives is holy.
> (*VDA* 8.9–10)

Blake in *Visions* has created a heroine unequalled in English poetry before or since. Oothoon not only defines and defends her own sexuality rather than waiting for Prince Charming to interrupt her nap, and not only attacks patriarchal ideology root and branch, but outflanks everyone in her poem for intellectuality and spirituality, and is intellectual and spiritual precisely because she is erotic. Shakespeare's comic heroines, though witty and sexy, are of course not intellectuals, much less revolutionaries. The Wife of Bath strongly resembles Oothoon as a voice of "experience, though noon auctoritee" who "spekes of wo that is in marriage," celebrates sexuality as such and female sexuality in particular, and lectures to the Apollyon of Judeo-Christian misogyny from his own texts. Yet she lacks Oothoon's generosity, and has been locked by men's contempt into a perpetuation of the war of the sexes. (If, though, we amend the portrait of the Wife as she appears in the Prologue by that "imaginative portion" of her which is her Tale, we have something different. Here perhaps is the Wife as she would be—neither offensively-defensively bawdy, nor angrily polemical, but lively and charming—telling the wish-fulfilling story of a rapist enlightened and reformed, of male violence, ignorance and pride transformed by the "sovereyntee" of feminine wisdom and love.) Hawthorne's Hester Prynne comes close to being what Oothoon is, even to the point of foreseeing that "in Heaven's own time, a new truth would . . . establish the whole relation between man and woman on a surer ground of mutual happiness."[7] But Hawthorne cannot sustain or elaborate the vision he glimpses, and sends Hester back in the end to her knitting, her works of charity, and a lifelong celibacy which—unlike Oothoon's—is supposed to be voluntary.

Blake number two appears later than Blake number one, and shifts his psychological principles from an essentially sociopolitical to an essentially mythic base. Beginning with *The Book of Urizen,* engraved in 1794, and throughout his major prophecies, the poet relies on an idea of humanity as originally and ultimately androgynous, attributing the fall of man and what John Milton called "all our woe" not to female narcissism but to specifically male pride, male competitiveness, or male refusal to surrender the self, and depicting a fallen state in which sexual division—lapse of unity between male and female as one being—is the prototype of every division within the self, between self and other, and between humanity and God.

The mythology of these poems posits a hero who is both Great Britain and all mankind, and who lives in Eternity or Eden as one of a family of Eternals who collectively compose One Man, Christ. Albion's "Human Brain," the equivalent of Jung's collective unconscious, houses four energetic Jungian Zoas, each of whom has a feminine counterpart or emanation. At Man's Fall, precipitated in *Urizen* by Urizen's pride, in *The Four Zoas* and *Milton* by rivalry between Urizen and Luvah, and in *Jerusalem* by Albion's selfish refusal to maintain erotic union with his saviour and his insistence on moral virtue, Albion lapses into what Blake variously calls sleep, death and disease, and what the rest of us call human history. The Zoas simultaneously lapse into lower forms and mutual conflict instead of harmony, and are disastrously divided from their emanations. As the late Blake formulaically puts it, "The Feminine separates from the Masculine & both from Man." Bodies grow around them, inimical "To the embrace of love":

> that no more the Masculine mingles
> With the Feminine, but the Sublime is shut out from the Pathos
> In howling torment, to build stone walls of separation compelling
> The Pathos. to weave curtains of hiding secresy from the
>   torment.
>
>   (*J* 97.10–14)

At the close of his three longest poems Blake imagines an apocalypse in which selfhood is relinquished and male and female are reunified:

> And the Bow is a Male & Female & the Quiver of the Arrows of Love
> Are the Children of this Bow: a Bow of Mercy & Loving-Kindness: laying
> Open the hidden Heart in Wars of mutual Benevolence Wars of Love
> And the Hand of Man grasps firm between the Male & Female Loves.
>
>   (*J* 97.12–15)

To say that Blake's emanations resemble what Jung calls the anima is to say that they represent a man's interior "female part," the "life-giving aspect of the psyche" and the "a priori element in his moods, reactions and impulses, and whatever else is spontaneous in psychic life."[8] As a positive figure the Blakean emanation like the Jungian anima is a benevolent guide to the unconscious life. As a negative figure she is seductive and destructive. She seems also to represent a man's emotionality, sensuousness, sensitivity, receptivity—all that makes him potentially effeminate—which in a fallen state he rejects or believes to be separate from himself, and must recover if he is to gain psychic wholeness. According to Jung, of course, an individual man changes and develops during the course of his lifetime but "his" anima does not. She remains static, and his only problem is to accept her existence as a portion of himself. What is particularly fascinating about Blake, then, is that he invents not one but a set of female beings, each appropriate to the Zoa she belongs to, each with her own personality and history of transformations, not radically different from the personalities in highly symbolic fiction and drama, and able to shed light very often on characters we thought we knew as well as on larger issues of sexual complementarity.

The first figures we encounter in *The Four Zoas,* for example, are Tharmas and Enion—humanity's Sensation—in the midst of a marital quarrel. Tharmas and Enion are bucolic characters of the sort that the wheels of history run over: good but not too bright, easily confused. We may recognize their like in mythic pairs like Baucis and Philemon, Deucalion and Pyrrha, and the Wakefield Noah with his farcically shrewish wife. Fictionally, and especially when a sentimental English novelist needs a pair of innocent parent-figures, they are legion: they are Sterne's Shandies, Goldsmith's Vicar and Mrs. Wakefield, and a troop of Dickensian folk like the Micawbers and Pockets, Casby (nicknamed "The Patriarch") and Flora, and perhaps most interestingly, the Gargeries of *Great Expectations.*[9] Across the Atlantic, they stumble through the fiction of writers like W.D. Howells and John Steinbeck. What Tharmas lacks when he loses Enion is his own sense of coherence. Without her he is a frantic and suicidal "flood" of feelings. What she lacks without him is resistance to pain. In her fallen form she becomes a grieving Demeter-figure who laments the sufferings of all earthly creatures,[10] and Blake gives her some of his best lines:

Why does the Raven cry aloud and no eye pities her?
Why fall the Sparrow & the Robin in the foodless winter?
(*FZ* I.17.2–3)

It is an easy thing to triumph in the summers sun
And in the vintage & to sing on the waggon loaded with corn
It is an easy thing to talk of patience to the afflicted
To speak the laws of prudence to the houseless wanderer . . .
It is an easy thing to laugh at wrathful elements
To hear the dog howl at the wintry door, the ox in the slaughter house moan . . .
While our olive & vine sing & laugh round our door & our children bring fruit & flowers
Then the groan & the dolor are quite forgotten & the slave grinding at the mill
And the captive in chains & the poor in the prison & the soldier in the field
When the shattered bone hath laid him groaning among the happier dead.
It is an easy thing to rejoice in the tents of prosperity
Thus could I sing & thus rejoice, but is is not so with me.
(*FZ* II.35.16–36.13)

Enion gives birth to Los and Enitharmon, the Eternal Prophet and his Muse, who from the start are as arrogant and self-absorbed as their parents are humble and selfless. Enitharmon espouses parent-abuse:

To make us happy let them weary their immortal powers
While we draw in their sweet delights while we return them scorn
On scorn to feed our discontent; for if we grateful prove
They will withhold sweet love, whose food is thorns & bitter roots.

(FZ I.10.3–6)

Soon she turns these arts on her twin and consort, becoming a seductive and maddening tease. She is the muse who won't come across, taunting the poet with failure and giving her alliance to Reason (Neoclassicism, let us say) instead of Prophecy, while forbidding the poet to love anyone but herself. As a couple, the Los and Enitharmon who are united "in discontent and scorn" uncannily resemble the self-destructive, sullen, jealous, incestuous or quasi-incestuous couples in novels like *Wuthering Heights, Women in Love,* and *The Sound and the Fury:* novels which in the light of Blake we can read as visions of a primitive creative energy thwarted by the impossibility of creativity in a culturally collapsed world they never made. Enitharmon is also La Belle Dame Sans Merci, she is Pip's Estella, or Lady Brett, or Marlene Dietrich in *The Blue Angel;* which is to say that she is the feminine agent of male sexual humiliation, who is herself governed by *ennui.*

A third couple is Urizen and Ahania: Reason and the Faith or Idealism necessary to it. Early in *The Four Zoas,* Urizen as cosmic architect places Ahania in a zodiacal shrine and burns incense to her. Here we have Blake's version of the "pedestal," and of that neo-Platonically inspired sexual reverence which prefers ladies pure, exalted and static rather than adjacent and active. When Ahania is uncomfortable in her shrine and tries to give her spouse some advice about returning to Eternity, he seizes her by the hair, calling her "Thou little diminutive portion that darst be a counterpart," and throws her out of heaven, declaring "Am I not God? Who is equal to me?" *(FZ* III.42.21–43.9). Without Ahania, Urizen is Doubt instead of Faith, and degenerates in the course of *The Four Zoas* from Prince of Light, to tyrannic parody of Milton's God, to William Pitt opposing the Bread Bill of 1800, to the Dragon Form of Antichrist. Ahania falls from being a sky goddess who opened her mouth once too often to "the silent woman" about whom feminist critics are presently writing a good deal.[11] Until just before the end of *The Four Zoas* Ahania has nothing further to say. As "the furrowed field" she is a figure of complete submission. We should compare her possibly to those other victims of exacerbated and anxious male intellect, Hamlet's Ophelia and Faust's Gretchen.[12]

Luvah and Vala, last of the Zoas and Emanations, are in their unfallen form lover and beloved, the Eros and Psyche of Man. Fallen, Luvah is born into this world as the revolutionary babe and flaming youth who must become a sacrificed god in epoch after epoch, while Vala is the *dolorosa* who, believing she loves him, always sacrifices him.

As all Blake readers know, Vala is one of Blake's most complicated characters. Her name means "vale" as in "valley," and as Nature she is the valley of the shadow of death, the declivity of the female genitals, and the membranous "veil" which preserves virginity, as well as the "veil" covering the tabernacle of the Old Testament. Like the chapel in "The Garden of Love" and the "chapel all of gold," she stands at the intersection between corrupt sexuality and institutional religion; thus she is also the veil of the temple which was rent when Jesus died, for Vala is the Nature we worship when we should worship Christ, she is Fortuna, Babylon, the Great Whore, enemy of Jerusalem. Where Enitharmon is a tease and a betrayer, Vala is the "Female Will" incarnate as killer. She is the chaste mistress who withholds favors so that her lovers will become warriors, and she is the blood-spattered priestess who with a knife of flint cuts the hearts out of men—all the while protesting that she craves nothing but Love. So powerful a figure is she that I expect we see at least as much of her in popular culture—where she is the voluptuous pinup on barracks walls, and she is the lady in black leather who will punish you—as in conventional fiction and drama. Pornography magazines offer us endless reproductions of Vala-Babylon, and, in the most high-chic phases of fashion design, the ideal fashion model is "cruel" Vala.

If we judge by Mario Praz' exploration of the "tormented, contaminated beauty" and "femme fatale" in western literature, this type of female seems—at least prior to Swinburne—to have been more extensively treated by French than by English writers.[13] Ste.-Beuve, Gautier, Baudelaire adore her. For Swinburne, she becomes the Venus of "Laus Veneris," Faustine, and Mary Stuart. But if we look earlier, she certainly figures in Jacobean drama, and in at least in one play of Shakespeare's.

Late in *Jerusalem,* one of Vala's avatars has a warrior-lover whom she craves to possess completely. "O that I could live in his sight," she says; "O that I could bind him to my arm" (*J* 82.44). Concealing him under her veil, she wishes him to become "an infant love" at her breast. When she opens the veil, revealing "her own perfect beauty," her lover has become "a winding worm." Blake hopes at this moment to show that Female Will is ultimately self-defeating. The winding worm is a further degeneration of helpless infancy, so that her wish has become true beyond her intention, as in folktales. The worm is also the phallic worm (cf. Yeats' "Chambermaid's Song," where "Pleasure has made him / Weak as a worm") and the devouring worm of the grave. The parallel story is of course *Antony and Cleopatra.* There, too, Woman reduces Warrior to absurd infantile dependency, out of pure erotic possessiveness. She then dies by the instrument of a worm that she describes as an infant—"the baby at my breast / That sucks the nurse asleep (V.ii.308–309) and that she croons to as lover. Without the aid of Blake, we might not think to identify the asp in *Antony and Cleopatra* as the last essence of Antony himself. With Blake, the identification seems compelling. At the same time, with the aid of Shakespeare, we may see Vala more clearly as the fallen form of female desire.

As the individual characters of Zoas and Emanations differ, so do the plots of their reconciliations. Los-Enitharmon's begins earliest in *The Four Zoas,* and involves a channeling of their arrogant energy through suffering. Following the binding of Urizen they have sunk, exhausted, to their nadir, "shrunk into fixed space . . . Their senses unexpansive" (V.57.12–18). Redemption starts with the painful birth of Orc, and the grief that follows the Los-Enitharmon-Orc Family Romance. Though repentance and sorrow over their mutual failure to free Orc are apparently useless, Enitharmon's heartbreak (V.63.10–14) triggers a process of imaginative re-expansion and re-unification that continues through the complex episodes of Spectre-Shadow and Spectre-Los reunions (VIIa.81.7–86.14) and the "six thousand years of self denial and of bitter contrition" during which Los builds Glogonooza and Los and Enitharmon finally labor together as partners in the Art which gives regenerate form to all of life (VIIa.90.2–57). At the opening of Night

IX "Los and Enitharmon builded Jerusalem weeping" and at no point thereafter are separated. In the final two pages the regenerate "dark Urthona" has reclaimed them both.

Reunion of the other Zoas and Emanations completes the Eternal Man's awakening and resumption of control over his warring "members." Ahania revives at the moment of Urizen's rejuvenation. She bursts with excess of joy, sleeps a winter and returns in spring as Kore, and finally takes her seat "by Urizen" (i.e., not enshrined) "in songs & joy." Next, when Orc's passion burns itself out, Albion takes the somewhat-charred Luvah and Vala in hand and admonishes them: "Luvah & Vala henceforth you are Servants obey & live" (IX.126.6). They enact their obedience first in the ensuing pastoral episode, with its idyllic evocation of a new Golden Age, and then in the Last Vintage, where human grapes are orgiastically crushed in the wine-presses of Luvah. The episode concludes with Luvah and Vala described as a couple linked to the seasons; together they sleep, wake, and are "cast . . . thro the air till winter is over & gone" while the "Human Wine" they have made "stood wondering in all their delightful expanses" (IX.137.30–32). Finally Tharmas and Enion, first pair to be seen in collapse and last to be seen regenerate, also undergo a double transformation. They are initially reborn into Vala's garden as naive and wayward children, as befits their innocent character. But a fully renewed and humanized Enion and Tharmas embrace and are welcomed by the Eternal Man (IX.132.10–133.1) to the final feast.

For the Blake who conceived of humanity as androgynous, the division of Zoas from Emanations signified human disorder and disaster. His poetry describing sexual division is some of the most anguished in the language. By the same token, re-couplings precipitate and are accompanied by all the images for joy and order Blake knew: a seasonal cycle culminating in harvest, vintage and communal feast; a painful bread-making and wine-making which issues in happiness; music and "vocal harmony" concluding in human "conversing"; and a beaming morning sun.

To trace the lineaments of Blake number three, we must return to the very outset of the poet's career, and the extraordinary lyric "How sweet I roamed from field to field," where an unidentified winged speaker is lured and trapped by "the prince of love." The poem is in a quasi-Elizabethan diction, but with the swoon of eroticism and ecstatic surrender we associate with Keats. Keatsian too are the lushness and fertility of the natural setting and the painful close:

> With sweet May dews my wings were wet,
>   And Phoebus fir'd my vocal rage;
> He caught me in his silken net,
>   And shut me in his golden cage.
>
> He loves to sit and hear me sing,
>   Then laughing, sports and plays with me;
> Then stretches out my golden wing,
>   And mocks my loss of liberty.

Un-Keatsian is the ambivalent gender of the speaker and the personification power of love as male not female. Although the theme of romantic enthrallment of a woman by a man is relatively unusual in English poetry, Irene H. Chayes argues convincingly that the speaker is Psyche and the manipulator of "silken net" and "golden cage" is Eros.[14]

But in later versions of this scenario, the instruments of entrapment and enclosure—net, cage, locked box—will be the sexually symbolic props of females who imprison males. "The Crystal Cabinet," "The Golden Net" and "The Mental Traveller" are all versions of this theme, and the "Woman Old" of the last of these is a brilliant portrayal of the *vagina dentata* in action, for she torments male vitality simultaneously by nailing and piercing, and by binding and catching. As if correcting his own earlier naiveté, one of Blake's *Notebook* poems asks rhetorically "Why was Cupid a Boy?" and answers that the illusion of a male Cupid who inflicts sexual suffering "was the Cupid Girls mocking plan," part of a scheme to keep real boys who "cant interpret the thing" unsuspecting while she shot them full of darts (E 470). Along similar lines, "My Spectre Around Me" envisages a war between the sexes dominated by female pride, scorn, jealousy and lust for "Victory" imaged as possession and enclosure: "Living thee alone Ill have / And when dead Ill be thy Grave." The solution is a Spectral threat of rejection and retaliation:

> Till I turn from Female Love
> And root up the Infernal Grove
> I shall never worthy be
> To step into Eternity
> And to end thy cruel mocks
> Annihilate thee on the rocks
> And another form create
> To be subservient to my fate.
>
> (E 468)

This brings the Emanation round, for it is either she, or Emanation and Spectre in duet, who "agree to give up Love" for "the world of happy Eternity."

Among the engraved poems, "To Tirzah" is a furious repudiation of female sexuality in its maternal aspect as that which encloses and divides man from Eternity. To appreciate the impact of "To Tirzah" in its original context we should probably see it as the contrary poem to "A Cradle Song" in *Innocence*. Where in *Innocence* a mother sings lullingly to a sleeping infant of the "sweet" smiles and tears that Jesus as "an infant small" sheds and shares with herself and the child, in *Experience* the child responds, ironically using Jesus' adolescent rejection of Mary (John 2.4) for his punch line:

> Thou Mother of my mortal part
> With cruelty didst mould my Heart,
> and with false self-deceiving tears
> Didst bind my Nostrils Eyes & Ears.

> Didst close my Tongue in senseless clay
> And me to Mortal Life betray.
> The Death of Jesus set me free,
> Then what have I to do with thee?

A second strong repudiation is *Europe,* where erotic entrapment both maternal and sexual, the former expressing itself as possessive, the latter as seductive manipulation of male desire, takes place so that "Woman, lovely Woman! may have dominion" during the corrupt centuries of Enitharmon's reign. Here Enitharmon's "crystal house" is analogous to the crystal cabinet, and within it there is a constant claustrophobic movement of nocturnal binding, circling, cycling, broken only by the dawn of European revolution.

How well do these poems fit the Blake who praises "gratified Desire" and insists that "Energy is the only life and is from the body"? Rather poorly, I think. However allegorically we interpret the thing, sexual love in these poems is neither gratifying nor capable of gratification, and the poet consistently associates "sensual enjoyment" with cruelty, imprisonment, illusion and mortality instead of liberation, vision, and immortality. Morton Paley has pointed out that Blake's Lambeth books involve "a sort of involuntary dualism, a myth with implications that in some ways conflicted with his own beliefs. Blake's intuition of the goodness of the body in general and of sexual love in particular had not weakened . . . but . . . the Lambeth myth seems to imply that physical life is inherently evil."[15] If, in other words, we have one Blake for whom physical life is type and symbol of spiritual life and fulfilled joy in one leads us to the other, there is also a Blake for whom body and spirit are as irreconcilably opposed as they are for any Church Father. But the contradiction is exacerbated rather than resolved in the later books, where the anatomical image of the enclosure vastly expands to become a whole world, the realm of Beulah, a dreamy moony place presided over by tender females, which is both comfort and trap.

To a fallen and depleted consciousness, Beulah is the source of poetry and our one hope of returning to Eden. The "Daughters of Beulah" are reliably compliant "Muses who inspire the Poets Song" or nurse-figures who comfort and protect the weary and distressed. That "Contrarieties are equally true" in Beulah makes it seem an obvious advance over single vision and Newton's sleep. Yet as another Crystal Cabinet writ large, Beulah inevitably means confinement, limitation, illusion. It can never mean Infinity. Where Eden is fourfold and human, Beulah is merely threefold and sexual, the vacation spot for beings who cannot sustain the strenuous mental excitement of Eden and need "repose":

> Into this pleasant shadow all the weak & weary
> Like Women & Children were taken away as on wings
> Of dovelike softness, & shadowy habitations prepared for them
> But every Man returnd & went still going forward thro'
> The Bosom of the Father in Eternity on Eternity.
>
> (*M* 31.1–5)

Of the double potentialities of Beulah, benign yields to malign in successive works. In *The Four Zoas,* Beulah is purely protective. *Milton* begins to emphasize not only its pleasantness but also its delusiveness. In *Jerusalem,* where the Daughters of Beulah have been replaced as muses by a single male muse and lover, "the Saviour . . . dictating the words of his mild song," Blake firmly identifies "the lovely delusions of Beulah" (*J* 17.27) with the terrors of sexuality. Thus Vala, claiming precedence over the Savior, hypnotizes Albion with her concave allure and her usurped phallic power:

The Imaginative Human Form is but a breathing of Vala
I breathe him forth into the Heaven from my secret Cave
Born of the Woman to obey the Woman O Albion the mighty
For the Divine appearance is Brotherhood, but I am Love
Elevate into the Region of Brotherhood with my red fires

(*J* 29.48–30.1)

Responding to Vala's triumph, Los laments:

What may Man be? Who can tell! But what may Woman be?
To have power over Man from Cradle to corruptible Grave.
There is a Throne in every Man, it is the Throne of God
This Woman has claim'd as her own & Man is no more! . . .
O Albion why wilt thou Create a Female Will?
To hide the most evident God in a hidden covert, even
In the Shadows of a Woman & a secluded Holy Place

(*J* 30.25–33)

Beulah itself seems at fault, in Los's agonized cry:

Humanity knows not of Sex: wherefore are sexes in Beulah?

(*J* 44.3)

And again, anticipating Keat's yearning description of a work of art "all breathing human passion far above:"

redeem'd Humanity is far above
Sexual organization; & the Visions of the Night of Beulah

(*J* 79.73–4)

For, as Blake in his own persona tells us, however tender and pleasant and full of "ever varying delights" the "time of love" passed in Beulah may be, where "every Female delights to give her maiden to her husband" and

The Female searches sea & land for gratification to the
Male Genius: who in return clothes her in gems & gold
And feeds her with the food of Eden, hence all her beauty beams

(*J* 69.17–19)

Love in Beulah inevitably brings a depletion of energy and the advent of jealousies, murders, moral law, revenge, and the whole panoply of inhuman cruelties the poet has taught us to struggle against. In visionary contrast, Blake imagines a love that transcends sexuality because it is a mingling of male with male:

I am in you & you in me, mutual in love divine:
Fibres of love from man to man thro Albions pleasant land . . .
I am not a God afar off, I am a brother and friend;
Within your bosoms I reside, and you reside me.

(*J* 4.7–19)

Such is the opening promise of the Saviour, and if in Eternity "Embraces are Cominglings from the Head even to the Feet" (*J* 69.43), we well may wonder whether such embraces can ever occur between male and female. For if the Blake who celebrates desire sees it as equally distributed between genders, the Blake who fears desire sees sexuality in general and sexual threat in particular as a female phenomenon. This third Blake gives us an array, culminating in *Jerusalem*, of passive males subject to females who seduce, reject, betray, bind, lacerate, mock and deceive them. After *Visions of the Daughters of Albion*, though Blake continues strenuously to oppose the idea that woman's love is *sin,* he increasingly describes it as *snare.* There is no comparable depiction of males seducing and betraying females.

This brings me to Blake number four, who is perhaps not quite a classic misogynist—though he sometimes sounds like one—but someone who believes that the proper study of woman is the happiness of her man, and who cannot conceive of a true woman in any but a supportive, subordinate role. In the margin of his 1789 edition of Lavater's *Aphorisms on Man,* Blake wrote, "Let the men do their duty & the women will be such wonders, the female life lives from the light of the male, see a mans female dependents, you know the man" (E 585). Females, in other words, may be wonders, but only if men are: and to be female is to be dependent.

Examining Blake from this point of view, and returning to *Visions,* we notice that Oothoon is good, and she is wise, but she is completely powerless. So long as her menfolk refuse enlightenment, she will be bound hand and foot, imprisoned in a passivity which she does not desire but to which she must submit. Looking at *The Four Zoas,* we see that Enion and Ahania are likewise good—indeed, they represent precisely the goodness of selfless love and compassion—but passive, while Enitharmon and Vala are active and evil. In *Milton* and *Jerusalem* the story is the same: female figures are either powerful or good; never both. The late prophecies may even constitute a retreat from the point Blake arrived at in *Visions,* for the better the late females are, the more passive, the more submissive and obedient they also are.[16] When Ololon finds Milton, she tearfully apologizes for being the cause of Natural Religion. And when Milton concludes his splendid final speech on "Self-annihilation and the grandeur of Inspiration" with a peroration against the "Sexual Garments, the Abomination of Desolation," Ololon responds by dividing into the six-fold Virgin who dives "into the depths / Of Miltons Shadow as a Dove upon the stormy sea" and a "moony Ark" who enters into the fires of intellect

> Around the Starry Eight: with one accord the Starry Eight became
> One Man Jesus the Saviour. Wonderful! round his limbs
> The Clouds of Ololon folded as a Garment dipped in blood
> (*M* 42.9–11)

At the climax of *Jerusalem* there is a similar self-immolative plunge when "England" awakes on Albion's bosom. Having blamed herself for being "the Jealous Wife" who has caused all the troubles of the poem:

> England who is Brittania enterd Albions bosom rejoicing
> Rejoicing in his indignation! adoring his wrathful rebuke.
> She who adores not your frowns will only loathe your smiles
> (*J* 95.22–4)

But this somewhat gratuitous-seeming passage lacks—since we have not met "England" until now—the systematic quality of Blake's treatment of his chief heroine.

The poet's final and most fully-idealized heroine "is named Liberty among the sons of Albion" (*J* 26.3–4) yet we seriously mistake Blake's intention if we think Jerusalem is herself a free being, or even a being capable of volition. She is the City of God, bride of Christ, and man's Christian Liberty, to be sure, but that is only in Eden, and even there she does not act; she simply is. What happens to Jerusalem within the body of the poem at no point involves her in action or in protest. At its outset she is withheld by Albion from "the vision & fruition of the Holy-one" (*J* 4.17) and is accused of sin by Albion and Vala. Unlike Oothoon she does not deny the accusation, nor does she defend her own vision with anything like Oothoon's exuberance. Patiently, meekly, she explains and begs Love and Forgiveness from her enemies. That is her last initiative. Subsequently she is rejected as a whore, cast out, imprisoned, driven finally to insanity, and becomes wholly incapable even of remembering her original self without being reminded of her origins by the voice of her pitying and merciful God. Even this comfort does not help; for at the poem's darkest moment, just before the advent of the Covering Cherub, Jerusalem passively receives a cup of poison from the conquering Vala (*J* 88.56).

The final movement of *Jerusalem* evokes its heroine twice, when "the Universal Father" speaking through "the vision of Albion" echoes the Song of Solomon:

Awake! Awake Jerusalem! O lovely Emanation of Albion
Awake and overspread all Nations as in Ancient Time
For lo! the Night of Death is past and the Eternal Day
Appears upon our hills: Awake Jerusalem, and come away
(*J* 97.1–4)

and when the poet's vision of "All Human Forms" is complete:

And I heard the Name of their Emanations they are named Jerusalem
(*J* 99.5)

Yet however amorous, however reverential our attitude toward this "persecuted maiden"[17] redeemed, we do not and cannot encounter the "awakened" Jerusalem directly. As *A Vision of the Last Judgment* explicitly tells us, and as the whole of *Jerusalem* implies, "In Eternity Woman is the Emanation of Man; she has no Will of her own. There is no such thing in Eternity as a Female Will" (E 552). If we wonder what the Emanative role in Eternity is, Blake has already told us:

When in Eternity Man converses with Man, they enter
Into each other's Bosom (which are universes of delight)
In mutual interchange, and first their Emanations meet . . .
For Man cannot unite with Man but by their Emanations . . .
(*J* 88.3–9)

Is femaleness, then, ideally a kind of social glue? Susan Fox argues that although "in his prophetic poems Blake conceives of a perfection of humanity defined by the complete mutuality of its interdependent genders," he nevertheless in these same poems "represents one of these equal genders as inferior and dependent . . . or as unnaturally and disastrously dominant," so that females come to represent either "weakness" or "power-hunger."[18] Anne Mellor has observed that Blake's ideal males throughout the major prophecies are creative and independent while his ideal females "at their best are nurturing . . . generous . . . compassionate . . . all welcoming and never-critical emotional supporters," and that "in Blake's metaphoric system, the masculine is both logically and physically prior to the feminine."[19] But at its most extreme, Blake's vision goes beyond proposing an ideal of dominance-submission or priority-inferiority between the genders. As a counter-image to the intolerable idea of female power, female containment and "binding" of man to mortal life, Blake wishfully imagines that the female can be re-absorbed by the male, be contained within him, and exist. Edenically not as a substantial being but as an attribute. Beyond the wildest dreams of Levi-Strauss, the ideal female functions as a medium of interchange among real, that is to say male, beings.

And what are we as readers to make of Blake's contradictions?[20] Morris Dickstein, noting the shift from the "feminism of *Visions* to his later stress on "female Will," calls it "a stunning change that seems rooted less in politics than in the nearly unknown terrain of Blake's personal life."[21] Diana George believes that Blake became entrapped in a culturally mandated sexual typology which he initially intended to "redeem."[22] Although all our anecdotal material about the Blakes indicates that Catherine adored her visionary husband even when he was not bringing home the bacon, much less adorning her in gems and gold, marital friction looks like a reasonable source for many *Notebook* and other poems. Perhaps, too, Blake had a model for Oothoon in Mary Wollstonecraft, whose vigorous equal may not have been encountered in his other female acquanitances after Wollstonecraft's death.[23] At the same time, we should recognize that the shift in Blake's sexual views coincides with other ideological and doctrinal transformations: from a faith in political revolution perhaps assisted or exemplified by Art to a faith in Imagination as that which alone could prepare humanity for its harvest and vintage; from what looks like a love of nature that makes him one of the great pastoral poets in the English language and extends as far as *Milton,* to a growing and finally absolute rejection of nature and all fleshly things; and from an imminent to a transcendent God.

Yet to say that Blake's views moved from X to Y would be an absurd oversimplification. It would be truer to say that X and Y were with him always—like his Saviour—in varying proportions, and that the antagonism between them is the life of his poetry. One of the idols of our tribe is System, a Blakean term signifying a set of ideas bounded by an adhesive inflexible consistency, cognate of the "bounded" which its possessor soon loathes, the "Circle" that any sensible God or Man should avoid, and the "mill with complicated wheels." If "Unity is the cloke of Folly" in a work of art, we might make it our business as critics not only to discover, but also to admire, a large poet's large inconsistencies—particularly in an area like the meaning of sex, where the entire culture, and probably each of us, in the shadows of our chambers, feels profound ambivalence.

If "without contraries is no progression," I think we should neither be surprised nor dismayed to find in Blake both a richly developed anti-patriarchal and proto-feminist sensiblity, in which love between the sexes serves as a metaphor for psychic wholeness, integrity, and more abundant life, and its opposite, a homo-centric gynophobia in which heterosexual love means human destruction.[24] "If the doors of perception were cleansed everything would appear to man as it is, infi-nite." What then if we concede that Blake's vision, at least part of the time, was fogged to the degree that he could perceive Man as infinite but could not perceive Woman as equally so? Blake understood that it is impossible for any prophet finally to transcend historical time. He understood so of Isaiah and Ezekiel, he understood the same of John Milton. "To give a Body to Error" was, he believed, an essential service by mighty intellects for posterity. We might, with gratitude for this way of comprehending great poetry, see him as he saw his precursors. To paraphrase Emerson and the *Gita,* when him we fly, he is our wings.

NOTES

1. Northrop Frye, *Fearful Symmetry* (Princeton: Princeton Univ. Press, 1947), p. 14.

2. Quotations are from David V. Erdman, ed., *The Poetry and Prose of William Blake* (New York: Doubleday, 1970); henceforth cited as E.

3. I am disagreeing at this point with Morris Dickstein's otherwise excellent essay, "The Price of Experience: Blake's Reading of Freud," in *The Literary Freud,* ed. Joseph Smith (New Haven: Yale Univ. Press, 1980), pp.67–111. Dickstein (pp.95–96) sees "The Garden of Love" as "angry polemical simplification," arguing that the speaker "thinks of repression in terms of a very simple etiology: *They* have done it to him," and that there is no question of "delusion or projection" here. A persuasive reading of the poem's Oedipal dimension is in Diana George, *Blake and Freud* (Ithaca: Cornell Univ. Press, 1980), pp. 104–106.

4. For a harrowing account of the phenomenon of the youthful harlot in nineteenth-century England, see Florence Rush, *The Best-Kept Secret: Sexual Abuse of Children* (Englewood Cliffs, N.J.: Prentice-Hall, 1980), ch. 5.

5. W.H. Auden, "Psychoanalysis and Art To-day" (1935), in *The English Auden,* ed. Edward Mendelson (New York: Random House, 1977), p. 339.

6. Analysis of Freud's rationalist and scientific pessimism, versus Blake's imagina-tive and artistic optimism, is a primary theme in *Blake and Freud,* which argues that in other respects the two men's diagnoses of western man's psychosexual ills were close to identical. Politically of course Freud remained conservative; the close parallels be-tween Blake and Reich as radical psycho-political thinkers are discussed in Eliot Katz, "Blake, Reich and *Visions of the Daughters of Albion,*" unpub.

7. *The Centenary Edition of the Works of Nathaniel Hawthorne,* vol. 1 (Ohio State Univ. Press, 1962), p. 263.

8. C.G. Jung, "Archetypes of the Collective Unconscious," in *Collected Works,* ed. Herbert Read, Michael Fordham, Gerhard Adler and W. McGuire, trans. R.F.C. Hull, Bollingen Series (Princeton: Princeton Univ. Press, Bollingen Series XX, 1967–78), vol. 9, part 1, p. 27. Jung also discusses the anima and the anima-animus "sacred marriage" in "Two Essays on Analytical Psychology" (vol. 7) and "Aion: Researches into the Phenomenology of the Self" (vol. 9, part 2). Among his less predictable parallels to Blake is Jung's idea that the anima-animus marriage is always accompanied and completed by the figure of a Wise Old Man—who I am ready to presume is "Old" in the same sense that Albion is an "Ancient" Man; i.e., he is Urmensch, not elderly. Among the critics who identify anima with emanation are June Singer, *The Unholy Bible: A Psychological Interpretation of William Blake* (New York: Putnam, 1970), p.

212, and W. P. Witcutt, *Blake: A Psychological Study* (Port Washington, N.Y.: Kenni-kat Press, 1946), pp. 43ff. Christine Gallant, in *Blake and the Assimilation of Chaos* (Princeton: Princeton Univ. Press, 1978) disagrees, arguing that although "the anima in Jungian psychology is a personification in a symbol, or in an actual human being, of those aspects of his unconscious of which a man is most ignorant, usually his emo-tional, irrational qualities," Blake's emanations are not animae because "if they were . . . they would have characteristics as differentiated as those of their Zoas" (pp. 53–54). It is my contention that they do. Although Jung in general diverges from both Freud and Blake in uncoupling psychological issues from socio-historic ones, he de-parts from Freud and coincides with Blake in at least three major respects: his insis-tence on the validity of spirituality in human life, his belief in a collective unconscious, and his relatively non-phallocentric exploration of female identity.

9. That Deucalion-Pyrrha and the Noahs are flood-survivors who renew the human race, and that the fallen Tharmas-Enion are identified with water and Tharmas in Night III struggles to take on Man's form, is a coincidence I do not pretend to understand but feel obliged to notice. My *primary* point here is that these couples are all parental, and all naive. The relation of Dickens' Gargeries to Tharmas and Enion seems to me particularly charming in that Joe Gargery is rather a perfect Tharmas throughout, but is given two wives by Dickens—as it were to parallel the quarrelsome and the redeemed Enion.

10. Gallant (p. 54) notes the Poseidon-Demeter / Tharmas-Enion parallel (author coincidence) and points out that the questing Demeter disguised herself as an old woman.

11. See, for example, Mary Daly, *Beyond God The Father* (Boston: Beacon Press, 1973), Marcia Landy, "The Silent Woman," in *The Authority of Experience,* ed. Arlyn Diamond and Lee Edwards (Amherst: Univ. of Massachusetts Press, 1977). Susan Griffin, *Woman and Nature: The Roaring Inside Her* (New York: Harper and Row, 1978), Sandra M. Gilbert and Susan Gubar, *The Madwoman in the Attic* (New Haven: Yale Univ. Press, 1979), chaps. 1 and 2. The contention of these and other feminist writers in America, England and France is that western religion and philosophy, by consistently associating power and authority with masculinity, have deprived women of access to authoritative speech and muted their ability to "voice" female experience authentically. The critique of rationalism in such works for the most part tallies very well with Blake's.

12. Ophelia's selfless "O what a noble mind is here o'erthrown" speech nicely resembles Ahania's memory of "those sweet fields of bliss / Where liberty was justice & eternal science was mercy (*FZ* III.39.12–13). Later, when Hamlet has rejected her and slain her father (cf. Urizen's rejection of Ahania and his defiance of Albion), Ophelia's "speech is nothing." Both Ophelia and Gretchen, of course, express pro-found admiration for their lovers' intellects.

13. Mario Praz, *The Romantic Agony* (1933; rpt. Cleveland: World Publishing Co., 1956), pp. 28ff, 189ff. Among Praz' many valuable observations is a remark on Ste.-Beuve which is particularly relevant to the Vala-Jerusalem relationship: "Whenever it happens that a writer feels admiration for [female] passionate energy—particularly if this energy have fatal results . . . it is always the diabolical . . . who ends by occupying the whole stage and causing her angelic rival . . . to appear a mere shadow" (p. 191).

14. Irene H. Chayes, "The Presence of Cupid and Psyche," in *Blake's Visionary Forms Dramatic,* ed. David V. Erdman and John E. Grant (Princeton: Princeton Univ. Press, 1970), pp. 214–43.

15. Morton D. Paley, *Energy and the Imagination: A Study of the Development of Blake's Thought* (Oxford: Clarendon Press, 1970), p. 90.

16. A partial exception is the prophetic figure of Erin in *Jerusalem,* yet in a sense Erin is an exception that proves the rule; for though her voice is inspirational without passivity or subordination, she remains undeveloped as a character, lacking the internal struggles and self-transformations of the other major figures in the poem.

17. The term is from Praz, who suggests Clarissa and Sade's Justine as two examples of the type.

18. Susan Fox, "The Female as Metaphor in William Blake's Poetry," *Critical Inquiry* 5 (Spring 1977), 507.

19. Anne K. Mellor, "Blake's Portrayal of Women," *Blake/An Illustrated Quarterly* 16 (Winter 1982–83), 148–155.

20. For some readers, of course, no contradiction worth noticing exists. Consider, for example, the following: "Some modern women may have much to object to in Blake's latest thought about the relations between the sexes. But it is hard to believe that *l'homme moyen sensuel* would reject the hearty bread and full-bodied wine the late Blake is offering him. Or his wife either, for that matter: 'let men do their duty & the women will be such wonders.' " Such is Jean Hagstrum's pleasant conclusion in "Babylon Revisited, or the Story of Luvah and Vala," in *Blake's Sublime Allegory: Essays on the Four Zoas, Milton and Jerusalem,* ed. Stuart Curran and Joseph Anthony Wittreich, Jr. (Madison: Univ. of Wisconsin Press, 1973), p. 118. David Aers, in "William Blake and the Dialectic of Sex," *ELH* 44 (1977), 500–14, feels that in *Visions* Blake "may have slipped toward an optimistic, idealistic illusion in his handling of Oothoon's consciousness. The illusion lies in assuming that revolutionary consciousness can ever be as uncontaminated by dominant structures and ideologies as Oothoon's appears to be" (p. 505). By stressing female will in later poems, Blake "is casting out the vestiges of optimistic delusions," having discovered that "it is utopian and undialectical to imagine a female consciousness like Oothoon's" (p. 507). Since Aers does not seem to reflect that Oothoon's inventor himself must have been as "uncontaminated" as his invention, and that Los in *Jerusalem* seems likewise, I take Aer's position to be that we can believe in a male uncontaminated consciousness but that it is undialectical to believe in a female one.

21. Dickstein, pp. 77–78.

22. *Blake and Freud,* chap. 6, includes this argument in a larger discussion of Blake's treatment of "the feminine."

23. See Alicia Ostriker, "Todd, *Wollstonecraft Anthology,*" *Blake/An Illustrated Quarterly* 14 (1980–81), 129–31.

24. The mirror image of this view appears in a number of contemporary lesbian feminist works. See, for example, Griffin, pp. 207–27.

William Wordsworth

Wordsworth remains at the center of romantic criticism and scholarship, as during the first decades of the nineteenth century when he was the focal point of the principal literary-political controversies. Every year more essays and monographs are published on him than any of the other poets of his epoch, a good number even by nonromanticists, such as Gerald Bruns, whose "Wordsworth at the Limits of Romantic Hermeneutics" (1989) is a valuable contribution to criticism of *Lyrical Ballads*. Recently the poet attracted still another biography, this by Stephen Gill, *William Wordsworth: A Life* (1989), an excellent supplement to Mary Moorman's *William Wordsworth: A Biography* (1957–65) and Mark Reed's indispensable *Wordsworth: The Chronology of the Early Years, 1770–1799* (1967) and *Wordsworth: The Chronology of the Middle Years, 1800–1815* (1975).

Over the past twenty years, furthermore, publication of the Cornell Wordsworth edition has retextualized the Wordsworth canon. This edition's aim, which runs against standard textual-editing principles, is to provide the earliest full versions of significant Wordsworth texts to supplement (perhaps to supplant) the final revised versions, which have long been available. As a consequence, many undergraduates now read familiar Wordsworth poems in forms unlike those their predecessors knew. Jack Stillinger's cautionary essay, "Textual Primitivism and the Editing of Wordsworth" (1989), may signal renewed debate if not a reversion to later texts, but so far the primitivists prevail.

The Prelude remains the chief magnet for Wordsworthian criticism, especially because it lends itself both to new-historicist commentaries (on which see the headnote to Johnston's essay), and to Freudian psychological analysis. And, as Arac so usefully elucidates, no work is better suited for revising both the earlier twentieth-century "humanistic" interpretation of Wordsworth *and* its replacement by rhetorical critics of the late sixties and early seventies. The Cornell edition's recovery of early versions of the poems, moreover, has sparked careful and penetrating reexaminations of Wordsworth's most celebrated shorter poems and opened some of the least regarded ones to rewarding new scrutiny. Among such studies one might note, for example, Mark Jones's "Interpretation in Wordsworth and the Provocation Theory of Romantic Literature" (1991), which

demonstrates how interpretations *within* Wordsworth's poems can
serve as a model and rationale for our contemporary interpretations.

We note one omission from our Wordsworth section, which testifies
complexly to the current situation in studies of the poet. We offer no
essay on the "Ode: Intimations of Immortality," which may be
Wordsworth's most extensively discussed major lyric. The reasons for
this are varied. In many cases significant work on the great Ode has
become so heavily contextualized that it has outgrown the confines of
a book like this one. The intertextual, dialogical analyses of the Ode's
engagements with Coleridge's and other work found in Lucy Newlyn's
Coleridge, Wordsworth, and the Language of Allusion (1986), Paul
Magnuson's *Coleridge and Wordsworth: A Lyrical Dialogue* (1988),
and Gene W. Ruoff's *Wordsworth and Coleridge: The Making of the
Major Lyrics, 1802–1804* (1989) are not readily extractable. In
*Wordsworth and the Enlightenment: Nature, Man, and Society in the
Experimental Poetry* (1989), Alan Bewell stresses Wordsworth's
indebtedness to eighteenth-century anthropological speculations for his
depiction of the child as philosopher. Jeffrey C. Robinson's *Radical
Literary Education: A Classroom Experiment with Wordsworth's "Ode"*
(1987) is a substantial and interesting monograph and encircles the
poem from a variety of perspectives. Helen Vendler's "Lionel Trilling
and the Immortality Ode" (1978), which takes off from Trilling's
celebrated and influential essay of fifty years ago is long and densely
argued, and does not represent the redirections we illustrate in this
book. Other distinguished commentaries, which any student of the
Ode should consult, are by scholars represented elsewhere in this
book. See Jerome Christensen's " 'Thoughts That Do Often Lie Too
Deep for Tears': Toward a Radical Concept of Lyrical Drama" (1981);
Geoffrey H. Hartman's " 'Timely Utterance' Once More," in *Rhetoric
and Form: Deconstruction at Yale* (1985); relevant chapters in Frances
Ferguson's *Wordsworth: Language as Counter-Spirit* (1977); Marjorie
Levinson's *Wordsworth's Great Period Poems: Four Essays* (1986); and
Peter J. Manning's *Reading Romantics: Text and Context* (1990).

KENNETH R. JOHNSTON

The Politics of "Tintern Abbey"

Although Kenneth R. Johnston's most substantial contributions to Wordsworthian studies are his comprehensive analyses of the various stages in the composition of the poet's unfinished masterwork in *Wordsworth and "The Recluse"* (1984), and although he would not describe himself as a new historicist, his important essay on "Tintern Abbey" dramatizes most of the characteristics of romantic new historicism. He is concerned here, as elsewhere, with how contexts affect texts, both in their presence and (in the case of "Tintern Abbey") by their absence. The concern extends to how texts work within contexts—how a poem appearing in the anonymous *Lyrical Ballads* of 1798, for example, differs from the same poem appearing in the 1800 edition of *Lyrical Ballads,* which emphasizes in its preface poetry's social relations.

One new-historicist tendency missing from Johnston's piece is deference to Frankfurt school Marxism, emphasized by Marjorie Levinson in her "New Historicism: Back to the Future" (1989). New historicists begin from the oldest tradition of Wordsworthian criticism, dating back to the poet's own day—the accusation of "anti-climax," denunciation of the change in both poetic skill and political morality in the poet's later years, this falling off attributed to his "betrayal" of his early interlinking of more progressive poetic and political priniciples.

New historicists, however, give this established tradition two special twists. First, political ideology for them supersedes all else. For new historicists, Wordsworth's principal and almost exclusive concern was the French Revolution, with his agonized apostasy from his original sympathies being the determinative event of his career. When in 1974, for example, Karl Kroeber, credited Wordsworth with being driven by an ecological vision, he observed that such a vision had definite political implications, that from its origins in the seventeenth-century landscape representation had been a politicized mode. But for the new historicists references to the natural world are primarily a screen for more fundamental ideological motivations, which, repressed, shape all other impulses and interests. Hence the importance of "displacement," currently our criticism's most fashionable term. As Johnston argues, "Tintern Abbey" is "already political," and because it is "one of the most powerfully *de*politicized poems in the language" it is necessarily "a uniquely political one."

The most controversial aspect of this popular approach is its emphasis on the silences of a text. Thus Marjorie Levinson, in her

From *The Wordsworth Circle* (1983): 6–14. Reprinted with the kind permission of *The Wordsworth Circle.*

essay "Tintern Abbey" (1986), which is generally congruent with Johnston's reading, argues with impressive vehemence that it is the absence of any reference to the French Revolution (along with the failure to mention the vagrants who congregated around Tintern Abbey) that should determine our understanding of the poem. A clue to this line of thought is provided by Johnston's observations on the poem's date, which he and Levinson believe Wordsworth associated with the fall of the Bastille nine years before.

This essay is also characteristic of current scholarship in its interest in the Wordsworth of the 1790s. Johnston's current work in progress is a biography of young Wordsworth. Among other recent studies shedding new light on the poet in this decade, see James K. Chandler, *Wordsworth's Second Nature: A Study of the Poetry and Politics* (1984); David V. Erdman, *Commerce des Lumières: John Oswald and the British in Paris, 1790–1793* (1986); and Nicholas Roe, *Wordsworth and Coleridge: The Radical Years* (1988).

Wordsworth's "Lines, Written a few Miles above Tintern Abbey, On Revisiting the Banks of the Wye During a Tour. July 13, 1798," is not usually considered a political poem, but if we shift from "political" to "social," and thence to the still more general "moral," we find ourselves on familiar grounds of interpretation. The entire poem may be said to turn upon the fulcrum of Wordsworth's assertion that he has "learned / To look on nature, not as in the hour / Of thoughtless youth; but hearing oftentimes / The still, sad music of humanity" (88–91). Most critical interpretations focus on the beginning or end of this process rather than its turning point: i.e., on Nature's "beauteous forms" or on the transcendentally sublime insights they lead to, when "we see into the life of things" (49). But each of the poem's five verse paragraphs contain strong language of social responsibility that lends value to Wordsworth's enjoyment of landscape—otherwise a morally neutral datum—and allows him to build toward quasi-religious assurances. Thus these knots of social language are essential to the reputation "Tintern Abbery" deserves and has long enjoyed, of a secular poem that gives us something to believe in. In its own cultural context, the poem enacts a process whereby a fashionable intellectual pastime—the cultivation of picturesque views—becomes transcendentally important, precisely by virtue of *not* being an escapist pleasure, but a socially responsible one.[1]

But there are many tensions inherent in this process, directly parallel to the more obvious tensions in the topic sentences of each of the poem's paragraphs, and generally identifiable with the over-arching drama of Wordsworth's work (especially *The Prelude*): how to present the growth of his mind as a continuous, uninterrupted, fundamentally unthreatened sequence, or, to show how love of Nature leads to love of Mankind. In socio-political terms, this problem requires that the connection between landscape-viewing and religious belief be non-violent, certainly non-revolutionary, and possibly even non-political, insofar as politics, the art of the possible, must be practiced in the arena of the improbable and the uncertain. Preliminarily, we can identify some of the strains to which Wordsworth subjects the idea of political maturity even in the poem's central fulcrum, the sonorously impressive lines on "the still, sad music of humanity."

There is the slight oddity of displacement between verbs, *looking* on nature while *hearing* that sad music. Is it a recall to duty or a fading echo? And *how* has he "learned" to do this? Not the process, but its beginnings and endings (Before and After) are represented most in the poem. The adverbs and adjectives multiply qualifications. "Hearing oftentimes—but how often is that? And what kind of music is "still, sad music"? It sounds more like the *andante* of a Brahms symphony than the *allegro* of a Romantic one by Beethoven, where we might hear, rather than "still, sad music," the agitated angry noise of human suffering. Furthermore, why is music so obviously calm as "still, sad music" further qualified as being "nor harsh nor grating," especially when, as John Hodgson has excellently observed, "harsh" and "grating" certainly seem appropriate to the human sounds represented elsewhere in the poem: "the din of cities," "the sneers of selfish men," and "greetings where no kindness is?"[2] What is being so carefully protected from harsh grating in a nonetheless necessary process of *chastening* and *subduing?* Probably, by way of a preliminary answer, the egoism of the creative artist, fearful of being overborne by other legitimate claims on his genius.

Certainly some of these questions are unfairly loaded, and go too far beyond the text, which after all is what it is, and is not required to supply an exact demonstration of the relation of aesthetic experience—whether landscape viewing or poetry writing (or reading)—to social responsibility and ultimate values. Nonetheless, the poem itself provokes such questions, and if in what follows I seem often to go outside the poem and to imply that Wordsworth is neglecting or sublimating unpleasant associations, it's not to suggest that he like any poet can't write the poem he wants to write, but that he himself has imbedded it with language which simultaneously invites and resists probing, opening up just those areas of concern that it determinedly seeks to elide or contain in more manageable terms. Overall, this dialectical tendency in the social language of "Tintern Abbey" is directly parallel to what is to many readers its most impressive dramatic achievement, its way of making affirmative statements of belief while urging itself along by a constant series of very tentative, not to say negative, qualifications: "If this / Be but a vain belief," "somewhat of a sad perplexity," "Nor perchance, / If I were not thus taught," etc.

The more appropriate question would be to determine how "the still, sad music of humanity" is represented *in the poem?* A partial answer has already been suggested, in Hodgson's gloss on "harsh" and "grating". But I want to consider Wordsworth's representations of humanity in "Tintern Abbey" from a variety of perspectives: the progress of the text itself, Wordsworth's actual and literary experiences during his Wye tours, the poem's place in *Lyrical Ballads* and in relation to Wordsworth's contemporaneous work on *The Recluse,* and in the context of his other learning processes combining nature and humanity between 1793 and 1798.

We hear the "still, sad music of humanity"—i.e., see representations of human beings and human emotions—in two basic variations of a single phenomenon: of elision, mutation, or restriction. In the first, descriptive paragraph, human phenomena constitute fully half the description, but are presented in a consistently specialized way that connects them—blurs them, one might say—as *undisturbingly* as possible into the beautiful surrounding natural landscape. Secondly, in each of the subsequent verse paragraphs, the fulcrum or tonic note of human music is heard within a very narrow yet very intense range of notes, which is generalized, broadened or crescendoed, at the poem's center into "the still, sad music of humanity." In paragraph two, it is "the din of towns and cities" and "hours of weariness—preliminarily generalized into "the heavy and the weary weight / Of all this unintelligible world." In three, it is "the fretful stir / Unprofitable, and the fever of the world." In four, it is "still, sad music" itself, very much subordinated to Wordsworth's description of his earlier youthful pleasures in nature and his quasi-metaphysical paeans to it in the present. And in paragraph five it is "evil tongues, / Rash judgments . . . the sneers of selfish men, / . . . greetings where no kindness is, [and] all / The dreary intercourse of daily life," subsequently generalized to "solitude . . . fear . . . pain . . . grief" (I. 143). Taken all together, these are not very great human evils that go to make up "the still, sad music of humanity," and do not specifically include the tragic associations we inevitably supply to that sonorous phrase, such as poverty, famine, disease, war, or all the irrevocable losses of love and life, irreversible, unmerited, and uncontrollable suffering which are inescapable in the human condition. At the risk of being gratuitous and unfair, we might rather generalize the specific representations of human suffering in "Tintern Abbey" as the lonely feelings of rejection suffered by a sensitive person in the conditions of intense competitive work in urban markets, where gossip, hasty judgement, jealousy, and smooth hypocrisy all contribute to the feverish pace at which one's business fails to go along as profitably as one wishes. Or, to gloss this last set of "Lines" in *Lyrical Ballads* from the first, the "Lines / Left upon a Seat in a Yew-tree," the experiences of human life represented in "Tintern Abbey" sound very much like those of a

> youth . . . led by nature into a wild scene
> Of lofty hopes, [who] to the world went forth . . .
> knowing no desire
> Which genius did not hallow; 'gainst the taint
> Of dissolute tongues, and jealousy, and hate,
> And scorn—against all enemies prepared,
> All but neglect. The world, for so it thought,
> Owed him no service; wherefore he at once
> With indignation turned himself away,
> And with the food of pride sustained his soul
> In solitude.
> (13–24)

THE PICTURESQUE AND THE UNPICTURESQUE AT TINTERN ABBEY

We are all familiar with the rhetoric of interconnection in the first paragraph, most fully analyzed by Colin Clarke,[3] by which Wordsworth connects past to present, spirit to matter, man to nature, and other variations of "connect[ing] / The landscape with the quiet of the sky." Indeed, frequent teaching of the poem produces a sort of occupational hazard in this respect, until its descriptive qualities seem much less representational than diagrammatic, so subtle, varied, and insistent are Wordsworth's buried repetitions and partial oxymorons throughout. Less often remarked is Wordsworth's "unobtrusive" debt to Wiliam Gilpin's guidebook, *Observations on the River Wye . . . made in the Summer of 1770* (published

1781).[4] The debt is most obvious in three particulars of his description: 1) The "orchard-tufts" losing themselves "among the woods and copses," 2) the "hedge-rows hardly hedge-rows," and 3) the smoke at the end of the paragraph, of which Gilpin says, "the smoke, issuing from the sides of the hills, and spreading its thin veil over a part of them, beautifully breaks their lines, and unites them with the sky."[5] More generally, Gilpin's cultivation of memory bears close comparison with Wordsworth's; at the twilight conclusion of the Tintern Abbey segment of his tour, he says such moments are "very favorable to imagination," producing "landscapes, perhaps more beautiful, than any, that exist in nature . . . formed from nature . . . treasured up in the memory . . . called into these imaginary creations by some distant resemblances, which strike the eye in the multiplicity of evanid surfaces, that float before it."[6]

My point in adducing Wordsworth's use of Gilpin is not to belabor his indebtedness: doubtless he improves on Gilpin, and being borrowed by Wordsworth is the best thing that ever happened to Gilpin. Rather, I am interested in the use Wordsworth did *not* make of Gilpin, in light of the fact that his knowledge of Gilpin's guidebook is demonstrably so strong, arguing perhaps for his carrying it with him on the tour (in 1793 or 1798 or both), or having Gilpin's phrases so firmly in mind that he could make unconscious use of them in describing similar scenes. What Wordsworth did *not* use from Gilpin, except perhaps very obliquely, pertains especially to the second half of the first paragraph—its human or social half. In the last six lines of the paragraph, Wordsworth combines into a pleasant picturesque image two distinctly unpleasant aspects of the landscape around Tintern Abbey, noted by Gilpin and by another contemporary guidebook of 1793 which David Erdman has unearthed:[7] 1) the extensive charcoal manufacturing which produced the smoke about whose source Wordsworth could hardly have been "uncertain" (as well as the heavily commercial aspect of the river at that point due to shipping traffic), and 2) the pervasive and disturbing presence of beggars, gipsies, and vagabonds in and around the abbey. These are represented by Wordsworth as "vagrant dwellers in the houseless woods," where "vagrant dwellers," besides appearing as a conventional picturesque detail (so too the smoke) also partakes of the oxymoronic quality elsewhere in the paragraph (e.g., "pastoral farms"): In what sense can a "dweller" be a "vagrant"? And what does "houseless" add—or take away—from such a construction? His immediately following surmise, "Or of some Hermit . . . ," removes possibly unsettling associations, since a hermit in his cave is a man at home (albeit a very marginal man, socially speaking). This internally corrective supposition parallels "these hedge-rows" swiftly becoming "hardly hedge-rows, little lines / Of sportive wood run wild." Both of these unattractive associations—industrial smoke and social outcasts— might very well account for Wordsworth's insistently placing his poem "a few miles above Tintern Abbey," a placement that he reminds us of three times before we have finished reading four lines of the poem (by the title, by line 4, and by his footnote to 1. 4).[8]

As Mary Moorman notes, Tintern Abbey "was a dwelling-place of beggars and the wretchedly poor" (M.I.403). These beggars made a very strong impression on Gilpin; nearly half of the pages he devotes to Tintern Abbey are given over to them, in a sort of unwilling digression. His tone in general is fastidious, not to say mincing, as he recommends one viewing-station and criticizes another, reminding us that cultivating the fashion of the picturesque was predominantly an upper-middle class, conservative pastime, and an eminently non-political or even escapist one. He facetiously proposes, for example, taking a hammer to certain corners of the Abbey to give it a more appropriately ruined appearance. Nonetheless the simple honesty of his clergyman's intelligence quite breaks through his aestheticizing framework when he come to the beggars, even as he tries to account for them with conventional moral assumptions (this is the same Gilpin whose only complaint against the picturesqueness of Grasmere was that it lacked banditti[9]). "The poverty and wretchedness of the inhabitants were remarkable," he says; they lived in "little huts, raised among the ruin;" they had "no employment, but begging: as if a place, once devoted to indolence, could never again become the seat of industry" [a Protestant slap at Catholic decadence]. "The whole hamlet" of beggars congregated at the gate, some begging outright, others offering "tours" of the ruin's most interesting spots. Gilpin and his party followed one of these: "one poor woman [who] could scarce crawl; shuffling along her palsied limbs, and meagre, contracted body." She leads them to what she says was the "monk's library," but "it was her own mansion," and "all indeed she meant to tell us was the story of her own wretchedness; and all she had to shew us, was her own miserable habitation. We did not expect to be interested; but found we were. I never saw so loathsome a dwelling . . . a cavity between two ruined walls; which streamed with unwholesome dews. . . . not the merest utensil, or furniture of any kind. We were rather surprised, that the wretched creature was still alive; than that she had only lost the use of her limbs."[10]

I submit that such a powerfully ambiguous passage, standing out markedly from its bland surrounding contexts in Gilpin, and reinforced by direct experience, must have had an enormous impact on Wordsworth, as landscapeviewer, as author of *Lyrical Ballads,* and as prospective author of *The Recluse,* with its philosophical "views of Nature, Man, and Society . . . of considerable utility" (*LEY,* 212, 214). And I think he went to great lengths—greatly artistic lengths—to prevent such powerful associations and experiences from overbearing his poem, by recasting such beggars as "vagrant dwellers in the houseless woods," and further distancing them into the Hermit at home in his cave, where he belongs, sitting by his fire, alone.

It may be objected that the poem is not set at Tintern Abbey, but a "few miles above" it.[11] Insofar as this is poetically true (even if not literally so), I may only be supplying background contexts to the poem. But we must also recall that Tintern Abbey was the focus of all such tours up the Wye, for Gilpin as well as Wordsworth, and that the Wordsworths were at the abbey every single day of their tour, arriving, departing, passing, or visiting.[12] The point of all such tours was to view *ruins in landscape,* not just landscape alone—a point underscored by the fact that in Gilpin's guidebook the ratio of illustrations of ruins to those of landscapes without ruins is three-to-one. Furthermore, though the poem's original title said "*written* a few miles above Tintern Abbey," Wordsworth later changed this to "composed," to take cognizance of the fact that he finished it as he descended into Bristol at the end of their "four or five" day tour. And, just as we all refer to the poem as "Tintern Abbey," so did Wordsworth and his circle, as evidenced most recently in Beth Darlington's edition of Wordsworth's love letters to his wife, where he speaks of "the Tintern Abbey, . . . of all my Poems the one [in] which I speak of it will be the most beloved by me."[13] There have been various attempts over the years to connect or detach the abbey from the poem, but these have been mostly concerned with reinforcing or downplaying the religious associations it would lend.[14] My point stresses, not its religious associations, but the troubling, painful notes its human, social implications would introduce into "the still, sad music of humanity."

To return, in conclusion of this point, to Gilpin's description of the crippled beggar woman, think how many of Wordsworth's *Lyrical Ballads* recapitulate Gilpin's stance when confronted by her: "all indeed she meant to tell us was the story of her own wretchedness." Compare the Female Vagrant: "She ceased, and weeping turned away, / As if because her tale was at an end." Compare the forsaken Indian woman: "Too soon, my friends, you went away; / For I had many things to say." And think how much of Wordsworth's own learning "to look on nature, not as in the hour / Of thoughtless youth" derives from following out the implications of Gilpin's unwilling expression of surprise: "we did not expect to be interested; but found we were." Wordsworth composed basically two kinds of poems for *Lyrical Ballads:* "views" or "pictures" of suffering humanity (roughly, his "ballads") and "lyrics" of meditation upon natural beauty (his five sets of "Lines" in the collection, from those left on the yew-tree seat to those composed above Tintern Abbey). The "views" or ballads of suffering are presented quite barren of commentary or explanation, except for a strong, repeated, but unspeci-fied injunction to *thought,* as in, "Now *think,* ye farmers all, I pray, / Of Goody Blake and Harry Gill." The "Lines," by contrast, are full of meditation and explanation about the source and meaning of human appreciation of natural beauty, but quite vague and unspecified about its social significance, except for the sense of sharp and even contradictory contrast, as in, "Have I not reason to lament / What man has made of man" "Tintern Abbey" in a way brings these two discrete modes together, when Wordsworth says he has "learned to look on na-ture, not as in the hour / Of *thoughtless* youth." But, though it admits more of "the still, sad music of humanity" into its meditations, it nevertheless radically downplays it, proportionate to "all that we behold / From this green earth; of all the mighty world / Of eye, and ear."

This proportion, or disproportion, within "Tintern Abbey," and between the two kinds of poems Wordsworth contributed to *Lyrical Ballads,* is explicable within the context of the work Wordsworth considered his main task in 1798, writing of *The Recluse,* to which the composition and collection of *Lyrical Ballads* was very much incidental. By the time he composed "Tintern Abbey," Wordsworth had written 1300 lines of *The Recluse,* consisting mainly of the poems now known as "The Ruined Cottage," "The Old Cumberland Beggar," the lines on the Discharged Veteran which conclude Book IV of *The Prelude,* and, probably, "A Night-Piece."[15] More important, however, is the fact that he had, by July, *stopped* working on *The Recluse,* and the most powerful reason for his stopping, on the basis of internal interpretation, is precisely his failure to integrate the sufferings of Marga-ret, the old Cumberland Beggar, and the Discharged Veteran with scenes of natural beauty like those described in "A Night-Piece," or to satisfactorily establish the connection between landscape viewing and social responsibility which is implicit in the frames around "The Ruined Cottage" and the Discharged Veteran—i.e., the connection between their aesthetic, way-wandering young narrator and the bleak human figures or stories he unexpectedly meets of the road. Wordsworth's poems in *Lyrical Ballads* are successful, relative to his failure on *The Recluse,* because they present separate, discrete, freestanding images of human suffering on the one hand, and meditations upon natural beauty on the other. He had, so far, failed to coordinate such images with such meditations in his masterwork, *The Recluse,* and he had to work very carefully in his most ambitious poem in *Lyrical Ballads* lest their failure to relate, to integrate, overcome and break down that poem as well. Hence the modulated chords of "the still, sad music of humanity." Of course, the integration of aesthetic experience to social responsibility is still the largest legacy—or piece of unfinished business—which the Romantic movement has bequeathed to the modern world, and our modern institutionalized academic structures (including scholarly journals) for instruction and research into the nature and meaning of artistic experience have as their major justification, in mass democratic societies, the claim to be doing just that.

FROM POLITICAL LONDON TO PICTURESQUE TINTERN

The presence or absence of beggars in poems was not necessarily a political fact in 1798, however much it may seem so today. It was more of a religious fact, having to do with parish relief rates and poorhouses, which, though not without political implications in a society with an established church, was mainly a local problem, not a national one, and certainly not yet a matter of international political ideologies. But mention of *The Recluse* does touch upon the widest sort of implications for explaining human suffering, since, with its themes of Man, Nature, and Human Life, it was to have been a means of rescuing the young intellectual radicals of Wordsworth's generation from the selfish cynicism into which they were sinking as a consequence of the failures of the French Revolution.[16] Furthermore, while *The Recluse* was not exactly an ideological poem, it was certainly a philosophical one, and was, in effect, the habitation and the name of the ideal of a philosophically interpretive, and philosophically *interpretable,* poem which motivated much of the greatest work of both Wordsworth and Coleridge. Although the idea of such a grandly philosophic masterwork undoubtedly came to Wordsworth from Coleridge, Wordsworth had not been innocent of grand plans before he met Coleridge, and the grandest of these was a project whose scope very much resembles that of *The Recluse:* his detailed discussions between 1792–95 with his best friend *before* Coleridge, William Mathews, for a liberal journal of politics and literature, to be called *The Philanthropist.* Some examination of this project, and some speculation on its possible realizations, will lead us back to the second large aspect I have noted in the representation of "the still, sad music of humanity" in "Tintern Abbey": the intense but narrow range of human ills by which it is characterized.

Wordsworth's description of the various departments he wanted to include in *The Philanthropist* give a good idea both of its ambitious scope and of likely reasons for its failing to appear. It would include 1) general political news and comment, 2) essays on morals and manners and "institutions whether social or political," 3) essays for instruction and amusement, particularly biographical sketches of such libertarian heroes as Milton, Sidney, and Turgot, 4) essays on taste and criticism, and works of imagination and fiction, 5) reviews, 6) "some poetry," selected on a decidedly conservative editorial policy (given Wordsworth's later reputation as an innovator)—no original compositions, to avoid the "trash" investing other journals, and 7) reports of parliamentary debates and selected state papers (*LEY* 125–26).

Given this enormous load of contents, it is not surprising that Wordsworth's and Mathews' plans for *The Philanthropist* should fail to materialize, nor to hear Wordsworth say, somewhat grandiloquently, in November, 1794, that "The more nearly we approached the time fitted for action, the more strongly was I persuaded that we should decline the field." But did they entirely abandon it? Even in the letter in which he gives it up, Wordsworth says he is so "emboldened" by Mathews' description of the possibility of finding work on an opposition newspaper "that I am determined to throw myself into that mighty gulph [i.e., London literary journalism] which has swallowed up so many, of talents and attainments infinitely superior to my own." By February of 1795, he was back in London in company with Mathews and several other old Cambridge "friends of liberty," congregating around the temporarily famous figure of William Godwin, author of *Political Justice.* And on March 16, 1795, appeared in the first issue of an actual journal called *The Philanthropist; or Philosophical essays on politics, government, morals and manners,* published "by a society of gentlemen." Of this actual *Philanthropist,* Moorman says it was of "extreme radical opinion [and] ran for six months, when Pitt's 'Gagging Acts' must have killed it. It was scurrilous in style and contained nothing which could have issued from the pen of Wordsworth" (M.I, 256n3).

I am very grateful to Moorman for pointing out the existence of the real *Philanthropist,* but I must indicate that even her description of it is not quite accurate. It ran for eleven, not six, months (through January 25, 1796), was not extremely radical in opinion (but rather liberal Whiggish, manifesting the "Spirit of 1688" which had been revived to greet the French Revolution and to push for further parliamentary reform in England), and contained many things which could have come from the mind or pen of Wordsworth—*if* we imagine him working in the special circumstance of a group effort by young liberal university gentlemen publishing a popular journal for the enlightenment of the masses, a group in which he would have been a decidedly junior, apprentice member. This actual *Philanthropist* was, for the most part, a Godwinian, anti-war, opposition paper. Such sentiments as, "All improvements are slow and progressive," are pure Godwinism. it contained some bumptious propraganda verse on contemporary abuses ("Bob Shave the King," against Pitt's tax on wig powder), but the imitations of Juvenal's satires which Wordsworth was writing during this same period (which he was later very eager to hush up) would have done just fine in *The Philanthropist.* For the most part it mixed lengthy extracts from standard Whig texts (e.g., Trenchard's *History of Standing Armies in England*) with original essays, the best of which are written in clear, simple, argumentative prose, based on traditional principles of British constitutionalism, and opposing the war with France not on revolutionary "French principles" but on the expeditious grounds of the war's damage to English peace and prosperity because it interfered with free trade and the expansion of the empire—and also because it inflicted hardship on the lower classes. Thus the politics of the actual *Philanthropist* of 1795–96 very much resemble the politics of the proposed *Philanthropist* of 1792–94. Although both might have been considered "radical" in the hysterical political climate in London after the declarations of war (mass meetings, extremist plots, Treason Trials, paid government informers), it was certainly not treasonous, *nor activist,* and could be characterized as "a very safe little journal," as E.P. Thompson has described another Wordsworth friend's provincial journal, *The OEconomist,*[17] a description which would also fit yet another of his friend's plans for yet another similar journal, Coleridge's *The Watchman* of 1796. When Wordsworth and Mathews were discussing the political slant of their proposed Philanthropist, Wordsworth said, "I recoil from the bare idea of a revolution," and the actual *Philanthropist* is not a revolutionary journal, but one aimed precisely at avoiding revolution by advocating economy in public administration and "gradual and constant reform" of profligate ministerial abuses.

Almost all that is known of Wordsworth's whereabouts in London in 1795 is that he was a frequent visitor at Godwin's. They first met at a large tea party on February 27 (M.I.; *CEY*)—a tea party which, in the hypothesis I am developing, has all the marks of an organizational meeting. There was Godwin, the tutelary genius and celebrity to act as a magnet and inspiration for the large group of ambitious young literary gentlemen three or four years out of college: Wordsworth, Mathews, James Losh (the friend from *The OEconomist,* and also the friend who received on of the first notices of *The Recluse*), and other ex-Cambridge friends of Wordsworth's, Tweddell, Raine, Thomas Edwards (who would work with STC on *Watchman*), Higgins, and French (M.I. 263–64). More important, there were, between Godwin and these young men, three men in particular—William Frend, George Dyer, and Thomas Holcroft—who were all experienced publicists in radical-reformist causes. Frend and Dyer were, more-over, former faculty members or family friends of Wordsworth and others in the younger group, and their presence as managers in a joint enterprise would be very flattering and impressive to their protegés. Frend had been removed from his Cambridge tutorship in 1792 for his conversion to Unitarianism, and from his fellowship in 1793 for writing a political and religious tract of liberal, moderate persuasion: *Peace and Union Recommended to the Association Bodies of Republicans and Anti-Republicans* (1793).[18] Holcroft was a different kettle of fish, irascible and erratic, one of the heroes of the day by virtue of his almost accidental inclusion in the famous Treason Trial of 1794, and, coincidentally, author of a condescendingly cool review of Wordsworth's first two published books, *An Evening Walk* and *Descriptive Sketches* (1793).

In sum, without going into all the many biographical details that variously link these people together, I hypothesize that the mix looks right for a publishing venture by a society of young, ambitious, and unemployed university gentlemen. And the title, *Philanthropist,* was in 1795 virtually a Godwinian code-word, the inevitable abstract personification, common to 18th century journals (cf. *The Spectator*), of Godwin's key noun: Benevolence. I propose that London was too small a town in 1795 for such a group of genteel intellectual philosophic reformers as met at Godwin's house in February not to overlap somehow with the "society of gentlemen" who brought out the first issue of *The Philanthropist* in March; indeed, it is questionable whether any other group could have published so thoroughly Godwinian a journal. I hypothesize not so much Wordsworth's composition of particular passages in the journal, but his place among the legwork errand boys of the enterprise: gathering the extracts from Trenchard's *Standing Armies* or Robinson's *Political Catechism,* writing up drafts—stimulated by meetings at Godwin's—of current topics, and experiencing the unpleasant sensation of having his drafts heavily edited by his former teacher, Frend, his former schoolteacher's friend, Dyer, and his former reviewer, the "extremely candid" Holcroft (as Lamb later described him). Furthermore, I connect Wordsworth's likely reaction to this experience with his letters to Mathews about their proposed *Philanthropist,* where he expresses the easiest sort of confidence about achieving a simple, lucid prose style with practice (cf. his actual, crabbed prose style in the *Letter to the Bishop of Llandaff,* 1793), and I contrast this with his hesitations about actual newspaper work as he comes to London, preferring solitary composition of occasional pieces of commentary to covering parliamentary debates, because of "being subject to nervous headaches, which invariably attack me when exposed to a heated atmosphere or to loud noises . . . with such an excess of pain as to deprive me of all recollection" (*LEY,* 138).

The most specific places in *The Philanthropist* where I would argue for the presence of Wordsworth's hand are two essays—one signed "W."—where the topic is the use of genius or talent in the face of widespread human suffering. The implicit argument—or subtext—of these essays is to draw parallels between England's ignoring its talented young men and its insensitivity to the hunger and homelessness of the rural lower classes, as if to assert, 'If only I could achieve greatness, so could all of humanity.' If not exactly a unique topos of argument, it is nonetheless a highly specialized one. Both of these essays concentrate more on poverty's effect on the human mind than on its bodily ills, as do Wordsworth's "views" of human suffering in *Lyrical Ballads,* and both extend such effects to the entire character of a nation. As "W" says, "familiarity with this kind of wretchedness has also an injurious effect upon the minds of the higher orders."[19] To anticipate, I hypothesize that in "Tintern Abbey" we see some of Wordsworth's efforts to modulate such injurious effects.

Not only does this hypothesis allow us to give a more concrete location to Wordsworth's flirtation with Godwinism in the 1790s (otherwise adequately covered by Harper and Legouis[20]), it also provides an active, real context for his narrow but intense range of expressions for human evils in "Tintern Abbey": "lonely rooms," "the din of towns and cities," "hours of weariness," "the fretful stir / Unprofitable, and the fever of the world," and, especially, "evil tongues, / Rash judgments . . . the sneers of selfish men, . . . greetings where no kindness is, . . . [and] all / The dreary intercourse of daily life." For this is the kind of emotional context my hypothesis suggests: heated discussions, intense arguments, differences of editorial opinion pressures of deadlines and securing copy, peer pressure and rivalries, oversight by slightly senior former teachers whose success and achievements could not be denied, even as (in Wordsworth's case) the suspicion dawned that he was a much better writer but *not* a better journalist, the need to find some employment, the eagerness to succeed, all underlined not only by the heady atmosphere of political liberty unleashed by the French Revolution, but, more to the point, the exciting danger of working on an opposition newspaper in wartime, which was underlined by the danger of treason trials—though for such young gentlemen the danger was less of imprisonment or transportation to Botany Bay than the almost equally frightening danger of damaging *their* individual publishing prospects, and messing up the development of their *careers.*

"Tintern Abbey" is not the only poem in which Wordsworth generalizes about human evil from a narrow base of negative emotions. I have already cited the "Lines" left on the yew-tree seat. The portions of Book X of the 1805 *Prelude* dealing with his London experiences of this time ("Dragging all passions . . . / Like culprits to the bar"), could as well describe editorial arguments at Godwin's house as internal arguments with himself. And in the portions of "Home at Grasmere" composed in 1800—as Book First of Part First of *The Recluse*—he defends his removal to Grasmere as not the escapist fantasy of a self-indulgent aesthete but as a realistically responsible decision, since human beings in Grasmere are just as bad as human beings elsewhere (i.e., in cities). But we note again the specificity of the evils by which he conveys this: "selfishness and envy and revenge, / Ill neighbourhood . . . flattery and double-dealing, strife and wrong" (436–38), in contrast to the poem he intends to write, *The Recluse*, which will keep "clear . . . of all ill advised ambition and of pride" (884–885). The range of powerful generalization that Wordsworth sustains from this narrow base is all the more important when we consider that the "W" of *The Philanthropist,* confronting much more directly the mental evils of extreme poverty and deprivation, was inevitably if unwillingly driven into veiled threats of violent revolution: "I forebear the direct application of these sentiments to our own country: if my premises be true, its prospects cannot be very bright. The state of the lower orders, I am persuaded, marks more than any other circumstance, the state of a country; that of the lower orders here is certainly deplorable. Let us hope that their relief is within the reach of ordinary means; for the application of extraordinary means to remedy the evil, the hardiest cannot anticipate without dread. Yours [sincerely], etc., W."

To return to "Tintern Abbey," we may say that insofar as it describes a process of learning "to look on nature not as in the hour of thoughtless youth, but hearing oftentimes the still, sad music of humanity," it is a process very different from the implicit disruption of picturesque context which occurs in Gilpin's guidebook, or the one that is explicit in *The Philanthropist.* Like "still, sad music," this learning is represented as smooth, continuous, and unbroken, not disruptive, violent, uncertain, or threatening. This is why it must be "nor harsh nor grating, though of ample power to chasten and subdue." Harsh, grating music might break the music of the poem, might cause the poem to break down, and open up the gaps in the fabric of thought, or society, such as those that "W" could only anticipate with dread.

Inevitably, this address to the politics of "Tintern Abbey" sounds critical of Wordsworth, and to a certain degree it is. But not to a fundamental degree: I wish him to have been neither a political journalist nor a revolutionary activist, and his shift of enthusiasm away from the French Revolution is a shift that almost all European intellectuals underwent in greater or lesser degree. Nor am I suggesting that "Tintern Abbey" should somehow be "more" political—that Wordsworth should have more forthrightly included some ruins—human or architectural—in his landscape "a few miles above Tintern Abbey." Rather, I am saying that the poem is already political, that its necessary social fulcrum is everywhere present (if narrowly defined), that the beggars are there, as "vagrant dwellers in the houseless woods," and that this necessary political element opens the poem up to further appreciation if we press appropriately on the language Wordsworth himself provides, aided by information outside the poem. Undeniably, Wordsworth engages in some retrenchment in presenting the mediating social terms of his learning process; we may call this his conscious artistic control or his unconscious psychological sublimation, or a little of both. This is part of the cost of his becoming a poet, and the price of "Tintern Abbey's" being the poem it is: moving without fundamental breaks from the beautiful landscape toward seeing into the life of things, with Nature as "the soul of all my moral being." Indeed, it is part of the triumph of the poem to be able to include as full a representation of this process as it does—in comparison, for example, with Wordsworth's tendency elsewhere in the *Lyrical Ballads* to divide his poems into powerful narratives of human suffering (that only vaguely imply "thought") and equally powerful meditations about the interrelation of Mind and Nature (that only vaguely refer to "what man has made of man"). I am as impressed by Wordsworth's honesty in allowing the socio-political tensions of his poem to show through as by the parallel rhetorical statement of doubt ("If this be but a vain belief") that organize his final affirmations.

CODA: THE DATE OF "TINTERN ABBEY"

The date of "Tintern Abbey" may bear importantly upon its political sublimations. The standard account is that William and Dorothy left Bristol on July 10 and returned on July 13; the poem being inspired, composed, and completed during most of these four days.[21] However, Wordsworth in later life spoke of a tour "four or five" days (Fenswick Note), and the rate of progress which he and Dorothy would have had to maintain to complete the entire tour (from Bristol past Tintern to Goodrich Castle and back) in four days has been calculated as twenty miles per day, even granting two stretches they covered in the sightseeing boats which plied a lively tourist trade between Ross-on-Wye and the Wye's mouth at Chepstow.[22] This may not seem much to such super-human walkers as the Wordsworths now appear to us lazy moderns, though it works out to three miles per hour if we assume eight full hours of steady walking, making allowance for time stopped for refreshment, time spent inspecting ruins (the main business of such popular excursions as the Wye tour), and the fact that Dorothy, however energetic, would necessarily have been a genteel young lady hiking in long skirts and none-too-comfortable shoes. Moreover, Wordsworth's description of another walking tour, his summer jaunt across Europe in 1790 with Robert Jones (which also began, coincidentally on July 13; cf. *Prelude* VI.355–57), consistently emphasizes their lightning speed and astonishing rate of progress. Yet my calculation of stages of this journey (from Mark Reed's *Chronology of the Middle Years*) shows them to have been approximately twenty-five miles per day—essentially the same as the Wye's tour's—covered by two young men aged 20, rather than a brother and a sister, aged 28 and 26. My wife and I tested these hypotheses by some "feet on" research in August, 1982, and though satisfied that the Wordsworths could have accomplished the circuit in four days, we are certain that five days would have been more comfortable. (The day deserving most suspicious scrutiny is the Wordsworth's third day, a 27-mile walk down the whole course of the trip, from Goodrich Castle through Monmouth past Tintern to Chepstow—and thence back up the river to Tintern to spend the night.) Given Wordsworth's literalism, there is not much reason to doubt that he dated the poem of the day he finished writing it. But there is every reason to suppose he looked at it long and hard the next day (it was at the printers with the rest of *Lyrical Ballads* by July 18), and, with that same literalism, thanked his Muse it was already finished. But it is intriguing to suppose that the tour took one day longer than we think, and that Wordsworth, in light of other contemporary socio-political associations we can find lurking beneath the calm surface of its "still, sad music," turned its clock back twenty-four hours, to avoid setting off the powerful buried charges that would be exploded if this locodescriptive meditative landscape poem concluding his new volume of poems, were to have been entitled, "Lines / Written a Few Miles Above Tintern Abbey, On Revisiting the Banks of the Wye During a Tour. July 14, 1798."[23] Though "Tintern Abbey" may never come to be regarded as a political poem, it may well be, in light of these interpretive possibilities, one of the most powerfully *de*politicized poems in the language—and, by that token, a uniquely political one.

ADDENDUM—1993

Since this essay first appeared, several others have been published, to such an extent that one might now refer to "The 'Tintern Abbey' Debate." The issue in the debate is more methodological than interpretive, turning on the kinds of evidence that are admissable when we interpret a historical document in terms of its context. The participants in the debate work from various sets of assumptions—historicist, deconstructionist, intertextual, and formalist—to ask how permeable a text is, or can be made, to phenomena (including other texts) that we know lie just outside its margins. What is or should be the effect, for example, of our knowledge that Wordsworth carried William Gilpin's *Tour of the Wye Valley* with him in 1798? This is a relatively uncontroversial example. The debate has tended to focus more heatedly on socioeconomic and political factors in the Wye Valley and in Wordsworth's career that are not mentioned in "Tintern Abbey," particularly the vagrants living in the ruins and the local iron industry. The most controversial position has been staked out by Marjorie Levinson, "Insight and Oversight: Reading 'Tintern Abbey'," in her *Wordsworth's Great Period Poems*, pp. 14–57. Levinson in effect argues for the poem's maximum permeability, not only to contemporary facts about the Wye Valley but also to the history of its institutions: the communitarian ideal of the Cistercian monastery, for example, relative to Wordsworth's personalistic focus. Most subsequent entries in the debate have tried to qualify Levinson's claims to a greater or lesser degree. But her position received an advance endorsement (so to speak) from its summarized appearance in Jerome McGann's *The Romantic Ideology*, pp. 84–88, as an example of the role historicist scholarship can play in exposing the assumptions of a past artistic ideology, especially how that ideology is reproduced in successive generations of critical (McGann would say, "naive") interpretation. Other essays in the debate include, to date: M. H. Abrams, "On Political Readings of *Lyrical Ballads*" (1990); Robert Brinkley, "Vagrant and Hermit: Milton and the Politics of 'Tintern Abbey' " (1985) and " 'Our Chearful Faith': On Wordsworth, Politics, and Milton" (1987); David Bromwich, "The French Revolution and 'Tintern Abbey' " (1991); Mark Edmundson, "Criticism Now: The Example of Wordsworth" (1990); and Thomas McFarland, "The Clamour of Absence: Reading and Misreading in Wordsworthian Criticism" (1992). Taken together, these essays provide an excellent introduction to current theoretical issues in Wordsworthian and Romantic studies, focused around the instance of a well-known text. The present essay, while anticipating Levinson's approach, does not go as far as she does in holding Wordsworth's poem responsible for what it excludes, ignores, or overlooks. But I do assume the interpretive "interest" (to use an ambiguous Wordsworthian word) of much of the same data she cites.

NOTES

1. Carl Woodring has recently traced in "Tintern Abbey" a movement from Pictur-esque to Sublime, stressing its "sublimity of humble human feelings," and comparing its "still, sad music" to the "still, small voice" of God in Old Testament prophecy ("The New Sublimity in 'Tintern Abbey,' " in *The Evidence of the Imagination*, ed. Reiman, Jaye, & Bennett [1978], pp. 86–100). My conclusions are similar, though in many instances our interpretations of textual details are so different we may be said to have arrived at agreement by opposite routes.

2. *Wordsworth's Philosophical Poetry, 1797–1814* (1980), p. 38.

3. *Romantic Paradox* (1962), pp. 39–53.

4. Mary Moorman, *William Wordsworth: The Early Years* (1957), p. 402; cited hereafter in text as "M.I."

5. In his general valuation of the inter-penetration of cultivated and uncultivated land, Wordsworth follows Gilpin: the artist "wishes that these [property] limits must be as much concealed as possible . . . that the lands they circumsribe, may approach, as near as may be, to nature—that is, that they may be pasturage" (p. 30). Specifically, Wordsworth's "hedge-rows . . . little lines of sportive wood" follow closely Gilpin's discussion of the border shrubs planted by a Mr. Morris at Persfield (*below* Tintern, incidentally): though causing "the most pleasing riot of imagination," such "paltry" improvements are but "splendid patches, which injure the grandeur, and simplicity of the whole," and their "formal introduction" should be avoided in favor of "wild underwood" (pp. 40–42).

6. Gilpin, p. 45.

7. "A Note on a Guide to Tintern Abbey," *TWC*, 8 (1977), 95–6.

8. "With a sweet inland murmur" (1.4); Wordsworth's note ends with the same phrase as his title: "The river is not affected by tides *a few miles above Tintern.*" There is considerable evidence available to caution us against taking too literally any of Wordsworth's statements in, or about, the poem (see Notes 11 and 21). The Wye ceases to be appreciably affected by tides very close to Tintern, perhaps less than a mile above it; tourist officials cite Tintern as *the* limit, for convenience.

9. I am grateful to Pamela Woof for this information, offered during an expert tour of "The Discovery of Lakes," an exhibition of picturesque landscape paintings mounted in the Wordsworth Museum, Grasmere.

10. Gilpin, pp. 35–37.

11. See Note 8. Geoffrey Little argues that the Wye landscape described in the poem bears more similarity to the areas Wordsworth visited on his first tour in 1793, much further up the valley (" 'Tintern Abbey' and Llsywen Farm," *TWC*, 8 [1977], 80–82).

12. If the tour took four days (see Note 21), they arrived at Tintern on the first day, departed from it on the second, passed by it on the third (returning to spend the night there), and departed from it on the fourth.

13. *The Love Letters of William and Mary Wordsworth* (1981).

14. Peter Brier, "Reflections on Tintern Abbey," *TWC*, 5 (1974), 5–6.

15. For an interpretive overview of Wordsworth's work on *The Recluse*, see my "Wordsworth and *The Recluse:* The University of Imagination," *PMLA*, 97 (1982), 60–82.

16. "I wish you would write a poem . . . addressed to those who, in consequence of the complete failure of the French Revolution, have thrown up all hopes of the amelio-ration of mankind. . . . It would do great good, and might form part of *The Recluse*"

(Coleridge to Wordsworth, *Collected Letters of Samuel Taylor Coleridge,* ed. Earl Leslie Griggs, 6 vols. [1956–1971], 1:527).

17. E.P. Thompson, "Disenchantment or Default?," in *Power and Consciousness,* ed. O'Brien and Vanech (1969), p. 169.

18. For a full account of Frend, see Frida Knight, *University Rebel: The Life of William Frend, 1757–1841* (1971). At the university disciplinary hearings on his dismissal, the Cambridge undergraduates strongly supported him, Coleridge prominent among them (Dictionary of National Biography); in 1789, he made a summer walking tour of France and Switzerland, returning with glowing reports of the new republic— such enthusiasm from a widely admired young faculty member may have helped stimulate Wordsworth to make essentially the same tour the following year.

19. *The Philanthropist* (London: Printed and sold by Daniel Isaac Eaton, Printer and Bookseller to the Supreme Majesty of the People, at the Cock and Swine, No. 74, Newgate Street, December 14, 1795), in *Early British Periodicals* (1972), University Microfilms, reel 244.

20. G. M. Harper, *William Wordsworth* (1916), I, 223–73; Émile Legouis, *The Early Life of William Wordsworth* (1897), pp. 221–78.

21. John Bard McNulty, "Wordsworth's Tour of the Wye: 1798," *MLN,* 60 (1945), 291–95; M.I., 400–07; Mark Reed, *Wordsworth: The Chronology of the Early Years* (1967), pp. 243–44.

22. McNulty, p. 293n.3.

23. J. R. Watson, while accepting the July 13 date, subjects it to interpretation that support my suppositions. Besides emphasizing the date's importance for Wordsworth as personal anniversary (because of the landing at Calais in 1790), he points out that on July 13, 1793, *exactly* five years before, Marat had been murdered in his bath by Charlotte Corday (the event which led most directly to Robespierre's rise to power), adding that Wordsworth, if he did indeed revisit Paris in autumn 1793, would've been aware of the great propaganda value the Jacobins had derived from this assassination, principally by David's famous painting, presented to the Convention on November 14, 1793 ("A Note on the Date in the Title of 'Tintern Abbey,' " *TWC,* 10 (1979), 379–80).

The Economy of Lyric:
The Ruined Cottage

The following selection abstracted from Alan Liu's book, *Wordsworth: The Sense of History* (1989), displays the interaction of new-historicist thinking with interest in the early versions of Wordsworth's poems. If displacement is taken as a dominating feature of Wordsworth's poetry, a conscientious critic must reconstruct specifically (not abstractly) what does not appear in the poem. And that will carry the critic, as it carries Liu, into detailed historical analyses not merely of the poet's psyche but also of the macropolitical and microeconomic life of his society. Such analyses require the critic to consult whatever version of the text is closest to the historical moment in which the poem took shape rather than a later, "final" form.

Our brief and heavily edited excerpt from Liu's very long and heavily annotated book does no justice to his broadest political discussions, which represent Wordsworth's anxieties at his psychic complicity in the tragic violence of the French Revolution and its principal "totalitarian" product, Napoleon. But Liu's treatment of "The Ruined Cottage" not as "a poem of humanity" but as a "capitalization upon inhumanity" illustrates his basic method. This brings together the biographical details of the poet's life at the time of composition with a definition of the social-political-economic forces impinging upon him then. With "The Ruined Cottage" Liu identifies the poet's anxieties about mismanaging the legacy left him by Raisley Calvert as concentrating his awareness of the deleterious effects of industrialization, whose effects on weavers like Robert, whose desertion of his wife is the crux of the tale, is of decisive importance to the poem's shape and tone. Thus for Liu the tragedy of the poem is its demonstration that labor, which had once signified the value of household economy, is being transformed into wage-value, becoming a dehumanizing activity.

Persuasive as Liu's learned presentation is, we must note that its very vigor has recently provoked an impressive counterargument. The charge is that Liu, along with other new historicists such as Levinson and McGann, having lost sight of Wordsworth's primary concern with natural phenomena, distort the fundamental character of the poet's sociopolitical commitments. This case is eloquently presented in Jonathan Bate's

From *Wordsworth: The Sense of History* (Stanford: Stanford University Press, 1989), pp. 314–332, 335–336, 337–338, 340–341, 343–349. Reprinted with the permission of the publishers, Stanford University Press. Copyright © 1989 by the Board of Trustees of the Leland Stanford Junior University.

Romantic Ecology (1991), which in its bold challenge to the discourse of displacement has probably defined the major battle zone of Wordsworthian criticism for the remainder of this century.

. . . In a passage from *The Ruined Cottage,* MS. B, later applied to himself in *The Prelude,* 3.141–44, Wordsworth hawks the Pelar's talents as follows:

> In all shapes
> He found a secret and mysterious soul,
> A fragrance and a spirit of strange meaning.
> Though poor in outward shew, he was most rich;
> He had a world about him—'twas his own,
> He made it—for it only lived to him
> And to the God who looked into his mind.
>
> (ll. 83–89)

This, we might say, is the original Romantic patent for the icon antedating even the Keatsian rift of ore. Following the lead of Marc Shell, Kurt Heinzelman, and R. A. Shoaf, who have explored the economics of the imagination,[1] I suggest that the best approach to the absent cash flow between culture and poetry in *The Ruined Cottage* will be to follow a figure of "richness" so central to the understanding of poetic talent from the Romantics to the New Critics that I believe it is actually the ground. If we can track the figure to its contemporary ground—that is, if we can remove "richness" from the sphere of imagery in order to let it tell us from a literal perspective *about* imagery—then we will be able to arrive at a standard by which to relate cultural and poetic value.

Given the fact that the value of "rich" poetry seems absent, what historical value constituted the ground of such absence? What economy underwrote the "iconomy" of lyric?[2]

The history of the value of absence may be blocked out as follows: if rich imagery is not secured upon any cash visible in normal usage, then it must be secured upon *lack* of cash. Such lack, I suggest, marked a value of industrial economy that did not yet have form for Wordsworth except as "debt." Or rather, it had no form except as Wordsworth captialized upon debt by strange speculations of imagery until the inhumanity of actual capitalization could seem to disappear. *The Ruined Cottage,* I fear, is not a poem of humanity. It is a capitalization upon inhumanity. A specific kind of capitalization, that is, is the historical form of Wordsworthian humanity. Endorsing a transition in the industrial method of the contemporary Lakes and in the poet's own livelihood at the time even as it looks away from such transition, *The Ruined Cottage* is one of the strongest cases of the denial, the overdetermined and precise absence, that is the poet's sense of history.[3]

Careful definition of the economy of debt is necessary before we can detail the Wordsworthian capitalization. The leading indexes of this economy in the poem are Robert, whose vocation defines a crux in contemporary industry, and the Poet, whose entrance in existential "toil" defines a corresponding crux in Wordsworth's own industry of writing. As intimated by the etymological link between "textitles" and "texts," as well as by such stock metaphors as the "warp and woof" of verse, Robert's weaving and Wordsworth's writing are really one labor I will call "textualization."[4] Whereas the Pedlar indexes the sun as the blinding source of reality, Robert and the Poet point to a different kind of sun: a strangely hollow "purse of gold."

Wordsworth is careful to detail Robert's status both before and after his ruin. An "industrious," "sober and steady" weaver with the by-occupation of gardening (ll. 172–84), Robert lapses into unemployment for reasons itemized in three steps. The poem depicts a general economic depression "some ten years ago" caused by bad harvests and "the plague of war" (ll. 185–96), adds that a "fever seized" Robert after two years and "consumed" all his savings (ll. 196–205), and finally recapitulates the calamity of general depression with stress on unemployment: "As I have said, 'twas now / A time of trouble; shoals of artisans / Were from their daily labour turned away" (ll. 205–7). The result is that Robert ends in a state of permanent unemployment. Becoming fretful and unbalanced, he increasingly absents himself from home (ll. 234–36) and finally deserts Margaret to enlist in the army for a "purse of gold" (ll. 320–23).

Upon close examination however, Wordsworth's explanation is puzzling in its overdetermination. . . . We need to establish as accurately as possible Robert's vocational situation. It is not unlikely, after all, that Wordsworth had technical knowledge of the weaving profession. While a schoolboy in Hawkshead, he often entered spinners' cottage and "admired the cylinders of carded wool which were softly laid upon each other" (quoted in MM, 1:24). He probably also saw weavers' homes because textiles and clothmaking were Hawkshead's second leading nonagricultural occupation, and he knew at least one weaver, John Martin, well enough to go fishing with him.[5] (It is also possible that he read John Dyer's *The Fleece* by the time of *The Ruined Cottage*.) But it will be sufficient to assume only what seems certain: whatever his acquanintance with techne, Wordsworth understood profoundly the ethos of weaving as the traditional exemplar of British labor. If we require more detail ourselves, it will be in the service of reproducing the poet's own deeper brand of familiarity.

First, we can be certain that Wordsworth conceived Robert as a traditional wool, as opposed to cotton, weaver. Among other evidence: the cotton industry was so new that it did not arrive in substantial form in the Lakes until the last decades of the eighteenth century ("cottons" still commonly referred to the area's trademark coarse woolens).[6] Woolen manufacture had been divided for centuries between two systems of production: the "household" domestic industry of Yorkshire and the North (including the Lakes) and the "putting-out" domestic industry of the West Country around Bristol and the Racedown-Alfoxden area (where Wordsworth wrote MSS. A and B of *The Ruined Cottage*). In the Northern system, to start with, a weaver controlled all the factors of production. He bought his own wool, carded and spun it at home with the aid of his family (and sometimes apprentices), worked it upon his own loom, and then sold the product to the clothier.[7] After fulling and dyeing, the clothier then distributed the product either through middlemen to stores or—and this will have special bearing for us—through an extensive network of peddlers directly to the rural public. Wordsworth's Pedlar with his "pack of winter raiment" (l. 192) is typical of contemporary peddlers in selling primarily women's clothes and accessories on an economically significant scale (on peddlers and the textile trade in the North, see Lipson, p. 90).

From this system arose the famous character of Northern weaving: "independence."[8] When operating above a certain scale, weavers who held land by freehold or customary tenure, owned both wool and loom, and controlled an in-house pool of labor tended to keep producing even if a depression meant that their products could not be sold for some time. As the Northern weavers represented themselves to Parliament in 1806, "Winter or summer, bad trade or good, we go on straight forwards" (quoted in Lipson, p. 78). By their own account, indeed, Northern weavers were so independent that their universe seemed to know no economic other at all. A petition of the Northern weavers to Parliament in 1794 pictured them as men "who, with a very trifling capital, aided by the unremitting labour of themselves, their wives and children, united under one roof, decently and independently have maintained themselves and families" (quoted in Lipson, p. 70).

Another way to measure "independence" is to observe that Northern laborers traditionally saved up a special kind of free-standing credit. Study of Lake District probate inventories and wills by J. D. Marshall shows that until the middle of the eighteenth century Northern laborers—including weavers—were dedicated savers who preferred to invest profit in credit instruments (bills, bonds, and mortgages) rather than new goods and services transcending traditional standards of comfort (e.g., clocks or expensive funerals).[9] Such credit, however, had a status more like treasure—a pure accumulation symbolizing "independence"—than of exchange value. It did not seem to imply a corresponding amount of debt as well. As Marshall observes, the striking evidence of the inventories is that, except in the case of the hill areas of rapidly industrializing Kendal, there was substantially more credit in the Lakes than debt ("Agrarian Wealth," p. 511 and table I on p.509; see also his "Kendal"). Who, then, owed money to the creditors?

Part of the mystery is explained by assuming that some credit was in the form of bills and bonds taken by agencies outside the Lakes, though contradictory evidence shows an extreme localism of credit (Marshall, "Agrarian Wealth," p. 511). But an additional hypothesis can be suggested: the formal recording process undervalued debt because it was conceptually different from, rather than simply the obverse of, credit. Northern weavers, we know, characteristically bought their wool on loan, but such debts necessary for production were individually very small.[10] Moreover, while profit was invested in credit instruments with long maturities, small debts incurred in production—even if extended over the month or so necessary to loom one batch of wool—existed on a different time scale, a subsistence schedule of week-by-week debit and repayment (Lipson, p. 79). In short, credit piled up visibly, but debt stretched thinly throughout working life in a different kind of space and time. The practical reason for such debt to fall out of the recording process is that the records available to us cover only estates above a certain level of wealth in which the overhead debt required for production was proportionally small.[11] Much of the missing debt in the Lake District must hide in the unrecorded operating costs of the lower yeomanry and the laborers. The conceptual corollary of this circumstance is that however much the small debts extending throughout working life added up to a high overall debt level, Lakes society as a whole—at least in the prosperous mid-century—estimated debt as insignificant except in the case of marginal producers. Such debts were no more than operating expenses, a sort of static noise of economic existence with no impact worth recording. *In the Northern system of labor as epitomized by weaving, debt was invisible.*

In the Bristol-area putting-out system, by contrast, the weaver worked at home usually upon his own loom, but it was the clothier who owned the wool, had it spun and carded, and contracted it to the weaver. The clothier then paid piece-rate for the woven product before selling it through the same network of middle-men and peddlers.[12] The sum was that the weaver worked in a nascent wage system not yet fully differentiated from the piece-rate system of payment. Such a system made crucial what Northern industry deemphasized: the essential indebted-ness upon which production floated. In contemporary economic thought, indeed, a putting-out economy was analytically identical with debt financing. As Adam Smith argued, "In all arts and manufactures the greater part of the workmen stand in need of a master to advance them the materials of their work, and their wages and maintenance till it be compleated" (I: 73—74). While the weaver controlled other factors of production, in other words, he could acquire materials only as an "advance" from the clothier. Unlike his Northern counterpart, then, who accumu-lated profit as what I have called free-standing credit, the putting-out weaver earned only unsavable subsistence, a continual refinancing of labor drawn upon capital controlled by the other. Indeed, only in such a system did there appear a true economic other. The social distance between wealthy clothiers and poor weavers was much greater than in the North (Lipson, pp. 13–20) and expressed itself in perennial disputes over weavers' embezzlement of wool (Lipson, pp. 59–61). *In the putting-out economy, indebtedness, or dependence on capital advanced by the other, was central.*

The application we can make of the facts of weaving is as follows. Wordsworth situates Robert in a crux *between* the traditional economies of weaving. We notice to start with that Robert resides both in the Lakes and in the Bristol sphere of influence. The poem's opening prospect with its southern "uplands" and "northern downs" clearly locates Robert in the Lakes of *An Evening Walk*, and the fact that Margaret later need not worry about eviction suggests specifi-cally that he is a Lake District yeoman holding his land by freehold or customary tenure.[13] But Robert also has clear ties with the West Country near Bristol from which, according to the Fenwick note on *The Excursion*, Book I, Wordsworth collected much of his local color (*RC*, p. 476). We know that Robert inhabits an unenclosed common covered with "bursting gorse" (ll. 18–25), for example, and that sheep cross his threshold and garden in his absence (ll. 388–94, 461). These details depict the area around Racedown, where the Wordsworths walked up gorse-covered Pilsdon Pen and themselves had trouble keeping livestock out of the garden (MM, I: 282–84).[14]

Correspondingly, Robert's industrial situation is double. While he lives within the orbit of Northern "independence," he is also victimized by a method of produc-tion resembling the Bristol-area putting-out system. Even after being idled, we notice, Robert "tasks" himself in ways confirming his Northern habits:

> The passenger might see him at the door
> With his small hammer on the threshold stone
> Pointing lame buckle-tongues and rusty nails,
> The treasured store of an old houshold box,
> Or braiding cords of weaving bells and caps
> Of rushes, play-things for his babes.
>
>   (ll. 224–29)

"Braiding" and "weaving" as if in a dream of occupation, he relives an "independent" career whose whole goal was to save a free-standing credit of "treasured store." His psychological decay begins only after a discovery that would be traumatic to any Northern saver: "the little he had stored . . . Was all consumed."

Yet Robert also certainly works according to something like the putting-out system. A first hint is the fact that he does not buy his own wool. Even in times of distress, we notice, Margaret does not help Robert by spinning or carding; indeed, she later subsists on the much more impoverished by-occupation of spinning flax (ll. 495–502).[15] Robert must be "advanced" wool already spun and carded. Confirmation of Robert's dependence on the capitalist other comes when Wordsworth recounts that it was "A time of trouble; shoals of artisans / Were from their daily labour turned away." The implication is that Robert depends for employment on others with the power to "turn him away." MS. A is even more specific: "Shoals of Artisans / Were from the merchants turn'd away" (with "daily labour" entered interlinearly above "merchants"; *RC*, p. 87). The ultimate marker of such dependence on capitalists, perhaps, is the "purse of gold" Robert at last accepts. In a sense, the purse of gold is the poem's imagination of a wage. In the economy of debt, the self mortgages itself for a wage and then disappears, in total indebtedness, into the armies of the other.

Robert thus exists at a troubled crux in the structure of industry. The historical significance of such crux is that it marks transition: Robert is the poem's paralyzed imagination of the shift by century's end from Northern to Bristol-area systems.[16] In fact, depression caused by bad harvests and war—as well as such regional factors as Yorkshire's increasingly successful competition against the Lakes[17]—did cause unemployment in Lake District wool weaving as well as a distortion of the whole system in the direction of the putting-out method. Weavers operating above a certain scale remained self-sufficient, but others saw their "independence" disappear as depression raised the static noise of operating debt above the threshold of significance. Poorer weavers subsisted entirely on a week-by-week supply of wool bought on credit and paid for upon delivery of the woven fabric to the clothier. In a depression, clothiers were often slow to pay for finished work or to extend credit (Lipson, pp. 70–71, 78), and weavers therefore had to use savings to buy wool if they wished to work at all.[18] Any interruption in the weaver's ability to work or market his product, and so to refinance himself, would thus indeed have left him unable to start up again except in complete indebtedness to a capitalist. We might look once more at Robert's illness:

A fever seized [Margaret's] husband. In disease
He lingered long, and when his strength returned
He found the little he had stored to meet
The hour of accident or crippling age
Was all consumed.

(ll. 201–5)

As in the actual case histories Marshall records of debt-ridden yeomen in the Lakes afflicted by illness ("Domestic Economy," p.215), Robert's "seizure" would realistically have put him out of business. But the real seizure consuming his living by sinking him irrecoverably into debt was financial. "The finances of many a family," Marshall observes, "might be miserably disorganised by prolonged illness on the part of its head or its members" (p. 215). . . .

Only after early May 1797 did Wordsworth truly understand the nature of debt. By the time he responded to Richard's demand for an accounting, he had already received another, more unsettling demand. Part of the £460 he owed their relatives in Whitehaven came due when his cousin, Robinson Wordsworth (who was planning to marry, insisted that £250 be paid back. . . .

What Wordsworth suddenly glimpsed, we might say, was an expanding universe of debts—Montagu's, William's, Richard's, and, at the outer periphery, Lonsdale's—each inscribed within the orbit of larger debts. (The largest of all, of course, was the national debt, which sources available to Wordsworth put at some £397 million in 1797; see *Oeconomist* I: 98–99.) In such a universe, there could be no endowment pure and simple. There could only be something like a sinking fund marking the intersection of monies collectible and payable. . . .

The Ruined Cottage in its earliest form (MS.A) evolved from March to June 1797 when the debt to Robinson Wordsworth was freshest in Wordsworth's mind. MS.B then developed from January to early March 1798, just in time to be offered to Cottle along with *The Borderers* and *Salisbury Plain* in Wordsworth's first major scheme to publish for money. Of the poems collated together in this package, indeed, *The Ruined Cottage* was the only one substantially written during the encounter with personal debt. We thus arrive precisely at the moment of *The Ruined Cottage* upon a crisis in Wordsworth's industry of writing parallel to that of weaving. Weaving and writing: the partners of textualization together entered the economy of debt.

Now we can account more fully for the "layoff of the signifier" in the poem's structure of humanity. Labor, we remember, was once the signifier of a value immanent in household economy: humanity. As framed between the labors of weaving and writing, such humanity was an "independent" textuality. But in the moment of economic crisis, labor became part of sign-structure displaced from the independent household—and industrial sign-structure in which, as Saussure has suggested, wages became the signifier and labor itself the signified.[19] Before labor could signify humanity, in other words, it now had to await the outcome of a previous adjustment of meaning, or negotiation of wage-value, occurring wholly outside the household. Labor, we might say, became intertextual, and what was once the value of domestic humanity opened out into the inhuman value or cash of the economic other.

What capitalist, with what funds can allow the labors of textualization to produce even in debt the text of humanity?

Peddling has been de-emphasized in readings of *The Ruined Cottage* as an occupation whose only significance is that it is peripatetic. But I believe the specifically vocational status of peddling is crucial. Not in a superficial or loose sense, but deeply and precisely, peddling is the Wordsworthian capitalization. It is a capitalization of ruin not the less identifiable for being denied. . . .

Peddling is Wordsworth's black-market capitalism, his itinerant speculation mandating a poetry of repressed or denied economy. I enter as evidence the actual status of peddling at the time. By the end of the century, and especially in the English Northwest, peddling had become precisely a parallel economy akin to a black market. Wordsworth, we know, knew the peddling trade remarkably well even before he had heard of James Patrick of Kendal and introduced him into the Pedlar's biography in 1801–2 (*RC*, p. 26). In the Fenwick note on *The Excursion*, he remembers a peddler ancestral to Patrick:

> At Hawkshead also, while I was a schoolboy, there occasionally resided a Packman (the name then generally given to this calling) with whom I had frequent conversations upon what had befallen him & what he had observed during his wandering life, &, as was natural, we took much to each other; & upon the subject of *Pedlarism* in general, as *then* followed, & its favorableness to an intimate knowledge of human concerns, not merely among the humbler classes of society, I need say nothing here in addition. (*RC*, p. 478)

There is even the possibility that "Pedlarism" undergirds *The Ruined Cottage* so thoroughly that the tale of Margaret and Robert could have been generated solely from the circumstances of Hawkshead peddlers. One of the six peddlers Wordsworth might have known at Hawkshead, according to T. W. Thompson, was related to a weaver the poet also knew and had once joined the army, and one had a wife named Margaret (pp. 207, 239–45).

Such familiarity with "the subject of *Pedlarism* in general" allows us to deduce that Wordsworth almost certainly knew of the Parliamentary controversy over peddlers in 1785–86, precisely when he was in Hawkshead. Changing regulation of the peddler's trade had stabilized in 1697 with the imposition of a barely enforceable system of licensing and taxation (Lipson, pp. 90–93). In 1785, however, a campaign suddenly began to persuade the House of Commons to ban the living of the nation's 1400 or so peddlers entirely by revoking or withholding their licenses. The motive was to compensate retailstore merchants—the competitors of peddlers—for a new tax. From spring 1785 to the following spring, scores of petitions on both sides of the issue came before the House. Among these, a disproportionately high number originated in the North country of Lancashire and the Lake District (especially Kendal and Westmorland generally, but also Cumberland).[20]

The debate can be summarized as follows, where "no" to the proposal to ban peddling was argued not only by peddlers but sympathetic farmers, weavers, wholesale merchants, and clergy, and "yes" exclusively by town retail-store merchants (cf. Lipson, pp. 91–93). *No:* peddlers (also known as hawkers, chapmen, and scotchmen) were a "useful Class of People" in the North, where distribution of cloth goods to rural customers would otherwise be much hampered. More than useful, peddlers were absolutely necessary. Without them, innumerable existing debts owed by rural customers to peddlers and, through peddlers, to merchants (some of whom circulated many thousands of pounds of goods at a time in this fashion) would become uncollectible and so plunge "Thousands of worthy Families in Distress and Ruin." Finally, peddlers were dealers of "Integrity and Uprightness" who stemmed what would otherwise be a rampant black market of "contraband Goods" detrimental both to merchants' profits and tax revenues.[21]

Yes: peddlers were "unfair" competition for retail outlets because they practiced "fallacious" advertisement and other flimflam, paid no parochial taxes, and could not be held to strict account for the licensing fees they did owe. Moreover, peddlers were not really useful in the Northern distribution system because they merely took trade away from "Retail Shops now established in all Parts of the Country." They were also so far from being necessary because of the credit line they controlled that they actually harmed all merchants because of "the Uncertainty of the Returns of Hawkers" and the fact that many were "profligate Tradesmen [who], in Contemplation of Bankruptcy, become intinerant for the sole Purpose of defrauding their honest Creditors." Finally—and this was a constant refrain—peddlers were *themselves* black marketeers engaged in "Smuggling," distribution of "stolen Goods," and "illicit Traffic" in general.[22]

Because peddlers lived on the outer fringe of documentation, the truth of the matter is hard to determine. But the lack of proper documentation is itself a clue to the deep truth of the controversy: peddlers were holdovers from a system of production and distribution that, in the transition to modern production by wage labor and distribution by retail outlet, became objectionable precisely because it represented the undocumented, unaccountable, and unregulated. Controlling in their informal way an extensive credit line, they stood for a recalcitrant unaccountability of debt, a refusal to make debt financing emerge from traditional Northern invisibility into the institutionalized form of the wage system. In other words, in an economic age of legitimate wage workers and merchant-capitalists, peddlers were unclassifiable except as dangerous "vagrants." They were reminders of an old Northern system now seen as itself an extralegal black market secreted within lawful business.

Wordsworth reverses the locus of legitimacy in *The Ruined Cottage*, but retains peddling in its black-market capacity. Traditional Northern economy is fixed as legitimate; capitalization as illegitimate; and peddling as the occupation that smuggles capitalization irrepressibly within. As the supertext of MS. B tells us, the Pedlar in his youth disregarded his father's advice to become a schoolmaster and took up what may seem the most disinterested of all trades: peddling (*RC*, pp. 175–77). In the 1801–2 revisions in MS. D, where the father (now a stepfather) is himself a schoolmaster (*RC*, p. 331), Wordsworth will emphasize that the son's vocation is so disinterested as to be wholly avocational. Because "he had an open hand / That never could refuse whoever ask'd / Or needed," the Pedlar "was slow / In gathering wealth" (*RC*, p. 359).[23] But such neglect of his father's business in books, as teaching might be called, is really a repression that smuggles the occupation of brokering textuality inside as preoccupation. Dealing in textiles and at one point in the supertext of MS.B in poetic texts as well (he "fitted to the moorland harp / His own sweet verse," "many a ditty"; *RC*, p. 191), the Pedlar is indeed the "itinerant speculator" of textuality. His talent is to capitalize secretly the labors of weaving and writing. He is the middleman, intertextual dealer, or interpreter of the text of "humanity" who allows the debt or absent value of the text to be pocketed as "riches" by that special economic other, the reader.

Now we can account for the poem's riches. In the Pedlar's youth, there was a primal "textuality" to be negotiated. As the supertext tells us, the Pedlar exchanged all his actual earnings for books (*RC*, p. 161) and "greedily . . . read & read again" (*RC*, p. 163). He also conned the book of Nature, a larger ledger of the riches to be gained from a ghostly, absent value of textuality. In a 1798 draft in the Alfoxden Notebook (DC MS. 14) later transferred to *The Prelude*, Wordsworth thus deems "not profitless these fleeting moods / Of shadowy exaltation" when the Pedlar strove for gain from the "ghostly language of the ancient earth" (*RC*, p. 119). The net gain from early dealings in textuality, the supertext of MS.B then adds, consisted of "accumulated feelings" that "press'd his heart / With an

encreasing weight" (RC, p. 169). The Pedlar capitalized upon textuality so success-
fully, we might translate, that he banked in his heart emotions recollectible, with
interest, in tranquillity. With such funds available, "He could afford to suffer /
With those whom he saw suffer" and in "best experience he was rich" (*RC*, p.
183). Or to cite again the passage about the Pedlar later applied to Wordsworth
himself in *The Prelude:*

> In all shapes
> He found a secret and mysterious soul,
> A fragrance and a spirit of strange meaning
> Though poor in outward shew, he was most rich
>   (ll. 83–86)

The maturity of the Pedlar's riches is then the hidden currency or black money
of imagery. Appreciation of spear-grass, in other words, is akin to speculation in
wheat futures with the exaggeration, as in the case of hoarders and cornerers
generally, that it is the total absence of wheat that the Pedlar most appreciates.
The Pedlar had "an eye / So busy," Wordsworth says (ll. 268–69). The eye is
precisely the Pedlar's instrument of business, his jeweler's loop or—to invoke
Shell's study of the mythic origin of money and its ability to make property visible
or invisible at will—his Gyges's Ring (pp. 11–62). Designed as the consummate
instrument of exchange, the Pedlar's eye is in the business of seeing traditional
cultural values disappear and the intertextual marker, debt-note, or "image" of
such values appear instead.[24] The crowning speculation of his eye is the tale of
Margaret, which, because it is "hardly clothed / In bodily form" (ll. 292–93)
virtually invites the capitalist of textuality to work his deal of imagery. . . .
    If there is one evaluation upon which I would be content to rest this chapter, it is
that money does indeed matter deeply and *legitimately* to poets, not just because
everyday subsistence demands attention by right of reality but because everyday
dealings infiltrate purely poetic imagery itself through shuttlings of mimesis work-
ing all the more powerfully the stronger the denial. If we cannot appreciate poetic
peddling as it mimes the unscrupulous processes of contemporary economic his-
tory without stigmatizing such peddling—without compounding the poetry's de-
nial with our own—then "appreciation" is too limited a response. A fuller reading
would follow the initial stage of appreciating a poem's own declared values with a
twofold process at once depreciative and reappreciative. A perspective that is
truly critical, perhaps, requires at last something like a con man's bait-and-switch
practiced in reverse: look once more at imagery and see the sun depreciate into a
mere guinea; look twice and appreciate the deeper fact that the world of spending
and getting has always itself been shot through with what Heinzelman calls
"mythic force" (*Economics of the Imagination,* p. 13). Such, after all, is the core
sense of Heizelman's expansive book as well as of Shell's work: economy exerts so
powerful a hold over everyday imagination because it is a *primary* poetics of the
imagination. Economics tosses the coin of golden hope and brass fear, illusion and
disillusion; and in the Platonic cave that is the speculative imagination, such is all
the sun there is. If the "dreaming man" or Pedlar in Wordsworth's poem plays the
con game of the "sidelong" glance, then a fully critical appreciation must not so
much avoid the shifty glance of ideology—for that would be to attempt to look

outside history—as con the poem's values in reverse. The imagery that the poem appreciates, we should finally depreciate as a precondition of critical reading; and, inversely, the economy that the poem's imagery depreciates, we should learn to re-appreciate—but without any illusion that our own idols of the marketplace (such terms as "capital," "labor," or "value" approaching at times the reified abstractions Bacon attacked) are less ideologically implicated than Wordsworth's idols *denying* the marketplace.[25]

To allow us to read certain values in order to re-appreciate them, I conclude, must be the true use of a poem like *The Ruined Cottage,* for "use" is a concept necessarily suspended between the horizons of the text "in itself" and of the reader. . . .

NOTES

1. See R. A. Shoaf, *Dante, Chaucer, and the Currency of the Currency of the Word: Money, Images, and Reference in Late Medieval Poetry* (Norman, Okla., 1983). I regret that Shoaf's study did not appear in time for me to assimilate it fully. His analysis of the economics of reference in light of the theology of the Image provides a prolegomenon to what I only touch upon in this chapter: the insistent nostalgia of faith that makes both the Romantic "image" and New Critical "icon" chalices for what T. E. Hulme called "split religion." Particularly apropos as well is Shoaf's study of the narcissistic image—within whose endless hall of mirrors reference is lost—as a danger to be overcome by an act of faith patterned either after Dante's transcendental self-imaging or Chaucer's other-imaging. It is the complex sin and salvation of the Pedlar (as well as Wordsworth's "egotistical sublime" in general) to be caught perpetually in a flirtation with narcissism, in the unstable vector or dialectic between the Dantesque and the Chaucerian.

Also relevant are works that have appeared in the burgeoning field of economic approaches to Romanticism and Wordsworth since I wrote this chapter. Highly consonant with my chapter, for example, is [Marjorie] Levinson's essay on "Spiritual Economics" in "Michael" (now chap. 2 in her *Wordsworth's Great Period Poems*), which not only addresses centrally the issue of symbolic as opposed to material value but touches upon one of my subthemes: the value-laden relationship of Wordsworth's characters to artifacts and utensils. Levinson's introduction of the Akedah analogy in discussing the spiritualization of economy also extends the religious direction of inquiry. Other works that I have lately had a chance to consult include Gary Harrison's dissertation on the discourse of poverty in Wordsworth, Mark Schoenfield's unpublished essay on the theory of property in *The Excursion,* Susan Eilenberg's essays on "Michael," and the papers by Lee Erickson, Charles Rzepka, John Hodgson, Kurt Heinzelman, and Raimonda Modiano in the sessions on "The Value of Romanticism" at the MLA convention in San Francisco, Dec. 28, 1987 (the sessions also included papers on broader or less directly related issues of criticism and value by Robert M. Ryan, Kim Blank, and Herbert Lindenberger).

RC = William Wordsworth, *"The Ruined Cottage and The Pedlar,"* ed. James Butler (Ithaca, N.Y., 1979). All subsequent references to the two poems, including MSS, are to this edition.

2. For Nicole Oresme's false etymology assimilating "economics" to the "icon," see Shoaf, pp. 168–69, 191.

3. Cf. Jerome McGann's brief treatment of the poem with its conclusion that " 'The Ruined Cottage' is an exemplary case of what commentators mean when they

speak of the 'displacement' that occurs in a Romantic poem" (*The Romantic Ideology: A Critical Investigation* [Chicago, 1983], pp. 82–85).

4. There is intriguing but incomplete evidence to suggest that the link between the textile and text trades is more than simply poetic metaphor. Initiating research into book subscription lists in eighteenth-century Britain, Laslett and the Cambridge Group for the History of Population and Social Structure reported that by far the largest (and, by inference, most literate) group of book owners in their Scottish examples were weavers. In one extensive list, for example, 31 percent of subscribers were weavers; in another, 41 percent were weavers (Peter Laslett, "Scottish Weavers, Cobblers and Miners Who Bought Books in the 1750s," *Local Population Studies* 3 [Autumn 1969]). As Laslett notes, shoemakers were "a very bad second" to weavers despite having the reputation of being "the best read and the most independent in outlook of the craftsmen of earlier times" (p. 10). It is uncertain, however, whether the conclusions drawn from these select cases can be safely generalized.

MM = Mary Moorman, *William Wordsworth: A Bibliography*, 2 vols., vol. 1, *The Early Years, 1770–1803* (Oxford, 1957).

5. Textiles and clothmaking ranked behind only leathercrafts in the nonagricultural occupations of Hawkshead (J. D. Marshall, "Agrarian Wealth and Social Structure in Pre-Industrial Cumbria," *Economic History Review*, 2d series, 33 [1980]: 515). On John Martin, see T. W. Thompson, *Wordsworth's Hawkshead*, ed. Robert Woof (London, 1970), pp. 206–7.

6. Moreover, it would have been hard to imagine a cotton weaver *unemployed* before the first setbacks in 1799 foreboding the end of cotton handlooming's "golden age" from 1788 to 1803. See C.M.L. Bouch and G. P. Jones, *A Short Economic and Social History of the Lake Counties: 1500–1830* (Manchester, 1961). Hereafter cited as *LC1*. Bouch and Jones trace the arrival of the cotton industry in the Lakes (*LC1*, pp. 266–68). On the traditional strength of the Lakes in coarse woolens or "cottons," see *LC1*, pp. 134–36, 263. On the boom and crash in cotton handlooming, see Duncan Blythell, "The Hand-Loom Weavers in the English Cotton Industry During the Industrial Revolution: Some Problems," *Economic History Review*, 2d series, 17 (1964): 339–53; see also Neil J. Smelser, *Social Change in the Industrial Revolution: An Application of Theory to the Lancashire Cotton Industry, 1970–1840* (London, 1959), 129–57.

7. On the Northern household system specifically in the Lakes, see *LC1*, pp. 132–41, 143–44, 236. A more general sketch of the Northern "domestic" system may be found in E. Lipson, *The Age of Mercantilism*, vol. 2 of *The Economic History of England*, 5th ed. (London, 1961), 69–93. The terms "household" and "domestic" appear to be somewhat plastic in economic history. "Domestic" indicates that work was done in the home as opposed to factory. By "household domestic" system, I mean to distinguish the Northern form of the domestic system from the Bristol-area form. Lipson suggests calling the Northern system—which was akin in spirit, if not organization, to the older guild system—a "primitive" form of the Bristol-area system (p. 69n). Of course, the Northern and Bristol-area systems overlapped to some degree (see *LC1*, p. 143). J. D. Marshall and M. Davies-Shiel provide a useful, step-by-step description of the whole process of Northern textile production (*The Lake District at Work: Past and Present* [Newton Abbott, U. K., 1971], 19).

8. Bouch and Jones observe the "independence of the weaver" and suggest its somewhat mythic or "illusory" nature (*LC1*, p. 143). See also Lipson p. xlv. E. P. Thompson gives the best reading of the ideology of weaving "independence" as it reached its tragic complication in the early nineteenth century (*The Making of the English Working Class* [Harmondsworth, 1968], 271–74).

9. Marshall, "Agrarian Wealth," esp. pp. 510–11, 514, 518–20. See also J. D.

Marshall, *Old Lakeland: Some Cumbrian Social History* (Newton Abbott, U.K., 1971), 41–48; "The Domestic Economy of the Lakeland Yeoman: 1660–1749," *Transactions of the Cumberland and Westmoreland Antiquarian and Archeological Society,* n.s., 75 (1975): 275–82"; and "Kendal in the Late Seventeenth and Eighteenth Centuries," ibid., pp. 188–257. See also G. P. Jones, "Some Sources of Loans and Credit in Cumbria before the Rise of Banks," ibid., pp. 282–92, and C. E. Searle, "Custom, Class Conflict and Agrarian Capitalism: The Cumbrian Customary Economy in the Eighteenth Century," *Past and Present* 110 (February 1986): 117. The probate inventory was "a list of movable personal goods, credits, and debts compiled under oath by the friends and neighbors (appraiser or apprisers) of a person newly deceased, as a central part of the process of proving a will" ("Agrarian Wealth," p. 506).

10. The probate inventories show lists of debts in "tiny sums" owed by weavers to spinners for yarn (Marshall, "Agrarian Wealth," p. 514). Also see Lipson for the "method of credit" in the textile trade that was "one of the reasons for the survival of the domestic system" in the North (p. 79). On the small size of many loans among the Lakeland yeomanry in general, see Marshall, "Domestic Economy," p. 217.

11. Marshall comments on the problem of what the probate inventories leave out of consideration ("Agrarian Wealth," pp. 505, 507; "Domestic Economy," p. 191).

12. On the textile industry of the West Country or Bristol area, see Lipson, pp. 11–54; and on the way the putting-out system resembled the wage system, Lipson, esp. p. 31.

13. Robert's residency in the Lakes is bolstered in the poem's later versions, where Wordsworth sets the Poet's childhood meetings with the Pedlar in Hawkshead (beginning in MS.D; *RC,* p. 327). Supposing the Poet to be the same age as Wordsworth himself these meetings may be imagined to occur in the mid to late 1780s, precisely at the outset of Robert's troubles ("some ten years gone"). Since the Pedlar is relatively settled in Hawkshead during the Poet's childhood, Wordsworth probably conceived Robert as living nearby and certainly in the North within a few days' walk.

14. Nearby Alfoxden, site of the early 1798 work on MS.B, was also set amid countryside covered with furze (gorse) (Dorothy Wordsworth, *Journals of Dorothy Wordsworth: The Alfoxden Journal 1798; The Grasmere Journals, 1800–1803,* ed. Mary Moorman, 2d ed. [Oxford, 1971], 5, 10. Hereafter cited as *DWJ*).

15. As emphasized by Wordsworth himself in MS. E, where he alters "flax" to "hemp" and adds that Margaret "gain'd / By spinning hemp, a pittance for herself" (*RC,* p. 440; see Jonathan Wordsworth, *The Music of Humanity: A Critical Study of Wordsworth's "The Ruined Cottage"* [New York, 1969], 24–25). Working ten or eleven hours a day, a flax spinner of the time earned what one contemporary observer remarked was the "very inconsiderable" sum of four pence (*LC1,* pp. 242–43). See also Marshall, "Domestic Economy," p. 195.

16. E. P. Thompson charts this crossover with characteristic force and clarity: "We may simplify the experience of the years 1780–1830 if we say that they saw the merging of [most types of weavers] into a group, whose status was greatly debased—that of the proletarian outworker, who worked in his own home, sometimes owned and sometimes rented his loom, and who wove up the yarn to the specifications of the factor or agent of a mill of some middleman" (p. 271)

17. A. E. Musson, *The Growth of British Industry* (London, 1978), 86–89.

18. Individual case studies of yeomen or merchants in the Lakes allow us to gain a feel for the degree to which the economy of "independence" was saturated by small debt transactions whose enabling climate of trust could be threatened during a depression. G. P. Jones, for example, records the case of Abraham Dent of Kirby Stephen, an eighteenth-century shopkeeper, brewer, wine seller, and merchant hosier: "Being a

prudent merchant he kept a record of purchases by customers who did not pay cash down, the entries being crossed out when payment was made, which sometimes happened on market day. The time taken to clear the account was often only a week or two but in some cases was a year or longer. Dent as a rule needed time to settle with the suppliers of the goods he sold and was ordinarily allowed six or seven months. He discharged his obligation by paying the suppliers' agents or representatives when they called in Kirkby Stephen or occasionally when he himself called on the supplier" ("Some Sources," p. 291).

19. In linguistics, "as in the study of political economy, one is dealing with the notion of *value*. In both cases, we have a *system of equivalence between things belonging to different orders*. In one case, work and wages; in the other case, signification and signal" (Ferdinand de Saussure, *Course in General Linguistics,* trans. Roy Harris, ed. Charles Bally and Albert Sechehaye, with Albert Reidlinger [La Salle, Ill., 1986], 80). See Kurt Heinzelman on this passage (*The Economics of the Imagination* [Amherst, Mass., 1980], 9–10), as well as on the modern divorce in meaning between "work" and "labor" (pp. 146–47).

20. The importance of the issue to the Lakes can be gauged from the fact that the single speech Sir Michael Le Fleming made in the House of Commons prior to 1790 was an address supporting the ban on peddlers (Valentine, p. 527). Le Fleming's view of wandering packmen thus paralleled his harsh view of such wandering trespassers of property as Wordsworth and Coleridge.

21. *Journals of the House of Commons* 40 (1785) and 41 (1786). For petitions from the Lakes, see 40:1018, 1030–31; and 41:337, 470. For others, see 40:1007–8, 1017–18, 1020, 1026, 1039–40, 1042, 1042, 1052, 1059 (repeated page numbers represent separate petitions). My quotes are drawn from, in order of citation, 40:1031, 1059, 1031; 41:337. Many of the petitions repeat parts of others verbatim, thus indicating a fairly high level of national organization.

22. *Journals of the House of Commons* 40 (1785). For petitions from the Lakes, see 40:1091, 1091. For others see 40:1078, 1090, 1091–92, 1109, 1114, 1114, 1117–18, 1118, 1120–21, 1124, 1137–38. My quotes are drawn from, in order of citation, 40:1117, 1078, 1091, 1090, 1109, 1091, 1091, 1109. Again, many of the petitions repeat parts of others.

23. If I read the complex revisions correctly, these lines were entered interlinearly in 1801–2 over 1799 material in MS. D and then subsequently deleted with vertical pencil strokes.

24. Marx's comment on imagery is suggestive: "Being the external, common medium and faculty for turning an image into reality and reality into a mere image, . . . money transforms the real essential powers of man and nature into what are merely abstract conceits and therefore imperfections—into tormenting chimeras—just as it transforms real imperfections and chimeras—essential powers which are really impotent, which exist only in the mind of the individual—into real powers and faculties" (*The Economic and Philosophic Manuscripts of 1844,* ed. Dirk J. Struick, trans. Martin Milligan [New York, 1964], p. 169; quoted in Marc Shell, "The Golden Fleece and the Voice of the Shuttle," in *The Economy of Literature* [Baltimore, 1978], 41–42).

25. Very relevant to my concerns here and throughout my discussion of Wordsworth's imagery is W.J.T. Mitchell's *Iconology: Image, Text, Ideology* (Chicago, 1986), which appeared subsequent to the writing of this chapter. Mitchell's general approach of investigating the ideological and cultural forces shaping the perceived relation between images and words—as well as many of his particular insights—greatly extend and expand upon my focus on peddling poetry. Esp. apropos are Mitchell's excellent chapters on the politics and ideology of the image in Lessing,

Burke, and Marx. Also relevant to my present, brief speculations about evaluation are Barbara Herrnstein Smith's essays on literary value—to which I must also make belated reference (thanks to Michael Warner of Northwestern University for bringing Smith's work in this field to my attention). See esp. her "Contingencies of Value," *Critical Inquiry* 10 (1983): 1–35, which includes a section on "The Economics of Literary and Aesthetic Value." The entire notion of literary value—as it is presently being reevaluated at the level of both economic and philosophical speculation—is undergoing a renascence. I have recently attempted to give some notice of this by organizing the Wordsworth-Coleridge Association sessions for the 1987 MLA convention on "The Value of Romanticism I: Wordsworth, Coleridge, and Romantic Money" and "The Value of Romanticism II: Romanticism and Evaluation."

DAVID SIMPSON

Figuring Class, Sex, and Gender: What Is the Subject of Wordsworth's "Gipsies"?

David Simpson elaborates a cogent, judicious use of the concept of displacement, whose significance in the general tide of new-historical criticism we touched upon in the preceding headnote. Simpson is an inveterately revisionary (and self-revisionary) critic. The following essay from *South Atlantic Quarterly* (1989) reflects on (and against) the extended treatment of "Gipsies" in Simpson's own *Wordsworth's Historical Imagination: The Poetry of Displacement* (1987), which itself develops insights foreshadowed in his earlier *Wordsworth and the Figurings of the Real* (1982). Simpson's essay is situated at one of the busiest (and most hazardous) intersections in romantic studies, the one where class runs into gender (or Marxism into feminism). These investigations are continued in his recent *Subject to History: Ideology, Class, Gender* (1991). Simpson comments wryly about his 1987 analysis of the poem: in "around thirty printed pages" it "said (I still think) a good deal about class without saying a word about gender, a blindness that would be remarkable were it not for the humbling ordinariness of the most likely explanation: that when I wrote the first account I was not a parent, and I have since become one."

Simpson's concern in both readings is to determine the underlying source of what Coleridge identified as the "mental bombast" of the poem, which is for Simpson a hysterical overreaction to the (apparent) sloth of the gypsy band. Where his earlier reading had traced the response to a class-based attraction to and repulsion by the unbridled liberty of this outlaw society, the new reading catches overtones of sexual fear and envy as well. In addition to fatherhood and its altered domestic circumstances, of course, Simpson has been moved by a substantial body of feminist commentary on issues of gender and sexuality, to which he (like most male romanticists) has come later rather than sooner. His essay shows especially the impact of Gayatri Spivak's work of the 1980s, gathered in *In Other Worlds: Essays in Cultural Politics* (1987), Margaret Homans's *Women Writers and Poetic Identity: Dorothy Wordsworth, Emily Brontë, and Emily Dickinson* (1980), several of the essays from Anne K. Mellor's influential edited volume, *Romanticism and Feminism* (1988), and the work of Mary Jacobus (see Headnote, Selection 12).

Much of Simpson's work on the anxieties of Wordsworth's poetry has centered on the experimental poems from *Lyrical Ballads*. For an

From *South Atlantic Quarterly* 88, no. 3 (1989): 541–567. Copyright © 1989 by Duke University Press. Reprinted with permission of the publisher.

alternative theorization of Wordsworth's controversial ballads, readers should consult Don H. Bialostosky's *Making Tales: The Poetics of Wordsworth's Narrative Experiments* (1984), which presents a less conflicted poet in much firmer control of his motivations, medium, and materials. Bialostosky's most recent book, *Wordsworth, Dialogics, and the Practice of Criticism* (1992), is an extended examination of, meditation upon, and occasionally caustic critique of directions in Wordsworth criticism in our time. Although certain to be controversial, the work provides solid evidence both of the centrality of Wordsworth studies to academic criticism and of why Wordsworthian criticism matters culturally and intellectually today.

Perhaps nothing in the field of feminist criticism arouses more debate than the relative claims of class, sex, and gender for interpretive priority. One position, identified as "essentialist feminism," holds that an unmediated biological determination, or sex (to specify at once the sense in which I shall continue to use the term) is the first principle of analysis and the primary determining influence upon personality and writing. In the sphere of literary criticism, this position produces, for example, the assumption that all writings *by* women must also and in an essential sense be *about* women. Among the various positions that present themselves as near-absolute alternatives to this essentialist feminism, we may locate classic Marxism, a tradition largely made up of males, for which class struggle or mode of production is the primary determination. And somewhere in the middle is the rapidly growing discipline of Marxist feminism, which tends to privilege "gender" as the principle of analysis; that is, it holds that figurations of the masculine and the feminine are determined by discourse and ideology, often to the degree that sex can only be known or thought of as already gender, already formed into historically determinate patternings. The exponents of these various positions tend to debate each other within a professional subculture whose own highly divided system of labor renders that debate unnecessarily absolute. We find ourselves pressed to think of Marxism versus feminism, class versus gender, and so forth, as if the categories of the subjects attending could be assumed identical to the objects attended to. But it is perhaps within the operative conventions of Marxist feminism that these self-imposed boundaries can be and should be most often transgressed, with the aim of seeking a genuine synthesis.

In the limited field of Wordsworth criticism, we are fortunate to be able to build upon an exemplary essay by Gayatri Spivak, first published in 1981, which argues that the poet's self-imagined "imagination" is constituted not simply by his displacement of the events of the French Revolution, but also of the sexual autobiography that was for him always and entirely a part of his experience of revolutionary France.[1] Spivak finds in the later books of *The Prelude* the "textual signs of a rejection of paternity" and a submerged narrative principle in "the most remotely occluded and transparently mediating figure" of woman.[2] This analysis, premised upon the poet's traumatic memory of his abandonment of Annette Vallon and of their illegitimate child, Caroline, powerfully explains the energy behind a poem that projects as its ideal reader a sexually disappointed male companion, Coleridge, and as its idealized inspiration a mothering nature and a sister whose own sexuality is distanced both by an identity with that nature and by the at least manifest security provided by the incest taboo. The poet's own wife, his companion in ongoing and legitimate acts of paternity, is hardly mentioned, along with their children, whom Wordsworth, we may infer from other sources, loved deeply and in the usual way.

Spivak's thesis has a force that extends well beyond *The Prelude*. The subject of the present essay is a much less well known poem, and the dramas of class and gender which it illuminates, I think, in exceptionally specific ways. "Gipsies" has not had much critical attention. Keats, Hazlitt, and Coleridge all commented upon it, but David Ferry is the only other precursor I know of to my own recent account.[3] That account, which runs to around thirty printed pages, said (I still think) a good deal about class without saying a word about gender, a blindness that would be remarkable were it not for the humbling ordinariness of the most likely explanation: that when I wrote the first account I was not a parent, and I have since become one. I argued there for "Gipsies" as the transcription of an insecurity both empirical and ideological; for a Wordsworth who was, in 1807, unsure both of the economic plausibility of a poetic career and of its place in any publicly validated language of social approbation. Anxious about whether poetry would pay as well as about whether it mattered to anyone, Wordsworth produced in this poem a hysterically oxymoronic declaration of desire and fear, love and hate, identification and disavowal—a bourgeois schizophrenia that is precisely articulated through the narrator's adoption of the persona of Satan as Milton had made it available for literary-historical reincarnation. I argued that Wordsworth both envied and despised the gypsies: envied their prelapsarian harmony and freedom from the demands of a complex economy founded in work and career, while despising their idleness and inertia, their willful refutation of the imperatives of property and labor. Here is the poem, in its 1807 version:

> Yet are they here?—the same unbroken knot
> Of human Beings, in the self-same spot!
>   Men, Women, Children, yea the frame
>   Of the whole Spectacle the same!
> Only their fire seems bolder, yielding light:
> Now deep and red, the colouring of night;
>   That on their Gipsy-face falls,
>   Their bed of straw and blanket-walls.
> —Twelve hours, twelve bounteous hours, are gone while I
> Have been a Traveller under open sky,
>   Much witnessing of change and chear,
>   Yet as I left I find them here!
>
> The weary Sun betook himself to rest.
> —Then issued Vesper from the fulgent West,
>   Outshining like a visible God
>   The glorious path in which he trod.
> And now, ascending, after one dark hour,
> And one night's diminuation of her power,
>   Behold the mighty Moon! this way
>   She looks as if at them—but they
> Regard not her:—oh better wrong and strife

Better vain deeds or evil than such life!
　The silent Heavens have goings on;
　The stars have tasks—but these have none.[4]

I should not, it now seems to me, have needed any special prompting to register the overtly sexual implication of the "unbroken knot," an implication I missed entirely in my eagerness to develop it as the image of a paradisal social contract. That prompting could well have come, indeed, from placing the rhetoric of this poem within the contested vocabulary deployed by various among Wordsworth's contemporaries to describe the innovations resulting from the events of 1789, which brought Wordsworth himself into contact with a liberty that was as much sexual as political. In his "Letter to a Member of the National Assembly" (1791) Edmund Burke had, for example, imaged the argued subversion of French political life as the result of carnivalesque energies that were both countercultural and sexual. He saw a legislation controlled by a motley crowd of "shameless women . . . keepers of hotels . . . pert apprentices . . . shop-boys, hair-dressers, fiddlers," and others like them, and displacing from authority the "dull, uninstructed men, of useful, but laborious occupations." The irony is so strained as to become unironic, as if Burke cannot command a voice in which the outcasts and *sans-culottes* are not indeed more appealing than the virtuous men of substance they have replaced. Burke almost admits as much in a passage strikingly emblematic of what I take to be Wordsworth's ambivalent attitude to the gypsies:

> . . . the retrograde order of society has something flattering to the dispositions of mankind. The life of adventurers, gamsters, gypsies, beggars, and robbers is not unpleasant. It requires restraint to keep men from falling into that habit. The shifting tides of fear and hope, the flight and pursuit, the peril and escape, the alternate famine and feast of the savage and the thief, after a time, render all course of slow, steady, progressive, unvaried occupation, and the prospect only of a limited mediocrity at the end of long labor, to the last degree tame, languid, and insipid.[5]

Burke's image of a community that has to be actively restrained from choosing the gypsy life certainly suggests that he did not perceive bourgeois self-discipline to be by any means well-established. For Wordsworth, who could not even be sure of a career that would be steady and progressive, and who definitely feared the fate of a limited mediocrity, that self-discipline must have been more than usually inefficient. George Dyer, after all, had included in his *Dissertation on the Theory and Practice of Benevolence* (1795) an extended discussion of the poverty and distress afflicting men of letters, which he saw as widespread enough to require the setting up of benevolent societies to assist them. Poets who began in gladness did indeed, it seems, stand threatened with despondency and madness; they might reasonably prefer to be pagans in outworn creeds, or gypsies, rather than to remain as slaves to such an uncertain future. The economic discourse of the times included, we may recall, Adam Smith's famous request that the free circulation of labor be encouraged rather than inhibited by parish laws and the appeal of a dear, perpetual place. So why not embrace, with Satanic self-assertion, the life of wandering that one might well be forced into anyway?

This life includes, as I now see, the experience of a liberty that is not just political but also sexual. The "unbroken knot" is not just the image of a prelapsarian community that Wordsworth wishes at once to join and to disrupt; or to disrupt because he cannot join, by converting leisure to work and sociability to solitude, conquering preclass solidarity by bourgeois discipline. As the social syntax of the poem's opening speaks for a triple consciousness—I want to join, I cannot join, I don't want to join—so too does the sexual. To the popular mythologies antithetically casting gypsies as at once thieves and vagrants but also lovers of freedom and independence, we must add those which cast them, antithetically, as seducers and libertines but also as the practitioners of an uncomplicated and guilt-free sexuality.[6] And, in the sexualized reading of the "unbroken knot," we may find a paradox very similar to that which informs the socioeconomic reading. On the one hand, it is a hymen, an intact maidenhead that the narrator wants and fears to penetrate. On the other hand, it is an image of sexual coupling, of bodies already intertwined, as they have been, apparently, for twelve whole hours, while the industrious poet has been going about his tasks. Gypsies were familiarly associated with excessive sexual energy (because they did not have to work?), as, for instance, when Shakespeare has Cleopatra convicted of "a gypsy's lust." And Shakespeare's texts prefigure exactly the two senses of "knot" for which I am arguing here. Thus we have (among other examples), Marina's "virgin knot" in *Pericles* and Othello's hideously cynical reference to that "cistern, for foul toads / To knot and gender in."[7] (To this we may add, for what it is worth, the vulgar British expression "get knotted.")

What might this double reading, this apparent syndrome of overdetermination, have meant to Wordsworth? Sexuality is indeed everywhere in his poetry, but almost always displaced firmly from any overt human embodiment. His exemplary rape narrative describes an expedition to gather nuts ("Nutting"), and in *The Prelude* (1805) his guilt-interrupted coital vocabulary is worked into an account of stealing someone else's boat. In Wordsworth's poems, lakes have bosoms, and trees and hills compel moods of enjoyment and desire, but people seldom do. The displacements are so massively apparent as to be almost ignorable, and so far displaced as to seem inexplicable. And, as it happens, they proliferate with particular density in that subsection of the *Poems* of 1807 in which Wordsworth first, and with some deliberation, published "Gipsies": a group of thirteen poems collected together under the title of *Moods of My Own Mind*. In "The Sparrow's Nest," which Wordsworth meant to come immediately after "Gipsies" in the order of the volume (though in the first edition it actually came before it), the speaker is cast as recalling the "home and shelter'd bed" of a bird's nest his own "Father's House."[8] Brother and sister would visit this nest, and the brother remembers his sister's reaction in terms that are startlingly suggestive of a displaced response, at least in his own diction: "She look'd at it as if she fear'd it; / Still wishing, dreading to be near it." In the poem's narrative, it is this same sister who has given the poet his descriptive talent and the emotions upon which it is based: receptivity, sensitivity, and love. Her own (possibly imagined) attitude to the nest, at once wanting and dreading contact, is the very ambivalent position that males often attribute to the female, both proverbially (she said no but she meant yes) and theoretically (as in the model of penis envy). And it is, noticeably, the same ambivalent position that the speaker of "Gipsies" occupies in relation to the society of wanderers—despising them but wanting to be one of them.

Another of the *Moods of My Own Mind* is the famous lyric "I Wandered Lonely

As a Cloud," which has the narrator discovering a "wealth" that is removed entirely from the public sphere (and thus from both the anxieties and rewards of a system of exchange) and to be enjoyed only (or most enduringly) in "the bliss of solitude."[9] In another poem, the small celandine's loss of the elastic power of swelling and shrinking provides poetic material for a meditation upon mortality in terms that recall (albeit in the mood of serious melancholy) the grave obscenity of the poets of John Donne's generation.[10] Again, in the debate between nightingale and stockdove, the poet declares a preference for the second, and thus for a song ". . . of love with quiet blending, / Slow to begin, and never ending"—something very much akin, perhaps, to the unbroken intercourse of the gypsy camp. Other poems in the series record Dorothy's disciplining of the young William's predatory ardor ("To a Butterfly"), and image the voice of the seldom-seen cuckoo as the perfect sign of an infinite desire ("To the Cuckoo"), a desire innocent because unacted.

These are hints of the richness of the poems in *Moods of My Own Mind* for an understanding of the dramas of displaced (sexual) languages in this section of the 1807 volume. The sequence ends with another complex meditation upon Hesperus, Satan, sunset, and the desire to trespass (unreproved) beyond the mortal condition, a condition conventionally imaged in the very sexual acts to which it must finally put an end. Woman, home, shelter, and security are the signs whose occasional erasure, as in "Stepping Westward," could allow Wordsworth to tolerate the idea of eternal solitude and perpetual social isolation, but to which he is also compelled to return in the language of longing and desire. All of these poems, and others, play upon the language of "Gipsies" as it reciprocally plays upon them to constitute an incipient logic of sexual anxiety, secretly intelligent if not consciously coherent.

What is the operation of this intelligence in "Gipsies"? Why is there a positive-negative imaging of the sexual as well as of the social contract that seems to pertain in the camp? The site seems almost bestial, with its "bed of straw," a place where animals (or vegetables) might repose, given home and shelter only by the oddly and entirely impermanent "blanket-walls." The gypsies are specified as ignoring the male and female cosmic principles, sun and moon, that divide the bourgeois life into the proper cycles of work and leisure, day and night. The lunatic, the lover, and the poet are all compacted in this poem; but where exactly does the lover fit?

The relation between gender and class could in principle be construed as a structure either of coordination or of subordination. That is, we might find that one of the terms subsumes or digests the other, contradicting its claims to interpretive priority by proving its own primary status as cause; or, we might end up with a model within which both terms operate in such a cooperative and mutually determining way that it seems impossible to isolate the one as the cause of the other. There is considerable evidence for suggesting that in the particular case of this poet, and this poem we are dealing with a structure of coordination, one in which class and gender anxieties are mutually interdetermining and reinforcing.

Recently there has been a quite extraordinary efflorescence of research on the subject of Wordsworth and gender. Most of this has surely not been conceived cooperatively, but the common concerns and approaches serve to remind us that we are all to some degree as the times are, and that there is an identifiable community of questions that a number of critics are addressing, even if there is no consensus about their proper solutions. In an important essay on the gender codes of "Tintern Abbey," John Barrell argues that the poem's complex syntax and high density of abstract nouns would have been taken as inviting the attentions of a capable reader who could only have been an educated male of the middle ranks of society or above.[11] All female readers, and all readers of the lower orders, were supposed incapable of the intellectual efforts required to comprehend such language; they could not successfully synthesize particular images under general concepts, nor hold onto the logic of dependency that marks complex syntax. Thus Wordsworth's apparently nostalgic recollection of his own "thoughtless youth," in which he was content with the immediate gratification of particularities, images that youth as a feminine moment which he has transcended. The concluding appeal to Dorothy for confirmation of what he "was once" positions her condescendingly as outside the republic of letters because she is unable to "reduce the data of experience to abstract categories."[12]

Barrell's argument is essential for our further understanding of the relation between gender and class at the moment of Wordsworth's writings. The gap between simply descriptive and abstractly complex language (to be negotiated only by educated males like the poet and Coleridge) becomes a version of the experience of the sublime, which was frequently (as by Kant) limited to those possessing prior cultivation, and which in this case is enjoyed not least as it affirms the social distance between the lower ranks of rustics and women, and the ideal (male) reader. One does not have to agree that "Tintern Abbey" performs this transformation of an ideologically feminized youth into an alternatively masculinized authority in order to endorse Barrell's explanation of what it seems to attempt. Readers will disagree about whether they find in the poem a consolidated male selfhood or an ungendered abyss of uncertainty. But Barrell is surely convincing in his specification of the rhetorical field within which the poem is situated. His argument is, moreover, very much compatible with the most authoritative analysis of the sociohistorical dramas of the poem, that offered by Marjorie Levinson.[13] Levinson has shown the degree to which the displacement of the immediate landscape of the Wye valley (vagrants in the ruined abbey itself, barges on the river, iron ore mines along its banks) is paralleled by the poem's covertly avowed relation to the downward trajectory of political events in France after 1789. And, in light of the findings of Spivak and Heinzelman, we cannot avoid searching out, here also, a place for Annette Vallon, herself by actual nomination a "little valley" (*vallon*) who/which must be considered a part of any adequate explanation of Wordsworth's fascination with vales and valleys, both as places to hide (veils) and as places to wander within—a locus *chosen* indeed, and at more than one level of motivation. That Wordsworth is in some urgent way lamenting not just the course of events in the public sphere in France, but also the demise of a private experience, his love for Annette, his fathering of Caroline, and his guilt at leaving them behind, now seems unignorable, and helps to explain what I would argue to be the desperation of the aspiration toward educated male mastery that this poem's language seeks to achieve. It also, I think, suggests that the final imaging of Dorothy, the sister and the female, as the icon of what William "was once," is overdetermined by the specter of the abandoned woman and female child. So too is the image of nature as the lost, previously experienced medium of immediate gratification, satisfaction *not* very confidently projected into a protes-

tant future founded in a hoped-for consolatory recollection of a "now" that spon-
sors only confusion at the moment of writing.

Following Barrell, we can see that the at least attempted self-establishment at
the end of "Tintern Abbey" is not just by way of Dorothy, but also by way of the
poetic construction of a preliterate female. In this context, the placing of this
poem at the end of the first edition of *Lyrical Ballads* (1798) comes to seem
especially significant. Not for nothing, perhaps, have generations of readers and
critics pronounced that this is the "major" poem of the volume, and that it fore-
casts a "maturity" that the less elevated earlier ballads do not prefigure. For it may
be that Wordsworth and Coleridge's joint entry into the literary marketplace of
1798 is in fact prefigured (in the preparation of the volume) and concluded (as one
reads through it) by the marginalization of the exemplary female, who may be a
worshipful or proleptic companion but who can never be a reader. What is the
energy behind this gesture? Are we dealing with a standard male insecurity of
universalist dimensions? Or do we have here a syndrome particular to the genera-
tion of 1800, or perhaps to male poets, or perhaps to Wordsworth alone? Our
conclusions cannot be conclusive, but the connections are intriguing.

In another recent essay, Marlon Ross has suggested that the "myth of masculine
self-possession" is economically generated.[14] As the market was felt to be passing
out of the control of any single writer, so the compensatory *assertion* of control,
the gesture of self-possession, becomes all the more emphatic, eventually to the
point of hysteria. For Ross, it is only a male companion or reader who can confirm
the market value of a writer's work: this indeed perfectly describes the place of
Coleridge, and the near erasure of Mary, in *The Prelude*. Following Ross's lead, I
would suggest that the hypermasculine rhetoric that constitutes itself through the
subordination of the female is expressive of an economic as well as an arguably
sexual anxiety. The female is not just the female, but also an image of the market,
the unstable and unpredictable and finally uncontrollable place where the poet
must be recognized but which he also despises and fears. The position of comfort-
able male self-establishment into which Wordsworth seeks to write himself must
be won not only from the female but also from the marketplace which she repre-
sents or is represented by.

Now we are getting closer, I think, to an understanding of why Wordsworth's
gendered languages are so often transcribed at the full pitch of the hyperbolic—
the rape of the nut trees, the heaving of the stolen boat (followed by the coun-
terintuitive phallic uprearing of the admonitory mountain), and the hysterical
reaction to the "unbroken knot" of gypsies. We cannot say—that is, we have no
clear evidence for saying—that his paranoid relation to the literary marketplace is
prior to and determining of his transcription (and perhaps his experience) of the
sexual and the feminine. What we can say is that the syndrome is overdetermined,
and that there is no sure way of establishing (and arguably no need to establish) a
hierarchy of primary cause and effect when all of these determinations—class,
sexuality, economic anxiety, the desire for public recognition—work together
within what seems to be a coherently structured textual transcription of alien-
ation.[15] The market is fickle, potentially depraved, and intransigently alien to the
emergent ideology of internalization as the measure of proper poetry; so too, in
the canonical language that Wordsworth rekindles for all that is threatening (and,
in another voice, all that is desired), are women. Sonia Hofkosh has noted that the

Romantics came more and more to conceive of their culture in feminized terms. The writer becomes a lover, subject to unpredictable acceptance or rejection, so that "the feminine figure variously reflects and reiterates the culture's challenge to the fantasy of autonomous creativity."[16] In this way the feminine figure must stand both for what is desired and for what is rejected: rejected indeed *because* desired, because provocative of the uncomfortable experience of desire itself. And Stuart Curran, in a remarkable and important essay, produces this case to the level of the empirical by arguing that in the 1790s there were many more female than male novelists and dramatists, and that women poets were becoming more and more prominent.[17] If Curran is correct to find in the works of Charlotte Smith the exemplary precursor of poetic mannerisms that "in a few years were to become identifiably Wordsworth's,"[18] then we must suspect the pressure of an identification that was not at all limited to the poet's confessed *youthful* admiration for the works of Helen Maris Williams (again, recall the imaging of Dorothy as an icon of William's youth), but which must have persisted at least throughout his early and middle career: the pressure of the female precursor. It is then quite astounding to recall that the model for the suppressed tale of Vaudracour and Julia, in which Wordsworth famously circled around and "represented" the painful truths of abandonment and illegitimate paternity in his own life, was itself a literary prototype written by a woman—Helen Maria Williams.[19] Wordsworth's half-confessed and half-repressed sin against the female (mother and daughter) is erected upon the textual priority of a female writer! If the feminine is thus within the Wordsworthian poetic psyche, at the level of the production of writing, at the same time as it threatens that production from without, in the sphere of consumption (whether as the potentially literate Dorothy or as the generally feminized medium of the market), then the hysteria that seems to mark so many of the sexualized moments of that writing will not seem so surprising.

Hence, perhaps, the emptiness that one can choose to read in the langauge of "Tintern Abbey": not the record of a discourse of abstraction mastered by an educated male speaker, and thus inviting the parallel mastery of other such readers, so much as a language caught between the comforts of the empirically particular and the suprematism of the abstract sublime—a language that offers no conpanionship and promises no social identity. Susan Wolfson, in her recent essay on the Wordsworths, finds in Dorothy's poetry the "figurings of a community in which the self has a place, but not the privileged place, and in which shared lives and values shape and sustain individual desire."[20] But if that community were premised on the rhetoric of femininity, one can see why William could not, for reasons both autobiographical and intersubjectively historical, have spoken in his "own" voice within it. Making a figure in the market must have seemed to require individuality, solitude, originality—to such a degree that the collaborators on the first edition of *Lyrical Ballads* refer to themselves, in the advertisement to that volume, as "the author."[21] The rhetoric of community (and of the feminine) could figure only as an alternative forever lost (nature, youth, immediacy) or as a resolution infinitely deferred. And the rhetoric of mutability must always have been threatening even as it was invoked.[22] Dorothy poeticized herself, implicitly, as a floating island, and found in change and death the comfort of participation within the "one duteous task" of a nature larger than any single human being.[23] For William, in his poems, the accounts of experiences of floating seem to have been a lot less comforting. Clouds, boats, butterflies, and musical sounds may float, and the poetic persona may engage sympathetically with them in various ways. But the passage that most obviously parallels the language of Dorothy's poem occurs in his recollections, more strongly worded in the 1805 than in the 1850 *Prelude,* of his vague and loosely indifferent time at Cambridge:

Rotted as by a charm, my life became
A floating island, an amphibious thing,
Unsound, of spongy texture, yet withal
Not wanting a fair face of water-weeds
And pleasant flowers.[24]

Dorothy must have founded her poem (written around 1832) on this passage, which she had copied, read, or had read to her no doubt many times. Perhaps she meant it, at some level, as a rebuke of William's dread of an impermanence that she herself had so long experienced, and in precisely the spheres of life to which William's language so often refers: public recognition, economic security, and sexual gratification.

For all these reasons we can imagine why, in the structured constellation of languages that describes and determines William's attitudes toward resolution, independence, class, career, and sexual identity, the categories of masculine and feminine labor cannot be brought into any harmonious conjunction. In the language of "Gipsies," the knot must be either hymeneal and forever unbroken (absolute alienation supporting a structure of desire) or eternally copulative, as if in a paranoid reenvisioning of the fates of Paolo and Francesca. Kurt Heinzelman quite properly takes us back to the garden of Eden, and in particular to *Paradise Lost* (by way of the inevitable imbalance of male and female production and reproduction as theorized by Malthus), when he points out that Eve's request for the institution of a system of divided labor, which commits her to the very solitude that Satan will exploit, is prompted by her inability to avoid sexual distraction in the presence of her consort. As Heinzelman puts it, "undivided labor leads to sexual dalliance."[25] The double reading of the first line of "Gipsies," which may intimate absolute chasity (virginity) or rampant sexual indulgence, is prefigured in the Miltonic narrative where it seems that there is no way out of the double bind of sexual desire. Eve distances herself in order to work, only to incur her fall and the consequent fall of Adam, itself motivated by desire and resulting in a further emphasized gap between gratification and melancholia in the postlapsarian sexual experience. The bonds between man and woman, both of cooperative labor and of sexual harmony, are forever broken. Wordsworth's experience of a market which seemed to require (if current findings are to be trusted) the strong individuation of an ideological masculinity must have reemphasized and perhaps even reshaped whatever determinations we might imagine to have been already in place at the level of sex or gender. The narrative of *The Prelude* represses the reproduction of children, whether legitimate or illegitimate, in order to describe the production of the exemplary poetic imagination, with which they apparently have nothing in common. To Wordsworth's inevitable guilt at the birth of Caroline to Annette, we can now add, by way of explanation, the awkwardly undeniable fact that biological reproduction depends upon a labor (if that is the word) that cannot be thought of as other than cooperative, unless it be weighted toward the female rather than the male agency. And if the very production of poetry were at some level sensed as founded upon female precursors, and were aimed at a market also imaged in feminized terms, then we can see that there might have been no place for a Wordsworthian masculinity except one constituted by the rhetoric of alienation. The narrator of "Gipsies" perhaps articulates exactly this alienation in the confused gendering of his self-positioning. He is like the sun, traveling for twelve whole hours, and like Vesper, in following the sun in his own glorious (self-glorifying) path. These are both masculine agencies: entirely effaced from explicit reference is the identity of Vesper with Venus, the goddess of love, and in her other incarnations, of chastity and gardens (Wordsworth was, at the time he met the gypsies, in the middle of redesigning the garden at Coleorton). But the feminine identification does appear in the narrator's identification with the moon. He, like the moon, is looking at the gypsies, but is also, like the gypsies, looked *upon* by the moon. The implication is that he, unlike them, does "regard" the moon, with which he is also partly identified. For the overaffirmation of industry and propriety is, we have seen, the symptom of a deep discomfort, of an instability aptly defined by the attributions of the "mighty moon" within a field of representations that are entirely feminine. Narrator-as-moon then becomes a figure subject to flux and mutability, one who has himself suffered one day's "diminution" of his powers, a mortal in the marketplace rather than an immortal in the heavens.

Returning to the gypsies themselves, we return to a group wherein labor is so far from being divided that it seems not to exist at all, and where the pursuit of leisure and pleasure appears to be untroubled and unmodified by the diurnal cycle so important to the industrious imagination (as it was in Milton's paradise even before the fall). As the sexes are undifferentiated in this "unbroken knot," connected and not alienated, so too are children included in a grouping that appears to the poet persona to negate the ordering of the generations as well as of the sexes: "Men, Women, Children, yea the frame / Of the whole Spectacle the same!" The reproduction of the species is not, in this community, a divisive or alienating process, as it has been for Wordsworth; children too are framed within the spectacle, another component in the gypsy community that renders it so traumatically distinct from the poet's own.

The conflation of the gypsies with a sexual transgression that may afflict Wordsworth so forcibly because it can for them apparently be experienced as *non*transgressive is further enhanced by the imaging of vagrant life in *The Prelude*. In my earlier account I discussed the connection between "Gipsies" and the retrospective narrative of Wordsworth's leaving Cambridge, when he became one who

> pitched my vagrant tent
> A casual dweller and at large, among
> The unfenced regions of society.[26]

On his walking tour of France in 1790, he and his companion had lived "Unhoused beneath the evening star" and enjoyed "in late hours / Of darkness, dances in the open air." The initial appeal and subsequent disavowal of these "dances of liberty" are perfectly captured in this wise-after-the-event autobiography by invoking the morally ambivalent imagery of the gypsy life.[27] Wordsworth is of course alluding to the sociopolitical ramifications of the aftermath of 1789, first welcomed and later disavowed. But we cannot avoid reading that "liberty" as permitting the relaxation of sexual as well as of political codes. Similarly, in the famous sonnet, "liberty" becomes not the lightening of a burden but itself a "weight," as Wordsworth compares his choice of the sonnet form to the decision of nuns who choose the convent, thereby not only avoiding the demands of making a career in the world, but also putting themselves beyond the reach of sexual experience.[28] Too much liberty has had negative consequences for the French nation, but also for William and Annette, and for those near to them. The "love-knot" that enters the displaced narrative of Vaudracour and Julia in the 1805 *Prelude,* and which remains more elliptically in the published text of 1850, is then doubly entwined with the "unbroken knot" of "Gipsies," as a knot that should and should not be broken, and one which is both the property of an inviolate woman and the result of her defloration. The same doubleness characterizes Wordsworth's other uses of the term. On the one hand, we have the admired "social knots" of *The Excursion,* and on the other hand a strongly negative image of postrevolutionary French politics as made up of "hissing factionists with ardent eyes / In knots, or pairs, or single."[29]

Describing the French radicals as snakes brings to bear the full weight of the Christian tradition of demonization, intimating sins that are at once political, metaphysical, and sexual. The same range of reference informs the language of "Gipsies," mediated of course through the narrator's self-dramatization as Satanic voyeur. Reading on from the "unbroken knot," it is the "self-same spot" that continues the allusion to a sexual-locational impropriety. Here is Othello again, to Desdemona: "Thy bed, lust-stain'd, shall with lust's blood be spotted."[30] The famous spots of time are all, for Wordsworth, associated with guilt and loss; and in this poem the displaced rhyme of "deep and red" with "bed" produces a gloss on the opening pairing of "knot" and "spot" that is distinctly sexual. It invokes either the blood of defloration (the broken knot), or that of menstruation or procreation (under the aegis of the "mighty moon").

It is a sexual scene that is here at once witnessed and provoked or imagined by a narrator who is both inside and outside the plot he describes or invents. He adopts toward this sexual scene the same antithetical stance that he projects toward all the other scenes that the poem invokes. Just as he speaks for and against bourgeois values (labor, property, career), and from a place that may be read as with or without sin, so too is the sexual narrative poised between two apparently different resolutions in a moment of indecision that seems not so much self-excusing as paranoid (because innocence points to what is inevitably about to happen, not to what can be avoided). Having recognized the place of a sexual scene in the poem, it would be easy to decide that the motivation is in some simple sense "found," and to announce that it devolves, once again, from the trauma of the abandoned woman and fatherless child. But the sexual scene is also overdetermined, and not to be thought of as necessarily a single event or association. William, Annette, and Caroline were not the only failed family group in Wordsworth's life. His mother had died when he was eight, and his father when he was thirteen. In 1805, two years before "Gipsies," John Wordsworth had gone down with his ship, occasioning both immense grief and immense guilt in the poet-brother.[31] Wordsworth wrote then to his other brother, Richard: "God keep the rest of us together! the set is now broken."[32] Wordsworth was born into what became a broken set: endogamous as well as exogamous relations both shattered. Nature's boon had not been generous.[33] And here we may figure in also the drama of his relation to a sister, a relation that both represented and substituted for those other paradigms

of failure or transgression. Many years later, De Quincey wrote of Dorothy that
" 'Her face was of Egyptian brown'; rarely, in a woman of English birth, had I
seen a more determinate gypsy tan.' "[34] He knew he was quoting from one Words-
worth poem about a gypsy, perhaps we should infer a reference to another, to
"Gipsies." For, if others besides De Quincey had noted Dorothy's complexion
and imaged it in the same way (remember, again, those "wild eyes," eyes that
John Thelwall also described as "ardent"), then the simultaneous rejecting and
desiring of the unbroken knot becomes the exact profile of an incest fantasy.[35] The
gypsy-sister stimulates a desire that must ever seem about to be, because it is not
permissible; or a rejection that is absolute, insofar as she is imagined to have
sexual relations with anyone else.

One could go on. But enough has been said to suggest that the categories of
both class and gender are so internally multiple and polymorphic that they are
never quite themselves. It is hard to speak of *the* one or *the* other, harder still to
pin down an exclusive relation of cause and effect operating between particular
versions of each. How could we expect to prove that anxieties about career, about
money, about the literary marketplace, must have determined how Wordsworth
generated the gender codes in his language? Alternatively, how can we be sure
that it was a sexual trauma that was already in place before those other, so-
ciohistorical pressures supervened? And what would that sexual trauma be? An-
nette, William's parents, Dorothy, all of these? The evidence does not by any
means speak for itself, since so much of it is in writing, and we have no way of
establishing the superior explanatory potential of one kind of writing over an-
other. The letters of both William and Dorothy are full of financial concerns and
details, which appear to have been almost obsessive for brother and sister through-
out their early and middle years. In the dry prose describing the events of daily
life, these economic concerns do not appear overlain or codetermined by the
erotic, as they are in "Gipsies." But this does not prove anything about the
relative authenticity of either genre. One could decide that the realist authority of
the letters is superior to that of a conventionalized poetry; or, one could decide (as
literary critics traditionally have decided) that poetry is "deeper" and reveals
more than everyday prose. There is just no way of knowing, or even of asking the
question, without the initiating invocation of an a priori theory. What we can say is
that the differences of emphases in these writings, and between the letters and this
poem, can be read as already within a composite language that specifies monetary,
class, and gender anxieties each in terms of the others. (So, for instance: a
nonbourgeois poet, say Byron, would be less likely to have the same concerns
about the income potential of poetry, and its place in the public sphere, which
might produce a different presentation of gender, and so forth. A change in one
determination at once affects the others.)

In the case of "Gipsies," I am now fairly confident that to talk about the fear-
desire syndrome in the poem means that one must talk about both the so-
ciohistorical and the sexual. But it would be implausible to pronounce as a
matter of necessity that it is always such overdetermination that produces the
language of poetry. Even Wordsworth, after all, wrote hundreds of lines that
seem to respond not at all to these particular obsessions, and others that presum-
ably respond to different pressures. There are no guarantees of absolute coher-
ence. Indeed, it might be better to assume incoherence in a career that lasted as
long as Wordsworth's lasted. Perhaps the often-sensed quietude of the later

writings has something to do with a change in the relation of the sexual to the economic. Perhaps financial security and a measure of fame meant that the burden of sexual guilt became less anxious, because unreinforced by other anxieties. These are speculations. (And one might speculate also about a change in the sex drive itself, a change that is in part at the level of nature.) Leaving them aside, let me discuss these findings as they inform the debate about class and gender within the Marxist tradition, before offering some thoughts on the difficult question of nature.

In the cause of explaining the popularity of Freud and Freudianism in early twentieth-century Europe, Vološinov argued that it is "first and foremost" in the sphere of sexuality that the "disintegration of an official ideology is reflected."[36] Because it is always difficult to verbalize sexuality, these particular verbal structures are the first to register the collapse of an ideology (capitalism, in the case of Freudianism). In a related though not quite similar argument, Bakhtin (whom many believe to have authored some of the books published under Vološinov's name) contends that it was in the emergence of class from preclass societies that sexuality became both discursively apparent and experientially complex. What was previously "realistic and straightforward" then became subject to sublimation: sexuality became "love."[37] Both of these arguments propose determinate relations between class and gender (understanding gender as the specific form of sexuality). But both have problems. Bakhtin seems to invoke a period of preclass innocence, a moment when "straightforward" bodily functions could be experienced without the complexities imposed by discourse. But he does not tell us what these straightforward relations were—whether, for example, they involved the subordination of woman to man, or the competition between everyone and everyone. He does not, in other words, speculate about any natural element in the cultural creation of gender. This suggests that we should read him as implying that the passage from preclass to class society does not so much *create* as modify or intensify a condition of nature/culture that is already there, already in place. And this instability in his analysis means that the exact relations of class to gender cannot be specified. Vološinov's argument is more specific to a moment in recent history that is arguably continuous with that of Wordsworth's "Gipsies," within an extensive model of modernity. The question we might have of his analysis concerns his assumption that sexuality is *always* difficult to represent in verbal form. Where does this difficulty come from, if not from an element of nature that is presented here as an assumption rather than as part of the analysis itself? And if it is to be part of the analysis, at what point can that nature be articulated as something that is not already culture?

It would be plausible to end this essay right here, with the declaration that we cannot, in principle, and need not, in practice, go beyond this understanding of the oneness of sex and gender in a knot that cannot be unraveled. Whether we call ourselves Marxists, materialists, or feminists, the problems of trying to go beyond seem insurmountable. For dialectical materialism, the attempt itself could come only from a misunderstanding, as Lukács, for instance, makes clear:

> Nature is a societal category. That is to say, whatever is held to be natural at any given stage of social development, however this nature is related to man and whatever form his involvement with it takes, i.e., nature's form, its content, its range and objectivity are all socially conditioned.[38]

Thus the impingement of nature upon human nature is perceptible only insofar as it has already been worked upon by human agency, whether by labor, thought, or gesture. Lukács is not merely revealing a questionable belief in the transformational powers of labor, for his emphasis conforms with that which we find in various non-Marxist philosophies, which agree that what we know of nature appears only as knowledge because it is either compatible with (Kant) or itself the creation of (various post-Kantians) preexistent forms, whether of the mind or in language. These philosophies differ from Marxism in attributing the transformation of matter to fixed systems (in mind or in language) rather than to the labor process, which transforms both subject and object through the temporal experience of work. But they agree with Marxism about the unavailability of a nature that is not already worked upon by something.

So there are very good reasons why we are in such a state of limbo when we try to set about an analysis that assumed the separability of sex and gender (reasons that are further compounded when we add in other elements of the historical). But at least one recent attempt has been made to articulate such separation, that of the Italian Marxist Sebastiano Timpanaro. Timpanaro offers a breakdown of the nature/culture relation in terms that seem to appease both Marxism and Darwinism. Nature is not eternal, but only seems so because its rate of transformation is usually so much slower than that of human social formations. It is always changing, and changing in reciprocal interaction with the human sphere, but in comparison to everything else it seems enduring, and can be imaged as such by the alienated imagination (of which Wordsworth would, as it happens, be a good example). Within the conventions of literary criticism and response, this syndrome makes it possible, for example, for us to identify with something in the Homeric poems that seems to transcend the utterly different social and historical conditions that separate the modern reader from the producer of these writings. Kings, laws, empires, and modes of production have come and gone, but jealousy and aggression remain recognizable. A medieval love lyric remains intelligible because people still fall in and out of love in generically similar ways.[39] These habits, if they change, do so at extremely slow rates.

These examples of the Homeric and the medieval are not especially happy ones, since one might reasonably object that the continuity we think we sense here in the sphere of the sexual is a false continuity, and one that would indeed disappear as soon as we attend seriously to the place of all of the other determinations that position and even define the sexual itself. As soon as we involve the Homeric sexuality with the conventions of the *oikos,* or the medieval poem with the architectures of Christian allegory, there is no place for an unmodified nature.

But there is another dimension of Timpanaro's argument that cannot be so comfortably deflected. Central to his definition of a "materialism" that contemporary Marxisms have ignored for far too long is the conviction that "experience cannot be reduced either to a production of reality by a subject (however such production is conceived) or to a reciprocal implication of subject and object." This means that we "cannot deny or evade the element of passivity in experience: the external situation which we do not create but which imposes itself upon us." Timpanaro does not mean that this passivity is simply biological, nor does he propose it as more than an essential *element* in knowledge and experience. But he does insist that our biological limits must constrain our aspirations, especially our hedonist ones.[40]

One might imagine sex, as a biological configuration, as one of these limitations of nature, along with mortality. But it is one thing to understand this as a general setting of limits to desire; it is quite another to propose that there is a determinate *textual* manifestation of this principle of limitation that is apparent as such to analysis. We do not have a method for describing the appearance of natural determinations in language that is not subject to the familiar skepticisms. Freudian, Marxist, and feminist approaches all offer such methods, but always become least convincing when they commit themselves to arguing from a priori necessity. Take, for example, the Marcusian fallacy, which insists on principle that the natural forces of Eros and Thanatos cannot be "dissolved into problems of class struggle," that there is an inevitable "metasocial dimension," and that art always invokes that dimension.[41] No one would doubt the general existence of limits to experience imposed by Eros and Thanatos; but everyone must doubt whether they operate in recognizably or meaningfully similar ways at all times in all places. There seems, indeed, no way, with our present resources, that we can identify a general, intersubjective rule for the conversion of arguably natural conditions into textualized forms. It does not even seem that we have been able to come up with convincingly objectivist arguments for this same conversion as operative within any single human subject. But to say this is not to say that such analysis is always and forever impossible; and it is certainly not to say that class, sex, and gender are always and forever composed by the same process of interdetermination. It may be, nonetheless, that we must abandon at least for now any attempt to propose (rather than attempting to discover) these things as separate, giving up, for example, on the idea that there "is" such a thing as "sex" that is more than merely anatomical; something essential that marks all human subjects before they are worked upon by culture and history. One reading of Freud's explanation of the dreamwork is that there is simply no predicting how a particular subject will negotiate or figure the relation between the biological or physiological and the general sphere of description and demonstration. Not only is every analysis case-specific; there is no a priori assurance that the "same" subject will behave in similar ways through time (hence, after all, the legitimacy of the cure). Nor does the fact that we may not be continuously identical subjects simply mean that we are always and entirely the product of an external "history"; for that history cannot be assumed to operate in any way that bypasses the whole range of subjective syndromes, from the physiological to the psychological.

I have pursued this indeterminate account of the question of nature simply to make clear that when we pride ourselves on demonstrating, for example, that there is no way to speak of either gender or class without speaking also of the other, we should refrain from declaring absolutely that there can never be anything else to say. It is convenient for those of us who operate within disciplines whose focus is upon material that is always textual, and mostly textualized in the same ways, to assume that it is only language and/or the symbolic order and/or ideology that give shape to the otherwise inchoate impulses that we might wish to call "sex." One familiar and extreme nominalistic conclusion from this would be that all possible forms for the appearance of sex (as sexuality or gender) are already in place, already organized. This may be true, but cannot be assumed, least of all since the historical dimension of determination is itself constantly changing. (Let me be explicit here: I deny the notion of an obligatory inertia imposed by bureaucracy or institutions or "culture" in general.) The last thing a materialist analysis should do would be to proclaim as a matter of theoretical certainty that nothing can ever be discovered that is not already latent in *our* ways of seeing, most of all in a world where there is no "us."

In the particular context of feminisms, these reflections seem to me to suggest that we cannot yet answer the question about an exact place for sex (nature) within an inclusive analysis of determinations. It may be utopian to imagine that we could ever do so. For we are a long way from understanding whether it is possible, at any level of determination, to describe either a nature that works independently of culture, or a biology that is at every point already within a constitutive intersubjective history. Furthermore, the notion of nature does not presuppose that nature itself be a constant (being a woman, being a man), either between different human subjects or between different moments in the life of the same subject. Those who avoid these questions by assuming the direct, unmediated appearance of a *natural* condition (being a woman, or a man) as a *textual* phenomenon would be missing the point of this essay if they found any comfort in it. If essentialist feminism defines itself, at its extreme, precisely by its exclusions of the determinations of culture and history, then it will deserve to be thought of as the feminism of the right. Marxist feminism, as presently developing, seems to me to offer the most capacious methodology for the articulation of a relation between sex, class, and gender. But it cannot, I think, afford to regard the question of nature as once and for all out of court. The debate has often been falsely closed by declarations of the identity of language and experience. To say that if there is an experience outside language, then knowing it for what it really is becomes a problem *because* of language, is one thing (and this is what I have been saying in my reading of "Gipsies"). To say that there is *no* experience outside language is quite a different statement. To a degree that I at least find suspicious it confirms us in a belief in the sufficiency of textual analysis, of what *we* (literary critics) do; as if texts are all we know on earth, and all we need to know. Thus do the disciplines that we have made rise up against us in the classic process of reification. Thus do analyses that would be posited as incomplete (as this of "Gipsies") appear instead as closed, confirming that sex is gender, all is class, and evermore shall be so. We are professionally suspicious, and rightly so, of the discoveries that science claims to make, and of the languages in which they are announced. But it might be helpful for us to ponder whether all forms of being in the world are textualized in the same ways, or even textualized at all.

NOTES

1. Gayatri Spivak, *In Other Worlds: Essays in Cultural Politics* (New York, 1987), 46–76. Other important accounts of the place of sex and gender in Wordsworth include Margaret Homans, *Women Writers and Poetic Identity: Dorothy Wordsworth, Emily Brontë, and Emily Dickinson* (Princeton, 1980); and Mary Jacobus, "The Law of/and Gender: Genre Theory and *The Prelude*," *Diacritics* (Winter 1984): 47–57. Most recently, Kurt Heinzelman has read the public language of the 1802 sonnets as incorporating and displacing anxieties about paternity and sexual impropriety, in "The Cult of Domesticity: Dorothy and William Wordsworth at Grasmere," in *Romanticism and Feminism,* ed. Anne K. Mellor (Bloomington, 1988), 52–78, especially 62–65.

2. Spivak, *Other Worlds,* 47, 76.

3. David Ferry, *The Limits of Mortality: An Essay on Wordsworth's Major Poems*

(Middletown, Conn., 1959); David Simpson, *Wordsworth's Historical Imagination: The Poetry of Displacement* (London, 1987), 22–55.

4. William Wordsworth, *Poems, in Two Volumes, and Other Poems, 1800–1807,* ed. Jared Curtis (Ithaca, 1983), 211–12.

5. *The Works of the Right Honorable Edmund Burke* (Boston, 1866), 4:4–5, 10–11.

6. Instanced, for example, in the popular ballad "The Gypsy Laddie," variants of which are recorded in *The English and Scottish Popular Ballads,* ed. Francis James Child (New York, 1957), 4:61–74.

7. William Shakespeare, *Anthony and Cleopatra,* 1.1.10, *Pericles,* 4.2.147, *Othello,* 5.2.62–63.

8. Wordsworth, *Poems,* 213. Wordsworth had already arranged and numbered the poems, and sent off his instructions to the printer, when he added in three extra poems, one of which was "Gipsies," with strict attention to their placement. The printer did not adopt these suggestions, and Wordsworth appears not to have queried the printed text, which has "Gipsies" coming after "The Sparrow's Nest" instead of before it, as he had wished. See *Poems,* 28–29, 55, 211.

9. That this language may be seriously interpreted as speaking for a predicament analogous to onanism is argued forcefully, in the case of Keats, by Marjorie Levinson in *Keats' Life of Allegory: The Origins of a Style* (Oxford, 1988). Levinson argues for a coherent relation between class instability, economic frustration, and lack of public visibility in Keats's career, all imaged in his repeated references to wasteful and solitary pleasures.

10. Wordsworth, *Poems,* 209.

11. John Barrell, *Poetry, Language and Politics* (Manchester, 1988), 137–67.

12. Ibid., 160.

13. Marjorie Levinson, *Wordsworth's Great Period Poems: Four Essays* (Cambridge, 1986), 14–57.

14. Marlon B. Ross, "Romantic Quest and Conquest: Troping Masculine Power in the Crisis of Poetic Identity," in Mellor, ed., *Romanticism and Feminism,* 26–51.

15. Gayatri Spivak's formative essay, "Sex and History," in *Other Worlds,* does seem to privilege the sexual as the *origin* of Wordsworth's attitude to the historical; the private predetermines the public sphere. This was an admirable corrective to a critical tradition that had been very happy to ignore or marginalize the sexual dimension; but I propose here an at least temporary suspension of the model of cause and effect, which can, it seems to me, be resurrected only after careful and skeptical analysis, if at all.

16. Sonia Hofkosh, "The Writer's Ravishment: Women and the Romantic Author— The Example of Byron," in Mellor, ed., *Romanticism and Feminism,* 94. Frank Lentricchia has recently raised very similar questions about American modernism as dramatizing the "cultural powerlessness of poetry in a society that masculinized the economic while it feminized the literary." See his important "Patriarchy against Itself: The Young Manhood of Wallace Stevens," *Critical Inquiry* 13 (1986–87):766.

17. Stuart Curran, "The I Altered," in Mellor, ed., *Romanticism and Feminism,* 185–207.

18. Ibid., 202.

19. Jacobus, "Law of/and Gender," 53, reminds us of this, and refers us back to F. M. Todd, *Politics and the Poet* (London, 1957), 219–25.

20. Susan J. Wolfson, "Individual in Community: Dorothy Wordsworth in Conversation with William," in Mellor, ed., *Romanticism and Feminism,* 147–48.

21. William Wordsworth, *Lyrical Ballads, with a Few Other Poems* (London, 1798), ii–iii, v.

22. In *Wordsworth and the Figurings of the Real* (London, 1982), I argued for Wordsworth's attempt to describe a place for the imagination that was neither fixed nor formless, neither hopelessly reified nor amorphously volatile. In terms of the present argument, one might identify the pole of absolute feminity-community with the formless end of the spectrum, as Wordsworth envisaged it.

23. *The Poetical Works of William Wordsworth,* ed. E. de Selincourt (Oxford, 1940–49), 4:162.

24. William Wordsworth, *The Prelude, 1799, 1805, 1850,* ed. Jonathan Wordsworth, M. H. Abrams, and Stephen Gill (New York, 1979), 1805, 3:339–43.

25. Heinzelman, "Cult of Domesticity," 61.

26. Wordsworth, *Prelude,* 1805, 7:60–62.

27. Ibid., 6:380–82.

28. Wordsworth, *Poems,* 133.

29. Wordsworth, *Prelude, 1805,* 9:558, 57–58; 1850, 9:555; *The Excursion,* 5:88.

30. Shakespeare, *Othello,* 5.1.36.

31. See my *Wordsworth and the Figurings of the Real,* 31–34, 37–38.

32. *The Letters of William and Dorothy Wordsworth: The Early Years, 1787–1805,* ed. E. de Selincourt (Oxford, 1967), 540.

33. The quotation is from Milton, who describes an ideal world of natural nurture made up of

Flowers worthy of Paradise which not nice art
In beds and curious knots, but nature boon
Poured forth profuse on hill and dale and plain.

See *Paradise Lost,* ed. Alastair Fowler (London, 1971), 4:241–43. This play on not/knot seems prophetic of Wordsworth's "nice art," most of all for a poet who was, when he met the gypsy band, on his way to Nottingham. In a letter of 15 February 1807, Dorothy implies that Milton afforded the family a constant consolation at this time—exactly the time of the composition of "Gipsies." William quotes from book 4 in another letter of May 1807. See *The Letters of William and Dorothy Wordsworth: The Middle Years, Pt. I, 1806–11,* ed. E. de Selincourt (Oxford, 1969), 133, 148.

34. *The Collected Writings of Thomas De Quincey,* ed. David Masson (Edinburgh, 1889–90), 2:238.

35. John Thelwall refers to Dorothy as "the maid / Of ardent eye" who "sweetens" William's "solitude" in his "Lines Written at Bridgewater," printed in his *Poems Written Chiefly in Retirement* (Hereford, 1801), 130–31.

36. V. N. Vološinov, *Freudianism: A Marxist Critique,* trans. I. R. Titunik (Bloomington, 1987), 90.

37. *The Dialogic Imagination: Four Essays by M. M. Bakhtin,* ed. Michael Holquist, trans. Caryl Emerson and Michael Holquist (Austin, 1981), 213.

38. Georg Lukács, *History and Class Consciousness: Studies in Marxist Dialectics,* trans. Rodney Livingstone (Cambridge, Mass., 1971), 234.

39. Sebastiano Timpanaro, *On Materialism* (London, 1980), 43–44, 50, 52.

40. Ibid., 34, 55, 61.

41. Herbert Marcuse, *The Aesthetic Dimension: Toward a Critique of Marxist Aesthetics* (Boston, 1978), 16, 24.

JONATHAN ARAC

Bounding Lines: The Prelude *and Critical Revision*

This selection from Jonathan Arac's 1979 essay was later incorporated into his book, *Critical Genealogies: Historical Situations for Postmodern Literary Studies* (1987). In this conclusion to his cogent and comprehensive survey of the "rewriting of *The Prelude* from 1798 to the present," Jonathan Arac clearly defines the "rhetorical models" of description and analysis that most romantic critics, not just those focusing on *The Prelude,* now strive to refine and extend, struggling with the problem Arac describes as that of "totality and representation," how to reconcile a major literary work's wholeness with its localized textures. And in tracing the principal contours of a major poem's critical history, Arac foregrounds what our earlier selections and headnotes may have somewhat obscured, the degree to which recent criticism has emphasized the psychological. Wordsworth's autobiographical poem about the development of his imaginative powers obviously pulls every commentator in this direction, a direction congenial to most of us today. Even historical studies, as is shown by the use of the term "displacement," tend now to be founded on presuppositions of modern psychology, which is perhaps why *The Prelude* not only remains central to romantic criticism but also, as Arac says, significantly contributes to "defining the contours of recent literary study."

Arac's work spans and assimilates a number of recent critical tendencies: deconstruction, poststructuralism, and new textual studies. It is most closely associated with the *boundary 2* Group, so-called after the influential journal in which this essay and much other advanced criticism first appeared. The group's work is represented by such critical studies as Paul Bové's *Destructive Poetics: Heidegger and Modern American Poetry* (1980), Daniel O'Hara's *Romance of Interpretation: Visionary Criticism from Pater to de Man* (1985), and W. V. Spanos's *Repetitions: The Postmodern Occasion in Literature and Culture* (1987), as well as the special double issue of *boundary 2,* volume 7, numbers 2 and 3 (1979), edited by Bové, which contains this essay.

From *boundary 2* 7, no. 3 (1979): 31–48. Copyright © 1979 by Duke University Press. Reprinted with permission of the publisher.

. . . I have tried to suggest ways of reading the circle, the journey, *The Prelude* itself that differ from those of *Natural Supernaturalism* not only to further an understanding of Wordsworth that I find more humane although less grand but also because the current criticism of Wordsworth engages fundamentals of practice and method. The issue I shall arrive at is the problem of spatial form, but I am taking a long way round to reach it.

Our current context for understanding *The Prelude* is defined by the appearance about fifteen years ago of works by Herbert Lindenberger, M. H. Abrams, and Geoffrey Hartman.[1] Despite several notable English essays, New Criticism had not much attended to *The Prelude,* and these works look toward a different practice of literary study.[2] They have so thoroughly reoriented Wordsworthian criticism as to overshadow the books of David Perkins and David Ferry, which hinted at a valuable turning toward *The Prelude* within the orbit of New Criticism.[3]

Our new way with Wordsworth came under the sign of comparative literature, engaging emphases at once more theoretical, more international, and more historical than those associated with New Criticism. Our wish for a "new literary history" and our current concern with methods of critical inquiry are both prefigured in this eruption within the criticism of Wordsworth. Paradoxically, this innovation came through engagement with the old German philological tradition. Hartman dedicated his book to the memory of Erich Auerbach, Abrams's essay draws on Auerbach for its climactic argument, and Lindenberger relates *The Prelude* to *topoi* studied by E. R. Curtius. All three locate Wordsworth in the history of European rhetoric. Hartman begins by isolating the romantic figure of "surmise," derived from the classical *"fallor . . . an"* construction. Lindenberger devotes his first chapter to *"The Prelude* and the Older Rhetoric" and goes on to define Wordsworth's new "rhetoric of interaction." Abrams connects the sublime and matter of fact in Wordsworth through the Christian rhetoric of *sermo humilis,* derived from the low style in which the Bible sets forth the greatest matters.

These new emphases altered the tradition of criticism of Wordsworth. Through their relation to these new studies, several older essays came into new prominence—those by A. C. Bradley, Matthew Arnold, and Walter Pater, all English critics who worked at joining the new thought and writing of Germany to native concerns.[4] Arnold and Bradley are accepted as the two poles of Wordsworthian criticism, and one may see Abrams and Hartman as their heirs.[5] Bradley's darkly philosophical, brooding poet, hostile to "sense" and verging on apocalypse,[6] has an affinity to Hartman's Wordsworth that is well known because Hartman himself notes it. Rejecting Wordsworth's "philosophy," Arnold in contrast looked back to Wordsworth for a consoling joy that forecasts Abrams's argument. In considering the necessity for poetry to engage with *"life"* and not rest in mere formalism, Arnold draws a figure from Epictetus. Perfection of form bears the same relation to life that "inns bear to home": "As if a man, journeying home, and finding a nice inn on the road . . . were to stay forever. . . . Man, thou hast forgotten thine object; thy journey was not *to* this, but *through* this." But "a poet like Wordsworth," Arnold concludes, "prosecutes his journey home" by choosing to sing "Of truth, of gradeur, beauty, love, and hope. . . . Of joy in widest commonalty spread."[7] Arnold shares Abrams's master figure and his central focus on the "Prospectus" to *The Recluse.* Arnold does not, however, claim that Wordsworth actually reaches home, only that he is en route, and I take this as a critical judgment, not merely as a matter of Arnold's writing before the publication of "Home at Grasmere."

Pater has had less impact because he does not fix an image of Wordsworth. Likewise the multiple approaches of Lindenberger's book have prevented it from consolidating a clear position in the critical tradition. But iconoclasm may help evade the impasse of strongly etched but opposite images. Can we set them into an active relation with each other that is not merely synthetic? Just as Lindenberger will follow one strand at a time of *The Prelude* and not strive for one coherent picture, so Pater emphasizes that "sometimes" Wordsworth felt a pure, imaginative solipsism, in which "the actual world would, as it were, dissolve and detach itself, flake by flake." "At other times," however, he felt a pantheistic "spirit of life in outward things, a single, all-pervading mind in them, of which . . . even the poet's imaginative energ[ies] are but moments" (W, 54–55). Pater presents the variety and mobility of writing in *The Prelude* without, like Abrams, demanding a harmonious resolution to a triumphant plot, without, like Hartman, insisting upon a fierce, debilitatingly self-conflicting struggle. At best such a strategy of reading encourages a fresh sensitivity to more of the poem than would one prepared to find only a single story.

Yet how can we read the work as a whole without fixing an image? This problem vexes the reading of nineteenth-century novels as well as poetry. For realistic fiction works by eroding conventional forms, which are set up only to be undermined. If one "stands at a distance" from such a work, it seems the very image of what it is attacking. Apart from local texture, *Don Quixote* looks a heroic romance, *Madame Bovary* a love story. And when the technique of realism is less ironic than these and more allegorical, depending like Thackeray or George Eliot on the sequence of larger units—so that any portion of such a plural work may show only one emphasis—the issue becomes ever more difficult. Nonetheless, attention to rhetoric (in its largest sense of how words are made to work) offers some resistance to seduction by the image.[8]

Pater implies one possible rhetorical reading of *The Prelude* in analyzing the problems of means and ends (which have already engaged us in thinking through the relation between *The Prelude* and *The Recluse* and then in following Wordsworth's meditations on epitaphs). Pater suggests that the way we relate means to ends is the "type or figure under which we represent our lives to ourselves." He offers three instances: that which subordinates means to end, "a figure, reducing all things to machinery"; that which justifies the end by the means—"whatever may become of the fruit, make sure of the flowers and the leaves"; that in which "means and ends are identified" (W, 60–62). These figures correspond to metonymy, synecdoche, and metaphor, and they offer rhetorical models for the major intellectual elements of *The Prelude*: the metonymic "reducing" of associational psychology ("an unrelented agency / Did bind my feelings even as in a chain" [III, ll. 168–69]); the synecdochic organicism of pantheistic totality (that "grows Like harmony in music" and "reconciles Discordant elements" [I, ll. 340–43]); the metaphoric leap of pure imagination that achieves identity without mediation ("the light of sense / Goes out, but with a flash" [VI, ll. 600–01]).

These rhetorical models support Lindenberger's reading of *The Prelude* in terms of three separate organizing principles: a memoir of facts in order (a metonymic reading Lindenberger ascribes to the nineteenth century); the principle of which "Wordsworth himself was most aware . . . the threefold pattern of early vision, loss, and restoration," modeled on the "traditional cycle of paradise, fall, and redemption" (Abrams's synecdochic, Hegelian reading); and a third principle that "stands at odds with the other two, for . . . it recognizes no beginning, middle, or end" (OWP, 190–91). This third principle, metaphoric in its eclipse of mediation, Lindenberger calls "repetition," drawing from Kierkegaard's critique of Hegel (OWP, 196–97). A fourth principle would find an unbridgeable gap between means and end. The end, or origin, would not exist, but our consciousness of its absence would nonetheless define our life as medial. I have tried reading *The Prelude* along this line, to challenge the dominance of the second.

Even if rhetorical analysis helps prevent fixation on an image, the German philosophical tradition which has made rhetoric available to us for the study of Wordsworth has problems of its own. Although to Americans they are both German Romanists, Auerbach and Curtius each felt strong distress at the work of the other. Auerbach criticized Curtius's *European Literature and the Latin Middle Ages* for its fundamentally unhistorical method, for neglecting Christian innovations and choosing a topical, synoptic emphasis on classical continuity.[9] This criticism bears directly on the opposing positions of the two men toward modernism. Auerbach was strongly disturbed by modernism, despite his acute comments on it in *Mimesis* and his recognition that his own method bore the marks of modernity. Curtius, however, wrote early defenses and interpretations of Joyce, Eliot, and others.[10] He casts his own *European Literature* into modernist spatial form, describing it in terms of "aerial photography" and "spiral ascent."[11] Auerbach's *Mimesis* remains resolutely chronological, striving to articulate disturbances and breakthroughs. Although Auerbach's crucial conception of figuralism shows a resemblance to spatial form, Christian figuralism is only a phase in the overall history Auerbach pursues.[12] In *Natural Supernaturalism* Auerbach's topics are put to use, but the work follows Curtius's organization, deliberately echoing the "spiral form" it finds in romantic writing.[13] Thus through the German heritage from Hegel, Abrams comes to the formalist cancellation of time that he shares with the New Critics, despite their other differences.[14]

I wonder, however, if a more resolute focus on rhetoric, on language in action, can evade the totalizing opposition of spatial versus temporal. Recent rhetorical studies have undermined a similar dichotomy, Roman Jakobson's polarizing of metaphor and metonymy, by recalling us to the necessary interplay between the two in any articulated work (since to rest wholly at one pole is to suffer an aphasia).[15] Is it any more possible wholly to segregate space and time, any more than Wordsworth's 1850 revision of the boat-stealing wholly segregates the elements? In contrasting Homer to the Bible, the first chapter of *Mimesis* sets in motion the terminology of space and time. The "complete externalization" [16] and "foregrounding" in *The Odyssey* create a static icon in which all time is present, while in the Bible matters of history, formation, and development in relation to divine will determine what is presented and how (M, 14–15). Auerbach argues (as he will later of *Ulysses*) that *The Odyssey* may be analyzed structurally (M, 11, 487) but that only in the Bible is the temporality of interpretation necessarily present (M, 12).[17] Yet within Auerbach's text the critical metaphors follow an opposite line as well. Connections in the Bible are "vertical," in Homer horizontal (M, 14). The parts of Homer's world link contiguously, metonymically, as the text moves along the syntagmatic axis that marks the flow of language in time; in the Bible, however, the leap of metaphor relates a human event to its paradigm in divine Providence. "History" (M, 15 ff.), as in the Bible, is seen from a perspective that lifts up every moment into eternal significance, while the Homeric icon, complete at every moment, from moment to moment metamorphoses.

In the palimpsest of our cultural history the languages of space and time are both inscribed. A purifying revision, or retranscription, that tried to straighten out the tangles of these lines, to free us from our need to read between them, would no doubt like Wordsworth achieve some fresh moments and new emphases. But would it ultimately do better? The "peculiar relation of mutual supplementation," by which minor terms become major and opposites complete, or replace, each other, saved Wordsworth from the complacency of *The Recluse;* his position was never wholly "made up" but always liable to displacement. This is the interest of his situation. Would our life be more interesting if we stepped out from between the lines, released by omitting "all cross-currents, all friction . . . everything unresolved, truncated, and uncertain" (M, 16)? That is, if we willed ourselves from history into legend?

NOTES

1. Herbert Lindenberger, *On Wordsworth's "Prelude"* (Princeton: Princeton Univ. Press, 1963); M. H. Abrams, "English Romanticism: The Spirit of the Age," in *Romanticism Reconsidered,* ed. Northrop Frye (New York: Columbia Univ. Press, 1963), pp. 26–72 (the first major step toward *Natural Supernaturalism*); Geoffrey H. Hartman, *Wordsworth's Poetry, 1787–1814* (New Haven: Yale Univ. Press, 1964). Future citations of Lindenberger's book will be abbreviated OWP.

2. F. R. Leavis, "Wordsworth," in *Revaluation* (1936; rpt. Harmondsworth: Penguin, 1972), pp. 145–64; G. Wilson Knight, "The Wordsworthian Profundity," in *The Starlit Dome* (1941; rpt. London: Oxford Univ. Press, 1971), pp. 2–24; William Empson, "Sense in The Prelude," in *The Structure of Complex Words* (1951; rpt. Ann Arbor: Univ. of Michigan Press, 1967), pp. 289–305.

3. David Perkins, *The Quest for Permanence* (Cambridge: Harvard Univ. Press, 1959), chs. 1–3; David Ferry, *The Limits of Mortality* (Middletown: Wesleyan Univ. Press, 1959).

4. Matthew Arnold, "Wordsworth" (1879), in *Essays in Criticism,* Second Series (1888; rpt. London and New York: Macmillan, 1896), pp. 122–62; A. C. Bradley, "Wordsworth," in *Oxford Lectures on Poetry* (1909; rpt. Bloomington: Indiana Univ. Press, 1961), pp. 99–148; Walter Pater, "Wordsworth," in *Appreciations* (1889; rpt. London and New York: Macmillan, 1897). Future citations will be abbreviated W.

5. On Bradley and Arnold, see M. H. Abrams, "Introduction: Two Roads to Wordsworth," in *Wordsworth: A Collection of Critical Essays* (Englewood Cliffs: Prentice, 1972), pp. 2–4.

6. *Oxford Lectures on Poetry,* pp. 130–34.

7. *Essays in Criticism,* pp. 144–47.

8. See Paul de Man, "The Rhetoric of Temporality," in *Interpretation: Theory and Practice,* ed. C. S. Singleton (Baltimore: Johns Hopkins Univ. Press, 1969), pp. 173–209. De Man's "Intentional Structure of the Romantic Image" (1960), in *Wordsworth: A Collection of Critical Essays,* pp. 133–44, further demonstrates the impact of European rhetorical analysis on the criticism of Wordsworth.

9. See Erich Auerbach's reviews, *MLN,* 65 (May 1950), 348–50; and *Romanische*

Forschungen, 62 (1950), 237–45, reprinted in *Gesammelte Aufsätze zur romanischen Philologie* (Berne and Munich: Francke, 1967), pp. 330–38.

10. See "James Joyce and his Ulysses" (1929) and "T. S. Eliot" (1927 and 1949), in E. R. Curtius, *Essays on European Literature,* trans. Michael Kowal (Princeton: Princeton Univ. Press, 1973), pp. 327–99. Note the adumbration of later theories of spatial form in Joyce: "In order really to understand *Ulysses* one would have to have the entire work present in one's mind at every sentence" (p. 353).

11. Ernst Robert Curtius, *Europäische Literatur und Lateinisches Mittelalter* (Berne and Munich: Francke, 1948), p. 10 ("Luftphotgraphien"), 384 ("spiraliger Aufstieg"). See *European Literature and the Latin Middle Ages,* trans. Willard R. Trask (1953; rpt. New York and Evanston: Harper, 1963), pp. ix, 381. These motifs from the "Foreword" and "Epilogue" recur throughout. On Curtius's Joycean "perspectivism," see Arthur R. Evans, Jr., "Ernst Robert Curtius," in *On Four Modern Humanists* (Princeton: Princeton Univ. Press, 1970), p. 142.

12. On figuralism and spatial form, see Joseph Frank, "Spatial Form: An Answer to Critics," *Critical Inquiry,* 4 (Winter 1977), 237.

13. M. H. Abrams, "Rationality and Imagination in Cultural History," *Critical Inquiry,* 2 (Spring 1976), 450.

14. Curtius and Auerbach specifically align their enterprises with Hegel, *European Literature,* p. 4, and "Epilegomena zu *Mimesis,*" *Romanische Forschungen,* 65 (1953), 15.

15. Roman Jakobson, "The Metaphoric and Metonymic Poles," in *Fundamentals of Language* (The Hague: Mouton, 1956), pp. 76–82; for a sample undermining, see J. Hillis Miller, "The Fiction of Realism" in *Dickens Centennial Essays,* ed. Ada Nisbet and Blake Nevius (Berkeley: Univ. of California Press, 1971), pp. 123–26.

16. Erich Auerbach, *Mimesis,* 2nd ed., trans. Willard Trask (1953; rpt. New York: Doubleday, 1957), p. 2. Future citations will be abbreviated M.

17. Auerbach remained uneasy with these strong contrasts. See "Epilegomena zu *Mimesis,*" p. 2.

"Splitting the Race of Man in Twain": Prostitution, Personification, and The Prelude

The following selection only feebly indicates the range of Mary Jacobus's book from which it is excerpted, *Romanticism, Writing, and Sexual Difference* (1989). Yet we hope it may suggest the breadth of concerns that have been opened up in romantic criticism by the maturation of feminist studies. Few passages of equal brevity could so successfully manifest the persuasive radicalism with which intelligent feminist criticism compels us to rethink, and reimagine, very familiar critical issues. To put the matter as simply as possible, can one conceive of any celebrated Wordsworthians of the past focusing an essay on *The Prelude* on prostitution?

As we pointed out in our general introduction, despite the work of critics like Jacobus, feminist criticism of romantic poetry has only recently begun to gather force. While we expect the next decade to produce a substantial body of such work equivalent to hers in its revitalizing power, it is probably asking too much to expect the kind of rhetorical efficacy Jacobus displays: "To save the boy, Wordsworth has to get rid of the mother." Much of her persuasive power derives from the clarity with which she perceives and vividly delineates central issues, in this case defining sexual difference as "the most repressed aspect of *The Prelude*." Illuminating as this is of Wordsworth's poem, it has obvious resonances throughout romantic literature, in which what Jacobus calls "the personification of the romantic woman" serves as one kind of defense against female sexuality.

'Every Jack will have his Jill.'[1] With what he calls 'This utopian and "romantic" proverb', Geoffrey Hartman begins a gnomic essay 'On the Theory of Romanticism'. An authorized gloss might run: 'Every intellectual desire will finally find its scholastic fulfilment.'[2] The role of woman (Jill) is to put man (Jack) in possession of his desire. High Romantic critical quests might be said to have been waylaid by this enchanting and discriminatory plot (also known as 'Natural Supernaturalism'); the metaphoric consummation or spousal union of masculine mind and feminine nature haunts A. O. Lovejoy's Romantic heirs, giving M. H. Abrams's shaping narrative its underlying form (that of the History of Ideas) and lingering on in Hartman's 'romantic' proverb.[3] As Gayatri Spivak has pointed out, the

From *Romanticism, Writing, and Sexual Difference: Essays on "The Prelude"* (Oxford: Oxford University Press, 1989), pp. 206–215. Copyright © Mary Jacobs 1989. By permission of Oxford University Press.

elision of sexual difference, or occlusion of woman, is a by-product of the Romantic master-plot.[4] Domesticated by her role in the Great (male) Tradition, Jill settles down with Jack in Dove Cottage to raise their brood of Romantic daughters; in the Romantic family, the only good daughter is a dutiful one (Dora), or a dead one (Kate—'Surprised by joy . . .').

I want to try to sketch a different Romantic plot, as well as an alternative profession for the Romantic daughter. What if the mind addressed its courtship, not to nature, but to the city (in Wordsworth's poetry, a city of dreadful art)? And what if the Romantic quester is accosted by a voice that speaks shamelessly, not from the world of the dead (*Siste viator*) but from the *demi-monde?* What if the long journey home were that of a prodigal daughter instead of the Romantic son and heir in Abrams's story? I have in mind the possibility of a prostituted and indiscriminate Romanticism, perhaps infected by the French disease. Hartman's essay asks us to make allowance 'for the seductive presence of romance motifs' in Romantic poetry, akin to the use of the *persona* in neo-classical and modern poetry.[5] My concern in this chapter is with the seductive presence of persons, or rather personifications, in Wordsworth's poetry, and with the turn towards Romance, or Spenserian allegory, which signals that seduction.[6] My argument will be not only that high Romanticism depends on the casting out of what defines its height—figurative language, and especially personification—but that the characteristic form of this figure is a Romantic woman. The fate of personification (the outcast of Romantic figuration) and of prostitution (the outcast of spousal verse) tells us how these rhetorical and figurative schemes are constituted and at what price. My example will be Mary of Buttermere in Book VII of *The Prelude,* and the girl prostitute, Ann of Oxford Street, from De Quincey's *Confessions of an English Opium-Eater;* my route will be digressive, accosted by the wandering forms of Romantic error (figured here as Milton's Spenserian allegory of Sin and Death), and I will conclude with a brief encounter with the economics of autobiography.

THE MAID OF BUTTERMERE

On the face of it, sexual difference seems the most completely repressed aspect of *The Prelude.* Except for the Vaudracour and Julia episode, later excised, the theme of sexual desire is either banished to the realm of the pastoral or else thoroughly domesticated. Mary of Buttermere, to whose seduction Wordsworth alludes in Book VII, prompts the improbable pre-seduction fantasy that 'we were nursed . . . On the same mountains' (vii. 342–3)—risking Johnson's testy objection to Milton's similarly pastoral fiction in *Lycidas* ('For we were nursed upon the self-same hill', l. 23): we *know* they never drove afield together. In Book XI the same pre-Freudian view of the nursery crops up in connection with the virginal Mary Hutchinson, here named as 'Nature's inmate'; 'Even like this maid', Wordsworth insists, he loved nature ('nor lightly loved, / But fervently') without being enthralled by the later tyranny of the eye which he terms a 'degradation' (xi. 213, 223–6).[7] And, in Book XIII, Dorothy Wordsworth is invoked as 'Child of my parents, sister of my soul' (xiii. 211); here, as always in Romantic poetry, the motif of brother–sister love (whether overtly incestuous or not) swiftly assimilates sexual difference to narcissistic identity. No less than the maid and the wife, the sister simultaneously figures the repression of sexuality and the refusal of sexual difference. Women are all the same (as the young Wordsworth).

Romantic women routinely appear in *The Prelude* at moments when Words-
worth wants to emphasize the continuity of his mature poetic identity with an
imaginary latency period, or undifferentiated sexuality, belonging to his Lake
District boyhood. Far from being emblems of sexual difference, they function
precisely as defences against it. Just as nature, at the opening of Book XI, inter-
poses itself 'betwixt the heart of man / And the uneasy world—twixt man him-
self . . . and his own unquiet heart' (xi. 17–19),[8] so the purified and purifying
figure of woman interposes itself healingly between man and his own unquiet, pre-
existing, inner division. But there is one important exception. In Book VII of *The
Prelude,* what I will call the Maid of Buttermere sequence—beginning with an
account of the Sadler's Wells melodrama, 'The Beauty of Buttermere', and ending
approximately a hundred lines later with the words 'I quit this painful theme'—
introduces a figure whose traumatic effect is to split 'the race of man / In twain'
(vii. 426–7).[9] Like the beggars of London, the figure of the prostitute is almost
synonymous with late eighteenth-century representations of the city. But Words-
worth's circuitous approach to the overwhelming visibility of prostitution at this
period (in 1803, estimates put the number of London prostitutes between 50,000
and 70,000) suggests an internal obstacle to broaching 'this painful theme'.[10] His
compulsively digressive returns to the same point of fixation—rather as Freud, in
his essay on 'The Uncanny', relates his own involuntary return to the red light
district of an unknown city—signal one effect of that traumatic 'splitting'; namely,
repression. Or, as Blake puts it at just about the time of Wordsworth's first
encounter with London, the Romantic family is blighted by the harlot's curse.

The most common literary form taken by the uncanny is doubling. Mary of
Buttermere raises the spectre of a theatrical other, or dark interpretess, whose
urban fall shadows her Lake District purity. Wordsworth's brief account of 'The
Maid of Buttermere' as presented on the London stage in 1803,

> how the spoiler came, 'a bold bad man'
> To God unfaithful, children, wife, and home,
> And wooed the artless daughter of the hills,
> And wedded her, in cruel mockery
> Of love and marriage bonds.
>   (*Prel.* vii. 323–7)[11]

introduces his 'memorial verse' on the bigamously unmarried mother, a personal
recollection of the real Mary Robinson as he and Coleridge had met her during
their walking tour of 1799 ('in her cottage-inn / Were welcomed, and attended on
by her', vii. 327–46). This tribute, he writes, 'Comes from the poet's heart, and is
her due'; it makes amends for her immodest stage career. But her image cannot be
laid so easily, rising up in the poet's path like an unexorcized ghost when he
attempts to resume his interrupted account of the London theatre:

> These last words uttered, to my argument
> I was returning, when—with sundry forms
> Mingled, that in the way which I must tread
> Before me stand—*thy image rose again,*
> Mary of Buttermere!
>   (*Prel.* vii. 347–51; my italics)

The unmarried mother comes athwart the poet like the 'unfathered vapour' of imagination in Book VI, halting him in the time of writing with the crisis of interpretative confusion which has been identified by Weiskel and others with the Romantic Sublime.[12] Here, however, an encounter with the 'unfathered' or unfathering Oedipal Sublime is replaced by an unlaid female apparition who blocks further poetic progress. The unsuccessful exorcism has to be repeated a second time in the succeeding lines ('She lives in peace . . . Without contamination does she live / In quietness . . . Happy are they both, / Mother and child!', vii. 351–4, 359–60)—but this time with an added sacrifice. Her new-born and unfathered child sleeps in earth ('Fearless as a lamb') in order that Mary may live on 'without contamination' as the Mary Magdalene of *The Prelude*. The infant's burial tranquillizes her unquiet life, allowing her to stand in for the purified, pre-sexual, Lake District poet (himself, one might note, the parent of an 'unfathered' child). This hushing up of the sexual drama is effected by making Mary no longer—or again not yet—a mother, still emphatically the *Maid* of Buttermere.

But the matter of sexuality cannot be laid to rest quite so easily as the babe. Or, someone, somewhere, is always getting laid. As if *The Prelude* were a Spenserian narrative in which the moment of interpretive difficulty produces an insistent doubling of allegorical persons, Duessa splits off from Una. In this theatrical city, how are we to recognize the difference between the Maid of Buttermere and a Sadler's Wells prostitute, between a Romantic woman and a painted theatrical whore?

> foremost I am crossed
> Here by remembrance of two figures: one
> A rosy babe, who for a twelvemonth's space
> Perhaps had been of age to deal about
> Articulate prattle, child as beautiful
> As ever sate upon a mother's knee;
> The other was the parent of that babe—
> But on the mother's cheek the tints were false,
> A painted bloom.
> (*Prel.* vii. 366–74)

In the semiotics of sexuality, 'painted bloom' is the sign of solicitation, and solicitation the sign of shamelessness; Sadler's Wells (like Drury Lane and Covent Garden, notoriously the haunt of prostitutes at the end of the eighteenth century) brings together anti-theatrical and sexual prejudices in one scene. But what about the rosy babe, who, we might note, differs in three important respects from Mary of Buttermere's dead, ungendered, new-born infant? He is alive, he is specified as male ('The lovely boy', vii. 396), and he is no longer 'infans' (i.e. he has been prattling for about a year). Not the mother ('scarcely at this time / Do I remember her', vii. 394–5) but this beautiful boy becomes the focus of Wordsworth's 'remembrance'. I want to emphasize the displacement from mother to child, since it will help to refine one common reading of the episode: namely, that it allows Wordsworth to depict himself as ultimately uncontaminated by the fall into writing or representation which London symbolizes in Book VII of *The Prelude*. And, once more, we should notice the disappearance of the mother during the decontamination process.

This mother-and-child pair, obviously parodic of the duo in the 'Blessed the infant babe' passage, implies a theory of pre-Oedipal relations previously unglimpsed in *The Prelude*—that of gathering dangerous passions from one's mother's eye; a theory, in fact, of maternal seduction. If the mother seduces, the child must be 'stopped' ('through some special privilege / *Stopped* at the growth he had', vii. 401–2; my italics), presumably lest he grow up gay as the result of a too-loving mother, like Freud's type of the homosexual artist, Leonardo da Vinci. Wordsworth fondly imagines the boy spared this fate, 'as if embalmed / By Nature',

> destined to live,
> To be, to have been, come, and go, a child
> And nothing more, no partner in the years
> That bear us forward to distress and guilt,
> Pain and abasement . . .
> (*Prel.* vii. 400–6)

We can glimpse here the shadow cast by an earlier family romance or incestuous primal scene. If the mother is Sin, accosting Wordsworth on his journey as she accosts Milton's Satan *en route* for chaos, then the final tendency of 'the years / That bear us forward' is not so much homosexuality as Death, Milton's name for Sin's incestuously conceived and incestuous son. Arrested development becomes the only alternative. This arrest or stoppage, it hardly needs pointing out, not only precludes growing up as distressed and guilty as the rest of us; it precludes the growth of a poet.

Like the Winander Boy in Book V, the embalmed child is arrested in a moment of indeterminacy, a pause that suspends him between mimic hootings or 'articulate prattle' on the one hand, and on the other the silent writing or reading of his own epitaph which Wordsworth characteristically undertakes at such self-reflexive moments.[13] Here a structure of address sketches the temporal relations between the two pairs (Mary of Buttermere with her nameless infant, and the painted woman with her rosy boy), installing Wordsworth himself in loving commiseration with his own future:

> he perhaps,
> *Mary,* may now have lived till he could look
> With envy on *thy* nameless babe that sleeps
> Beside the mountain chapel undisturbed.
> (*Prel.* vii. 409–12; my italics)

In these lines the poet in the time of writing addresses a purified Mary (the Mary of his Lake District past), just as the unembalmed, unstopped city boy might look with envy (*invidia*) on her nameless babe—a babe imagined as not only immune to time (euphemistically asleep), but immune to the division which besets all subjects, especially what has come to be known as the subject in language; hence, a babe immune to sexual division.[14] The unstopped boy occupies the same position as the guilty, autobiographically split Wordsworth who is also subject to growth; but his fall has been displaced on to the forgotten mother. The reason why the mother is scarcely remembered 'at this time' is that she has been cast out—in the Kristevan terms which I will elaborate later, 'abjected'—so that Wordsworth can throw in his lot with the 'embalmed' and separate self figured by the beautiful boy. In order to save the boy, Wordsworth has to get rid of the mother.

It is not surprising, then, that the residual form taken by the mother is that of the prostitute. Cast out, she becomes (by a neat symbolic reversal) an outcast. As if possessed by its own internal momentum, the sequence digresses yet again from its theatrical context, this time to invoke the earlier journey when Wordsworth, *en route* from the Lake District to Cambridge in 1787, first heard and saw a cursing prostitute,

> for the first time in my life did hear
> The voice of woman utter blasphemy—
> Saw woman as she is to open shame
> Abandoned, and the pride of public vice.
> (*Prel.* vii. 417–20)

The Prelude represents the effect—or affect—as 'immense', a permanent and founding split in the autobiographical subject that is simultaneously trauma and repression:

> Full surely from the bottom of my heart
> I shuddered; but the pain was almost lost,
> Absorbed and buried in the immensity
> Of the effect: a barrier seemed at once
> Thrown in, that from humanity divorced
> The human form, splitting the race of man
> In twain, yet leaving the same outward shape.
> (*Prel.* vii. 421–7)

A pain 'absorbed . . . in the immensity / Of the effect' sounds remarkably like the pain of castration anxiety before naked female sexuality as Freud describes it—in his account, a pain buried by the immense effects of fetishism. Even as sexual difference is recognized, it is denied or disavowed by means of a defensive 'splitting' (what might be termed the both/and defence).[15] The barrier permits a 'divorce' which paradoxically allows the subject not to confront difference structured as division or as equally unacceptable alternatives (the either/or trauma). Characteristically, the fetishist clings to a representation associated with the last moment before his sight of the apparently castrated mother. Here that representation is 'the human form', or rather, 'man'—the ostensibly undifferentiated (male) body which serves as the measure of Romantic humanism while serving also to deny sexual difference.

Splitting becomes the means to defend an imaginary bodily integrity, warding off castration anxiety by means of the fantasy of organic wholeness with which Romantic humanism is invested, whether its subject is man or simply his imagination. In the context of Book VII of *The Prelude,* the book of representations, the painted or fallen woman becomes an emblem of representation itself, allowing Wordsworth to cling to the (here perilously sustained) fiction of a self that is not the subject of, or in, representation (and hence inevitably split). 'The overthrow / Of her soul's beauty' (viii. 432–3)—we might note that Wordsworth's soul is regularly feminized in *The Prelude*—is the ostensible trade-off for Wordsworth's immunity to division; but the female body is the actual price paid, since the overthrow of the prostitute's soul means the throwing over of her body. In other words, the passage allows us to see how the fetishistic compromise works for men (splitting keeps them whole), but only, and contradictorily, at the expense of women (splitting creates the division fallen/unfallen, and thus institutes a denigrated class). Once this compromise between incompatible ideas has been effected, Wordsworth can move on from the 'Distress of mind [that] ensued upon this sight' (vii. 428) to a more manageable 'milder sadness'. 'In truth', he writes, 'The sorrow of the passion *stopped* me here' (vii. 434–5; my italics). This stoppage is so effective that Wordsworth can finally 'quit this painful theme' (vii. 436)— shut his eyes to division—and return to his account of the London stage. 'Stopped' is the same word used of the beautiful boy's arrest ('through some special privilege / Stopped at the growth he had', vii, 401–2). It halts Wordsworth by returning him in fantasy to the moment before the distressing and anxiety-inducing sight of sexual difference. We should also notice that Wordsworth's insistence on the child being father to the man (the *post hoc ergo propter hoc* recipe for embalming infants) allows him to adopt the myth of nature as Romantic Mother without ever confronting maternal desire, whether the mother's for and in him, or his own for the mother. To call sexual difference the most completely repressed aspect of *The Prelude* amounts to saying that it is put a stop to, whether by the fiction of Natural Supernaturalism, or by systematic domestication, or, as here in Book VII, by being cast out in the figure of the prostitute. . . .

NOTES

1. G. Hartman, *The Fate of Reading and Other Essays* (Chicago and London, 1975), 277.
2. Personal communication.
3. See M. H. Abrams, *Natural Supernaturalism* (New York, 1971).
4. G. Spivak, 'Sex and History in *The Prelude* (1805): Books Nine to Thirteen', *Texas Studies in Literature and Language*, 23 (1981), 336.
5. Hartman, *The Fate of Reading*, pp. 277–8.
6. I am indebted to Steven Knapp, *Personification and the Sublime: Milton To Coleridge* (Cambridge, Mass., and London, 1985), for suggesting the relation between allegorical romance and Romantic attitudes to personification.
7. These lines belonged originally to drafts connected with 'Nutting', where 'Nature's inmate' presumably referred to Dorothy. See *The Prelude*, ed. de Selincourt, rev. Darbishire, p. 612.
8. *Prel.* xi. 17–19 also belonged originally to drafts connected with 'Nutting'; see ibid. 610.
9. See also L. Kramer, 'Gender and Sexuality in *The Prelude:* The Question of Book Seven', *ELH* 54 (1987), 619–37, for a detailed psychoanalytic reading of the Maid of Buttermere episode in relation to Wordsworth's larger repression of the theme of sexuality, and to related issues of representation figured in Book VII by the city; I am grateful to Professor Kramer for the opportunity to read his essay while working on my own.
10. See A. Parreaux, *Daily Life in England in the Reign of George III* (London, 1966), 122–8, 134–40. For a fuller account of prostitution in 18th-cent. London, see Fernando Henriques, *Prostitution and Society* (2 vols.; London, 1962–1968), ii. 143–91.

During the 18th cent., London was said to have twice as many prostitutes as Paris; in 1789, the West End alone contained an estimated 30,000 prostitutes (see ibid. 144). For literary representations of the prostitute, see also J. B. Radner, 'The Youthful Harlot's Curse: The Prostitute as Symbol of the City in 18th-Century English Literature', *Eighteenth Century Life*, 2 (1976), 59–63.

11. As Kenneth R. Johnston writes, pointing out the anachronism whereby Wordsworth introduces a play which he not only did not see in the 1790s but may not in fact have seen later, 'Wordsworth's oddly self-implicating account of *The Beauty of Buttermere*' seems to block his narrative and thematic progress as well: see *Wordsworth and The Recluse,* pp. 160–3. For Mary Robinson, see also D. H. Reiman, 'The Beauty of Buttermere as Fact and Romantic Symbol', *Criticism,* 26 (1984), 139–70.

12. See e.g. Thomas Weiskel, *The Romantic Sublime* (Baltimore, 1976), 173–5, 200–4.

13. See Neil Hertz, *The End of the Line* (New York, 1985), 218–19, for what he calls 'structures of minimal difference' in relation to the Winander Boy episode.

14. The term *invidia* is Lacan's, as elaborated by R. Young, 'The Eye and Progress of his Song: A Lacanian Reading of *The Prelude*', *Oxford Literary Review,* 3 (1979), 78–98; for the connection between this passage and the 'Blessed the Infant Babe' passage in Book II, see esp. pp. 89–90.

15. See S. Freud, 'Fetishism' (1927): 'what happened [in the case of the fetishist] . . . was that the boy refused to take cognizance of the fact of his having percevied that a woman does not possess a penis . . . It is not true that, after the child has made his observation of the woman, he has preserved unaltered his belief that women have a phallus. He has retained that belief, but he has also given it up. In the conflict between the weight of the unwelcome perception and the force of his counter-wish, a compromise has been reached . . .', *The Complete Psychological Works of Sigmund Freud,* trans. and ed. J. Strachey, xxi. 153–4.

Samuel Taylor Coleridge

If Coleridge's poetry does not attract the same volume of research and comment as Wordsworth's, the tendency in recent years to move away from the old view of Wordsworth as in some sense a creature (at times even a rather monstrous one) of his younger friend's superior critical intelligence has increased appreciation of Coleridge's accomplishments in their own right. This process, a key contribution to which was Don H. Bialostosky's "Coleridge's Interpretation of Wordsworth's Preface to *Lyrical Ballads*" (1978), reaches one kind of fulfillment in Paul Magnuson's essay, with its focus on Coleridge's unique political entanglements as providing an essential context for "Frost at Midnight." Karen Swann's essay on *Christabel* carries us further into the social dynamics of the interplay between "creation" and "reception." An excellent complement to Swann's essay is Charles Rzepka's lucid Lacanian analysis of *Christabel* as revelatory of the poet's complex relations with his own family, now available in his useful book *The Self as Mind: Vision and Identity in Wordsworth, Coleridge, and Keats* (1986).

Our choice of Raimonda Modiano's article on *The Ancient Mariner* requires some explanation, despite the essay's obvious excellence, for it appeared earlier than many pieces in this collection. In our view it marks an intriguing turning point in the voluminous criticism of Coleridge's most famous poem, pointing to the fashion in which feminist attitudes were to reorient our understanding of every kind of romantic poem, while also suggesting the need to examine with fewer prejudices of conventional rationalism the effect of genuine religious commitments upon artistic practice. Modiano's essay, furthermore, interestingly anticipates current concern (deriving in good measure from the increasing availability of first-rate texts) with different versions of the poem. Characteristic of this focus is Jerome McGann's essay "The Ancient Mariner: The Meaning of Meanings," now available in his book, *The Beauty of Inflections: Literary Investigations in Historical Method and Theory* (1985). As valuable for a broad understanding of the significance of romantic revisings is Jack Stillinger's "Multiple Versions of Coleridge's Poems: How Many *Mariners* Did Coleridge Write?" (1992). (The answer to Stillinger's question is sixteen—at least.) Other significant reconsiderations of the poem include Homer Obed Brown's "Art of Theology and the Theology of Art: Robert Penn Warren's Reading of Coleridge's *The*

Rime of the Ancient Mariner" and Jonathan Arac's response, "Repetition and Exclusion: Coleridge and New Criticism Reconsidered," both of which appeared in *boundary 2* (1979).

Our Coleridge section ends with Gene W. Ruoff's "Romantic Lyric and the Problem of Belief," which argues that although modern criticism has readily appropriated many of Coleridge's esthetic precepts, it has systematically minimized doctrinal aspects of his poetry. Ruoff uses as his test case a lyric that is simultaneously one of Coleridge's earliest poems (written by 1796) and one of his latest (receiving its final revisions in 1828). The essay's critical method depends upon retrieving and even accentuating internal dissonances between the poem's voices, arguing for a dialogical and consequently rhetorical consideration of their completing claims.

The Politics of "Frost at Midnight"

Although Magnuson's essay manifests today's critical bias toward the historical, it also reflects the rather subtle because diffuse effect of "reader-response" theories. Magnuson's dialogic approach, which he carefully distinguishes from Bakhtin's, is like most of the best commentary of this kind (such as Cooper's discussion of the shipwreck in *Don Juan* in the next section) undoctrinaire in affirming how readerships may shape the constitution of a poem. For that reason, perhaps, one feels a special cogency in Magnuson's demand that we recognize how *all* the immediate circumstances through which a poem comes into being determine what it has meant and therefore can mean. In this particular case, what has consistently been treated as a "conversation poem" relevant principally to the poet's psyche is shown to be deeply enmeshed in and affected by specific political pressures on Coleridge, the poem's meanings being significantly determined by the relation of its themes and figures to the public discourse in which it participated. The result of this demonstration is, as Magnuson says, "not necessarily to develop a clear meaning for it," but, rather, substantially to increase its fascinating complexities by, for example, showing how issues in it of patriotism and domestic affection have less to do with biographical facts than ideological debates.

Magnuson's essay is one of a forthcoming collection on canonical romantic poems in the public context of the debates on the principles and events of the French Revolution. They argue that poems commonly read as subjective products of a poet's individual sensibility are strongly mediated by the public discourse they enter. Other essays discuss Coleridge's *Ancient Mariner,* Wordsworth's *Poems in Two Volumes* (1807), Byron's *Don Juan,* and Keats's "Ode on a Grecian Urn." This book has in common with Magnuson's earlier book, *Coleridge and Wordsworth: A Lyrical Dialogue* (1988), the theme that location is crucial to reading a poem and that to change a poem's context is to change its significance, sometimes radically.

I would like to begin with a quotation, which I take to be representative of common opinion on Coleridge's Conversation Poems and his mystery poems. In his Clark Lectures, published in 1953, Humphry House remarked:

> It has been observed by Dr. Tillyard how very unpolitical "The Ancient Mariner" is. "Frost at Midnight" (dated February 1798—that is, while the "Mariner" was being written) is, if possible, less political still. (85–86)

From *The Wordsworth Circle* (1991): 3–11. Reprinted with the kind permission of *The Wordsworth Circle*.

House argues that at the time that these poems were being written Coleridge began to divide his poetical interests, writing some poems with explicit political content and others that do not contain a word of politics. In other words, the comparison of either "Frost at Midnight" or "The Ancient Mariner" with other poems written or published at the same time, "The Visions of the Maid of Orleans" or "Fears in Solitude" for example, demonstrates that Coleridge was liberating his genius from the mundane impediments of topical literature.

I will elaborate an argument that "Frost at Midnight" is a political poem if it is read in the dialogic and public context of Coleridge's other poems and the political debates of the 1790's. A comparison of "Frost at Midnight" with other Coleridge poems yields a conclusion contrary to House's. But before I ask about the significance of a Romantic lyric, I want to ask about its location: Where is it? and Who conspired to put it there? The method that I will follow argues that a lyric's location determines its significance, and to change a poem's location is to change its dialogic significance, sometimes radically. "Frost at Midnight" was written in late February 1798. It is commonly read as an intensely subjective, meditative lyric written in isolated retirement and reflecting the isolated consciousness of its author; or it is read in the context of Coleridge's other Conversation Poems such as "The Eolian Harp" and "This Lime-Tree Bower," and it echoes the themes of those poems with which it was grouped as "Meditative Poems in Blank Verse" in *Sibylline Leaves* (1817); or it is read in the context of Wordsworth's lyrics, particularly "Tintern Abbey." But it was first published in the fall of 1798 as the final poem in a quarto volume that began with two explicitly political poems: "Fears in Solitude" and "France: An Ode." These two poems were also written early in 1798, and "France: An Ode" was published in the *Morning Post,* April 16. The quarto was published by Joseph Johnson, the radical bookseller, in the early fall after Coleridge met him in late August or early September while he was on his way to Germany with Wordsworth (*CL,* I:417–8, 420).

I propose to locate "Frost at Midnight" in the context of the other poems in the volume and to locate the volume in the context of the political debates conducted in the popular press. My more general interest is in the ways in which context determines dialogic significance, and I certainly do not intend to argue that "Frost at Midnight" must be read in these contexts or that the reading that I will suggest is the only, or even the best, reading. In a reading of a poem as an isolated, integral, and individual poem, the process of interpretation relies only upon the poem itself; in the variety of dialogic reading that I am offering, the meaning of a poem depends upon the meanings of its themes and figures that exist in the public discourse before the poem is written. I will be comparing Coleridge's poems with other written material that is not often considered in a traditional explication; I draw upon the political pamphlets and political journalism, which implies that a Romantic lyric participates in the ordinary language of the day. For this contextual reading there is no distinction between an aesthetic language that is unique and separate from ordinary language. And in dealing with the dialogic relations of lyric poetry and political journalism, my dialogic method differs from the theory of Bakhtin, who places primary emphasis upon the multiplicity of voices within a single work.

To put all this in a simpler way: I will be looking at the public Coleridge and the public location of the poem. Our reconstructions of Coleridge in this century are based upon the publication of his notebooks and letters, by our knowledge of the scholarship that has traced his reading, and by our knowledge of his later career.

None of these were available to his contemporaries, whose comments make the history of the reception of the poem and whose debates constitute the context of its publication. The story of its public context and reception, I think, is a particularly complex instance of tendentious interpretation and deliberate misrepresentation. To conduct an inquiry into the publication and reception of the poem is not necessarily to develop a clear meaning for it. Significance remains as slippery as it is for other critical approaches. It partakes, in other words, of the rhetoric of public debate rather than the rhetoric of symbolism and allegory by which it is usually discussed.

For a reading of "Frost at Midnight" in the public dialogue, the crucial dates are those of the composition of the volume in late August or early September 1798, when Coleridge first met Joseph Johnson. The dates of the writing of the poem are relatively insignificant, because the purposes of publication are more important than Coleridge's original intentions in drafting the individual poems. To publish, in the 1790's, was inevitably to enter a public debate. In August, when the volume was composed, both author and publisher were under attack from the press and the government. Joseph Johnson, whose name appeared boldly on the title page, had been placed on trial in the Court of the King's Bench and convicted on July 17 for selling Gilbert Wakefield's *A Reply to Some Parts of the Bishop of Llandaff's Address to the People of Great Britain.* His indictment reads in part: "Joseph Johnson late of London bookseller being a malicious seditious and ill-disposed person and being greatly disaffected to our said Lord the King . . . wickedly and seditiously did publish and cause to be published a certain scandalous malicious and seditious libel. . . ." Although he had been found guilty, sentencing was postponed for many months for obvious reasons. At the hearing on his sentence, he would have to produce evidence of his good behavior in any plea for leniency. His sworn statement at the hearing claimed "that where he could take the liberty of doing it, he has uniformly recommended the Circulation of such publications as had a tendency to promote good morals instead of such as were calculated to mislead and inflame the Common people."[1]

Since the end of 1797, Coleridge himself had been under attack in the *Anti-Jacobin,* which began publication as a weekly in November to attack the opposition press. It published on July 9, 1798 a satirical poem called "New Morality, or the promised Installation of the High Priest of the Theophilanthropists," in which Coleridge was ridiculed along with Southey, Charles Lloyd, and Charles Lamb for being both Jacobins and atheists, followers of the French deist La Réveillère Lépeaux, a member of the Directory, who proposed replacing Christianity with a form of Deism called Theophilanthropy.

behold . . .

The Directorial Lama, Sovereign Priest—
Lepaux—whom Atheists worship—at whose nod
Bow their meek heads—the Men without a God.
Ere Long, perhaps, to this astonished Isle,
Fresh from the Shores of subjugated Nile.
Shall Buonaparte's victor Fleet protect
The genuine Theo-philanthropic Sect—
The Sect of Marat, Mirabeau, Voltaire,
Led by their Pontiff, good La Reveillere.
Rejoiced our Clubs shall greet him, and install

The holy hunch-back in thy Dome, St. Paul
While Countless votaries thronging in his train
Wave their Red Caps, and hymn this jocund strain.

(ll. 314–28)

On August first James Gillray published an elaborate caricature of the worshippers of Lépeaux based on the poem. At one side is the figure of Lépeaux based on the poem. At one side is the figure of Lépeaux, standing on a footstool preaching to a group of votaries which includes three dwarfs holding copies of the *Morning Post*, the *Courier*, and the *Morning Chronicle*. Behind Lépeaux are three allegorical figures of starving Justice with a raised dagger, Philanthropy squeezing the earth with a deathly embrace, and Sensibility with what appears to be a bleeding heart. Facing Lépeaux is a Cornucopia of Ignorance, from which flows a torrent of pamphlets and journals, two of which are being read by asses and carry the titles "Southey's Saphics" and "Coleridge's Dactylics." Lamb and Lloyd appear in a corner as a frog and toad croaking from a volume called "Blank Verse by Toad and Frog" (I do not know who is toad and who is frog). It is clear from both text and caricature that Southey and Coleridge were the most important Jacobin poets. Wordsworth and Blake were, of course, nowhere to be seen. Thus a volume apparently presenting simultaneously the author and publisher of "Fears in Solitude" as both patriots and Christians would tend to take the heat off both. The volume would be a public defense against attacks upon both that had been made merely weeks before the volume was composed.

The public debate that the volume entered was composed of a rhetoric of purposeful duplicity, distortion, and personal attack, and Coleridge was constantly in the sights of the *Anti-Jacobin,* which contains many attacks on him although often Coleridge is not mentioned by name. One of its major aims was to expose the errors in the liberal press, which it ranged under three categories: lies, misrepresentations and mistakes. Its Prospectus promised to present "Lies of the Week: the downright, direct, unblushing falsehoods, which have no colour or foundation whatever, and which at the very moment of their being written, have been known to the writer to be wholly destitute of truth." Yet its own rhetoric was that of parody and distortion. The early numbers contained essays on Jacobin poetry, whose major targets were Southey and Coleridge. In its number for December 18 it included a parody of Southey's "The Soldier's Wife: Dactylics." First, Southey's poem printed from his *Poems* of 1797.

Weary way-wanderer languid and sick at heart,
Traveling painfully over the rugged road,
Wild-visag'd Wanderer! ah for thy heavy chance!

Sorely thy little one drags by three bare-footed,
Cold is the baby that hangs at thy bending back,
Meagre and livid and screaming its wretchedness.

* Woe-begone mother, half anger, half agony,
   As over thy shoulder thou lookest to hush the babe,

* This stanza was supplied by S. T. Coleridge.

The *Anti-Jacobin*'s parody is prefaced by the following comment: "Being the quintessence of all the Dactylics that ever were, or ever will be written."

> Wearisome Sonnetteer, feeble and querulous,
> Painfully dragging out thy demo-cratic lays—
> Moon-stricken Sonnetteer, "ah! for thy heavy chance!"
>
> Sorely thy Dactylics lag on uneven feet:
> Slow is the Syllable which thou wouldst urge to speed,
> Lame and o'erburthen'd and "screaming its wretchedness!"

The next stanza, indicated only by a lines of asterisks, is omitted with the following note: "My worthy friend, the Bellman, had promised to supply an additional Stanza but the business of assisting the Lamp-lighter, Chimney-sweeper, &c with Complimentary Verses for their worthy Masters and Mistresses, pressing on him at this Season, he was obliged to decline it." The Bellman is, of course, Coleridge, who had published *The Watchman,* and the reference to the lamp-lighter may be an allusion to the practice of the French Revolutionaries of hanging their victims on lamp posts.

Not only was Coleridge's poetry parodied in the *Anti-Jacobin,* but his journalism was ridiculed as well. An article in the *Morning Post* for February 24, recently identified as Coleridge's by David Erdman in his edition of *Essays on His Times,* was quoted in the *Anti-Jacobin* on March 5. Coleridge had written that "The insensibility with which we now hear of the most extraordinary Revolutions is a very remarkable symptom of the public temper, and no unambiguous indication of the state of the times. We now read with listless unconcern of events which, but a very few years ago, would have filled all Europe with astonishment." The *Anti-Jacobin* quoted this passage with some errors and commented: "Where he found this 'insensibility,' we know not unless among the Patriots of the Corresponding Society;—for our parts, we have a very lively feeling of the transaction [the entry of the French armies into Rome], which for perfidy and inhumanity, surpasses whatever we have yet seen or heard of." Later in his article Coleridge had written "In the midst of these stupendous revolutions, the Nobility, Gentry, and Proprietors of England, make no efforts to avert that ruin from their own heads, which they daily see falling on the same classes of men in neighbouring countries." The *Anti-Jacobin* sniffed in response to this: "Never, probably, in any period, in any Country, were such efforts made, by the very descriptions of men this worthy tool of Jacobinism has pointed out as making no exertions."

In March and April 1793 government pressure upon dissent forced the radical press to become more circumspect and duplicitous in its rhetoric. When Coleridge published "France: An Ode" as "The Recantation" in the *Morning Post,* Daniel Stuart's editorial policy had been shifting against French militarism. Coleridge's ode was prefaced by this note: "The following excellent Ode will be in unison with the feelings of every friend to Liberty and foe to Oppression: of all, who admiring the French Revolution, detest and deplore the conduct of France toward Switzerland." As David Erdman says in his introduction to *Essays on His Times,* "Both editor and poet, in their different ways, recanted while saying that they did not, and oscillated more than they recanted" (*EOT,* I, lxxxi). One week after Coleridge's "Recantation" was published, the *Anti-Jacobin* gloated that the *Morning*

Post "has wisely shrunk from our severity, reformed its Principles in some material points, and in more than one of its last columns, held language which the Whig Club and Corresponding Society will not soon forgive" and concluded "If we could but cure this Paper of its inveterate habits of Lying and Swearing, and give it a few notions of *meum* and *tuum,* we should not despair of seeing it one day an English Opposition Paper."

The *Anti-Jacobin,* however, could claim only some of the credit for the changes of the *Morning Post.* The government had turned up the heat on the paper. The occasion of the government pressure, and the occasion of Coleridge's "Fears in Solitude," as Erdman recounts it, was the arrest on March 1 of John Binns, of the London Corresponding Society and two members of the United Irishmen. They were apparently in possession of papers proposing a French invasion of Ireland. Within a week the *Morning Post* printed accounts of the arrest, and Daniel Stuart was summoned before the ministers to reveal his sources of information. Stuart's editorial policy became more cautious. In these instances the dialogue into which Coleridge's poems enter is conducted by the affirmations and denials, the accusations and defenses, and the distortions and misrepresentations in the continuing battle between the liberal papers and the *Anti-Jacobin.* The early attacks against Coleridge did not mention him by name. Some readers, of course, would have recognized that Coleridge was the Bellman in the parody of Southey's "The Soldier's Wife." It would have been more obvious that the *Morning Post* was responding to various pressures in the shift of its editorial policy and, since Coleridge signed "France: An Ode" with his own name, that he was a part of the shift. But the shift was not his alone.

"Fears in Solitude," which was written at the same time as this exchange between the *Morning Post* and the *Anti-Jacobin,* returns the accusations about the rhetoric of public discourse. "Lying and Swearing" were not confined to the liberal press. While Coleridge's poem attacks Britain for slavery, greed, and war fever, its major theme is the violation of the ninth commandment against baring false witness, which he called "one scheme of perjury." In the Sixth Lecture on Revealed Religion, Coleridge had anticipated these complaints by arguing of government itself that

> There is scarcely a Vice which Government does not teach us—criminal prodigality and an unholy Splendor surrounds it—disregard of solemn Promises marks its conduct—and more than half of the business of Ministers is to find inducements to Perjury! Nay of late it has become the fashion to keep wicked and needy men in regular Pay, who without scruple take the most awful oaths in order to gain the confidence which it is their Trade to betray.[2]

Coleridge's immediate target of criticism here is the abuse of the system of government spies, from which he was later to suffer himself, and the bribery of witnesses in criminal cases, but his complaints are resonant of the agitation against the Test Acts which predates the Revolution. Thus both Coleridge and the *Anti-Jacobin* agreed that political dialogue was conducted by duplicity. The truth of duplicity was adopted by both parties.

Perhaps the cruelest attack upon Coleridge came in 1799 when the satirical poems from the *Anti-Jacobin* were republished with a note that Coleridge has "left his country, become a citizen of the world, left his little ones fatherless, and his wife destitute." Most likely, this is an intentional echo of the accusations made against Rousseau, who ignored and disavowed his natural children. In *The Friend* for June 8, 1809 Coleridge answers these accusations:

> Again, will any man, who loves his Children and his Country, be slow to pardon me, if not in the spirit of vanity but of natural self-defence against yearly and monthly attacks on the very vitals of my character as an honest man and a loyal Subject, I prove the utter falsity of the charges by the only public means in my power, a citation from the last work published by me, in the close of the year 1798, and anterior to all the calumnies published to my dishonor.[3]

Coleridge then includes a lengthy quotation from "Fears in Solitude." Since he cited the "Fears in Solitude" volume in his defense in 1809, it seems reasonable to me to think that he thought of it in the same way in 1798. If, indeed, Coleridge's self-defense began in 1798 and not later when he had changed his political allegiances, his later self-defense must be regarded in a different light. His self-defense in 1798 was not, as it later appeared, an effort to change the record to cover up his youthful radicalism, to rewrite his youth, but rather it was a necessary self-defense, done at the moment of pressure from both the press and the government, and done in concert with others who themselves were under similar pressure.

That Coleridge's volume was designed to answer criticisms of himself and Johnson is confirmed by the first notices printed in the *Analytic Review* (Dec. 1798), which was published by Johnson: "Mr. C., in common with many others of the purest patriotism, has been slandered with the appellation of an enemy to his country. The following passage [from "Fears in Solitude"], we presume, will be sufficient to wipe away the injurious stigma, and show that an adherence to the measures of the administration is not the necessary consequence of an ardent love for the constitution." Of "Frost at Midnight" the reviewer said that the poem does "great honour to the poet's feelings, as the husband of an affectionate wife, and as the father of a cradled infant." The review might almost be considered the official publisher's interpretation of the volume, like the puffs we all conspire to write today. The publisher reads the author as a patriot, who can prove that he is a patriot because he is not an atheist. "Fears in Solitude" calls upon his countrymen to rise and defeat the impious French. "France: An Ode" deplores French aggression while retaining admiration for the Revolution. And "Frost at Midnight" concludes with six lines that were later deleted. The "silent icicles" will shine to the moon

> Like those, my babe! which, ere to-morrow's warmth
> Have capp'd their sharp keen points with pendulous drops,
> Will catch thine eye, and with their novelty
> Suspend thy little soul: then make thee shout,
> And stretch and flutter from thy mother's arms
> As thou would'st fly for very eagerness.

The public and dialogic significance of "Frost at Midnight" in the fall of 1798 was that it presented a patriotic poet, whose patriotism rested on the love of his country and his domestic affections. Coleridge specifically instructed Johnson to send a copy of the volume to his brother, the Reverend George Coleridge. As the reviewer in the *Monthly Review* (May 1799) put it, "Frost at Midnight" displays "a pleasing picture of virtue and content in a cottage," hardly a penetrating critical comment of interest to us in these days of deconstruction and hermeneutics, until one recognizes that the word "content" implies the negation of its opposite. Coleridge is not discontent, not ill-disposed to the existing state of society; he is not, therefore, seditious.

Considering the political intentions of the volume, intentions that were present in 1798 and not constructed later to hide a youthful radicalism, is it possible to draw conclusions about Coleridge's political principles and ideology as they appeared in the public discourse in 1798? Isn't the public dialogue that "Frost at Midnight" enters full of duplicity? Does not the volume intend to present Coleridge both as a loyal patriot who loves his country and as a devoutly religious man, on the one hand, and on the other as one who continues to support the ideals of liberty that he has always held? The evidence of the volume along with the letter that Coleridge sent to his brother George in March that he had "snapped [his] squeaking baby-trumpet of Sedition" (*CL*, I, 397) suggest that the invasion of Switzerland and government pressure upon Stuart had forced him to change his views. In this private letter he announces that

> I deprecate the moral & intellectual habits of those men both in England & France, who have modestly assumed to themselves the exclusive title of Philosophers & Friends of Freedom. I think them at least as distant from greatness as from goodness. If I know my own opinions, they are utterly untainted with French Metaphysics, French Politics, French Ethics, & French Theology. (*CL*, I, 395)

Considering Coleridge's 1795 Lectures, this comment is less of an apology or an announcement of new views as it is a confirmation of his original positions. In the same letter he comments upon his public persona:

> I am prepared to suffer without discontent the consequences of my follies & mistakes —: and unable to conceive how that which I am, of Good could have been without that which I have been of Evil, it is withheld from me to regret any thing: I therefore consent to be deemed a Democrat & a Seditionist. A man's character follows him long after he has ceased to deserve it . . . (*CL*, I, 397)

At the same time that Coleridge claims to have converted to being a loyalist, he admits willingness to be considered a democrat and seditionist. In part, the volume *Fears in Solitude* wants to have it both ways. Its author as a public figure is both a friend of liberty and a loyal patriot.

At the same time that he seemed to recant his former praise of the French Revolution, he continued to publish poems in the *Morning Post* expressing some sympathy with France. For instance on July 30 he published "A Tale," the story of the mad ox, which, as a note explains, represents the French Revolution:

> An ox, long fed on musty hay,
>   And work'd with yoke and chain,
> Was loosen'd on an April day,
> When fields are in their best array,
> And growing grasses sparkle gay
>   At once with sun and rain.

> The grass was sweet, the sun was bright
> > With truth I may aver it;
> The beast was glad, as well he might,
> Thought a green meadow no bad sight,
> And frisk'd,—to show his huge delight,
> > Much like a beast of spirit.

> 'Stop, neighbours, stop, why these alarms?
> > The ox is only glad!'
> But still, they pour from cots and farms—
> 'Hallo!' the parish is up in arms,
> (A hoaxing-hunt has always charms)
> > 'Hallo! the ox is mad.'

The ox is chased through the town:

> The frightened beast ran through the town
> > All follow'd, boy and dad,
> Bull-dog, parson, shopman, clown,
> The publicans rush'd from the Crown,
> 'Halloo! hamstring him! cut him down!
> > They drove the poor ox mad.[4]

The poem concludes with the admission that now the beast of the Revolution is indeed mad and must be controlled, as does "France: An Ode," but the attitude toward the Revolution is quite different. "France: An Ode" had portrayed the Revolution rising like the allegorical figure of wrath, not the animal gladness of the ox:

> When France in wrath her giant limbs uprear'd
> And with that oath which smote earth, air, and sea,
> Stamp'd her strong foot and said, she would be free. . . .

The picture of the ox liberated in gladness and goaded to madness displays both a greater sympathy with France and a liberal attitude which, as Carl Woodring points out, Whigs and Friends of Freedom had held for some time.[5] One wonders at the degree of recantation that has has actually gone on.

The language of politics in Coleridge's dialogue with the reactionary press is tempered to suit the intentions of those who use and abuse it. If Coleridge seems to oscillate and to move easily from side to side, it is in part because his writing was entering a public discourse of duplicity, one in which his works were certain to be misread and mistaken. While the conservatives who attacked him and the other radicals could parade without ambiguity their principles and ideology, the radicals including Coleridge were forced to be more cautious. Coleridge's oscillations could be reread as the acrobatic feat of remaining in the public debates, when other radical voices had been silenced or exiled.

At any given moment and with any given utterance in the public debates, its terms are complex and even contradictory. And because of the surrounding context, each utterance is unique in the complexity of its dialogic significance. For an obvious example, the word "patriotism" is about as ambiguous as one could want.

"Fears in Solitude" was reviewed in the *Analytic* as displaying the "purest patrio-tism." And the *Monthly Review* (May 1799) echoed the evaluation: "Of his country he speaks with a patriotic enthusiasm, and he exhorts to virtue with a Christian's ardor . . . no one can be more desirous of promoting all that is impor-tant to its security and felicity." But what does "patriot" mean? In the first edition of his *Dictionary,* Dr. Johnson defined a patriot as "one whose ruling passion is the love of his country," but in the fourth edition he added a contrary definition: "a factious disturber of the government." A correspondent to the *Anti-Jacobin,* who signed himself "A Batchelor" had his own definition: "By pretty long habit of observation, I have at length arrived at the skill of concluding from a man's politics the nature of his domestic troubles" (Jan. 1, 1798). The inflamed passions and gloomy dispositions of those who are discontent are caused by sexual frustra-tion. The Batchelor concludes that "A Patriot is, generally speaking, a man who has been either a Dupe, a Spendthrift, or a Cuckhold, and, not unfrequently, all-together." Clearly the Batchelor has been reading Swift's *Tale of A Tub* and thinks of a patriot as someone whose height of felicity is being a "fool among knaves" and whose acquisitions include the perpetual "possession of being well deceived," and whose great achievements in new systems and conquests can easily be traced to sexual frustration. Curiously enough, in a somewhat different and Miltonic key, Coleridge agrees with the Batchelor's analysis. In "Fears in Solitude," he accused both radicals and conservatives: "We have been too long / Dupes of a deep delusion." Among those deceived Coleridge includes the radical iconoclasts as well as the conservative idolaters, who demand total submission to the present system of government. The volume thus presents Coleridge as a patriot but what kind of patriot? Both of course, depending which of Coleridge's readers is doing the reading.

Another related, and more complex, set of political keywords surrounds the domestic affections in "Frost at Midnight." Does the love of landscape and family form the basis of a patriotism similar to Burke's or does it lead to a love of all mankind that is characteristic of radical writing? The question of the value of patriotism of this sort enters the public discourse on the French Revolution with Dr. Richard Price's sermon "A Discourse on the Love of our Country, Delivered on November 4, 1789" before the society to "commemorate the Revolution in Great Britain." Price's thesis argues that the love of one's country is not based on "the soil or the spot of earth on which we happen to be born . . . but that community of which we are members . . . who are associated with us under the same constitution of government." He argues that any love of one's own country "does not imply any conviction of the superior value of it to other countries, or any particular preference of its laws and constitution of government." Finally he concludes that "in pursuing particularly the interest of our country, we ought to carry our views beyond it. We should love it ardently, but not exclusively. We ought to seek its good, by all the means that our different circumstances and abilities will allow; but at the same time we ought to consider ourselves as citizens of the world, and take care to maintain a just regard to the rights of other countries. . . ."[6] In response to Dr. Price, Burke's *Reflections on the Revolution in France* countered that the inheritance of monarchy went hand in hand with the inheritance of property, and that the love of one's country and government is bound to the love of one's family:

By a constitutional policy, working after the pattern of nature, we receive, we hold, we transmit our government and our privileges in the same manner in which we enjoy and transmit our property and our lives. . . . In this choice of inheritance we have given to our frame of polity the image of a relation in blood, binding up the constitution of our country with our dearest domestic ties, adopting our fundamental laws into the bosom of our family affections, keeping inseparable and cherishing with the warmth of all their combined and mutually reflected charities, our states, our hearths, our sepulchres, and our altars. (Butler 40)

In Coleridge's 1795 Introductory Address, he, like Burke, grounds benevolence and patriotism in the domestic affections, but his definition of benevolence as universal is precisely the opposite of Burke's:

The searcher after Truth must love and be beloved, for general Benevolence is a necessary motive to constancy of pursuit; and this general Benevolence is begotten and rendered permanent by social and domestic affections. Let us beware of that proud Philosophy, which affects to inculcate Philanthropy while it denounces every home-born feeling, by which it is produced and nurtured. The paternal and filial duties discipline the heart and prepare it for the love of all mankind. The intensity of private attachments encourages, not prevents, universal Benevolence. (*Lect.* 46)

The thought is repeated in Lecture Three, where it introduces a criticism of Godwin:

Jesus knew our Nature—and that expands like the circles of a Lake—the Love of our Friends, parents, and neighbors lead[s] to a love of our Country to the love of all mankind. The intensity of private attachments encourages, not prevents, universal philanthropy—the nearer we approach to the Sun the more intense his Rays—yet what corner of the System does he not cheer and vivify. (*Lect.* 163)

Coleridge's immediate criticism in these passages is not of Burke, but of Godwin's "proud philosophy" and his indifference to personal and domestic affections. In the next paragraph he ridicules the "Stoical Morality which disclaims all the duties of Gratitude and domestic Affection" and addresses Godwinians (like Thelwall, to whom he used the same words in a private letter): "Severe Moralist! that teaches us that filial Love is a Folly, Gratitude criminal, Marriage Injustice, and a promiscuous Intercourse of the Sexes our wisdom and our duty. In this System a man may gain his self-esteem with little Trouble, he first adopts Principles so lax as to legalize the most impure gratification and then prides himself on acting to his Principles" (*Lect.* 164–65). Coleridge's consistent rejection of materialism, atheism, and the libertinism in liberty separates him from Godwin, Thelwall and other radicals, but that does not mean that his invocation of the domestic affections places him in Burke's camp. For Burke the domestic affections form the basis of the British Constitution, a decidedly national allegiance, while Coleridge views them as the basis of a universal benevolence and a love of all mankind. The *Anti-Jacobin,* not surprisingly, takes Burke's and not Coleridge's position. In "New Morality" Coleridge's image of the sun for the love of mankind is turned against him. The "universal man"

> through the extended globe his feelings run
> As broad and general as th'unbounded Sun!
> No narrow bigot he—his reason'd view
> Thy, interests, England, ranks with thine Peru
> France at our doors, he sees no danger nigh,
> But heaves for Turkey's woes th'impartial sigh;
> A steady Patriot of the World alone,
> The Friend of every Country—but his own.
> (ll. 107–14)

In the eyes of the defenders of tradition and prejudice, Coleridge then should stand in the ranks with Dr. Price and his followers who ask

> What has the love of their country hitherto been among mankind? What has it been but a love of domination; a desire of conquest, and a thirst for grandeur and glory, by extending territory, and enslaving surrounding countries? What has it been but a blind and narrow principle, producing in every country a contempt of other countries, and forming men into combinations and factions against their common rights and liberties . . . ?" (Butler 25–26)

Finally, in the first of the series on Jacobin poetry, the *Anti-Jacobin* ticks off its characteristics:

> The Poet of other times has been an enthusiast in the love of his native soil.

> The Jacobin Poet rejects all restriction in his feelings. His love is enlarged and expanded so as to comprehend all human kind.

> The Old Poet was a Warrior, at least in imagination; and sung the actions of the Heroes of his Country, in strains that 'made Ambition Virtue,' and which overwhelmed the horrors of War in its glory.

> The Jacobin Poet would have no objection to sing battles too—but he would make a distinction. The prowess of Buonaparte indeed he might chaunt in his loftiest strain of exultation. There we should find nothing but trophies, and triumphs, and branches of laurel and olive, phalanxes of Republicans shouting Victory, satellites of Despotism biting the ground and geniuses of Liberty planting standards on mountain-tops.

"Frost at Midnight" as a portrait of the domestic affections enters this debate in 1798, but how was it possible for a reader in 1798 to know whether what the *Monthly Review* called this "pleasing picture of virtue and content in a cottage" reflects the ideology of Price, or Burke, or Coleridge, or Lépeaux, or Paine, or Priestley, or Bishop Berkeley? Is the public Coleridge the Watchman, the Bellman, or the lamp-lighter, the patriot or the Jacobin, a Christian or a theophilanthropist? Coleridge's and Johnson's friends would have read the "content in a cottage" as portraying the domestic affections as the ground for universal benevolence. Coleridge clearly hoped that his brother would have read it in an opposite way, as a rejection of sedition and atheism. The *Critical Review* (Aug. 1799) wouldn't buy it at all: "But those who conceive that Mr. Coleridge has, in these poems, recanted his former principles, should consider the general tenor of them. The following passage is not written in conformity with the fashionable opinions of the day," and then the reviewer quotes from "Fears in Solitude." The *Anti-Jacobin* may have read the references in "Frost at Midnight" to the "eternal language, which thy God / Utters" as an allusion to Paine's *Age of Reason:* "The Word of God is the creation we behold: And it is this word . . . that God speaketh universally to man" (*Lect.* 95n). In 1799, when the *Anti-Jacobin* republished "New Morality" it included a footnote that described Coleridge as "an avowed Deist," which to their Church-and-King crowd meant that Coleridge was an atheist and a follower of Paine. Combined with their ungenerous note about his going to Germany and leaving his family destitute, the note interprets Coleridge as a Jacobin in the camp of Rousseau, Godwin, and Paine.

These issues of patriotism, content, and domestic affections have little to do with the facts of biography. They are parts of a crucial political struggle, keywords in an ideological debate. Their various meanings existed long before Coleridge wrote "Frost at Midnight," and when he did write it, he was certainly aware of their meanings, because he himself had contributed to the debate as early as 1795. To put it another way, Coleridge's references to the domestic affections had nothing to do with his own domestic affections and everything to do with the public discourse. The language of "Frost at Midnight" in 1798 is the creation of that public discourse, not the creation of private circumstances or private meditation. "Frost at Midnight" is a private poem with public meanings because it has a public location. Its language is defined by the rhetoric of public oratory, not the rhetoric of symbolism and allegory, a language that takes its significance from the allusiveness of the dialogue, not from the referentiality of its figures. Since it was placed in 1798 in the public dialogue, it cannot represent rural retirement as an evasion of political issues, although it is certainly evasive. Nor does it represent a desire to escape from history. Rather, by becoming public, it enters history because it enters the debates that constitute history and that motivate action. It is not the private meditation of an isolated consciousness, but the testimony of a public figure. "Frost at Midnight" is a poem that is changed by its public context.

How would "Frost at Midnight" be read with this context in mind? In traditional symbolic readings the images and figures are explicated, first of all, by reference to other figures in the poem itself and perhaps by reference to Coleridge's other poems or philosophical writings. In the form of dialogic reading that I am suggesting, the images are glossed by their meanings within the public discourse and its political language. If this method is to have any value, it should have a practical effect on the readings of poems, yet all I can do here is to suggest some significantly different readings of portions of the poem that the context provides. The reference to "abstruser musings" becomes a problem. In a symbolic reading Coleridge is alone in his cottage in the silence of the night quite removed from the intrusive presence of sensible activity and permitted to think philosophically about the activity of nature, the ministry of frost and its ultimate cause and purpose. Yet in the public context "abstruse" thinking sounds suspiciously like the kind of abstraction and metaphysics that Burke saw as part of the origin of the Revolution: "I cannot stand forward and give praise or blame to any thing which relates to human actions, and human concerns, on a simple view of the object, as it stands stripped of every relation, in all the nakedness and solitude of metaphysical abstraction" (Butler 8). What after all could Coleridge be thinking about so abstrusely?

He is vexed and disturbed with the extreme calm, a calm that indicates its opposite, activity and audible language. In a symbolic reading of the poem, the language of nature troubles him, and he wishes to be able to read that language symbolically, but his phrase "the numberless goings on of life" signifies that the vitality of natural and human life is indistinct. But "Frost at Midnight" is preceded by two political poems that worry specifically about war and invasion. In the context of those poems, how could the phrase mean anything else but the present political anxieties. Within the poem itself the "numberless goings on of life" are asserted to be present in "Sea, hill and wood"—the elements of nature; but in the context of the first two poems, the potential invasion by sea changes the reference of the phrase.

Why is not the relation between the calm and the vexation in "Frost at Midnight" the same as it is at the beginning of "Fears in Solitude" when calm and retired solitude turns abruptly to thoughts of war: "it is a melancholy thing / For such a man, who would full fain preserve / His soul in calmness, yet perforce must feel / For all his brethren." "Fears in Solitude" concludes with a return to calm that provides a location for continued thoughts of human sympathy:

> O green and silent dell!
> And grateful, that by nature's quietness
> And solitary musings all my heart
> Is soften'd, and made worthy to indulge
> Love, and the thoughts that yearn for human kind.

If one reads the entire volume of "Fears in Solitude" as a single composition, why are not the "abstruser musings" of "Frost at Midnight" precisely the same as the "solitary musings" that conclude "Fears in Solitude?" If the two are the same, and if the thoughts of humanity and universal benevolence at the end of "Fears in Solitude" remain with Coleridge throughout the volume, then the "abstruser musings" of Frost at Midnight" may well be precisely the kind of thinking that Burke feared.

Let me select one more example of an important phrase that becomes richer because of the context. Toward the end of the poem Coleridge hopes that Hartley will be able to "see and hear / The lovely shapes and sounds intelligible / Of that eternal language, which thy God / Utters. . . ." God is the "Great Universal Teacher." But whose universality are we talking about? My preferred traditional answer is that Coleridge is alluding to the divine visible language of nature that Bishop Berkeley writes about in *Alciphron* and to which Coleridge himself alludes in a note to "This Lime-Tree Bower" when he explains to Southey that "I am a Berkleyan:"

the great Mover and Author of nature constantly explaineth Himself to the eyes of men by the sensible intervention of arbitrary signs, which have no similitude or connexion with the things signified; so as, by compounding and disposing them, to suggest and exhibit an endless variety of objects differing in nature, time, and place; thereby informing and directing men how to act with respect to things distant and future, as well as near and present. In consequence, I say, of your own sentiments and concessions you have as much reason to think the Universal Agent or God speaks to your eyes, as you can have for thinking any particular person speaks to your ears.[7]

For the purposes of my contrast, it is a matter of some indifference whether other traditional readers might wish to quote Spinoza or Priestley as the source of Coleridge's lines. If the poem is located within a political context, universality becomes a problem. What is the universal teacher teaching? The works of Tom Paine or the works of Edmund Burke?

In his review of the *Biographia,* Hazlitt said of Coleridge's political writings: "His style, in general, admits of a convenient latitude of interpretation."[8] With some modification Hazlitt's words can be used to conclude. Coleridge's latitude wasn't merely convenient; it was necessary. If Coleridge was dodging, it was because the heat was on him, and his associates Stuart and Johnson, from the government and the hostile press. As we know, it is common for those who try to maintain opposition in times of repression to speak in a kind of double talk; it is the nature of public discourse. The latitude that Hazlitt observed does more than measure the poles of his political oscillations. It also describes a field of possible contexts in which his poetic and political utterances were received and read, the contexts that determined how they would be read, and the context that determined the dialogic significance of "Frost at Midnight" in 1798.

NOTES

1. Quoted in Gerald P. Tyson, *Joseph Johnson: A Liberal Publisher* (Iowa, 1979) 159–61.

2. *Lectures On Politics and Religion,* ed. Lewis Patton and Peter Mann (Princeton and London, 1971) 221, hereafter abbreviated *Lect.*

3. *Biographia Literaria,* ed. James Engell and W. Jackson Bate (Princeton and London, 1983) I: 68n; *The Friend,* ed. Barbara Rooke (Princeton and London, 1969) II: 23.

4. "A Tale," later reprinted as "Recantation: Illustrated in the Story of the Mad Ox," is here reprinted with the corrections listed in David Erdman's "Unrecorded Coleridge Variants," *Studies in Bibliography* 11 (1958): 154.

5. Carl Woodring, *Politics in the Poetry of Coleridge* (Wisconsin, 1961), 141.

6. Marilyn Butler, ed., *Burke, Paine, Godwin and the Revolution Controversy* (Cambridge, 1984) 25–6. Peter Swaab spoke on some of these same issues in his talk "Wordsworth and Patriotism" at the Wordsworth Summer Conference, July 1990.

7. *Berkeley: Essay, Principles, Dialogues,* ed. Mary Whiton Calkins (New York, 1929) 370.

8. "Coleridge's Literary Life," *The Complete Works of William Hazlitt,* ed. P. P. Howe (London, 1930–34) 16:129.

Literary Gentlemen and Lovely Ladies: The Debate on the Character of Christabel

This selection might well be considered the second half of Swann's companion essay, "*Christabel:* The Wandering Mother and the Enigma of Form" (1984), which focuses more on analysis of the poem in itself. Our selection, however, illustrates how some recent critics, particularly those with a feminist orientation, have begun to utilize detailed analyses of poems' receptions to bring to light the socially determined ambitions and anxieties that went into their creation. Swann is particularly interested in how Coleridge's self-conscious play with elements of popular sensationalism, most familiar in "Gothic" romance, evoked from sophisticated readers of his time "hysterical" responses. Those responses, Swann shows, reveal the unstable socio-intellectual situation into which '*Christabel*' entered, a situation that reflected the ambiguous relation of "serious" and "popular" literature, in which the empowered establishment defended its position by condemning generic impurity as gender impropriety. This defense, however, betrays the vulnerability of the critical arbiters.

Swann's essay is representative of younger critics' mode of attack on problems of the material, historical circumstances in which romantic poems came into being. These critics readily deploy psychoanalystic insights into how individuals and their social milieus are mutually self-creating to explore the social significance of the textual instabilities on which deconstructionists have fastened attention. Swann thus perceives romantic audiences' overreactions as revelatory of Coleridge's daring/fearful exploration into the relation "of cultural processes" and (fantasized) "feminine erotic experience." So here a "feminist" criticism is scarcely identifiable as such, because it has evolved so far from any limited polemical origins, but without losing its power to establish radically new perspectives on familiar materials.

Often when Coleridge discusses *Christabel*, his poem becomes a lady whose character needs protecting or explaining. In April 1803, writing to Sara Coleridge from London, he boasts of Sotheby's interest in the poem:

> To day I dine again with Sotheby. He ha[s] informed me, that ten gentlemen, who have met me at his House, desired him to solicit me to finish the Christabel, & to

From *ELH* 52, no. 2 (Summer 1985): 397–418.

permit them to publish it for me/ & they engaged that it should be in paper, printing, & decorations the most magnificent Thing that had hitherto appeared.—Of course, I declined it. The lovely Lady shan't come to that pass!—Many times rather would I have it printed at Soulby's on the true Ballad Paper/—[1]

Refusing Sotheby and the ten gentlemen, Coleridge stands on his literary principles: a ballad is a popular form, and it would be politically and aesthetically inappropriate to publish one in a guinea volume. But with a shift symptomatic of his and his critics' writing on *Christabel,* he frames the genre question in the poem's own terms, playfully casting its *literary* character as a *feminine* character. Posing as a Baron-like protector of maiden innocence, he asserts that his *Christabel* shall not become a Geraldine, making up in "magnificence" for what she has lost in honest virtue.

The Baron is not the only role Coleridge plays here. His soliciting "ten gentlemen" recall Geraldine's "five ruffians," the anonymous and plural abductors who eventually deposit her under Christabel's tree. Like the story Geraldine tells to Christabel, Coleridge's tale is itself a solicitation, an attempt to convince Sara that this latest flight from home has yielded professional if not financial returns. He simply plays his enchantress as a flirt—a heartless flirt, one might add, noticing the way he flaunts his power to attract monied gentlemen. He leads Sara to hope for his capitulation, then drops her flat with his protest that a lady's good character cannot be bought; he charms her with a glimpse of a world from which she is excluded—a world where gentlemen make deals and dine together, and where *he* is attractive because he possesses a certain "lovely Lady." Despite what he tells his wife about the lady's good character and his own honorable intentions, Coleridge is toying here with the unstable, charming character of *Christabel.*

This essay addresses the question of *Christabel's* generic status. Coleridge's letter to Sara Coleridge might seem at best a negative example of how to go about such an inquiry: defining the proper literary form of his poem, Coleridge quite improperly comes under the sway of its fictional content, conflating the poem with its "lovely Lady," and incorporating that feminine character into the dramas of real life. This negative example, however, is also a good example of his and his contemporaries' habitual ways of writing about *Christabel.* When the poem was finally published in 1816, its reviewers attacked it on literary grounds, declaring it an improper *kind* of poem. Their terms, however, had more to do with gender than genre: the lady, they declared, was immodest and improper, and its author, not simply "unmanly," but an "enchanted virgin," a "witch," and an "old nurse."

My analysis of the debate on *Christabel's* character will dwell on the poem's peripheries. The first two sections of this essay explore Coleridge's references to his poem's disturbingly ambiguous status and his reviewers' scandalized responses to the poem. I propose that men of letters reacted hysterically to *Christabel* because they saw the fantastic exchanges of Geraldine and Christabel as dramatizing a range of problematically invested literary relations, including those between writers and other writers, and among authors, readers, and books. By feminizing the problem critical discourse on *Christabel* both played out and displaced the excessive charges of these literary relations: it cast impropriety as *generic* impurity, and then identified this impurity with dangerously attractive feminine forms—the licentious body of Geraldine, and more generally, of the poem *Christabel.* The final sections of the essay argue that the feminization of the terms of the debate on *Christabel* repeats, in an exemplary way, a strategy habitually adopted by high culture when defending its privileges. *Christabel* can be located in the context of Coleridge's writings on a variety of ghostly exchanges between observers or readers and representations. Coleridge's thinking about perception suggests that what is at stake in these exchanges is the identity and autonomy of the subject in relation to cultural forms; a footnote to the *Biographia Literaria* on circulating library fare indicates that it is ladies' literature—the derogated genres of romantic fiction—which conventionally represents this threat in the discourse of literary gentlemen. *Christabel*'s connections with Gothic romance account for the conventionality of the critics' responses to the poem; its exposure of their hysterical defenses accounts for its exemplary power among Coleridge's poems of the supernatural.

I

Perhaps Coleridge's only uncontroversial definition of *Christabel*'s literary character is in chapter 14 of the *Biographia Literaria,* where he classifies the poem with others whose "incidents and agents were to be, in part at least, supernatural."[2] But his intention here is to lay old controversies to rest, and his emphases are on harmony—disquietingly so. According to him, the idea of the *Lyrical Ballads* presented itself to two minds working as one—mutually possessed minds, if we care to edge his description toward the concerns of *Christabel:* "The thought suggested itself (to which of us I do not recollect) that a series of poems might be composed of two sorts." Describing his and Wordsworth's respective tasks, Coleridge implies that the difference between the two collaborators hardly amounts to more than an accident of light or shade: his poems were to give a "semblance of truth" to supernatural incidents, while Wordsworth's would "give the charm of novelty to things of every day" and thus "excite a feeling analogous to the supernatural." "With this view," he continues, "I wrote 'The Ancient Mariner,' and was preparing among other poems, 'The Dark Ladie,' and the 'Christabel,' in which I should have more nearly realized my ideal, than I had done in my first attempt." If in the end his poems came to seem like "heterogeneous" material, the reasons were purely circumstantial: "But Mr. Wordsworth's industry had proved so much more successful . . . that my compositions, instead of forming a balance, appeared rather an interpolation of heterogeneous matter" (*BL,* 2:6).

Several chapters later, though, Coleridge hedges on *Christabel*'s character and charges the poem with introducing discord into his life. Although professing surprise that a work which "pretended to be nothing more than a common Faery Tale" should have excited such "disproportionate" responses, he himself clearly attaches "disproportionate" significance to *Christabel*. His account of the "literary men" who "[took] liberties" with it before it went on "common sale" but failed to defend it in 1816 identifies that date as a major divide: whereas in the past "[he] did not know or believe that [he] had an enemy in the world," now he must reproach himself "for being too often disposed to ask,—Have I one friend?" (*BL,* 2:210–11). Pointing to the date of *Christabel*'s publication as a great rupture in his life, Coleridge plays a role he had created more than sixteen years before—the Baron, betrayed into solitude by "whispering tongues [that] poison truth."

Actually, from the very beginning Coleridge had difficulty keeping *Christabel* in proportion—or rather, he was always happy to exaggerate its proportions. Already by 1799 he was casting it as controversial, disruptive of generic categories and collaborative efforts alike. *Christabel* would be an "improper opening poem" for that year's *Annual Register,* he explains to Southey:

> My reason is—it cannot be expected to please all/ Those who dislike it will deem it extravagant Ravings, & go on thro' the rest of the Collection with the feeling of Disgust—& it is not impossible that were it liked by any, it would still not harmonize with the *real-life* Poems that follow. (*CL,* 1:545)

Whatever *Christabel*'s character here, it is emphatically *not* the decorous, modest character of a "true ballad," nor the "common" character of a "Faery Tale," nor yet the character of a poem of the supernatural, if the latter is meant to "balance" with the poems of real life.

This hyperbolic account of the poem's reception is of course more indicative of Coleridge's extravagance than *Christabel*'s—he is amusing Southey at the expense of an overnice reading public, and lightening with bluster a tacit admission that *Christabel* will not be ready in time for the *Annual Register.* His remarks were prophetic, however, not only of the poem's reception in 1816, but also, of Wordsworth's response to it in 1800, when after the second edition of the *Lyrical Ballads* had already gone to press he decided to pull *Christabel* from the volume.[3] The *Biographia* account of the great collaborative project suppresses *Christabel*'s role in its disintegration—*Christabel* was the poem that made Wordsworth realize that the poetry of real life and the poetry of the supernatural do not "balance." Explaining his decision to Longman & Rees, Wordsworth emphasizes the "impropriety" of including a poem that does not harmonize with the others: "A Poem of Mr. Coleridge's was to have concluded the Volumes; but upon mature deliberation, I found that the Style of this Poem was so discordant from my own that it could not be printed along with my poems with any propriety" (q. in *CL,* 1:643). His words fulfill Coleridge's predictions of 1799, and contradict the *Biographia*'s explanation of Coleridge's "heterogeneity"—*quality,* not quantity, makes his work discordant.

Wordsworth's tone—his defensive or exasperated emphases on *mature* deliberation," "*so* discordant," "*any* propriety"—hints at personal as well as literary differences between the two men; perhaps 1800, not 1816, was the year that *Christabel* was instrumental in sundering friendships. In contrast, Coleridge's account of the same event tempers personal discord. It also produces some strange, Christabellian effects. Writing to Josiah Wedgewood shortly after the decision, Coleridge seems to parrot Wordsworth's accusation of "discordancy": *Christabel* was "discordant in its character" with the *Lyrical Ballads,* he explains. At the same time, he bestows a character of generosity on his friend and vicarious praise on himself by passing on Wordsworth's extravagant appreciation of the poem's excellencies: "My poem grew so long & in Wordsworth's opinion so impressive, that he rejected it from his volume as disproportionate both in size & merit"— sentiments so discordant with Wordsworth's letter to Longman that we suspect Wordsworth of speaking them under compulsion, or Coleridge of putting words into his friend's mouth (*CL,* 1:643).

Although Coleridge's claims about his poem generally address its literary improprieties, a measure of its extravagance would seem to be its capacity to disrupt the boundaries between literature, commentary, and real life. Asserting *Christabel*'s problematic literary status, Coleridge conflates the poem with the extravagant, ambiguous Geraldine, the character *in* the poem who excites desire and disgust, and introduces discord into apparently harmonious circles; describing the poem's origin in a collaborative endeavor and its receptions in 1800 and 1816, he produces muted versions of *Christabel*'s story of an uncanny exchange and a friendship "rent asunder," and recreates, in the register of his own telling, the slippages of identity that mark the exchanges of Geraldine and Christabel. Reading Coleridge's accounts of *Christabel,* we begin to feel that all the characters involved—the "literary gentlemen" through whom he ventriloquizes his fluctuating, extravagant responses to his poem, the poem he employs as a go-between in his extravagant relations with other gentlemen, and the figure of the author, who appears by turns as the Baron and an enchantress—acquire the curious status of Geraldine, a figure from fantasy or dream who intrudes into daytime existence.[4]

Like all uncanny effects, Coleridge's apparent possession by *Christabel* is a motivated and gainful loss of control, allowing him to perform, domesticate, and manipulate the charged relations of his literary life. His strategy is most overtly one of domestication, of course, when he casts his poem as a woman—as a "lovely Lady" whose character must be defended, as the "other woman" in his sparring with Sara Coleridge, or as a doubtful character with whom gentlemen "take liberties." The lady becomes the locus of rhetorical and erotic play, when, disarmingly, Coleridge figures his lapses of authorial control as capitulations to extravagant femininity, or renders the exchanges of poems among literary gentlemen as the movements of a scandalous woman from man to man. *Christabel* circulates licentiously, captivating readers and tainting its author with its femininity. Flaunting his poem's impropriety, but coyly withholding it from "common sale," he presents himself as both master and possessor of its charms.

Even Coleridge's more hysterical performances with *Christabel* figure and control the operations of fantasy in literary life. In an oddly explicit accession to the poem's femininity he becomes its mother, in 1801 producing the second part of *Christabel* with "labor-pangs" in competition with Sara's delivery of Derwent: announcing the double event in a letter to James Tobin, he relegates his wife's labors to a postscript (*CL,* 1:623). Later, writing to De Quincey, he associates his poem's publication, its "embodiment in verse," with birth and death: *Christabel* "fell almost dead-born from the Press" (*CL,* 5:162).[5] When he holds it in "suspended animation," however, it has the virulent life of fantasy.[6] Repossessing the poem after Wordsworth rejected it in 1800, Coleridge enacted a possession as lurid and extreme as the enchantments of *Christabel*—an illness he dramatizes in numerous letters to his friends as a hysterical pregnancy. It began with a symbolic castration, inflamed eyes and boils on the scrotum;[7] the next "9 dreary months" or more he passed with "giddy head, sick stomach, & swoln knees," his left knee at one point " '*pregnant* with agony' as Mr Dodsley says in one of his poems" (*CL,* 2:745, 748). During one of his "confinements," he reports, "one ugly Sickness has followed another, fast as phantoms before a vapourish Woman" (*CL,* 2:729, 725).[8] Flirting now with actual madness, but still performing the woman for an audience of gentlemen, he figures his strange entanglement with literature as the apparent duplicity of the female body when it is pregnant with child or with the vaporish conception of the "wandering mother" or womb. Inhabiting him as an alien, internal body, his poem constitutes him as a female hysteric who cannot "tell," but can only enact the intrusion of fantasy into real life.

II

Christabel engaged the fantasy lives of more than a narrow circle of literary gentlemen. In 1799, Coleridge imagined his apparently "extravagant Ravings" exciting the equally extravagant response of "Disgust," which he predicted would cling to the reader even after he had finished reading the poem. Urging Coleridge to publish the poem in 1815, Byron attests to its excessive, clinging "hold": "[the poem's details] took a hold on my imagination which I never shall wish to shake off" (q. in *CL*, 4:601). When the poem came out the next year the critics described it as "ravings," hysterically assessing poem and author in a Christabellian vocabulary of dream and possession.[9] Frequently they attribute its strange, singular character to its author's wild confounding of genres, styles, and intentions. *Scourge*, for example, criticizes the poem's blending of "passages of exquisite harmony" with "miserable doggrel"; in a similar vein, the *Augustan Review* complains that "there are many fine things [in the poem] which cannot be extracted, being closely connected with the grossest absurdities" (*RR*, 2:866, 1:36). But the vocabulary of poetic decorum easily becomes the vocabulary of sexual, and particularly feminine, decorum: when *Christabel*'s reviewers protest that "poetry itself must show some modesty," or criticize the poem for merely "affecting" simplicity, they capitalize on that play (*RR*, 1:239–40). Like Coleridge, they hint that *Christabel*'s extravagances are more than rhetorical, and have a peculiarly feminine character.

Moreover, just as in Coleridge's imagined scenes, the extravagant, sexual character of *Christabel* proves to be contagious. In the hands of the critics, the author's poetic license becomes more-than-poetic "licentiousness": "In diction, in numbers, in thought, . . . Mr. Coleridge's licentiousness out-Herod's Herod," the *Champion* protests, while *Farrago* claims that "on no occasion has Mr. Coleridge appeared in so degraded and degenerate a light as in the present publication" (*RR*, 1:269, 2:546). Coleridge's breaches of decorum are not simply "unmanly," they feminize him: his "epithets of endearment, instead of breathing the accents of manly tenderness, are those of the nurse," charges *Scourge;* according to others, he tells an "old woman's story," and is himself acting the part of an "enchanted virgin" or a "witch" (*RR*, 2:866, 1:214, 1:373, 2:531). Reading *Christabel* would seem to draw one into a charmed circle where all the participants have the taint of affected, licentious femininity. Even the poem's real-life readers are feminine, according to the *Anti-Jacobin* reviewer. Professing bewilderment at the poem's success despite the universally scathing reviews, he concludes that the ladies must be responsible: "for what woman of fashion would not purchase a book recommended by Lord Byron" (*RR*, 1:23).

If, pursuing *Christabel*'s character, we ask the critics why *Christabel* became the poem they loved to hate, we might choose William Hazlitt's review in the *Examiner* as our focus; one of the earliest, it set the tone for subsequent notices. From the very first lines of his essay, Hazlitt adopts a strategy of diminishment against *Christabel* and its author. The review begins with some biting comments on the "mastiff bitch," regularly cited by critics as an example of the poem's "doggrel."

Appealing to "gentlemen" to share his contempt for her impotence ("Is she a sort of Cerberus to fright away the critics? But—gentlemen, she is toothless!"), he reduces the poem's impropriety to toothless naughtiness, its author to a buffoon (*RR*, 2:530–31). Then, still on the subject of Coleridge's caprice, he makes a spectacle of withered femininity for a second time. Quoting the scene of Geraldine's undressing, he pauses to supply a missing line:

> The manuscript runs thus, or nearly thus:—
> "Behold her bosom and half her side—
> *Hideous, deformed, and pale of hue.*"

> This line is necessary to make common sense of the first and second part. 'It is the keystone that makes up the arch.' For that reason Mr. Coleridge left it out. Now this is a greater physiological curiosity than even the fragment of *Kubla Khan.*

The "sight to dream of, not to tell" ought simply to be *told*, Hazlitt protests, deploring "Mr. Coleridge"'s power play while trumping him with a line from his own manuscript. The reviewer's quarrel with the author is rendered as a battle for control of Geraldine: the author conceals her bosom from view, and the critic unveils it again. As when he made sport of the "mastiff bitch," Hazlitt implicates poem and author in the fate of the impotent female, reducing the former's obscurity to a transparent mystery, and the latter's motives to a "physiological curiosity," a deformity like Geraldine's.

So far, Hazlitt's tactics have been similar, not just to those he imputes to *his* "Mr. Coleridge," but also to those Coleridge adopts when he uses the poem's feminine subject to domesticate its impropriety, and then employs the poem as a third character in his relations with other literary gentlemen. In the last paragraph of the review, however, *Christabel* threatens to escape its bounds. Here, Hazlitt's description of *Christabel*'s hold on the reader's mind recalls Byron's approbation of the "hold" he "never shall wish to shake off":

> In parts of *Christabel* there is a great deal of beauty, both of thought, imagery, and versification; but the effect of the general story is dim, obscure, and visionary. It is more like a dream than a reality. The mind, in reading it, is spell-bound. The sorceress seems to act without power—*Christabel* to yield without resistance. The faculties are shown into a state of metaphysical suspense and theoretical imbecility.

Hazlitt implies that interpretive mastery involves locating a source of power and meaning in the text. *This* poem, however, is obscure in its treatment of volition, depicting sorceress and victim in mysterious communion. Disclosing a radical complicity between actor and yielder, good and evil, the exchanges between Christabel and Geraldine confound the logical and moral categories the reader attempts to bring to bear on the poem, throwing his faculties into a state of "metaphysical suspense and theoretical imbecility." Thwarted in his effort to interpret, he becomes "bound" passively to imitate the relation between Christabel and Geraldine in his own relation to the story.

Continuing his final remarks about *Christabel*, though, Hazlitt rescues this hypothetical reader from impotence by providing him with a dual focus of moral outrage—an unnamed, unsavory content, "something disgusting at the bottom of the subject," and a willful author at the bottom of it all:

The poet, like the witch in *Spenser,* is evidently

"Busied about some wicked gin."—

But we do not foresee what he will make of it. There is something disgusting at the bottom of his subject, which is but ill glossed over by a veil of Della Cruscan sentiment and fine writing—like moon beams playing on a charnel-house, or flowers strewed on a dead body. Mr. Coleridge's style is essentially superficial, pretty, ornamental, and he has forced it into the service of a story which is petrific.

Many readers of this review, including Coleridge himself, have speculated that Hazlitt has "something" specific in mind here—something he *could* tell, but won't. Rumor has identified him as the source of a scandalous report that Coleridge intended to unmask Geraldine as Christabel's male lover.[10] But significantly, at this point Hazlitt does not band with other "gentlemen" to deride the poem's impropriety as sophomoric naughtiness, nor does he simply identify Geraldine's deformity as the suppressed "keystone" of the poem. Rather, bursting into rhetorical flower at just the moment he purports to descry "something . . . at the bottom" of *Christabel,* he gives the impression that there is more to the poem than is in his or Coleridge's power to declare. In this Gothic scenario, Geraldine's body is not the "keystone" to the poem's obscurity, but a figure of the problem: Hazlitt displaces her character onto both poet and poem, metaphorizing the former as a "witch," and the latter as a veiled, horrific site. "Something" which cannot be figured is "disgusting" or "petrific" "at the bottom" of that site, in the poem's nether regions—"something" which ought to be well hidden, but is only "ill glossed over." Hazlitt's rhetoric suggests that he is now seeing the poem, not as a woman who has been or could be had, but as a potent figure of castration, a Medusa. His "scandalous" rumor, then, is a subterfuge masking the *real* scandal of *Christabel*—that Geraldine is a woman.

But Hazlitt, who put down these clues, may have prepared a trap. Certainly, the movement of the whole paragraph suggests that this melodramatic scene of a horrific, buried "something" is a feint. For it follows an acknowledgment that there is *nothing* "at the bottom" of *Christabel*—no single source of power or significance: "The sorceress seems to act without power; *Christabel* to yield without resistance." This "nothing" is not the lack psychoanalysis allots to women, but a strange overdetermination which creates disturbances in the register of metaphysics as well as sexuality. Hazlitt suggests that the obscure and compelling logic of *Christabel,* effecting displacements of identity and power which reveal the affinity of apparent opposites, is the logic of dream or fantasy; that the danger of this "dim, obscure, and visionary" poem is that it threatens to hold the reader as if it were his *own* dream or fantasy. He holds this imagined experience of complete surrender to *Christabel* within bounds, however, by almost immediately transforming the poem's unsettling, uncentered power into a disgusting "something" obscurely visible behind a veil of language and sentiment, thus reducing to its sexual content power he has just described as having philosophical as well as erotic dimensions: he contains this power in the "bottom" and invites us to declare it female. Although it suggests that *Christabel* is potent and horrific, Hazlitt's melo-drama, which associates the poem with a derided genre (the Gothic) and gender (the feminine), actually reduces it as fully as did his play with the "mastiff bitch."[11]

Like Coleridge, Hazlitt cannot or will not "tell" what is enchanting or distress-ing about *Christabel.* Instead he objectifies the poem as a feminine body, in a move which allows him to disentangle matters of intellect from matters of desire to some extent; admitting the pull of, and stridently defending himself against, this body, he charges his writing with the libidinal possibilities he has contained. *Christabel* has subterfuges of its own, however. In a sense it is the poem which contains its critics, whose two responses to it—a spellbound accession to play and a petrified and petrifying refusal of exchange—are figured in the text. When Hazlitt asserts manly judgment against a feminized author and poem at the close of his essay, he only substitutes one form of impotency for another, shedding the role of a mute, enthralled Christabel to become the Baron, whose world is a "world of death."[12]

Turning now to Coleridge's writing on perception, on circulating library litera-ture, and on the poetry of the supernatural, we see him exploring, in a range of situations, how individuals and culture produce "bodies"—hallucinated "reali-ties," but also literary genres, bodies of literature. *Christabel* figures the responses it elicits because in the poetry of the supernatural, Coleridge is dramatizing and manipulating a conventional or "bound" relation between certain kinds of figures and certain kinds of responses; particularly, he is examining the way certain bodies conventionally function to objectify a problematic response to representation.

III

"Disgust" is the response Coleridge and his reviewers most frequently attached to *Christabel.* When at the end of his review Hazlitt attempts to shake off the poem's hold, he locates "something disgusting"—something like a body or a corpse—under its decorative surface. His gesture is dismissive: the disgusting body is elsewhere. During the years 1799–1801 Coleridge was already predicting that his poem would inspire "disgust," but the investigations he was pursuing at the time into "disgust" and related sensations would have prompted him to insist on the complicity of mind and body, and self and elsewhere, in disgusted response. "Define Disgust in philosophical Language—.—Is it not, speaking as a material-ist, always a stomach-sensation conjoined with an idea?" he asks, and answers, Humphry Davy in January of 1800: the object of disgust is "always" an already-internalized "idea" (*CL,* 1:557). Just a day later, writing to Thomas Wedgewood about a similar sensation, he implies an even more thorough entanglement of physiological and ideational entities and processes in certain responses: "Life were so flat a thing without Enthusiasm—that if for a moment it leave me, I have a sort of stomach-sensation attached to all my Thoughts, like those which succeed to the pleasurable operation of a dose of Opium" (*CL,* 1:558). In this description of the conjoined response, Coleridge's analogy to the "dose" implies that even a terminological distinction between "sensation" and "idea" may distort: perhaps the very "sensation" of difference between mind and body is one stage in a self-perpetuating economy of desire. "Disgust" is not the mind's critical pronounce-ment on a body (although it may masquerade as such), but a symptom of the subject's mourning or revulsion for the lost, mutual pleasures of mind and body.

Two notebook entries, also from the *Christabel* period, allow us to link the complex response Coleridge was pursuing to a category, or genre, of representation. In one, Coleridge describes yet another "unpleasant sensation"—this time, a response to the confusion of physical bodies and ideational elements in an observed scene:

> Objects, namely, Fire, Hobs, and Kettle, at the first Look shone apparently upon the green Shrubs opposite to the Parlour, but in a few seconds acquired *Ideal* Distance, & tho' there were of course no objects to compare that Distance by, the Shrubbery limiting the view, yet it appeared *indefinitely* behind the Shrubbery—/ I found in looking an unpleasant sensation, occasioned as I apprehend from the distinctness of the Shrubbery, and the distinct shadowyness of the Images/ (*N*, 894)

Here, in a different context, is the difficulty of locating "something . . . at the bottom"—and the "unpleasantness," too, for Coleridge's sensation would seem to be occasioned by an idle attempt to do just that. When he first looks out the parlor window he perceives a variety of "Objects" existing relatively in the same space: images from the room in which he sits shine "upon" the shrubs outside. But "in a few seconds," prompted by what he knows—that "Images" are the immaterial derivatives of real objects—he sorts real things from images, locating the latter in "Ideal" space: they seem "*indefinitely* behind" the shrubbery. Thus he comes to identify two mutually exclusive perceptual fields in a single field of view; furthermore, his separation of material and "Ideal" elements according to what he knows about representation contradicts what he sees, two "distinctnesses," and other knowledge he possesses: the objects he has placed indefinitely behind the shrubs outside are actually *inside* the room. Paradoxically, then, the very speculative activity that attempted to grasp the scene leads to the vertiginous play of objects and representations, inside and outside, and even of perception, speculation, and sensation. For as Coleridge's attempts to grasp the scene result in its oscillation between warring interpretive possibilities, the scene itself comes to represent a queasy "sensation": he seems, first to "find" his bodily "sensation," and then to "apprehend" his understanding, outside of him.

This experience is something like reading *Christabel*, judging from its reader's accounts and our knowledge of what it is about—*Christabel*'s readers become caught up in the interactions of a "real" lady and a possibly more fantastic lady, and they seem to "find" their own spellbound or disgusted reactions to this exchange figured in the poem. The second notebook entry we will consider, related to the first and to *Christabel* by its attention to a "ghost" image, suggests why some people might find such an experience distressing enough to want to ward it off:

> Ghost of a mountain—the forms seizing my Body as I passed & became realities—I, a Ghost, till I had reconquered my Substance (*N*, 523)

Like *N* 894, *N* 523 describes a confrontation between the "real"—here, "my Body"—and an optical projection; once again, the scene's power, now rendered as mortal, is a redounding effect of speculative operations idly performed by the subject. He identifies the image of the mountain as a "ghost" or "form," apportioning it to the category of immaterial, ideal representations, and opposing it to (his own) body or substance. But the "ghost of a mountain," an image projected onto mist by the sun, is a "real" optical phenomenon. Working from the logic of the narrated event, we could propose that the observer's apprehension of the ghost's autonomy effects a crossing of the terms he has used to secure his relation to the scene: the "ghost" preempts or "seizes" body, while the "I" becomes derivative, a "ghost." This crossing is not a simple reversal. At once a projection and an invested "form," but detached, apparently deriving neither from an empirical ground nor from the subject, the "ghost" become "reality" acquires the status of a hallucination. "Seizing . . . Body"—snatching away body from the subject, but also, introjecting its body into "*my* Body"—it effects a split between "my Body" and "I." Simultaneously displaced and colonized by fantasy, the "I" is seized with an intuition that identity is derivative, a "ghost" of the body.

These two notebook entries share a structure and an effect: both conjoin physical bodies and optical or material images, and in each, a scene provokes speculative operations which finally betray the observer into a possessing, destabilizing reading of his own activity. Together, these two entries allow us to construct a category or genre of problematic representations—of representations which disrupt the very idea of category by exposing the arbitrariness of the fundmental categories of "inside" and "outside," "self" and "world." For in these two encounters, the spectator apprehends that the physical shell of the body is no guarantee of the subject's autonomy and difference; and that representations—scenes, images, and ideas, including, perhaps, the "ideas" of body, substance, reality—are in some sense material and primary, constitutive of subjects and objects. Finally, subject, representation, and the specular configuration that embodies their difference are all revealed to him as the same *kind* of structure, invested constructions of the real, or fantasies—"sensation[s] conjoined with . . . Idea[s]," or, in Freud's terms, "fiction[s] cathected with affect."[13]

Christabel, which figures the responses it provokes, would seem to be related to this genre of representations. But of course it is more conventionally placed in the class "literature." Within *this* class, *Christabel* and the problematic representations we have just been discussing are related, at least by Coleridgean association, to the family or gender of genres which represent conventionality in nineteenth-century critical discourse. For tellingly, when Coleridge describes the experiences of bookworms in a long, whimsical, and self-revealing footnote to the *Biographia Literaria,* he relies on a figure from optics, the *camera obscura,* to illustrate how circulating library literature takes over, not so much life, as fantasy life:

> For as to the devotees of the circulating libraries, I dare not compliment their *pass-time,* or rather *kill-time,* with the name of *reading.* Call it rather a sort of beggarly day-dreaming, during which the mind of the dreamer furnishes for itself nothing but laziness, and a little mawkish sensibility; while the whole *materiel* [sic] and imagery of the dose is supplied *ab extra* by a sort of mental *camera obscura* manufactured at the printing office, which *pro tempore* fixes, reflects, and transmits the moving phantasms of one man's delirium, so as to people the barrenness of a hundred other brains afflicted with the same trance or suspension of all common sense and all definite purpose. (*BL,* 1:34)

There are only shades in this underworld—a literary subculture, confined by Coleridge to a note "at the bottom" of the *Biographia's* legitimate matter. Here, through the mediation of a "sort of mental *camera obscura*" a delirious brain "people[s] the barrenness" of brains as ghostly as its own with representations, in a travesty of authentic literary experience. The *camera obscura* mass-produces fantasy life for consumers who receive it, not because it sounds depths of communal experience, but because they are too ennervated even to supply the purely conventional details of their own daydreams.

The *camera* comes between minds which mirror each other: author and public share the same afflictions, "trances or suspensions of all common sense and all definite purpose"—aimlessness coupled with vague expectancy, "mawkish sensibility" lacking material and imagery on which to fasten. This last is supplied *ab extra,* being simply the materiality of the printed book, or more fundamentally, of its systems of narrative codes and signs. These effect the translation of trancelike or suspended mental states into the plots and characters of circulating library literature—into the "sensationalist" "ghost" stories of Gothic romance and into the literature of "sensibility," tales of "suspense" whose stock characters languish, wander without "definite purpose," mysteriously fall into trances and can't stop repeating themselves. Like the parlor window of *N* 894 and the mist of *N* 523, a true *camera obscura* effaces its own materiality, producing an apparently ungrounded image—an uncannily material, non-derivative representation. Coleridge's analogy attributes to bad books a like capacity both to conceal the means of production and to betray the materiality of the objectified product. In the charmed circle he constructs, readers find their minds "peopled" with apparently unmediated representations of their own mental lives, with their phantasms made uncannily "material."

Even as he deplores the "*kill-time*" of novel reading, the literary man of the *Biographia Literaria* participates in the play of mirrors he describes. As the footnote continues he goes on to include the activity he "dares not" call "reading" within "that comprehensive class characterized by the power of reconciling the two contrary yet co-existing propensities of human nature, namely, indulgence of sloth, and hatred of vacancy," and then launches into an extensive catalogue of species belonging to the same genus: "gaming, swinging, or swaying on a chair or gate; splitting over a bridge, smoking; snuff-taking; . . . &c&c&c." "&c&c&c": could attacks on bad literature by literary men be numbered among the mildly pleasurable, wanton, marginal, and thoroughly conventional activities comprising the genus "kill-time"? Coleridge's prose hints at certain affinities between men of letters and circulating library devotees. It, too, might seem to have been produced in response to the combined pressures of "indulgence of sloth and hatred of vacancy": his taste runs to excess and repetition, even to the baroque—he jingles and alliterates, multiplies clauses and subspecies, and overreaches what is generally considered decorous in sentence and footnote length. And through much of the note he seems under the spell of a metaphorical and "mental" *camera obscura*—the only "material" image in his long and wayward account of a captivating and aimless pleasure.

The writer's peculiarly complicitous engagement with this scene prompts us to consider the figure of the *camera obscura* as the *Biographia Literaria*'s fantastic projection or "ghost." It is intended to illustrate the subject of fantasy life, "a sort of beggarly day-dreaming," and thus could be thought of as being thematically opposed to the "real" matter of the *Biographia*. The text at the top of the page is a narrative of time lived, of intellectual undertakings actively pursued along lines endorsed by culture; the note below depicts time killed or suspended in activities having no significance or returns for the self. But of course the "real" life of the *Biographia* is the life of the mind, particularly as it has been lived through books, rather than any palpably material "reality," and despite the author's protests, the scene at the bottom of the page represents both a species and a construction of the genus "reading," rather than its opposite. Judging from these very protests, the scene is a construction—an objectification—of something fantastic or uncanny in this literary man's interest in literature.[14]

Indeed, this attack on mass culture strikes us as self-revelatory—a mock exorcism of a peculiarly Coleridgean spook. It seems to have a direct and obvious relation, for example, to a life which we know was exceptionally and self-destructively given over to addictive kill-times. A "library cormorant" whose appetite for romance was particularly keen, Coleridge may have constructed this sense of rapt absorption in order to reject it extravagantly, dramatizing in the relation of speaker to scene how the memory of the "pleasurable operation of a dose" might acquire the negative, morally charged affect of distaste or disgust. Alternatively, the footnote can be read as an oblique acknowledgment that there is something fantastic about the *Biographia Literaria*'s relation to the received ideas of a "legitimate" cultural tradition—evident in its author's obvious anxiety about questions of originality and priority, and, more bizarrely, in his apparent incapacity or refusal to recognize boundaries between his writing and that of others.

But although this note may strike us as characteristic of Coleridge's writing at its most distinctive or eccentric, his derogatory representation of ladies' literature also "fixes, reflects, and transmits" once more a moving fantasy of his day. In yet another coincidence of the individual (and in this case, highly personalized) and the received, Coleridge's manner of speaking about popular literature engages and burlesques a polemic against the vitiation of culture by tainted literary forms carried on by his contemporaries, and, before them, by Burke and Johnson. By the common consensus of literary men, popular literature, including circulating library fare, is set over and against authentic intellectual activity as its travesty. It is aligned with the mechanical reproduction of conventions and the proliferation of commodities, and with the falsely or unnaturally inspirational "dose" which circulates a taint of diseased sexuality through a body of increasingly dependent and emasculated consumers, most of whom were of course female to begin with. Apparently confirmed by a market of "real" products and consumers, this happily and indignantly excoriated representation of mass culture is at the same time high culture's ghostly representation of its own processes, a depiction of the transmission of knowledge as the circulation of fantastically invested materials.[15]

IV

The language of Coleridge's footnote circulates around *Christabel*. The second part of the poem was conceived after a "dose" that peopled "barrenness" according to its author, who then imagines it as infinitely reproducible ("I would rather have written Ruth, and Nature's Lady than a million such poems," he confesses to Davy after *Christabel* was rejected from the *Lyrical Ballads* [*CL*, 1:643, 632]); he isn't sure how to classify *Christabel* but knows to exclude it from the category of "real-life" poems, a genus whose boundaries he suggests it has the capacity to disturb. Its readers responded to it with hysterical attacks of the sort burlesqued in Coleridge's note. Almost all of them connected the poem's disturbing character to its licentious femininity, one even going so far as to suggest it appeals only to the devotees of Lord Byron. To suggest that these terms and postures are conventional does not answer the question of why *Christabel* excited the response it did, but perhaps helps to explain the coincidence between Coleridge's perception of the poem and the way it was received: he must have suspected that *Christabel* would be regarded as belonging to a tainted category of literary endeavor.

Christabel, then, is not just a ghost story, but also the "ghost" of literature: men of letters perceive it as belonging to a body of literary products which figure the possibility that books are fantastic representations exercising a dangerous attraction for the subject. We should not imagine that the typical man of letters's relation to this category of goods is straightforwardly defensive, however. For the scenario of the *camera obscura* translates the energy of systems that drive the subject into libidinal energy, which circulates back to "one man," and, eventually, to the man of letters and the body of his text. The scene encysts a state of pleasurable indeterminacy, where representations transmit "doses" of fantasy from devotee to languid devotee, whose "hundred [feminine] brains" are loosely but gratifyingly oriented toward the potentate who "peoples [their] barrenness." The speaker closes off this circle from "time" and his literary life, and then by his self-ironic admission of his complicity in it charges his own discourse with libidinal possibility: this is not "real" literature, and yet literature and literary men are always flirting with the dangerous and heady attractions of fantasy. And surely, both Hazlitt and Coleridge seem at their most seductively interesting to the critic when by hysterically charged attack or coy self-betrayal they reveal their attraction to a charmed circle, whether that represented by Christabel in the arms of Geraldine, or that of the circulating library.

Modulated just a little, Coleridge's attack on lending library culture becomes the famous account of his role in the *Lyrical Ballads,* an experiment he is anxious to legitimize in the *Biographia Literaria:*

> [M]y endeavors should be directed to persons and characters supernatural, or at least romantic; yet so as to transfer from our inward nature a human interest and a semblance of truth sufficient to procure for these shadows of imagination that willing suspension of disbelief for the moment, which constitutes poetic faith. (*BL,* 2:5)

The terms he used earlier to protest the devotees' absorption are here employed to describe the ideal reader's generosity: if successful, he will procure "for the moment" ("*pro tempore*") the reader's "suspension of disbelief" (a "suspension of all common sense") for his "shadows of the imagination" ("phantasms"). But as a formerly excluded experience of books is admitted to the genus "reading," a new category, actual madness, is produced as a figure of that which is at once other than literature and literature's internal possibilities and limit. If readers are deluded by the "shadows" of his poetry, Coleridge implies, it may be because in real life they have actually confounded shadow and substance and come under the spell of hallucinated realities:

And real in *this* sense [supernatural incidents] have been to every human being who, from whatever source of delusion, has at any time believed himself under supernatural agency.

"For a moment" the reader of supernatural poetry may touch the perimeters of madness. The experience is not limited to one genre; even Wordsworth, Coleridge's writer of real-life poems, "for short spaces of time" plays with shadows, as any good poet might. Describing the figure of the poet in the 1802 preface to the *Lyrical Ballads,* Wordsworth suggests he must be something of a madman—and something of a Christabel:

Nay, for short spaces of time perhaps, [the poet might] let himself slip into an entire delusion, and even confound and identify his own feelings with [those of his characters].[16]

In moments of imaginative generosity, of voluntary relinquishments of self to fictions, writers and readers flirt with the possibility of going too far—of losing their "Substance" to a "ghost," of "letting themselves slip" into delusions which could become difficult to escape, of acceding to "holds" they might "never . . . wish to shake off." In these moments the subject touches a perpetually bracketed, continually displaced representation of literature's fantastic appeal, a "moving phantasm" of Coleridge's discourse and a discourse about literature in which he participates.

Coleridge's poems of the supernatural illustrate mental states, including states where the mind comes under the sway of a hallucinated "reality." When "for the moment" a reader of these poems suspends disbelief and gives himself over to representations, he touches madness—doubling, in his own relation to fiction, the very condition the poem dramatizes. But although *all* the poems of the supernatural are intended to produce this effect in the reader, it is *Christabel* which most alarms its public. Coleridge's account in the *camera obscura* footnote of the circulating library devotees casts the pleasure one takes in certain kinds of books as a feminine pleasure: the implicit message is that to read is to behave like a woman, an axiom the man of culture might find both alarming and alluring to contemplate. I would propose that Coleridge explores the relation between cultural processes and (fantasized) feminine erotic experience in *Christabel,* a poem which dramatizes hysteria, conventionally figured as the flights of a "wandering mother," which alienates female subjects from their own speech. To "tell" the story of *Christabel,* a narrator or narrators—we cannot tell if we hear one voice or two—resurrect the ghosts of genres as apparently disparate as Spenserian romance and pulp fiction; they reenact and tumble into the exchanges of Christabel and Geraldine, and suggest that the subject's relation to cultural forms is hysterical.[17] It may be a measure of the poem's success that many of its contemporary readers responded to it like hysterics who "cannot tell" what ails them—who could only repeat its effects in the manner of Byron, Scott, and a host of other imitators and parodists of the poem, or, like Hazlitt, resist its effect by hysterical defense.

NOTES

1. *Collected Letters of Samuel Taylor Coleridge,* ed. Earl Leslie Griggs (Oxford: Clarendon Press, 1956–71) 2:941 (hereafter cited as *CL*).

2. *Biographia Literaria,* ed. J. Shawcross (Oxford: Oxford Univ. Press, 1907) 2:5 hereafter cited as *BL*).

3. This episode is discussed by Marilyn Katz in "Early Dissent Between Wordsworth and Coleridge: Preface Deletion of October, 1800," and by James Kissane in " 'Michael,' 'Christabel,' and the *Lyrical Ballads* of 1800." Both articles appear in *The Wordsworth Circle* 9.1 (1978).

4. My reading of *Christabel*'s capacity to disturb and to influence Coleridge's literary relationships is indebted to Reeve Parker's essay, " 'O could you hear his voice!': Wordsworth, Coleridge, and Ventriloquism," in *Romanticism and Language,* ed. Arden Reed (Ithaca: Cornell Univ. Press, 1984).

5. In 1801, Coleridge was also thinking of the poem's "birth" as a death: he marked *Christabel*'s and Derwent's simultaneous appearance with a spate of notebook entries about dead or dying children which have interesting connections with his post-partum feelings about *Christabel* as well as with his sickly child: in one, he recalls a local woman's expression of relief at parting with a "little Babe one had had 9 months in one's arms"; in another, he quotes from the *Star* a description of a drowned infant, a spectacle &c" whose "flesh was more yielding to the touch than is either necessary or agreeable to describe"—a "sight to dream of, not to tell" (*The Notebooks of Samuel Taylor Coleridge,* ed. Kathleen Coburn [New York: Bollingen Series: Pantheon Books, 1957–73] 1:814, 809 [hereafter cited as *N*]).

6. Coleridge's descriptions of his relation to the poem come from the preface to *Christabel:*

> Since the latter date [1800], my poetic powers have been, till very lately, in a state of suspended animation. But as, in my very first conception of the tale, I had the whole present to my mind, with the wholeness no less than the loveliness, of a vision; I trust that I shall yet be able to embody in verse the three parts yet to come.

In Coleridge's account it is the author's "powers," not the poem, which have existed "in a state of suspended animation"; but my shift is, if not excused, at least precedented by his own.

7. See, for example, Coleridge's letter to Davy, January 11, 1801 (*CL*, 2:662–63).

8. See also *CL*, 2:731–32, 735–36, 739. For a more extended discussion of this period and these letters see Jerome Christensen, *Coleridge's Blessed Machine of Language* (Ithaca: Cornell Univ. Press, 1981), 76–81. Christensen focuses on the grandiose philosophical claims that appear in the letters I have been quoting, relating them to attempts, described in the *Notebooks,* to derive knowledge and perception from infantile experience of the mother.

9. Variously, they liken it to "a strange fantasy," "a nightmare," a "symptom" of madness, and the "ravings of insanity." These reviews are all printed in *The Romantics Reviewed,* edited, with introductions, by Donald H. Reiman (New York: Garland, 1972). I have just quoted from 1:239, 2:470, and 1:36 (hereafter cited as *RR*).

10. For Coleridge's speculations, see *CL*, 4:917–18. This rumor found its boldest public expression in a parody printed in 1818, which took up the story of *Christabel* nine months after Geraldine's first visit, with the heroine in the advanced stages of pregnancy (*Christabel,* by "Morgan O'Doherty," published in *Blackwood's Edinburgh Magazine* 5 [April–September 1819]: 286–91).

11. This strategy—of reducing the poem to *just* a Gothic tale of terror—repeats tactics conventionally used on the Gothic itself. In "The Character in the Veil: Imagery of the Surface in the Gothic Novel" (*PMLA* 96 (1981): 255–70), Eve Kosofsky Sedgwick describes a prevalent critical tendency to read the Gothic as a literature of "depth and the depths," and argues that this reading is blind to the Gothic novel's thematic insistence on surfaces as "quasi-linguistic" carriers of sexuality: to see the Gothic in terms of a convention of surfaces and depths is to repress the possibility that (one's own) identity and responses are conventional. Coleridge's and Hazlitt's readings of *Christabel* suggest that one moment—itself highly conventionalized—in this repressive strategy is an imagined accession to the logic of contaminative linguistic experiences; the glimpse of this threat to the self's autonomy becomes a pretext for a hyping up of an attack on the (supremely conventional) literature of buried things.

12. Like the Baron, who in a moment of confusion imagines separating "souls / From the bodies and forms of men," and like Perseus, Hazlitt takes cutting measures to reassert the implicitly hierarchical categories of thought that allow one to "tell" he dissevers surface from "bottom," decoration from content, and life and play from death and stasis. Then, almost as if to acknowledge his affinity with Sir Leoline, as a coda to his review of *Christabel* he attaches lines which he calls "the one genuine burst of humanity" in the poem, lines he claims show what the author can do when "no dream oppresses him, no spell binds him." The passage he has in mind describes the ruined friendship of Roland de Vaux and the Baron. I excerpt what I suspect moves him most:

> They stood aloof, the scars remaining
> Like cliffs which had been rent asunder;
> A dreary sea now flows between,
> But neither heat nor frost nor thunder
> Shall wholly do away, I wean,
> The marks of that which once had been.

My selection is not arbitrary. Not only Hazlitt, but virtually every contemporary reviewer of *Christabel,* no matter what his opinion of the poem as a whole, cites these "manly" lines with approval. It almost seems to be a conspiracy of gentlemen—to find, in a poem which describes a mysterious contract between two women, so much to admire in these lines about manly friendship unambiguously "rent asunder."

13. Freud's formulation is quoted by Jean Laplanche and J.-B. Pontalis in their essay "Fantasy and the Origins of Sexuality," which appears in the *International Journal of Psycho-Analysis* 49 (1968): 1–18. My own understanding and use of the term "fantasy" is indebted to this work.

14. Indeed, part of the joke is that what is at the top of this particular page differs very little from what is at the bottom. Coleridge is describing how the continual perusal of periodical literature has weakened the memory of the reading public. It is *this* public from which the devotees have been excluded.

15. In "Concepts of Convention and Models of Critical Discourse" (*NLH* 13 [1982] 31–52), Laurence Manley proposes that conventions have a "quasi-objective status for the people who share them, a formulation that would seem to bear on my suggestion that the "genre" of ladies' literature has the status of a cultural fantasy in Coleridge's day.

16. *Lyrical Ballads* 1798, ed. W. J. B. Owen (Oxford: Oxford Univ. Press, 1969), 166.

17. I discuss the poem more thoroughly in my essay "*Christabel:* The Wandering Mother and the Enigma of Form," forthcoming in *Studies in Romanticism.*

Word and "Languageless" Meanings: Limits of Expression in The Rime of the Ancient Mariner

Raimonda Modiano's critique of *The Ancient Mariner* centers on the significance of discrepancies between experience and the recounting of experience even "by a most believing mind," in short, on possible inadequacies of language. It particularly challenges critical interpretations that have viewed the poem in the light of closed religious or philosophical systems, of whatever variety. This focus manifests a pervasive critical preoccupation of our time. Failure of language is of course a starting point for deconstructionists, but with Coleridge's ballad it must be a concern of even the most "traditional" critics because, as Modiano demonstrates, the adequacy of language is a central dramatic issue in *The Ancient Mariner*. She concentrates on the contradiction between the Mariner's sensorial, concrete language when immersed in the memory of his personal suffering and his more conventionally metaphoric language when engaged in explanatory social discourse. This contradiction poses starkly the paradox of the incommunicability of the story the Mariner is compelled to try to tell.

The paradox Modiano so effectively articulates lays the ground for a romantic solution to the problem of the inadequacy of language that critics have only very recently begun to take seriously. The romantics conceived the possibility of linguistic efficacy if readers were willing to risk belief in its possibility, to recognize that the "decreative" ironies of a text might also provide the basis for recreative readerly acts. This is the ground of Rajan's "reconstructive" reading in our Shelley section of *The Triumph of Life* as well as the essay on Coleridge's poem "The Eolian Harp," Gene W. Ruoff's "Romantic Lyric and the Problem of Belief," which follows in this section. It is also the subject of an important forthcoming article in *Studies in English Literature* by John Axcelson describing reconstructive aspects of Coleridge's "constitutive irony" in *The Ancient Mariner*, and is touched upon by John Hodgson in *Coleridge, Shelley, and Transcendental Inquiry* (1989). Such understandings are built upon such shrewdly perceptive analyses as Modiano's of essential discrepancies between experience and discourse so provocatively embodied in Coleridge's poem.

From *Modern Language Quarterly* 38, no. 1 (March 1977): 40–61. Copyright © 1977 by the University of Washington. Reprinted by permission of the publisher.

With its first appearance in *Lyrical Ballads* (1798), *The Rime of the Ancient Mariner* emerged as a perplexing and highly controverisal poem. To Coleridge's contemporaries it seemed a "rhapsody of unintelligible wildness and incoherence," occasionally redeemed by passages of unusual craftsmanship.[1] To modern readers the poem is neither absurd nor spoiled by "great defects" of diction, character, and morality, and certainly no one today would want to call it a "Dutch attempt at German sublimity," as Southey mockingly described Coleridge's venture (*Coleridge: The Critical Heritage*, p. 53). Yet although readers no longer dispute the coherence and quality of the poem, they hardly agree on what it means. *The Ancient Mariner* has been variously interpreted as a sacramental vision of crime, punishment, and salvation; as a nightmarish tale of senseless suffering; as a discourse on prayer; as a parody of the Christian doctrine of atonement; as an elaborate structure of occult symbolism; as a poetic workshop for Coleridge's later metaphysics; and as a prophetic allegory of Coleridge's personal life.[2]

The myriad of critical interpretations points to a fundamental center of ambiguity in the poem. In his narrative the Mariner conspicuously relies on Christian rituals and beliefs, and yet the Christian doctrine fails to explain his world of excessive suffering and irrational events. Much of the Mariner's fate seems bleakly absurd, and yet he moves in an ordered universe where crime leads to suffering, however disproportionate, and blessing brings about redemption, however temporary. Natural forces such as the sun and the moon appear to form unified symbolical patterns, but contrary to what Robert Penn Warren once tried to demonstrate, not everything good happens under the moon and everything bad under the sun. The poem teasingly gravitates toward coherent systems of thought, and yet no mythic or philosophical tradition, be it Christian, Egyptian, Neoplatonic, or the like, is large enough to contain it.

The Ancient Mariner raises special problems of interpretation because while it involves us in a series of captivating incidents and continuously tempts us to decipher some meaningful order which holds them together, it draws its dramatic action not from events as such which correspond to any one particular world view, but from the manner in which a deeply troubled character, laboring under various delusions, fears, and anxieties, is able to reconstruct a painful episode of his past. The poem does not offer an objective account of an adventurous voyage at the time when it originally occurred, but merely a later *version* of that voyage told by an old and lonely man who can neither explain nor fully describe what happened to him on a "wide wide sea."[3]

From Coleridge's own statements about the composition of *The Ancient Mariner* and from the testimony of his contemporaries, it appears that Coleridge intended to explore precisely the discrepancy between actual experience and the recounting of experience by a character with a "most believing mind."[4] Until late in his life Coleridge maintained his view that the true subject of a supernatural poem is the mentality of its narrator and the circumstances that cause him to confuse reality with his distorted apprehension of it. In a notebook entry written in 1830, Coleridge points out that, to insure the credibility and success of a supernatural tale, the poet "of his free will and judgement" must do "what the Believing Narrator of a Supernatural Incident, Apparition or Charm does from ignorance and weakness of mind,—i.e. mistake a *Subjective* produce (A saw the Ghost of Z) for an objective fact—the Ghost of Z was there to be seen." The poet must also take into account the psychological forces that play upon the witness of an unfamiliar object, namely, "the magnifying and modifying power of Fear and *dreamy* Sensations," the "additive and supplementary interpolations of the *creative* Memory and the inferences . . . of the prejudiced Judgement," which tend to slip into and are "confounded with the *Text* of the actual experience."[5]

My interest here is to investigate some aspects of the discrepancy between the experience the Mariner is likely to have undergone and his subsequent account of it. I shall pay particular attention to the Wedding Guest's controlling influence on "the additive and supplementary interpolations" of the Mariner's "*creative* Memory" and the inferences of his "prejudiced Judgement." I would also like to show that language itself, although it is the only means by which the Mariner can relive his past, finally binds him to an inaccurate view of it. In many ways *The Ancient Mariner* draws our attention to the distance between private history and its narratives, between attempted "texts" and "the thousand indescribable things that form the whole reality of the living fuel."[6] The poem tests the limits of man's power to convey through language the inner life of self which is intrinsically mysterious, prerational, and mute; it points to "the inadequacy of Words to Feeling, of the symbol to the Being" (*Notebooks,* II, 2998).

For the moment I would like to mention two hints by which the poem alerts us to this question. When the Mariner kills the Albatross, he not only alienates himself from nature, his shipmates, and God, but also loses his speech:

And every tongue, through utter drought,
Was withered at the root;
We could not speak, no more than if
We had been choked with soot.

(135–38)[7]

Consequently, the Mariner remains silent during most of the action recorded in his tale. In Part III, upon apprehending the oncoming bark, he performs a sacrificial gesture to regain speech, biting his arm to draw blood. But the words he is able to utter ("A sail! a sail!" [161]), words of hope and salvation, so blatantly conflict with the events that follow that the Mariner immediately reverts to his mute mode of perceiving, dreaming, enduring. Like Christabel after her enigmatic encounter with Geraldine, the Mariner is cursed with the extinction of language. Indeed, how is one to name and encode that most bizarre apparition of a spectral bark with a deathly crew on it? The Mariner's world is full of sights "to dream of, not to tell." But although the Mariner, like Christabel, suffers the pain of inexpressible solitude after the contact with an unfamiliar world, he carries an even greater burden: all his life he *must* tell a story about an experience that has deprived him of a corresponding language, a story that will inevitably disclose its limitations.

This is one of the central paradoxes of the Mariner's situation. He can relieve himself of his inner agony and retain his sanity after his return from the vast solitudes of the ocean only by shaping an otherwise formless, incomprehensible, and unbearable past into a structured narrative with a beginning, climax, ending— and a moral lesson as well. Despite its inadequacies, language provides the Mariner with the means of expression and conceptual categories by which he can make sense of his experience and share it with an auditor. But through the very process of turning his recollections into a tale that must account for his endless wandering, and must also be credible to an auditor, the Mariner endows his past with a coherence and meaning which it did not originally possess. At an uncertain hour, the narrative that has temporarily given form and value to the Mariner's life is doomed to disintegrate, and his labor to "bring back fragments of former Feeling" begins anew (*Notebooks,* III, 3420).[8]

Coleridge gives us yet another clue to the poem's concern with the disparity between discourse and experience. In 1817, when he revised *The Ancient Mariner* for *Sibylline Leaves,* he added an explanatory gloss which, allegedly, was meant to clarify the poem's geographical and moral directions. Wordsworth regarded the gloss as a superfluous afterthought, and later critics have likewise had difficulties in defining its function. Recently, William Empson has made a strong case against the inclusion of the gloss in modern editions of *The Ancient Mariner,* for he believes that it is nothing but a "parasitic growth" which makes nonsense of the poem.[9] It is true that, as Empson demonstrates, the gloss tends to misrepresent the poem by translating its ambiguities into simplistic equations. For example, the speaker of the gloss attributes the persecution following the killing of the Albatross to the Mariner's breach of the laws of hospitality, which hardly explains the cause of the Mariner's torment. To justify the presence of spirits in the Mariner's narrative, the speaker pedantically refers the reader to a scholarly source (gloss to lines 131–34), and later he conveniently identifies the spirits animating the dead crew as a "troop of angelic spirits, sent down by the invocation of the guardian saint" (gloss to lines 346–53). Are we to agree with Empson that the gloss should be discarded as an entirely mistaken frame of reference for the poem, composed by a poet who had fallen out of sympathy with his earlier ideals and grown more conventional in his old age? I think not, for one good reason: the incongruities between the gloss and the Mariner's tale are much too obvious not to become suspect. It is hard to imagine that Coleridge could have misunderstood his own work to such a degree or that he would have compromised his artistic standards in order to suit the orthodox norms of the public of his time.[10] Clearly, Coleridge did not want us to take the moralistic judgments proposed in the gloss at their face value. Rather, he uses the gloss to show what can happen to a work if clarity and secure moral explanations replaced its vastly nebulous universe, if the poet were to write exactly as people like Mrs. Barbauld expected him to write.[11]

It would, however, be a simplification to regard the gloss merely as Coleridge's answer to contemporary critics and reviewers who found *The Ancient Mariner* offensively obscure and lacking in moral sentiments. For one thing, the speaker of the gloss is not hopelessly unperceptive; in some instances he understands quite well the psychic factors that influence the Mariner's acts.[12] Perhaps we can gain a fuller sense of the persona of the gloss through a comparison with Carlyle's *Sartor Resartus.* Like Teufelsdröckh's editor, the narrator of the gloss approaches a strange piece of imaginative literature from a rational position which is bound to be inadequate and is exposed for its inefficiencies. And like Carlyle's editor, the speaker of the gloss shows a capacity for imaginative growth and is drawn into the center of the hero's world to the point of stylistic imitation.[13] And yet, very much like Carlyle's editor, the speaker can grow only so much in the direction of the hero's values, so that his distinctive sensibility is always in view.[14]

The gloss, in effect, duplicates and is meant to highlight a particular situation dramatized in the poem. Within the narrative the Mariner tries to communicate to a conventionally-minded auditor a deeply personal experience of his past; in the gloss an editor tries to make that same experience accessible to readers who may share the biases of the Wedding Guest. Although the editor is often entranced by the strange fortunes that befall the Mariner, his responsibility toward the public makes him adopt a more sensible and ethical approach to the Mariner's story, an approach that results in gross misrepresentations. But the Mariner's need to maintain a dialogue with the Wedding Guest forces him to adopt the same approach with similar disadvantages. It is the Mariner who winds up his tale with a perfectly orthodox moral which contrasts with the pain and inexplicable suffering he had described all along. Thus, the editor's overt practice of translating the Mariner's narrative into a public language of familiar beliefs reflects a less perceptible process by which the Mariner gradually produces a socially acceptable account of his voyage. This process has as its source the Wedding Guest's resistance to the Mariner's tale.

The confrontation between the Mariner and the Wedding Guest is one of the most obvious features of surface plot in the poem, so obvious, in fact, that few critics have cared to discuss its significance at any length. The Mariner's unusual character has so absorbed critics that the minor appearance of the Wedding Guest has slipped by unattended. A few have tried to rescue him from neglect, showing that he, like the Mariner, is capable of conversion and changes from a stubbornly conventional man to a "sadder and wiser" member of his community.[15] But no matter how generous we want to be with the Wedding Guest, it is the Mariner who engages our interest, and although one might want to know to what extent he influences the Wedding Guest's life, it is more important to investigate whether the Wedding Guest affects the Mariner in any way or, rather, whether the Mariner is affected by his own compulsion to speak to the Wedding Guest.

Critics have not sufficiently recognized the Mariner's vulnerable susceptibility to the Wedding Guest, in part because they have mistakenly seen their relationship as one of the master-pupil kind. The Mariner is often taken to be the impersonated figure of the artist-missionary who wants to inform the kirk, hill, and lighthouse top of the shore. From this perspective the Wedding Guest is reduced to a frivolous and naïve man who must be taught that there are more things on earth than marriage feasts. But the Mariner does not simply have a mission; he has a fate as well. When he meets the Wedding Guest, he has one possession: a story. His monomania, his sole mode of being, is an oral recapitulation of a devastating experience of his past. Unless his ghastly tale is told, he can never escape, not even momentarily, the most "woful agony" (579). The Mariner desperately needs the Wedding Guest, because through his confession he hopes to wrench himself free of his painful loneliness and find some continuity between the chaos of his past life and the Wedding Guest's world of communal rituals. His need for the Wedding Guest is so urgent that at the beginning he resorts to physcial force to make him listen to his tale. His dependence upon the Wedding Guest's continuous attention will significantly influence the very way in which he shapes his narrative, as I shall show in the following discussion.

To my knowledge, no critic has noticed that an abrupt shift takes place in the Mariner's story when the Wedding Guest interrupts him in Parts IV and V of the poem. In each case, and more prominently in the latter, the Mariner interpolates calm scenes of beauty in a context that does not assimilate them. Preceding the Wedding Guest's intervention in Part IV, for instance, is the scene of the Mariner's shipmates dropping dead one by one, each turning his face with a "ghastly pang" and cursing the Mariner "with his eye" (212–23). This gruesome moment is followed, after the Wedding Guest's outburst of fear and the Mariner's haunting cry of loneliness, by a return to the scene of death which, surprisingly, becomes quite attractive to view:

> The many men, so beautiful!
> And they all dead did lie:
> And a thousand thousand slimy things
> Lived on; and so did I.
>
> (236–39)

Having previously witnessed the pang of death in the sailors' eyes, one would expect to see ugly faces distorted by pain rather than serene bodies merging quietly with the general calm of life. The incongruity of this scene is intensified by the fact that in the stanzas immediately following, the beauty of death vanishes completely and in its stead terror creeps in. There is nothing aesthetically pleasing about the sight of a "rotting deck" on a "rotting sea" (240–43), or of "cold sweat" melting from dead limbs (253–54). What is it, then, that causes the Mariner's brief and rather unnatural perception of beauty? It is possible to speculate that, given the proximity of this scene of restful calm to the Wedding Guest's intervention, it might be in some way related to it. This suggestion gains support from the fact that, with the next intervention of the Wedding Guest in Part V, a parallel though much more emphatic change occurs in the Mariner's narrative from supernatural horror to humanized beauty.

Before the Wedding Guest interrupts him in Part V, the Mariner relives one of the most frightening episodes of his past. The dead sailors suddenly rise like ghosts, without speaking or moving their eyes. They begin to work the ship as "they were wont to do" (338), but their motions are lifeless and their silence eerie. The sailors are indeed "ghastly," as the Mariner describes them (340), and their miraculous reanimation is even more horrifying than their previous dying (341–44). At this point the Wedding Guest breaks in, voicing his anxiety; to placate his fears, the Mariner provides him with the following explanation:

> 'Twas not those souls that fled in pain,
> Which to their corses came again,
> But a troop of spirits blest.
>
> (347–49)

Although the Wedding Guest might buy this explanation, the reader will not and should not. The metamorphosis of the "ghastly crew" (340) into a disembodied troop of angelic spirits is much too obvious a tour de force to be credible. It looks like a "supplementary interpolation" prompted by the Mariner's need to respond to and pacify the Wedding Guest. It is important to note that the lines just quoted were not part of the original composition of *The Ancient Mariner;* Coleridge inserted them in 1800 when he revised the poem for the second edition of *Lyrical Ballads.* Empson uses this example to demonstrate how Coleridge manages to ruin his work by trying to cover up its unchaste strangeness (*Coleridge's Verse,* pp. 45–46, 61–62). But to read the passage this way is to lift it out of its dramatic context and forget that it is the Mariner who speaks it, not Coleridge. When Coleridge added these lines in 1800, he made another important change in the original text: in the second version, the Wedding Guest addresses himself to the Mariner just before the blest spirits enter into the Mariner's tale.[16] Viewed from this perspective, the lines do not emphasize Coleridge's orthodox leanings; rather, they identify the Wedding Guest as a source for the Mariner's orthodox vocabulary. They indicate that the presence of the Wedding Guest forces the Mariner to mold his unfamiliar past into a more conventional and communicable story. The lines also establish a link between the intervention of the Wedding Guest and the following episode of enchanting sights and sounds, a link that is vaguely suggested in the 1798 text.

Since this episode is central to my thesis, I shall quote it in full and examine it in detail:

> For when it dawned—they dropped their arms,
> And clustered round the mast;
> Sweet sounds rose slowly through their mouths,
> And from their bodies passed.
>
> Around, around, flew each sweet sound,
> Then darted to the Sun;
> Slowly the sounds came back again,
> Now mixed, now one by one.
>
> Sometimes a-dropping from the sky
> I heard the sky-lark sing;
> Sometimes all little birds that are,
> How they seemed to fill the sea and air
> With their sweet jargoning!
>
> And now 'twas like all instruments,
> Now like a lonely flute;
> And now it is an angel's song,
> That makes the heavens be mute.
>
> It ceased; yet still the sails made on
> A pleasant noise till noon,
> A noise like of a hidden brook
> In the leafy month of June,
> That to the sleeping woods all night
> Singeth a quiet tune.
>
> (350–72)

This is a beautiful reverie, but it remains a reverie nonetheless, a distorted apprehension of the Mariner's existence on the ocean. It is difficult to believe with J. B. Beer that the episode marks the culmination of the Mariner's process of regeneration, the completion of his vision of the ideal universe "which was only prefigured to him in the sight of the moon and the water-snakes" (p. 162). Nothing happens to the Mariner himself at this time. He is able to apprehend harmonious sounds, but that does not transform him in the way the blessing of the water snakes did. The act of blessing had immediate and major psychic effects on the Mariner: "the self-same moment" (288) he could pray, the Albatross fell off his neck, he was able to sleep, and he was released from thirst. No such positive consequences follow from the Mariner's entranced vision of sweet sounds. The ship moves on quietly for a while, "Yet never a breeze did breathe" (374)—a statement with an ominous ring in view of previous scenes of terror when motion took place "Without a breeze, without a tide" (169). Indeed, no sooner does the sun fix itself upon the bark than the Mariner is knocked down senseless by the ship's sudden bound.

There is a fundamental difference, both in the manner of the Mariner's composition and in its content, between the scene of blessing and that of divine music. In the former instance the Mariner's experience takes in beings which inhabited his world all along: the slimy water snakes. He can therefore focus on them sharply and perceive them vividly. Although, as he declares, no human tongue could describe their beauty, he is able to represent in detail their shapes, colors, and movements. In the latter example, on the other hand, the Mariner has difficulties in identifying the things he perceives. Unable to determine the source of the sounds he hears or their exact quality, he proceeds to name them through a series of analogies, constantly shifting the terms of comparison. The sounds come to him now mixed, now one by one; they seem to originate from the song of a skylark or other little birds and resemble in turn the collective tune of "all instruments" or the individual voice of a lonely flute, an angel's song, or a hidden brook. The whole scene is cast in an unreal light. Nothing is what it is but seems to be like something else. Moreover, all the terms of this rich metaphoric exchange come from a realm that is essentially foreign to the ocean. (There are no skylarks on the ocean.) It is quite apparent that the Mariner borrows the metaphors composing his aural reverie from a landscape that belongs entirely to the Wedding Guest's shore world. Only in this world would one normally hear sounds of skylarks, lonely flutes, or hidden brooks, and would such time references as "the leafy month of June" have any significance. For the Mariner whose ship is stalled on a silent sea, time extends indefinitely, and conventional month-counts have ceased to matter.

It appears, then, that the Wedding Guest's intervention in Parts IV and V of the poem occasions a sudden shift of narrative perspective in the Mariner's tale which meliorates the horror of previous scenes. This shows that the Mariner's story is a composite of his past and present, of the time of his voyage and the time of dialogue about it. At crucial moments the present invades the Mariner's past, clouding his memory of what that past really was, giving him fantasies of little birds exchanging "sweet jargoning" in the midst of a grotesque spectacle of bodies that mimic the actions of live men. The episode of angelic sounds makes two important suggestions: one, that the Wedding Guest has a direct impact on the course of the Mariner's story, and two, that the Mariner's tale and the life behind it do not always coincide. The episode also reveals the Mariner's particular habit of metaphoric expression which will eventually distance him from his own past, leaving him in the end with a dry moral that falls flat even on the Wedding Guest's ears. As I shall show in the rest of the chapter, the Mariner is subject to linguistic forces which finally defeat him, mocking the pride he takes in his "strange power of speech" (587).

A close look at the vocabulary of the poem indicates that the Mariner resorts to two modes of language which, though mixing with each other, remain relatively distinct. When he is deeply immersed in his past and oblivious to his auditor, he speaks in a language that is primarily sensorial and concrete. Objects and actions are named as they are perceived without taking on conceptual meanings external to their immediate experiential value. On the other hand, when the Mariner is influenced by a social situation—a debate with his shipmates, a dialogue with the Wedding Guest, or a discussion between two spirits apprehended from a trance— he tends to use a language that does not merely record objects but assigns them meanings dependent upon a system of shared mythology.

For convenience I would like to label the former type as the language of self and the latter as the language of social discourse. A complex process of transfer from one type of language to the other governs the development of the Mariner's narrative. As the Mariner departs from the shore and advances toward the climactic event of his journey, the encounter with the specter-bark, his tale gradually empties itself of metaphors which link him to the safe public world he has left behind. After the intervention of the Wedding Guest in Part IV, this process reverses itself. The Mariner is increasingly tempted to find Christian equivalents in his mysteriously demonic universe and begins to draw upon orthodox analogies to characterize unqiue experiences. The language of metaphor, however, has dangerous pitfalls. By using metaphor, one may easily end up being used by it; that is, one may cease to distinguish between models of comparison and the reality they were meant to illustrate.[17] This is, I believe, what happens to the Mariner. Having borrowed his terms of description from the Wedding Guest's world in order to make himself understood to his listener, the Mariner soon begins to confuse it with his own world, and in the end he identifies himself completely with the public values represented by his auditor.

In Part I, the Mariner uses a mixed language which contains both vivid pictorial and auditory imagery and conventional perceptions of Christian heritage. To say that the ice is "As green as emerald" (54) and sounds "Like noises in a swound" (62) is to establish an analogy in which both terms belong to the same level of physical reality and which functions to intensify the sensory qualities of the objects perceived. On the other hand, to say that the ship drove fast "As who pursued with yell and blow / Still treads the shadow of his foe" (46–47), or that the arrival of the Albatross was "hailed . . . in God's name," as "if it had been a Christian soul" (65–66), is to build up a quite different kind of analogy which refers particular objects to concepts of a well-established tradition ("foe," "God's name," "Christian soul"). When at the end of Part I the Wedding Guest invokes "God" to "save" the Mariner from the "fiends" that plague him (79–80), he expresses himself precisely in the language of that tradition.

These two types of analogy illustrate the linguistic trends I wish to trace here, one based on concrete perceptions of individual objects, the other on more abstract and conceptual interpretations of events. Both trends recur throughout the poem, but their frequency and distribution vary from part to part. In Part II, for instance, the action of sensory language is more intense than in Part I, where it frequently mixes with the language of social discourse. This mixture is due in part to the Wedding Guest's interruption and in part to the circumstance that the Mariner still speaks collectively for himself and his shipmates. As the Mariner becomes an isolated voice after killing the Albatross, and his ship enters an unknown world ("We were the first that ever burst / Into that silent sea" [105–106]), unusual events begin to happen, all demanding an acute sensory awareness. The ship is stopped in the midst of a "copper sky" (111), "As idle as a painted ship / Upon a painted ocean" (117–18); an infinitude of water surrounds the crew only to remind them of their thirst; slimy things crawl upon the sea, and the water burns at night "like a witch's oils," "green, and blue and white" (129–30).

Despite the increase of sensory data, the language of social discourse is not extinct in this section of the poem. It occurs before the Mariner's advent into the silent sea, toward the beginning of Part II. Here the shipmates gather to discuss the Mariner's act of shooting the Albatross. They refer to it in turn as "hellish" (91) and "right" (101), appealing to conventional though opposite moral absolutes. In the midst of this debate the Mariner notices the rising of the sun: "Nor dim nor red, *like God's own head,* / The glorious Sun uprist" (97–98; my italics). There are many different suns and moons in the poem, some more symbolic than others. The sun that rose upon the right at the beginning of Part II is a merely physical sun engaged in its daily activities. But the sun of this passage is primarily a symbolic object; it is a Christian sun and glorious. The point I want to stress is that in the context of a social dialogue, the Mariner's perception of the surrounding universe is conceptualized. As soon as the dialogue is over, the narrative turns to sensory objects and immediate experiences of physical suffering (unbearable thirst, the withering of speech organs).

The language of social discourse reasserts itself at the end of Part II, where the Mariner directs his attention to his shipmates. He detects "evil looks" in their faces and finds the Albatross hung around his neck instead of the cross (139–42). The exchange of the cross for the slain Albatross summons again the Christian doctrine as a mythological frame of reference. But this replacement does not simply establish a symbolic association between the Albatross and Christ; it also marks the Mariner's separation from a world represented by the cross, a world of redemptive suffering and just order. In Part III, this separation grows wider. As the specter-bark approaches the ship from a distance, the Mariner's universe becomes increasingly mysterious and its morality increasingly dubious. The fact that his fate is decided by an irrational fortune game played by frightening and alien figures undermines the logic of a Christian world view, as Edward Bostetter convincingly demonstrates (see note 2). The Mariner still attempts ritualistic invocations to protective powers ("Heaven's Mother send us grace!" [178]) and gestures of sacrifice to regain speech (the biting of his flesh), but these prove to be meaningless. Familiar assumptions about reality, such as "a sail is a ship which means people which means aid," are no longer functional in a universe policed by Death and Life-in-Death. The very nature of knowing has become problematic.

By the time the Mariner encounters the specter-bark, he is completely divorced from communal ties: he has been separated from nature, from his shipmates, from God, and from language itself. Significantly, his narrative loses many of its conceptual referents to an established order and marks his immergence into a private world which has no correlation to reality as commonly understood. The episode of the encounter with the specter-bark is composed of a series of concentrated and fast-moving actions, and the Mariner uses strikingly unusual analogies to describe them:

A speck, a mist, a shape, I wist!
And still it neared and neared:
As if it dodged a water-sprite,
It plunged and tacked and veered.
                    (153–56)

And straight the Sun was flecked with bars,
(Heaven's Mother send us grace!)
As if through a dungeon-grate he peered
With broad and burning face.
                    (177–80)

Are those *her* sails that glance in the Sun,
Like restless gossameres?
                    (183–84)

And every soul, it passed me by,
Like the whizz of my cross-bow!
                    (222–23)

Although they contain words that connote social or metaphysical concepts (dungeon, soul), these analogies are essentially concrete. The reference to a dungeon grate emphasizes the physical appearance of the sun. Likewise, the last analogy focuses not on the metaphysical status of the sailors' departing souls, but on their movement and quality of sound.

After the intervention of the Wedding Guest in Part IV, a change in the Mariner's use of language becomes noticeable. Although the narrative maintains stretches of sensory descriptions (the sight of the water snakes in the moonlight, for instance), a different mode of discourse begins to emerge. The narrative moves from a world commanded by Death and Life-in-Death to one where a "saint" is supposed to "take pity" on the Mariner (234), and finally does, as the Mariner interprets it, when he blesses the water snakes. The Mariner turns to traditional concepts, such as heaven, hell, and religious rituals of blessing and praying. He had previously described his experiences through the action of physical objects; now he resorts to familiar metaphors ("My heart as dry as dust" [247]) or to analogies that appeal to an orthodox mentality:

An orphan's curse would drag to hell
A spirit from on high;
But oh! more horrible than that
Is the curse in a dead man's eye!
                    (257–60)

This is not the way the Mariner projects horror in Part III. In this passage he insists that his experience is horrible through a conspicuous social rhetoric. He refers to "An orphan's curse," to "hell," to spirits "from on high," and uses conventional phrases such as "the curse in a dead man's eye." These lines do not advance the action of the narrative or add new descriptive details; instead, they offer an explanation that demands the exercise of a traditional imagination. The Wedding Guest, for example, might understand the Mariner's situation if he were to think of an orphan's curse and accept the fact that a curse in a dead man's eye is even more horrible. As this example shows, there are parts of the Mariner's narrative in which he does not describe anything new but reflects on his experience, and these parts tend to attract a social mode of discourse. The same thing happens at the end of Part IV, where the Mariner explains the blessing of the water snakes as the merciful act of a saint, and at the beginning of Part V, where he attributes the long-awaited sleep to "Mary Queen" of Heaven.

In Part V we are plunged again into the center of acute sensory perceptions and dynamic action. Refreshed by rain during sleep, the Mariner awakes to an animated landscape of explosive fireflags, dancing stars, roaring wind, and torrential rain. He continues to observe the activity of nature and the ghostly reanimation of the crew until the Wedding Guest interrupts him. As the Mariner's dream soliloquy is shattered ("It had been strange, even in a dream, / To have seen those dead men rise" [333–34]), his narrative takes an orthodox turn which conceptualizes and tames his previous account of events. What follows is the episode of sweet sounds already discussed, where we find metaphors drawn from a common stock of religious vocabulary ("And now it is an angel's song, / That makes the heavens be mute"), as well as from a hospitable shore landscape.

From this point on, the rich sensorial language and swift-moving narrative of earlier episodes give way to a more pronounced trend of social discourse.[18] The end of Part V and the beginning of Part VI consist of a rather long dialogue between two spirits which recasts the entire sequence of calamities suffered by the Mariner in the light of Christian morality. The killing of the Albatross is related to the Crucifixion, and the Mariner's subsequent punishments are interpreted as a trial of "penance" (398–429). The dialogue prefigures both the concepts and the conventional rhythms of the Mariner's concluding moral; lines like " 'He loved the bird that loved the man / Who shot him with his bow' " (404–405) sound close to

> He prayeth best, who loveth best
> All things both great and small;
> For the dear God who loveth us
> He made and loveth all.
> (614–17)[19]

The Mariner soon adopts the Christian explanation provided by the two spirits and believes that he is in a world where crime leads to punishment and penance to salvation. When he sees the hermit on the shore, he hopes to be released from his sin through the ritual of confession: "He'll shrieve my soul, he'll wash away / The Albatross's blood" (512–13).

As the Mariner approaches the shore, elements of a familiar landscape and concepts of a familiar world begin to invade his narrative. The wind feels "Like a meadow-gale of spring" (457), and the sailors' bodies, which were "flat, lifeless and flat" (488), are miraculously transformed into a "heavenly sight" of seraphs (492–93). Even when the Mariner concentrates on physical objects and actions, he uses a language that is more commonplace than before. Analogies such as "The harbour-bay was clear as glass" (472), "Like one that hath been seven days drowned / My body lay afloat" (552–53), or "But swift as dreams, myself I found / Within the Pilot's boat" (554–55) are pale and lack the unusual imaginative quality of previous images such as sails "Like restless gossameres" or souls rushing by like the whizz of the crossbow.

I do not mean to claim that the distinction between sensory and conceptual language has mathematical precision. My purpose has been to point out some linguistic strategies employed in *The Ancient Mariner* to show the modifications undergone by individual experiences during the process of their transfer into verbal structures which make possible the communication between speaker and listener. I have also tried to establish a critical perspective from which the Mariner's concluding moral no longer appears as a feeble tag unconnected with the content of his story, as critics have often argued. The moral represents the culmination of a tendency that is apparent throughout the Mariner's tale and is only given a more emphatic form toward the end. As I have shown, the Mariner erects orthodox structures out of unorthodox experiences when he interprets events or when the Wedding Guest claims his attention. The Mariner is in many ways a Wedding Guest himself, and his exchange with his auditor reflects an inner conflict. Like the Wedding Guest, the Mariner desires to make sense of chance and irrationality in terms of accepted myths in order to maintain control over an experience that borders on madness. In light of the changes that occur in the Mariner's narrative when his auditor interrupts him in Parts IV and V, it is not at all surprising that the Mariner, when he reaches out for the Wedding Guest for the first time, utters a moral extracted from the codes by which the Wedding Guest leads his life. The irony of the Mariner's fate is that, while trying to overcome the resistance of the Wedding Guest by exposing his auditor to a more imaginative way of thinking and at the same time by drawing closer to this values, the Mariner succeeds in alienating both himself and the Wedding Guest from their own respective worlds.[20] When the Mariner delivers his closing moral, the Wedding Guest is "stunned" and "of sense forlorn" (622–23), a state hardly suitable for the wise lesson of love and prayer the Mariner tries to teach him. He has been initiated indeed into a universe where God "Scarce seemed . . . to be" (600), and naturally he goes neither to the marriage feast nor to the church.[21] On the other hand, the tale which ends with the moral is a tale gone wrong for the Mariner too, and he is the first to feel it. The memory of green ice, slimy water snakes, and the revengeful specter-bark continues to haunt the mind and demands a new story. But every time the Mariner beginns his tale again, trying to seize upon his past as firmly and urgently as he commands a Wedding Guest to listen, he is bound to fall into the same trap of dialogued experience and to construct a narrative that will provide a Christian abstract of a far more mysterious and in part untranslatable episode of his past.

The search for an adequate medium of expression that could accommodate the deepest demands of the self without sacrificing either the authenticity of the artistic product has a long and tortuous history in Coleridge even prior to the composition of *The Ancient Mariner,* and it forms the subject of many reflections in his later work.[22] Coleridge's views on the suitability of language to self-expression and to the representation of fundamental intuitions gained through the imagination are not consistent, varying according to his moods and the specific purpose of his arguments. At times Coleridge regards language as a potent and elevated means of articulating the poet's visionary perceptions of reality. As "the medium of all Thoughts to *ourselves* of all Feelings to others, & partly to ourselves," language partakes of "the two things mediated," participating in the unified entity which it represents (*Notebooks,* III, 4237). Coleridge agrees with his contemporary, the philologist Horne Tooke, that words are the wheels of intellect, "but such as Ezekiel beheld in 'the visions of God.' . . . Whithersoever the Spirit was to go, the Wheels went, and thither was their Spirit to go; *for the Spirit of the living creature was in the wheels also.*"[23] But this great credit granted to language is often undermined by Coleridge's gloomy awareness of the abstractness of words and their power to chain, distort, and impoverish the experiences of the self.[24] In one notebook entry he says:

> It is the instinct of the Letter to bring into subjection to itself the Spirit.—The latter cannot dispute—nor can it be disputed for, but with a certainty of defeat. For words express generalities that can be made *so* clear—they have neither the play of colors, nor the untranslatable meanings of the eye, nor any of the thousand indescribable things that form the whole reality of the living fuel. (*Notebooks,* III, 4350)

Like other Romantic writers, including Wordsworth and Shelley, Coleridge believed in the existence of a prelinguistic level of consciousness which cannot be fitted into any one objectified verbal structure.[25] The poet's innermost feelings and impressions are, as he puts it in a notebook entry, "languageless." Words convey "generalities, tho' some less than others," and they "not only only awake but really involve associations of other words as well as other Thoughts—but that, which I see, must be felt, be possessed, in and by its sole self!" (*Notebooks,* III, 3401). The stronger the desire to possess an emotion or image in its unadulterated form, the more frustrating it is to try to break through the abstract network of language. Who, Coleridge asks,

> has deeply felt, deeply, deeply! & not fretted & grown impatient at the inadequacy of Words to Feeling, of the symbol to the Being?—Words—what are they but a subtle *matter?* and the meanness of Matter must they have, & the Soul must pine in them . . . O what then are Words, but articulated Sighs of a Prisoner heard from his Dungeon! powerful only as they express their utter impotence! (*Notebooks,* II, 2998)

To escape the prison of language, Coleridge tries out various means of nonverbal representation only to discover that while they supplement language, none of them is a fit measurement for the noblest parts of one's nature:

> Without Drawing I feel myself but half invested with Language—Music too is wanting in me.—But yet tho' one should unite Poetry, Draftsman's-ship & Music— the greater & perhaps nobler certainly all the subtler parts of one's nature, must be solitary—Man exists herein to himself & to God alone/—Yea, in how much only to God—how much lies *below* his own Consciousness. (*Notebooks,* I, 1554)[26]

If poetry, drawing, and music together fail to communicate the voice of self, what can one expect from language alone? Moreover, how does one share with readers or listeners impressions which they have never experienced in their own lives, "material Objects, Landscapes, Trees, &c they have never seen"? "Assuredly, the impressions received by the words are very faint compared with the actual impression—it is but a dim abstract at best—and most often a Sort of *tentative process* now by this analogy, now by that, to recall the reader to some experiences, he must have, tho' he had not attended to them" (*Notebooks*, III, 3947). The Mariner too draws upon the resources of analogies to make himself intelligible to the Wedding Guest, but what he offers his auditor is an imperfect copy of an inimitable original. The actual impressions and memories of his past cry out for words. The inner anguish generates the tale, and the tale once told perpetuates the anguish. The Mariner is trapped in a Sisyphean labor to articulate his solitary voyage on a "wide wide sea."

NOTES

1. See Charles Burney's unsigned review in the *Monthly Review* of June 1799, in *Coleridge The Critical Heritage*, ed. J. R. de J. Jackson (New York, 1970), p. 56. Richard Haven has done a useful study of the reception of *The Ancient Mariner* in its time in "The Ancient Mariner in the Nineteenth Century," *SIR*, 11 (1972), 360–74.

2. The following references list the authors of these views in the order in which they have been mentioned: Robert Penn Warren, "A Poem of Pure Imagination," *Kenyon Review*, 8 (1946), 391–427; Edward E. Bostetter, "The Nightmare World of *The Ancient Mariner*," *SIR*, 1 (1962), 241–54; Malcolm Ware, "*The Rime of the Ancient Mariner*: A Discourse on Prayer?" *RES*, 11 (1960), 303–304; William Empson, "The Ancient Mariner," *CritQ* 6 (1964), 298–319; J. B. Beer, *Coleridge the Visionary* (London, 1959); Irene Chayes, "A Coleridgean Reading of 'The Ancient Mariner,' " *SIR*, 4 (1965), 81–103; and George Whalley, "The Mariner and the Albatross," *UTQ*, 16 (1947), 381–98.

3. Lionel Stevenson believes that we should read *The Ancient Mariner* as we read one of Browning's dramatic monologues: "In understanding such a dramatic monologue we must always begin by separating in our own mind two distinct elements—the events as they really occurred, and the coloring given to those actual events by the mentality and prejudices of the dramatic character who speaks" (" 'The Ancient Mariner' as a Dramatic Monologue," *Personalist*, 30 [1949], 41).

4. Coleridge points out that "the excellence aimed at" in *The Ancient Mariner* "was to consist in the interesting of the affections by the dramatic truth of such emotions, as would naturally accompany such situations, supposing them real. And real in *this* sense they have been to every human being who, from whatever source of delusion, has at any time believed himself under supernatural agency" (*Biographia Literaria*, ed. John Shawcross, 2 vols. [Oxford, 1907], II, 5). From De Quincey we learn that, as Wordsworth informed him, Coleridge's plan was to compose "a poem on delirium, confounding its own dream-scenery with external things, and connected with the imagery of high latitudes" (*Collected Writings of Thomas de Quincey*, ed. David Masson, 14 vols. [London, 1896–97], II, 145). A recent interpretation of *The Ancient Mariner* based upon Coleridge's original conception of the poem can be found in Paul Magnuson, *Coleridge's Nightmare Poetry* (Charlottesville, 1974), pp. 50–84.

5. *Inquiring Spirit*, ed. Kathleen Coburn (London, 1951), p. 191.

6. *The Notebooks of Samuel Taylor Coleridge*, ed. Kathleen Coburn, 3 vols. (London, 1957–), III, 4350; hereafter cited *Notebooks*, with appropriate volume and item numbers.

7. All quotations of poetry are from volume 1 of *The Complete Poetical Works of Samuel Taylor Coleridge*, ed. Ernest Harley Coleridge, 2 vols. (Oxford, 1912).

8. This is from a moving notebook entry in which Coleridge tries to establish a linguistic connection with external objects and memories of his past: "O! Heaven! one

thousandfold combinations of Images that pass hourly in this divine Vale, while I am dozing & muddling away my Thoughts & Eyes—O let me rouse myself—If I even begin mechanically, & only by aid of memory look round and call each thing by a name—describe it, as a trial of skill in words—it may bring back fragments of former Feeling—For we can live only by feeding abroad."

9. *Coleridge's Verse: A Selection,* ed. William Empson and David Pirie (London, 1972), p. 43.

10. Coleridge was an inveterate opponent of public taste. After the unfavorable critical reception of *The Ancient Mariner,* he began to think about the unreliability of public judgments and planned to write an essay about it. Max F. Schulz believes that Coleridge's disparaging opinions on public taste caused his conflict with Wordsworth when the two poets agreed to have a critical preface for the second edition of *Lyrical Ballads* ("Coleridge, Wordsworth, and the 1800 Preface to *Lyrical Ballads*," *SEL,* 5 [1965], 619–39).

11. Coleridge's well-known answer to Mrs. Barbauld's complaint that *The Ancient Mariner* contained no moral is recorded in his *Table Talk* (May 31, 1830): ". . . as to the want of a moral, I told her that in my own judgement the poem had too much; and that the only, or chief fault, if I might say so, was the obtrusion of the moral sentiment so openly on the reader as a principle or cause of action in a work of such pure imagination. It ought to have had no more moral than the Arabian Nights' tale of the Merchant's sitting down to eat dates by the side of a well and throwing the shells aside, and lo! a genie starts up, and says that he *must* kill the aforesaid merchant, *because* one of the date shells had, it seems, put out the eye of the genie's son" (*Specimens of the Table Talk of the Late Samuel Taylor Coleridge,* ed. Henry Nelson Coleridge, 2 vols. [London, 1835], II, 155–56).

12. The moon gloss to lines 263–76 is one such instance. The editor is able to articulate here the unconscious process which precedes and prepares for the Mariner's seemingly abrupt blessing of the water snakes. In a most poetic commentary the editor shows that, through an unconscious act of identification with the journeying moon, the Mariner apprehends—however dimly—the possible harmony that can exist between a traveler and his surroundings. The imaginative quality of the moon gloss has been recognized by Huntington Brown, among others. "Who but a poet," asks Brown, "can write of 'the journeying moon and the stars that still sojourn'?" ("The Gloss to *The Rime of the Ancient Mariner,*" *MLQ,* 6 [1945], 322). Brown is one of the few critics who take into account the interplay of the gloss and the poem and the full dramatic personality of the editor. My point of view differs from Brown's in that I find Coleridge's attitude toward the editor much more ironic and critical than Brown seems to acknowledge.

13. In Part III of *The Ancient Mariner,* the editor's comments reproduce quite well the tempo of the Mariner's narrative. The editor is no mere observer here and does not indulge in his usual lengthy explanations. He responds to events in brief, emotional phrases such as "A flash of joy" or "Like vessel, like crew!" This is also the only time when he asks a question, wondering, as does the Mariner, about the strange bark that comes into view (gloss to lines 167–70).

14. Carlyle's use of the editor in *Sartor Resartus* is clearly a much more self-conscious device and forms a more integral part of the structure of the whole work than does the gloss to *The Ancient Mariner.* It is also important to note that the relationship between the editor and Teufelsdröckh is a controversial issue in Carlyle criticism. Some critics see a progressive elimination of the gap between the two characters and a gradual fusion of their originally antithetical points of view. See G. B. Tennyson, *Sartor Called Resartus* (Princeton, 1965); and Walter L. Reed, "The Pattern

of Conversion in *Sartor Resartus*," *ELH*, 38 (1971), 411–31. My position is similar to that taken by George Levine, who claims that the tension between the editor and Teufelsdröckh is constant throughout the book (*The Boundaries of Fiction: Carlyle, Macaulay, Newman* [Princeton, 1968], chap. 1).

15. See Charles A. Owen, Jr., "Structure in *The Ancient Mariner*," *CE*, 23 (1962), 261–67; and Ward Pafford, "Coleridge's Wedding-Guest," *SP*, 60 (1963), 618–26.

16. In the 1798 text, this episode is followed rather than preceded by the Mariner's conversation with the Wedding Guest. The conversation extends to ten lines which alter substantially the relationship between the Mariner and the Wedding Guest from the way it appears in the revised version of the poem. The Mariner willingly addresses himself to the Wedding Guest, trying to win him over with wise words which announce his moral at the end: "Listen, O listen, thou Wedding-guest! / 'Marinere! thou hast thy will: / 'For that, which comes out of thine eye, doth make / 'My body and soul to be still.' / Never sadder tale was told / To a man of woman born: / Sadder and wiser thou wedding-guest! / Thoul't rise to-morrow morn. / Never sadder tale was heard / By a man of woman born." Coleridge's elimination of these lines in favor of a rather short exchange between the Mariner and the Wedding Guest initiated by the Wedding Guest himself shows that by 1800 Coleridge was a better master of his verse and was able to discard awkward rhythms and unnecessary duplication of lines, and that he also conceived of a wider rift between the Mariner and the Wedding Guest. In the 1800 text, the Wedding Guest, far from acquiescing in the Mariner's plea, opposes the bizarre descriptions of his tale. The Mariner, on the other hand, does not appear to be conscious of the Wedding Guest until he is interrupted by him, nor is he willing to implore his auditor to listen, as he does in the earlier version. It is possible to argue that by 1800 Coleridge's confidence in the potential reconciliation of artist and society was much shaken, partly because of the negative reception accorded *The Ancient Mariner*, partly because of his growing estrangement from Wordsworth. It is also possible to speculate that Coleridge intuited a direct connection between the Mariner's reverie and the intervention of the Wedding Guest and therefore decided to restructure his narrative.

17. An interesting study of this proces has been done by Colin Murray Turbayne in *The Myth of Metaphor* (Columbia, S.C., 1970).

18. Max F. Schulz points out that in the final sections of *The Ancient Mariner* Coleridge's narrative control weakens considerably: "The last three sections devote a large percentage of the tale to recording the conversation of the polar spirit's fellow daemons, the actions of the seraph band, and the life and sentiments of the hermit and of the mariner. In all three instances, exposition, Gothic claptrap, and moral edification replace narrative progression" (*The Poetic Voices of Coleridge* [Detroit, 1963], p. 62).

19. Gayle S. Smith has analyzed in detail the moral stanzas of *The Ancient Mariner* and has shown that both in meter and diction they are monotonous and contrast with the poem's larger narrative design ("A Reappraisal of the Moral Stanzas in *The Rime of the Ancient Mariner*," *SIR*, 3 [1963], 42–52).

20. A reversal of roles takes place between the Mariner and the Wedding Guest which maintains the original distance between the two characters. While at first the Mariner acts irrationally toward a conventional Wedding Guest, in the end it is the Wedding Guest who is "of sense forlorn" (623), and the Mariner is the one who becomes conventionally wise. This reversal of roles can be grasped at the level of language. While the Mariner moves from a concrete language of sensory perception to a more abstract one, the Wedding Guest moves in the opposite direction. If in Part I the Wedding Guest speaks of God and fiends, by Part IV he has acquired a language

that is purely perceptual and quite imaginative: " 'I fear thee, ancient Mariner! / I fear thy skinny hand! / And thou art long, and lank, and brown, / As is the ribbed sea-sand. / I fear thee and thy glittering eye, / And thy skinny hand, so brown' " (224–29).

21. The last stanza of the poem has been commonly used by critics as evidence for the Mariner's success in affecting the Wedding Guest's life. Yet there are deeper implications in this stanza which have to do with the effect of time on both characters. The lines state not only that the Wedding Guest becomes a "sadder and a wiser man" (624) through contact with the Mariner, but also that with the passing of one day much of the darker and more ambiguous content of the Mariner's tale gets lost. A man who is slightly mad can wake up "wise" the next day. Time alters, domesticates, and moderates the strangeness and intensity of painful experiences, because from a distance in time man can rationalize the alien and the terrifying. Unlike the Wedding Guest, the Mariner does not need a day, but only the time during which he completes his story to draw wisdom out of a stunning experience.

22. The tension between a language generated by solitary experiences of the self and one called upon by the poet's participation in the world of social action first emerges in Coleridge's conversation poems. Richard Haven has analyzed the stylistic differences between the socialized rhetoric of the opening and final sections of these poems and their climactic passages, when specific things are no longer defined in relation to abstract ideas but are assimilated into a visionary whole which dissolves the barriers between perceiver and the immediate object of perception (*Patterns of Consciousness* [Amherst, 1969], chap. 2).

23. The quotation is from Coleridge's Preface to *Aids to Reflection;* see Coburn's note to entry 4237.

24. Frank Lentricchia, "Coleridge and Emerson: Prophets of Silence, Prophets of Language," *JAAC,* 32 (1973), 37–46, attributes Coleridge's ambivalent conception of language to his divided allegiance to Kant, who believed in the uniqueness of the aesthetic activity, and to Schelling, who assumed the unity of cognitive, artistic, and ethical functions in the all-encompassing intuition of the absolute, the ground of the oneness of subject and object. In keeping with the Kantian spirit, Lentrichhia suggests, "an object whose value is unique and purely immanent to its mode of existence must be brought into existence by a creative imagination that exercises its power wholly within an artistic medium, an imagination that belongs exclusively to the poet and that resists the transcending intuition as well as the conceptual and moral faculties" (p. 39). From a Schellingian perspective of transcendental monism, the direct and unmediated apprehension of the absolute is a self-sufficient and all-inclusive experience that defies rational or linguistic categories. Any translation of such an experience into language will unavoidably destroy the purity of the original intuition. For an informative discussion of the distrust of language inherent in the epistemological premises of transcendental idealism, see Arthur O. Lovejoy, *The Reason, the Understanding, and Time* (Baltimore, 1961), esp. pp. 35–41.

25. The powerlessness of language to convey the artist's most intense emotions and visionary grasp of some transcendent force in the universe is a theme that recurs in nearly all of Shelley's major poems as well as in some of his prose essays. "How vain is it to think," Shelley warns us in his *Essay on Life,* "that words can penetrate the mystery of our being! Rightly used they may make evident our ignorance to ourselves, and this is much." In a famous passage of *A Defence of Poetry,* Shelley points out that "the mind in creation is as a fading coal. . . . when composition begins, inspiration is already on the decline, and the most glorious poetry that has ever been communicated to the world is probably a feeble shadow of the original conceptions of the poet" (*Shelley's Prose,* ed. David Lee Clark [Albuquerque, 1954], pp. 172, 294). For Words-

worth's notion on the limitations of language, see Stephen K. Land, "The Silent Poet: An Aspect of Wordsworth's Semantic Theory," *UTQ,* 42 (1973), 157–69.

26. Coleridge's anticipation of Freudian concepts can be found in many of his notebook entries; see Coburn's notes to *Notebooks,* I, 44, 1552; II, 2302, 2495, 2638, 2930. An interesting comment on the suppressive power of conscious behavior and the revenge of the "under-consciousness," as Coleridge calls it (coming remarkably close to Freud's terminology), occurs in a letter written by Coleridge in 1811 (*Collected Letters of Samuel Taylor Coleridge,* ed. E. L. Griggs. 6 vols. [Oxford, 1956–71], III, 310).

GENE W. RUOFF

Romantic Lyric and the Problem of Belief

Since his first published essay on romantic poetry and poetics,
"Wordsworth on Language: Toward a Radical Poetics for English
Romanticism" (1972), Gene W. Ruoff has been urging the recognition
of essential differences between Wordsworth's and Coleridge's poetic
theories and practices. This interest reaches its fullest development in
Ruoff's major contribution to romantic studies, *Wordsworth and
Coleridge: The Making of the Major Lyrics, 1802–1804* (1989). There
Ruoff provides a sometimes speculative step-by-step narrative of the
intertextual geneses of the poems that have become known as the
Intimations Ode, "Resolution and Independence," and "Dejection." A
significant force in the final formation of the texts, he argues
somewhat unfashionably, may be attributed to how they ultimately
engage major issues in Western religious culture.

The current essay comes from Ruoff's edited volume, *The
Romantics and Us* (1990), which reflects on the mutual entanglements
of romantic and modern poetics. His essay is concerned with the
inabilities of modernist criticism (or romantic criticism under the sway
of modernism) to admit issues of conflicting belief into its readings of
texts. The essay's opening analysis of our cultural situation (written
before the epidemic of religious and ethnic butchery in the Balkans
and parts of the former Soviet Union and before Patrick Buchanan's
ringing declaration of "cultural war" at the 1992 Republican National
Convention) has lost little of its currency. Employing a method
adapted from Bakhtinian dialogics as its basis for a new reading, the
essay finds "that conflicting beliefs are wholly functional elements of
'The Eolian Harp,' and that discussions which evade, minimize, or
otherwise trivialize them cannot do Coleridge or the poem justice."

The problem could be worse. At last report, Shelley has not been condemned to
be reborn so that he can be rekilled for the milk-hearted progressivism of *The
Revolt of Islam,* and the creeping evolutionism of Keats's *Hyperion* has escaped
even the keen eye of the Texas Committee to Keep Textbooks Safe for Texans.
That these fanciful instances hardly violate the recent spirit of public discourse
about arts and letters, whether the issue at hand has been the fictive representa-
tion of the wives of Mohammed, the revision of the core curriculum at Stanford,
the improper display of the American flag at the Art Institute of Chicago, or
federal funding for art works deemed sexually or religiously offensive, suggests
the temper of our times. It may point to one reason why the rift between the

From *The Romantics and Us,* ed. Gene W. Ruoff (New Brunswick, N.J.: Rutgers University
Press, 1990), pp. 288–302. Copyright © 1990 by Gene W. Ruoff.

literary academy and the common reader is larger today than it has been in my academic lifetime, by the beginning of which questions of belief in literature had been largely shoved aside, however unresolved.

My title recalls an essay published just over thirty years ago by M. H. Abrams, "Belief and the Suspension of Disbelief," which appeared in *Literature and Belief,* the volume of proceedings of the English Institute meeting for 1957.[1] Reexamination of the topic seems timely, because we are experiencing in romantic studies clear signs that the cultural moment represented in the brilliant work of the past three decades, elaborating the expansive prophetic and spiritual mission of romantic writing, has passed. That work is emblematized for the academic reader in Abrams's learned and literate study, *Natural Supernaturalism* (1971), which has also attracted its share of lay readers. Its influence has been even more pervasive as it has been filtered through the great classroom text of which Abrams is general editor, *The Norton Anthology of English Literature,* now in its fifth edition. There Abrams himself has orchestrated the introduction of the romantics to several generations of college freshmen and sophomores. Even at its most persuasive, such work feels dated, an emanation from a kinder and gentler age of ecumenical readings and ecumenical hopes. That age was characterized in the larger intellectual sphere by the powerful syncretism of scholars like Joseph Campbell, Mircea Eliade, and Northrop Frye. In their various ways, and whatever their reservations about mythic criticism per se, many critics who flourished from the fifties through the seventies attempted to accommodate romantic texts to a sense of capacious spirituality, consistently undervaluing polemical dissonances in search of higher spiritual harmonies.

Our problem today may be not that these understandings have suddenly proved faulty, but that history has left their project behind. The age of ecumenicism, which had followed a solid Wordsworthian program in accentuating experiential and spiritual affinities while diminishing credal differences, is dead. Ecumenicism itself, which had seemed a turning point in the history of religions—perhaps an evolutionary growth—now appears to have been a narrowly based cultural detour given crucial energy by the memory of a war that had written in blood the frightening destructive potential of secular and sacred zealotry. The rush of enthusiasm inspired by Vatican II has become the faintest of memories, as any broadening of Roman doctrine lies wrecked on the shoals of the women's movement in developed countries and population explosion, famine, and radical politics in the third world. Holy wars rage in the Middle East. Our major growth industries in American religion are rigidly sectarian faiths, which know their truth and know it loudly. As dogmatic religion revives, humanism grows increasingly secular. The response of many younger critics to the spiritualized humanism of an older generation of scholars is a counter-humanist critique of all pieties, often conducted from post-Freudian or post-Marxist perspectives.

In looking again at the question of belief in poetry we do not have to reinvent the wheel. Gerald Graff's 1970 study, *Poetic Statement and Critical Dogma,* astutely reviewed the intellectual underpinnings of a half-century of diverse critical theory and practice which, for all its other powers and other benefits, had left us unable to deal not only with questions of belief in poetry, but with the presence and function of propositional or assertive language itself.[2] Graff's target at that time was the broad spectrum of organicist criticism, running from the practical neo-Coleridgeanism of I. A. Richards through the mythopoeics of Frye and others, which he collectively dubbed "mythotherapies." Graff had in mind a body of sweeping, widely accepted, and lightly examined claims about the nature of literature and literary experience: that a work's content is inseparable from its form; that its meaning cannot be paraphrased, because poetry is itself a mode of knowledge; that its ideas, values, and beliefs are dramatic enactments, and consequently make no truth-claims; and that a work of literature cannot be evaluated by criteria extrinsic to itself. Cleanth Brooks organized the 1957 English Institute program on belief; his contribution was "Implications of an Organic Theory of Poetry," an essay which remarks almost in passing that "critics of quite various persuasions" have accepted poetry's "special kind of unity" as "an empirical fact."[3]

Graff's book, which doubts throughout this "empirical fact," could hardly have been less timely. It called for a battle which was never to be fought on its terms: the anti-organicist polemic which took hold was to be conducted in the name of deconstruction, which even more radically challenged questions of referentiality in poetry. Deconstruction charges organicism with confusing the wish for the deed in attributing representational as well as creative power to literature. From its perspective, poetry constructs neither a transcendent reality nor a self-sufficient fictive reality, but a pseudo-reality that only patches over deep rifts in culture, society, and the self. The proper mission of criticism, then, is not to demonstrate and celebrate the higher unity poetry brings into being, but to unveil its illusions, to de-construct its constructions. More recently the new historicism has extended this challenge, as it pursues the socio-economic grounding, the material base, of what some of its practitioners call "romantic ideology." As practiced by Jerome McGann, Clifford Siskin, and others, this critique is as attentive to the ways in which we have characteristically read romantic texts as it is to the texts themselves.[4] Because romantic ideology is always at some remove from the conscious constructions of a text, questions of belief, even of intention, are not instrumental to its investigations. If organicism found the sacred lurking behind the secular, and deconstruction the abyss papered over by the sacred, new historicism finds the political lurking behind everything. For all our methodological sophistication, so often befuddling to general and academic readers alike, we remain unable to face the specter of doctrine in poetry: our eyes go funny and we cease reading. I address here only one manifestation of this problem in romantic lyric and suggest a few of its consequences for our criticism, our teaching, and our loss of public audience for poetry.

My example is Coleridge's "The Eolian Harp." In "Coleridge's 'A Light in Sound': Science, Metascience, and the Poetic Imagination" (1972), Abrams judged it a "flawed example" of the greater romantic lyric, the central poetic type he had so persuasively described several years earlier: "There are instances of stock diction and standard moral parallels . . . , and the concluding verse paragraph strikes the modern reader as a timid and ineptly managed retreat to religious orthodoxy from the bold speculation of the middle of the poem."[5] Still, the poem has been very important to postwar formulations of romantic aesthetics. According to Abrams in "Structure and Style in the Greater Romantic Lyric" (1965), its expanded version of 1796 "established, in epitome, the ordonnance, materials, and style of the greater [romantic] lyric," the form of poem that begins with a

> determinate speaker in a particularized . . . setting. . . . The speaker begins with a description of the landscape; an aspect or change of aspect in the landscape evokes a

varied but integral process of memory, thought, anticipation, and feeling which remains closely involved with the outer scene. In the course of this meditation the lyric speaker achieves an insight, faces up to a tragic loss, comes to a moral decision, or resolves an emotional problem. Often the poem rounds upon itself to end where it began, at the outer scene, but with an altered mood and deepened understanding which is the result of the intervening meditation. (76–77)

No other single formulation of the practices of romantic lyric has been so influential as this, and none has proven so compatible with continuing lyric practice in this century.

In an earlier essay Abrams had described both the surface properties and the spiritual and metaphysical grounding of "The Correspondent Breeze: A Romantic Metaphor" (1960), while all but avoiding "The Eolian Harp"—surely as seminal in its figural as in its formal aspects—in his numerous examples of the trope. The reason for this elision becomes clear in "Coleridge's 'A Light in Sound,' " which rounds off what we might call his "Eolian Harp" trilogy. The problem Abrams has with the poem is its foregrounding, through the retraction of its palinode, the problem of belief. This troubles Abrams on behalf of "the modern reader," who presumably is more at home with "bold speculation" than "religious orthodoxy." What is less fully articulated is the extent to which the poem's self-confutation threatens Abrams's entire project of understanding the properties of romantic lyric, especially in Coleridge's fully elaborated version, 1828 and after.

The questions raised by Abrams cannot be discussed meaningfully without a reading of the poem, in this case a reading which will highlight rather than evade the way in which issues of belief function in it. "The Eolian Harp" begins in a mood of mild erotic languor marked by a heightened, but essentially passive, sensory luxuriance:

My pensive Sara! thy soft cheek reclined
Thus on mine arm, most soothing sweet it is
To sit beside our Cot, our Cot o'ergrown
With white-flower'd Jasmin, and the broad-leav'd Myrtle,
(Meet emblems they of Innocence and Love!)
And watch the clouds, that late were rich with light,
Slow saddening round, and mark the star of eve
Serenely brilliant (such should Wisdom be)
Shine opposite! How exquisite the scents
Snatch'd from yon bean-field! and the world *so* hush'd!
The stilly murmur of the distant Sea
Tells us of silence.

Everything about the initial scene bespeaks passivity, from the postures of the lovers to the speaker's acceptance of traditional moral emblematism of nature. Meanings need not be sought, because this world is complete.

The second verse paragraph turns by association from the one sound which has confirmed the silence of the scene, the "murmur of the distant sea," to the eolian harp, "that simplest Lute, / Placed length-ways in the clasping casement," which will register plastically the changes in the breeze, setting in motion the poem's meditative excursion:

                                                  hark!
      How by the desultory breeze caress'd,
Like some coy maiden half yielding to her lover,
It pours such sweet upbraiding as must needs
Tempt to repeat the wrong! And now, its strings
Boldlier swept, the long sequacious notes
Over delicious surges sink and rise,
Such a soft floating witchery of sound
As twilight Elfins make, when they at eve
Voyage on gentle gales from Fairy-Land,
Where Melodies round honey-dropping flowers,
Footless and wild, like birds of Paradise,
Nor pause, nor perch, hovering on untam'd wing!

The poem moves into story-making here, as its speaker goes beyond the fixed analogies of the opening verse paragraph to develop a chain of associative comparisons. The breeze is to the harp as the masculine lover is to the maid, implicitly as Coleridge is to Sara. He is the force, she the response. In this mode of erotic dalliance, the maid's upbraidings encourage the lover, leading at last to full erotic engagement: "the long sequacious notes / Over delicious surges sink and rise." As the poem reaches this emotional pitch, its analogies shift, and the harp no longer reflects the human content of the scene, which is abruptly displaced, perhaps transcended. The notes of the harp, "a soft floating witchery of sound," now suggest a world beyond the moment, a world of elves, fairies, and mythological creatures. That complete and self-sustaining environment of the opening stanza has come to be merely proleptic to an alternative reality. Leaving casuality aside, we might observe that the movement to this alternative realm has coincided with the depersonalization of the poem's opening situation; as the speaker's active powers are exercised, "pensive Sara" becomes anything but thoughtful, objectified into an amalgam of generic coy maid and passive harp.

    The poem moves immediately from its playful invocation of quaint superstitions, which are self-limiting, into a powerful metaphysical claim, which is not:

O! the one life within us and abroad,
Which meets all motion and becomes its soul,
A light in sound, a sound-like power in light,
Rhythm in all thought, and joyance every where—
Methinks, it should have been impossible
Not to love all things in a world so fill'd;
Where the breeze warbles, and the mute still air
Is Music slumbering on her instrument.

The first four lines of this passage are a late interpolation, first appearing in the errata of *Sibylline Leaves* (1817), and included in the text proper in 1828 and after. For Abrams and most other interpreters, these four lines are very near the core of the poem's difficulties.

    The central purpose of Abram's 1972 essay is to unpack these four lines of "The Eolian Harp," demonstrating the astonishing degree to which they interweave continuing threads of Coleridge's mature thought on nature and supernature. For Abrams they obviously constitute a signature passage. Adapting Coleridge on Wordsworth, we might say that if we were to encounter them running wild in the deserts of Arabia, we should immediately shout aloud, "COLERIDGE!" Here is the way Abrams frames his concluding citation of the lines:

> The poet breaks through sensation into vision, in which the phenomenal aspects of the landscape, its colors, music, and odors, are intuited as products and indices of the first manifestations of the creative Word, gravitation and light, in whose multiform unions all nature and life consist; and he goes on to celebrate the world's song of life and joy, which sounds through the wind-harp, in which the silent air is merely music unheard, and of which the subject is the one Life that, in marrying all opposites, also weds the single consciousness to the world without. (190)

For Abrams, the passage just given is at the heart of Coleridge's achievement as a poet and thinker. He begins and ends his essay with reflections upon it, claiming at one point that "every reader feels [it] to be the imaginative climax of the poem." Indeed, his essay implicitly rewrites the poem to make this utterance climactic and terminal as well as central. But within the poem itself, of course, the passage remains embarrassingly medial.

The third verse paragraph begins with yet another displacement. This time the movement of the speaker's consciousness is not upward toward a higher range of experience, but away in space and time:

> And thus, my Love, as on the midway slope
> Of yonder hill I stretch my limbs at noon,
> Whilst through my half-clos'd eye-lids I behold
> The sunbeams dance, like diamonds, on the main,
> And tranquil muse upon tranquillity;
> Full many a thought uncall'd and undetain'd,
> And many idle flitting phantasies,
> Traverse my indolent and passive brain,
> As wild and various as the random gales
> That swell and flutter on this subject Lute!

While Sara had before been the lute, played upon by the lover-harpist, Coleridge has now replaced her in the role of that "subject" instrument. Not incidentally, Sara has disappeared from the scene as it is imagined, or remembered, or both. It is no longer sunset but midday. Sara's cheek is no longer on Coleridge's arm, and it is his limbs which are stretched upon the "slope / Of yonder hill." From playing her, his "indolent and passive brain" has come to be played upon by random thoughts. From being an object of attention, Sara has receded to become an object of address, abandoned but unseduced—a singularly mortifying predicament for the heroine of what looked as though it was going to be a seduction poem.

Or maybe it remains a seduction poem, while its temptations shift from sexuality to metaphysical speculation. I give here both the climactic verse paragraph of its speculative movement and the beginning of the palinode, so that the critical problem the work poses is clear:

And what if all of animated nature
Be but organic Harps diversely fram'd,
That tremble into thought, as o'er them sweeps
Plastic and vast, one intellectual breeze,
At once the Soul of each, and God of all?

But thy more serious eye a mild reproof
Darts, O belovéd Woman! nor such thoughts
Dim and unhallow'd dost thou not reject,
And biddest me walk humbly humbly with my God.
Meek Daughter in the family of Christ!
Well hast thou said and holily disprais'd
These shapings of the unregenerate mind;
Bubbles that glitter as they rise and break
On vain Philosophy's aye-babbling spring.

Abrams sees clearly enough from Coleridge's vantage point the dangers in this speculative train that necessitate its rejection. Even expressed hypothetically, the passage

> opens a possibility that filled Coleridge with metaphysical terror: the world-view he called "Pantheism." That is, the passage threatens to absorb a transcendent and personal Creator of the world, without remainder, into an Indwelling Soul of Nature, . . . which informs all the material universe and constitutes all forms of consciousness. . . . Coleridge's "intellectual breeze" even suggests a regressive form of the religion of Nature in which the unifying presence is a sacred wind or divine breath. (162)

Thomas McFarland, so often our best commentator on Coleridge's religious thought, describes the repudiated lines as "an example of pure Neoplatonic Spinozism." For McFarland, Spinoza represents one of the oscillatory poles of Coleridge's thought—Kant was the other—in which the struggle between pantheism and Christianity is continually restaged. Because McFarland adduces Coleridge's poetic text within the context of a book which is about belief, designed to illuminate the writer's entire theological project, he is comfortable with the turn the poem has taken, as the voice of the intellect and of Spinoza "is immediately counter-balanced by the voice of the heart and of Christianity."[6] The poem is a specific manifestation, then, of a conflict that runs throughout Coleridge's intellectual career.

Abrams's concern goes beyond historical elucidation of the passage. It is not enough for him or for his modern reader that the conflict expressed was an abiding one for Coleridge. The question is whether the poem makes its conflict real for us, or whether it is finally a disruptive intrusion, "timid and ineptly managed," that mars a poem. Abrams seems to have two concerns. The first is whether Coleridge's retraction does not in fact come from outside the poem, interjecting an issue that has little to do with the conduct of the poem itself. In this case Coleridge would be acting as his own non-poetic reader, rejecting a line of poetic thought because of personal doctrinal adhesions.[7] The second is whether the palinode must be taken as canceling not just the "organic Harps" and "intellectual breeze," which have come immediately before, but also "the one Life within us and abroad." As I read him, Abrams would in a pinch sacrifice the bauble of the lute, but his essay contests all assaults on "the one Life."

Our first recourse in addressing these questions can remain within the legal limits of modernist/romantic aesthetics by staying within the confines of the poem, attending to its rhetorical strategies. The role of Sara requires particular attention, because she is credited with providing the doctrinal check on its speculations. Interestingly enough, she is not allowed to voice her concerns, which Coleridge purports to read in the "mild reproof" of her "more serious eye." Coleridge's handling of the situation allows him to have it both ways: to attribute the motivation for his turn to orthodoxy to another person (who has, after all, been sitting there all along), but still to control the terms of the rebuff. Indeed, we know from McFarland (166–167) that Coleridge was conducting this debate with himself in his correspondence, using almost identical language, in the mid-1790s, close to the time he wrote the first version of the poem to include the palinode. Why, then, is Sara there?

In describing the form of the greater romantic lyric, Abrams noted that its "determinate speaker . . . carries on, in a fluent vernacular which rises easily to a more formal speech, a sustained colloquy, often with himself or with the outer scene, but more frequently with a silent human auditor, present or absent" (76–77). Abrams's priorities are revealed even in the structure of his sentence: he is finally interested in the colloquy with the self and/or scene, not any possible colloquy with the human other of the poem, even while admitting that a determinate addressee is normative. Nor, we might add, are these auditors invariably silent. Witness Wordsworth's "Resolution and Independence," which is not mentioned in the essay on the greater lyric, though a prime candidate for the form in every other respect, and think of "Expostulation and Reply" and "The Tables Turned," which if not "greater" lyrics, are frequently marginalized as "doctrinal" poems.

What I am suggesting is an incipient dialogical tendency in romantic lyric which subtly undermines claims for the self-sufficiency of either the individual poetic imagination or the monological lyric, greater as well as smaller. This dialogical quality governs the thematic development of "The Eolian Harp" and generates its theological conflict. Sara is more than a fictive convenience providing a beginning, turn, and end. She is that pole of the poem which represents human personality, the affectional life, and the present moment. Put simply, she is the embodiment of difference in the poem—sexual difference, human difference, temporal difference, ideological difference—against which its massive drive for unity strains.

The first verse paragraph is filled with minute, personalized, individualized particularities: "My . . . Sara"; "thy . . . cheek"; "mine arm"; "our Cot, our Cot o'ergrown"; "white-flower'd Jasmin"; "broad-leav'd Myrtle"; "yon bean-field."[8] The central meditation of the poem erases all difference, even perceptual difference ("A light in sound, a sound-like power in light"), in pursuit of a higher unity, "the one Life." Loving "all things" is poised against loving those individual things which began the poem, including Sara herself. If "all of animated nature / Be but organic Harps diversely fram'd," there is finally *no* difference, and the merely carnal, the merely affectionate, the merely sensual, and the merely personal are irrelevant. The drive of Coleridge's speculation is toward an ever more expansive sense of divine immanence, "one intellectual breeze, / At once the Soul of each, and God of all." The power of the poem lies in its discovery that immanence is alienating, that that which is everywhere can in fact be nowhere. The divinity it seeks is so depersonalizing and dehumanizing that the great marriage that Abrams celebrates, of "the single consciousness to the world without," is at war with the marriage of one man and one woman.

If we can read past the doctrinal truisms of the response imagined in Sara's "more serious eye," that glance through which she reasserts her personal presence, we will find it superbly balanced against Coleridge's speculations. To bid her husband to "walk humbly with . . . [his] God" is to reassert divine personality and specifically human characteristics; *walking* itself resonates against the recumbent *lying* posture of the speculative movement, acknowledging a world of effort which "the one Life" elides. Addressing Sara as "Meek Daughter in the family of Christ" reasserts the familiality of devotion, the humanity of worship. The poem's use of formulaic language in this section, language which is communally accessible and easily sharable, stands in sharp contrast to the brilliant singularity of the language of its earlier speculations. The poem has discovered paradoxically that hunger for immanence begets absence and alienation, and that acceptance of transcendence is the key to presence:

> For never guiltless may I speak of him,
> The Incomprehensible! save when with awe
> I praise him, and with Faith that inly *feels*.

The "Incomprehensible"—here divinity in all its austere transcendence—is twice renamed in the surrounding lines by the personal pronoun "him." This nominal sequence, "him . . . The Incomprehensible. . . . him," expresses graphically the poem's closing insistence on the inseparability of transcendence and personality. Its recovery of personality is then extended to the speaker, "me, / A sinful and most miserable man, / Wilder'd and dark," and it restores those other individual blessings, presented as gifts and possessions, which had been threatened by speculation: "Peace, and this Cot, and thee, heart-honour'd Maid!"

My reading of the poem has attempted to work from within to determine the way in which it grounds its confrontation of beliefs. Its historical validity may be measured by the degree to which it confirms McFarland's observations about the strains within Coleridge's thought as he participated in the contemporary controversy over pantheism, the *Pantheismusstreit*, the ambivalences of which set "Pantheism against Theism. Atheism against Christianity. Personality against the outer world. The head against the heart" (166). I would further argue, though, that one does not have to share or even honor the body of belief attributed to Sara in order to apprehend the dialogic of the poem. If the conflict between transcendence and immanence allows one entry, so do its conflicting modes of perception, of depiction of nature, and of love. Who among us has not at some time surmised that what Sara's eyes are really saying is "Shut up and kiss me," called to mind Don Juan's uncomfortably analogous fits of adolescent nature-worship, and entertained the possibility of a parody from Sara's perspective akin to Anthony Hecht's "The Dover Bitch," that magically funny riposte to Matthew Arnold's somber meditations?

My point is that conflicting beliefs are wholly functional elements of "The Eolian Harp," and that discussions which evade, minimize, or otherwise trivialize them cannot do the poem or Coleridge justice. Modern criticism's avoidance of belief, which often claims its warrant from Coleridge's own strictly circumscribed "willing suspension of disbelief for the moment, which constitutes poetic faith,"[9] distorts and enervates the romantic achievement. The dialogic of a poem like "The Eolian Harp" calls for an equally dialogical criticism, which is willing both to enter fully into a work's theological and metaphysical positions and to provide its best reasoned responses to Coleridge's open invitation, "What if?" What if this assertion were true? What would follow from it? What are its consequences for human life? In its final form of 1828, "The Eolian Harp" completes its own profound critique of "the one Life," which it had begun more than thirty years before. By coming to judgment on the conflicting beliefs it has embodied, it should encourage a criticism which will grant them equal seriousness, which might well include the seriousness of opposition which does not masquerade as aesthetics.

A purely aesthetic criticism of poems like "The Eolian Harp" is insufficient, however dense and compelling the historical detail with which it buttresses one side of its poetic argument. Its procedures reveal more about our need to bring romanticism within the compass of modernism than about the poetry itself. Of course such criticism is not entirely averse to dramatic conflict, upon which it purports to thrive. But it seems able to accept this conflict only when it can be made part of a positive, progressive, expansionist dialectic, incorporating all elements into some higher unity. It balks at embracing a poetic dialogic which is equally capable of rejecting beliefs which, however attractive, compelling, or characteristic of the age, are found somehow inadequate. "The Eolian Harp" may be the cleanest case we have of such conflict, and for this reason it may finally be one of the less interesting. I argue elsewhere that other central lyrics, such as Wordsworth's Intimations Ode and "Resolution and Independence," require equally rigorous examinations of their most quintessentially "romantic" sections, which seldom receive sustained critical attention.[10] Our inability to attend to unbridgeable conflicts of belief in romantic lyric is one of the clearest measures of the difference between the romantics and us. At the same time, it marks the distance between us, as academic readers, and the rest of us—them, as we are wont to think of that substantial portion of the world's population for which belief, creed, and doctrine remain central determinants for action. This is a distance we might find it worth narrowing.

NOTES

1. M. H. Abrams, ed., *Literature and Belief: English Institute Essays, 1957* (New York: Columbia University Press, 1958).

2. Gerald Graff, *Poetic Statement and Critical Dogma* (Evanston, Illinois: Northwestern University Press, 1970). Graff has recently refined his critique of anti-propositional literary theory, although he now prefers the term "anti-assertional" as more technically accurate; see "Literature as Assertions," in *American Critics at Work: Examinations of Contemporary Literary Theories,* ed. Victor A. Kramer (Troy, New York: Whitstone Publishing Co., 1984), 81–110.

3. Cleanth Brooks, "Implications of an Organic Theory of Poetry," in *Literature and Belief,* 63.

4. See especially Jerome J. McGann, *The Romantic Ideology: A Critical Investigation* (Chicago: University of Chicago Press, 1983), and Clifford H. Siskin, *The Historicity of Romantic Discourse* (New York: Oxford University Press, 1988).

5. Abrams, *The Correspondent Breeze: Essays on English Romanticism* (New York: Norton, 1984), 159. Subsequent references to this and other essays by Abrams are to this collection and are given parenthetically. My analysis follows the text of "The Eolian Harp" of 1828 and after, as found in *The Complete Poetical Works of Samuel Taylor Coleridge,* 2 vols. (Oxford: Clarendon Press, 1912), 1:100–102. My discussion concentrates on Abrams because of his towering presence in romantic studies. For discussions of "The Eolian Harp" with similar concerns see William H. Scheuerle, "A Reexamination of Coleridge's 'The Eolian Harp,' " *Studies in English Literature* 15 (1975): 591–599; and Douglas B. Wilson, *Two Modes of Apprehending Nature: A Gloss on the Coleridgean Symbol, PMLA* 87 (1972): 42–52.

6. Thomas McFarland, *Coleridge and the Pantheist Tradition* (Oxford: Clarendon Press, 1969), 166.

7. I borrow here the terminology of I. A. Richards, *Practical Criticism: A Study of Literary Judgment* (London: Routledge and Kegan Paul, 1929), 16.

8. For a provocative discussion of the role of particularity in another of Coleridge's conversation poems, "Fears in Solitude," see Karl Kroeber, *British Romantic Art* (Berkeley: University of California Press, 1986), 85–93.

9. Coleridge, *Biographia Literaria,* ed. James Engell and Walter Jackson Bate (Princeton: Princeton University Press, 1983), 2:6.

10. Gene W. Ruoff, *Wordsworth and Coleridge: The Making of the Major Lyrics, 1802–1804* (New Brunswick, New Jersey: Rutgers University Press, 1989). See 147–154 for a reading of the rhetorical function of the old man-stone-seabeast passage of "Resolution and Independence"; see 229–260 for a reconsideration of the function of the myth of pre-existence in the Ode, which is at issue in Abrams's "Belief and the Suspension of Disbelief," 24–28.

Lord Byron

Most Byron studies of the past decade have derived, directly or indirectly, from the extraordinary scholarly accomplishments of two men, Jerome J. McGann, responsible for the impressive new edition of Byron's poetical works, and Leslie Marchand, who in his ninth decade completed his superbly accurate but entirely readable edition of Byron's letters. From these solid foundations critical respectability has been restored to the English writer most famous in his own day, and still in the non-English-speaking world the one British poet besides Shakespeare whose name is familiar. A thorough analysis of the virtual obliteration of Byron as a serious object of critical study in the middle of this century, a dismissal in which traditionalists such as M. H. Abrams, new critics, structuralists, and Yale formalists concurred, would make a fascinating contribution to our understanding of twentieth-century academic criticism. Here, however, we point only to one feature of the 1980s revival of interest in Byron's poetry, the perception of it as foretelling the nature and the significance of the dissolution of psychosocial boundaries so characteristic of late twentieth-century cultures. Probably central to this feature of Byron's achievements is what we now call his bisexuality. The importance of the poet's homoerotic tendencies was first emphasized by Leslie Marchand, and familiarized in 1985 by the publication of Louis Crompton's valuable book, *Byron and Greek Love: Homophobia in Nineteenth Century England* (1985).

The contemporary perception of Byron as uniquely gifted in representing new modes of interplay between sociopolitical pressures and the dynamics (particularly in regard to sexual resonances) of interpersonal relations has produced a reassessment of every aspect of his art, with a central focus on *Don Juan,* in our time at last recognized as a major document of British romanticism as well as a masterpiece of European literature. Among contributors to this revalorization one might mention Frederick L. Beaty's *Byron the Satirist* (1985) and Peter Graham's *"Don Juan" and Regency England* (1990). That *Don Juan* marked a decisive turn in Byron's relation to his public is established by William St. Clair's groundbreaking analysis, "The Impact of Byron's Writing: An Evaluative Approach," in the collection *Byron: Augustan and Romantic,* edited by Andrew Rutherford (1990), which deploys quantifiable data to demonstrate the transformation in Byron's popularity in midcareer from the literati to a more popular readership. Probably the most influential commentators, however, have been Peter J. Manning—for example his *"Don Juan and Byron's Imperceptiveness to the English Word"* (1979)—and Jerome J. McGann; the latter, in addition to his invaluable annotations to *Don Juan* in *The Complete Poetical Works* (1986), has added to his book *Don Juan in Context* (1976) several seminal essays, including "Byron, Mobility and the Poetics of Historical Ventriloquism" (1985), and more recently "My Brain Is Feminine: Byron and the Poetry of Deception," in *Byron: Augustan and Romantic* (1990). Also worthy of note are some carefully analytical essays by Paul Elledge, such as "Parting Shots: Byron's Ending *Don Juan I*" (1988), and Frederick W. Shilstone's *Byron and the Myth of Tradition* (1988).

ANDREW M. COOPER

Shipwreck and Skepticism: Don Juan *Canto II*

The foundation of Andrew Cooper's analysis in the following selection is his original insight into the importance of chance in *Mazeppa* as providing a forerunner for the more complex demands made upon readers by both substantive and stylistic contingencies in *Don Juan.* Contemporary critics are more comfortable with such "uncontrolled" material than their predecessors, which helps to explain the resurgence in Byron's popularity. And Cooper's focus enables him to define with admirable specificity the dynamics of the reader's intricate participation in the constituting of *Don Juan,* even how "the way we experience *Don Juan's* ottava rima" is decisive to what we help to make the poem mean.

Cooper thus exemplifies the best applications of "reader-response" criticism to romantic poetry, especially since his perspective is historical: how we today respond, he makes us understand, contrasts dramatically with Keats's shocked response. Particularly valuable here is the explanation of how the reader is involved even in the poem's lapses in taste, for example, when we are compelled to recognize of the shipwreck that "after so horrific an event, what remains to say? Only cant." This approach permits Cooper to arrive at a definition of Byronic skepticism as less philosophic rationalism than a "perpetual process of pragmatic adjustment," a definition congenial to most recent critics, particularly those like Anne K. Mellor who have concerned themselves with issues of "romantic irony": see her *English Romantic Irony* (1980). In addition to studies mentioned above in our general headnote on Byron, relevant criticism includes E. D. Hirsch's "Byron and the Terrestrial Paradise," in *From Sensibility to Romanticism,* edited by Frederick W. Hilles and Harold Bloom (1965); Robert Gleckner's *Byron and the Ruins of Paradise* (1967); Michael Cooke's *The Blind Man Traces the Circle: On the Patterns and Philosophy of Byron's Poetry* (1969); and Peter J. Manning's *Byron and His Fictions* (1978).

From *Keats-Shelley Journal* 32 (1983): 63–80. Reprinted by permission of Keats-Shelley Association of America, Inc.

"Life is, in itself and forever, shipwreck. To be shipwrecked is not to drown. . . .
Consciousness of shipwreck, being the truth of life, constitutes salvation."
Ortega y Gasset, "In Search of Goethe from Within"

Mazeppa, composed simultaneously with *Don Juan* Canto I during the late sum-
mer of 1818, constitutes in several respects a preliminary version of the shipwreck
episode in Canto II. In both cases a youthful adulterer undergoes a kind of descent
into Hell, finally awakens before a Nausicaa, and thereafter remains exiled from
his homeland. More important, Byron's active juxtaposing of different historical
contexts in *Mazeppa* sheds light on his considerably subtler manipulations of
ottava rima in *Don Juan. Mazeppa's* opening stanza, alluding to the recent fall of
Napoleon, introduces the poem as contemporaneous. The narrative, however,
takes place immediately following the battle of Pultowa in 1709; and within that
narrative, the old hetman tracks his "seventy years of memory back" to his "twen-
tieth spring," 1660 (lines 126–127).[1] The time-frames distance the reader from the
events of Mazeppa's story, yet by forming a continuum they implicitly connect us
at the far end. The effect is of a progressive historicism, as the intensely private
experience standing at the core of the narrative (virtually a nonexperience, since
Mazeppa loses consciousness at the nadir of his journey) is gradually subsumed
into a public context, becoming transformed from, first, the original, near-
solipsistic event itself, to the long stored-up memory of a single individual, to a
beguiling story intended for a small "band of chiefs" (line 44), to, finally, a poem
whose audience includes ourselves.

Mazeppa thus appears less a formal poetic object willed directly by an author
than a naturally evolved artifact inseparable from the surrounding contours of
European history. Those contours, moreover, are seen to be defined largely by
chance. *Contra* William Marshall, who ingeniously makes Mazeppa a parody of
Charles's common sense, the narrator's position is not "clearly anti-
providential," nor does Mazeppa express by contrast an "organized moral view
of the universe" according to which his rescue by the Cossack maid constitutes a
"providential intervention."[2] Quite the opposite, the moral of Mazeppa's tale is
that he was saved by an unforeseeable stroke of luck, the same luck that will
perhaps save Charles now. In devising a clever torture for Mazeppa, the Count
Palatine inadvertently raised him to power and so ensured his own defeat; by the
same token, the defeated Charles may also live to destroy his enemies.[3] The
narrator's remark about "the hazard of the die" (line 15) therefore tends to
support Mazeppa's affirmation of chance as a positive force. If you have hit
bottom, if the odds are "ten to one at least [for] the foe" (line 114), then even
random change can only help. This capacity to sustain ups and downs is what
makes man more than merely animal, despite his untamed passions, which the
wild horse plainly represents. Whereas the horse's unrelenting instinct for its
homeland proves self-destructive, Mazeppa, whose home is simply wherever he
happens to find himself (as shown in stanzas 3 and 4), survives his trek to love
again. Similarly, the reason "Danger levels man and brute" (line 51) is that it
brutalizes man; but of course danger is not the sole condition of human exis-
tence, and hence Mazeppa ridicules Charles for making war to the exclusion of
love (lines 126–142). Indeed, the satirical thrust of his tale is its tacit advice that,

since we all must suffer defeat sooner or later, it is better to have loved and lost than never to have loved at all and still to have lost.

Yet even random change has its limits; the dice may be fickle, but their permutations repeat. Thus the constant recurrence within the poem of rivers (the Borysthenes, the dark unnamed stream of fifty years past), horses (Gieta's, Mazeppa's Bucephalus, and the wild Tartarian courser), and an assortment of personal and military defeats suggests that, although meaningful causal connections between the individual occasions of experience may be impossible to determine, nevertheless life's various circumstances do unmistakably embody distinct patterns of contrast and resemblance. So the top and bottom of man's universe—paradise and death, love and brutalization—emerge from the narrative as fixed lineaments of experience without which it would lose self-differentiation and simply dissolve into the general flux. As random as an individual's life may be, it can never trespass those bounds beyond which lies the merely unimaginable: gods and dust.

Far more than even *Mazeppa, Don Juan* abounds with chance surprises, above all in the shipwreck episode of Canto II, where raw forces of nature solely propel the narrative. Subjugated by storms from without and starvation from within, man appears throughout the episode as a cipher lacking effective power to resist. A total newcomer to the larger world in which henceforth *Don Juan* takes place, Juan is here less a protagonist than just another sufferer scarcely to be distinguished from everybody else aboard ship. One recalls only his heroic stance, pistols drawn, before the rum-room (II.xxxv–xxxvi), and his tacit refusal to eat Pedrillo (II.lxxviii). The shipwreck, then, is Juan's rite of passage into "our nautical existence" (II.xii) on the sea of adventitious circumstance, the Deluge which precludes any direct return to Spain and Donna Inez. It serves to define the Stygian nadir of his new-found universe, much as the subsequent Haidée idyll defines its paradisal apex.

For Byron himself, moreover, it seems the decision to continue the poem beyond Canto I, apparently first designed as a separate poem like *Beppo*, involved an embarkation similar to his hero's.[4] The two well-known stanzas he added to the completed draft of Canto I make the parallel almost explicit:

No more—no more—Oh! never more on me
  The freshness of the heart can fall like dew,
Which out of all the lovely things we see
  Extracts emotions beautiful and new;
Hived in our bosoms like the bag o' the bee.
  Think'st thou the honey with those objects grew?
Alas! 'twas not in them, but in thy power
To double even the sweetness of a flower.

(I.ccxiv)

"Thou" evidently refers to Byron's reader. Assuming our ignorance of the melancholy truth he wishes to convey, the poet rejects the earlier first-person plural and addresses the reader directly. Yet the continuing second person of the next stanza reveals that Byron is really addressing his own heart, perhaps has been all along:

No more—no more— Oh! never more, my heart,
   Canst thou be my sole world, my universe!
Once all in all, but now a thing apart,
   Thou canst not be my blessing or my curse:
The illusion's gone for ever.

                (i.ccxv)

Ultimately, however, such distinctions fail, for Byron's heart and his implied readers are one and the same. His heart can no longer be his universe, because it now must take account of the larger world outside itself, the world of concrete human life existing beyond poetry and encompassing ourselves as actual readers. Hence *we* become the objects out of which the disillusioned poet will extract new emotional sustenance. The series of contexts that *Mazeppa* deployed as a framing device, then, *Don Juan* Canto II actively incorporates as a method of composition. The consequent relationships between Juan's occasion of shipwreck, the author's collateral expressions of skepticism, and finally the individual reader's subsuming experience of both, supply the subject of this essay.

Unexpected as it is, the shipwreck episode starts out open-ended. Anything might happen. Yet it is almost completely closed off at the other end, and Juan seems to escape through an orifice. This development stems from the way the law of attrition at sea logically works itself out: "Famine—despair—cold, thirst and heat, had done / Their work on them by turns" (ii.cii), to which one might add drowning, bad meat and delirium, overexposure, and sharks. If the one doesn't get you, the others will. The form of the episode is therefore a vortex of diminishing possibilities. Juan's situation grows progressively more cramped and isolated as he moves from the Seville aristocracy to a ship carrying approximately 250 people to a longboat containing 30. Within the longboat, Juan's refusal to turn cannibal distinguishes him from "all save three or four" (ii.lxxviii) who die anyway, leaving Juan the sole survivor. As the allusion to Dante's Ugolino suggests, cannibalism is the innermost ring of this Hell; Juan's solitary struggle with Ocean's "insatiate grave" (ii.cviii) is the nadir; like Dante he squeezes through it and emerges into a new world, Haidée's island.

Byron articulates the descent as a series of small mishaps in which hopes are raised only to be dashed. The episode begins in full expectation of a safe passage; but then "at one o'clock" the ship is suddenly about to sink (ii.xxvii). Then it appears the pumps will save them; but then they almost capsize in a squall (ii.xxx). Then there comes "a flash of hope once more" as the wind lulls with "a glimpse of sunshine" (ii.xxxviii); but then the storm renews and the boats must get out (ii.xlv). Then we learn that, as " 'T is very certain the desire of life / Prolongs it," "people in an open boat [can] live upon the love of life" (ii.lxiv–lxvi); but then we also learn that this will not suffice them indefinitely because "man is a carnivorous production. . . . He cannot live, like woodcocks, upon suction" (ii.lxvii). Then arrives a sleep-inducing calm that restores the survivors' strength; but then they awake and eat all their provisions (ii.lxviii). And so forth. The sequence suggests that events trick us into hope in order that we may be doubly defeated when they subsequently turn more dangerous yet. For the failure of each new promise of deliverance leaves the men not the same as before, but worse, because they have irrevocably used up one more chance for survival. " 'T is best to struggle to the last," advises the narrator, " 'T is never too late to be wholly wreck'd" (ii.xxxix)—

good advice, surely; and yet three stanzas later one discovers its terrific irony, as the pumps give out and the dismasted ship rolls "a wreck complete" (II.xlii). It is as though the struggle to keep it afloat only led to a greater devastation (in fact, they deliberately cut away the masts to avoid broaching). This almost systematic way in which various saving possibilities only serve to become fresh defeats distinctly conveys the impression of an impersonal, casually malignant power of circumstance gradually revealing itself through the course of the episode.

Yet as their situation worsens, the men hope all the more intensely. From the cannibalism to Juan's final arrival on the beach, the poem presents a series of auguries: the shower of rain, the rainbow, the white bird, the turtle. The episode begins with an objective narrative of suspenseful action telling with considerable show of authority exactly what the ocean did to the ship and what the crew is doing to save it (II.xxvii). The reality of the world "out there" is assumed; it may be inhuman and destructive, but one can still be confident of knowing how to handle an emergency. Later, however, the objective narrative virtually disappears—appropriately so, for no longer is anything taking place out there; inert, the survivors are not engaged in visible activity. The poem therefore shifts to a phenomenalistic presentation of their experience of reality, a realm in which belief, illusions, and symbolism play a vital part. Causality stands in abeyance; as the boat drifts, events seem to transpire without what Hume calls "necessary connexion," comprising instead simply an observed succession of independent phenomena (a rainbow, a bird, a turtle). In such a world, as in Coleridge's Ancient Mariner's, there is no reason for rational, purposive action because no likelihood exists that it will produce its intended effect. Mental activity such as hope appears at least as effective.

This is not to imply that the phenomenal world of the longboat survivors is experienced directly by the reader the way the Ancient Mariner's is. "We" are not in the longboat, "they" are: we see them through the narrative presentation. But this is just what we were *not* conscious of doing at the outset of the episode, when the narrative appeared objective. Now it is indeed a presentation and, moreover, a skeptical one. Says Byron of the rainbow: "Our shipwreck'd seamen thought it a good omen— / It is as well to think so now and then /. . . And may become a great advantage when / Folks are discouraged" (II.xciii). In their helplessness the survivors have made a possibly useful interpretation, no more or less. Byron's remarks are final, but they do not dispel our appreciation of how lovely the rainbow looked to "the dim eyes of these shipwreck'd men" (II.xci). Their hope, which interprets natural phenomena as evidences of things unseen, is a tentative form of faith. Furthermore, the comparison of the rainbow to "Quite a celestial kaleidoscope" (II.xciii) suggests that such faith, under the circumstances, is inevitable. Like a kaleidoscope, a rainbow is not simply seen, but seen *into*, for it is an optical illusion existing as object entirely in the eye of the beholder. Being all appearance, as it were, the rainbow is thus whatever the half-dead men in the longboat perceive it to be.

If we prefer the narrator's skepticism here, it is with awareness that he stands outside the longboat and can afford to be rational. Standing in "their" shoes (which anyway they have already eaten), we might well find skepticism to be just one more discouragement. The point about the survivors' providential attitude is that it is more pragmatic than rationalism. They shrewdly anticipate a twofold benefit from the turtle and the sacred-seeming white bird: the animals are regarded as both auguries and meat, and the two viewpoints do not conflict. After all, given a boatload of starving men, how else is a turtle evidence of heavenly concern but that it may serve to sustain life? Similarly, what makes the bird a "bird of promise" is partly its promise of becoming food. Had the Ancient Mariner done the natural thing with *his* white bird—eaten it—he might have spared himself much grief, for the killing in that case would not have been wanton.

Such pragmatism gets its force from the way we experience the form of *Don Juan*'s ottava rima. Much has been said on this score, with attention usually directed toward the closing couplet rhyme. Alvin Kernan has emphasized the "but then" movement of the poem, its vital unpredictability; for him, the wave-like "onward rush of life" that the poem imitates, "upward to a pause, and then a sweep away, is most consistently present in the stanza form. . . . The first six lines stagger forward, like the life they contain, toward the resting place of the concluding couplet and the security of its rhyme—and a very shaky resting place it most often is."[5] Edward Bostetter replies that the reader's expectations are not simply thwarted but renewed as curiosity; he proposes a complementary movement, "what next?" which "puts the emphasis on the anticipatory suspense."[6] What perusal of the poem's individual stanzas shows is that these two movements coalesce so as to deny readers an accustomed complacency. We are drawn into and then thrust out of each stanza, which thus forms a miniature vortex. We end where we began, but meantime have become consciously aware of experiencing a fiction. Then we suspend that consciousness and proceed to repeat the process by moving on to the ever-imminent next stanza. The vortex form of the *Don Juan* stanza is not, however, simply a stylistic version of the thematic "falling" first discerned in the poem by George Ridenour;[7] it is less the characteristic Romantic fall into reality or experience than a freely willed descent into a specifically literary self-awareness, into what both Jerome McGann and Peter Manning, borrowing a phrase from Wallace Stevens, term "the fictions of reality."[8] "The actions of the poem complete themselves in [the reader's] consciousness," says Manning;[9] yes, and they do so by directly exercising our moral imaginations. The questions Byron raises entail active examination of ourselves as social individuals. In Canto II he is not asking, "What would you do if stuck in a longboat with thirty others without food?"—as though unshipwrecked readers could give any answer that were not fantasy. The question lacks ballast; one wants to reply, "*I* would heroically save them all (but don't press me for details)." Instead Byron asks, "Exactly what *does* one do, having arrived at such a situation through force of circumstance?"—and what one does is, as usual in life, no one particular thing: not everybody eats Pedrillo. To repeat myself, "we" are not in the same boat as "them," but it is conceivable we could be because clearly their world much resembles ours. This consciousness of sharing the same context of possibilities as the shipwrecked men, without sharing even vicariously in their experience, is clarified by scrutinizing the individual stanzas themselves.

First consider stanza xxvii, the beginning of the end for all but Juan:

> At one o'clock the wind with sudden shift
>   Threw the ship right into the trough of the sea,
> Which struck her aft, and made an awkward rift,
>   Started the stern-post, also shattered the
> Whole of her stern-frame, and, ere she could lift
>   Herself from out her present jeopardy,

The rudder tore away: 'twas time to sound
The pumps, and there were four feet water found.

In poetry, the prototype for such a nautical *tour de force* was William Falconer's *The Shipwreck* (1762), an exciting first-hand account in which numerous professional-sounding marine terms are casually retailed in rhyming couplets. But Byron's stanza is effective as much by what it does not do as by what it does. It is all objective narrative, a sudden accumulation of events without any development. The wind shifts, and then no less then six violently active verbs happen to the ship one after the other; even the syntax, perfectly unextraordinary in itself, appears jerked about to fit the ottava rima. One realizes the helplessness of the ship, and the immense arbitrary power of the ocean that has evidently cuffed it. Appropriately, therefore, we find the birthday-snapper in the couplet rhyme is too damp to explode except matter-of-factly. Events have so overwhelmed the crew that it is not until line 7 that it manages to take defensive action; but even then, all the men do is discover still another way in which Ocean has anticipated them. So by forcibly failing to meet our expectations, this unusual stanza serves to reveal what, in fact, we expect of the usual *Don Juan* stanza: namely, that it begin with an objective narrative of events leading to description of an active human response, leading in turn to commentary by the narrator himself. Not coincidentally, this is the same pattern of development we saw take place within the episode overall: Canto II moves from an impersonal narrative of the sinking ship implying confidence in the reality of the world "out there," to a presentation of the survivors' subjective construing of that world, to Byron's disinterested but sympathetic statements of skepticism.

Stanza 1 I take to be the ottava rima model on which Byron elsewhere plays changes. It is a manipulation of narrative, but not to make any particular point. However, the manipulation involves several distinct shifts of perspective. We can enumerate them.

Some trial had been making at a raft,
   With little hope in such a rolling sea,
A sort of thing at which one would have laugh'd,
   If any laughter at such times could be,
Unless with people who too much have quaff'd,
   And have a kind of wild and horrid glee,
Half epileptical, and half hysterical:—
Their preservation would have been a miracle.

Lines 1–2) Objectively speaking, the raft is a futile effort. 3) So futile, the reader might find it ridiculous. 4) Now, however, we are grimly reminded that under the circumstances a raft is better than nothing. 5–7) And yet there is room for compromise between the two points of view: if you want to laugh, laugh with them, the hideous despairing drunks. 8) This line cuts off the lurid description of the laughter, itself slightly hysterical, by giving a blunt assessment of the raftsmen's chances. It thus repeats lines 1–2, only now it is the colloquial Byron speaking, not the impersonal narrative ("a miracle," not "little hope"). The stanza bends into the reader challenging us directly with the "If" of line 4. Then, with the concessional "Unless," it turns back toward the fictive scene, which however now seems real in that it ironically subsumes our own response to it;

with the introduction of "wild and horrid glee," the reader is forced to recognize that, under the pressure of actual shipwreck, his armchair amusement at the raft could well become something less pleasant. The intervention of Byron in line 8 completes the proof that we are not entitled to judge these people, only their chances for survival.

In the previous stanza, xlix, the same pattern was used first to suggest the existence of an evil Deity hidden in matter, then skeptically to show that people aboard a storm-beaten ship at least have good reason to believe so. The first four lines, with their hint of a reversed Genesis, present the uncreating God of Byron's "Darkness." (What makes the last line of stanza 1 so potent is partly its suggestion that the raftsmen need *two* miracles, one to save them, plus one to create the good God who might bother to do so.) But then this vision is attributed to "hopeless eyes" looking only at "the night." Yet there is no cynicism here, for it next appears that the night these people saw really did "grimly darkle o'er the faces pale, / And the dim desolate deep." The horror they imagined therefore was not *all* illusion, a point the narrator reinforces by affirming that "now Death was here." The skepticism cuts too deep to be cynical.

Too deep, perhaps, for those who see in stanza lv only a failure of good taste. Even Andrew Rutherford, author of the tough-minded "*Don Juan:* War and Realism," hits upon this stanza as "the only one . . . in which Byron lapses into a flippant derisive tone which would have been perfectly appropriate in *Beppo* but which constitutes a blemish, a breach of decorum, in his wonderful description of the wreck."[10]

> All the rest perish'd; near two hundred souls
>   Had left their bodies; and what's worse, alas!
> When over Catholics the Ocean rolls,
>   They must wait several weeks before a mass
> Takes off one peak of purgatorial coals,
>   Because, till people know what's come to pass,
> They won't lay out their money on the dead—
> It costs three francs for every mass that's said.

Certainly the lapse is there; yet in a sense it belongs as much to the reader as to Byron. For consider the context. As early as stanza xxxiv, the ship presents the spectacle of a *Walpurgisnacht:* "Some plundered, some drank spirits, some sung psalms / . . . Strange sounds of wailing, blasphemy, devotion, / Clamoured in chorus to the roaring Ocean." The spectacle intensifies once the sinking commences. We now become witnesses to a microcosm revealing the various ways in which men prepare to meet death: "Some went to prayers . . . / . . . Some looked o'er the bow; / Some hoisted out the boats," "Some lashed them in their hammocks; some put on / Their best clothes, as if going to a fair; / Some cursed the day on which they saw the Sun, / And gnashed their teeth," "Some trial had been making at a raft" (II.xliv–l). The ship sinks in a virtual apocalypse: "the sea yawn'd round her like a hell," "And first one universal shriek there rush'd / Louder than the loud Ocean . . . / . . . and then all was hush'd" (II.lii–liii). Or almost all: wind and ocean continue, and "at intervals there gush'd, / Accompanied with a convulsive splash, / A solitary shriek, the bubbling cry / Of some strong swimmer in his agony." In retrospect, an instant and utter apocalypse would have been a relief. Instead of anything so final, one ship went down. The point of Byron's bringing in the agonized drowning castaway of William Cowper's poem here is to provide some distance from this disaster, which is absolute in itself but limited; he shifts our perspective to the survivors in the longboat (II.liv).

To read the limpid elegiac opening of stanza lv, then, is to prepare for a eulogy: "All the rest perish'd; near two hundred souls / Had left their bodies." The second phrase is taken as a pathetic restatement of the first, recalling as it does the Ancient Mariner's "Four times fifty living men" whose "souls did from their bodies fly . . . / Like the whizz of my crossbow."[11] But it becomes a trick, for Byron proceeds, in a travesty of Coleridge's literalism, to belabor theological assumptions hidden in the phrase. The result is a satire of the eulogy we expected. For plainly the "leave-taking" of these men's souls was not the graceful affair such a formula implies. After so horrific a spectacle, what remains to say? Only "cant." If we realize this, then the circumspection with which we read that "Nine souls more went" in the cutter will steady us to accept lines otherwise unacceptable:

> They grieved for those who perish'd with the cutter,
> And also for the biscuit-casks and butter.
>
> (II.lxi)

"High thought / Link'd to a servile mass of matter" is Lucifer's Hamlet-like description of man in *Cain*.[12] Here the couplet performs the linkage.

We began this perusal with stanza xxvii, an objective account telling precisely what happened to the ship the moment the wind shifted. We end with lovely, allusive stanza lxxxiv:

> And that same night there fell a shower of rain,
>   For which their mouths gaped, like the cracks of earth
> When dried to summer's dust; till taught by pain,
>   Men really know not what good water's worth;
> If you had been in Turkey or in Spain,
>   Or with a famish'd boat's-crew had your berth,
> Or in the desert heard the camel's bell,
> You'd wish yourself where Truth is—in a well.

By contrast with meat, which must be hunted and killed, the rain shower comes spontaneously as a gift. Like Truth, water is valuable essentially; it is free, yet under the circumstances it makes these men "rich" (II.lxxxvi). Chiefly, though, it is the biblical quality of the poetry that makes the rain so much resemble grace or manna. Lines 2–3 echo the thought that man is dust of the earth, his life a summer's day; there is a deep, melancholy sympathy for this fiery dust who feels his thirst so urgently. Almost immediately, however, this developing awareness of the boatcrew's universality begins to become rationalized by the philosophy of suffering introduced in lines 3–4. Line 5 goes a step further and addresses us directly; taking us outside the narrative, it establishes a global context for thirst in which "a famish'd boat's-crew" is but a local instance. Their predicament is not essentially different from that of others whose thirst we find small difficulty in imagining. The joke at the end becomes effective by our recognizing that it is our universal experience of water's preciousness that makes us identify it with Truth in the first place. This is the same pragmatism we met with earlier in the providential turtle. The allusiveness that functions as pathos in lines 1–3 thus becomes an explicit intellectual point in line 8—almost, but not quite, the butt of a joke. The rain shower *has* really seemed like grace; but it is no wonder that it should.

Clearly, Byron's skepticism is less a definite philosophic rationalism than a perpetual process of pragmatic adjustment. Hence it completes itself only in the reader's mind (not the narrator's, whose thought, however various, remains determined by what Byron actually wrote), as over and over we are made to confront, examine, and revise our own prior responses to the poem. To a skepticism so paradoxically thoroughgoing in its tentativeness, an affirmation any less indirect is bound to appear merely self-approving. As Peter Manning points out:

> *Don Juan* baffled contemporaries and incurred accusations of cynicism because its first readers did not realize that Byron had transferred the locus of meaning from within the poem outside to them. Pope draws his audience into a compact of solidarity against the fools he presents—the Dunces, the Timons, the Sir Balaams. In Byron, however, the object of satire is not a fictive, representative character, but the false assumptions in the individual reader that his reactions to the poem bring to the surface.[13]

So with regard to the shipwreck episode, what is most striking about first readers' reactions is not their horror, but specifically their mortification, as though they felt Byron had personally duped them somehow. All protest their excruciated "consciousness of the insulting deceit which has been practised upon us. . . . Every high thought that was ever kindled in our hearts by the muse of Byron . . . every remembered moment of admiration and enthusiasm is up in arms against him"—thus the *Blackwood's* reviewer.[14] Keats—whom *Blackwood's* held anathema—less prissily expresses the same sense of betrayal; in Severn's report he flung the book down, exclaiming that Byron had evidently grown so jaded "that there was nothing left for him but to laugh & gloat over the most solemn & heart-rending scenes of human misery; this storm of his is one of the most diabolical attempts ever made upon our sympathies. . . ."[15] Such reactions are quite accurate in their way. Most of the stanzas just examined contain a development whose challenge to the reader could easily be construed as mockery or betrayal. As stanza l shows no less than lxxxiv, *Don Juan* elicits pathos not for the sake of pathos alone, but in order that we may consider its appropriateness within a particular context. Normally, this entails the intervention of the narrator whose irony, as in the stanza Rutherford singled out, can seem even to unmoralizing modern readers like the devilish laughing and gloating Keats imagined. Among contemporaries it appears that only Shelley, applying the arguments of *Areopagitica*, was able to grasp how the poem locates its meanings within the individual reader, thus making his response a direct moral act. "You unveil & present in its true deformity what is worst in human nature," he wrote Byron, "& it is this what the witlings of the age murmur at, conscious of their want of power to endure the scrutiny of such a light."[16]

Byron's implicit rejection of the cannibalism, the aspect of the shipwreck it remains to consider, follows from the premium *Don Juan* places upon the socialized individual. That the cannibalism is to be regarded as a moral issue appears from the fact that somebody is killed. Nevertheless the reader is not allowed to pass judgment, and the narrator judges the event only by its consequences.

'T was not to be expected that [Juan] should,
Even in extremity of their disaster,
Dine with them on his pastor and his master.

'T was better that he did not; for, in fact,
   The consequence was awful in the extreme;
For they, who were most ravenous in the act,
   Went ranging mad—Lord! how they did blaspheme!
And foam, and roll, with strange convulsions rack'd,
   Drinking salt-water like a mountain stream,
Tearing, and grinning, howling, screeching, swearing,
And, with hyæna-laughter, died despairing.

                    (ii.lxxviii–lxxix)

The "extremity" to which they resort is repaid in kind by the consequence being "awful in the extreme"; but holier-than-thou readers who believe the cannibals got what they deserve must immediately confront a mock-serious distortion of themselves: "Lord! how they did blaspheme!" The narrator here is holier than anybody, and as a result seems merely hypocritical: "Kill and eat people if you must, but swearing like that is an affront to society. Cannibalism thus appears as "man's worst—his second fall," the fall of civilized man into barbarism;[17] the last two lines describe primarily the behavior of monkeys. This is Byron's societal version of Coleridge's Death-in-Life. Yet the Ancient Mariner sucked only his own blood, whereas Byron's boatcrew in much the same situation—compare the calm at stanza lxxii with that in *The Rime* Part ii—choose to sacrifice a victim to their vampiric surgeon.[18]

Leading as it does to madness and "a species of self-slaughter" (ii.cii), the cannibalism is seen to be a socialized form of suicide. Unlike hope, "the desire of life [that] / Prolongs it" by binding "people in an open boat" into a hardy little community (ii.lxvi), the killing and eating of Pedrillo is an act of cynicism. It is the individual's capitulation to his instinct for self-preservation at any cost, a desire of life murderous in the event. In the boat the men "lay like carcasses; and hope was none, / . . . They glared upon each other . . . And you might see / The longings of the cannibal arise / (Although they spoke not) in their wolfish eyes" (ii.lxxii). Like original sin, the longings arise and intensify from within; motionless, the men are visibly regressing into barbarism (apparently they have lost the power of speech); "like carcasses" is how they now perceive one another. It would appear that Byron's survivors see only the low half of what Lucifer saw, the "servile [and serviceable] mass of matter." Moreover, having consumed Pedrillo, "as if not warned sufficiently," the men next dispense with democratic lottery and like a wolfpack fix upon the master's mate "As fattest" (ii.lxxx–lxxxi). Their dehumanization emerges vividly in the next stanza: "At length they caught two Boobies and a Noddy, / And then they left off eating the dead body" (ii.lxxxii). Previously the feast possessed a certain macabre gusto (ii.lxxvii); now it seems genuinely necrophilic, an impression heightened by the ensuing reference to Dante's Ugolino. With the reappearance of normal food sources, normal standards of edibility resurface, and the other meat is recognized with horror as the damaged corpse of Pedrillo.

Cannibalism, then, represents the furthest reach from Spanish society, the barbaric inner ring of Hell below which lies the merely animal, Juan's struggle with Ocean. In a parody of the Genesis God's prolificness, Byron shows the survivors' day-by-day exhausting of their provisions; finally on "the seventh day" (I.lxxii), the day God created man and gave him life, the boatcrew kills the Christly Pedrillo and consumes him. Yet this Hell opens up within a group of ordinary, civilized Europeans. The reader looks down into it from the circle of his own values, which are the same—hence the encapsulated quality of the whole episode. The cannibalism is barbarism localized as an unlikely but genuine possibility occurring within a broader social context that, though it usually escapes barbarism, nevertheless cannot control the force of circumstance that makes barbarism always a danger. Pedrillo's skillful euthanasia by a doctor we may regard as Byron's *reductio* of a runaway principle of enlightened rational self-interest, his own Modest Proposal to the Malthusians in the audience.

Juan's heroism in the shipwreck is his Promethean persistence in civilized values that he knows, implicitly to be greater than his own personal annihilation or suffering. " 'No! / 'T is true that death awaits both you and me, / But let us die like men, not sink / Below like brutes" (II.xxxvi), he tells the whiskey-craving crew, and silently proves his credo in the nasty crucible of the longboat. Unlike the others, he resists "the savage hunger which demanded, / Like the Promethean vulture" (II.lxxv), the sacrifice of Pedrillo. For Byron, civilized man is a Prometheus who internalizes the vulture that gnaws him. Barbarism occurs when the individual looses his personal vulture to gnaw upon somebody else; inside and outside then merge, and the individual actually becomes his vulture. The cannibalism is Byron's literalization of this myth of the modern Prometheus; the bestial deaths that result, simply the natural penalty for so uncivil a "pollution" (II.lxxv; the word translates the Aeschylean *miasma,* or blood-guilt, which as E. R. Dodds remarks, "is the automatic consequence of an action, belongs to the world of external events, and operates with the same ruthless indifference to motive as a typhoid germ"[19]). No matter then that "None in particular had sought or planned it," the cannibalism is inevitably self-defeating.

Admittedly, Juan's persistence may be ingenuous, but it reflects nonetheless a vigilant sensitivity to the possibilities for true, unspecious survival—that is, for Byron, survival "like a gentleman," without compromise. The change of mind whereby Juan finally eats his favorite spaniel shows not only that his forbearance of Pedrillo is something more than fastidiousness; it also attests his moral continence under even the most trying conditions. When it comes to the crunch, we see, the profligate Juan is able to make the crucial discriminations between the moral and the sentimental, the human and the merely animal, seeing which of them is inessential and expendable and which not. It is no coincidence that Byron's manipulation of his readers through the ottava rima involves us in discriminations of the same kind. Not that Juan is therefore a directly exemplary figure, but his behavior during the shipwreck does illustrate the same resolute pragmatism we discovered in stanzas l–lxxxiv. This we may summarize as follows. Hope for the best, and act accordingly, but do not expect this or that consequence to follow or you will soon despair. To doubt something, on the other hand, is not to believe it is impossible, but only unlikely; far from necessarily conducing to despair, every doubt thus contains in itself the hopeful germ of a possibility. Or as bold Mazeppa put it, the battle lost, his forces routed, and himself surrounded by an enemy "ten to one at least": "What mortal his own doom may guess? / Let none despond, let none despair."[20] The shipwreck episode of *Don Juan* represents Byron's exploration of the ellipsis between these two statements, the first skeptical, the second affirmative, and his laying bare the moral fabric that connects them.

NOTES

1. *Byron: Poetical Works,* ed. Frederick Page, rev. John Jump, 3rd ed. (London: Oxford University Press, 1970), pp. 341–342. All subsequent quotations of Byron's poetry are from this edition.

2. William H. Marshall, *The Structure of Byron's Major Poems* (Philadelphia: University of Pennsylvania Press, 1962), pp. 120–124.

3. Comparison of *Mazeppa* lines 417–422 ("For time at last sets all things even. . . .") with the letter to Lady Byron of 5 March 1817 suggests Byron identified his own position after the separation with that of Mazeppa: "For myself I have a confidence in my Fortune which will yet bear me through—['Chance is more just than we are']—the reverses which have occurred—were what I should have expected. . . .—However I shall live to have to pity you all . . . time & Nemesis will do that which I would not—even were it in my power remote or immediate.—You will smile at this piece of prophecy—do so—but recollect it.—it is justified by all human experience—no one was ever even the involuntary cause of great evils to others—without a requital—I have paid and am paying for mine—so will you." *Letters & Journals,* ed. Leslie A. Marchand (London: John Murray, 1976), v, 181. See also the letter to Lady Byron of 18 November 1818.

4. See Jerome McGann, Don Juan *in Context* (Chicago: University of Chicago Press, 1976), pp. 59–61. The fullest account of *Don Juan*'s composition is Truman Guy Steffan's in *The Making of a Masterpiece: Byron's* Don Juan, Vol. I of *Byron's* Don Juan: *A Variorum Edition,* 2nd ed. (Austin: University of Texas Press, 1971). See esp. pp. 362, 365–367.

5. Alvin Kernan, *The Plot of Satire* (New Haven: Yale University Press, 1965), pp. 176–179.

6. *Twentieth Century Interpretations of* Don Juan, ed. Edward E. Bostetter (Englewood Cliffs, N.J.: Prentice-Hall, 1969), p. 14.

7. George Ridenour, *The Style of* Don Juan (New Haven: Yale University Press, 1960).

8. Peter J. Manning, *Byron and His Fictions* (Detroit: Wayne State University Press, 1978), Chapter 7; and Jerome McGann, Don Juan *in Context,* pp. 111–112, 156, Chapter 8 passim. The reader's cyclical experience of *Don Juan*'s stanzas resembles William James's account of the process by which truths become verified: "Truths emerge from facts; but they dip forward into facts again and add to them; which facts again create or reveal new truth, and so on indefinitely. The facts themselves are not *true.* They simply *are.* Truth is the function of the *beliefs* that start and terminate among them." *Pragmatism: A New Name For Some Old Ways of Thinking* (1907; Cambridge, Mass.: Harvard University Press, 1975), p. 108.

9. Manning, *Byron and His Fictions,* p. 260.

10. Andrew Rutherford, *Byron: A Critical Study* (Stanford: Stanford University Press, 1961), p. 172. Rpt. in *Twentieth Century Interpretations,* pp. 51–62.

11. *Coleridge: Poetical Works,* ed. E. H. Coleridge (1912; rpt. Oxford: Oxford University Press, 1973), p. 196.

12. *Cain* II.i.50–51.

13. Manning, *Byron and His Fictions,* p. 260.

14. "Remarks on Don Juan," *Blackwood's Magazine*, 5 (August 1819), 512–518. Rpt. in *Byron: The Critical Heritage*, ed. Andrew Rutherford (New York: Barnes & Noble, 1970), pp. 166–172.

15. *The Critical Heritage*, p. 163.

16. Letter of Shelley to Byron, 21 October 1821, in *The Critical Heritage*, p. 197. Compare Byron's letter to Murray of 1 February 1819: "I maintain that it is the most moral of poems—but if people won't discover the moral that is their fault not mine." *Letters & Journals*, vi, 99.

17. *Childe Harold's Pilgrimage* iv, 97; cited in McGann, Don Juan *in Context*, pp. 146–147.

18. Pedrillo's death is a comment on the earlier assertion that "the desire of life / Prolongs it":

> . . . this is obvious to physicians,
> When patients, neither plagued with friends nor wife,
>   Survive through very desperate conditions,
> Because they still can hope, nor shines the knife
>   Nor shears of Atropos before their visions:
> Despair of all recovery spoils longevity.
> And makes men's miseries of alarming brevity.
>
>   (ii.lxiv)

For Pedrillo, it was not the knife of Atropos that shone before his vision, but the surgeon's scalpel that glimmered before his eyes; the men have tried to take fate into their own hands. It is hard to know what McGann means when he claims of the stanza that "even in the doctor/patient context one is forced to concede the virtues of despair. As Byron suggests, it 'makes men's miseries of alarming brevity. . . .' In Byron's view, if anything is human—like hope and despair, for example—it will serve human ends, sometimes well, sometimes equivocally, sometimes badly" (Don Juan *in Contest*, pp. 164–165). But something that serves human ends badly does not really serve human ends at all. Thus for the cannibals the "virtues of despair" are nonvirtues. Far from simply offering the men relief from a painful existence, the cannibalism gives them the worst of both worlds: *more* suffering (despair, insanity, and convulsions rolled into one), and death as well. Such misery is "alarming" indeed.

19. E. R. Dodds, *The Greeks and the Irrational* (Berkeley: University of California Press, 1951). p. 36.

20. *Mazeppa,* lines 114, 853–854.

SUSAN J. WOLFSON

"Their She Condition": *Cross-Dressing and the Politics of Gender in* Don Juan

Susan J. Wolfson's essay on cross-dressing takes as its starting point McGann's observation in "Byron, Mobility and the Poetics of Historical Ventriloquism" (cited in our general note to this section) that Byron's is a poetry of social reflection—a complementary aspect of which is explored in Marina Vitale's "The Domesticated Heroine in Byron's *Corsair* and William Hone's Prose Adaptation" (1984). But Wolfson of course extends McGann's fundamental insight significantly. Although concentrating on gender relations and gender preconceptions, Wolfson carries her analysis beyond these specific issues—important as they are in *Don Juan*. She shows that these crossings exemplify a larger challenging of "conventional expectations and customary boundaries" of many kinds, all of which serve to articulate what contemporary critics find most fascinating in Byron's poem—its "cultural contradictions and personal self-divisions."

Aside from its self-evident interest in gender studies and cultural criticism, Wolfson's essay is an example of what she calls "soft-core" deconstruction—criticism concerned with dismantling hierarchy and difference—which also goes by some harsher names in sterner deconstructive circles: "weak deconstruction," "timid deconstruction," and "opportunistic deconstruction." In this community of interests Wolfson's work takes its place in a growing body of recent criticism. See, for example, Terry Castle's "Eros and Liberty at the English Masquerade, 1710–90" (1983); Jerome Christensen's "Perversion, Parody, and Cultural Hegemony: Lord Byron's Oriental Tales" (1989); Caroline Franklin's " 'Quiet Cruising over the Ocean Woman': Byron's *Don Juan* and the Woman Question" (1990); Marjorie Garber's *Vested Interests: Cross-Dressing and Cultural Anxiety* (1991); Diane Hoeveler's *Romantic Androgyny: The Woman Within* (1990); and Katherine Kernberger's "Power and Sex: The Implication of Role Reversal in Catherine's Russia" (1980).

I

Don Juan, like much Romantic writing, displays numerous demarcations of sexual difference. Indeed, there is a notable contradiction between the poem's social politics, which despite an aristocratic allegiance, tend to satirize prevailing ideologies, and its sexual politics, which often reflect a conventional masculinism.[1] Some

From *ELH* 54 (1987): 586–617.

have summoned issues of the latter to make categorical claims about Byron and his contemporaries. Questions of gender are certainly fundamental; evidence of Byron's—and many others'—sexism and patriarchal bias is clear and compelling. Yet I wish to revise some of the categories advanced in some recent feminist readings of English Romanticism by showing that Byron's sexual politics are neither persistent nor consistent. Even granting the notoriously adept ironies of *Don Juan,* its politics of sexual difference prove remarkably complex and unstable. At times they are governed by the general satirical perspective of the poem; at other times they clash with Byron's pronounced liberal politics; and at still others they appear scarcely fixed—even within their own frame of reference. Signs that seem clear markers of difference can become agents of sexual disorientation that break down, invert, and radically call into question the categories designed to discriminate "masculine" from "feminine."

This sense of dislocation is provoked in a variety of ways, but with particular agitation in instances of cross-dressing. Such agitation, not surprisingly, can generate a conservative counterreaction—a series of defensive maneuvers to reinscribe sexual orthodoxy. Even so, the energies released in such instances are central to Byron's writing, not only illuminating the codes that govern the behavior of men and women, but becoming a means of exploring new possibilities as well. The cross-dressings of *Don Juan* also, and undeniably, reflect a more private, and more privately coded, issue: Byron's homoeroticism. Louis Crompton's recent study, *Byron and Greek Love,* offers a lucid and powerful examination of Byron's literary and social behavior from this perspective, especially in relation to Georgian and Regency homophobia. My essay concentrates on Byron's representations of heterosexual politics, which, sensitized by his homosexuality, turn personal experience outward into a critical reading of the discourses of sexual difference and sexual ideology that permeate his age.

II

Traditional distinctions of gender and corresponding habits of judgment are everywhere apparent in Byron's writing. A woman may be written off with the prescription of "a looking-glass and a few sugar plums . . . she will be satisfied."[2] If her gaze turns to man, he must guard against the peril to his security. "Love" in *Don Juan* is personified as a gallant male (9.44), but its female embodiments in the Sultana Gulbeyaz or the Empress Catherine are dangerous; and in Queen Elizabeth, love is so "ambiguous" in method and so incompatible with the exercise of political power, that she disgraces both "her Sex and Station" (9.81).[3] "Hatred," not coincidentally, is pure female treachery, a spidery woman with a "hundred arms and legs" (10.12). Even if "woman" in this poem escapes such extreme representations, it is only towards an unpredictable chaos of activity:

> What a strange thing is man! and what a stranger
>   Is woman! What a whirlwind is her head,
> And what a whirlpool full of depth and danger
>   Is all the rest about her!
>   (9.64)

Man may be strange, but woman is both stranger than he and ultimately a stranger to him and his world. Thus, if as Peter Manning remarks, "Juan's education is his experience with women," *Don Juan* remains concerned about that economy, for female padagogy, even when its curriculum is "that useful sort of knowledge . . . acquired in nature's good old college" (2.136), is of dubious value.[4] " 'Tis pity learned virgins ever wed / With persons of no sort of education," the narrator muses, with Byron's line-break momentarily suggesting an even more radical solution to the summary lament, "Oh! ye lords of ladies intellectual, / Inform us truly, have they not hen-peck'd you all?" (1.22). This couplet may be Byron's most famous; it is significant that the point of its texty wit is the reduction of women's intellect to an instrument to torture a lord. When it is not so precise, women's learning is treated as an easily exposed pretension: "Men with their heads reflect on this and that— / But women with their hearts or heaven knows what!" (6.2). Their capacity for "sober reason" is so easily compromised that it is impossible, the narrator smirks, to know what "can signify the site / Of ladies' lucubrations" (11.33–34). Those subject to sharpest sarcasm are, predictably, "The Blues"—a "tribe" whom even Juan ("who was a little superficial") can conquer, and with no more than a light continental style "Which lent his learned lucubrations pith, / And passed for arguments of good endurance" (11.50–52). Of the two orders of pretension, Juan's escapes derision because Byron allows him to recognize the hoax, indeed to participate in the self-parodies of his author, who could on occasion refer to "his masterpieces" as "his elucubrations."[5]

Byron shows his narrator preferring women who behave in accord with conventional models—for example, Haidée and Zoe nursing Juan "With food and raiment, and those soft attentions, / Which are (as I must own) of female growth" (2.123). Similarly, the Sultana Gulbeyaz is most affecting, to Juan and the narrator alike, when her "imperial, or imperious" manner (5.110) succumbs to the female heart, as when, for instance, she is moved to tears by Juan's own. If her rage at Juan's refusal to love on command reminds the narrator of King Lear's in intensity, he is struck by how "her thirst of blood was quench'd in tears," which he deems "the fault of her soft sex" and the conduit through which "her sex's shame broke in at last. . . . it flow'd in natural and fast." He is glad to note that on such occasions "she felt humbled," adding that "humiliation / Is sometimes good for people in her station" (5.136–37). For then, "nature teaches more than power can spoil, / And, when a *strong* although a strange sensation, / Moves—female hearts are . . . genial soil / For kinder feelings, whatso'er their nation" (5.120). Byron's textual variants imply that tutelage by "nature" yields a political corrective as well: thus moved, Gulbeyaz not only "forgot her station," but may be addressed as a "Poor Girl."[6]

If tears mark the female here, they are still part of that world of woman's strangeness, and not always susceptible to certain interpretation. For what looks "natural" also has the effect of manipulating male sympathy, and we have just heard that women such as Gulbeyaz may "shed and use" tears "at their liking" (5.118). Tellingly, Juan finds that his resistance to sexual exploitation "Dissolved like snow before a woman crying" (5.141). By contrast, men's tears, the narrator is certain, are true "torture," agon rather than art. "A woman's tear-drop melts, a man's half sears, / Like molten lead, as if you thrust a pike in / His heart to force it out" (5.118). Men's tears reflect a wholly unsuspect emotion: when one of the shipwrecked crew "wept at length," the narrator assures us it was "not fears / That made his eyelids as a woman's be"; he weeps in pure pity for "a wife and children" (2.43).

The subject of tears is a synecdoche for the demarcations of gender that inflect the world of *Don Juan,* and one instance of how its narrator generates masculine self-definition by contraries and oppositions. These dynamics are typically represented as a contest between masculine and feminine will, in which female manipulation is represented as inimical to male independence and power. Significantly, the suspicion of calculation in Gulbeyaz's tears and their effect in mastering Juan's resistance recall the arts Donna Julia deploys to deflect interrogation by her husband, even as she conceals her lover in her bed. Byron's narrator, in solidarity with the cuckold, dons a voice of moral outrage at the whole gender. "Oh shame! / Oh sin! Oh sorrow! and Oh womankind! / How can you do such things and keep your fame, / Unless this world, and t'other too, be blind? / Nothing so dear as an unfilch'd good name!" (1.165). Byron, whose own name was tainted by sexual scandal, is perhaps a little irked by the female art of having it both ways. Thus of Lady Adeline, a later variation on Julia, he has his narrator remark, "whatso'er she wished, she acted right; / And whether coldness, pride, or virtue, dignify / A Woman, so she's good, what does it signify?" (14.57). Her security depends on remaining an opaque or perpetually intractable signifier to masculine intelligence, and her social power derives from such finesse: she acts the "amphibious sort of harlot, / '*Couleur de rose,*' who's neither white nor scarlet," and who, with a "little genial sprinkling of hypocrisy," may become one of the "loveliest Oligarchs of our Gynocrasy" (12.62, 66). This is a rhyme Byron liked, for he summons it again to advise all who would "take the tone of their society" to "wear the newest mantle of hypocrisy, / On pain of much displeasing the Gynocrasy" (16.52). The hostility that sharpens the point of these pairings can be heard in Byron's self congratulating claim to be neither surprised nor distressed on hearing of women's aversion to *Don Juan:* "they could not bear it because it took off the *veil* [of their] d[amne]d sentiment. . . . They hated the book because it showed and exposed their hypocrisy," he says, and he seems to have enjoyed provoking Teresa Guiccioli's dislike of "that ugly *Don Juan.*"[7]

Yet if these numerous apostrophes to and declarations about the arts of women, as well as the narrator's insistence on "their" hypocrisy, seem to divide the world of *Don Juan* securely along lines of gender, Byron's concentration tugs at a network of affiliations. Even to say "*our* Gynocrasy" implies a certain pride of identification. Indeed, in the stanza from Canto 12 quoted above, the third rhyme word, significantly, is "aristocracy"—as if Byron were signalling his awareness that women are culpable of nothing more than disclosing the master-trope of all social success. They play of rhyme itself is relevant, for if, as the narrator remarks with faint condescension, "There's nothing women love to dabble in / More . . . Than match-making in general: 'tis no sin" (15.31), Byron has him do so in matched words, a sign of his own love of match-making in the general society of language. There is an even more pronounced affinity of interest to challenge the supposition that hypocrisy is all "theirs": hypocrisy may be a moral fault, but it is also artful acting, and the narrator's confessed pleasure in performances both literary and social implicates him in a similar masquerade. It is interesting that Princess Caroline would apply the same term to Byron that his narrator applies to women: "He was all *couleur de rose* last evening."[8] These cross applications are not exactly "cross-dressing," but they indirectly participate—for the fashion, if not the material, is the same. Thus it is only half-sarcastically that Byron's narrator admits, "What I love in women is, they won't / Or can't do otherwise than lie, but do it / So well, the very truth seems falsehood to it"; their artifice is natural, and so their lies are true. And in a world where all pretenses to truth seem to veil the artifices of ideology, women's hypocrisy may, paradoxically, be the most honest behavior of all: "after all, what is a lie? 'Tis but / The truth in masquerade" (11.36–37). By Canto 16, in fact, Byron's narrator is praising his female muse as "The most sincere that ever dealt in fiction" (2), and reflecting this quality in the "mobility" of women such as Adeline who, in adapting to the performative requirements of any occasion, are not playing "false," but "true; for surely, they're sincerest, / Who are strongly acted on by what is nearest" (97).

Byron makes some attempt to distinguish the male poet and his muse from the behavior of such women, for mobility, his narrator says, is "A thing of temperament and not of art" (16.97), and a habit that may leave its possessor more "acted on" than acting—while his poem, presumably, is a thing of art alone. He implies that distinction elsewhere in his claims that it is "ladies' fancies" that are "rather transitory" (10.9), and "feminine Caprice" that inspires their "indecision, / Their never knowing their own mind two days" (6.119, 117). And of course, the poem's definitive figure of mobility is Lady Adeline. Even so, mobility is not the sure index of gender that tears are. Byron in fact added a note to the poem in Adeline's defense, as if to balance the masculine bias of Juan's external perspective on her "playing her grand role" (and thus prone to "doubt how much of Adeline was *real*" [16.96]) with a more sympathetic assessment: mobility is "an excessive susceptibility of immediate impressions," he explains, and "though sometimes apparently useful to the possessor, a most painful and unhappy attribute" (*CPW*, 5:769). This gloss seems more than sympathy; it has the sound of psychological self-pleading. Thus it is not surprising to hear from Thomas Moore that Byron "was fully aware not only of the abundance of this quality in his own nature, but of the danger in which it placed consistency and singleness of character" (*CPW*, 5:769). Lady Blessington comments that the "mobility of his nature is extraordinary, and makes him inconsistent in his actions as well as in his conversation"—a quality Hazlitt observes in *Don Juan* itself, summoning a term that suggests cross-dressing: the "great power" of this poem, he proposes, lies in Byron's ability to "turn round and *travestie* himself: the drollery is in the utter discontinuity of ideas and feelings."[9]

In Byron's experience, it seems clear, mobility is an epic renegade, loyal to no sex, itself showing mobility across gender lines. George M. Ridenour in fact discerns in Adeline's mobility "another version of that growing urbanity Byron has so praised in his hero himself: 'The art of living in all climes with ease' (15.11)," and he extends this art to include the narrator's acknowledged facility at playing "the *Improvvisatore*" "amidst life's infinite variety" (15.19–20).[10] This last allusion to the arts of Shakespeare's Cleopatra, which in their "infinite variety" defeat the attritions of "custom" (2.2.241), further perplexes discriminations of gender. Not only does Byron have his narrator apply the infinite variety of her art to his own general view of life, but it is worth recalling that Cleopatra's various repertoire includes the fun of cross-dressing: "I . . . put my tires and mantles on him, whilst / I wore his sword" (2.5.21–23).[11] With this borrowing, Byron fashions a kind of psychic cross-dressing for his narrator; not coincidentally; Byron's very language for "mobility" appears to have been converted from Madame de Staël's description of feminine consciousness in her popular novel, *Corinne*.[12]

As the issue of mobility suggests, *Don Juan* at times complicates the language of gender in ways that focus on the definition of self in gendered society, and may even expose the political investments of those definitions. Such preoccupation in Byron's poetry with "the social structures of its rhetoric," as Jerome J. McGann argues, works to reflect "the audience's character . . . back to itself so that it can 'reflect' upon that reflection in a critical and illuminating way."[13] That dynamic is especially active in the social and linguistic cross-dressings of *Don Juan,* for these figures not only concentrate the energies of Byron's satire, but compel our attention to those crucial discriminations through which the masculine and the feminine have been culturally defined, and through which men and women have been psychologically compelled and historically confined. Social cross-dressing includes both the "odd travesty" of Juan in the slave market "femininely all array'd" (5.74, 80) and "her frolic Grace—Fitz-Fulke" disguised as the ghost of the Black Friar (16.123); it also involves the less obvious but equally significant covering of Juan by female clothes—first by Julia, then by Haidée and Zoe. Linguistic cross-dressing materializes in transfers of verbal property, such as the narrator's calling himself "a male Mrs. Fry" (10.84), or Antonia's references to Juan as a "pretty gentleman" with a "half-girlish face" (1.170–71), corroborated by the narrator's descriptions of his hero as "a most beauteous Boy" (9.53), "feminine in feature" (8.52), who dances "like a flying Hour before Aurora, / In Guido's famous fresco" (14.40). These transfers also include the application of masculine-toned terms to women: the Sultan desires a "handsome paramour" (6.91); Empress Catherine is "handsome" and "fierce" (9.63)—her behavior "a kind of travesty" as one critic remarks, and so in the most fundamental sense, for "travesty" is a linguistic kin of "transvestite." (Suggestively, another reader discerns Catherine's origins in a male historical figure, the Ali Pasha, who implicitly feminized Byron by paying great attention to his beauty.)[14] An even more complex exchange of the properties of gender plays in the comment that Juan dances "Like swift Camilla" (14.39). The comparison may appear to feminize Juan, but it actually entertains a dizzying interchange of properties, for as a hunter and epic warrior, Camilla is associated with typically male pursuits. . . .

The fictions of *Don Juan* serve Byron in part as an outlet for homoerotic material in disguise, but its cross-dressings accomplish something else as well, for they put his imagination in touch with heterosexual politics by animating a set of social signifiers that challenge conventional expectations and customary boundaries of demarcation. Some of these transfers and transgressions emerge as farce, but not exclusively, for Byron implicates them in deep (if not fully sustained) counterplots that perplex the terms "male" and "female"—both politically and psychologically construed—and thereby unsettle, even dismantle, the social structures to which gender has been assimilated. The result of these transsexual poetics is a qualified but potent redefinition of conventional sexual politics, for gender symbolism, as Natalie Zemon Davis remarks, "is always available to make statements about social experience and to reflect (or conceal) contradictions within it."[15] Thus the spectacle of Juan "femininely all array'd" in the slave market works to foreground female restriction and vulnerability, while the figures of women "masculinized" through social power or costume disguise emerge with the energy of self-direction and the force of sexual assertiveness. These transfers allow Byron to inscribe a language of cultural contradiction and personal self-division in which what has been habitually denied to one sex gets projected in terms of the other. And while the figures on both sides of these transfers are often made to seem absurd or anomalous, it is their very anomaly that makes palpable the ideology by which conventional codes are invested, maintained, and perpetuated.

It is fitting that *Don Juan,* an infamously impure poem assayed in terms of generic convention, should yield related transgressions of gender that may, in Jacques Derrida's words, test "identity and difference between the feminine and masculine." That test is a provocative one, for as Derrida notes, to cross the "line of demarcation," whether in terms of gender or genre, is to "risk impurity, anomaly or monstrosity."[16] To the extent Byron imports words such as "handsome" and "feminine" across conventional lines of demarcation, he speculates about such risks; but he also shies away from the full consequences by restabilizing these transgressions from the full consequences by restabilizing these transgressions with plots of correction. For Julia's "handsome eyes"—like Austen's "handsome" Emma Woodhouse or Hemingway's "handsome" Margot Macomber—suggest theft or impropriety of character, and all three writers set their problematically self-possessed women into plots that conclude in their submission to male power and authority. Byron's tendency to conserve a traditional character within potentially subversive cross-dressing is also legible in the image of Kaled, who in *Lara* accompanies her lover disguised as his page. Kaled's hand seems "So femininely white it might bespeak / Another sex, when matched with that smooth cheek," even though "his garb, and something in his gaze, / More wild and high than woman's eye betrays; / A latent fierceness" (1.576–80). Byron underscores the tensions implicit in the convention of the disguised page (which in English literature is at least as old as Sidney's revised *Arcadia*) by having "his" behavior everywhere recall that of a wife or lover: "mute attention, and his care . . . guessed / Each wish, fulfilled it ere the tongue expressed" (556–57). Finally, as Lara dies, Kaled's emotions overwhelm restraint, and her true "sex confest": "Oh! never yet beneath / The breast of man such trusty love may breathe! / That trying moment hath at once reveal'd / The secret long and yet but half conceal'd" (2.513–17). Murray's edition of *Lara* gives a special prestige to the moment, in fact, by printing an engraving of the scene (see *CPW* 3, facing page 250). Byron's plots of correction and restoration not only counter but may even be compelled by the transfers he has entertained within them, for his experiments with the codes of gender are radical in their implications, and potentially chaotic in their social and psychological consequences. . . .

III

The condition of "something wanting" [in Lord Henry] was normally ascribed in the dominant discourses of Byron's era to the female rather than the male, and the corresponding linguistic habits are evident enough in the culture of letters in which Byron came of age—even in writers of such opposite sexual politics as Alexander Pope and James Fordyce on the one side and Mary Wollstonecraft on the other. Pope's Epistle "To a Lady, of the Characters of Women" assumes, for instance, that "Most Women have no Characters at all" (2), and though it concludes, as the Argument promises, with a "Picture of an esteemable Woman, made up of the best kind of Contrarieties," Pope can describe that "best kind" only as an aesthetic enhancement of the male character: "Heav'n, when it strives to polish all it can / Its last best work, but forms a softer Man" (271–72).[17] Catherine Macaulay ponders this construction of the feminine in her *Letters on Education,* with a specific scrutiny of the linguistic conventions so incorporated:

> when we compliment the appearance of a more than ordinary energy in the female mind, we call it masculine; and hence it is that Pope has elegantly said *a perfect woman's but a softer man.* And if we take in the consideration, that there can be but one rule of moral excellence for beings made of the same materials, organized after the same manner, and subjected to similar laws of Nature, we must either agree with Mr. Pope, or we must reverse the proposition and say, that *a perfect man is a woman formed after a coarser mold.* The difference that actually does subsist between the sexes, is too flattering for men to be willingly imputed to accident, for what accident occasions, wisdom might correct.[18]

Both Pope's "Epistle" and Macaulay's critique of the ideology of masculine and feminine are potent points of reference for Wollstonecraft in *A Vindication of the Rights of Woman.* Yet her linguistic politics are inconsistent in ways that anticipate Byron's ambivalent plays with the conventions of gender in *Don Juan.* Sometimes her analysis is as sharp as Macaulay's, especially when the subject is Macaulay herself: "I will not call hers a masculine understanding," she insists, "because I admit not of such an arrogant assumption of reason."[19] But her Introduction, though its scrutiny of linguistic convention is as scrupulous as Macaulay's, reflects and perpetuates those conventions even as their application is called into question:

> I have heard exclamations against masculine women. . . . If by this appellation men mean to inveigh against their ardour in hunting, shooting, and gaming, I shall most cordially join in the cry; but if it be against the imitation of manly virtues, or more properly speaking, the attainment of those talents and virtues, the exercise of which ennobles the human character, and which raise females in the scale of animal being . . . [may they] every day grow more and more masculine. (8)

Wollstonecraft retains "masculine" as the nobler term, and in order to "render my sex more respectable members of society," she works a style that deliberately shuns "pretty feminine phrases, which the men condescendingly use to soften our slavish dependence." She spurns typically feminine dresses of thought—not only "pretty superlatives" but all "fabricating," "polish," and "dazzle"—to advance the "simple unadorned truth" of "masculine and respectable" conduct (9–11). In these sentences Wollstonecraft is at least self-conscious about the conventional language of gender, but elsewhere in *A Vindication* she seems to credit gendered terms by habit. Criticizing present codes of heroism, for instance, she complains that these favor "effeminacy" over "fortitude" (145). And she imagines "that the few extraordinary women who have rushed in eccentrical directions out of the orbit prescribed to their sex, were *male* spirits, confined by mistake in female frames" (35). Even of Macaulay, she implies gender is an obstacle to be overcome: "in her style of writing . . . no sex appears, for it is like the sense it conveys, strong and clear" (105). These usages, in effect, reinforce the orthodoxy of Fordyce's *Sermons to Young Women* (published the same year as *A Vindication,* 1792), which categorize as "masculine women" those who would share activities that are "properly the province of men"—"war, commerce, politics, exercises of strength and dexterity, abstract philosophy, and all the abstruser sciences."[20] Fittingly, though with a different stress, Mary Hays's memoir of Wollstonecraft would note the "high masculine tone" through which the "power and energy of thought" in *A Vindication* are conveyed.[21]

Don Juan at times perpetuates these linguistic and social conventions, but like Wollstonecraft, Byron intermittently calls attention to their codes in ways that provoke critical scrutiny. His attitudes are never of a piece, and often self-contradictory within the same stanza. This changefulness at once reflects the active power of his questioning of the "she condition," even as it suffers from the ambivalence afflicting those who would inaugurate or sympathize with such questions. Fluctuations of compassion and nervous scorn can be read in the very passage in which Byron has his narrator ponder the "she condition." He begins in tones of mock sympathy and blame, but within a few lines these become expressions of genuine sympathy:

> Alas! Worlds fall—and Woman, since she fell'd
>   The World (as, since that history, less polite
> Than true, hath been a creed so strictly held)
>   Has not yet given up the practice quite.
> Poor Thing of Usages! Coerc'd, compell'd,
>   Victim when wrong, and martyr often when right,
> Condemn'd to child-bed . . .
>
>   (14.23)

His sympathy modulates into a self-conscious contemplation of sexual politics and policy:

>   who can penetrate
>   The real sufferings of their she condition?
> Man's very sympathy with their estate
>   Has much of selfishness and more suspicion.
> Their love, their virtue, beauty, education,
> But form good housekeepers, to breed a nation.
>   (14.24)

Wollstonecraft herself could have written the next stanza:

> The gilding wears so soon from off her fetter,
>   That—but ask any woman if she'd choose
> (Take her at thirty, that is) to have been
> Female or male? a school-boy or a Queen?
>   (14.25)

If Pope's Epistle assumes that "ev'ry Lady would be Queen for life" and shudders at the thought of "a whole Sex of Queens! / Pow'r all their end" (218–20), Byron's summary question guesses that any woman might prefer the lot of a schoolboy—the lowest of males—to that of a queen, the highest of females. But he allows the issue to diffuse as he returns his narrator to the more familiar ground of sexist mocking: " 'Petticoat Influence' is a great reproach, / Which even those who obey would fain be thought / To fly from, as from hungry pikes a roach" (14.26). Potential political commentary then evaporates into a digression on the "mystical sublimity" of the petticoat (14.26–27). Yet the evasion itself is revealing; the analogy of hungry pikes and their prey that Peter Manning remarks is indeed worth attention—not the least for renewing an earlier image of Englishwomen as unholy "fishers for men" (12.59).[22] Though the vehicle shifts, the tenor is the same: women are always the predators.

Despite the narrator's reversion to antifeminist bitterness, Byron's willingness to have him meditate on the "she condition" is a striking one, for it not only allows a male voice to confirm the validity of a woman's earlier lament—namely Julia's—but now invests that grievance with intersexual authority. Writing to Juan, Julia had complained that if

> Man's love is of man's life a thing apart,
>   'Tis woman's whole existence; man may range
> The court, camp, church, the vessel, and the mart,
>   Sword, gown, gain, glory, offer in exchange
> Pride, fame, ambition, to fill up his heart. . . .
> Man has all these resources, we but one,
> To love again, and be again undone.
>
> (1.194)

Not only does Byron's ventriloquy through Julia express a sympathetic understanding of the limits imposed on "woman's whole existence," but Julia's letter may actually have female authority—its voice inhabited by the language of both Jane Austen and (like the meditation on mobility) Madame de Staël.[23] Though still reflecting the terms of difference authorized by his culture, in his effort to address the "she condition," to hear and render its voices, Byron attempts a critical perspective, one that allows him to reveal and explore the ideological implications of those terms.[24]

That exploration is helped by Byron's capacity for owning what amounts to a 'he" complicity in the "she condition": even as the narrator of *Don Juan* rails against marriage, Byron has him admit that not only do women invest "all" in love, but that "man, to man so oft unjust, / Is always so to women" (2.199–200). Byron himself informs an "incredulous" Lady Blessington that "men think of themselves alone, and regard the woman but as an object that administers to their selfish gratification, and who, when she ceases to have this power, is thought of no more, save as an obstruction in their path." His terms for assessing difference still inscribe a hierarchy: men enjoy the privilege of power, women the honor of a higher moral place: "women only know evil from having experienced it through men; whereas men have no criterion to judge of purity of goodness but woman"; "I have a much higher opinion of your sex than I have even now expressed," he adds (*Blessington*, 196)—a remark that his Italian mistress, Countess Teresa Guiccioli, underscored in her own copy of Blessington's *Conversations of Lord Byron*. These critiques reflect ideological myths of course, but their psychological reflex in Byron is revealingly self-critical. In the privacy of his journal he remarks: "There is something to me very softening in the presence of a woman,—some strange influence, even if one is not in love with them,—which I cannot at all account for, having no very high opinion of the sex. But yet,—I always feel in better humour with myself and every thing else, if there is a woman within ken" (*BLJ*, 3:246). Conventional polarities and traces of habitual opinion notwithstanding, one is struck by the implication that "the presence of a woman" seems necessary to Byron, both for his sense of self-completion and for his sense of integration with the world at large. He wants a heroine.

That psychological undercurrent to Byron's critique of the sexual politics that underwrite the "she condition" exerts a nervous force however—especially when that critique is articulated by cross-dressings, for these inversions and reversals not only erode male privilege, but inhabit plots in which such erosion is associated with images and threats of death. The dissolution of male power is apparent enough in the loss of male attire and the quasi-transvestism that ensues in Juan's romances with Julia and Haidée. Julia "half-smother'd" a naked Juan in her bedding to hide him from her husband's posse; it is a naked and half-dead Juan for whom "Haidée stripp'd her sables off" to make a couch—"and, that he might be more at ease, / And warm, in case by chance he should awake," she and Zoe "also gave a petticoat apiece" (2.133). Though not overtly transvestite, these coverings still compromise Juan's manhood, for each, while protective, also marks him as passive and dependent, the property of a woman's design. Significantly, after being discovered by Alfonso, Juan cannot recover his clothes, but must escape "naked" (188) into the night. That reduction is also suggested by the garments Juan, "naked" once again, receives from Haidée, for though these are men's, the apparel does not proclaim the man: the "breeches" in which she "dress'd him" are rather "spacious" (probably her father's) and more tellingly, she neglects to supply the real signifiers of male power—"turban, slippers, pistols, dirk" (2.160). With both Julia and Haidée, Juan remains a "boy" (Catherine too, we learn, "sometimes liked a boy," "slight and slim," preferring such "a boy to men much bigger" [9.47, 72]), and Byron underscores the corresponding impotence not only by confronting Juan with a genuine threat of death from the men betrayed by these affairs, but by masculinizing the women. Julia is given an uncommon bearing of "stature tall," complemented by a "brow / Bright with intelligence" and "handsome eyes" (1.60–61). Haidée's stature is "Even of the highest for a female mould . . . and in her air / There was a something which bespoke command" (2.116). The implicit maleness of this manner is confirmed when she confronts her father: protecting Juan, "Haidée threw herself her boy before"; "Stern as her sire" (Byron revises the adjective from "calm" [*CPW*, 5:216]), "She stood . . . tall beyond her sex . . . and with a fix'd eye scann'd / Her father's face. . . . How like they look'd! the expression was the same. . . . their features and / Their stature differing but in sex and years" (4.42–45). Sexual difference is less remarkable than the display of common traits across gender lines, for Haidée and Lambro differ less from each other than both differ from the "boy" Juan—a term applied several times in this episode (2.144, 174; 4.19, 38).

All these inversions of socially prescribed character fuel a lethal economy, as if Byron worried that to indulge such transgressions were to tempt self-cancellation— a psychological updating of the well-known injunction of Deuteronomy dear to Stubbes and other chroniclers of abuses: "The woman shall not wear that which pertaineth unto a man, neither shall a man put on a woman's garment: for all that do so *are* abomination unto the LORD" (22:5). A feminized Juan always invites death into the poem, whether in the form of threats to his own life or to the lives of those implicated in his travesties. "Juan nearly died" (1.168) from affairs with Julia and Haidée, and they exact full wages: the passionate Julia is sentenced to life-in-death in a convent; Haidée's nurturing of Juan is allied with figures of death, and she herself dies.[25] The threat is nearly perpetual: when Gulbeyaz discovers her designs for Juan as odalisque usurped by his harem bedpartner, she issues a warrant for both their deaths, and Catherine's appetites all too soon reduce her "beauteous" favorite to "a condition / Which augured of the dead" (10.39). So, too, after his first sighting of the Black Friar's Ghost—itself a patent spectre of death—Juan and Fitz-Fulke look "pale" (16.31); the morning after discovering her within that "sable frock and dreary cowl" (16.123), Juan appears "wan and worn, with eyes that hardly brooked / The light"; Her Grace seems scarcely better—"pale and shivered" (17.14). Byron's "Memoranda" on the Murray manuscript scrap in fact reveals a suggestive linkage: "The Shade of the / Friar / The D[ea]th of J[uan]" (*CPW*, 5:761). All these presages and figures of death suggest that Byron senses fatal consequences when the law of gender is violated: the annihilation of self in both its social identity and psychological integrity.

In assessing Byron's apprehension of such consequences, it is useful to turn briefly to Keats, for his "feminine" flexibility of ego is often compared, for better or worse, to Byron's "masculine" force of self-definition. In commenting on Keats's "deficiency in masculine energy of style," Hazlitt, for one, cites Byron's racy violations of social propriety to sharpen his case.[26] Even to Keats, Byron's bold inscriptions of self—"Lord Byron cuts a figure," he says—are a felt contrast to his own "poetical Character," a "camelion" of "no self . . . no identity."[27] This chameleonism bears on the question of gender, for as Keats puts it, such self-effacement allows "as much delight in conceiving an Iago as an Imogen"—showing, in effect, ability to negate what some modern feminist critics call "masculine" self-assertion. Thus, sharing Hazlitt's sense of gender, Erica Jong, Adrienne Rich, and Margaret Homans all have perceived in Keats qualities they identify and value in women writers. Speculating that Keats's humble origins and poverty correspond to "certain aspects of women's experience as outsiders relative to the major literary tradition," Homans exempts him from classification with poets of the dominant masculine tradition, who typically construct "the strong self from . . . strong language." Rich, in the course of explaining the "female" ability to "lose all sense of her own ego" and exercise "tremendous powers of intuitive identification and sympathy with other people," cites Keats's term "Negative Capability." Jong summons the same term to declare that "feminism *means* empathy . . . akin to the quality Keats called 'negative capability'—that unique gift for projecting oneself into other states of consciousness."[28] And albeit with a different emphasis from Hazlitt's, there is an implied contrast to masculinism such as Byron's, whose poetry "simply exaggerates . . . societal experience" Homans says: "the men are even bolder, the ladies even more beautiful and passive, in Byron than in life" (8).

What is interesting is how slippery such distinctions become as soon as one applies any kind of pressure. The issues are not clearcut. *Don Juan* offers scant evidence of the sexual politics Homans describes—Byron in fact thought he was being "true to Nature in making the advances come from the females" (*Medwin*, 165). This may be sexism in a different form, but the difference is crucial, for the dynamics of power that seemed to Byron to be "natural" in English Regency Society run significantly counter to the politics feminists such as Homans ascribe to him: "I am easily governed by women," Byron confesses (*Medwin*, 216); and protesting *Blackwood's* charge that he treated women "harshly," he replies: "it may be so—but I have been their martyr.—My whole life has been sacrificed *to* them & *by* them" (*BLJ*, 6:257). Nor are Keats's sexual politics unproblematic. Like Byron in some moods, he condescends to "the generallity of women" as creatures "to whom I would rather give a Sugar Plum than my time"; he derides the bluestockings as do Byron and Hazlitt; and with a puerile fear of sexual self-discovery, he ridicules the "Man in love" (*KL*, 1:404; 2:187–88). His unassertive male ego, moreover, typically finds poetic correlatives not in figures of sexual equality, but in tales of young men dominated—sometimes fatally so—by powerful women: recall Venus and Adonis, Circe and Glaucus, Cynthia and Endymion, Moneta and the poet-dreamer, Lamia and Lycius, "Fanny" and her poet-lover. Indeed, such tales (as his letters show) are in many ways the reflex of a sexism that is hostile, adolescent, and more deeply entrenched than Byron's for want of the intimate friendships with women that complicate Byron's attitudes. . . .

IV

The two most extended episodes of transvestism in *Don Juan*—Juan's conscription as an odalisque and Fitz-Fulke's appropriation of a friar's habit—show Byron's effort to explore the arbitrariness of male privilege in an economy of sexual commodities. Both derive their energy from the inversion of that privilege, and both provoke Byron's ambivalence about the cost. Behind both, too, is Byron's participation in the institution of the "Cavalier Servente," the accepted escort and socially tolerated lover of a married woman. Byron could sometimes comment on the system in quasi-feminist terms, deeming Serventism a byproduct of the way Italian fathers treat their daughters as commodities to be sold "under the market price"—that "portion" of their assets "fixed by law for the dower." The successful bidder was often a man older than the father himself (Teresa Guiccioli's husband, for instance, was about three times her age). With "such a preposterous connexion," Byron exclaims, "no love on either side," extramarital romance was necessary, indeed inevitable (*Medwin*, 22). That is not the whole story, of course, for as Cavalier Servente to Teresa Guiccioli, Byron felt acutely the inversion of sexual privilege to which he was accustomed in England, an inversion that may have been doubly disturbing for bringing into prominence his intrinsic passivity with Regency women: in Venice "the *polygamy* is all on the female side. . . . it is a strange sensation," he remarks (*BLJ*, 6:226).

This wavering between defensiveness and feminist analysis in relation to Serventism thoroughly informs Juan's experience in the Turkish court. Here Byron partly redresses Venetian imbalances, for the polygamy is all on the male side: that Gulbeyaz is one of four wives and fifteen hundred concubines makes her purchase of Juan seem minor in comparison. Yet by placing Juan in women's clothes and in the roles of a sex-slave, Byron does more than simply invert the cultural norm; he allows Juan's debasement to reflect in excess the customary status of women as objects of barter and trade in a male-centered economy. Behind Juan's shocked discovery at learning he is the property of a Sultana who asks only "Christian, canst thou love?" and who "conceived that phrase was quite enough to move" (5.116), one senses Byron's own discomfort at having actually become "a piece of female property" in his relationship with Teresa Guiccioli

(*BLJ,* 7:28): "the system of *serventism* imposes a thousand times more restraint and slavery than marriage ever imposed," he laments to Lady Blessington (180). And he feels particularly taxed by the erosion of time and autonomy that his "defined duties" required (*BLJ,* 7:195). The mistress's word is "the only law which he obeys. / His is no sinecure. . . . Coach, servants, gondola, he goes to call, / And carries fan, and tippet, gloves, and shawl," the narrator of *Beppo* reports, describing the role of this "supernumerary slave" (the noun was originally "gentleman" (*CPW* 4:141]) in terms that tellingly figure such bondage as a species of transvestism: he "stays / Close to the lady as a part of dress" (40). As if to inflict his own lot on his hero, Byron considered submitting Juan to the "ridicules" of being "a Cavalier Servente in Italy" (*BLJ,* 8:78), a role he has him rehearse in Russia. And when he comments on his hero thus as "man-mistress to Catherine the Great" (*Medwin,* 165), he reveals his agitation about the radical cost of these inversions: degraded to sexual property, Juan has to be regendered.[29]

Juan had, of course, been something of an illicit or smuggled piece of property in his affairs with Julia and Haidée; but the spectacle of him as woman's property is particularly compelling "in his feminine disguise" (6.26) because Byron now makes his loss of power coincide with loss of male identity. The slave market itself is an omen, for in addition to being for sale, the "boy" Juan (5.13)—"an odd male" in more ways than one—gets paired with an "odd female" in an allotment in which everyone else is paired "Lady to lady . . . man to man" (4.91–92). Indeed this odd couple is linked only after the captors decide not to link Juan with one of the "*third* sex" (86), a castrato who inspires "some discussion and some doubt" if such a "soprano might be deem'd to be a male" (92). The precarious security of Juan's gender in the marketplace becomes yet more vulnerable when he is purchased by a eunuch and ordered to dress himself in "a suit / In which a Princess with great pleasure would / Array her limbs" (5.73). The narrator conspires in this travesty, not only by insisting on referring to Juan as "her"—"Her shape, her hair, her air, her every thing" (6.35; itself a parody of Shakespeare's Troilus on "fair Cressid": "Her eyes, her hair, her cheek, her gait, her voice" [1.1.54]—but also by teasing at Juan's latent affinities with the feminine odalisques "all clad alike" (5.99).[30] For in such company, Juan's difference is scarcely apparent: indeed "his youth and features favour'd the disguise" (5.115), and "no one doubted on the whole, that she / Was what her dress bespoke, a damsel fair, / And fresh, and 'beautiful exceedingly' " (6.36)—that last phrase further dressing Juan in Coleridge's phrase for Christabel's first sight of Geraldine.

Yet Byron's total treatment of Juan cross-dressed, though it exposes the politics of sexual property, ultimately contains its subversive impulses by subsuming them into renewed expressions of male power. That agenda is anticipated by Juan's steadfast adherence to the grounds of his identity: Byron allows him the dignity of protesting to his purchaser "I'm not a lady," and of worrying about his social reputation if "it e'er be told / That I unsexed my dress" (5.73, 75). It is only Baba's threat that he will be left with more unsexed than his dress if he does not cooperate that produces compliance, even as Juan declares his "soul loathes / The effeminate garb" (5.76). Juan's statements of resistance to the effeminate find an even stronger ally in Byron's narrative politics, which, as often happens with male transvestism in literary and theatrical tradition, give the occasion over to farce, yet another means of restabilizing the apparent sexual radicalism of Juan regendered.[31] The political implications of Juan's effeminate garb dissipate into a high-camp parody of the trappings of female subjection. Juan even has to be coached "to stint / That somewhat manly majesty of stride" (5.91). The Englishman who befriends him in the slave market sounds the cue as he favors Juan with a jesting version of Laertes' caution to Ophelia—"Keep your good name"—and Juan and the narrator merrily play along: "Nay," quoth the maid, "the Sultan's self shan't carry me, / Unless his highness promises to marry me" (5.84). And when the Sultan takes a shine to Juan's beauty, Juan shows how well he has learned to mimic feminine manners: "This compliment . . . made her blush and shake" (5.156). And quite beyond such campy playfulness, Byron actually reverses the seeming impotence of Juan's travesty by introducing another kind of potency: Juan discovers he is not so much an unsexed man as a newly powerful woman. "Juanna" immediately becomes the center of attention and rivalry in the harem; all the girls want "her" to share their beds. This turn of events affords Juan a novel indirection by which to find directions out, for as the only phallic woman in the harem, he discovers a world of sexual opportunity. Clothes make the man.[32]

Juan's success as a phallic woman is all the more significant for its relation to a set of psychological and cultural contexts that are particularly potent for Byron. The psychological matrix has been studied by Otto Fenichel, who argues that some forms of transvestism are the behavior of a man who fantasizes about being a woman with a penis. Elaborating this view, Robert J. Stoller claims that the male transvestite "does not question that he is male," nor is he "effeminate when not dressed as a woman"; the transvestite, in fact, "is constantly aware of the penis under his woman's clothes, and, when it is not dangerous to do so, gets great pleasure in revealing that he is a male-woman."[33] In *Don Juan* phallic womanhood is made to seem a lucky effect rather than the premise of Juan's transvestism, but Byron's letters suggest an impetus for such luck. The relevant issue is Stoller's proposal that the transvestite man senses "the biological and social 'inferiority' of women" and knows "that within himself there is a propensity toward being reduced to this 'inferior' state" (215)—a propensity Byron displays in Juan's "feminine" characteristics as well as in his affairs with Julia and Haidée. Both Fenichel and Stoller argue that the transvestite invents the fantasy of a "phallic woman" either to remedy his feminine tendencies, or to assert a superior presence in his relations with strong women. In fact, Stoller goes on to say, the "prototype" for this figure "has actually existed in his life—that is, the fiercely dangerous and powerful woman who has humiliated him as a child" (215), namely his mother, whom the male transvestite at once identifies with and supersedes. This analysis may seem to some to be the myth of a male-authored and male-centered psychoanalytic tradition, but it is for that very reason so appropriate in Byron's case, coinciding remarkably not only with Juan's mother, the tyrannical Donna Inez, but with Byron's picture of his own mother in his letters: "Mrs. Byron furiosa," a "tormentor whose *diabolical* disposition . . . seems to increase with age, and to acquire new force with Time (*BLJ,* 1:93–94; 1:75). Byron's sense of his vulnerability is clear enough in his reports of her behavior and his own corresponding hostility: "I have never been so *scurrilously* and *violently* abused by any person, as by that woman, whom I think, I am to call mother" (1:66); "she flies into a fit of phrenzy upbraids me as if I was the most undutiful wretch in existence. . . . Am I to call this woman mother? Because by natures law she has authority over me, am I to be trampled upon in this manner?" (1:56).[34] Byron's fantasy of Juan-the-phallic-woman at once reclaims "authority" from "natures law" and redresses a psychic grievance by imagining, as Stoller puts it, the possibility of "a better woman than a biological female" (177).[35]

Because the biological female in Juan's case is a Sultana, Byron's promotion of Juan from odalisque to phallic woman invests transvestism with a political significance that exceeds the realm of specific psychic grievance. Such potential is implicit in Stoller's incidental remark that "sanctioned transvestic behavior" is frequent "at carnival times, at masquerade parties" (186), behavior with which Byron was familiar, having attended "masquerades in the year of revelry 1814" (*BLJ,* 9:168) and the Venice Carnival in 1818 and 1819. Even so sanctioned, the sexual inversions of the carnival, as Davis points out, were ambiguously productive. On the one hand, they could "clarify" the structure of hierarchical society in the very process of reversing it; these occasions offer a controlled "expression of, or a safety valve for, conflicts within the system" that operate, ultimately, to contain energy and reinforce assent. On the other hand, "festive and literary inversions of sex roles" could also excite "new ways of thinking about the system and reacting to it," and so "*undermine* as well as reinforce" assent to authority, and destabilize political structure—especially through "connections with everyday circumstances outside the privileged time of carnival and stage-play." Male transvestism, it turns out, is a particularly potent form of connection: aware that women were deemed susceptible to irrational behavior and so given some legal license for misbehavior, men resorted to transvestite cover, hiding behind the female dress when they wanted to challenge authority or engage in outright rebellion. "Donning female clothes . . . and adopting female titles" could even energize and "validate disobedient and riotous behavior by men." Davis notes a number of "transvestite riots" in Britain between the 1450s and the 1840s.[36] As a member of Parliament whose maiden speech passionately opposed the Frame-breaking bill (which specified the death penalty), and whose sarcastic "Ode to the Framers of the Frame Bill" was published (anonymously) a few days later in the *Morning Chronicle,* Byron knew about at least one such instance: the riot in April 1812 at Stockport, during which steam looms were smashed and a factory burned, led by "two men in women's clothes, calling themselves 'General Ludd's wives', "[37] He may also have recalled that the Edinburgh Porteous Riots of 1736 featured men in women's clothes, led by one "Madge Wildfire." Certainly by the time he was writing cantos 5 and 6 of *Don Juan,* he knew Scott's representation of these riots in *The Heart of Midlothian* (1818), spearheaded by a "stout Amazon"—a term Byron applies to "bold and bloody" Catherine, that "modern Amazon" (9.70, 6.96).[38]

The figure of the phallic woman not only redeems that character of Juan in female garb, but reduces Gulbeyaz, the biological woman who would exercise "male" political and sexual power in this episode. For at the same time that Juan is newly empowered by his female attire, Byron's narrative abases the "imperious" woman by whom he had been abased: the episode ends with the Sultana's will subverted and her character refeminized. When we first meet her, she is an interesting "mixture . . . Of half-voluptuousness and half command" (5.108), but the destiny of biology—"Her form had all the softness of her sex" (5.109)—prevails. Not only can she not command Juan, but having been outwitted by him and his harem bedpartner, she is reduced to a caricature of a woman scorned. Her culpability in commanding Juan's sexual service, moreover, is not something Byron cares to impose on the men in his poem who command women's bodies: in a later canto, he makes crude comedy out of geriatric rape. After the sack of Ismail, "six old damsels, each of seventy years, / Were all deflowered by different Grenadiers" (a couplet Mary Shelley refused to copy), and certain "buxom" widows who had not yet met the conquering army, we are told, were "heard to wonder in the din . . . 'Wherefore the ravishing did not begin!' " (8.130, 132).[39]

Nor surprisingly, such a heavy-handed restoration of male power does not settle the sexual politics of the poem. Byron renews the whole question with Fitz-Fulke's impersonation of the Black Friar, an episode that restages and makes more flexible the issues of transvestism and female appropriation of male property. In contrast to the Sultana's thwarted attempt to exercise male sexual prerogative, Fitz-Fulke's transvestism, even in the figure of a friar whose ghost is hostile to the sexual productivity of the House of Amundeville, is a relatively successful strategy. Byron may be recalling the chimerical behavior of Caroline Lamb, who sometimes visited him "in the disguise of a carman. My valet, who did not see through the masquerade, let her in," Byron recalls; when "she put off the man, and put on the woman . . . Imagine the scene" (*Medwin*, 216–17). Fitz-Fulke's disguise carries a similar force of surprise, giving her already aggressive sexuality an opportunity for bold initiative as she temporarily escapes conventional constraints on her behavior. Feminized men in *Don Juan* are typically objects of contempt or subjects for farce, but masculinized women are almost always figures of erotic desire, and Byron's characterization of English society makes it clear why some women might desire male prerogatives: women's whole existence is limited to gossip and social intrigue; marriage is the only game in town and an unmarried man the only game worth the pursuit; and for a woman to wield any kind of power is to risk men's derision as one of the scheming "Oligarchs of Gynocrasy" (12.66). Fitz-Fulke's cross-dressing releases her from these circumscriptions, affords an outlet for desire, and grants her a kind of "male" power of action within the existing social structure. Indeed, it aligns her with male power, for quite beyond her plotting against Juan, Byron allows the art signified by her disguise to operate as a witty deconstruction of the duplicitous political arts practiced by the men of that world—those "Historians, heroes, lawyers, priests" who put "truth in masquerade" (11.37), and whose example inspires the narrator to urge Juan to "Be hypocritical . . . be / Not what you *seem*" (11.86).

Fitz-Fulke's transvestite behavior draws even fuller energy and ideological significance in this respect from the highly popular institution of the masquerade, at which, Terry Castle reports, transvestism was not only frequent, but frequently suspected of encouraging "female sexual freedom, and beyond that, female emancipation generally." Indeed, in the world of the eighteenth-century English novel, Castle argues, the masquerade episode is "the symbolic theater of female power," for here women usurp "not only the costumes but the social and behavioral 'freedoms' of the opposite sex." As in Byron's transvestite episodes, there are conservative checks and balances: from the novelist's overall perspective, Castle suggests, the masquerade offers a way to indulge "the scenery of transgression while seeming to maintain didactic probity. The occasion may be condemned in conventional terms, yet its very representation permits the novelist, like the characters, to assume a different role."[40] Byron's version of such "probity" is typically not a matter of attitude, but an inference of those larger narrative patterns which "correct," or at least remain nervous about, the different roles played out in his episodes of transvestite transgression. Yet because

Fitz-Fulke's disguise has less to do with the specific hypocrisies of the Gynocrasy than with the general ways of the world, her manipulations yield an ambiguously potent narrative. If, as Byron's narrator remarks, that "tender moonlight situation" in which she and Juan discover each other "enables Man to show his strength / Moral or physical," he remains coy both about who the "Man" is—the girlish Juan or the transvestite Fitz-Fulke?—and about what actions, and by whom, exemplify "moral or physical" strength. He merely remarks that his is an occasion on which his hero's "virtue" may have "triumphed—or, at length, / His vice." His "or" is not much help either, for insofar as virtue (in the Latin sense of manly power) may reveal itself in "strength / Moral or physical" (even if the bawdiness of "at length" favors physical vice), Byron's phrasing compounds rather than resolves the question. The issue is managed only by a provisional deferral, a decision to retract his narrator's powers of speech: this "is more than I shall venture to describe;— / Unless some Beauty with a kiss should bribe" (17.12). That seduction is and remains merely potential, for the narrator soon becomes as silent as Juan himself, who is a thoroughly ambiguous signifier in the wake of his seduction: only his "face" can be called "virgin" and even that looks "as if he had combated" (17.13–14).

With the categories of virtue and vice, strength and weakness, activity and inactivity, male reticence and female determination, male coyness and female arts thus perplexed, Byron has his narrator "leave the thing a problem, like all things" (17.13).[41] If the "masculine tradition" is, as Homans remarks, typically manifested by "the masculine self dominat[ing] and internaliz[ing]" an otherness "identified as feminine," Byron's participation in such a tradition, as is his habit, is animated by critical self-consciousness: the sexual politics that inform *Don Juan* at once expose their ideological underpinnings and qualify the potential subversiveness of these exposures with strategies to contain the risks posed to male privilege.[42] The cross-dressings of *Don Juan* are thus significant not so much for showing the poem's male hero appropriating and internalizing female otherness (indeed, his very name implies a parody of that masculine tradition), as for provoking the poem's readers to attend to what happens—politically, socially and psychologically—when women and men are allowed, or forced, to adopt the external properties and prerogatives of the other. Byron's poem does not, finally, escape the roles fashioned and maintained by his culture, but it does explore the problems of living with and within those roles. And by doing so in the heightened forms of transvestite drama and verbal cross-dressing, Byron foregrounds the artifice that sustains much of what we determine to be "masculine" and "feminine"—a strategy at once cautious and bold, through which he engenders the world of *Don Juan* and generates its elaborate plays against the codes and laws of gender.

NOTES

I wish to thank Ronald L. Levao and Peter J. Manning for especially helpful discussion at several stages of this project.

1. Leslie A. Marchand, in *Byron: A Biography* (3 vols., New York: Knopf, 1957), remarks that Byron "had always been most successful with girls below his social and intellectual level . . . who flattered his ego and looked up with awe at his title" (1:330). Similarly, Louis Crompton, in *Byron and Greek Love: Homophobia in 19th-Century England* (Berkeley: Univ. of California Press, 1985) suggests that Byron's favoring of

the "pederastic" form of homosexuality over the "comrade" form corresponds to an overall sexual politics that "preferred aristocracies to democracy and hierarchies to egalitarianism" (239).

2. *Medwin's "Conversations of Lord Byron"*, ed. Ernest J. Lovell, Jr. (Princeton: Princeton Univ. Press, 1966), 73. Hereafter cited as *Medwin*.

3. Quotations of *Don Juan* , as well as of other poems, follow *Lord Byron: The Complete Poetical Works*, 5 vols., ed. Jerome J. McGann (Oxford: Clarendon Press, 1980–86). In the parenthetic references in my text, I note canto and stanza for *Don Juan;* for other poems, I give canto and line number; a number alone, unless the context of the paragraph suggests otherwise, designates stanza number. Citations of the edition itself hereafter are given as *CPW* with volume and page.

4. Peter J. Manning, *Byron and His Fictions* (Detroit: Wayne State Univ. Press, 1978), 180.

5. *His Very Self and Voice: Collected Conversations of Lord Byron*, ed. Ernest J. Lovell, Jr. (New York: Macmillan, 1954), 249.

6. See *CPW*, 5:279 and 5:284, respectively.

7. *His Very Self and Voice*, 452 and 299 respectively; compare *Byron's Letters and Journals*, 12 vols., ed. Leslie A. Marchand (Cambridge: Harvard Univ. Press, 1973–1982), 8:147–48. Cited hereafter *BLJ* by volume and page.

8. Marchand (note 1), 1:382.

9. *Lady Blessington's "Conversations of Lord Byron"*, ed. Ernest J. Lovell, Jr. (Princeton: Princeton Univ. Press, 1969), 47; hereafter cited as *Blessington*. Hazlitt, "Lord Byron," *The Spirit of The Age* (1825), reprinted in *The Complete Works of William Hazlitt*, ed. P. P. Howe, 21 vols. (London: J. M. Dent, 1930–34), 11:75. *Travestie* (Hazlitt's italics) abbreviates *transvestire* (the OED in fact gives the "odd travesty" of Juan in woman's garb as an instance of *travesty* meaning "alteration of dress"). Shelley is inclined to describe Byron's style in terms that play at a similar sense: of the same canto in which Byron makes Juan an odalisque, he writes, "the language in which the whole is clothed—a sort of chameleon under the changing sky of the spirit that kindles it" (*Letters 1818 to 1822*, ed. Roger Ingpen, 331; vol. 10 of *The Complete Works of Percy Bysshe Shelley*, 10 vols., ed. Roger Ingpen and Walter E. Peck [New York: Charles Scribner's Sons, 1926]).

10. George M. Ridenour, *The Style of Don Juan* (New Haven: Yale Univ. Press, 1960), 164–65.

11. My quotation follows the Arden edition of *Antony and Cleopatra*, ed. M. R. Ridley (Cambridge: Harvard Univ. Press, 1956).

12. Ridenour comments on the similarity, 165–66. See also Jerome J. McGann's discussion of "mobility" in *Don Juan* ("Byron, Mobility and the Poetics of Historical Ventriloquism," *Romanticism, Past and Present* 9 [1985]: 66–82)—the terms of which bear on the question of gender, insofar as the poem does not confine this "psychological attribute and [its] social formation" to women such as Adeline, but "specifically calls attention to the relation of mobility to the structure of the artist's life" (69–71).

13. McGann, "Byron, Mobility," 69.

14. See Ridenour (140) for the remark about Catherine's "travesty," and Cecil Y. Lang for a discussion of Catherine and Juan as "masks" for Ali Pasha and Byron ("Narcissus Jilted: Byron, *Don Juan,* and the Biographical Imperative," *Historical Studies and Literary Criticism,* ed. Jerome J. McGann [Madison: Univ. of Wisconsin Press, 1985]: 143–79).

15. Natalie Zemon Davis, "Women on Top," *Society and Culture in Early Modern France* (Stanford: Stanford Univ. Press, 1975), 127.

16. Jacques Derrida, "La Loi du Genre" / "The Law of Genre," tr. Avital Ronell

(*Glyph Textual Studies* 7 [Baltimore: Johns Hopkins Univ. Press, 1980]: 221, 203–4. Further citations appear parenthetically.

17. The parentheses give line numbers; quotations follow *Epistle 2* of *Epistles to Several Persons* (*Moral Essays*), vol. 3, part 2 of *Poems of Alexander Pope*, ed. F. W. Bateson; 6 vol. series ed. John Butt (New Haven: Yale Univ. Press, 1961). In *Alexander Pope* (New York and London: Basil Blackwell, 1985), Laura Brown discusses the "misogyny" of this Epistle in relation to its poetics of difference: women "serve to shore up the notion of a stable, morally determinate identity for men . . . by their eminently transparent, clearly despicable characterlessness" (101–7; I quote from 106).

18. Catherine (Graham) Macaulay, *Letters on Education, With Observations on Religious and Metaphysical Subjects* (London: C. Dilly, 1790), Part 1, Letter 22: 204.

19. Mary Wollstonecraft, *A Vindication of the Rights of Woman*, ed. Carol H. Poston (New York: Norton, 1975), 105. Further citations are given parenthetically.

20. 1.272; quoted by Ralph M. Wardle, *Mary Wollstonecraft: A Critical Biography* (Lawrence: Univ. of Kansas Press, 1951), 140–41.

21. Mary Hays, "Memoirs of Mary Wollstonecraft," *The Annual Necrology, 1791–8* (London: 1800): 422–23; reprinted in Poston (see note 19), 211–12.

22. Manning (note 4), 247.

23. Truman Guy Steffan and Willis W. Pratt, the editors of *Byron's Don Juan, A Variorum Edition* (4 vols., Austin: Univ. of Texas Press, 1957) cite *De L'influence des passions* (1796) and *Corinne, ou l'Italie* (1807), chapter 5 (1:45). McGann remarks that the same position "is memorably stated by Anne Elliot in Jane Austen's *Persuasion* . . . which [Byron's publisher] Murray published, and which he may very well have sent to Byron, not long before this passage was written" (*CPW*, 5:680).

24. Even *Blackwood's Edinburgh Magazine*, which charges Byron with "brutally outraging all the best feelings of female honour, affection, and confidence," admires Julia's "beautiful letter," printing stanzas 94–97, and regretting only the "style of contemptuous coldness" applied in stanza 98 to "the sufferings to which licentious love exposes" some women ("Remarks on Don Juan," vol. 5 [Aug. 1819]: 512–18; my quotations are from 512, 516–17; Donald Reiman thinks John Gibson Lockhart is the reviewer [*The Romantics Reviewed: Contemporary Reviews of British Romantic Writers* (New York: Garland, 1972), B: 143]).

25. For a compelling reading of Haidée in these terms, see Manning: "enveloping protection becomes suffocation, and what were only undertones in Juan's affair with Julia become prominent" (186).

26. In his essay "On Effeminacy of Character" (1822) Hazlitt declares esteem for "a manly firmness and decision of character," and discusses Keats as a summary case of "effeminacy of style, in some degree corresponding to effeminacy of character" (*Table Talk: Opinions on Books, Men, Things*, 2 vols., [London: Henry Coburn, 1822] 2:199–216; I quote in order from 215, 212, 214–15). *Blackwood's* more pointedly—and suggestively for the terms of the issues I address—deems Keats's poetry "a species of emasculated pruriency . . . the product of some imaginative Eunuch's muse within the melancholy inspiration of the Haram" (vol. 19 [1826] Preface xxvi; J. R. MacGillivray identifies the reviewer as Lockhart's new successor, John Wilson: *Keats: A Bibliography and Reference Guide with an Essay on Keats' Reputation* [Canada: Univ. Of Toronto Press, 1949], xliii). Even Leigh Hunt, Keats's loyal defender, remains sensitive to the charge. He concedes that Keats's "natural tendency to pleasure, as a poet, sometimes degenerated, by reason of his ill health, into a poetical effeminacy. . . . His lovers grow 'faint' with the sight of their mistresses"; but he also makes a point of

citing the sonnet on Chapman's Homer as "a remarkable instance of a vein prematurely masculine" (*Lord Byron,* 219 and 214, respectively).

27. *The Letters of John Keats,* 2 vols., ed. Hyder E. Rollins (Cambridge: Harvard Univ. Press, 1958), 2:67 and 1:386–87, respectively; hereafter cited as *KL* by volume and page.

28. Margaret Homans, *Women Writers and Poetic Identity* (Princeton: Princeton Univ. Press, 1980), 240, notes 25 and 33, respectively. Adrienne Rich, "Three Conversations," *Adrienne Rich's Poetry: Texts of the Poems, the Poet on Her work, Reviews and Criticism,* ed. Barbara Charlesworth Gelpi and Albert Gelpi (New York: Norton, 1975), 115. Erica Jong, "Visionary Anger," *Ms.* 11, 1 (July 1973): 31.

As this brief array of comments may suggest, Keats is a provocative figure in the discourses of gender. In the nineteenth century he had the curious but striking effect of making everyone who knew him or wrote about him acutely sensitive to definitions of manhood—that is, what it is to fulfill the conventional figure and behavior of fully empowered citizenship in patriarchal society. A counter-movement to the numerous charges of Keats's effeminacy appears in the equally obsessive efforts of Keats's admirers to insist on his manliness or to qualify the ambiguities. Leigh Hunt is an early voice in the motions of defense that were conducted throughout the nineteenth century, and the issues are still active in the polemics of recent biographies over the accuracy of various portraits of Keats: see Aileen Ward (*John Keats: The Making of a Poet* [New York: Viking, 1963], 89) and W. J. Bate (*John Keats* [Cambridge: Harvard Univ. Press, 1963], 113). A still more recent development in these negotiations of Keats and gender is offered by Margaret Homans's suggestive reading of Keats into the Romantic ideologies of the "masculine" in relation both to Keats's sense of powerlessness vis-à-vis supposedly powerful women (a deft updating of the nineteenth-century complaint about Keats's swooning heroes) and to his fear of being stigmatized by the real powerlessness of women themselves in nineteenth-century England ("Keats and Women Readers," a paper delivered at the English Institute, 1986).

29. The sexual ideology behind remarks such as this is so emphatic that it affects even a reader such as Cecil Lang (note 14), who is otherwise impressed by the "revolutionary" aspect of *Don Juan* "in transferring sexual aggression to the female figures": Lang retains conventional terms of evaluation, speaking of aggressive women as "sexual predators," but crediting aggressive men with "an assertion of sexuality"; similarly, he describes Juan as Catherine's "male whore," as if the role were implicitly female and Juan something of a degenerate transvestite in such a position (152, 153, 158). The politics of this episode are discussed by Katherine Kernberger ("Power and Sex: The Implication of role reversal in Catherine's Russia," *The Byron Journal* 8 [1980]): "Byron recognizes that long habituation has made women's social situation seem natural; only an inversion of the traditional distribution of power can indicate the effects of sexual subordination" (42); "This inversion is unsettling; behaviour we tolerate as "*natural*" in one sex looks odd in the other. . . . Sexual relations are exposed as merely political" (49).

30. My quotation follows the Arden edition of *Troilus and Cressida,* ed. Kenneth Palmer (New York and London: Methuen, 1981).

31. Contemporary reviews were divided over the evaluation of Julia's sexual aggressiveness, but were uniformly amused by Juan's adventures in the harem. For a relevant discussion, see Jane W. Stedman ("From Dame to Woman: W.S. Gilbert and Theatrical Transvestism," *Suffer and Be Still: Women in the Victorian Age,* ed. Martha Vicinus [Bloomington: Indiana Univ. Press, 1972], 20–37), who notes that post-Elizabethan male theatrical transvestism is "not the simple convention of boys playing serious

feminine roles" ("in fact, this is the one sort of transvestism not found"), but routinely took the form of farce and grotesque parodies. I quote from p. 20.

32. This episode of transvestite opportunity may have been inspired by the resource-fulness of Byron's friend, Colonel Mackinnon: "Byron was much amused by Mac-kinnon's funny stories, one of which was later supposed to be the basis of *Don Juan,* V: Mackinnon disguised himself as a nun in order to enter a Lisbon convent" (*The Reminiscences of Captain [Rees Howell] Gronow,* [1862], 85–86, quoted in Lovell (note 5), 612 n. 39). The anecdote seems, in addition, to offer a fantasy continuation of Juan's aborted romance with Julia.

33. Otto Fenichel, "The Psychology of Transvestitism" (1930); reprinted in *The Collected Papers of Otto Fenichel,* First Series (New York: Norton, 1953) 1:167–80 (I refer to 169); Robert J. Stoller, *Sex and Gender: On the Development of Masculinity and Femininity* (New York: Science House, 1968), 176–77. It is worth noting Stoller's conservative bias in assessing the issue: he assumes, for instance, that to feminize men with women's dress is to humiliate them (185) and he describes as "effeminate" behav-ior that of any father "overly loving and 'maternal' to his small children" or that of any man "oversolicitous to other people and thrillingly responsive to the universe of art" (179). Further citations of Stoller are given parenthetically.

34. For a perceptive discussion of Byron's relationship with his mother and its literary consequences, see Manning, 23–55 and 177–99.

35. Also referring to Stoller, Sandra M. Gilbert studies various "costume drama[s] of misrule" in modern literature with an aim to showing how "the hierarchical princi-ple of an order based upon male dominance / female submission [gets] recovered from transvestite disorder" ("Costumes of the Mind: Transvestism as Metaphor in Modern Literature," *Writing and Sexual Difference,* ed. Elizabeth Abel [Chicago: Univ. of Chicago Press, 1982]: 193–219). Elaine Showalter, too, refers to Stoller in a witty and perceptive essay on how the figure of the "phallic woman" in the male feminism of the 1980s underwrites power, usurping and in effect marginalizing the feminism it seems to endorse ("Critical Cross-Dressing: Male Feminists and The Woman of The Year," *Raritan* 3:2 [Fall 1983]: 130–149). For a theoretical assessment of the treatment of transvestism in this essay, Gilbert's, and Shoshana Felman's "Rereading Femininity" (*Yale French Studies* 62 [1981]: 19–44, see Mary Jacobus, *Reading Woman: Essays in Feminist Criticism* (New York: Columbia Univ. Press, 1986), 5–24.

36. Davis (note 15), 130–31, 142–43, 147–50.

37. See E. P. Thompson, *The Making of the English Working Class* (London: Victor Gollancz, 1965), 567.

38. For Byron's references to Scott's novel, see *BLJ,* 9:87, 10:146, 11:46. The riots are represented in chapters 6 and 7.

39. Andrew Rutherford (while finding these stanzas "very funny") laments Byron's "abandonment of the standards of morality on which his satire has been based," for he frivolously refuses "to face the horror of mass rape, or even indeed of individual cases. Byron attacked Suvarov for callousness, for seeing men in the gross, but here he is himself prepared to think of women in the same way . . . to withhold in treating rape the moral sensitivity that he had shown in treating deaths in battle" (*Byron: A Critical Study* [Stanford: Stanford Univ. Press, 1961], 179).

40. I quote, in order, from "Eros and Liberty at the English Masquerade, 1710–90," *Eighteenth-Century Studies* 17 (1983–84): 164, and "The Carnivalization of Eighteenth-Century English Narrative,"*PMLA* 99 (1984): 909, 912. Castle is interested in the way masquerade "represented a kind of institutionalized disorder, one that served both as a voluptuous release from ordinary cultural prescriptions and as a stylized comment on them"; she suggests that "the carnivalesque sexual reversals of masquerade may have

contributed, in however a minor form, to incipient feminist sentiment in the late eighteenth century" ("Eros and Liberty," 159, 175). In the theater itself, women such as Byron's acquaintance Sarah Siddons assayed serious male roles (Siddons played Hamlet in Dublin). For other instances, see Stedman (note 31) and Frank W. Wadsworth, "Hamlet and Iago: Nineteenth-Century Breeches Parts," *Shakespeare Quarterly* 17 (Spring 1966): 130–39.

41. If, as Castle argues, the masquerade episode has the effect of introducing "a curious instability into the would-be orderly cosmos of the eighteenth-century English novel" ("Carnivalization," 904), the transvestite episodes of *Don Juan* reflect a world that presumes no such order, but is, as Anne K. Mellor puts it, "founded on abundant chaos; everything moves, changes its shape, becomes something different" (*English Romantic Irony* [Cambridge: Harvard Univ. Press, 1980], 42).

42. I quote Margaret Homans (note 28, p. 12) for a representative description of the masculine tradition.

Setting Byron Straight:
Class, Sexuality, and the Poet

This brief excerpt is from one of several valuable essays by Jerome
Christensen dealing with Byron and his times. Another, closely related
article, "Theorizing Byron's Practice: The Performance of Lordship
and the Poet's Career," appeared in the special issue of *Studies in
Romanticism* edited by Karl Kroeber, *Beginning Byron's Third
Century*. Our selection here also illustrates how the importance of
Byron's homoeroticism (and the attitude toward it in the England of
his day), opened up especially by Louis Crompton's research and
commentary, is currently perceived as crucial to the special quality of
Byron's literary achievements. Christensen combines sophisticated
poststructural analyis with experimental biographical criticism, showing
how homosexuality helped Byron to establish a literary sense of
identity, and from this base argues cogently that an important aspect of
the poet's genius consists in a radical openness to experiences that
many others would have found overwhelming. One should not
overlook, however, Christensen's note 14, which draws attention to Sir
Walter Scott's perhaps superior consciousness of the social and
political complexities with which Byron was entangled. Finally, we
must remark on how Christensen's and Wolfson's essays are mutually
reinforcing, both adding depth and detail to what all critics are coming
to recognize as Byron's extraordinary "mobility," just as Christensen's
and Cooper's essays are complementary in their meticulous
articulations of the complexity of the interplay between ideological and
psychosocial forces that dominate Byron's later poetry.

Both in what she affirms and in what she denies Mary Wollstonecraft contributes
to that discursive practice in which, as Theodor Adorno writes, "the network of
the whole is drawn ever tighter, modelled after the act of exchange. It leaves the
individual consciousness less and less room for evasion, performs it more and
more thoroughly, cuts it off *a priori* as it were from the possibility of differencing
itself as all difference degenerates to a nuance in the monotony of suppy."[1] The
categories with which Wollstonecraft engages gender and class difference are
strength and mobility: aristocratic strength becomes male mobility. By no accident
those are the historically sanctioned terms for characterizing the figure, event, and
text called Lord Byron. The text of Lord Byron is the test of difference in the
Romantic period—whether it need be straightened out and adjusted to the net-

From *Literature and the Body,* ed. Elaine Scarry (Baltimore: The Johns Hopkins University
Press, 1988), pp. 125–140, 148–157.

work of exchange or whether by some evasion it can separate itself from that very code by which it becomes recognizable.

Here is a scene of fascination framed by Byron in a letter from Greece to his former traveling companion John Cam Hobhouse:

> At Vostitza I found my dearly-beloved Eustathius—ready to follow me not only to England, but to Terra Incognita, if so be my compass pointed that way. . . . The next morning I found the dear soul upon horseback clothed very sprucely in Greek Garments, with those ambrosial curls hanging down his amiable back, and to my utter astonishment and the great abomination of Fletcher, a *parasol* in his hand to save his complexion from the heat.—However in spite of the *Parasol* on we travelled very much enamoured, as it should seem, till we got to Patras, where Strané received us into his new house where I now scribble.[2]

However enamored, this lord, unlike Wollstonecraft's more scrupulous voluptuary, displays a rather breezy detachment. Although there can be little doubt that Byron's first genital intimacy with boys occurred during his first trip to Greece, and probably with Eustathius, this moment seems no more unmediated than any other. Indeed, the tableau is *about* mediation. The gaze is mediated by its doubling between the abominated expression of Fletcher and the quizzical esteem of Byron. The lyrical freeze frame concatenates with additional moments and even, as the epistolary format implies, other minds. The gaze is subordinated to an exchange, and the exchange is ultimately referred to a moment of production, "I now scribble."

What is being produced? First, a discourse of what has come to be called "liberation"—a liberation that runs the scale between sex and politics and that combines in supposedly mutual benefit both agent and object. The tag "Greek love" does not euphemize this bond. Lord Byron learned his homosexuality from books—old books. One of the most impressionable students of the classics the English public schools have ever formed, Byron invested sexual desire only in Greek boys. For Byron "Greek love" means love of Greeks.[3]

The liberation of homosexual desire only becomes possible after desire has been sexualized, which in turn, as Foucault has argued, depends on the hypothesis of repression. Generalized, the repressive hypothesis permits the fluent translation of the domain of sexuality into nationality. Only the repression of the Greek by the Turk allows for the possibility of his liberation; it renders him an equivocal being and makes him interesting. For Byron the Turkish occupation of Greek soil is homologous with the parasol covering Eustathius's fair skin. The sexual body of the boy is produced as the effect of that which covers and corrects it. Byron desires the boy only insofar as the body is repressed—he desires "him" as sign.[4]

Let me be precise here. The convergence of a certain discourse of golden-age innocence and truth with the ocular evidence of a repression by the despotic Turk *constitutes* Byron's homosexuality. Evidence of repression orients and organizes his inchoate political and erotic impulses, which then become *homosexual,* retrospectively. For us, not for him. Byron never intimated that he had been a homosexual before leaving England, nor even after he had indulged with Greek boys did he suggest that he had left something undone in his relations with John Edleston, the Cambridge choir boy toward whom he frankly acknowledged a love "violent, although pure" (*BLJ* 8:24).[5] Greek love could not be practiced with English lads.

Moreover, the love of the sentimental liberator can never confess to its violence and so can never be pure.

The repressive hypothesis is well meaning; it gives Byron a purpose, some good work to do. He will liberate himself; he will liberate the Greek—or, as Jerome J. McGann puts it, neatly hybridizing the "isms" natural supernatural and Oriental: Byron becomes "obsessed with the idea of renewal of human culture in the west at a moment of its deepest darkness. This means for Byron the renewal of the value of the individual person, and the renewal of Greece as an independent political entity."[6] But this is surely a misrecognition. Lord Byron believed in no such thing as "human culture," nor did he cherish the idea of a transhistorical individual whose value fluctuated like the funds. He did, at times, however, project a *specific* form of renewal or liberation, as in this note to *Childe Harold* II: "The English have at last compassionated their Negroes, and under a less bigoted government may probably one day release their Catholic brethren; but the interposition of foreigners alone can emancipate the Greeks, who, otherwise appear to have as small a chance of redemption from the Turks, as the Jews have from mankind in general."[7]

Lord Byron's messianism is less Christological than feudal. He imagines the redeemed purity of the Greek as the gift of a chivalrous knight, who magnanimously presents the repressed with *their* emancipation as a corollary of the revival of *his* mythic past. Subjected to the repressive hypothesis, difference (historical, geographical, subjective) is thematized as the consequence of a lost or stolen original purity, which the sentimental liberator will profess to *return* to the Greek, but which he is actually *donating for the first time*. Eustathius and the Greeks are engendered by the dream of their emancipation—a story that produces their bygone freedom as the alibi for the representational practice of the liberator, in the same way as the pure white body of the boy is the alibi for the parasol—for the signifier that constitutes him as a sign and shadows him forth as an object of desire. Byron can imagine freeing the Greeks, but he cannot imagine the Greeks free:

> The Greeks will never be independent; they will never be sovereigns as heretofore, and God forbid they ever should! but they may be subjects without being slaves. Our colonies are not independent, but they are free and industrious, and such may Greece be hereafter. (*CPW* 2:201)[8]

It is a telling coincidence that Byron scribbles his Greek love at "Patras," for the colonization that Byron calls freedom is a form of patronage. That Byron's relations with boys were established along lines of patronage has not gone unnoticed,[9] but the sentimental structure of such relationships has. Its flavor can be sampled in the 1807 letter to Elizabeth Pigott in which Byron writes of the *"Chaos of hope & Sorrow"* into which he has been thrown by his separation from John Edleston, described as his "protege," who is committed to entering a "mercantile house in Town" on Lord Byron's interest. The dismal denouement of this relationship (during his voyage Byron was doubly shocked by the news that the urbanized Edleston had been accused of "indecency" and that soon after he had died of consumption) was partially the result of the misprision attendant on the attempt to maintain patronage as a mediatory fiction between men of different social classes and between a schoolboy world of "violent, although pure" love and the tranquil gloom of a countinghouse. Once the doomed Edleston (who, in the iconography of nineteenth-century medievalism, played Lady of Shalott to Lord Byron's Lancelot) left the safety of Cambridge, he and Byron ceased to meet. So distant did they become that Edleston's revival of the fiction of patronage in response to Byron's crass misreading of an earlier appeal seems embarrassingly abject: "At present I must beg leave to repeat that [it] is only the favor of your Lordship's *personal* Influence and Patronage [not money] which I humbly presumed in my last as well as now,—to request."[10]

The transactions with Edleston are an extreme example of a characteristic mode in Byron: the structure and ethos of patronage, usually bedecked in the finery of chivalric *noblesse,* were invoked to reconstruct and normalize contacts with men and women that were in their happening invisible, fluid, even anarchic. By "invisible, fluid, even anarchic," I mean what Lord Byron's crony Scrope Berdmore Davies meant when, upon departing from a stay at Newstead Abbey, he jotted the note, "This whole week passed in a delirium of sensuality."[11] Davies, like Byron, has impressive claims to authority on such matters, having spent his schooldays at Eton, where as a Kings Scholar he was housed with roughly fifty other lads in a dormitory room where, as his biographer describes it, "between the hours of 8 o'clock at night, when they were locked in, and 7 o'clock the next morning when they were released by the Head Master's servant the boys were left totally to their own devices."[12] We have no way of knowing what those devices were. No doubt there was "cruel bullying and sexual malpractices," but the "total lack of privacy" for the individual had the consequence of conferring privacy or, better, complete invisibility on the dreamlike, delirial world of boys, each and all with their peculiar devices. If this world can be described as the "other face of the 18th century, the face unglimpsed in Jane Austen's novels, brutal, filthy, and corrupt," it can only be once the eighteenth century has been given a recognizable face by such writers as Austen.[13] Only then, in a self-consciously *nineteenth* century, could this region of delirium, unreadable according to the Malthusian and Benthamite schemata, be given the physiognomy of the other, corrupt and brutal, in order that it could be redeemed for the future by Christian muscle and chivalric myth.

Hours of Idleness, Byron's first book of poems, situates itself at the divide (called the "Rubicon" in the Preface) between minority and legal maturity and eagerly contributes to the general cultural project of recasting the invisible world of dirty little boys in terms of the regulative format of chivalric romance. The cultural plot is expounded with intelligence and wit by Mark Girouard in the *Return to Camelot.*[14] But Girouard does not observe what "Lord Byron Minor" failed to see: that not only was the consequence of seeing, remembering, schooldays their annihilation, but also this medievalist strategy was so readily available because it repeated with remarkable fidelity the monarchic attempt to control the bullyings and sexual malpractices among the nobility that was the policy behind the royal institution of tournaments and heraldic codes in the thirteenth century (henceforth the nobles' devices would never be totally their own).[15] It would be some time before Lord Byron would come to understand nostalgia as a form of suicide.[16]

Lord Byron's attempts both to memorialize the delirial world of his youth and to contain similar possibilities in the present are epitomized by his relations with Nicolo Giraud, singled out among the "sylphs" with whom Byron "rioted" at the

Capuchin monastery at Athens. "I am his 'Padrone' and his 'amico,' " Byron writes, "and the Lord knows what besides" (*BLJ* 2:12). About Giraud we know little more than what Byron tells us, but the switching between "Padrone" and "amico" is wholly characteristic of Byron, who in his first public appearance as poet split his poetic persona between Julius Caesar and William Cowper, as well as between the reluctant commander of "To the Earl of Dorset" and the stripling friend of "To the Earl of Clare." This oscillation would remain a constant threat to the stability of the Byronic poetic subject (see, for example, the wavering between a jolly democracy and a melancholy despotism in the opening of *The Corsair*), until in *Don Juan* the undecidable priority between "Padrone" and "Amico" becomes the whirligig on which character and narrator ride in outlandish parody of chivalrization and its discontents.

For the roving Lord of 1810, however, who is unconnected by anything but debts to the world of men in which he has, despite himself, grown up, freeing the Greeks is a profession of sorts. So is writing about it. The pursuit of boys may satisfy diverse aims, but "the end of all scribblement is to amuse" (*BLJ* 2:20). And if it is arguably the case that Byron could not have coitus with any boys while Hobhouse, an "enemy to fine feelings & sentimental friendship" (*BLJ* 2:155), was around, it is certainly true that Byron could not write to Hobhouse with Hobhouse around. The departure of Hobhouse is ultimately less important for allowing Byron to have the experience than it is for enabling Byron to represent the experience, tantalizingly, for an audience of intimate male friends.

In his book *Byron and Greek Love,* Louis Crompton sets Byron's Eastern journey against the background of a Cambridge circle (which included Byron, Hobhouse, and Charles Skinner Matthews) knit by what he calls a "homosexual bond." "In a sense," Crompton observes, "the three share what would today be called a gay identity, based on common interests and a sense of alienation from a society they must protect themselves from by a special 'mysterious' style and mutually understood codes."[17] Crompton refers to an exchange between Byron and Matthews on the eve of the former's embarkation with Hobhouse for the East. Byron writes,

> I take up the pen which our friend has for a moment laid down merely to express a vain wish that you were with us in this delectable region, as I do not think Georgia itself can emulate in capabilities or incitements to the "Plen. and optabil.—Coit." the ports of Falmouth & parts adjacent—We are surrounded by Hyacinths & other flowers of the most fragrant [na]ture, & I have some intention of culling a handsome Bouquet to compare with the exotics I hope to meet in Asia. (*BLJ* 1:206–7)

Matthews replies by congratulating Lord Byron "on the splendid success of your first efforts in *the mysterious*, that style in which more is meant than meets the Eye." He goes on to encourage Byron in his "Botanical pursuits" and decrees "that everyone who professes *ma methode* do spell the term which designates his calling with an *e* at the end of it—*methodiste*, not method*ist*, and pronounce the word in the French fashion. Every one's taste must revolt at confounding ourselves with that sect of horrible, snivelling, fanatics."[18] Though barely utterable, the code is easily deciphered: "Hyacinths" are boys; the Latin abbreviation "Plen. and optabil.—Coit." is from *The Satyricon* and refers to "full and to-be-wished-for intercourse."[19]

Rather than the formation of a gay sense of identity in response to real or imagined persecution, this bit of correspondence describes the deliberate formation of a *literary* sense of identity, a shared sense of what Matthews calls a profession. The profession is formed by the positing of a particular kind of sexual experience as that which, because it cannot meet the eye, underwrites everything that can. Of greater importance than the wished-for coitus is the idea of it. Rendered jokingly as the pursuit of a natural history of all beautiful boys, that idea makes possible both the ritual exchange of pens between Hobhouse and Byron, anticipating their literary collaborations, and the economical style of the "mysterious," which forecasts the darkly implicative portrayal of a character who unites "the eager curiosity of youth with the fastidiousness of a sated libertine" that was to be the first literary fruit of Byron's pilgrimage.[20] The linkage of the mysterious style with the broodings of the Byronic hero connect it to the gothic motif of the "unspeakable," which, as Eve Kosofsky Sedgwick has incisively remarked, was in the Romantic period "a near-impenetrable shibboleth for a particular conjunction of class and male sexuality."[21] In *this* context the mysterious style, if almost unutterable, is most significant as that which is highly writable. It has all the conspicuous visibility and fluent transmissibility of a code, which here operates not primarily to hide something but as a kind of trademark to identify an association of senders and receivers. The "mysterious style" enables a profession; it is what Defoe, speaking of brewers, Swift, speaking of stockjobbers, Coleridge, speaking of contemporary critics, or Byron, speaking of publishers, would describe as the cant of the trade.[22] Its jargon artificially creates the body of traders, establishing the line between inside and outside, forming the basis for and boundaries of association. Their "mysterious style" binds these three Cambridge students together in what is a professional organization that *elects* not to speak its name.

The jargon of homosexuality expresses what Jacques Lacan calls a "formal fixation, which introduces a certain rupture of level, a certain discord between man's organization and his *Umwelt,* which is the very condition that extends indefinitely his world and his power."[23] In the case of these men, the jargon of homosexuality produces a specific kind of paranoiac knowledge in the service of a distinctive literary identity. The extension of world proceeds imperially according to the metonymic association of subjects: boys, Greek boys, Greeks, the Orient. Although it may be appealing to regard this as the sort of project in which the poet carries with him relationship and love, K. J. Dover's distinction between "legitimate" and "illegitimate" eros shames such vanity. Among the ancient Greeks, according to Dover, the legitimacy that was conferred on a philanthropic relationship between an *erastes* and his youthful *eromenos* was sharply contrasted with "gross misbehaviour for monetary payment [which] is the act of a hubristes and uneducated man."[24] Although there is no evidence that Lord Byron, "Padrone and amico," was ever so vulgar as to offer money directly for sex, Nicolo Giraud, Eustathius's replacement in Byron's affections, was employed as "dragoman and Major Domo" (*BLJ* 2:29), a position that almost certainly entailed payment in love *and* money. But more important than specific acts of monetary payment is the imperial conception of a tour that would induce Byron to describe himself as a very Caesar of sexuality (*BLJ* 2:14). That hubristic orientation is first established by the jocular denomination of boys as "Hyacinths & other flowers." Botany is not just a convenient metaphor; it is the privileged metaphor for the instrumentality of metaphor—for the way natural bodies can, à la Rousseau in *The Reveries,* at once be "loved" and regarded as specimens, can be cathected, collected, and then inserted into books which, like Hobhouse's memoires and *Childe Harold*, are then sold as commodities on the open market (Byron speaks of his Greek boys as his "antiques" [*BLJ* 2:29]). The process by which a formal fixation underwrites both a literary identity and a hubristic extension of cognitive and rhetorical power would seem to vindicate Wollstonecraft's vision of "bodies of men who must necessarily be made foolish or vicious by the very constitution of their profession."[25]

The jargon of homosexuality furnishes not only a subject but also a way to write about it. Professing homosexuality, Matthews decrees, means professing *ma methode,* which in turn entails adopting a certain style—epitomized by the addition of an *e* to "method." The *e* is the letter of affection and affect, both the sign and the act of male bonding. In its capacity to charm, Matthews's *e* resembles the "naked letter" of romance with which, according to Richard Hurd, Gothic poets enchanted their readers or, closer to home, the *a* with which Jacques Derrida neologized *"differance,"* at once volatilizing the text of Western metaphysics and spellbinding a generation of literary critics.[26] But *differance* is not *methode.* By Frenching and feminizing English method, Matthews's supplemental letter merely translates it into a new, fetching, but altogether functional uniform. Unnaked, the letter is a device by which romantic force can be made recognizable and put to work as the no-nonsense instrument of interest. In the moment of its institution, the code, ostensibly meaningful, masking from all but initiates the existence of forbidden sexual desires, is rendered as the meaningfulness *of* the ostensible, the letter that invites but does not require decoding, like a style. Following Matthews, we may hazard the neoclassical maxim that for these men homosexuality is nature methodized. Having said that, however, the revision naturally follows that for these writers homosexuality is style methodized. . . .

NOTES

1. Theodor W. Adorno, *Prisms*, trans. Samuel and Shierry Weber (Cambridge: MIT Press, 1982), 21.

2. *Byron's Letters and Journals,* ed. Leslie A. Marchand, 12 vols. (Cambridge: Harvard University Press, 1973–82), 2:66. Subsequent references to *BLJ* will be indicated by volume and page number in the text.

3. Byron's romantic classicism was not, of course, his own invention; it has a pedigree that extends backward to the Jacobins and refracts through Napoleon. The Napoleonic career was always before Byron, whose own politico-sexual itinerary could be described as a mock-Bonapartism. See, for example, Lord Byron's attempt to resolve disputes among his tenants on his return from the East: "But I shall not interfere further (than like Buonaparte) by diminishing Mr. B's *kingdom,* and erecting part of it into a *principality* for Field Marshal Fletcher!" (*BLJ* 2:52).

4. Besides Foucault, my analysis heavily depends on Jean Baudrillard's *For a Critique of the Political Economy of the Sign,* trans. Mark Poster (St. Louis: Telos Press, 1981), esp. chap. 3, "Fetishism and Ideology."

5. In denying that Lord Byron was initiated into homosexuality before departing from England, I am rejecting Louis Crompton's revisionary reading of the texts surrounding the supposed advances made to Byron by Lord Grey de Ruthyn, tenant of Newstead Abbey, during Byron's visit with Grey in 1804. Differing from Byron's biographers Leslie A. Marchand and Doris Langley Moore, Crompton argues that the

available evidence supports the inference that some sexual contact occurred (*Byron and Greek Love: Homophobia in 19th-Century England* [Berkeley: University of California Press, 1985], 81–85). The strong evidence of repulsion disables Crompton's case, though it is not, I would argue, repulsion toward homoerotic contact. Byron was disgusted not by the sexual nature of Grey's advances but by the advancing nature of Grey's sexuality. In the same letter to his mother in which Byron mysteriously refers to Grey as his "inveterate enemy," he boasts, "But however the way to *riches* to *Greatness* lies before me, I can, I will cut myself a path through the world or perish in the attempt. Others have begun life with nothing and ended Greatly. And shall I who have a competent if not a large fortune, remain idle, No, I will carve myself the passage to Grandeur, but never with Dishonour" (*BLJ* 2:49 [sic]). All other evidence of Byron's relations with boys shows him in the active role. To imagine him in the pathic with the tenant of his ancestral home is to promote an incredible aberration—particularly in one who is strongly afflicted with status anxiety and who takes his erotic patterns from the Greeks. My reservations are similar, though less strenuous in regard to Cecil Y. Lang's claim that there was a sexual liaison between Byron and the Ali Pacha on Byron's trip East (see "Narcissus Jilted: Byron, *Don Juan,* and the Biographical Imperative," *Historical Studies and Literary Criticism,* ed. Jerome J. McGann [Madison: University of Wisconsin Press, 1985], 143–79). Lang's ingenuity, which promises to disseminate the Byronic text in a radical and exciting way, tempts belief. Unfortunately that ingenuity is yoked to the quaint thesis that the biographical method is not, as Brooks and Warren once taught, irrelevant to interpretation. Who out there is arguing? But there is more than one biographical method, and, like Crompton's, Lang's reduces to decoding: he wants to use facts to get through the poetry to *the* fact (what the Ali Pacha actually did to Lord Byron, how *Don Juan* would really have ended). It is not the seductiveness of the Ali Pacha I deny—he could be politically and sexually accommodated to the interpositional model of Greek love described in notes 19 and 20 below. If Byron did have sexual relations with Ali Pacha, he did it for love of the Greeks. Regardless, I reject the sentimental commitment to the liberation of the referent that Lang's argument entails—Lang's insistence that "it" all comes down to one thing in the end. On the investment in the ethical distinction between active and pathic roles among the ancient Greeks, see K. J. Dover, *Greek Homosexuality* (New York: Random House, 1978), passim.

6. Jerome J. McGann, *The Beauty of Inflections: Literary Investigation in Historical Method and Theory* (Oxford: Clarendon Press, 1985), 260. Cf. Maurice Godelier's comment that "the image of Asia stagnating for millennia in an unfinished transition from classless to class society, from barbarism to civilisation, has not stood up to the finding of archaeology and history in the East and the New World. . . . What was born in Greece was not civilisation but the West, a particular form of civilisation which was finally to dominate it while all the while pretending to be its symbol" ("The Concept of the 'Asiatic Mode of Production' and Marxist Models of Social Evolution," in Anthony Giddens, *A Contemporary Critique of Historical Materialism* [Berkeley and Los Angeles: University of California Press, 1981], 87). Cf. the review of *Childe Harold's Pilgrimage* in the *Monthly Review* of May 1812, which after quoting Byron's patronizing remarks about the Greeks' need for interposition, observes that "perhaps [Lord Byron] rather under-rates the value of the co-operation of the natives, which would certainly be essential on such an occasion" (*Romantics Reviewed,* ed. Donald A. Reiman [New York: Garland, 1972], B:4:1734).

7. *The Complete Poetical Works,* ed. Jerome J. McGann, 4 vols. (Oxford: Clarendon Press, 1980–86), 2:202. Hereafter cited parenthetically as *CPW* by volume, canto (where appropriate), and line number. Sexualized, Byron's notion of the "interposi-

tion" of himself between the aggressor Turk and victimized Greek, giving and receiving, would be diagnosed as bivalently sadomasochistic, especially if contrasted with the strikingly similar, overtly sexual gesture of liberation proposed by Lytton Strachey who, when asked at the 1916 inquiry into his claims to be a conscientious objector, "What would you do if you saw a German soldier attempting to rape your sister?" replied, "I should try and interpose my own body" (Michael Holroyd, *Lytton Strachey: A Critical Biography,* 2 vols. [New York: Holt, Rinehart & Winston, 1967–68], 2:179). Both Strachey's known homosexual preference and the incest taboo restrict the function of "interpose" to the provision of a masochistic buffer rather than a sadomasochistic hinge.

8. Byron's liberation of Eustathius amounted to a substitution of a "green shade" for "that effeminate parasol"—a change in inflection but no reconstitution of the boy's sign-value (*BLJ* 2:7). Not that the change in inflection, accent or color is insignificant. Neil Hertz addresses the element of hysteria in the debates regarding the proper shape of the ideologically charged Phrygian cap, which veered between a drooping, emasculated/ing, Asiatic, Medusa-like model and the more than Roman cone shape (Neil Hertz, *The End of the Line* [New York: Columbia University Press, 1985], 179–91). Although there is, I think, a fair analogy between parasol/shade and droopy cap/cone cap, it would be too farfetched to mention were it not that the two articles of clothing are linked in one of the most influential colonialist fantasies in the English language, *Robinson Crusoe.* An account of the political, economic, racial, and sexual themes invested in Crusoe's goat-skin parasol and cap is given in Derek Walcott's brilliant *tour de force Pantomime*, staged in New York City, 1986–87.

9. See Doris Langley Moore, *Lord Byron: Accounts Rendered* (London: John Murray, 1974), 89, and Crompton, *Byron and Greek Love,* 152.

10. Moore, *Lord Byron,* 90.

11. T. A. J. Burnett, *The Rise and Fall of a Regency Dandy: The Life and Times of Scrope Berdmore Davies* (London: John Murray, 1981), 36.

12. Ibid., 14.

13. Ibid. Because the "face unglimpsed" is no face at all, perhaps it would be more accurate to note that in *Northanger Abbey,* for example, Austen gives a face to the other side of the eighteenth century and "romantically" names it "Gothic." Both the countenancing of the other as Gothic and the denial that Gothic plots bear any relation to actual circumstances are part and parcel of the near-hysterical denial by Henry Tilney, Catherine Morland's patron, that there could be anything unglimpsed in a society so elaborately contrived for the ends of surveillance as contemporary England: "Does our education prepare us for such atrocities? Do our laws connive at them? Could they be perpetrated without being known, in a country like this, where social and literary intercourse is on such a footing; where every man is surrounded by a neighbourhood of voluntary spies, and where roads and newspapers lay every thing open?" (chap. 24).

14. Mark Girouard, *The Return to Camelot: Chivalry and the English Gentleman* (New Haven: Yale University Press, 1981), 163–76. Girouard's history could be read as an extended commentary on Scott's account in the General Preface to the Waverley Novels of the schoolboy "bicker" in which neighborhood brawled with neighborhood and class battled class in a brutal melee on the streets of Edinburgh, until, magically, "a lady of distinction presented a handsome set of colours," eradicating peculiar devices by chivalrizing one and all. Scott's recollection, offered with an aplomb that almost disarms criticism, not only craftily deploys all the motifs and devices we have been addressing, but is characteristically self-conscious about the social and political implications of their deployment.

15. Maurice Keen, *Chivalry* (New Haven: Yale University Press, 1984), 86–90, 125–34.

16. Cf. Girouard's account of the humiliating failure of the Eglinton Tournament in 1839 (*Return to Camelot*, 87–110).

17. Crompton, *Byron and Greek Love*, 129. In his usage Crompton does not clearly distinguish between the terms "homosexual" and "gay." John Boswell incisively frames the terminological issue in his *Christianity, Social Tolerance, and Homosexuality* (Chicago: University of Chicago Press, 1980), where he defines "homosexuality" as comprising "all sexual phenomena between persons of the same gender, whether the result of conscious preference, subliminal desire, or circumstantial exigency," and "gay" as referring to "persons who are conscious of erotic inclination toward their own gender as a distinguishing characteristic or, loosely, to things associated with such people" (44). Although Boswell is clearer, his definitions increase rather than diminish the ambiguity. "Gay" by this definition is a trope; it need not be sexual at all. Its relation to homosexuality is fundamentally contingent. For an admirable, historically nuanced discussion of the variations in homosexual identity that were constructed in the nineteenth century, see Jeffrey Weeks, *Sex, Politics and Society: The Regulation of Sexuality since 1800* (London: Longman, 1981), 108–17.

18. Crompton, *Byron and Greek Love*, 127–29.

19. Crompton mentions that the code was first deciphered by Gilbert Highet in 1957 at the request of Leslie A. Marchand (128). That it remained mysterious for so long has more to say about the decline of classical education than it does about the inherent difficulty of the code.

20. But not the only fruit. In a later letter Byron jokingly promised a treatise on sodomy (*BLJ* 1:208). During the journey the friends hatched the project of launching a literary journal to be called the *Bagatelle* (allowing glimpses of the cat in the bag?). The Wollstonecraftian characterization of Childe Harold appears in George Ellis's review for the *Quarterly* in March 1812 (*Romantics Reviewed*, B:5:1991).

21. Eve Kosofsky Sedgwick, *Between Men: English Literature and Male Homosocial Desire* (New York: Columbia University Press, 1985), 95.

22. For Defoe on jargon, see *The Complete English Tradesman in Familiar Letters*, 2 vols. (1727; rept. New York: Augustus Kelley, 1969), 1:26–34; for Swift, *Examiner* (November 2, 1710), *The Works of Jonathan Swift*, ed. Thomas Roscoe, 6 vols. (New York: O'Shea, 1865), 3:454; for Coleridge, see *Biographia Literaria*, ed. James Engell and W. Jackson Bate, vol. 7 of *The Collected Works of Samuel Taylor Coleridge*, gen. ed. Kathleen Coburn, 2 vols. (Princeton: Princeton University Press, 1983), 1:60–67 and 2:109–10. Here is a frustrated Lord Byron addressing his publisher John Murray: "Indeed you are altogether so abstruse and undecided lately—that I suppose you mean me to write—'John Murray Esqre. a *Mystery*' a composition which would not displease the Clergy nor the trade.—" (*BLJ* 9:168).

23. Jacques Lacan, "Aggressivity in Psychoanalysis," in *Ecrits: A Selection*, trans. Alan Sheridan (New York: Norton, 1977), 17.

24. Dover, *Greek Homosexuality*, 47.

25. Mary Wollstonecraft, *A Vindication of the Rights of Woman* (London: Dent, 1929), 21.

26. Richard Hurd, *Letters on Chivalry and Romance* (1762; rept. Los Angeles: Augustan Reprint Society, 1963), 113. Jacques Derrida, "Differance," in *Speech and Phenomena: And Other Essays on Husserl's Theory of Signs*, trans. David B. Allison (Evanston: Northwestern University Press, 1973), 129–60.

PETER J. MANNING

The Nameless Broken Dandy and the Structure of Authorship

This short chapter is from Peter Manning's splendid collection of essays, *Reading Romantics: Text and Context* (1990), which seeks to reconnect literature with the motives from which it springs and the social relations within which it exists. Although brilliantly displaying how in *Beppo* Byron's self-refashioning articulates the intricate play of gender, literary professionalism, social rank, and the institution of literature, this essay cannot represent the breadth and significance of Manning's many contributions to romantic criticism, especially his commentaries on Wordsworth and Byron, during the past few years. Yet the chapter does exemplify a major contemporary mode of critical analysis, of which Manning is one of the most skilled practitioners. This links a carefully elaborated sociopolitical "locating" (to use Magnuson's term) of a particular poem to overarching principles of human psychology. Such analyses enable us to see familiar material— here *Beppo*—in an entirely new fashion and forces us to reevaluate our critical presuppositions. Manning's practice, moreover, is distinguished by a subtle sympathy with the works he examines; in the present instance his critique deploys a mixture of self-conscious skepticism with impassioned engagement analogous to the Byronic manner he defines and explains.

For Francis Jeffrey, writing in *The Edinburgh Review* in 1818 an appropriately unsigned notice of an anonymously published poem narrated by "a nameless sort of person, / (A broken Dandy lately on [his] travels" (st. 52),[1] Byron's *Beppo* was "absolutely a thing of nothing."[2] For Jerome McGann and other modern critics, it is "probably the most crucial single work in the entire canon."[3] At once trivial and critical to that trajectory of a name that we call a career, *Beppo* presents a series of paradoxes which begin and end with the authorless status of its first appearance.[4]

To set this nothing in perspective it is useful to consider an earlier instance of play between the naming *in,* and the anonymity *of,* a text: Byron's outburst of disappointment at the abdication in April 1814 of that other figure who signed himself NB, not so much his alter ego as his alter image, in whom he saw his reflection and with whom he was joined in popular view as the type of the Promethean genius.[5] The *Ode to Napoleon Buonaparte,* which Byron wrote in heat and Murray published with speed to capitalize on sensational news, opens:

From *Reading Romantics: Text and Context* (New York: Oxford University Press, 1990), pp. 145–162.

'Tis done—but yesterday a King!
　And arm'd with Kings to strive—
And now thou art a nameless thing
　So abject—yet alive!
Is this the man of thousand thrones,
Who strew'd our Earth with hostile bones,
　And can he thus survive?
Since he, miscall'd the Morning Star,
Nor man nor fiend hath fall'n so far.

The failure of his hero nobly to have committed suicide fuels Byron's indignation: by preserving his life, Napoleon has paradoxically destroyed his name. As Lucifer was "miscalled" the Morning Star, so the judgments of those who praised Napoleon are exposed by his craven conduct. In a journal-entry Byron confessed that he was "utterly bewildered and confounded," and the threat to his own identity produced a dispersal of voices notable even in his habitually echoing prose. In the space of a page, Byron invokes Otway's *Venice Preserved;* Shakespeare's *Antony and Cleopatra, Hamlet,* and *Macbeth;* Juvenal's and Johnson's "Vanity of Human Wishes"; Milo; Sylla; Charles V; Amurath; and Dionysius at Corinth. Many of these found their way into the *Ode* (*BLJ* III, 256–57). Byron, however, was wrong: Napoleon sought exactly the exchange of life for name Byron wished of him. Although Byron had already written his poem and did not know it, Napoleon attempted to poison himself on April 12 but survived.[6] That the apparent revelation of intrinsic character was thus based on a mistake only emphasizes the mirroring circuit in which the "name" is suspended.

Once the *Ode to Napoleon Buonaparte* passed from the poet to his publisher the names of both Byron and Napoleon were governed by the laws, commercial and legal, of trade. Byron's instructions to Murray reveal the various conventions upon which authorship depends. Byron sent the poem as a gift on April 10, telling Murray that he "might print it or not as you please"; later the same day, he added that "if deemed worth printing" it should be "*without* a name," but admitted that he had "no objection to it's [sic] being *said* to be mine." The diffidence was a polite fiction: Byron knew that the topicality of the subject and the celebrity of the author ensured publication, and Murray knew that Byron wanted it, providing him proofs within a day. These Byron immediately corrected and returned, reiterating that "[i]t will be best *not* to put my name to our Ode but you may *say* openly that it is mine": speech thus permitted authorship to be known and profited from while not yet acknowledged. "[W]e will incorporate it in the first *tome* of ours that you find time or the wish to publish," Byron told Murray; as the repeated use of "our"indicates, copyright fixed authorship in the exchange of author and publisher (*BLJ,* IV, 94).[7]

Even as Byron and the *Ode* float within the "*channel* of publication" (*BLJ,* IV, 104), so within the poem the representation of Napoleon, once seated upon "The throne of the world" (*BLJ,* III, 256), was shaped by the tax code. Finding that the early editions of the *Ode* were subject to the stamp duty levied on pamphlets of less than a sheet, Murray requested further stanzas. Byron complied, furnishing three more, though displeased with them; the addition of the current fifth stanza to the third edition, however, seems to have served the purpose, and the new stanzas were never used in Byron's lifetime. Subsequently, in spite of Byron's expressed desire that they be omitted, they became the conclusion of the received text.[8] Editors and regulations motivated as much by political censorship as revenue considerations thus triumphed over Napoleon and Byron, the exemplars of Romantic will.

I begin my chapter on *Beppo* with this episode because it suggests the interplay of authorship with the conditions of production and replaces the static opposition between the proper name and anonymity with a fluid continuum. In the *Ode* Byron had loftily consigned Napoleon to Elba: "Then haste thee to thy sullen Isle, / And gaze upon the sea" (st. 14). Self-exiled from England, Byron, after a brief stay in Switzerland, made for Venice, "as it has always been (next to the East) the greenest island of my imagination" (*BLJ*, V, 129). Pleasurable as Venice was, Byron disclosed a melancholy truth in fashioning a narrator who describes himself as a nameless, broken dandy. The scandal of the separation had ended Byron's reign as the darling of Whig society, and *Manfred* and the third and fourth cantos of *Childe Harold* had won not a name but notoriety.

Beppo is anonymous in a deeper sense as well. As critics rightly observe, it marks the pivot in Byron's turn on the Romantic excesses of his generation. He repeated to Moore in 1818 what he had told Murray in 1817: "I . . . said, that I thought—except [Crabbe and Rogers]—all of '*us youth*' were on the wrong tack" (*BLJ*, VI, 10). Moore shrewdly saw this deprecation as a tactic to confirm his own eminence: "being quite sure of his own hold upon fame he contrives to loosen that of all his contemporaries, in order that they may fall away entirely from his side, and leave him unencumbered, even by their floundering."[9] Indeed, a manifesto that alludes to the ceaselessly devious Falstaff does not so much clarify as fruitfully mystify Byron's poetic program. If Byron declared "I certainly am a devil of a mannerist—& must leave off" (*BLJ*, V, 185), he sought to escape the style that had brought him fame only to devise another that would extend his grip on the public. Some reviewers, unaware of the authorship of *Beppo,* took it as a satire on Byron, which indeed it was, but the new Byron to succeed the repudiated one would be not the true voice of feeling so much as it was another modulation in the relations existing between the historical Byron, his reading, his publisher, and the audience and critics of this and his prior texts. The emerging self of *Beppo* (and subsequently of *Don Juan)* evolved within a network that enabled the expatriate Byron to remake his name even as it restricted how he could do so. *Beppo* is a text in which the issue of anonymity is primary, not accidental.

I overstate the case in order to contrast it to a biographical reading of the poem. In 1968 Jerome McGann asserted, "Everything in *Beppo* orbits around Byron; it is the figure of Byron, both as an artist and (more importantly) as a human being, which determines both the form and significance of the details."[10] In an excellent introduction to his edition of the manuscript, McGann in 1986 still argues that "The tale is [Byron's] vehicle for transmitting what is essentially a very personal poem."[11] I should like to invert the terms: the self acquires its image—not its essence—by telling tales that negotiate or, to use a more Byronic term, navigate impersonal structures.

Byron came to speak in the voice of *Beppo* by a series of mediations. He happily credited W. S. Rose and John Hookham Frere's *The Monks and the Giants* with having displayed for him the possibilities of the *ottava rima* stanza, and through them he returned to the Italian originals of the style, many of whom he knew already: Pulci, Berni, Casti.[12] If the chivalric romance that the pseudony-mous Whistlecrafts had put forward was *A Prospectus and Specimen of an Intended National Work,* Byron's elaborately artificial Italian comedy might well seem its anti-national antipodes. Such stanzas as those on the suspension of Habeas Corpus (sts. 47–49) illustrate why Byron told Murray that *Beppo* has "politics & ferocity, & won't do for your Isthmus of a Journal," the conservative *Quarterly Review (BLJ,* VI, 9), but the poem's manner was itself read politically, as the denunciation of Byron's "cosmopolitan liberality" in the notice of *The British Review* attests. Declaring that *Beppo* came "reeking from the stews of Venice," William Roberts connected it to the growth "of a denationalizing spirit" in English society since the French Revolution, a symptom of the "decay of that masculine decency, and sobriety, and soundness of sentiment, which, about half a century ago, made us dread the contagion of French or Italian manners."[13] From the smug center of British chauvinism where he locates himself Roberts astutely specifies Byron's allegiances, and the association of suspect politics with gender impropriety is one to explore further.

Two triangles map the contours of *Beppo:* that of Laura, the Count, and Beppo *in* the poem, and that formed *outside* it by the poet, the poem, and his audience. The outer one inflects the plot which it encloses—as digression overwhelms narrative—because, as W. P. Elledge has argued in a brilliant essay, Byron's eye remains anxiously on the England from which he had parted.[14] Nothing better illustrates the apparently merely arbitrary constellations through which self-representation is composed than the treatment of William Sotheby.[15]

Byron finished a first draft of *Beppo* in eighty-four stanzas on October 10, 1817; to that matrix he added in the next two weeks five stanzas expanding his attack on "bustling Botherby" and his coterie of bluestockings. I quote the first, in which Byron cites the absence of a Botherby as a special advantage of the confinement to which Turkish women are subject:

> No solemn, antique gentleman of rhyme,
>   Who having angled all his life for fame,
> And getting but a nibble at a time,
>   Still fussily keeps fishing on, the same
> Small "Triton of the minnows," the sublime
>   Of mediocrity, the furious tame,
> The echo's echo, usher of the school
> Of female wits, boy bards—in short, a fool![16]

In his very lack of necessary relationship to the story of *Beppo* and seemingly fortuitous arrival in the text Sotheby focuses the literary dynamics that the poem exposes. The previous spring in Rome Byron had received what he called "a scurvy *anonymous* letter" together with a marginally annotated copy of the Italian edition of his *Prisoner of Chillon* volume. "The dog" might have been "right enough" to judge "that out of ten things—eight were good for nothing," Byron told Murray, but the anonymity of the letter incensed him. Such unauthored, or unauthorized, criticism Byron took to violate "all the courtesies of life & literature": "he should put his name to a note—a man may *print* —anonymously—but not write letters so" (*BLJ,* VI, 24, rearranged).

The distinction Byron draws between the codes of (private) life and (public) literature, between presence and text, however, collapsed. Murray evidently mentioned the lampoon to Sotheby, who denied responsibility for the incident that produced it. "As Mr. S says that he did not write this letter &c I am ready to believe him," Byron conceded to Murray, but the statement of the man was outweighed by the evidence of the text. Byron enumerated his reasons for having believed in Sotheby's authorship:

> firstly—similarity in the handwriting . . . 2dly. the *Style*—more especially the word "Effulgence" a phrase which clinched my conjecture as decisively as any coincidence between Francis & Junius—3dly. the paucity of English *then* at Rome . . . 4thly. my being aware of Mr S[otheby]'s patronage & anxiety on such occasions which led me to the belief that with very good intentions—he might nevertheless blunder in his mode of giving as well as taking opinions—& 5thly. the Devil who made Mr. S[otheby] one author and me another.

Despite Sotheby's explicit disclaimer Byron refused to retract his stanzas, and in so persisting he made clear that acts of interpretation, not intentional origins, affix a text to an author.

Byron continued:

> As to Beppo I will not alter or suppress a syllable for any man's pleasure but my own—if there are resemblances between Botherby & Sotheby or Sotheby and Botherby the fault is not mine—but in the person who resembles—or the persons who trace a resemblance.—Who find out this resemblance?—Mr. S[otheby]'s *friends—who* go about moaning over him & laughing? Mr. S's *friends*—whatever allusions Mr. S may imagine—or whatever may or may not really exist in the passages in question—I can assure him—that there is not a literary man or a pretender to Literature—or a reader of the day—in the World of London—who does not think & express more obnoxious opinions of his Blue-stocking Mummeries than are to be found in print— (*BLJ,* VI, 35)

This disingenuous apologia re-emphasizes the location of identity outside the self: Sotheby is Botherby if his friends say so. The identification "may or may not really exist" in *Beppo:* Byron disavows his intention while affirming it. The anonymous letter, denied by its putative author; the anonymous poem, written in English in Italian style; behind the fictional Botherby, the proper name Sotheby (but how, exactly?); behind the nameless narrator, Byron (but how, exactly?)—the figures and texts circulate, cut off from authors, among "literary men" and "pretenders to Literature."

Sotheby is also a point at which the triangles inside and outside the poem touch. The links may be seen as well in the tandem development of the ten stanzas Byron added to the original eighty-four-stanza matrix of his poem. Five are the description of Botherby, one the description of the speaker as "a nameless sort of person, / (A broken Dandy lately on my travels)" (st. 52), and two an expansion in the description of Laura's lover, the Count:

> He patroniz'd the Improvisatori,
>   Nay, could himself extemporize some stanzas,

Wrote rhymes, sang songs, could also tell a story,
   Sold pictures. and was skilful in the dance as
Italians can be, though in this their glory
   Must surely yield the palm to that which France has;
In short, he was a perfect cavaliero,
And to his very valet seem'd a hero.

Then he was faithful, too, as well as amorous,
   So that no sort of female could complain,
Although they're now and then a little clamorous,
   He never put the pretty souls in pain;
His heart was one of those which most enamour us,
   Wax to receive, and marble to retain.
He was a lover of the good old school,
Who still become more constant as they cool.

                      (sts. 33–34)

Botherby in the midst of "Blue-stocking Mummeries" and the dilettante Count, whose " 'bravo' was decisive, for that sound / Hushed 'academie' sighed in silent awe" (st. 32) but who waits docilely on Laura, are alike visions of the man of letters reduced to what Byron calls a "supernumerary slave, who stays / Close to the lady as a part of dress" (st. 40), a "piece of female property" (*BLJ*, VII, 28).

Byron's unease on this score is a repeated theme of his Italian years; what particularly matters here is an unacknowledged kinship between the Italian and English sites of the story. *Beppo* proceeds by contrasting Italian and English society, but at the point where they touch such binary oppositions disclose a muted equivalence. Let us return to the added stanzas on Botherby:

A stalking oracle of awful phrase,
   The approving "*Good!*" (by no means GOOD in law)
Humming like flies around the newest blaze,
   The bluest of bluebottles you e'er saw,
Teasing with blame, excruciating with praise,
   Gorging the little fame he gets all raw,
Translating tongues he knows not even by letter,
And sweating plays so middling, bad were better.

One hates an author that's *all author*, fellows
   In foolscap uniforms turned up with ink,
So very anxious, clever, fine and jealous,
   One don't know what to say to them, or think,
Unless to puff them with a pair of bellows;
   Of coxcombry's worst coxcombs even the pink
Are preferable to these shreds of paper,
These unquenched snuffings of the midnight taper.

Of these same we see several, and of others,
   Men of the world, who know the world like men,
S[co]tt, R[oger]s, M[oo]re, and all the better brothers,
   Who think of something else besides the pen;

But for the children of the "mighty mother's,"
  The would-be wits and can't-be gentlemen,
I leave them to their daily "tea is ready,"
Smug coterie, and literary lady.

(sts. 74–76)

Botherby is savaged on two retaled but distinguishable grounds. The first is that of gender: Botherby is excoriated for his effeminizing absorption—like the Count—in a circle of women, against which Byron sets a vision of male bonding, allying himself firmly with "all the better brothers." The second is rather an issue of the professionalization of literature: Botherby is *all author,* a man of letters who translates Latin and German, writes poems, produces dramas, and publishes tours. Against this image of career Byron sets himself as one of the aristocratic amateurs, "Men of the world, who know the world like men."

The two charges overlap, and their conjunction is revealing. These stanzas merge effeminization with professionalization, and Byron was acutely and ambivalently aware that his reputation with women had contributed greatly to the commercial success of *Childe Harold's Pilgrimage* and the Turkish tales. One illustration, discussed elsewhere in this book, is the brouhaha over the publications of *Stanzas to a Lady Weeping.* On January 22, 1814, Murray reported to Byron Gifford's opinion that "you ought to slip [the verses] quietly amongst the Poems in 'Childe Harold' " rather than annex them to *The Corsair,* where Byron intended them, because the tale "is to be read by women, and it would disturb the poetical feeling."[17] Not for nothing did Murray produce engravings of his handsome poet, a lord yet exotic, for purchasers to bind into their volumes of Byron's work, or urge him "to resume my old '*Corsair* style, to please the ladies,' " as Byron told Shelley in Italy. To Shelley's warm contempt for such pecuniary considerations Byron replied: "John Murray is right, if not righteous: all I have yet written has been for women-kind: you must wait until I am forty, their influence will then die a natural death, and I will show the men what I can do."[18]

"I have not written to please the women or the common people," Byron declared in the rush of popularity after the publication of *Childe Harold,* and the convoluted connections between gender, writing, and audience animate *Beppo.* To put it schematically: if professionalization is equated with the feminine, then Byron must doubly dissemble the literary venture, the attempt to establish his name on a new basis, that *Beppo* represents. The easy conversational manner upon which every reader has remarked needs to be understood against the structures of publication that it masks. Donning the pose of one who even from Italy knows more of the sayings of the London literati than Murray or Sotheby, Byron affirms his membership in the world from which he had parted; at the same time, dismissing Botherby and the bluestockings, Byron proclaims his masculine independence and denies his implication in the motives that drive professional authors.[19]

This strategy produces complex tensions, because the chat that obscures the trial of the market upon which Byron and Murray were embarked is another term for gossip—and gossip is traditionally associated with women.[20] If to characterize the inclusiveness with which *Don Juan* surveys the Europe of Byron's times Jerome McGann titles a recent essay "The Book of Byron and the Book of a World,"[21] I might perhaps indicate the miniature world of *Beppo* with an epigram from Rousseau scornfully cited by Mary Wollstonecraft in *A Vindication of the*

Rights of Woman: "The world is the book of women."[22] *Beppo* springs from a sexual anecdote, drawing us in with the fascination always exerted by "sinful doings" (st. 41), and swirling outward toward the comparative discussion of national *mores*.

In renouncing his magniloquent style in *Beppo* Byron also renounced heroism, or rather shrank it to the dimensions of the clever pun:

> Crush'd was Napoleon by the northern Thor,
>   Who knock'd his army down with icy hammer,
> Stopp'd by the *elements,* like a whaler, or
>   A blundering novice in his new French grammar;
>
>   (st. 61)

Heroism is not merely absent from the world of *Beppo* but rather thus deliberately excluded. The poem shifts from north to south, public to private, honor to shame (or at least scandal), from consolidating masculine power to the plural and the insinuating. In Canto 3 of *Childe Harold's Pilgrimage* Byron had portrayed Napoleon as the figure of antithetical extremes who disrupts the Aristotelean ethical mean; the "new French grammar" Napoleon wrote in making himself emperor, however, in turn yields to the elements not so much of nature as of Byron's own mocking linguistic facility. In place of the fatal determinism of the Byronic hero, there is the unfettered digressiveness of anecdote. This language is the weapon of the powerless, perhaps capable of achieving what masculine will cannot, perhaps only capable of reassuring those at the margins, as Byron in Italy was, of their freedom to comment. Unlike *Childe Harold's Pilgrimage* and the tales, concerned to impose on their audience the single, unique, dominant Byronic hero, the language of *Beppo*—not without, given Byron's withdrawal from England, a certain pathos—elaborates a community. The English "you" with which the narrator addresses and marks his distance from his readers plays off against integrating usages: "One of those forms which flit by us" (st. 13); "and really if a man won't let us know / That he's alive, he's *dead,* or should be so" (st. 35), "Our standing army, and disbanded seamen" (st. 49); and so forth. This presumption of agreement simultaneously creates a microcosm against the larger world and serves as the go-between of the private and public worlds.

Much as William Roberts became alarmed by the "decay of masculine decency" *Beppo* witnesses, so Francis Jeffrey, describing its style as "loquacious prattling" and "gay and desultory babbling," recognized Byron's intimate, easy language of intrigue and fashion as an appropriation from the opposite gender as society stereotypes it. The passing fancy of a pensioned "missionary author" to teach the harem-bound "poor dear Mussulwomen" "Our Christian usage of the parts of speech" (st. 77, rearranged) is one condescending imagining in the poem of a language of and for women; a richer one is the description of Laura:

> Laura, when drest, was (as I sang before)
>   A pretty woman as was ever seen,
> Fresh as the Angel o'er a new inn door,
>   Or frontispiece of a new Magazine,
> With all the fashions which the last month wore,
>   Coloured, and silver paper leav'd between

That and the title-page, for fear the press
Should soil with parts of speech the parts of dress.

(st. 57)

Byron's own similes of inn and magazine soil Laura by implicating her in the world
of commerce, but at the same time they mark the milieu his writing also inhabits
and turn us back to those female readers of magazines who shaped his success.

The virulence of Byron's attack on Sotheby and the bluestockings is a reflex of
the anxious fantasy at play in Byron's otherwise pleasurable immersion in Venice:
a fear that the male self is rendered precarious by the power of the woman-
dominated society of salons and *cavaliere servente* for which Laura stands in the
poem, and that of the audience of women readers outside it. Though the "name-
less broken Dandy" is undeniably male, "broken" suggests a ruin beyond the
financial, an impotence at once sexual and political. Consider, for instance, the
proliferation of feminine rhyme (as in the stanzas on the Count [e.g., sts. 31–34])
in that self-description:

But I am but a nameless sort of person
    (A broken Dandy lately on my travels)
And take for rhyme, to hook my rambling verse on,
    The first that Walker's Lexicon unravels,
And when I can't find that, I put a worse on,
        Not caring as I ought for critics' cavils;
I've half a mind to tumble down to prose,
But verse is more in fashion—so here goes.

(st. 52)

Or consider the difficulty of placing Byron's praise of Italian:

I love the language, that soft bastard Latin,
    Which melts like kisses from a female mouth,
And sounds as if it should be writ on satin,
    With syllables which breathe of the sweet South,
And gentle liquids gliding all so pat in,
    That not a single accent seems uncouth,
Like our harsh northern whistling, grunting guttural,
Which we're obliged to hiss, and spit, and sputter all.

(st. 44)

If the very next stanza, beginning "I like the women too," asserts a traditional
masculine identity, nonetheless Byron speaks a language throughout *Beppo* that
repeatedly emulates that "[w]hich melts like kisses from a female mouth." "His
heart was one of those which most enamour us," the narrator says of the Count in
the added stanza quoted above, seeming momentarily to cross the border between
genders and slip into identification with women and the oddly unstable sexuality
of "amorous / clamorous / enamour us" (st. 34). The more Byron disguises the
authorial venture through his amateurish and gossipy pose, in short, the more his
narrator verges on the feminine he scorns.

Yet analysis of this persona in terms of Byron's psychology, even of the bisexuality persuasively set forth by Louis Crompton,[23] should be contained within acknowledgment of the setting of *Beppo* at the time of Carnival. As the opening stanzas repeatedly insist, Carnival is a ritual of mask and masquerade, when "you may put on whate'er you like" (st. 5), and the shifting of identities it fosters Byron brings home to his readers by likening it to "Mrs. Boehm's masquerade" (st. 56) and comparing "the Ridotto" to "our Vauxhall" (st. 58). Carnival is the privileged moment of transgression, and, as Terry Castle has recently argued, the more complexly the assumed costume disrupts the usual sexual and hierarchical roles of its wearer, the more the opportunities for equivocation multiply. The transformation of Beppo into a Turk is less salient, and less disturbing, than Byron's own travesty. William Roberts's denunciation of the poem has a long history in the moralistic condemnation of such ambiguous and promiscuous events.[24]

To argue that beneath this voice we always hear Byron the Improviser is to beg the question of why this voice at this time. I suggest instead that the peculiarly suspended quality of *Beppo,* its focus hovering in the pairing of England and Italy, its nameless, sexually evasive narrator negotiating through his own verbal skill the engulfing power of women and the male violence lurking in the allusions to Othello, Macbeth, and Odysseus returning to slaughter the suitors, corresponds to a Byron wishing to remake his poetic identity and uncertain of the forces outside him that would determine it.

At the close of the poem Byron re-establishes the traditional sexual roles he has put into play by the treatment meted out to Laura.[25] If it is the traditional place of women to be silent, obedient, and chaste, Laura is none of these; indeed, in choosing a lover she has seized the masculine prerogative and reversed the exchange of women on which society is based. Laura wards off any embarrassing conflict between returning husband and faithful *cavalier servente* by her irrepressible curiosity about Beppo's foreign experience, but such defusion by language sounds the knell of male heroism, and Byron moves swiftly to subordinate her. Beppo, the narrator says, "threw off the garments which disguised him" and is rebaptized, restoring everyone to his and her "proper" place. In a gesture that realizes the male bonding against which Botherby has been set, Beppo "borrow[s] the Count's small-clothes for a day" (st. 98), and the final vision shows Laura trivialized and the men united:

> Whate'er his youth had suffered, his old age
>   With wealth and talking made him some amends;
> Though Laura sometimes put him in a rage,
>   I've heard the Count and he were always friends.
>   (st. 99)

This tableau nonetheless leaves unsettled the tensions of the poem. Laura functions all too evidently as the necessary link between the men, a link whose necessity explains the ensuing necessity to deny her importance. The uneasy secret is still visible: the male bond passes through women. Whatever we say about Byron the man here, for Byron the poet the audience of women remains inescapable, the clear distinction between himself and Sotheby, already breached in the similarities of Botherby and the broken dandy, impossible to maintain. Within the poem Byron exits by reminding us that he stands above the "nothing" he has narrated, fixing his priority to his story in a series of first-person clauses:

"*He* said that *Providence* protected him— / For my part, I say nothing" (st. 96); "trading / With goods of various names, but I've forgot 'em" (st. 97); "dinners, where he oft became the laugh of them, / For stories,—but *I* don't believe the half of them" (st. 99); culminating in the final indifference, "I've heard the Count and he were always friends" (st. 99). The function of *Beppo* was to kindle interest in a "Byron" different from those before seen, to intrigue readers into purchasing this new mode. By such explicit concluding gestures, Byron signaled that interest was to be focused not on his tale but on him, and on "his pen at the bottom of a page" (st. 99), the material agent of translation that makes of the book we buy a passport to an imagined authorial and richly oral presence. As Ross Chambers has suggested, such embedded reminders of the situation of the storyteller are characteristic of the new nineteenth-century conditions of literature in which the writer could only speculate on his diatant and unknown audience.[26] With direct communication defferred, Byron in Italy had to resort to arts of seduction uneasily like Laura's, and such wiles remain vulnerable: his aloofness to his story within *Beppo* apotropaically mimes that of the readers without, who might prove as immune to his charms.

The appeal of the name thus forms the salient question, and in *Beppo* only Byron will possess one. Beppo gives his to the tale, but as Byron told Murray in an appropriately belittling parenthesis, it is only a common diminutive, "(the short name for Giuseppe—that is the *Joe* of the Italian Joseph)" (*BLJ,* V, 269); the Count is merely "the Count"; Laura owes her name ostensibly to Byron's metrical convenience:

> A certain lady went to see the show,
>   Her real name I know not, nor can guess
> And so we'll call her Laura, if you please,
> Because it slips into my verse with ease.
>
>   (st. 21)

Despite this parade of freedom, the new name the success of *Beppo* won for Byron enmeshed him in the institution of literature that he scornfully epitomized in Botherby/Sotheby. Murray published *Beppo* in February 1818, Byron having thrown in the copyright with Canto IV of *Childe Harold* "to help you round to your money" (*BLJ,* V, 269). The sublime style and the colloquial style that inverted it were all one on Murray's ledgers. Byron's name first appeared on the fifth edition, already reached in April, but the acknowledgment reflected a weighing of commercial gain against fears of suit from Sotheby. "If you think that it will do *you* or the work—or *works* any good," Byron wrote Murray, "—you may—or may not put my name to it—*but first consult the knowing ones;*—it will at any rate shew them—that I can write cheerfully, & repel the charge of monotony and mannerism" (*BLJ,* VI, 25). Murray, no fool when it came to calculating where his interest lay, replied: "I have heard no word more from Mr. Sotheby; and as to my having ventured upon any alteration or omission, I should as soon have scooped one of my eyes out."[27]

If the reception won by his new production redefined Byron's name, so his name reciprocally guaranteed that the transformation would be noticed; in its review, the *Monthly Magazine* commented that it "should have passed over [*Beppo*] had not his lordship's signature commanded our attention."[28] Thus did Byron's publisher seal the new course of Byron's name; the aristocratic title remained implicated in, and dependent upon, the balance sheets of the book trade.

The matter does not quite end there. In a revision of the agreement for the sum to be paid for *Beppo,* Murray suggested to Byron that the copyright "cancel all former bookselling accounts between us *up* to that period" (*BLJ,* IX, 84). The transaction was a fitting one: in exchange for the books Murray had furnished Byron, the highly literary manuscript from which he made further profits. The cycle continued. "I have finished the First Canto (a long one, of about 180 octaves) of a poem in the style and manner of 'Beppo,' " Byron wrote Murray six months later, "encouraged by the good success of the same" (*BLJ,* VI, 67). Success produced success, and a new project, which would rewrite the Byronic self and extend the partnership—until, scandalized by *Don Juan* and *Cain,* Murray withdrew, and Byron's name became Hunt's. But that is another essay.

NOTES

1. All quotations from Byron's poetry are from *Lord Byron: The Complete Poetical Works,* ed. Jerome J. McGann (Oxford: Clarendon, 1980–). Hereafter cited as *PW.*

2. *Edinburgh Review* 29 (February 1818), as quoted in *Byron: The Critical Heritage,* ed. Andrew Rutherford (New York: Barnes and Noble, 1970), p. 122.

3. Jerome McGann, in *Shelley and His Circle 1773–1822,* Vol. VII, ed. Donald H. Reiman (Cambridge, Mass.: Harvard University Press, 1986), p. 247.

4. Readers will recognize here and throughout my indebtedness to Jerome Christensen, "Byron's Career: The Speculative Stage," *English Literary History* 52 (1985): 59–84.

5. One example of many, apposite here: in April 1817 Byron wrote to deny the assertion of an essay in a Venetian newspaper, purportedly translated from the Literary Gazette of Jena, that Napoleon was the protagonist of *Childe Harold III* "under a fictitious name." Byron declared that "Buonaparte is not the protagonist of the poem under any name," but the page he required to explain his attitudes suggests that if the essay was undeniably wrong, literally, it was right figuratively. *Byron's Letters and Journals,* ed. Leslie A. Marchand, Vol. V (Cambridge, Mass.: Harvard University Press, 1976), pp. 201–2. The volumes of this series, begun in 1973, are hereafter cited parenthetically in the text as *BLJ.*

6. See Felix Markham, *Napoleon and the Awakening of Europe* (New York: Collier, 1965), p. 126.

7. Not until the tenth edition did the *Ode* appear with Byron's name on it (*PW,* III, 456.

8. See *PW,* III, 456.

9. *The Journal of Thomas Moore,* ed. Wilfred S. Dowden, Vol. II (Newark: University of Delaware Press, 1985), p. 448.

10. Jerome McGann, *Fiery Dust: Byron's Poetic Development* (Chicago: University of Chicago Press, 1968), p. 288.

11. *Shelley and His Circle,* VII, 246.

12. See Peter Vassallo, *Byron: The Italian Literary Influence* (New York: St. Martin's Press, 1984).

13. *British Review* 11 (May 1818): 327–33, quoted in *The Romantics Reviewed,* ed. Donald Reiman (New York: Garland, 1972), Part B, 1:456.

14. W. Paul Elledge, "Divorce Italian Style: Byron's *Beppo,*" *Modern Language Quarterly* 46 (1985): 29–47.

15. Frederick L. Beaty compactly narrates the relations of Byron and Sotheby lying behind *Beppo* in Chapter 4 of his *Byron the Satirist* (DeKalb: Northern Illinois University Press, 1985).

16. This is stanza 73 of the Clarendon text; for the compositional history of the poem, see the apparatus to that edition; Vol. VII of *Shelley and His Circle;* and T. G. Steffan, "The Devil a Bit of Our *Beppo*," *Philological Quarterly* 32 (1953): 154–71, who first analyzed the Pierpont Morgan manuscript and from whom I take the term "matrix." The "bustling Botherby" of the manuscripts became "bustling Botherbys" in the first edition, which Byron let stand; thus, printer's errors, or publisher's caution, turn individuals to plural.

17. Samuel Smiles, *A Publisher and His Friends: Memoir and Correspondence of the Late John Murray,* 2d ed. (London: John Murray, 1891), I, 211. See Thilo von Bremen, *Lord Byron als Erfolgsautor,* Athenaion Literaturwissenschaft, Band 6 (Wiesbaden: Athenaion, 1977), p. 191.

18. *Recollections* of E. J. Trelawny, quoted in *His Very Self and Voice,* ed. Ernest J. Lovell (New York: Macmillan, 1954), p. 267. In "The Writer's Ravishment: Women and the Romantic Author—The Example of Byron," Sonia Hofkosh observes that Byron's "literary career is also the chronicle of a love affair," in which "the woman in the romance enacts the marketplace forces that contest the writer's exclusive claim to his work." *Romanticism and Feminism,* ed. Anne K. Mellor (Bloomington: Indiana University Press, 1988), pp. 93–114.

19. The third term of the identification "Count → Botherby," which Byron was at pains to suppress, is Byron himself, as "Presbyter Anglicanus" shrewdly point out in *Blackwood's Magazine* 3 (June 1818: 323–29: "We look below the disguise which has once been lifted, and claim acquaintance, not with the sadness of the princely masque, but with the scoffing and sardonic merriment of the ill-dissembling reveller beneath it. In evil hour did you step from your vantage-ground, and teach us that Harold, Byron, and the Count of *Beppo* are the same." Quoted in *Byron: The Critical Heritage,* ed. Andrew Rutherford (New York: Barnes and Noble, 1970), p. 129.

20. See Patricia Meyer Spacks, *Gossip* (New York: Knopf, 1985).

21. *The Beauty of Inflections* (Oxford: Clarendon, 1985), pp. 255–93.

22. *A Vindication of the Rights of Woman,* ed. Carol H. Poston (New York, Norton: 1976), p. 39.

23. *Byron and Greek Love* (Berkeley: University of California Press, 1985).

24. Terry Castle, *Masquerade and Civilization: The Carnivalesque in Eighteenth-Century English Culture and Fiction* (Stanford: Stanford University Press, 1986). I have also learned from Eve Kosofsky Sedgwick, *Between Men: English Literature and Male Homosocial Desire* (New York: Columbia University Press, 1985).

25. For a shrewd study of Byron's ultimately restabilizing playing with gender, see Susan J. Wolfson, " 'Their she condition': Cross-dressing and the Politics of Gender in *Don Juan*," *ELH* 54 (1987): 585–617. An instance particularly germane to *Beppo* is the "[Epistle to Mr Murray]" which follows it in Jerome McGann's Oxford Authors edition of Byron (Oxford: Oxford University Press, 1986). Written as a verse letter to Murray on January 8, 1818, its last three stanzas recall the conclusion of *Beppo* but display the relation of writing to women that Byron was concerned to establish *in propria persona:*

Now, I'll put out my taper
(I've finished my paper
  For these stanzas you see on the *brink* stand)
There's a whore on my right

For I rhyme best at Night
   When a C—t is tied close to *my Inkstand.*

It was Mahomet's notion
That comical motion
   Increased his "devotion in prayer"—
If that tenet holds good
In a Prophet, it should
   In poet be equally fair.—

For, in rhyme or in love
(Which both come from above)
   I'll stand with our "*Tommy*" or "*Sammy*")
But the Sopha and lady
Are both of them ready
   And so, here's "Good Night to you dammee!"

26. Ross Chambers, *Story and Situation: Narrative Seduction and the Power of Fiction* (Minneapolis: University of Minnesota Press, 1984).

27. Smiles, *A Publisher and His Friends,* I, 394. Letter of June 16, 1818.

28. *The Romantics Reviewed,* ed. Reiman, Part B, 4:1671.

Percy Bysshe Shelley

Our guess is that the most exciting intellectual criticism of romantic poetry in the 1990s will focus on Shelley, heralded perhaps by a rush of books at the end of the eighties, including Stephen B. Behrendt's *Shelley and His Audiences* (1989), Timothy Clark's *Embodying Revolution: The Figure of the Poet in Shelley* (1989), Jerrold E. Hogle's *Shelley's Process: Radical Transference and the Development of His Major Works* (1988), and Christine Gallant's *Shelley's Ambivalence* (1989), which makes good use of the psychological ideas of Klein and Winnicot. There seems at last to be assurance that an accurate and responsible complete edition will be produced under the editorship of Donald H. Reiman and Neil Fraistat. Such an edition should have the same positive impact that new editions have had on the criticism of Blake, Wordsworth, and Byron. The extraordinary extent of Shelley's reading in literature, combined with his wide-ranging intellectual curiosity, has always attracted philosophically inclined critics. The recently increased attention to the politics of the younger romantic poets caught in the post-Napoleonic reaction across Europe makes Shelley an obvious focus of study, exemplified in John Jay Baker's "Myth, Subjectivity, and the Problem of Historical Time in Shelley's 'Lines Written among the Euganean Hills' " (1989). G. Kim Blank's useful *Wordsworth's Influence on Shelley: A Study of Poetic Authority* (1988) is probably symptomatic of increasingly close examinations of the relations between the two generations of English romantic poets— a subfield still surprisingly little developed through careful and detailed criticism such as Blank's. Shelley's creative and critical faculties, moreover, tended to find their sharpest focus on problems of language, problems with which present-day critics feel most comfortable. But as our selection from Tilottama Rajan's recent book demonstrates, in some respects we are only now beginning to catch up with Shelley's radical innovativeness in linguistic manipulations, just as it is only recently that critics like William Keach have learned to do justice to the technical intricacy of his poetic artistry.

DONALD H. REIMAN

Shelley as Athanase

This selection from volume seven of the monumental *Shelley and His Circle,* first edited by Kenneth Neil Cameron and for the past two decades by Donald Reiman, seems to us representative of some of the best contemporary biographical work on the romantic poets, among which should be counted Richard Holmes's biography *Shelley: The Pursuit* (1976). Reiman, furthermore, attends carefully to the changes not only in Shelley's situation and personality but also to the evolution in his styles of self-presentation. The result is vivid delineation of a process of progressive self-fashioning inseparable from the poet's responses to the sociopolitical developments of his era. Here, too, Reiman would demonstrate for us Shelley's innovativeness, for he perceives the poet giving "influential form" to the "new idea" of the artist as "politically and socially an impotent outcast."

> Prince Athanase, whose philosophic studies Yeats identified with his own, . . . provided an alternate self-image to the "Alastor" persona during the nineties. As a poet of Intellectual vision, Yeats donned the mask of "Alastor" when he pursued his vision as beauty, but imitated Athanase when he sought it as wisdom.
> —George Bornstein in *Yeats and Shelley*

In the Commentary on the letter from Shelley to Ollier of December 23, 1819 (sc 554 [VI]), I mentioned that "the present location" of the manuscript of *Prince Athanase,* which Shelley enclosed in that letter, was "unknown to us."[1] That location, it turns out, was unknown to everyone until the manuscript appeared, with many other treasures, in the sale of rare books and fine manuscripts from the collection of the late David Joyce of Chicago.[2]

The emergence of this manuscript, hidden since 1918, is an event of some significance, and provides an opportunity to discuss the implications of Shelley's poem that in his holograph press-copy manuscript he clearly titled not "Prince Athanase" but "Athanase: A Fragment." Though Mary Shelley changed the title on the basis of allusions to the protagonist as "Prince" Athanase in other draft portions of the poem that Shelley had chosen not to publish, the title should, clearly, be revised to conform to Shelley's own explicit intention. (Nowhere in the 124 lines that Shelley sent to Ollier is Athanase referred to as a prince; the closest approach to conferring a title on the protagonist occurs in lines 37–38, where Athanase is described as "a child of Fortune & of Power / Of an ancœstral name the orphan chief"—that is, he is the heir of a rich and influential family.) Mary's

From *Shelley and His Circle VII* (Cambridge: Harvard University Press, 1986), pp. 110–132. Reprinted with permission of The Carl and Lily Pforzheimer Foundation, Inc.

change of title may have originated in her earlier transcriptions of fragments of the poem from Shelley's draft notebooks,[3] or it may have been an attempt to give the character of Athanase more distance from Shelley's own situation than Shelley felt it necessary to claim for himself when he sent "Athanase: A Fragment" to Ollier for anonymous publication.

The discrepancy between the title Shelley gave this poem in his press copy and the title under which it was printed raises more than one of the central issues relating to "Athanase" in general and to this manuscript in particular. These issues, beginning with the most concrete and specific, are as follows: First, since SC 582 is one of a very few surviving press-copy manuscripts of Shelley's poetry and one of the longest such manuscripts written entirely in Shelley's hand, what does it show about Shelley's preparation of his poetry for publication? Second, what is the relationship of the provenance of the manuscript to the poem's textual history? Third, what does "Athanase," Shelley's earliest extended use of *terza rima*, show us about his technical facility with that form; how does it relate to the versification of "Ode to the West Wind" and *The Triumph of Life?* Fourth, what do the portraits of Athanase and the maniac in *Julian and Maddalo* tell us about Shelley's interior biography in the second half of 1819? Fifth, is Shelley's study of Athanase intended as a self-portrait, or did Shelley intend Athanase as a beau ideal for a sensitive man's experience? Sixth, how does "Athanase" relate to the image of the poet found in Shelley's poems of earlier and later periods? Finally, what have been the effects of Shelley's portraits of Athanase and his kindred on later writers and on the course of English and American literature? The Commentary that follows SC 582 will discuss the first three of the above questions; in this essay I shall examine the last four questions, which I believe to be of substantial importance not only for Shelleyans but also for students of literature generally and the Romantic poetic tradition in particular.

SHELLEY AGONISTES

One conclusion, for those who accept the evidence presented in SC 531, Commentary, and SC 554, Commentary (VI) that both the maniac's self-revealing outpourings in *Julian and Maddalo* and "Athanase: A Fragment" were composed in the second half of 1819, is that the maniac and Athanase are self-portraits of Shelley at two stages of his psychological adjustment to his estrangement from Mary Shelley. Shelley's letters between the death of William on June 7, 1819, and August 15, 1819, are filled with lamentations and emotional reactions to his various difficulties, with passages unlike any he had written for years:

> Our melancholy journey finishes at this town. . . .—O that I could return to England! How heavy a weight when misfortune is added to exile, & solitude, as if the measure were not full, heaped high on both—O that I could return to England! . . .
>
>   I do not as usual give you an account of my journey, for I had neither the health or spirits to take notes. My health was greatly improving when watching & anxiety cast me into a relapse.[4]

> Our house is a melancholy one & only cheered by letters from England. . . .[5]

> Our misfortune is, indeed, a heavy one. . . . By the skill of the physician he [William Shelley] was once reanimated after the process of death had actually com-

menced, and he lived four days after that time.[6] This was, as you may think, a terrible reprieve. I had been slowly recovering a certain degree of health until this event, which has left me in a very weak state,—and Mary bears it, as you may naturally imagine, worse that I do.[7]

I ought to have written to you some time ago but my ill spirits & ill health has forever furnished me with an excuse for delaying till tomorrow. . . .
Mary's spirits still continue wretchedly depressed—more so than a stranger (tho' perhaps I ought not to call you so) could imagine—[8]

Then, in his letter to Hunt of August 15, 1819 (sc 531), in which he mailed *Julian and Maddalo* to England, while half-revealing and half-equivocating to Hunt about the breakdown in his communication with Mary, Shelley stated baldly his bitter disaffection from Godwin. This outburst (though patently calculated and controlled) apparently combined with the maniac's more revealing outcries in *Julian and Maddalo* itself to exorcise feelings in Shelley's psyche that had been merely hinted at in his letters of July and early August 1819. For from about August 16, 1819, when the Shelleys received the Hunts' long-delayed letter of July 14–August 4, 1818 (sc 486), together with John R. Wildman's portrait of Leigh Hunt, until almost the end of 1819, the complaints about low spirits and ill health suddenly vanish from Shelley's letters. To Hunt he is buoyant, to Peacock he is seriously but almost impersonally concerned about his literary plans and English political events.[9] To Charles Ollier he is first tight-lipped about Ollier's failure to correspond with him; later, when he hears from Ollier about the restricted sale of his writings and the impending attack in the *Quarterly,* he is determinedly undaunted; then, after seeing the text of the *Quarterly* article and at least part of Hunt's reply, he is—to use his own inappropriate description of the *Quarterly*'s remarks—"droll."[10] To the Gisbornes and Henry Reveley, the Shelleys' only confidants in Italy at this period, he is full of business advice and helpfulness on matters ranging from the financing of the steamboat to Henry's English composition.
In a paragraph that may serve to epitomize the spirit of Shelley's correspondence between August 16 and late December 1819, he writes to Maria Gisborne on October 14, 1819:

Let us believe in a kind of optimism in which we are our own gods. It is best that Mr. Gisborne should have returned, it is best that I should have overpersuaded you & Henry, it is best that you should all live together without any more solitary attempts—it is best that this one attempt should have been made, otherwise perhaps one other thing which is best might not have occurred, & it is best that we should think all this for the best even though it be not, because Hope, as Coleridge says is a solemn duty which we owe alike to ourselves & to the world—a worship to the spirit of good within, which requires before it sends that inspiration forth, which impresses its likeness upon all that it creates, devoted & disinterested homage.[11]

The ultimate parentage of Shelley's attitude is Stoic and accords with his earlier statements on how a man ought to face discomfort, ill health, and disappointment.[12] It also parallels his decorum and the "artfulness" of his correspondence.[13] Shelley in his letters (almost as much as in his artistically shaped poetry) channeled his emotions intellectually, saying not precisely what he felt but what he thought was either appropriate or rhetorically effective in the given situation. Shelley's portraits of himself as Julian, as the maniac, and as Athanase reflect various aspects, or even different stages in the development, of a new "self" that Shelley was showing to his friends in 1819.

Julian in *Julian and Maddalo* is Shelley the gentleman enthusiast, limited not only by a penchant for arguing doctrines as his sociable hobby but also by his inability to implement his beliefs in practice. Though he says, as he enters the madhouse and sees how the sound of music calms the inmates, "Methinks there were / A cure of these with patience and kind care" (lines 228–229),[14] it was Maddalo who had already provided the young stranger with "Busts and books and urns for flowers, / Which had adorned his life in happier hours, / And instruments of music" (lines 254–256) that produced the calming effect Julian witnessed. The reason Maddalo gives for his kindness, when Julian reminds him that the maniac "Had no claim, / As the world says" (lines 262–263), is that the maniac's claim was merely "the very same / Which I on all mankind were I as he / Fallen to such deep reverse" (lines 263–265). In the sequel to the maniac's ravings, it is Julian who, "urged by my affairs"—or, perhaps, to seek "relief / From the deep tenderness that maniac wrought / Within me" (lines 565–567)—leaves Venice the following morning (in spite of elaborate "dreams of baseless good" about how he might nurse the maniac back to sanity), while Maddalo takes the maniac and his now-chastened lover into his palace. Though lack of knowledge of the maniac's fate is thematically requisite for Shelley's poem, the character Julian must still be seen as a limited individual who might (for example) begin enthusiastically to raise money to restore the embankment at Remadoc and then, as soon as his personal affairs and/or desires dictated, leave the area precipitously long before his goal was, or could have been, achieved.

The portrait of the maniac, on the other hand, represents an inner side of Shelley—a vision of private psychic turmoil quite in contrast with the well-bred gentleman of affairs embodied in Julian. Unlike Julian, the maniac exists not in theories but in emotions; if Julian is the essence of the rational, liberal aristocrat, the maniac is the existential reality of a human being tortured at one and the same time by external circumstances and his own hyperacute sensibilities. For the maniac to characterize himself as "*Me*—who am as a nerve o'er which do creep / The else unfelt oppressions of this earth" (lines 449–450) is to highlight both life's oppressions and his own vulnerability to them. The maniac, seen in the context of the more objective frame story of Julian and Maddalo, is intended to arouse the reader's pity, not his sympathetic identification. But Julian (like Maddalo) can sympathize with him, for the maniac represents, in part at least, the secret inner man that Julian's urbane exterior hides from public view.

The portrait of Athanase shows the reuniting of Shelley's inner and outer selves embodied in the maniac and Julian. Shelley is as explicit on this point as he could have been without referring directly to *Julian and Maddalo*, for near the end of "Athanase: A Fragment" (lines 102–131) he speaks of the idle debates of Athanase's friends over the unknown cause of the young man's sorrows. The talk parallels that of Julian and Maddalo about the maniac (and that of Job's "friends"), and the last line ("And so his grief remained—let it remain—untold") exactly parallels the final lines of *Julian and Maddalo*, where, after Julian has urged Maddalo's daughter to tell him the maniac's secret, the young woman replies:

". . . if thine aged eyes disdain to wet
Those wrinkled cheeks with youth's remembered tears,
Ask me no more, but let the silent years
Be closed and ceared over their memory
As yon mute marble where their corpses lie."
I urged and questioned still, she told me how
All happened—but the cold world shall not know.

Inasmuch as Shelley insisted that the two poems should appear in the same volume, it even seems possible that the remarks in "Athanase" about how "this converse vain & cold" "galled & bit / His weary mind" (lines 130–131) were intended to suggest to Shelley's friends, such as Peacock—whose portrayal of Shelley's *Weltschmerz* in *Nightmare Abbey* Shelley had recently received with outward grace and courtesy—that such anatomization of his psyche and values was neither kind nor welcome. For those bred to the polite reticences of English upper-class manners, Shelley probably considered this hint enough to silence such painful talk. Peacock (though perhaps for quite different reasons) did not, in fact, portray Shelley again in his fiction until 1858–1860, when he recreated almost with reverence the young Shelley as the learned, chaste, and charming Algernon Falconer—a subject for admiration, not laughter. And Peacock's *Memoirs of Percy Bysshe Shelley* enunciates as its cardinal principle that Shelley, like all authors and their friends, was entitled to privacy: "No man is bound to write the life of another. No man who does so is bound to tell the public all he knows. . . . Neither if there be in the life of the subject of the biography any event which he himself would willingly have blotted from the tablet of his own memory, can it possibly be the duty of a survivor to drag it into daylight."[15] Peacock, as the second installment of his *Memoirs* shows, was cognizant of the deep feelings of sorrow or guilt that Shelley suppressed within himself. There he wrote:

> Harriet's untimely fate occasioned him deep agony of mind, which he felt the more because for a long time he kept the feeling to himself. I became acquainted with it in a somewhat singular manner.
> I was walking with him one evening in Bisham Wood. . . . when he suddenly fell into a gloomy reverie. I tried to rouse him out of it, and made some remarks which I thought might make him laugh at his own abstraction. Suddenly he said to me, still with the same gloomy expression: "There is one thing to which I have decidedly made up my mind. I will take a great glass of ale every night." I said, laughingly, "A very good resolution, as the result of a melancholy musing." "Yes," he said; "but you do not know why I take it. I shall do it to deaden my feelings: for I see that those who drink ale have none."[16] The next day he said to me: "You must have thought me very unreasonable yesterday evening?" I said, "I did, certainly." "Then," he said, "I will tell you what I would not tell any one else. I was thinking of Harriet." I told him, "I had no idea of such a thing: it was so long since he had named her. I had thought he was under the influence of some baseless morbid feeling; but if ever I should see him again in such a state of mind, I would not attempt to disturb it."[17]

Yet Peacock—who was certainly the most discreet among Shelley's friends and the one who most genuinely respected Shelley's reticence—within the year after this scene must have taken place not only made public fun of Shelley's relations with Harriet and Mary in the triangle involving Scythrop, Marionetta, and

"Stella" (Celinda) in *Nightmare Abbey,* but he even transmuted Shelley's remark about drinking "a great glass of ale" into the conclusion of that novel, in which, having lost both women to other suitors, Scythrop, who has threatened to blow his brains out with a loaded pistol, instead tells his servant: "Bring some Madeira."[18] If *Peacock* could, in 1818, be this insensitive to his friend's feelings, Shelley had little hope of reaching Hogg or Godwin or John Gisborne. The portrait of Athanase is Shelley's projection of his own emotional isolation resulting from his revulsion toward Godwin, the growing estrangement between himself and Mary, Charles Ollier's neglect, the repeated irresponsibility of the Hunts in all practical matters, and Peacock's callousness, as typified by *Nightmare Abbey.*[19]

The three central facts about Athanase, as Shelley approved his portrait in "Athanase: A Fragment," are: first, he is good and moral; second, he is unhappy; third, he is reticent. He was not burdened by "secret crime" or false ambition, or superstitious fears: "none than he a purer heart could have" (lines 13–25). Why, then, did he suffer? The question is posed again and again, but never satisfactorily answered in the fragment. Even in his love and labors "for his kind," he "unlike all others it is said, / . . . never found relief" (lines 34–36). The last ambiguous phrase is subject to being interpreted either as "his labors for others never ended" or "he found no satisfaction in helping others." In either case, the poem represents, perhaps, Shelley's deepest poetic exploration of his own motivations. In the ambiguity of endless or joyless service, he admits to himself that even his good works bring him no ultimate reward. Like John Stuart Mill discovering in 1827–1828 that he would not be happy even if all the social goals to which he had devoted his early life were to be realized, Shelley in "Athanase: A Fragment" admits the presence of the mid-life crisis (characteristic of ambitious people in their mid-thirties), which struck him early, in keeping with his consistent precocity. That Shelley could not so name or analyze this event does not invalidate the importance of his honesty in pinpointing it carefully enough to enable us to do so.

The general symptoms of the malaise Shelley experienced are those shared by many who commit themselves to a career or course of action and—whether they achieve the success they envisioned or encounter nothing but frustration in the endeavor—suddenly realize the ultimate futility of their efforts. Either the end proves to be illusory, or false, or has been lost in the means, or the rewards anticipated and won have cut the striver off from those people he most cares about. For Shelley to admit, as he seems to in "Athanase: A Fragment," that he received no satisfaction even from his service to others is an important revelation. For him to portray his friends as unfeeling and cruel would make him appear to be terribly paranoid, did we not possess such a full, substantiating record of his friends' behavior toward him and such a wealth of poetic self-portraits written under different conditions and in various moods.

PORTRAITS OF THE ARTIST

Shelley's self-portrait in "Athanase: A Fragment" is strikingly different from his earlier self-portraits, which depict the Shelleyan poet-hero as a man of great moral fortitude and resourcefulness. Let us look briefly at those early sketches.

In the poems of *The Esdaile Notebook,* Shelley included some self-portraits that reflect both his sense of isolation and impotence, and others (a preponderance, I believe) in which his sense of his own mission and his dedicated strength to accomplish it are paramount. "Death-spurning rocks!" expresses the sorrows of a "maniac-sufferer" who, like the youthful wanderer in *Alastor,* is tortured by his own memories, hopes, and fears and driven to the awesome forms of nature—towering rocks and wild moors. The poem ends, however, not with weeping and gnashing of teech, but with images and sentiments strongly prefiguring the end of *Adonais:*

> Shall he turn back? The tempest there
> Sweeps fiercely thro' the turbid air
> Beyond a gulph before that yawns.
> The daystar shines, the daybeam dawns.
> God! Nature! Chance! remit this misery—
> It burns!—why need he live to weep who does not fear to die?[20]

In such a poem the courage to face death in spite of the ultimate mystery of life—whether it is controlled by God, Nature, or Chance—gives a tone of affirmation, though the content itself is largely negative. In another early poem (dated by Shelley himself "1810"), the poet compares himself to a weak Lama; he has fallen victim to "the grasp of Religion," which, "fiercer than tygers," pursues and persecutes him.[21] Again, his courage and integrity enable him to plan at least to follow the advice of Job's friends—to curse religion and die. On the other hand, in such poems as "To Harriet: 'It is not blasphemy to hope' " and "The Retrospect" Shelley celebrates the strength he has gained from the love and companionship of Harriet, who has changed him from a lonely outcast to a dedicated spirit, strong and secure in purpose. In "On leaving London for Wales" Shelley denies that he is fleeing to Snowdonia to forget the social wrongs he has witnessed in London; rather, addressing Cambria, he declares:

> . . . the weapon that I burn to wield
> I seek amid thy rocks to ruin hurled
> That Reason's flag may over Freedom's field,
> Symbol of bloodless victory, wave unfurled—
> A meteor-sign of love effulgent o'er the world.
>
> .   .   .   .
>
> Let me forever be what I have been,
> But not forever at my needy door
> Let Misery linger, speechless, pale and lean.
> I am the friend of the unfriended poor;
> Let me not madly stain their righteous cause in gore.[22]

Here he is strong and able to maintain the struggle against the oppressors; his only fear is that he may be led by their outrages to turn to violence, thereby compromising the holy cause. The poem beginning "I will kneel at thine altar" (dated by Shelley 1809) is an account of Shelley's youthful dedication to "God, Love or Virtue."[23] In it, and in the later accounts of similar uplifting experiences recounted in "Hymn to Intellectual Beauty" and other poems, we find the real source of Shelley's sense of strength and purpose: the feeling of power derived from a firm conviction that he was on the side of Truth and Justice and that ultimately the Powers of the Universe itself would support his efforts on behalf of righteousness.

In *Queen Mab,* of course, the supportive power is personified in the fairy Mab, who represents (though she cannot totally embody) Necessity, the "mother of the world." Henry, the surrogate of the poet, has nothing to do except watch over the sleeping body of Ianthe, while her soul is whisked off in Mab's chariot to learn what Henry's soul already knows. Not only does the poet express no fear or uncertainty, but there is, apparently, nothing at all for *him* to learn. Shelley's point of view for *Queen Mab* was carefully chosen; there is a harmony between the poetic text and the teacherly tone of the elaborate notes (which contain far more words than the poem itself). Shelley in the flesh was less certain of truths than the Henry/Mab duo in the first poem to which he intended to attach his name. The stance is adopted to display a confidence that will capture the imagination of young aristocrats and persuade them to participate in the great adventure of liberal propagandizing, while at the same time assuring them that they will end up on the winning side.

Alastor pictures quite differently the results of an encounter between idealistic youth and eternal Truth: a surrogate of the poet withdraws from uncongenial society, studies the records of human history, and encounters the truth of existence in a flash of insight:

> He lingered, poring on memorials
> Of the world's youth, through the long burning day
> Gazed on those speechless shapes, nor, when the moon
> Filled the mysterious halls with floating shades
> Suspended he that task, but ever gazed
> And gazed, till meaning on his vacant mind
> Flashed like strong inspiration, and he saw
> The thrilling secrets of the birth of time.
>
> [lines 121–128][24]

But far from binding the young man closer to the human community (as Shelley had confidently predicted of his own dedication in "I will kneel at thine altar" and was to recount later in the Dedication to *Laon and Cythna*), the mystical encounter with truth causes the young man to ignore the sympathetic service of the Arab maiden and to wander off into Asia until "The spirit of sweet human love . . . sent / A vision to the sleep of him who spurned / Her choicest gifts" (lines 203–205) that filled him with undying restlessness. Thus Shelley, speaking both as author in the Preface and as the narrator who tells the youth's story, judges the youth and finds his life and death ultimately a tragic waste.[25] The lesson taught by the fate of the youthful visionary in *Alastor* is that insight is not enough—that, in fact, unless the man of vision can maintain sympathy with the human community, his fate is pitiable, not admirable. This lesson had been implicit in the poems of *The Esdaile Notebook* in which Shelley discussed his feelings of isolation before his union with Harriet; *Queen Mab* had focused on the opposite condition, in which a sympathetic union of lovers leads to strength and the spread of knowledge.

In *Laon and Cythna* (*The Revolt of Islam*) Shelley, of course, recombines the two elements essential to victorious living in his scheme of things: a true picture of the nature of human life and society, joined with supportive human love and sympathy. But during the period between *Alastor* and *Laon and Cythna*, he wrote two poems that throw into sharper focus the primacy of love over doctrine in

Shelley's thinking. "Mont Blanc" is notable as a statement about the limitations of human knowledge. On September 27, 1815, Shelley mentioned his copy of Sir William Drummond's *Academical Questions* (1805).[26] In a footnote to the Preface of *Laon and Cythna,* Shelley singles out Drummond's book ("a volume of very acute and powerful metaphysical criticism") as the sole exception to his judgment that "Metaphysics, and enquiries into moral and political science, have become little else than vain attempts to revive exploded superstitions, or sophisms like those of Mr. Malthus, calculated to lull the oppressors of mankind into a security of everlasting triumph."[27] Drummond's book is a detailed critique of contemporary schools of philosophy from the viewpoint of Humean or (to cite its classical antecedent) Academic Skepticism—that is, the skeptical philosophy originated by Pyrrho of Elis and taught in the New Academy by Arcesilaus, Carneades, and Cleitomachus, perpetuated by Cicero, and revived during the Renaissance by Montaigne and others.[28] There can be no doubt that Drummond's arguments strongly affected Shelley's thought; "Mont Blanc" is the first important record of that influence. The chief message of "Mont Blanc" is that human life and history are forever cut off from knowledge of the ultimate source of Power, symbolized by the cloud-hidden, silent top of Europe's highest mountain. No human philosophy or religion or system of government can honestly claim divine sanction. "Hymn to Intellectual Beauty," on the other hand, recounts the poet's encounter with *glimpses* of *shadows* of the unseen power—those brief moments of inspiration that the poet hopes, but cannot be certain, are divinely originated. From these fragmentary glimpses, the poet derives strength to dedicate himself to the service of mankind. Man, cut off from an absolute revelation of the ultimate reality, must therefore confine his realm of action to the area of human knowledge in which the welfare of sentient creatures is the highest good. The poet's final dedicatory goal is "To fear himself, and love all human kind."[29]

No longer could Shelley write from the point of view of the omniscient Queen Mab, looking down at antlike humans from a sublime standpoint on "the overhanging battlement" of her "Hall of Spells." After taking the cold bath of Drummond's philosophy in 1815–1816, Shelley wrote *Laon and Cythna* as an epic of human psychological growth and interaction, in which there are no appearances of a deus ex machina and in which sympathetic human love in its various manifestations—between Laon and Cythna, the Hermit and Laon, Cythna and her child, Cythna and the slave girls, Laon and his unnamed friend, and finally, Laon and Cythna once again—provides the full supportive apparatus that generates the moral progress of the action. The external universe does not visibly support the revolutionaries, though Cythna assures Laon that in time the natural cycle will bring forth the fruits of their martyrdom. The symbolic opening canto and last half of the concluding canto are not parallel to the cosmic certainties of *Queen Mab.* The events witnessed by the poet, and the journey to the Temple of "The Great, who had departed from mankind" are entirely separated from the actual narrative of Laon and Cythna. Their story is introduced, in fact, as "A tale of *human* power." The frame story derives, quite simply, from traditions of supernatural frame stories, such as the dream-vision. There is no direct intervention from the supernatural realm into the world of Laon and Cythna while they live.[30] Their destruction and the total suppression of their bloodless revolution illustrate the lesson of "Mont Blanc": far from interfering with mortal affairs, "Power dwells apart in its tranquillity / Remote, serene, and inaccessible" (lines 96–97).[31]

In *Rosalind and Helen* Shelley plays again upon the theme that mutual sympa-
thetic love between a man and a woman is at once the strongest support and the
most valuable fruit of moral and social regeneration. Lionel is strong and an
effective mental warrior against oppression even before he and Helen link their
fates. As Helen recounts, Lionel, who was, like Athanase, "of great wealth and
lineage high," experienced the sudden Shelleyan conversion:

>   there came
> Thy thrilling light, O Liberty!
> And as the meteor's midnight flame
> Startles the dreamer, sun-like truth
> Flashed on his visionary youth,
> And filled him, not with love, but faith,
> And hope, and courage mute in death. . . .
>   [lines 615–621]

And out of the strength of his encounter with this vision of "Liberty" and the love
he has had since his birth,

> He passed amid the strife of men,
> And stood at the throne of armèd power
> Pleading for a world of woe:
> Secure as one on a rock-built tower
> O'er the wrecks which the surge trails to and fro,
> 'Mid the passions wild of human kind
> He stood, like a spirit calming them;
> . . . .
> Joyous he was; and hope and peace
> On all who heard him did abide,
> Raining like dew from his sweet talk. . . .
>   [lines 629–635, 641–643][32]

But when the movement for reform is disastrously thwarted, Lionel's strength
fails him. He becomes exceedingly depressed and writes despairing poetry until he
and Helen meet. Then their love sustains them through his imprisonment by the
tyrannical authorities. When Lionel dies, Helen is comforted first by the devotion
of Lionel's mother and then, after the mother's death, by love for her own young
son. Thus reiterated throughout the poem (in somewhat different ways in Rosa-
lind's history) is the motif of sympathetic love as the sustaining motive force in
human life.

The fragmentary essay "On Love," written in July 1818, marks the first shift in
this message. Though the essay asserts the supremacy of sympathetic love, it
exhibits a desperate tone that already contains hints of the system's weakness. The
entire second paragraph, beginning "I know not the internal constitution of other
men" and ending "I have every where sought, and have found only repulse and
disappointment," suggests that Shelley realized by this date that he had counted
too heavily on human sympathy to replace the elusive divine love that appeared
only in those infrequent and shadowy visitations of the Spirit of Intellectual
Beauty.[33]

When Shelley, then, in "Lines written among the Euganean Hills"—a poem begun in the autumn of 1818, a few months after *Rosalind and Helen* was completed and "On Love" was drafted at Bagni di Lucca[34]—writes of existing in a world without human love, he was facing squarely a new dimension of despair that necessitated a reexamination of his basic psychic supports. The opening three verse-paragraphs of "Lines written among the Euganean Hills" speak of the need for "green isles" of momentary peace and calm to console man on his grim voyage "To the haven of the grave" (line 26). Even if in the grave "no heart will meet / His with love's impatient beat" (lines 28–29), there is no special fear in that, for

> Can he dream before that day
> To find refuge from distress
> In friendship's smile, in love's caress?
> [lines 31–33]

This outcry from a mood which Shelley himself characterized in his Advertisement to the *Rosalind and Helen* volume as "a state of deep despondency" is his first poetic expression since the days of the earlier poems in *The Esdaile Notebook* that human love is lacking in his life—that he feels cut off from sustaining affectionate sympathy. But in "Euganean Hills," the mood is lightened by the glorious Italian sunrise, by hopes for a political renewal in Italy, and by a quasi-mystical experience in which the poet's psyche seems merged with the plains, the surrounding mountains, the sky, and all living things into a moment of total peace and harmony.

By the time Shelley completed *Julian and Maddalo* in August 1819, the momentary relief afforded by infrequent visits from the spirit of delight no longer satisfied the poet's needs. Because the deaths of Clara and William Shelley[35] led to the loss of Mary's sympathy and affection and coincided with Shelley's awareness that his handful of friends in England were separated from him by more than miles, his entire value system, for which human love and sympathy provided the underpinning, was radically threatened. Mary's depression and the minor outrages committed by Godwin, Peacock, Ollier, and Hunt during 1819 had confirmed the inefficacy of human relations to provide Percy Bysshe Shelley with his raison d'être.

The vacuum created by the loss of human sympathy was filled eventually by Shelley's increasing dedication to the humane values recorded in great art, and his new credo was to be sung early in 1821 in *A Defence of Poetry*. In that work—as in *Epipsychidion, Adonais,* and *Hellas*—the idealistic humanist who feels most keenly the failure of mortal existence to fulfill his highest aspirations or his deepest needs receives compensation from experiencing the fellowship of his kindred spirits—the noble living and the noble dead—who have transmitted the records of their best and happiest moments across time and space through literature and the fine arts.

On Shelley's quest for a new set of values and a redefinition of love, "Athanase: A Fragment" represents a defensive strong point, a temporary armed camp of the soul from which the poet could portray in ideal colors both the ruins of his past hopes and his potentialities for creative growth. "Athanase" is a sentimental portrait embodying the poet's lament for the loss of his own hopes (aspirations that the reader may feel were unjustified) and his proud declaration that his head, though bloody, is quite unbowed and that he is superior to mere mortal pain. He looks at himself, moreover, as one of a kind—the only man of sorrows, the sole idealist acquainted with grief. This sense of total isolation gives the poem its most poignant and yet its falsest note, for it is obvious to even the most callow reader that Shelley's personal trials were not unique among mankind. Shelley himself, of course, must have recognized that even as he expressed himself, for an awareness of the growing sentimentality of the poem's final lines, as well as the weakness of some of the versification, gave ample reason for his breaking off the fragment and adding a note half-apologizing for the tone.

A BOOK OF MARTYRS

From seeing himself as a unique, isolated figure, Shelley turned in his later writings to identify himself with other idealists of the past and of his own age who had suffered exile, ostracism, or martyrdom, through either the blindness or the cruelty of their societies. Socrates, Jesus, Cain, Lucan, Dante, Rousseau, Milton (when old and blind), Chatterton, and Keats all figure prominently as exemplars of the fate of sensitive spirits who dared to pioneer for new and more creative solutions to human problems. And in giving such prominence to the trials of creative men who suffered the wrath of their contemporaries, Shelley gave memorable and influential form to the idea of the artist as a politically and socially impotent outcast, an image that was almost a new idea in English literature at the time but has since become a banality.

Because both Shelley and Keats died in exile, the entire image of the poet in England was changed for the later nineteenth century and the twentieth century. Until the time of the Romantics, many of the best English writers had been men of practical affairs engaged in significant public service, political or ecclesiastical (as witness the careers of Chaucer, Sir Thomas More, Sidney, Spenser, Donne, Milton, Herrick, Swift, Fielding, Burke, and Sheridan), or men who were prominent in their individual professions and were admired for their professional success (Shakespeare, Ben Jonson, Richardson), or men who through their literary prowess won recognition from other intellectuals, politicians, and statesmen alike (Dryden, Steele, Addison, Pope, and Dr. Johnson). Though the careers of Richard Savage, Christopher Smart, Cowper, and Burns seemed to point the way, the image of the poet as a tender and vulnerable individual who is hounded to an early death or driven mad by a cruel world does not really come to the forefront in England until the death of Chatterton provided a striking exemplum for the tale of a society hostile or indifferent to men of genius. Examples from Continental Europe—particularly Rousseau's *Confessions,* Goethe's *Sorrows of Young Werther,* and the (largely false) legend of Tasso's misfortunes—reinforced the native tradition, but it was Chatterton whom Wordsworth recollected during his despair on the heath in "Resolution and Independence," to whom Keats dedicated his poetic first fruits, and who persisted as a certral figure at least until the manhood of Robert Browning. But by the latter period, more forceful examples had come into prominence.

Wordsworth's controversy with the *Edinburgh Review* and Byron's tilting with and overthrow of Scotch Reviewers cannot be seen as a persecution of the poetic sensibility by a philistine society. They were, rather, political and literary wars of the kind that challenged and ultimately gave additional prominence to Milton, Dryden, Pope, and Dr. Johnson during their literary development. Coleridge's misfortunes were intertwined with the man's personal mixture of integrity and sycophancy and his subtle, often equivocating, prose style, and he not only played an influential role for years as a political journalist, but ultimately achieved great popularity and influence on the younger generation; there is no way to this day to be certain whether he was or was not unjustly treated by society at large. But the cases of Keats and Shelley—especially as depicted in the Preface and text of *Adonais*—provided the next generation of poets with a heightened consciousness of every slight and wrong and gave them a precedent to label each harshness by an authority, parental or governmental, as a plot against the creative spirit by forces of mediocrity and darkness. Arthur Hallam, Alfred Tennyson, and Richard Monckton Milnes among the "Cambridge Apostles" of the later 1820's imbibed the lesson and applied it to themselves and to writers in general. Browning identified himself with Chatterton, Keats, and Shelley through long years of obscure exile in Italy. The Rossettis, Clough, George Eliot, Swinburne, Hardy, Oscar Wilde, D. H. Lawrence, and G. B. Shaw all identified themselves more or less with the image of the artist as an outcast critic of society, though Shaw at least never let the feeling drive him into self-pity or isolation. Following them came Yeats, Joyce, and finally the colony of American expatriates in Europe in the twentieth century, including Frost, Eliot, Pound, Gertrude Stein, Hemingway, Fitzgerald, and Henry Miller, who in conjunction with such compatriots as Thomas Wolfe, Hart Crane, Sherwood Anderson, Sinclair Lewis, e.e. cummings, and John Dos Passos, who were also critical of their roots, strengthened the image of the creative writer as an exile alienated from and profoundly critical of the social, political, and religious environment out of which he had emerged.[36]

Twentieth-century English and American writers have, on the whole, accepted the experience of Chatterton, Coleridge, Shelley, Keats, De Quincey, and John Clare—reinforced both by more extreme examples among the French symbolists and by Freudian psychology—and reckoned that the writer must be an outcast from society, or be set apart by his involvement in political rebellion or sexual experimentation, or be crippled by alcoholism or drugs—that he must acquire a "wound" in order to draw the bow of his artistic craft.[37] That prevailing attitude is satirized by Hemingway in *A Moveable Feast* when the friends of T. S. Eliot rally in an attempt to rescue him from working in a bank; it is reflected in the ambiguous reaction of critics toward the "anomalies" of Wallace Stevens and William Carlos Williams, who pursued professional careers while writing some of the greatest poetry yet produced in America.

The truth of the matter for the English Romantics was that all, except Keats, had they been able to arrange it, would have undertaken some practical activity (as did Scott, Wordsworth, Lamb, Hunt, and Peacock) in political life, government service, or journalism. After Peacock was secure in his position at the East India Company, Shelley asked whether *he* could not be given a responsible post in the company's service in India. Peacock discouraged that particular idea because of the difficulties involved, but he suggested that some practical pursuit would be good for Shelley.[38] Shelley in 1819 undertook to finance Henry Reveley's building of a commercial steamship to ply between Leghorn and Marseilles, a venture that, had it not proved abortive, might well have made Shelley a shipping entrepreneur. But we need not speculate on what Shelley might have become; we need only examine his early career to see that he had set himself the primary goal of propagandizing English society into a bloodless revolution. Had this effort been successful during his lifetime, he was certainly ready to emulate Milton by assuming an active role in the new order. At least until late 1819, he did not envision himself as an eternal John the Baptist issuing calls to repentance from exile in the wilderness.

During most of Shelley's life he fervently desired to fill a position of responsibility and exercise practical influence—with all the pragmatic compromises that such activity might involve—to achieve reform. Only when Peacock had failed to make his mark on the literary milieu did he in "The Four Ages of Poetry" urge men of genius to turn their attention from poetry to practical activities; only when Shelley felt alienated *by* others and isolated from all effectual political and humanitarian pursuits did he create the ambiguous image of the poet as "a nightingale, who sits in darkness and sings to cheer its own solitude with sweet sounds."[39]

But Shelley, even in *A Defence of Poetry,* defends (as strongly as does Charles Lamb) "the sanity of true genius." For the Romantics, poets and creative artists were not, essentially, wounded men but whole men; Homer was a great poet not because of his blindness but because of his "triple sight," his insight into the nature of man on earth as well as in his private paradises and hells.[40] That doctrinaire twentieth-century critics consider an incapacity to compete in the everyday, practical world as a sine qua non for achievement as an artist is an aberration that would have shocked the Romantics and must be seen as foolishness in the longer perspective not only of English but Western cultural history, from the first Isaiah and the Greek dramatists through Virgil and Marcus Aurelius, Dante, Leonardo, Michelangelo, Erasmus, Bacon, Montaigne, Bach, Corneille, Descartes, Calderon, Velazquez, Goethe, Haydn, Schiller, Chateaubriand, and Manzoni. Indeed, throughout most of history, when the patronage of men of power was requisite for freedom to create, as well as for publication and fame, practical wisdom and necessity dictated that men who wished to create must be able to maneuver successfully in the larger world.

Only in bourgeois society, with its accompanying diffusion of wealth, power, and aesthetic interests, can the artist take his creations directly to the public marketplace and thereby dissociate himself from some system of governmental or quasi-feudal patronage. (Dr. Johnson's *Letter to Lord Chesterfield* [1755] marks the watershed moment in English literature, though Defoe and others had operated successfully years earlier.) Under the commercial system the writer could get his works accepted if he could find or create a reading public, and this is what, to a certain extent, Wordsworth and his contemporaries proceeded to do. In the modern world of xerography and offset printing, not even the conglomeration of major publishing houses into profit-and-loss subsidiaries of giant corporations can prevent a determined writer from seeking his public. And if a thousand self-appointed nightingales try to sing in darkness to cheer their own solitude, we can only hope that the loudest voice belongs to the nightingale with the greatest genius and the sweetest song. Otherwise, poetry may be destroyed by the myth of its own isolation from the larger intellectual world "Which is the world of all of us, & where / We find our happiness or not at all.[41]

Shelley himself made a serious effort to return to that larger world after he wrote "Athanase" in such works as *Hellas, The Mask of Anarchy, A Philosophical View of Reform,* and "Charles the First" and through such enterprises as the inception of *The Liberal.* That he was not finally successful probably was due more to his early death than to his failure to act. (Milton, after all, was in his thirty-third year before he left belles lettres to become a public controversialist.)

After Shelley rededicated himself, late in 1819, to the "worship of the spirit of good within," he sometimes stumbled but never again quite fell into the despairing sense of isolation depicted in "Athanase: A Fragment." Its existence, however, reminds us of the cost paid by Shelley for his dedication to that good spirit.

NOTES

1. *Shelley and His Circle,* ed. Donald H. Reiman, vol. 6 (Cambridge: Harvard University Press, 1973), 1102 fn. Citations of this series, hereafter designated SC, include vols. 5 (1973) and 7 (1986), in which this essay originally appeared. Shelley's poetry is cited from *Shelley's Poetry and Prose,* ed. Donald H. Reiman and Sharon B. Powers (New York: Norton, 1977), hereafter cited as *Shelley's Poetry.*
Shelly clearly designated the portion of the poem he copied and sent to Ollier for publication, "Athanase: A Fragment." Mary Shelley, publishing it in *Posthumous Poems* after she had gone through Shelley's rough drafts and found there the hero called *Prince* Athanase, titled it *Prince Athanase: A Fragment.* To distinguish among the various versions, we shall attempt consistency in citing: (1) the published version in *Posthumous Poems* as *Prince Athanase: A Fragment* (or, simply, *Prince Athanase*); (2) the fair-copy manuscript SC 582, as "Athanase: A Fragment" (or "Athanase"); and (3) the rough-draft version in Shelley's notebook now designated Bodleian Ms. Shelley e. 4, as "Prince Athanase."
2. *Literary and Historical Manuscripts, Autographs, Books, . . . : The Collection Formed by the Late David Gage Joyce* (*Hanzel Galleries, September 23–24, 1973, lot 150*).
3. SEE SC, vol. 7, p. 144, fn. 9.
4. To Peacock, Leghorn, June 20–21, 1819, in The Letters of Percy Bysshe Shelley, ed. Frederick L. Jones, 2 vols. (Oxford: Clarendon Press, 1964), vol. 2, p. 98; text checked against manuscript, in The Berg Collection, The New York Public Library.
5. To Peacock, ca. July 20, 1819; Shelley, *Letters,* II, 101.
6. Compare with this sentence the moving passage in *Adonais,* beginning with these lines in stanza 25, when Urania reaches the tomb of Adonais:

> In the death chamber for a moment Death
> Shamed by the presence of that living Might
> Blushed to annihilation, and the breath
> Revisited those lips, and life's pale light
> Flashed through those limbs . . .
> [lines 217–221]

Allusions to William Shelley's death and burial have previously been noted in *Adonais,* lines 438–441 and 469–471. But this further parallel suggests that part of the emotional power of the poem comes from Shelley's sorrow over the death of his young son, who was, in a much more extreme way than Keats, an inheritor of "unfulfilled renown" (line 397).
7. To Hogg, July 25, 1819; Shelley, *Letters,* II, 104.
8. To Amelia Curran, August 5, 1819; Shelley, *Letters,* II, 106–107.
9. The chief exception to this generalization, consisting of two nostalgic paragraphs in Shelley's letter to Peacock, August 24, 1819 (Shelley, *Letters,* II, 114), provides a clue to the depth of Shelley's otherwise overcontrolled emotions.
10. See Shelley, *Letters,* II, 126, and SC 543 (VI).

11. Shelley, *Letters,* II, 125. Charles E. Robinson, in "The Shelley Circle and Coleridge's *The Friend*" (*English Language Notes,* VIII, 1971, 269–274), identifies Shelley's source in Coleridge as *The Friend,* No. 5 (September 14, 1809).

12. For example: "all human evils either extinguish, or are extinguished by the sufferer., and I am now living with my accustomed tranquillity & happiness . . ." (*SC* 396, V, 196), and "It is not health but life that I should seek in Italy, & that not for my own sake—I feel I am capable of trampling on all such weakness—but for the sake of those to whom my life may be a source of happiness utility security & honour—& to some of whom my death might be all that is the reverse" (to Godwin, December 7, 1817; Shelley, *Letters,* I, 573).

13. For my definition and discussion of *artless* and *artful* correspondents, see SC 444, Commentary (see SC, vol. 5, pp. 436–437).

14. This and subsequent quotations from *Julian and Maddalo* are from *Shelley's Poetry,* pp. 118 ff.

15. Peacock, *Memoirs,* p. 40.

16. Though Peacock does not spell out the point of this remark, Peacock himself came over to Shelley's house at Marlow "to drink his bottle" (at Shelley's expense). See Mary Shelley, *Letters* (Bennett), I, 41.

17. "Memoirs of Percy Bysshe Shelley," in *The Works of Thomas Love Peacock,* ed. H.F.B. Brett-Smith and C. E. Jones, 10 vols. (London: Constable, 1924–1934), vol. 8, p. 40. Hereafter cited as *Memoirs.*

18. Edward DuBois, as we have seen, found the ending of *Nightmare Abbey* flat and unsatisfying (see SC, vol. 6, p. 755). But it is appropriate when it is recognized as a private allusion to this scene between Shelley and Peacock that remained vivid in Peacock's memory for another forty years.

19. Since reading Marilyn Butler's excellent *Peacock Displayed: A Satirist in his Context* (London: Routledge & Kegan Paul, 1979), I have reviewed the preceding paragraphs in the light of her contention that *Nightmare Abbey* does not portray Shelley's personal affairs in the triangle with Marionetta and "Stella." Using Dr. Butler's own evidence that Peacock parodies Godwin's *Mandeville* for its gloomy misanthropy and that "Stella" is identified with such literature, I think that Mary Shelley, "The author of *Frankenstein,*" is confirmed as the original of "Stella," just as Peacock's portrait of Harriet Shelley in his *Memoirs* of Shelley confirms *her* as the original of Marionetta. On the question of whether Peacock would go against what he (many years later) stated as his rule, I am convinced that Peacock's resentments, and those of other writers, sometimes emerge in spite of moral principles or even their personal interests. I am equally convinced that Peacock's much more favorable portrait of Algernon Falconer (who, as Butler points out, embodies one side of Peacock's ideal only at the *end* of *Gryll Grange*) is in part an attempt to compensate for his earlier injustice to Shelley, rather than a comment on Matthew Arnold's early poetry, as Butler would have it.

20. Percy Bysshe Shelley, *The Esdaile Notebook: A Volume of Early Poems by Percy Bysshe Shelley,* ed. Kenneth Neill Cameron (New York: Knopf, 1964), pp. 81–82.

21. Shelley, *The Esdaile Notebook,* pp. 123–124.

22. Shelley, *The Esdaile Notebook,* pp. 54–55.

23. Shelley, *The Esdaile Notebook,* p. 125. I agree with Cameron's commentary in *The Esdaile Notebook* in seeing this event as parallel to, rather than identifiable with, the cataclysmic experience recounted in "Hymn to Intellectual Beauty" and the Dedication to *Laon and Cythna* (pp. 250–254).

24. This and subsequent quotations from *Alastor* are from *Shelley's Poetry,* pp. 69 ff.

25. Though I accept aspects of Earl R. Wasserman's reading of *Alastor* (*Shelley: A*

Critical Reading, Baltimore: Johns Hopkins University Press, 1971, pp. 11–41), includ-ing his judgment that the narrator represents an essentially Wordsworthian perspec-tive, I do not accept his attempt to choose between the moral qualities of the narrator and those of the youth ("Visionary"), as though Shelley were Henry James and created an untrustworthy narrator. In fact, Shelley draws on Wordsworth's early, visionary poems (which he admired) to strengthen the moral credibility of the narrator, not to undercut him.

26. Shelley, *Letters,* I, 433.

27. *Laon and Cythna* (London: Sherwood, Neely, & Jones and C. and J. Ollier, 1818), pp. xi–xii.

28. See C. E. Pulos, *The Deep Truth: A Study of Shelley's Scepticism* (Lincoln: University of Nebraska Press, 1954), pp. 9–41. See also "Shelley's Treatise on Political Economy," *Shelley and his Circle,* VI, 946–947.

29. *Shelley's Poetry,* p. 95.

30. Shelley took the story of the sea-eagle that feeds Cythna in her cave, for exam-ple, from a story that Pliny in his *Natural History* records as a factual one.

31. *Shelley's Poetry,* p. 92.

32. Shelley, *Poetical Works* (OSA) p. 177.

33. See sc, vol. 6, pp. 633–647.

34. See Shelley's Advertisement and Mary's Note to *Rosalind and Helen,* in Shelley, *Poetical Works* (OSA), pp. 167, 188–189.

35. These two shocks came, we must remember, hard upon Shelley's legal loss of his other two children through the Chancery Court decision.

36. The roots of this alienated tradition in American literature are proportionately stronger and deeper, going back at least to Thoreau, Poe, Hawthorne, and Melville in their isolation from or reaction to the puritanism that had defined the early American experience; but note that such diverse major writers as Emerson, Whitman, Mark Twain, and Henry James viewed American society not as an enemy to be castigated but as a prize to be won.

37. Edmund Wilson's *The Wound and the Bow* has been the most influential docu-ment in this tradition since its publication in 1941. But in 1974, Richard Wollheim authoritatively refuted Wilson's amateur Freudianism out of Freud's own writings and rejoinders on the subject recorded in the *Minutes of the Vienna Psychoanalytic Society.* Wollheim argues, in a paper entitled "Neurosis and the Artist" (*TLS,* March 1, 1974, pp. 203–204), that Freud saw the artistic component of the writer's temperament not as a necessary correlative to neurosis or neurosis as basic to the artistic temperament. Rather, he saw creativity as a curative and sanative element tending to mitigate patho-logical tendencies. Wollheim writes, for example: "it is the intensity and inflexibility of a wish, not just its object, that brings about the existence of a neurosis. . . . the very fact that the artist can mould or shape his 'neurotic' material into a form that com-mands our interest and excites our curiosity is testimony to the fact that the material is not of pathological strength: or, to put it in a way which increasingly appealed to Freud, that it is not stronger than his ego can contain" (p. 204). Though Wollheim restates this proposition as: "artistic creativity is some kind of sign of freedom from neurosis," he denies at the same time that it is "possible to free oneself from neurosis through artistic creativity" because, "Just as the thesis that art is neurosis has a blurred conception of the neurosis, so the thesis that art is therapy has a blurred conception of art" (p. 204). Citing Lamb's essay "Sanity of True Genius," Wollheim writes: "it would be absurd . . . to argue from this that a good way of not going mad would be to be another Shakespeare" (p. 204). Wollheim concludes his important essay with these reflections on the corruption of Freud's ideas: "the massive struggle for new markets

for art . . . would seem to have imposed on art a new mission: that of carrying the comforting message that nothing is really disturbing, that the pathological has its charms. . . . Freud could have had no reason to anticipate . . . the way in which vulgarized views about the sickness of the artist have contributed to the sickness of art itself" (p. 204).

38. See Peacock's letter to Shelley dated October 1821 (*Works of Thomas Love Peacock,* vol. 8, pp. 225–226).

39. *Shelley's Poetry,* p. 486. In "The Nightingale Figure in Shelley's *Defence*" (*English Language Notes,* XVII [1980], 265–268), John F. Schell puts Shelley's image back in its context to argue that, whatever later artists and critics have tried to make of it, the image of the poet as a solitary nightingale does not refer to "the interaction of the artist and audience, or the role of the poet in society," but rather to the problem of finding 'a jury" of "his peers" to pass aesthetic judgment on the superior artist whose peers, "the selectest of the wise of many generations," can only be found scattered through history. Thus society at large hears not only a contemporary poet but every poet of the past as a hidden nightingale and responds to him "as men entranced by the melody of an unseen musician, who feel that they are moved and softened, yet know not whence or why? (*Shelley's Poetry,* p. 486); only the "selectest of the wise" know "whence or why" this influence thus improves society.

40. See Keats, "To Homer" (*The Poems of John Keats,* ed. Jack Stillinger, Cambridge: Harvard University Press, 1978, p. 264).

41. Shelley to Gisborne, April 10, 1822; Shelley, *Letters,* II, 406. Shelley is here misquoting three lines of Wordsworth's which later became lines 142–144 of *The Prelude,* Book XI. Lines 105–144 of this Book were first published, without title, in Coleridge's *The Friend,* No. 11 (October 26, 1809), p. 163. They were reprinted in the 1815 edition of Wordsworth's *Poems* with the title "French Revolution, as It Appeared to Enthusiasts at Its Commencement" (II, 69–71).

FRANCES FERGUSON

Shelley's Mont Blanc: What the Mountain Said

The following selections on one of Shelley's greatest lyrics illustrate a significant process in the development of romantic criticism which is most sharply delineated in the seventies' and early eighties' fascination with the topic of sublimity, perhaps most famously explored in Thomas Weiskel's *Romantic Sublime: Studies in the Structure and Psychology of Transcendence* (1976), and continued by Frances Ferguson in her recent *Solitude and the Sublime: Romanticism and the Aesthetics of Individuation* (1992). Ferguson, still most widely known in romantic studies for her book, *Wordsworth: Language as Counter-Spirit* (1977), wrote this essay while she was still working through a generally deconstructive interest in the materiality of language and how that issue redefines the sublime less in terms of natural greatness than in terms of an emphasis on shifting the unit of representation. She finds Shelley's principal purpose in *Mont Blanc* to be the aestheticizing of the natural world. The poem, in her words, works to "domesticate the material world for the purposes of aesthetics," to convert the natural "object into a found object." But for Shelley this process of symbiosis of mind and thing expresses love—the sublimity of the mountain is a product of the mind's capacity to love, the power to impute relationships.

Critics seem to have agreed on one thing about *Mont Blanc*—that it is a poem about the relationship between the human mind and the external world. After that, the debates begin—over whether the mind or the world has primacy, over whether "The veil of life and death" of line 54 has been "upfurled" or "unfurled" in line 53, over whether "but for such faith" in line 79 means "only through such faith" or "except through such faith," and so on.[1] It is not surprising that debates should have arisen, because the poem moves through a variety of different ways of imagining the mountain and the power of which it is symbolic (or synecdochic); and although the poet may do the mountain in different voices, the variety of conceptions and the rapidity with which they succeed one another are possible largely because the mountain is like the tarbaby in Uncle Remus and says nothing.

The question that arises, of course, is, How is the mountain's silence any different from the silence of the subjects of any other poem? Grecian urns are likewise silent; and nightingales may sing, but they do not talk. In the case of *Mont Blanc,* the interest lies, curiously enough, in the palpable improbability of

From *Romanticism and Language,* ed. Arden Reed (Ithaca, N.Y.: Cornell University Press, 1984), pp. 202–214. Copyright © 1984 by Cornell University. Used by permission of the publisher, Cornell University Press.

looking for anything but silence from the mountain, which is repeatedly seen as the ultimate example of materiality, of the "thingness" of things, so that its symbolic significance is quite explicitly treated as something added to that materiality.

At moments Shelley seems to be almost defiantly trying to think of the mountain (and the entire landscape connected with it) as a brute physical existence. Such an effort would have to be at least somewhat defiant, both because of the inevitable difficulty of trying to imagine anything completely without history and context (and thus associations) and because of the multiplicity of associations that had accrued to the idea of this mountain. Whereas it is crucial to the mountain's force as an example of pure materiality that it can never know that it is the highest mountain in Europe, it—and the vale of Chamonix generally—had, as Richard Holmes nicely observes, developed a reputation among the "travelling English" of the time "as a natural temple of the Lord and a proof of the Deity by design."[2] The famous story of Shelley's traveling through the region, entering his name in the hotel registers in Chamonix and Montavert, and listing his occupations as "Democrat, Philanthropist and Atheist" serves to indicate the level of his indignation at the way in which religion attributes spiritual qualities to a brute material object when it assimilates such an object to a proof of the deity by design.[3] It serves as well to suggest how difficult it is to think of the mountain as a merely physical object. For in his efforts to counter the myth of natural religion that is attached to Mont Blanc, Shelley does not destroy the mountain's symbolic value but merely inverts it.

To say that Shelley attempts to conceive Mont Blanc in terms of sheer physical force may sound like a movement toward recognizing a gap between signifier and signified and toward trying to accept the mountain not just as pure nonreferentiality. The mountain would function, in such an account, as a linguistic signifier that would reveal the ironic distance between its material presence and any possible signified. Yet I would argue that the poem insists, most importantly, on the inability of one's resting in such irony as it exhibits its own repeated failures to let Mont Blanc be merely a blank, merely a mass of stone: *Mont Blanc* leads to attempts to think of the mountain as physical and without metaphysical attributes, and fails; it attempts to imagine a gap between the mountain and the significances that people attach to it, and fails. But if one way of talking about the poem is to suggest that Shelley is here restricted because of the inadequacy of language, or the way in which language blocks one from saying certain things or certain kinds of things, the other side of that image of blockage—of the inability to break through—is a contrary movement made manifest by the way in which the relationships that are sketched out in the poem are not merely adequate but so abundant and well-fitting as almost to inspire claustrophobia. In this respect, the poem is more nearly akin to Wordsworth's lines about how exquisitely the human mind and the world are fitted to one another than even those lines that Harold Bloom and others have seen echoed in the opening section of *Mont Blanc*—the lines from "Tintern Abbey" in which Wordsworth speaks of having "felt / A presence that disturbs [him] with the joy / Of elevated thoughts . . . / A Motion and a spirit, that . . . / . . . rolls through all things" (ll. 93–102).[4]

Thus, although the motive behind the poem appears to be conceiving of Mont Blanc not just as the white mountain but also as a massive version of blankness— or "solitude / Or blank desertion" (*The Prelude*, I:394–95), the poem has already in its first few lines become a poem about the impossibility of seeing the mountain as alien. As Earl Wasserman observes, the "everlasting universe of things" is like the Arve flowing through the Ravine that is like the "universal mind," and the Ravine of "universal mind" and the Channel in which the brook of the individual mind flows merge with one another.[5] In the midst of all the convergence and congruence of the schema, however, Wasserman very convincingly notes a sensory overload in the image of the brook: "The simile, which has no significant function except to transform the mode of vision, by its very tautology opens the door to an abundance of supposedly external objects that exceed the requirements of the comparison, as though the tendency to conceive of images as external were too great for the poet to resist."[6]

Wasserman's central point here is that the poet conceives of metaphors in which he then finds "a remarkably consistent objective correlative for his metaphor for a total universe that is indifferently things or thoughts and that is located in the One Mind."[7] It is not, of course, particularly surprising that Shelley should see the scene, when he finally looks at it, in the terms in which he thought about it before he looked at it; what is, however, remarkable is not just that the interpretation and the perception are aligned with one another but that the various portions of the imagery are as well. The river, of necessity, fits the ravine perfectly—and in a way that makes it impossible to say which has priority and determines the other. Whereas a glass of water may be said to be prior to the water in it, in that its shape is one that any water in it must conform to, the course and shape of a riverbed may be said to be determined by the waters that flow through it just as much as the riverbed may be said to determine the course of the river. Yet it is not merely the river and the riverbed that are interdependent and mutually creative, for the height of the mountain and the depth of the ravine have an analogous relation to one another: there is a ravine—and a ravine this deep—because there is a mountain—and a mountain this high—and vice versa.

An additional complication appears, however, in the image of the brook that Wasserman describes as exceeding "the requirements of the comparison."[8]

> The source of human thought its tribute brings
> Of waters,—with a sound but half its own,
> Such as a feeble brook will oft assume
> In the wild woods, among the mountains lone,
> Where waterfalls around it leap for ever,
> Where woods and winds contend, and a vast river
> Over its rocks ceaselessly bursts and raves.
>   [II. 5–11]

The "feeble brook" is not described simply as a tributary to the "vast river"; instead, the river is said to "burst and rave" over its—the brook's—rocks, thus introducing the question of whether a brook is still a brook when a river runs in its channel. Although the question itself seems like a bad riddle, it forcibly demonstrates Shelley's procedure throughout the poem of insisting on the changeableness of the identity of any individual entity. For the brook, in becoming a part of the river, both loses its identity as a brook and transcends itself, gaining access to a forcefulness it never had as a "feeble brook."

We have here, in the cluster of images that are continually put into relation with one another, an elaborate schema of reciprocity. The universe of things exists to be perceived by the universal mind, so that the mind does not create things in its acts of perception but rather keeps the things of the world from going to waste. The river that courses along the channel of the brook enables the individual mind to participate in thought and sensation without ever having to originate them for itself. As we do not make up the world of things as we go along, so we do not discover all of human thought on our own. The relationship between the river and the brook may be seen not only as analogous to that between all of human knowledge and an individual knowing subject but also as similar to all human language in relation to an individual speaker.

It is, however, when the terms that are put into relationship with one another get proper names that the poem begins to flirt with relational punning. Bloom has stressed the importance of Shelley's addressing the ravine and the mountain as "Thou" and has seen it as emblematic of the poem's conjecturing "the possibility of a Thou as a kind of universal mind in nature."[9] Although there are no proper names in the first section of the poem, the second section offers not just the pronoun "Thou" but also the names "Ravine of Arve" and "Arve." The appearance of the names registers the shift from Shelley's imagining a schematic relationship for the ravine and the river to his seeing this particular ravine and this particular river. But the address to the ravine is repeated enough for it to become, as Wasserman might have said, "excessive." For when Shelley turns to look at and speak to the ravine, he calls it "thou, Ravine of Arve—dark, deep Ravine," and in the nomenclature "Ravine of Arve" is another way of suggesting the interdependence of the ravine and the river. There is also, however, a linguistic *tour de force*—or cheap trick—at work here: the river that has been imagined in the first section to "burst and rave" ceaselessly is identified as the Arve, so that the "Arve raves." And it of course turns out that the "Arve raves in the Ravine" (If you drop the article "the" from the previous clause, you have four words that are all contained in the letters of the word "ravine," and it might, with a bit of work, be made into another song for *My Fair Lady*.)

This species of relational punning underscores the symbiosis of things and mind, of river and ravine, that Shelley has earlier been sketching. Further, it raises some interesting questions about the status of language in the poem. Although the punning is a kind of technological trick with language, it is hard to see how this language can really be described as duplicitous, for all it does is reiterate the earlier message: thought takes the world of things to be inextricable from the mind; the actual perception of the scene confirms this message, in taking the river to be inextricable from the ravine, and at this point in the poem the language itself rather glaringly insists that the Arve exists because it is in the Ravine of Arve. The importance of the language trick lies not, however, in the fact that this language is human and might thus reveal the primacy of the human and the priority of the human mind. Rather, the anagram suggests the inevitability of any human's seeing things in terms of relationship.

The significance of this love language, moreover, goes beyond the familiarity built into a poet's addresses to the personifications that he creates. For the questions about epistemology that Wasserman has very convincingly seen to dominate the poem appear very different if epistemology is correlated with ontology on the one hand or, alternatively, with love. In the one account—that which continually seeks to align epistemology with ontology so that one's knowing always struggles to coincide with the real existence of what one knows—the adequacy of one's ability to know is always suspect. In the other account—that which aligns epistemology with love—emotional profligacy that continually postulates and assumes the existence of an interlocutor supplants any notion of matching one's knowledge with things as they really are.

In the remarkable fragment "On Love," Shelley approvingly remarks that "Sterne says that if he were in a desert, he would love some cypress."[10] In *Mont Blanc* Shelley falls in love with a ravine, a river, and a mountain not because of the nature of those objects but because of his own, his human, mind, which cannot imagine itself as a genuinely independent, isolated existence. Love is, he says,

> that powerful attraction towards all that we conceive, or fear, or hope beyond ourselves, when we find within our own thoughts the chasm of an insufficient void and seek to awaken in all things that are a community with what we experience within ourselves. If we reason, we would be understood; if we imagine, we would that the airy children of our brain were born anew within another's; if we feel, we would that another's nerves should vibrate to our own, that lips of motionless ice should not reply to lips quivering and burning with the heart's best blood. This is Love. This is the bond and the sanction which connects not only man with man but with everything which exists.[11]

When Shelley views the natural landscape, he immediately begins to speak familiarly to it, not just because poets traditionally personify natural objects and address them with terms of endearment, but because he cannot imagine himself without imagining an anti-type that will enable him to be assured of his own existence. For "the invisible and unattainable point to which Love tends," he says, is "the discovery of its anti-type; the meeting with an understanding capable of clearly estimating our own."[12]

Edmund Burke had identified as sublime not only the experience of contemplating enormous heights and depths but also, and most particularly, the experience of being isolated from other humans.[13] From one perspective, Shelley seems to provide a textbook example of how to experience the sublimity of Mont Blanc as he registers his consciousness of the mountain's force while appearing to speak from a condition of isolation (where no human aid can intervene between him and the mountain's power). It is from this perspective unremarkable that Shelley's account of the mountain continually recurs to the subject of its wildness, of its being a wilderness remote from all that civilization involves. By a peculiar twist, however, Shelley converts the isolation of the mountain from a threat into an opportunity—as if he were not so much alone with the mountain as "alone at last" with it. For the act of imagination or intellection by which he moves from the description of the portion of the mountain that remains hidden to him is an act of sympathy; although he speaks merely of the portion of the mountain that really exists, he in effect woos the mountain with an "imagination which . . . enters into and seizes upon the subtle and delicate peculiarities" that the mountain (if it were human) would have "delighted to cherish and unfold in secret."[14]

Thus Shelley's addressing the ravine and the mountain as "Thou" is only one aspect of the poet's effort to convert epistemological language into love language. For although *Mont Blanc* is a sublime poem upon a sublime subject, it projects an air of sociability. As soon as the poet depicts the "Dark, deep ravine," he provides it with companionship in the persons of "Thy giant brood of pines," those "Children of elder time" (ll. 920–21). Even when he imagines Mont Blanc as a fierce and ravening force, he cannot imagine it as a real desert; it is "A desart peopled by the storms" and a place where the poet immediately starts constituting a domestic circle as he asks, "Is this the scene / Where the old Earthquake-daemon taught her young / Ruin? Were these their toys?" (ll. 71–73).

Yet Shelley's famous letter to Thomas Love Peacock describing his first viewing of Mont Blanc makes the poem's love-longing for the mountain seem particularly one-sided, not just unrequited but positively scorned:

> I will not pursue Buffon's sublime but gloomy theory, that this earth which we inhabit will at some future period be changed into a mass of frost. Do you who assert the supremacy of Ahriman imagine him throned among these desolating snows, among these palaces of death and frost, sculptured in this their terrible magnificence by the unsparing hand of necessity, and that he casts around him as the first essays of his final usurpation avalanches, torrents, rocks and thunders—and above all, these deadly glaciers at once the proofs and symbols of his reign.—Add to this the degradation of the human species, who in these regions are half deformed or idiotic and all of whom are deprived of anything that can excite interest or admiration. This is a part of the subject more mournful and less sublime;—but such as neither the poet nor the philosopher should disdain.[15]

The logic by which Shelley regards the degradation of the humans in the vicinity as "more mournful and less sublime" than Buffon's theory that the entire earth will become "a mass of frost" may not be self-evident. But his central point here is that the deformity and idiocy of the inhabitants of the area are, quite literally, not sublime because such deformity and idiocy merely provide, in human form, a repetition of the mountain's role as pure materiality. Thus, although the mountain has the power to make these people less than human, that very power of oppression sets a limit to itself because it annihilates everything in the human that can understand the mountain's material aspect—with an understanding that Shelley speaks of in the fragment "On Love." Throughout *Mont Blanc*, Shelley's attention always moves from images of destructiveness to images of complementarity. In this sense, the poem appears to be almost an endorsement of Kant's remark that nothing in nature is sublime: "All we can say is that the object is fit for the presentation of a sublimity which can be found in the mind, for no sensible form can contain the sublime properly so-called."[16]

Shelley here focuses on a central paradox of the sublime—that we should take pleasure in the contemplation of anything that presents a threat to our tendency toward self-preservation. By falling in love with strenuous death, however, Shelley demonstrates the way in which nature's destructiveness is never centrally at issue in the experience of the sublime. Rather, because the human mind can attribute destructiveness to nature, nature needs us for it to be perceived as destructive and to continue to be destructive in any significant way. Thus *Mont Blanc* creates an image of sublimity that continually hypostatizes an eternity of human consciousness. Because even the ideas of the destructiveness of nature and the annihilation of mankind require human consciousness to give them their force, they thus are testimony to the necessity of the continuation of the human.

In the poem's first section, "woods and winds contend" (l. 10); in the second, "The chainless winds" (l. 22) come to hear the "old and solemn harmony" (l. 24) that they make with the "giant brood of pines" (l. 20). The perspective of the mountain, presented in the third section, is the perspective of eternity where "None can reply—all seems eternal now" (l. 75); and the fourth section offers the inverse of that eternal view—the perspective of mutability and mortality that sees that "The race / Of man, flies far in dread; his work and dwelling / Vanish . . ." (ll. 117–19).

These different sections, although obviously similar, do not offer merely different versions of the same message. If the struggle between "woods and winds" of the first section does not negate the possibility of seeing these same woods and winds creating a harmony between them, the relationship between the terms of eternity and mutability is even stronger. For it is not just that mutability and eternity are two different ways of conceiving time, but also that it becomes impossible for the poet to imagine eternity except in terms of mutability—the terms of generation in which earthquakes create epochs and broods of little earthquakes— or to image mutability except in the terms of eternity, in the form of a Power that "dwells apart in its tranquillity" (l. 96).

The poet begins the fifth and final section with a magnificent feat of calculated vagueness and understatement:

Mont Blanc yet gleams on high:—the power is there,
The still and solemn power of many sights,
And many sounds, and much of life and death.
[ll. 127–29]

The understatement registers, among other things, the poet's awareness that his thoughts about the mountain have not changed the universe—or even the mountain. He seems almost to struggle to see the mountain's continued existence as a reason for him to return to his struggle to see it in its materiality. Yet this final section of the poem recapitulates the earlier movement into a language that inexorably begins to treat the mountain landscape as *someone* to be understood not merely through the understanding but through an understanding that operates to complete and magnify its object through an aggrandizement Shelley calls love.

The mountain has "a voice" to "repeal / Large codes of fraud and woe" (ll. 80– 81) not because "The secret strength of things / Which governs thought" inhabits it but because the poet is its voice as he finds himself in the process of recognizing the impossibility of taking the material as merely material. Just as one can see the letters that go together to make up "Arve" and "Ravine of Arve" as an example of the material aspects of language but cannot see them as language without seeing them as implying something more than matter, so one can see the mountain as an example of materiality but cannot see it even as a mountain without seeing it as involving more than matter. The mountain can repeal "Large codes of fraud and woe" by making it clear that a love of humanity is easy if one can love a mountain that is physically inimical to man. And yet the final irony of the poem is that Shelley can conclude by asking the mountain his most famous question:

And what were thou, and earth, and stars, and sea,
If to the human mind's imaginings
Silence and solitude were vacancy?

[ll. 142–44]

With this question, he reminds the mountain that it needs him. The relationship between man and world has been painted in such a way as to make it clear that complementarity rather than direct communication is at issue in his version of language. But although he reminds the mountain of its need for him, his questions also have all the poignancy of a speech by a lover who still needs to argue his case. He may be a fit anti-type to the mountain, but he is still looking for a mountain who will understand him.

Even though the poem ends with a question directed to the mountain, Shelley's interest in Mont Blanc is, of course, predicated upon the impossibility of the mountain's ever taking any interest in him and answering. The mountain is matter, and its power resides to a very considerable extent in that fact; just as Milton's Eve was once "stupidly good," so matter is, in Shelley's account, "stupidly power-ful," and powerful more because of its stupidity than in spite of it. That is, its power depends upon its never being able to move out of the world of death. Because it can never be alive, it can never be subject to death; because it can never be conscious, it can never experience fear (or love or any other emotion, anticipatory or otherwise).

In light of the poem's final account of the mountain, the first four verse para-graphs might seem to represent a massive epistemological error and a mistake in love as well. For the first two verse paragraphs argue for resemblance between the human and the natural worlds in claiming that the same model can be used for both (the Arve is to the ravine as the "everlasting universe of things" is to the individual human mind) and in presenting the similarity between the two with a lover's air of pleasure in the discovery of himself in another. In this manner, Shelley addresses the ravine as if it were a version of himself:

Dizzy Ravine, and when I gaze on thee
I seem as in a trance sublime and strange
To muse on my own separate phantasy,
My own, my human mind. . . .

[ll. 34–37]

The reversion from thoughts of the ravine to thoughts of his own mind does not betoken any inappropriate narcissism but indicates, rather, the translation of the material to the human that is involved in any effort at making the scene intelligi-ble. As both the formal analogy and the poet's familiar address to the scene argue for the equivalence between the material and the human, Shelley pursues this thinking by analogy down its fallacious course as he attributes sublimity to the mountain in making it appear to transcend itself. Thus he speaks of the "Power in likeness of the Arve" as not like water but more than water as it comes "Bursting through these dark mountains like the flame / Of lightning through the tempest" (ll. 16–19) and of those "earthly rainbows stretched across the sweep / Of the etherial waterfall" (ll. 25–26) that refuse to occupy any single element or place;

the transfer of attributes from one element to another lends each an all-inclusiveness that none would have individually.

Of course, the phenomena that are presented as more than themselves because of the transfer of attributes *are* palpably more than themselves, in that the rainbow, while being an interaction of water and air, is made "earthly" whereas the waterfall produced by the passage of the water over the rocky earth is made "etherial." The distinct limit to the self-transcendence of these physical elements is, however, implicit in the conspicuous omission (for the moment) of the fire that emblemizes the animation of the elements. Although the water and the air, like the water and the earth, act together to produce a mutual self-transcendence of each, the crucial difference between these mutual magnifications and any real instance of sublime self-transcendence lies in the fact that these elements provide instances of action without representing agency.

If the apparent threat involved in any landscape that might be provocative of a sublime experience is that man (and mind) might be reduced to mere matter, the correspondent activity that occurs is that the poet's sublime account of Mont Blanc and the entire scene around it never allows matter to remain material but rather co-opts it or transmogrifies it by continually mistaking the activity of the material world for agency, by taking it to be as intentional as any human activity might be. Shelley insists virtually throughout the poem upon this confusion between activity and agency as he continually treats the mountain as a person (albeit a particularly large and powerful one). This programmatic confusion discloses a fundamental insight into the nature of sublime experience: in treating natural objects as occasions for sublime experience, one imputes agency (and therefore a moving spirit) to them. Although such imputation would, in other hands, perhaps be the basis for seeing the designedness of nature as an argument for the existence of God, for Shelley it instead identifies the sublime as the aesthetic operation through which one makes an implicit argument for the transcendent existence of man—not because man is able to survive the threat posed by the power of the material world but because he is able to domesticate the material world for the purposes of aesthetics by converting such a massive example of the power of the material world as Mont Blanc from an object into a found object. For what the sublime does for nature is to annex all that is material to the human by appropriating it for aesthetics. In this sense, Shelley in *Mont Blanc* discovers the same assertion of human power that Kant did when he distinguished between the sublime and the beautiful on the grounds that "we must seek a ground external to ourselves for the beautiful of nature, but seek it for the sublime merely in ourselves and in our attitude of thought, which introduces sublimity into the representation of nature."[17] At Mont Blanc, in the assertion of human power that any sublime experience represents, Shelley thus revamps the argument from design to redound to the credit of the human observer who converts the object into a found object, not merely matter but matter designed by its perceiver.

Moreover, in treating the sublime experience of Mont Blanc as not merely adapting the material to the purposes of the human and the supersensible (or spiritual) but as a discovery of the human in nature, Shelley collapses Kant's account of the "purposiveness without purpose" that we discover in aesthetic objects as he speaks of Mont Blanc as if it had purposes in relation to humans. Thus it is that the language of the poem continually moves from epistemological questions, questions of the poet's understanding, to love language in which all the questions are of his being understood.

NOTES

1. The best brief survey of the various debates about the poem appears in the notes to the poem in *Shelley's Poetry and Prose,* ed. Donald H. Reiman and Sharon B. Powers (New York: Norton, 1977), pp. 89–93.

2. Richard Holmes, *Shelley: The Pursuit* (London: Quartet Books, 1976), p. 342.

3. See Holmes's account, pp. 339–43.

4. Harold Bloom, *Shelley's Mythmaking* (Ithaca: Cornell University Press, 1969), p. 20. See also Bloom, *The Visionary Company* (Ithaca: Cornell University Press, 1971), p. 293.

5. Earl R. Wasserman, *Shelley: A Critical Reading* (Baltimore: Johns Hopkins University Press, 1971), pp. 221–38. Wasserman's reading remains, to my mind, the most impressive account of the poem.

6. Ibid., p. 224.

7. Ibid.

8. Ibid.

9. Bloom, *Shelley's Mythmaking,* p. 23.

10. *Shelley's Prose, or The Trumpet of a Prophecy,* ed. David Lee Clark (Albuquerque: University of New Mexico Press, 1954), p. 171.

11. Ibid., p. 170.

12. Ibid.

13. Edmund Burke, *A Philosophical Enquiry into the Origin of Our Ideas of the Sublime and Beautiful,* ed. J. T. Boulton (Notre Dame: University of Notre Dame Press, 1958), pp. 43 and 71.

14. Shelley's *Poetry and Prose,* p. 170.

15. *Letters of Shelley,* ed. F. I. Jones, 2 vols. (Oxford: Oxford University Press, 1964). 1, 499. Quoted in Bloom, *Shelley's Mythmaking,* p. 19, and in Holmes, *Shelley,* p. 340.

16. Immanuel Kant, *Critique of Judgment,* trans. J. H. Bernard (New York: Hafner, 1966), pp. 83–84.

17. Ibid., p. 84.

WILLIAM KEACH

Rhyme and the Arbitrariness of Language

Because such interest as Frances Ferguson's in the sublime is metaphysically oriented and founded on rather abstract linguistic theorizing, it tends to ignore the specific formal structuring by which sublime aestheticizing is achieved. Precisely that disregarded structuring becomes the focus of William Keach's more radically revisionary critique. His "return" to formalistic matters, however, is shaped by his acceptance of the importance of Ferguson's metaphysical-linguistic orientation. Thus where she remarks briefly on some punning, anagrammic details of the poem, his interest in "Mont Blanc" as a rhymed totality enables him to observe the special fashion in which Shelley "takes advantage of . . . the arbitrariness of linguistic signs" to make his formal artifice become "both a stay and a means of marking the chaos and blankness which are *Mont Blanc*'s special concern." In short, Keach specifies more exactly the sources and attributes of the sublimity to which Ferguson points, showing how rhyme is a resource "with which the poet verbally counters as well as encounters an experience of . . . sublimity."

Both Ferguson's and Keach's studies are poised against standard new-critical readings of *Mont Blanc,* such as Earl Wasserman's treatments of the poem in *The Subtler Language* (1959) and *Shelley: A Critical Reading* (1971) and Charles H. Vivian's "The One 'Mont Blanc' " (1955). If space permitted, we would have included G. Kim Blank's fine recent reading of the poem in *Wordsworth's Influence on Shelley* (cited in our headnote to this section), because his analysis builds on his predecessors' work by taking fully into account *Mont Blanc*'s relation to "Tintern Abbey"—thereby extending the significance of both Ferguson's and Keach's observations. The latter deserves another word of comment, for we suspect that *Mont Blanc* has frequently been taught in American college classrooms as if it were a poem in blank verse. When we survey the lengthy critical history of the poem, we are struck by the paucity of comment on the unusualness of the poem's rhyming. Analyses such as those of Keach manifest a revived attention to textual details that is distinctive of our epoch. The same kind of interest is visible, for one example, in Viscomi's essay in this collection, and for another example, in Brendan O'Donnell's splendidly comprehensive description of Wordsworth's use of multifarious poetic forms, *Numerous Verse: A Guide to the Stanzas and Metrical Structures of Wordsworth's Poetry* (1989).

From *Shelley's Style* (London: Methuen, 1984), pp. 194–200, 257–258.

'Before the chariot had begun to climb
  The opposing steep of that mysterious dell,
Behold a wonder worthy of the rhyme

'Of him who from the lowest depths of Hell
Through every Paradise and through all glory
  Love led serene . . .'
                                                    (469–74)

It is no accident that Shelley should rhyme on the word 'rhyme' in an allusion to Dante, nor was the decision to compose *The Triumph of Life* in terza rima an arbitrary one. But his decision some six years earlier that Mont Blanc was a wonder worthy of rhyme presents a much more challenging formal situation. Shelley's own note says that *Mont Blanc* 'rests its claim to approbation on an attempt to imitate the untameable wildness and inaccessible solemnity from which [his] feelings sprang'.[1] 'Untameable wildness' and 'inaccessible solemnity', without and within, both suggest that blank verse might have been the appropriate form for this subject. Wordsworth (in *The Prelude*), Coleridge (in the 'Hymn Before Sunrise, in the Vale of Chamouni')—and John Hollander too (in a wonderful parody of Shelley's poem called 'Mount Blank')[2]—all write about Mont Blanc in blank verse. But Shelley's poem, while creating the impression of blank verse with its massive periods and very frequent enjambment, uses rhyme in its 'attempt to imitate' an experience of the untameable and the inaccessible. Why?

The facts about rhyme in *Mont Blanc* are in themselves striking, particularly when measured against what must have been one of Shelley's formal models, Milton's *Lycidas*.[3] Of the 144 lines in *Mont Blanc,* only three end in words which have no rhyme elsewhere in the poem.[4] Three of the 193 lines in *Lycidas* are also unrhymed. There are only fifteen couplets in Shelley's poem, contrasted with thirty-four in Milton's (ten of these contain lines of different length), and six of the fifteen are relatively faint or imperfect. Curiously, however, two of these six imperfect couplets are repeated: 'for ever'/'river' in lines 9–10 are reversed as 'River'/'for ever' in lines 123–4; 'down'/'throne' in lines 16–17 are repeated phonetically though not semantically in 'down' / 'over-thrown' in lines 111–12. Even more curiously, there are eleven instances in *Mont Blanc* of words rhyming with themselves (usually over long stretches of verse), and in three of these eleven instances the same word appears in rhyming position not twice but three times.

One of the remarkable features of this extensive rhyming is the degree to which it is disguised or muted by enjambment. In the text Shelley published in 1817, seventy-three of the poem's 144 lines (one more than half) have no punctuation at the end. In *Lycidas,* by contrast, thirty-three of Milton's 193 lines are without terminal punctuation. In the *Defence* Shelley says of the language of Bacon's prose that 'it is a strain which distends, and then bursts the circumference of the hearer's mind, and pours itself forth . . . into the universal element with which it has perpetual sympathy' (*PP,* 485). The images Shelley uses about Bacon in this passage all have their parallels in the imagery of *Mont Blanc* (*burst* actually appears twice in the poem, at lines 11 and 18). There is much in the syntax and versification of *Mont Blanc* that invites us to apply these images—the recurrent Shelleyan pun on 'strain'; the activities of distending, bursting and pouring—to

Shelley's own style. But noticing the rhymes in *Mont Blanc* makes us think differently about the straining swell and flow of Shelley's lines. To treat the poem as if it were written in blank verse is to close our eyes, ears and minds to one of its greatest sources of poetic power.

There is no precedent for Shelley's crossing of extended blank-verse enjambment with irregular rhyme in a poem which raises such fundamental questions about the mind's powers and limitations. That he should rhyme with pervasive and provocative irregularity while going so far to create the feeling of blank verse is in keeping with a poem in which questions simultaneously propose and interrogate, in which the experience of blankness itself is both acknowledged and challenged. Considered from this inclusive perspective, rhyme in *Mont Blanc* is one important way in which Shelley's verbal imagination structures and shapes, without giving a closed or determinate pattern to, an experience which defies structuring and shaping. In a more specific sense, the cognitive play between or among rhyme words shows Shelley taking advantage of the way in which the very arbitrariness of linguistic signs he speaks of in the *Defence* can produce an expressive coincidence and thus a resource for a mind contending, ultimately, with its own and nature's blankness. There is no prior reason, for example, why 'waves' (2) and 'raves' (11) should rhyme. But they do, and the fact affords Shelley a distant yet powerful phonetic link that spans and condenses the relation in this opening verse paragraph between the mad rush of the 'vast river' and the 'everlasting universe of things' to which it metaphorically corresponds. As a dimension of poetic form wrought from the mysterious arbitrariness of language, Shelley's rhyme becomes both a stay against and a means of marking the chaos and blankness which are *Mont Blanc*'s special concerns.

In thinking about the purposes rhyme serves in *Mont Blanc,* we need to look at the way it functions both in terms of its own inherent possibilities and in relation to the syntax and rhythm of Shelley's periods. We must be careful not to isolate rhyme as the vehicle of the structuring, organizing intellect in easy contrast to the sweeping, impetuous emotional energy of the long, overflowing sentences: both are aspects of Shelley's 'attempt to imitate' an experience in which philosophical skepticism and impassioned intuition are held in suspension. Take the second couplet in the opening verse paragraph:

> Where waterfalls around it leap for ever,
> Where woods and winds contend, and a vast river
> Over its rocks ceaselessly bursts and raves.
>
> (9–11)

'For ever' and 'river' here seem at once to confirm the proposition with which the poem opens—'The everlasting universe of things / Flows through the mind' (1–2)—and yet to convey a certain probing openness, both because the rhyme is partial, imperfect (the imperfection stands out against the initial repetition of 'Where'/'Where'), and because the absence of any pause after 'river' leaves that line open to flow into the next. This couplet is again left open in part IV, where its reversal shifts the emphasis from 'river' to 'for ever' ('all seems eternal now' the speaker has said in line 75, after first taking in the summit of Mont Blanc). The couplet is followed by 'raves' in line 11, by 'waves' in line 125:

> and one majestic River,
> The breath and blood of distant lands, for ever
> Rolls its loud waters to the ocean waves,
> Breathes its swift vapours to the circling air.
>
> (123–6)

The last word in this passage, 'air', is part of what is perhaps the most striking group of postponed or suspended rhyme-words in *Mont Blanc*. Part II ends with the word 'there', with no immediate companion or echo: 'till the breast / From which they fled recalls them, thou art there! (47–8). That this line appears to be unrhymed is appropriate in a passage about the momentary, precarious apprehension of 'some faint image' (47) of the awesome, personified Ravine of Arve. But 'there' does eventually get its complement in the insubstantial 'air' at the end of part IV. Once this very distant rhyme has been completed, it is immediately confirmed at the end of the first line of part V: 'Mont Blanc yet gleams on high:— the power is there' (127). This is the only point in the poem where a couplet spans two verse paragraphs (although 'raves' and 'Ravine' between parts I and II, both of which contain anagrams of the name 'Arve', and 'feel' and 'streams' between parts III and IV, may seem to foreshadow such a spanning). Yet to link two separate sections together by rhyme in this way is also to pull the couplet apart: every resolution in *Mont Blanc* has at least an undertow of dissolution. The 'there'/'air'/ 'there' sequence is extended a few lines later in part V, but this time the sense of the passage cuts across even the tentativeness of those previous assertions that some presence is 'there': 'in the lone glare of day, the snows descend / Upon that Mountain; none beholds them there' (131–2). The internal rhyme in these lines ('glare'/'there') illuminates the discrepancy between the mind's power of perception and its limitations in gaining access to reality's ultimate source. The same daylight which renders things visible in the speaker's immediate realm of experience 'glares' upon the snows of Mont Blanc—but 'there', remote and apart from any beholder, daylight itself seems to lose all connection with human intellection.

The 'there' (48)/'there' (127)/'there' (132) pattern is Shelley's finest exploitation in *Mont Blanc* of identical rhyme, of a word rhyming (and re-rhyming) with itself. Homonymic rhyme (punning rhyme, *rime très riche*), in which entire rhyme-words are phonetically identical but semantically different, is a related but distinct phenomenon. Hollander assents to the prejudice against such rhyme when he argues that because of 'the crucial relation between the effect of word stress and the quality of rhyme in English . . . *rime très riche* is always in a sense, *rime pauvre*.'[5] But the two instances of it in *Mont Blanc* indicate how alert Shelley could be to the ways in which even flamboyantly fortuitous rhyme could help him mark the mind's response to the wild and the inaccessible. 'Throne' (17)/'overthrown' (112) is not a pure example (it is analogous phonetically, though not semantically, to 'form'/ 'deform' in *The Triumph of Life*), but given Shelley's politics it might appear to be a suggestive one. The suggestiveness is not, however, exactly predictable. Although earthly thrones, so often the embodiments for Shelley of 'large codes of fraud and woe' (81), are implicitly included in what will be 'overthrown' by the 'Power' in part IV as it flows down from its remote abode, that 'Power' has itself been imaged as occupying a 'secret throne'. So 'throne' stands distantly and indirectly in relation to 'overthrown' as subject, not object, a relation in keeping with Shelley's skeptical ambivalence towards the 'Power'. The fact that both 'throne' and 'overthrown' form imperfect couplets with 'down' (16, 111) further complicates the suggestiveness of this rhyme group.

The other homonymic rhyme in *Mont Blanc* affords a purer example of this phenomenon and more telling evidence of Shelley's resourcefulness in handling what would appear to be deliberately restricted verbal possibilities. At the beginning of part II, when he first names the Ravine of Arve as the immediate location of his experience, he addresses the ravine as 'Thou many-coloured, many-voiced vale' (13). Twelve lines later, when the first of these compound adjectives is expanded and particularized, the 'vale' becomes, or is seen to contain, a 'veil':[6]

> Thine earthly rainbows stretched across the sweep
> Of the ethereal waterfall, whose veil
> Robes some unsculptured image . . .
>
> (25–7)

'Poetry', Shelley says in the *Defence*, '. . . arrests the vanishing apparitions which haunt the interlunations of life, and veiling them, or in language or in form, sends them forth among mankind" (*PP*, 505). One is again tempted to follow this line of thought and figuration and apply the images in *Mont Blanc* to the poem itself, to see the 'ethereal waterfall' as a metaphor for the poem's own verbal veiling of what may be accessible only to momentary, vanishing intuition. The 'veil' in these lines, as so often in Shelley, has a double valence—it simultaneously conceals and reveals—and the movement from 'vale' to 'veil' is by no means entirely negative (compare the function of Iris and 'her many coloured scarf' in *The Triumph of Life*, 357). There is a sense in which this aspect of the 'vale' hides the 'unsculptured image' behind it; there is also a sense, partly enforced by the verb 'Robes', that the 'veil' is what makes this unspecified ('some'), uncreated image exists for the mind at all. Shelley's homonymic rhyme signals the precarious balance and interaction between skepticism and visionary imagination so important in this section and throughout the poem.

Rhyme in *Mont Blanc* is not, then, as 'wildly irregular' as it has been thought to be. It is sufficiently irregular to help evoke the 'untameable wildness' Shelley spoke of: some of the most interesting rhymes in the poem are so distant and so muted by distended syntax that the reader may find them as 'remote' and 'inaccessible' as Mont Blanc itself. With the three unrhymed lines Shelley's rhyme remains open, partly unresolved. Yet rhyme is there as one of the resources with which the poet verbally counters as well as encounters an experience of threatening power and sublimity. A glance at Shelley's final question, together with the sentence that precedes it, may help to confirm our sense of why he did not ask about Mont Blanc in blank verse:

>   The secret strength of things
> Which governs thought, and to the infinite dome
> Of heaven is as a law, inhabits thee!
> And what were thou, and earth, and stars, and sea,
> If to the human mind's imaginings
> Silence and solitude were vacancy?
>
> (139–44)

At the beginning of the poem, 'things' (1) became Shelley's first rhyme-word by finding its phonetic complement in 'secret springs' (4), a phrase which appears prominently and characteristically in the opening section of Hume's *Enquiry Concerning Human Understanding* as a metaphor for the unknowable first principle 'by which the human mind is actuated in its operations'.[7] Here at the end of *Mont Blanc*, 'things' finds a rhyme with a different, apparently less skeptical resonance in 'imaginings', although the difference diminishes when one takes in the immediate context of those words: the 'secret strength of things' in line 139; the if-clause and interrogative syntax surrounding 'the human mind's imaginings'. 'Thee' in line 140 forms a couplet with 'sea' and thus supports the initial 'And' through which the final question is joined logically to what precedes it. And does 'vacancy' belong in this rhyming sequence with 'thee' and 'sea'? It both does and does not: the '-cy' suffix rhymes with 'thee' and 'sea', but imperfectly, because it is rhythmically unstressed and because it is attached to the root *vacan(s)*. Shelley simultaneously draws that critical last word into and separates it from the central rhyme of the entire passage—'vacancy' seems both to yield to and to resist the rhyming power of the compositional will—and in the process he makes us conscious of the ambiguous categorizations on which rhyme depends in the first place.

The rhymes of *Mont Blanc* are part of Shelley's response to a landscape and to a philosophical tradition—'to the Arve's commotion, / A loud, lone sound no other sound can tame' (31–2), and to Hume's argument that the 'ultimate springs and principles' of phenomenal reality 'are totally shut up from human curiosity and enquiry', that the mind's attempts to make sense of them as necessity are nothing more than arbitrary impositions:

> every effect is a distinct event from its cause. It could not, therefore, be discovered in the cause, and the first invention or conception of it, *a priori*, must be entirely arbitrary. And even after it is suggested, the conjunction of it with the cause must appear equally arbitrary.[8] (*An Enquiry Concerning Human Understanding*, iv.1)

Shelley's irregular rhymes do not tame the wildness of a 'sound no other sound can tame', nor can they break the inaccessible silence at the summit of Mont Blanc. But they impose on his and our experience of both an order of language that accepts the arbitrary and submits it to the deliberations of art. They are part of the evidence the poem offers that the arbitrary connections of thought and language need not leave the 'human mind's imaginings' in vacancy.

NOTES

1. Shelley's note appears at the end of the Preface to *History of a Six Weeks' Tour through a Part of France, Switzerland, Germany, and Holland*, London, T. Hookham Jr, C. and J. Ollier, 1817.

2. The poem is in *Tales Told of the Fathers*, New York, Atheneum, 1975.

3. See Judith Chernaik, *The Lyrics of Shelley*, Cleveland, Case Western Reserve University Press, 1972, 288 n.4. She points out that the rhymes in the Bodleian MS. of *Mont Blanc* are more regularly interwoven than those of the 1817 printed text and suggests that 'Shelley may have been consciously striving in 1817 for the more irregular rhyme effects of *Lycidas*.' I refer here to the text of *Lycidas* in the *Complete Poems and Major Prose*, ed. Merritt Y. Hughes, New York, Odyssey, 1957. For excellent

accounts of Milton's rhyming in *Lycidas,* see Ants Oras, 'Milton's early rhyme schemes and the structure of *Lycidas*', *MP,* 52, 1954–5, 12–22, and Joseph A. Wittreich Jr, 'Milton's "Destin'd urn": the art of *Lycidas*', *PMLA,* 84, 1968, 60–70. Wittreich's analysis is particularly relevant to Shelley's rhyming in *Mont Blanc,* since he argues that Milton's 'encompassing scheme' is not confined to patterns within individual verse paragraphs but 'envelops the poem and its various parts in a massive unity' (61). *Lycidas* is listed among the poems read by Shelley and Mary Shelley in 1815, the year before *Mont Blanc* was written (*Mary Shelley's Journal,* 48).

4. The unrhymed words in *Mont Blanc* are 'forms' (62), 'spread' (65) and 'sun' (133). Neville Rogers, *The Complete Poetical Works of Percy Bysshe Shelley,* Oxford, Clarendon Press, 1975, II, 355, says that Locock also counted 'sky' (108) and 'world' (113) as rhymeless. But if we look at the poem as a whole, 'sky' (108) repeats 'sky' at the end of line 60 and rhymes with 'lie' (19, 54), 'by' (45) and 'high' (52, 70); 'world' (113) repeats 'world' at the end of line 49 and rhymes with 'unfurled' (53). *Lycidas* had traditionally been analyzed paragraph by paragraph, in which case there appear to be ten unrhymed lines. But looking at the total rhyme pattern of the poem as Wittreich does yields only three; see 'Art of *Lycidas*', 63, 69–70.

5. John Hollander, *Vision and Resonance: Two Senses of Poetic Form,* New York, Oxford University Press, 1975, 118. See Derek Attridge on the different functions of rhyme in English and French verse in 'Dryden's dilemma, or, Racine refashioned: the problem of the English dramatic couplet', *YES,* 9, 1979, 62–5.

6. Cf. David Simpson, *Irony and Authority in Romantic Poetry,* Totowa, N.J., Rowan & Littlefield, 1979, 233, n.15.

7. Ed. L.A. Selby-Bigge, rev. P.H. Nidditch, Oxford, Clarendon Press, 1975, 14. See also 30, 33, 42, 66. 'Secret springs' receives additional emphasis by forming the poem's first couplet with 'brings' in line 5. If this phrase is a Humean allusion, it developed late in Shelley's revisions; he wrote 'secret caves' both in the Bodleian draft and in the recently discovered fair copy. See Chernaik, *The Lyrics of Shelley,* 288, and Judith Chernaik and Timothy Burnett, 'The Byron and Shelley notebooks in the Scrope Davies find', *RES,* n.s. 29, 1978, 45–9.

8. Ed. Selby-Bigge, 30.

TILOTTAMA RAJAN

The Broken Mirror: The Identity of the Text in Shelley's Triumph of Life

This analysis of *The Triumph of Life* from Rajan's new book, *The Supplement of Reading: Figures of Understanding in Romantic Theory and Practice* (1990), is rewarding in diverse ways, but not least as a subsuming revision of her earlier study of the poem in *Dark Interpreter: The Discourse of Romanticism* (1980). Her critical self-refashioning, however, is peculiarly significant in deriving from and yet going decisively beyond Paul de Man's influential essay, "Shelley Disfigured," in *Deconstruction and Criticism* (1979). Rajan shows that *The Triumph of Life,* while essentially deconstructive in character, is not an exercise in self-erasure. Rajan's revision begins with her "post-deconstructive" principle that "the supplement of reading" is a process "in which the positive essence of the work must be grasped across the barrier of the text's negativity, and in which the reading does not simply complete the creative process but compensates for the destructive momentum of the latter" (*Supplement*, p. 25).

Rajan thus takes a important new step in advancing deconstructive criticism, moving it away from its simpler, and often nihilistic, manifestations toward possibilities of illuminating how poetry such as Shelley's is shaped by a process in which "negative statements are in their turn negated." This process, closely equivalent to the Blake's theologically derived concept of *kenosis,* reveals not the mere cancellation of inherited tropes that preoccupied de Man but also the more complex fashion in which obscurity may arise from the "shadow that futurity casts upon the present." Illustrated here again, therefore, is that absorptive encompassing by which scholarly criticism moves ahead, by adapting methods and ideas of previous critics even as it transforms them into new techniques for attaining new kinds of insight, insight both into how particular poems function and how those poems may be experienced in new social conditions.

Rajan's latest book demonstrates the powerful hermeneutic forces accessible to an imaginatively deconstructive critic. Rajan is able to define how Shelley criticizes even while making use of his literary tradition and to suggest how Shelley's participative critique *in* the poem facilitates an astute reader's capacity to create meanings of it, allowing us, as the poem's narrator is invited by Rousseau, to risk becoming actor rather than mere spectator.

From *The Supplement of Reading: Figures of Understanding in Romantic Theory and Practice* (Ithaca, N.Y.: Cornell University Press, 1990), pp. 323–349. Copyright © 1990 by Cornell University. Used by permission of the publisher, Cornell University Press.

At first sight, *The Triumph of Life* seems simply to dismantle the assumptions of *Prometheus Unbound*. Not only does it recapitulate negatively such motifs as the chariot of the hour; as a fragment it aborts meaning, where as theater *Prometheus* produced it. No analysis of the poem can now ignore the seminal essay by Paul de Man that sees the diegetic level of the text as preempting all attempts to approach it thematically. All interpretations of the poem hitherto have assumed that it 'says' something, that it has a content other than the processes of its own language. Such interpretations would include those of Bloom and Woodman, who make the poem didactic or apocalyptic, viewing it as a critique of Rousseau for having been seduced by nature and perhaps as a rejection of life in the manner of *Adonais*. But they would also include more recent ones like my own in *Dark Interpreter,* which deconstructs the binary oppositions crucial to earlier readings only to make the poem's indeterminacy the regenerative prelude to what it does not quite succeed in saying. My reading elides the fragmentary status of the poem and provides a hermeneutic completion for it by arguing that it is in the process of rehabilitating Rousseau. His shifting view of himself is thus explained by the fact that he is in transit from the Platonic repudiation of the phenomenal world associated with the sacred few to an existential embrace of life in which activity is its own Sisyphean reward.[1] Describing a range of interpretations that either view the movement of the poem as negative (a rejection of life) or positive (a discarding of old positions in order to work through to new ones), de Man dismisses them as captive to an idealizing genetic metaphor, which insists that there is psychological growth in the poem, that it moves toward some insight. Instead, he shifts his attention to its rhetoric, which he characterizes in terms of erasure, disfiguration, the syntax tying itself into a knot. In figuring the poem as a scene of reading in the larger setting of Western culture, de Man sees it as challenging the hermeneutic foundations of that culture, which represents reading as the recovery of something meaningful and its application to the life of the reader, and which thus places texts as spots of time to which we can repair for increased self-understanding.[2]

The power of de Man's essay lies in his exposure of the ways in which previous readings have made something out of the poem without attending to its most pervasive feature: the status of a language unable either to state or to perform anything that is not already different from itself. Yet it remains to be seen whether the poem's lack of 'identity' renders it 'unreadable' or brings into being a reconception of the supplement of reading. For one thing, de Man (as he would be the first to admit) *has* provided a 'reading,' by making form take the place of a vanishing content through a hypostasis of the poem's method. Or to put it differently, even this text, which asks to be approached diegetically rather than mimetically, has a referent, that referent being the process of the poem itself. If we grant that de Man has provided a reading, the issue raised by his concept of unreadability is not whether the poem has any meaning, but whether the way it foregrounds its own discourse invalidates its power to create something meaningful. Put differently, the issue is whether the poem still permits reading as it is understood by the developing tradition of hermeneutics discussed in this book. The greatest challenge to answering this question affirmatively is not the language of the posthumously printed text but the tangle of the manuscript in which Shelley himself left the poem. De Man does not refer to the manuscript except in passing, but it plays an important symbolic role in his reading, the mutilated text becoming a disfiguration of any attempt to read Shelley or to read Shelley as a paradigm of romanticism. As a synecdoche for Shelley's drowned body, which is inscribed in its last page, the manuscript thwarts our attempts to incorporate the scandal of disfiguration into literary history.[3] We could speculate that if de Man had discussed its details, it would have become the trace left by an irreducible aporia at the heart of language and the site of our submission to that aporia. Thus, any attempt to re-vision the poem's discourse must deal not only with its language but also with the intervention made by the manuscript in the institutional structures of literary criticism.

Our discussion of the poem will focus on how it functions: on its repetitions, its syntax, and on its foregrounding of speech over writing, as elements that create differences within the rhetoric of erasure, so that disfiguration is not just the effacement of figures but also the production of new figures. In many ways this discussion subsumes my own previous analysis, which saw Shelley's poem as generated by a process of self-revision. Crucial to that analysis was the unsettling of a pattern of binary oppositions by which earlier readings had schematized the poem so as to criticize Rousseau for participating in life. Such oppositions included those between the sacred few and the multitude that was not wise enough to avoid life (ll. 128–37, *SPP*); between the bards of elder time and Rousseau himself, whose lack of distance from the world he wanted to change resulted in his infecting his audience with his own misery (ll. 274–81, *SPP*); and most importantly between the two shapes, the shape all light generated by the spark with which heaven initially lit Rousseau's spirit, and the shape in the car that replaced it when he put on the "disguise" of life. There is no question that the text is profoundly ambivalent about "Life," and that that ambivalence disrupts not only the earlier view that the poem was written by a 'Platonic' rather than 'radical' Shelley,[4] but also the recent emphasis on its semiotic nihilism. But instead of embedding that ambivalence in a genetic narrative that absorbs aporia into the dialectic of Rousseau's (and the poet's) maturation, I will assume that my earlier reading is a heuristic construction. It must therefore be reinscribed in the text that generates it, and is present in the text only as a trace and not as what Godwin called the poem's 'tendency.' The details of this reading are less important than the linguistic processes that make it possible, while also generating the kind of reading provided by de Man. And these processes, too complex to be summed up in the term 'effacement,'[5] are in some form intrinsic to all poetic narrative, even though they may be foregrounded in this poem. But the details of the reading are also not unimportant. For the eschewing of the thematic in favor of the figural elides both the possibility that the nature of the figural may be altered by what we pick out as being (dis)figured, and the recognition that much Yale poststructuralism takes form as a thematics of figures: in other words, as a reading that can be challenged thematically as well as linguistically.

For the sake of convenience, we can divide the poem into three sections: an opening segment in which 'Shelley' falls asleep in a transfigured natural landscape only to witness its transformation into the dismal scene of the procession; a dialogue between him and Rousseau in which the latter describes in detail the significance of the same procession; and a dream narrative that describes an experience parallel to 'Shelley's' initial experience, namely, the transformation of the shape all light that Rousseau conceived at the moment of his creative birth into the shape in the chariot with its attendant procession. On the most obvious level the poem tells a characteristic romantic story about the collapse of illusion.

Its return (three times) to the procession emphasizes in an emblematic way the chariot that erases hope and the chain of historical figures without origin or end. But the fact that the poem's title does not specify whose triumph it details (that of Life over humankind, or the triumph that is life, the triumph of surviving) suggests that it cannot simply be reduced to its most traumatic images: the car that wipes out what preceded it as the shape obliterates Rousseau, and the procession of disfigured dancers who follow it. These are in turn the figures that de Man uses to represent figuration and must be set against other images whose presence suggests that language is a form of the unconscious, and that so far we have only succeeded in representing, not in understanding it. Among these other images are the car's "creative ray" (l. 533, *SPP*); the association of life with dance, music, and embroidery (ll. 98, 110, 142, 448, *SPP*); and the image of life as a cleaving apart that sculpts the "marble brow of youth," allowing form to emerge only through disfiguration (l. 523, *SPP*).

We can locate the poem's indeterminacy partly in its repetitions: the repetition of the procession; the repetition of 'Shelley' as Rousseau; the temporal repetition of Rousseau's life in the form of a retrospective narration; and finally the repetition of Rousseau's attempt to understand the core experience of the transformation of something beautiful into something hideous in the discursive form of a conversation with 'Shelley,' and in the symbolic form of a dream sequence unimpeded by conceptual filters. Because the poem is a dream, its repetitive organization suggests an incomplete attempt at mastery: an attempt that we repeat each time we interpret the poem. Blocking progress, the figure of reading as repetition halts any attempt at the teleological completion of the poem. But though repetition may be intended to confirm trauma, it also allows reading-again to become the production of differences. We do not repeat something in different words if we mean to say exactly the same thing. Repetition implies the insufficiency of what was said: we repeat because there is still something more to be said, something more to be read in the political unconscious whose shadows are mirrored in this poem. Moreover, the attempt to understand the poem's core experience is repeated by Rousseau at different stages of his life: as the young man who experiences the transformation of the shape, as the older man who remembers it, and as the subject in dialogue with Shelley, in conversation with a future that discloses new perspectives to him even as it seems to close itself against him. It is repeated by 'Shelley,' both as the autonomously later subject who sees the procession, and then as the subject in dialogue with the past who re-views the procession in his conversation with Rousseau. By repeating itself at different points on a personal and on a historical axis, by allowing these axes to intersect in different ways, the poem generates more than one perspective from which we can view it and gives to the repetition that is reading a complex and still unfinished historical dimension.

The Triumph is organized so as to foreground repetition on a narrative level and so as to make it a figure for understanding. But the poem's structure simply raises to a level of self-consciousness what is a feature of all extensive utterance: namely, a tendency to repeat along different axes, to illustrate concepts through figures or fables, or conversely to reduce symbols or narratives to conceptual paraphrases. We become aware of how the poem is complicated by such micrological repetitions in the very first segment. For the most part 'Shelley' describes the followers of the car with condescension and takes the view that their error is involvement in life. But his argument is constantly disarticulated by the figures he uses to convey it, this despite his attachment to similes, which maintain a formal commitment to the exact equivalence of image and referent. For instance, in dismissing the procession he tells us that it includes:

> All but the sacred few who could not tame
> Their spirits to the Conqueror, but as soon
> As they had touched the world with living flame
>
> Fled back like eagles to their native noon.
>
> (ll. 128–31, *SPP*)

This binary opposition between the multitude who are captivated by life and those who see through it is more explicitly unsettled in Rousseau's account of the procession. But even here it is undermined by the description of the sacred few as "fleeing," Thel-like, from the generative world, and by the fact that the noon of transphenomenal vision that they embrace only seems to be outside the temporal cycle. And on the other hand, the dancers in the procession are described with an energy and vitality that belies their portrayal as part of a sad pageantry. One example is the account of how they are destroyed by their own desire for life. To begin with, they are described as moths attracted by the light (ll. 153–54, *SPP*), but then they are paralleled to

> . . . two clouds into one vale impelled
> That shake the mountains when their lightnings mingle
> And die in rain.
>
> (ll. 155–57, *SPP*)

The second simile displaces the first by continuing its emphasis on self-destruction but making this a generative rather than a futile activity: productive of rain that will fertilize the land. This is only one example of how a statement is unraveled by its multiplied figurative repetition and how the process of articulation generates new perceptions about the car's followers which refigure the pageant of error as a vital and Dionysiac dance.

The dialogue of text and subtext in 'Shelley's' monologue generates quite naturally his repetition of himself in the person of Rousseau and his placing of himself in a dialogical setting. Rousseau seems at first to confirm 'Shelley's' rejection of life. But a measure of how unsettled his position is is the discrepancy between his initial advice to 'Shelley,' "Forbear / To join the dance" (ll. 188–89, *SPP*), and his later suggestion that involvement is the only means to understand it:

> "But follow thou, and from spectator turn
> Actor or victim in this wretchedness
>
> "And what thou wouldst be taught I then may learn
> From thee.—
>
> (ll. 305–8, *SPP*)

Nor does Rousseau's account of the procession simply duplicate 'Shelley's,' for the participants are now named and individualized, which makes it difficult to dismiss them as an anonymous multitude. The roll call of names, moreover, includes all the great figures of Western culture and leaves us wondering who the "few" who have avoided life might be. Bacon, compared in the manuscript to an eagle and thus imagistically linked to the sacred few,[6] is in the procession, as is Napoleon with his "eagle's pinion" (l. 222, *SPP*). But it now seems to be Bacon's error that like the sacred few he wanted more than the phenomenal world and tried to force "The Proteus shape of Nature" to yield him a truth (ll. 269–71, *SPP*). Socrates, once exempt from the procession, seems to enter it vicariously through Plato, who "Expiates the joy and woe his master knew not" (l. 255, *SPP*), as if Plato's very inferiority is a greater knowledge and Socrates' superiority a sin. Plato, moreover, has been conquered by "love" (l. 258, *SPP*), not something for which we can criticize him, especially since Socrates in avoiding woe was also ignorant of joy. Though repeating 'Shelley's' account of the procession, Rousseau's is actually quite different. One could do an extensive thematic analysis of the section, showing how as he speaks, Rousseau creates a space in which he can think and in which he can unravel not only his earlier radicalism but also his present condemnation of himself for having entered life. It is specifically the diacritical nature of dialogue which causes it to unsettle and generate penumbral positions, for the presence of the other person makes us recognize that we are other than what we are, and yet that we are not the other or the other's perception of us. But my concern is also with a character-istic linguistic feature of the poem, which complicates the movement of syntactic erasure. I have in mind the way in which negative statements are constituted on the trace of positive ones, or to be more precise, the way in which negative statements are in their turn negated, so as to produce the trace of something positive, though only as a shadow that futurity casts upon the present.

We notice how often the trace of self-assertion is masked within Rousseau's statement that he is *not* something, or to put it differently, how often erasure generates a construction, both in terms of syntax and in terms of the syntax of identity and action. A significant example is the passage on the bards of elder time, which has been edited differently by Mary Shelley and by Donald Reiman, thus raising the ancillary question of how the state of the manuscript affects our attempts to (de)construct the poem's significance. Mary Shelley's version, as Reiman's transcription indicates, was deleted, though less definitively than he implies. However, I begin with it partly because it was the text that most people read until Reiman published his reading text of the poem in the 1977 Norton critical edition. Moreover, given the unfinished state of this poem, in which conve-nient deletions are not always made and final intentions are hard to extract, no deletion can be sufficiently absolute to counteract the material force of the manu-script as a palimpsest in which the trace of an earlier version survives in emenda-tions that repeat and displace it. For instance:

"See the great bards of elder time, who quelled

"The passions which they sung, as by their strain
May well be known: their living melody
Tempers its own contagion to the vein

"Of those who are infected with it—I
Have suffered what I wrote, or viler pain!
And so my words have seeds of misery—

"Even as the deeds of others, not as theirs."
And then he pointed to a company.

(ll. 274–82)[7]

Grammatically, these lines are destabilized by a curious tension between Rousseau's statement that he is *not* the equal of the bards and the self-assertive position of the personal pronoun in l. 278, which prevents them from neatly settling into a representation of Rousseau as inferior. Entangled in the next line (279) is a sense that Rousseau has suffered more than the bards and thus is *not* as great as them, but also has lived at a greater intensity. Even more interesting are lines 280–81. They castigate Rousseau for writing words that have destructive consequences in the world of action and therefore are "not as theirs," not like the tranquilizing words of the bards. Yet this does not exhaust the meaning of "not as theirs," which dangles oddly at the end of the line, attempting to erase the forceful impression of what Rousseau *has* done by reintroducing the bards in a rather unprepossessing and pronominal way as something that Rousseau is not, through a word ("theirs") that has no clear antecedent in something actually achieved by the bards. To elaborate, it is not clear whether "theirs" refers to the words of the bards or to their deeds, which are not "as the deeds of others." And at this point we begin to recognize that perhaps the bards have no deeds, but only words, and that in this they are not like Rousseau, whose words reach out beyond the monastery of language. My point is that at no place in Rousseau's discourse are grammar and statement fully adequate to each other, so that the grammar paradoxically deconstructs the poem's logic of erasure, leaving a residue, a trace, that makes it different from itself.

What emerges from this analysis is that although the text is constantly erasing itself, that process is by no means unidirectional. In attempting to deny the value of his own work, Rousseau is unable to construct the bards as a positive counterpoint and instead reconstructs their position by telling us what it is not. The result of this double negation is to efface his self-rejection, but without immediately representing himself in a positive light. The double negation dilutes the force of the binary opposition by which Rousseau tries to measure his failure against the norm furnished by the bards. But on the other hand, the fact that his rehabilitation is initially no more than a syntactic trace, and the fact that his assertion of his own achievement is deferred to a passage some stanzas later (ll. 292–95, *SPP*) gives this self-assertion a tentative and supplementary quality. The vindication of Rousseau also leaves out something—which is perhaps why the manuscript could not be finished. We will return at the end of this chapter to the hermeneutic problems posed by the manuscript. But for the present it is worth noting that the line about which there is disagreement exists in three manuscript states: an 'original' state (already a reading that jumps from f. 33r. to f. 33v., omitting 'irrelevant' material) the version chosen by Mary Shelley, and the version (by no means final) chosen by Reiman. Set in between the two other versions of the line, the anxious negativity of the one we have just analyzed becomes all the more interesting:

1. Thus have my words been seeds of misery—
   Even as the deeds of others—*even as* theirs
   And then he pointed to a company

   [original; italics mine]

2. "And so my words have seeds of misery—

   "Even as the deeds of others, not as theirs."
   And then he pointed to a company,

   [Mary Shelley's version]

3. "And so my words were seeds of misery—
   Even as the deeds of others."—"Not as theirs,"
   I said—he pointed to a company

   [Reiman's version]

Reiman's version, to which we will return, breaks up line 281 and assigns the second half to 'Shelley' instead of to Rousseau (a questionable attribution, since the manuscript at no point uses quotation marks). In the 'original' version, (reconstructed by undoing Shelley's cancellations), it seems that Rousseau speaks the entire line and that its meaning is relatively straightforward: his words sow misery, like the deeds of others, "even as" the deeds of those to whom he then points. In the intermediate version Rousseau reassigns the antecedent of "theirs" from the company of despots to the bards: his words are like the deeds of others, and not as theirs (the words [?] of the bards [?]). In Reiman's version, which does not definitively replace the second one, the poem once again avoids the double negative. The words "not as theirs" are reassigned so that they neither support nor confuse the opposition between Rousseau and the bards. Rather, they prepare the way for Rousseau's later distinction between creative and destructive forms of power by having 'Shelley' differentiate Rousseau's verbal deeds from the actions of the despots: his deeds are "Not as theirs," not like the atrocities they commit. Somewhere in between an opposition that devalues Rousseau and an uncharacteristic response by 'Shelley' that rehabilitates him is Mary Shelley's version, a version that makes the positive a trace within the negative. In this interstice in Rousseau's speech, he emerges as the difference between a self-rejection in which he cannot find identity and a self-assertion whose lack of finality is evident in the fact that the poem continues, as if this is just one more figure cast on the "fragile glass" (l. 247, *SPP*) in which identity (dis)appears:

>   —"Their power was given
> But to destroy," replied the leader—"I
> Am one of those who have created, even

> "If it be but a world of agony."—
>   (ll. 292–95, *SPP*)

The self-displacing energies of speech are equally evident in Reiman's version of the passage, which seems at first to invalidate our reading. Removing the awkward phrase "not as theirs" from Rousseau's speech, Reiman tidies up what Rousseau says and allows it the neatness of a straightforward opposition. But the new version is no simpler, because the referent of what is now 'Shelley's' half-line intervention is less clear than we have made it seem, depending as it does on whether we connect the phrase to what precedes or to what follows it. We can take the antecedent of "theirs" to be the bards, in which case 'Shelley' seems to be confirming Rousseau's self-repudiation by adding to the latter's claim that his words are like vicious deeds a clarification that tells us that Rousseau's words are indeed unlike the words of the bards: "Not as theirs." Alternatively, we can take the statement as referring to the despots 'Shelley' proceeds to list, in which case he is dissenting from Rousseau's self-condemnation to observe that Rousseau's verbal deeds have not produced the misery created by tyrants and demagogues. It seems logical to connect 'Shelley's' intervention to what precedes it and to see him as condemning Rousseau, because that is what 'he' usually does. Moreover, it is Rousseau (not 'Shelley') who points to Caesar and Constantine, so that the list of despots does not seem to come as an illustration of 'Shelley's' statement. On the other hand, it is just as logical to connect 'Shelley's' intervention to what follows it, because it is after all he who recognizes tyranny for what it is, thus enabling Rousseau to make his subsequent distinction between creative and destructive power.[8] At issue is whether 'Shelley' repudiates or rehabilitates Rousseau, and the problem cannot be resolved because he seems to do both. Diverging from Mary Shelley's version in the assignment of words to characters, Reiman's version differs only in extending the entanglement of positive and negative from Rousseau to 'Shelley.' In the course of the dialogue Rousseau moves from self-rejection to a self-justification that, being an equal and opposite reaction, has no final authority. In his brief intervention, and in the silent meditation on tyranny that follows it, 'Shelley' exhibits a similar ambivalence produced, it would seem, by the tendency of extended discourse (whether silent or verbal) to revive the traces of what it does not say.

If the sense of poetry as difference emerges linguistically at the level of the poem's grammar and generically from its dialogue form, it is also presented mythopoeically in the scene of Rousseau's creative birth, where he imagines the shape all light that later becomes the destructive shape in the car. The background in which the shape appears is a complex intertexture of light and shadow, shadow and substance:

> "but all the place

> "Was filled with many sounds woven into one
> Oblivious melody."
> > (ll. 339–41, *SPP*)

Though this is apparently a scene of paradisal origins, oblivion alone makes us ignore that it is woven of many elements. Of particular interest throughout the poem are the figures of music and dance, but specifically in this passage of melody, for herein lies the deconstruction of Rousseau's oblivious perception of unity. We may think of Nietzsche's use of music in *The Birth of Tragedy* to symbolize the originary difference that is the ground of all systems of representation. But Shelley himself discusses music in the *Defence,* in terms of a vertical/referential axis and a horizontal/associative axis, which at another point he attributes separately to poetry and all the other arts, respectively. Harmony is the internal adjustment of sounds to their referents, but melody is the unschematized play of external and internal impressions over the mind (*SPP,* p. 480), a perpetual motion of impressions that develop relations among each other that interpose between conception and expression. Hume, similarly, had linked music to the interpresence of apparently separate elements within a syntagmatic chain. In discussing the passions, he compares the mind to a stringed instrument "where, after each stroke, the vibrations still retain some sound. . . . Each stroke will not produce a clear and distinct note of passion, but the one passion will always be mixed . . . with the other."[9] Rousseau's error, if we can speak of one, is to create a unitary form (a shape *all* light) out of this differential ground through an act of Orphic will. Or rather, since the shape seems autonomously generated by a combination of light and optics—by a process at once perceptual and natural—his error is to isolate the shape from its spatial and temporal context. For the apparently single shape emerges from a background of difference, as a moment in a process that consolidates and fixes an impression only to complicate it, threading "all the forest maze / With winding paths of emerald fire" (ll. 347–48, *SPP*):

> . . . "there stood

> "Amid the sun, as he amid the blaze
> Of his own glory, on the vibrating
> Floor of the fountain, paved with flashing rays,

> "A shape all light, which with one hand did fling
> Dew on the earth, as if she were the Dawn."
>   (ll. 348–53, *SPP*)

It seems clear that what is described here is the making of a figure through a process of substitution and displacement. To begin with, it is not the sun that we see, but the sun's image in a body of water that is confusingly a well or a fountain, in other words, the sun as constituted by reflection (ll. 345–46, 351, *SPP*). The shape is then generated by a series of synecdoches in which a diffuse and formless radiance imaged in the water is represented by an anthropomorphized sun described as "he," which in turn is represented by an inner, more focused female shape, metaphorically identified as the dawn, and as the dawn of a new era. There is indeed nothing unusual about a romantic poem's drawing attention to its construction of a myth. But here the process by which a myth is traced from its genesis in a moving army of metaphors and metonymies to its misprision as truth is presented as a hypnotism. Long before Rousseau explicitly perceives that the shape is not as simple as he takes it to be, the destructive effects of its formation are described:

> "And still her feet, no less than the sweet tune
> To which they moved, seemed as they moved, to blot
> The thoughts of him who gazed on them, and soon

> "All that was seemed as if it had been not,
> As if the gazer's mind was strewn beneath
> Her feet like embers, and she, thought by thought.

> "Trampled its fires into the dust of death."
>   (ll. 382–88, *SPP*)

As Rousseau allows himself to be captivated by the unitary shape that momentarily forms itself out of the play of differences, the ground of his creativity is erased. The sparks of his mind (1. 201, *SPP*), Shelley's image in the *Defence* for thought as a productivity, are trampled out as one idea is made to represent a differential complex of ideas and "All that was seemed as if it had been not." For as long as the mind is inhabited by a variety of different thoughts, as long as we remain aware that the dominant thought is constituted on the trace of what it does not say, the mind remains in Shelley's image both here and in the *Defence* a 'fountain' (1. 351, *SPP*), or more precisely a source of elements between which we can form new relations. Thus the creative oblivion Rousseau suffers in these lines is not something done by the shape to him, but rather something that he does to himself as he yields to the impossible desire to create a unity out of multeity. For the shape, as light, is not a fixed form but a moving army of particles. She is, moreover, a dancer, dancing "i' the wind where eagle never flew" (1. 381, *SPP*), beyond the grasp of those who reject the differential flux of life for the native noon of single rather than manifold vision. Those who will survive the dance of language dance with her, as Rousseau comes to do and enjoins Shelley to do. Those who abstract a single form from the dance, as Rousseau once did, find the spark of their creativity killed.

Even after his first encounter with the shape of his own mind ends with its disintegration, Rousseau's sense of what constitutes truth remains simple. Thus the unitary construction of the shape as 'all light' is now replaced with an equally partial perception of it as entirely destructive. Dimly, however, he is beginning to grow aware that the figures the mind constructs, whether negative or positive, contain the trace of their own difference from themselves:

"So knew I in that light's severe excess
The presence of that shape which on the stream
Moved, . . ."

"So did that shape its obscure tenour keep

"Beside my path, as silent as a ghost."
(ll. 424–33, *SPP*)

On a diegetic level, then, the poem, while essentially deconstructive, does not present a process of pure erasure. Rather, it shows us how the power of deconstruction at the heart of language actually produces meaning. The image of erasure crucial to de Man's analysis,[10] of the waves perpetually erasing the tracks of wolves and deer on the sand, is Rousseau's image, used with reference to what is chronologically the earliest segment of his life, to describe his initial sense of vertigo at the destruction of old positions (ll. 405–410, *SPP*). A variant of it turns up in Rousseau's dialogue with Shelley in the present, namely, the image of figures painted on a bubble (ll. 248–51, *SPP*). But if indeed the words are his,[11] he uses this image in response to a comment by Shelley, which he qualifies by pointing out that if cultural heroes are merely historical *figures,* this does not make them identical, erasable, reducible one to the other. Plato, he tells us, "Expiates the joy and woe his master knew not" and is uniquely different from Socrates. The poem does, to be sure, operate in terms of grammatical and conceptual displacements. But if this were purely a matter of erasure, we would feel a sense of loss at

Rousseau's inability to rest with his rejection of the phenomenal world, instead of feeling that the presence of other responses creates openings in the poem.

Paradoxically, then, *The Triumph of Life* is profoundly committed to the power of LOGOS, or rather DIA-LOGOS. If it deconstructs writing as an enduring monument by refusing to let Rousseau rest in peace, it valorizes speech as closer to a presence-as-difference. As writer, Rousseau had used the power of the published book as a means to fix meaning and achieve canonical status. But by the same token he was dead, catalogued like Adonais in the abode where the eternal are. Paradoxically, it is because 'Shelley' does not let him rest but deconstructs him that he comes to life, for to be deconstructed is to be read, and Rousseau is at least read, where 'Adonais' in some sense is killed with reverence. But more importantly it is through the power of speech that Rousseau returns to life, because until he speaks, he is simply a root in the hillside. The dialectic of author and reader, as Shelley dramatizes it here, is a complex one, which transforms writing into speech through a process in which the reader deconstructs the writer, but in which the writer also speaks back and in some sense deconstructs the reader. Two things occur in the extended interchange between 'Shelley' and Rousseau. Rousseau loses his authority over his own words in entering the circuit of reading: they can be appropriated in different ways by different readers, such dissemination being the price of the communication for which Shelley uses the image of the spark and of the acorn that contains all future oaks (*SPP,* p. 500). But 'Shelley,' too, loses his authority over his reading, which becomes part of the differential process of speech between writer and reader. He becomes what we might describe as a *lector* rather than a reader, following Barthes' distinction between the author who controls the circulation of meaning and the *scriptor* who is a function of his own language.[12] Though 'Shelley' does not recognize his changed status and does not speak again after Rousseau's account of his dream, such a shift seems implicit in the fact that Percy Shelley takes *both* author and reader out of contexts that may be thought to exist outside language (death in Rousseau's case, ordinary life in 'Shelley's'), and places them in a world of langauge.

The Triumph of Life is thus committed to speech and reading, to the human participation in the dance of words. Shelley's poem is characteristically romantic in actually valorizing speech, but speech (whether fictional, psychological, or political) is something very different from what Derrida criticizes in his distinction between speech (equated with a language that is self-identical) and writing (equated with difference and the loss of presence). For these terms Shelley substitutes an opposition between writing (equated with codification) and speech (equated with presence, but also difference). The written book offers a certain security, as something that confers on words the finality, recognition, and also the complacency of publication. But speech, which Rousseau engages in when he leaves the archives to encounter 'Shelley,' exposes and also revitalizes his words by placing them in a dialogical relationship with an other or with a world that dismantles and reconstitutes them. Nor is this view of speech confined to Shelley, for the renewed interest in Platonic dialogue evident in eighteenth-century British philosophy, in the hermeneutics of Schleiermacher and others, and in forms like the conversation poem, is at least potentially an interest in speech-as-difference: in speech as superior to writing because it is more fluid and indeterminate.

Similarly, the poem actually valorizes reading. In some sense it is, as de Man suggests, a deconstruction of reading, because it presents language as a process of repetitive expansion that unreads itself and therefore unreads any attempt at unitary interpretation. But this is only to say that it deconstructs the kind of allegorical reading, practiced by the character 'Shelley,' who tries to establish a one-to-one correspondence between figure and referent, to read the scene he witnesses into a book and out of his life. It is no accident that 'Shelley' uses simile rather than metaphor, that he describes the dance as a "just similitude" (l. 117, *SPP*), and that he tries to construe it in terms of literary conventions such as the medieval dream-vision and the Petrarchan triumph that will help him to label its characters and themes (ll. 40, 118, 176, *SPP*). But in a deeper sense the poem can be seen as developing a complex symbiosis between reading and deconstruction. As 'Shelley' reads Rousseau and more importantly as Rousseau reads himself, narrating the growth of his mind not to arrange and monumentalize his past like Wordsworth in *The Prelude* but to reread it, he unweaves his past self in such a way that his rereading unreads itself and creates a further language within language. It is, moreover, the fact that we can discover ever new relations within the poem that keeps us and future generations reading it. It is, of course, a far cry from this defense of reading to the one constructed by a traditional hermeneutics that sought to recover the original meaning of the text. We may discover how the poem functions as process but we do not discover its original meaning, any more than Rousseau, in recounting his past, is able to discover the original meaning of his life. Rather, we appropriate the poem to our own experience and create something meaningful out of it by participating in it, by becoming actors rather than spectators, and teaching the text what we would learn from it.

NOTES

1. Harold Bloom, *Shelley's Mythmaking* (1959; rpt. Ithaca, N.Y.: Cornell University Press, 1969), pp. 220–75; Ross Woodman, *The Apocalyptic Vision in the Poetry of Shelley* (Toronto: University of Toronto Press, 1964), pp. 180–98. Woodman's argument is characteristic of a certain phase of romantic criticism but is unlikely to represent his view now. Tilottama Rajan, *Dark Interpreter: The Discourse of Romanticism* (Ithaca, N.Y.: Cornell University Press, 1980), pp. 58–71.

2. Paul de Man, "Shelley Disfigured," in Harold Bloom, Paul de Man, et al., *Deconstruction and Criticism* (New York: Continuum, 1979), pp. 39–74. See esp. pp. 39–42, 44–46.

3. Ibid., p. 67.

4. I borrow this distinction from Milton Wilson, *Shelley's Later Poetry: A Study of his Prophetic Imagination* (New York: Columbia University Press, 1957), pp. 176–77.

5. For a discussion of the concepts of face and effacement, see de Man, "Shelley Disfigured," p. 46.

6. References to the manuscript are to Donald Reiman, ed., *"The Triumph of Life: A Facsimile of Shelley's Holograph Draft," The Bodleian Shelley Manuscripts: A Facsimile Edition, with Full Transcriptions and Scholarly Apparatus,* vol. I (New York: Garland, 1986).

7. Mary Shelley's version is reprinted in *The Complete Poetical Works of Percy Bysshe Shelley.* ed. Thomas Hutchinson (London: Oxford University Press, 1905).

8. This is how Reiman reads the passage in his notes to the Norton critical edition (*SPP,* p. 463n.).

9. David Hume, "Dissertion on the Passions," quoted by Engell, *The Creative Imagination: Enlightenment to Romanticism* (Cambridge, Mass.: Harvard University Press, 1981), p. 54.

10. De Man, "Shelley Disfigured," pp. 45–46.

11. Since there are no quotation marks in the manuscript, it does not follow that Rousseau speaks these words. It is just as possible that his part of the dialogue begins at l. 252.

12. Roland Barthes, *Image, Music, Text,* trans. Stephen Heath (New York: Hill and Wang, 1977), pp. 145–46.

Shelley's "Defence of Poetry"

Karl Kroeber concludes his survey of both literary and graphic arts in
in *British Romantic Art* with this analysis of the "Defence of Poetry."
He points out how Shelley's conceptions carry him toward central
"deconstructive" principles, as Rajan demonstrated in her essay.
Kroeber emphasizes that in anticipating even Foucault's "author-
function," Shelley refutes Thomas Love Peacock's pre-Auden
judgment that poetry makes nothing happen. Shelley's un-modernist
celebration of poetry depends on a strategy ignored not only by
Victorians and modernists, but even by some postmodern critics. He
argues that "poetry" is not merely to be defined as "aesthetic" but is
the efficient source of *all* cultural achievement. This explains his key
metaphor for the work of art as "a fountain for ever overflowing"
from which "new relations are ever developed." By treating this claim
as the basis for the romantics' determinative commitment
simultaneously to idealism and skepticism, Kroeber argues that if we
take the claim seriously we can perceive in an entirely new light the
fashion in which the romantics transformed their ideological heritage.
And we may thus better understand (in accord with Marilyn Butler's
observations on the difference between romantic and modernist art)
why these romantic attitudes have become alien to us.

What today seem shortcomings in early twentieth-century criticism of Romantic
art mostly originate in the pervasive influence of Modern art, which rejected or
reoriented many Romantic ideals. Critics came to think of Romanticism as either
something that had to be overcome for the truly Modern to emerge or as a
primitive, undeveloped version of what only in the twentieth century was fully
realized. The Romantics did, of course, initiate some ideas and techniques that
flowered more spectacularly later. But with the waning of Modern art, critical
attention veered toward the analysis of the complex play of processes responsible
for differences and divergencies between Modern and Romantic art. These might
be brought into sharpest focus by detailed study of the history of criticism, as a few
comments on one of the major critical documents of the Romantic era, Shelley's
"Defence of Poetry," may suggest.

Shelley's essay is too complicated to be analyzed adequately in anything less
than a monograph, and I make no pretense of explaining its intricacies, inconsis-
tencies, and pardoxes, most of them deliberate, for Shelley's view of his subject
urged him into a style "vitally metaphorical." Without enumerating his many

debts to earlier aestheticians and theorists of language, such as John Locke, Hugh Blair, and Adam Smith,[1] I focus on features in Shelley's argument that emphasize why we need to recast the terms in which Romantic art has been discussed for nearly a century.

Shelley's immediate purpose in the "Defence" is to refute the essay of his friend Thomas Love Peacock, "The Four Ages of Poetry," a clever piece that skillfully makes the case that poetry is useless in an advanced industrialized society. In simpler societies, says Peacock, poets are among the intellectual leaders, but as society becomes more complicated "intellectual power and intellectual acquisition have turned themselves into other and better channels," for poetry "can never make a philosopher, nor a statesman, nor in any class of life a useful or rational man."[2] "A poet," Peacock asserts, "in our times is a semi-barbarian in a civilized community," for "it is not to the thinking and studious, and scientific and philosophical part of the community, not to those whose minds are bent on the pursuit and promotion of permanently useful ends and aims, that poets . . . address their minstrelsy." As Shelley feared, Peacock's view has largely triumphed, so that even some artists and critics now take the triviality of art for granted.

With rhetorical shrewdness, Shelley seizes the offensive. Against Peacock's view that poetry does nothing, he asserts that poetry is the source of everything worthwhile in human life. He launches his attack from a distinction between reason and imagination, stressing the superiority of the latter, reason being "the enumeration of quantities already known," whereas imagination perceives "the value of those quantities." Reason is merely "mind *contemplating* the relations of one thought to another," but imagination is "mind *acting* upon those thoughts so as to colour them with its own light, and composing from them, as from elements, other thoughts, each containing within itself the principle of its own integrity" (p. 480).[3] Language rooted in imagination, what we would call poetic discourse, unlike rational discourse, "marks the before unapprehended relations of things" (p. 482), will "inevitably innovate" (p. 484), and "awaken and enlarge the mind itself by rendering [it] the receptacle of a thousand unapprehended combinations of thought" (p. 487). Only the language of imagination, which Shelley calls poetry, can create "forms of opinion and action never before conceived" (p. 495).

In identifying how innovations can occur, how originality in ideas, practical devices, and social orderings is possible, Shelley takes a position similar to Blake's in his argument in the series "There Is No Natural Religion." Blake stresses the hopeless circularity of explanations offered by "the calculating faculty." Like Blake, Shelley is aware that imagination, being "connate with the origin of man" (p. 480), cannot be defined by reduction to a brief formulation modeled on scientific equations. He delineates some of imagination's qualities and effects, not a few of which appear contradictory, so as to illuminate the process—and its mysteriousness—by which we may succeed in apprehending what previously we had been unable to apprehend.

Imagination for Shelley, as for the other Romantics, is inseparable from our nature as essentially social beings, one reason Shelley's "poets" include institutors of law, founders of civil life, and nonrhymesters like Bacon. Language "arbitrarily produced by the Imagination" (p. 483) practically effectuates its power. But this does not definitively decide the question of whether thought creates language, or language thought. The "vitally metaphorical" (p. 482) language of poetry revealing previously unapprehended relations and perpetuating their apprehension constitutes a true organizing of social intercourse, which always involves the interdependence of thinking and articulating. In the absence of imagination these interanimating structurings of relation become reified through the splitting apart, the disorganizing of conception and expression, a cliché being a final form of this division. Language thus disorganized hardens and desiccates as words become "mere signs for portions or classes of thought" (p. 482), functioning as signs, not symbols. Social life contracts into a torpid mass. The universe ceases to have meaning for us, individuals become hypocrites pledged to "the principle for us, individuals become hypocrites pledged to "the principle of Self, of which money is the visible incarnation" (p. 503), and disown their deepest desires and fears. These disavowals are writ large in the false arts that then flourish, arts that can only "affect sentiment and passion" (p. 491), appeal to a narcissistic hedonism, and pander to "caprice and appetite" (p. 491).

The sociohistorical direction of Shelley's thinking explains his paradoxical deployment of veil imagery. Poetry, he tells us, lays "bare the naked and sleeping beauty of the world" (p. 505). But each of Dante's words is a spark, "a burning atom of inextinguishable thought," many still "covered by the ashes of their birth" and still charged with a "lightning which has yet found no conductor," because "all high poetry is infinite. . . . Veil after veil may be withdrawn, and the inmost naked beauty of the meaning never exposed" (p. 500). The paradox of poetry revealing naked beauty yet never exposing its inmost naked beauty begins in Shelley's understanding that poetic accomplishments always emerge from specific historical conditions. A great poet such as Dante offers improvement or restoration to his society. But since genuine poetry is infinite, its potential can never be entirely realized. Dante's contribution to thirteenth-century Italian culture is not the limit of his attainment, some aspects of which could be realized only in the nineteenth century, still others only in the twentieth. Every unveiling initiates the possibility of another unveiling; so Shelley conflates processes we usually consider to be opposites, veiling and unveiling.

We must remember that in Shelley's view reification of language results not merely from repetition and routine but more significantly from those disownings and falsifications by which we conceal our true selves from ourselves. In unimaginative art, the only art that can flourish in the society Peacock idealizes, there appear "doctrines, which the writer considers as moral truths; and which are usually no more than specious flatteries of some gross vice or weakness with which the author in common with his auditors are infected" (p. 491). The dialogic drama between artist and audience that characterizes true art is reduced to a monologue in which the artist flatters his audience's prejudices. In contrast, great art exposes its audience to itself because "neither the eye nor the mind can see itself, unless reflected upon that which it resembles," inculcating not only "Self-knowledge" but also "self-respect" (p. 491). The argument that within our self-deceptions and disownings are possibilities for genuine self-respect recalls the crux of *The Cenci*: "knowing what must be thought," Beatrice wrongly shifts the accompanying "what may be done" into "what I must do" (1.2112), changing a psychic possibility into a willful imperative. Her decision leads to the "casuistry with which men seek the justification of Beatrice, yet feel that she has done what needs justification," as Shelley defines her tragedy (and all Romantic tragedy) in his preface to the play.

For the Romantics the veil of familiarity is a source of self-loathing, a sense of self-worthlessness whose social manifestations are prejudice, hatred, injustice, and feelings of impotence and whose intellectual consequences are the metaphysics of meaninglessness and an aesthetic that denigrates the value of art. The cornerstone of the Romantic ideal of self-revelation is that "Poetry is a mirror which makes beautiful that which is distorted" (p. 485)—or "disfigured," as Coleridge puts it in the *Biographia Literaria*. The acuity of Romantic psychological insight rests in this surprising blend of skepticism and idealism.

Shelley's observations sometimes anticipate trends in twentieth-century criticism. His comment that *Paradise Lost* "contains within itself a philosophical refutation of that system of which, by a strange and natural antithesis, it has been the chief popular support" (p. 498) carries him toward deconstruction, while his remark that Milton's poem and Dante's will someday serve, as Homer's epic now does, as the means of and reason for recovering an otherwise useless set of obsolete religious beliefs points toward an idea exploited in modern hermeneutics. Even more surprising, perhaps, are his thoughts about intertextuality and the irrelevance of the artist's person. Insisting on poets' lack of control, "speaking words which they understand not . . . and feel not what they inspire" (p. 508), Shelley approaches Foucault's author-function. But Shelley attributes the unimportance of the individual in imaginative exercise to inspiration—a power "*above* consciousness" (p. 486)—while psychoanalytic theory has led most of us to peer below. Working from the Romantic conception of the identity of invention and execution as essential to the exercise of the imagination, Shelley seizes as a key to the failure of imagination in modern life the refusal, originating in the Enlightenment, to consider art inspired, a rejection of the continuing testimony of artists that "their" creations are indebted to a power beyond their control. This point is crucial to Shelley's rebuttal of Peacock, for were Peacock to admit any significant form of inspiration, his argument would disintegrate.

The profound importance for Shelley of the possibility of inspiration is implicit in his comment on "sparks" of Dante's thought still "covered in the ashes of their birth," and is explicit in his famous comment that "the mind in creation is as a fading coal" (p. 503), so that the "most glorious poetry that has ever been communicated to the world is probably a feeble shadow of the original conception of the poet" (p. 504). That works we regard as totally successful—those of Dante, Shakespeare, and Homer—may be but weak realizations of what might have been accomplished is a daring conception, one to which Shelley is drawn by his conviction that poetry is not created by will. If a poem helps to liberate a reader from socially induced misconceptions, that effect is less the deliberately targeted achievement of the poet than a happy effect of the shadow of liberated vision that inspired him to write. It is this power beyond any individual's control that renders superior poetry "infinite," possessed of future effects beyond what even the greatest artist can predict. Thus the creative capacity itself manifests the evanescence of the eternal.

To understand Shelley's concept of inspiration, we must refrain from the current critical tendency to associate the term with mystical or vaguely transcendental activities. For the Romantics inspiration was not a communion with a transcendental source but a response to the actual nature of the cosmos. Blake and Shelley viewed inspiration or poetical genius as connate with the origin of man, and for them, as well as the other Romantics, poetry is not a special language but ordinary language used imaginatively.

The disastrous triumph of the "principle of self" in modern society, the diminished power of love, a "going out of our own nature" (p. 487), Shelley can unhesitatingly identify as founded in imaginative failure because, as emphatically as Blake, Coleridge, and Wordsworth, he links poetry and pleasure: "poetry is ever accompanied by pleasure" (p. 486); "the strength of the bucolic poets is that their work endows the sense with a power of sustaining its extreme delight" (p. 492); "poetry ever communicates all the pleasure which men are capable of receiving" (p. 493). Art begins in an "excess" of pleasure that "communicates itself to others, and gathers a sort of reduplication from that community" (p. 482), an idea exactly paralleled in Wordsworth's Preface to *Lyrical Ballads*. Conceived in pleasure, the work of art is indeterminate not because fragmented or inadequate but because it is like "a fountain for ever overflowing with the waters of wisdom and delight":

> After one person and one age has exhausted all its divine effluence which their peculiar relations enable them to share, another and yet another succeeds, and new relations are ever developed, the source of an unforeseen and an unconceived delight. ("Defence," p. 500)

Few critics in our time, however, do not work from the opposite premise, that art comes into being through injury or dislocation, a fault or fracturing of some kind, either psychological or sociological, perhaps both, and consequently, that the endless interpretability of a work of art is due not to its being a fountain forever overflowing but a *mise en abîme*. For the Romantics art is an ever self-renewing surplus; for us art is an unfathomable chasm. Yet if we view all literary works as inherently unstable we are positioned, as earlier twentieth-century critics were not, to appreciate the destabilizing vitality in Romantic art, although in our compulsive gazing into the abyss we have perhaps moved farther away from understanding art as "a fountain for ever overflowing."

NOTES

1. The best work on the Romantics' indebtedness to earlier language studies, and not merely in Britain, is Hans Aarslef, *From Locke to Saussure: Essays on the Study of Language and Intellectual History* (Minneapolis: University of Minnesota Press, 1982).

2. Thomas Love Peacock, *Memoirs of Shelley and Other Essays and Reviews,* ed. Howard Mills (New York: New York University Press, 1970), pp. 117–132; citations in this paragraph are from pp. 132, 130, 129, and 131.

3. For the "Defence" I follow the well-edited text in *Shelley's Poetry and Prose,* ed. Donald H. Reiman and Sharon B. Powers (New York: Norton, 1977), pp. 480–508; emphases throughout are mine.

John Keats

Keats is the most remarkable of the English romantic poets. His fame rests on a tiny amount of what he called "poesy," the skillful deployment of a few thousand words. His accomplishment appears even more impressive when one considers the vast quantity of criticism focused on his handful of marvelous poems. That so small a body of verse should survive, even thrive, under such a ponderous weight of commentary is amazing. Yet thrive it does—as everyone who teaches Keats rediscovers every year. To define the source of this extraordinary potency is the goal of every Keatsian critic. How can the hundredth reading of, say, the "Ode on a Grecian Urn" be perhaps more wonderful than the first?

This self-reviving quality of Keats's poetry may explain why, once he was fully accepted as canonical (and even during his tragically brief life his abilities were significantly recognized), there have been few drastic revisions in critical judgments of his work. Scholars are continuing, of course, to teach us more about the conditions of his life, Hermione de Almeida's recent encyclopedic display of Keats's knowledge of the medicine of his day, *Romantic Medicine and John Keats* (1991), being a specially impressive example. But the history of Keatsian criticism demonstrates most clearly the efficacy with which earlier critiques are absorbed into later ones. This critical evolution we illustrate both by presenting a sequence of commentaries on what has often been cited as Keats's "most perfect" lyric, "To Autumn," and by arranging other selections to illustrate processes of innovative critical indebtedness. By so doing, however, we have blocked ourselves from presenting valuable discussions of some of Keats's best-known poems, such as the famous odes, analyzed exhaustively by Helen Vendler, for example, in *The Odes of John Keats* (1983), "Lamia," recently reexplored interestingly by George C. Gross in his "*Lamia* and the Cupid-Psyche Myth" (1990), and the "Hyperion" poems.

Romance as Wish-Fulfillment: The Eve of St. Agnes

We have chosen a chapter from Stuart Sperry's *Keats the Poet,* which appeared in 1973, earlier than other selections in this volume, because it sharply illuminates how superior scholarly criticism endures by entering into the ongoing continuity of commentary. One has but to read Marjorie Levinson's recent meditation on *The Eve of St. Agnes* in *Keats's Life of Allegory* (represented by our next selection) to recognize how her views are anticipated by Sperry's succinct analysis. This is not to imply that Levinson's observations are superfluous or "un-original"; it is, rather, to suggest that the most "original" criticism is always mediated by the best criticism that has preceded it.

In 1973 Sperry, building on a conscientious reading of *his* predecessors (as his notes demonstrate), defined *The Eve of St. Agnes* as a poem of "wish-fulfillment." He observed that the work involved itself in a highly self-conscious critique of the romance form, "using and spoofing" its conventions. He showed how Keats exposed the "strategem to which poetic magic must resort" at his "belated" epoch in literary history, to produce a work of "inherent relativity" that leaves readers "charmed but also perplexed." Sperry thus delineated the contours that criticism of *The Eve of St. Agnes* for the next twenty years was to explore and redefine. In the past half decade, for example, nothing has attracted more attention than the topic of "romance," in all its meanings, especially questions of how poets such as Keats refigured, even deconstructed, received conventions and attitudes.

Many of the issues that arise in approaching *St. Agnes* revolve around the fundamental question of its tone. For Keats's contemporaries and the Victorians, most of whom in one way or another came under its spell, there was no mistaking the poem's "meaning." It was for them the essence of romance, a gorgeous bit of tapestry, full of color, tenderness, passion, and high feeling. Leigh Hunt thought it "the most delightful and complete specimen of [Keats's] genius" among the longer pieces, a poem standing midway between efforts like *Isabella,* at times more sensitive but feebler, and "the less generally characteristic majesty of the fragment of *Hyperion.*"[1] Modern criticism, with its distaste for such banalities, has by contrast dealt with the poem somberly and with a certain grim intellectual seriousness.[2] Yet *St. Agnes* is above all dramatic (Keats himself saw it as a step toward a

From *Keats the Poet* (Princeton, N.J.: Princeton University Press, 1973), pp. 199–220. Copyright © 1973 by Princeton University Press. Reprinted by permission of the publisher.

chief ambition, "the writing of a few fine Plays" [II, 234]); and while it tends to sacrifice depth of character to richness and suggestiveness of background, it skillfully achieves a rich interplay of dramatic emotions, a complex texture not lacking its own kind of playfulness, irony, and even humor. Of course we are seduced, along with Madeline, each time we return to the work, as we submit to its suggestions of mystery, the rapture of young love, and its high, romantic spell; that is all part of its deeper playfulness, and part, too, of its deeper point. Yet at the same time we are hardly unmindful that the machinery by which we are taken in is conventional, not to say thin. The castle, for all its monumentality, is shadowy, insubstantial. The dwarfish Hildebrand and old Lord Maurice (some of the "fine mother Radcliff" types Keats was himself particularly amused by [II, 62]) and their kinsmen, whose very dogs howl execrations, rage savagely, only to subside in the end into a harmless, drunken stupor, "be-nightmar'd" as if by fairies. There is the lovers' usual go-between, a tottering, cackling crone, and a solemn Beadsman, both of whom seem to dissolve simultaneously into ashes, along with the rest of the castle, when the lovers depart. There are dusky galleries, arched ways, silken chambers, and, near the end, a drunken porter and a bloodhound.

It is no wonder Keats found the poem "smokeable" (II, 174).[3] Yet it is not, at the same time, merely ingenious to suggest that our consciousness of artificiality, at times of deliberate contrivance, makes up a necessary part of our enjoyment of the work and constitutes a vital element in its effect. For if at first glance Keat's romance strikes us as thoroughly conventional in its melodrama, we are soon aware that the conventions it employs are hardly of a piece, indeed that they are used at times with beguiling inconsistency. Madeline is sober and demure, "St. Agnes' charmed maid" (192), rising, beneath her solitary candle's gleam, to pious observances. Yet the rites she must observe ("supperless to bed . . . Nor look behind, nor sideways" [51, 53]), while rooted in folk superstition, suggest a little child put to bed early with visions of sugar plums. Porphyro is soft-voiced and trembling, yearning for his lady in the darkness while loath to interrupt her slumbers. Yet he is brought on at the outset, crowding stage like a big Italian tenor, with unabashed hyperbole:

> He ventures in: let no buzz'd whisper tell:
> All eyes be muffled, or a hundred swords
> Will storm his heart, Love's fev'rous citadel.
> (82–84)

Even the element of mystery, or mystification, that pervades the poem is hardly of a piece. We begin with the somber, Christian devotions of the Beadsman, which lend at first a more serious color to the popular superstitions Madeline pursues. But it is not long before we are in a world of charms and dim enchantments, a world inhabited by elves and fairies. Religious ritual, the stately mysteries of high romance, the self-conscious theatricality of opera, and the improbabilities of folk legend and a child's fairy tale all proceed to merge impenetrably. However, if *St. Agnes* lacks the larger unity and cohesiveness that characterizes Spenser's world, if we are puzzled as to which species of "romance" it belongs, such doubts and questions make up an integral part of its effect and meaning.

All this is not to argue that in *St. Agnes* Keats was writing parody or burlesque. It is, however, to claim that in taking refuge from the contradictory pressures of the moment in the consolations of a new romance, he was dong so with heightened awareness of the tenuousness of the imaginative world into which he was withdrawing and with a view of the poet's role as conjurer that was at times ironic.[4] Like most of Keats's major efforts, *St. Agnes* is a poem about the etherealizing power of human desire and passion, a further attempt at the "material sublime." However the particular genius of the work lies in its comprehension of the kinds of evasiveness and disguise the imagination necessarily employs in accomplishing its transformation, an awareness of the poetic process as an act of sublimation now in some ways closer to its modern psychological sense than its older, chemical one. Although it is often taken as such, *St. Agnes* is not primarily a glorification of sexual experience or even, for all the condensed richness of its imagery, of the human senses.[5] It is, rather, an exceptionally subtle study of the psychology of the imagination and its processes, a further testing, pursued more seriously in some of the poet's later verse, of the quality and limits of poetic belief. More than anything else, perhaps, the element most central to the poem is its concern with wish-fulfillment, a fundamental aspect of romance that had fascinated Keats from the time of his earliest verse—often, as he himself was well aware (and as Byron, for one, pointed out with vulgar contempt) at the cost of particular embarrassments.[6] To describe *The Eve of St. Agnes* as a romance of wish-fulfillment is, of course, to expose oneself immediately to misunderstanding, for we are apt, even today, to regard that activity as artless, not to say simple-minded, whereas in actuality it is close to the root of creativity of human culture and the arts and never more compelling or intense than when acting through a consciousness of the kinds of reality it would alter or circumvent. A wish is double-natured: it lies somewhere between a desire and an act of will, an impulse and its realization, the unconscious and the conscious. It is, in fact, the imagination (in its broader romantic sense) that serves to mediate between the self-centered gratifications of phantasy and the awareness of human limitation, between the pleasure and reality principles, and which, by creating the grounds for an accommodation, defines the kinds of beauty or truth we find at any given moment acceptable or satisfying. What distinguishes *St. Agnes* at the point at which it occurs in Keats's career is the subtlety of its control over the psychological mechanisms of repression and release, the fact that the perspective it provides upon the reality it constructs is not simple but complex and continually shifting.

In visualizing *St. Agnes* as a poem of wish-fulfillment, one can hardly overlook either the defensive nature of its battlemented setting or the poem's whole nocturnal character. The major action itself suggests by analogy the way in which the defenses of consciousness are circumvented, the way in which, as in dreams, awareness begins to take its shape from the promptings of latent desire. Consider merely the plot. An ardent young lover abducts a lovely maiden from a closely guarded castle filled with rivals and violent enemies; and when at the end the two escape across the moors to some legendary home in the south, they make their way through chained and bolted gates, past watchmen overcome by drink and slumber. Porphyro enters furtively and by night and, with the help of a sole friend and intermediary, gains access to Madeline's chamber. Here he conceals himself. It is only when, after watching her enter, undress, fall into prayer and reverie, and prepare herself for bed, he hears the steady breathing of her slumber that he dares leave his hiding place. Despite the arguments of Stillinger,[7] the climax of the poem, the union of the two lovers, in no way resembles rape or even a seduction of any ordinary kind. For it is a part of Porphyro's task, as the overtones of stealth and anxiety make us feel, that he must not break the spell in which Madeline lies bound, that he cannot interrupt the current of her dreams, that merely to awaken her would be disastrous. He must rather, through the use of various suggestions— the feast of fruits and spices with its teeming odors, the music he plays on her lute, the sound of his voice, the touch, even, of his arm—*create himself* within her dream. The desire he represents and introduces must be partly disguised, partly transformed, in order to win admission to the dream where alone it can find fulfillment. How and where the two first met, how long they have known each other, the state of Madeline's affections, or even the degree of her awareness of Porphyro as a lover are all questions to which we are never given answers, although we are made to feel, somehow, that he has been implicitly in her thoughts almost from the start of the poem. But when she awakes, or half-awakes, from her dream (for the point is left deliberately ambiguous), she recognizes Porphyro, after a moment of painful confusion, not just as a mortal wooer in all his human limitations, but also as a part of her dream, a part of her vision and her desire, and she accepts him as her lover. There is an accommodation, one that is neither easy nor untroubled, between imagination and reality.

There is no need for elaborate Freudian analysis to see that the major action of the poem is essentially a drama of wish-fulfillment, a testimony to the power of human desire to realize itself, to transform awareness, and to gain a measure of recognition and acceptance despite the thousand restraints—fear, disbelief, denial, propriety—excluding it. Only in the dream and its processes—by extension the domain of romance, poetry, art—and the shelter they afford from waking consciousness is there any hope for the recognition and appeasement that the most fundamental kind of human energy and instinct insistently demand; for the dream is conditioned and informed by the same human desire it transfigures and fulfills.

Such a formulation enables us to see the poem plainly for what it is, and yet paradoxically could cause us to miss its real artistry. For if within the literature of English Romanticism *The Eve of St. Agnes* is a supreme example of art as wish-fulfillment, it is, nevertheless, as we have partly seen, a wish-fulfillment of an exceptionally practiced and self-conscious kind that gives the work its essential character. The poem, that is, achieves its magic, but only in such a way as to dramatize the particular tensions that oppose it and the kinds of device it must employ in overcoming them—repression, anxiety, disguise, censorship, sublimation. The very artistry that brings the dream swelling into reality draws our attention to itself in such a way as subtly to qualify, even to unsettle, its own effects. Once we go beneath the surface melodrama we discover a mixture of the naive and sophisticated, the sentimental and the disenchanted, fantasy and psychological realism.

II

"It shall be as thou *wishest*" (172) Angela tells Porphyro, and her words suggest the principle of causality within the lovers' universe the poem invites us to accept. Yet we are not introduced to Madeline or Porphyro directly; nor, as we discover at the beginning, are all forms of wishing equally efficacious. The inductions to the narrative poems and fragments of Keats's last great year are masterpieces of technique, and that of *St. Agnes* is no exception. The description of the Beadsman and the chapel's piercing cold prepares a series of contrasts the poem is steadily to develop and expand.

> St. Agnes' Eve—Ah, bitter chill it was!
> The owl, for all his feathers, was a-cold;
> The hare limp'd trembling through the frozen grass,
> And silent was the flock in woolly fold:
> Numb were the Beadsman's fingers, while he told
> His rosary, and while his frosted breath,
> Like pious incense from a censer old,
> Seem'd taking flight for heaven, without a death,
> Past the sweet Virgin's picture, while his prayer he saith.
>   (1–9)

Keats ingeniously begins his drama of wish-fulfillment by presenting a familiar form of sublimation that is introduced only to be rejected as ineffectual. As worshiper and adorer, the Beadsman prepares the way for Porphyro by establishing a contrast that is ironical; for his primary role requires a form of wishing—that is, prayer. Indeed the images that first surround him suggest a certain ardor and devotion, just as his breath, rising like incense, and the lamp he carries convey a kind of perfume, light, and warmth. Long practiced, however, in the rites of penitence and self-discipline, he restrains his feeling while his passion, channeled into the forms of religious worship, seems powerless to animate a host of images that are lifeless and unyielding. The virgin to whom he prays, however sweet, remains a mere picture. The emprisoned knights and ladies praying in their frozen oratories, reflect, through Keats's brilliant use of sculptural imagery, the harsh repression of human warmth and feeling, the note from which the poem commences and ascends. One may compare them with the carved angels of the ballroom who, eager-eyed and expectant as if animated by the music and festivities around them, seem virtually bursting from the stonework of the cornice into human life. At the most critical moment of the poem, the moment of Madeline's apparent withdrawal from her dream and her awakening, Porphyro kneels as if frozen by her bedside, "pale as smooth-sculptured stone" (297), only to derive a new and almost preternatural vitality by his acceptance as the consummation of her vision, as he melts "Into her dream" (320). Throughout the poem we find Keats using the imagery of sculpture to express the way feeling is arrested or repressed, then liberated and fulfilled in a new onrush of emotion.

There is a similar logic at work in the poet's use of musical themes and images. The contrast between the constraint of the Beadsman's world and the glow and movement of the ballroom culminates in the single moment when he passes through the little door—the indication of another range of experience:

> Northward he turneth through a little door,
> And scarce three steps, ere Music's golden tongue
> Flatter'd to tears this aged man and poor.
>   (19–21)

The image of tears, which drew Hunt's admiration and moved him to observe that "a true poet is by nature a metaphysician,"[8] defines a particular moment central to the poem's harmony. The image recurs twice at important turning-points in the poem—once when Porphyro first learns of Madeline's hopes for St. Agnes' night and again when Madeline weeps on awakening from her dream to observe her lover kneeling by her bedside—and thus perpetuates and extends, almost like a theme in music, the power of a single mood. In the Beadsman's sudden weeping we recognize an act of self-love, or, more exactly perhaps, self pity, an instant in which the restraints upon feeling are momentarily dissolved and the repressed desires and longings of the soul achieve an unexpected outlet to expression. The image thus defines, in a moment of sudden contrast, the gap that exists between desire and fulfillment, between potential and realization, a gap that, as the poem is to suggest, can be bridged only by a leap of the imagination. From the very beginning, then, Keats creates, almost as a kind of leitmotif, that specific quality of human yearning basic to the theme and structure of his poem. Nor should one overlook the fact that the Beadsman is moved to tears by music, for it serves to symbolize throughout the poem, as in the image of the "silver, snarling trumpets" (31) that summon and chide the guests, the power of aroused desire. Often, however, it is used, as in the great image of the ballroom, filled with "music, yearning like a God in pain" (56), to suggest emotion denied its full expression or unnaturally restrained. Whether it be the boisterous music from the revelers below that is silenced when the hall door closes, the hushed strains the trembling Porphyro plays so quietly on Madeline's lute, or the inner melody that Madeline, entering her chamber like "a tongueless nightingale," feels "paining" her side with longing for deliverance (205–206), music is throughout the poem a symbol of the tide of human feeling that seeks to overbear all efforts to contain it.

Despite the show of feeling that momentarily masters him and sets the keynote for the poem, the Beadsman turns his back upon the setting he has opened. He turns "Another way" (25), which is not the way the lovers take. As in the "Bright Star" sonnet, Keats moves toward the world of mortal rapture from an image of devout but cold and inhuman isolation. The Beadsman affords an effective transition to our first glimpse of Keats's heroine for further reasons. Both are bent on rites and meditation, for we find Madeline already engrossed by the ceremonies she intends to observe. Both shun the castle's glittering entertainment for prayer, fasting, seclusion, and the hope of their own visionary fulfillment. The same questions of truth and substantiality, moreover, surround the world to which each is drawn. Self-absorbed, Madeline does not seem to hear the music, yearning in desire; nor does she heed the ardent cavaliers, who approach her only to withdraw. She is oblivious to the looks of "love, defiance, hate, and scorn" (69) around her. While she dances, her eyes are "vague, regardless" (64); she is already engrossed by her imagination—

> Hoodwink'd with faery fancy; all amort,
> Save to St. Agnes and her lambs unshorn,
> And all the bliss to be before to-morrow morn.
> (70–72)

Paradoxically, however, the courtly festivities Madeline turns away from do not seem any more real than the world of her fancies. The revelers burst in

With plume, tiara, and all rich array,
Numerous as shadows haunting fairily
The brain, new stuff'd, in youth, with triumphs gay
Of old romance.

(38–41)

They seem ghostly, insubstantial, merely part of the trappings of "old romance," an outworn spell. As R. H. Fogle has justly observed, such effects are "complex and even self-contradictory," certainly "not the poetry of a simple romancer."[9] If we are tempted to view Madeline as the prey of her illusions, we are at the same time reminded that the framework of the entire poem, the conventions of romance themselves, are hardly above suspicion. From start to finish we are in a world of make-believe where our habitual distinctions between reality and illusion no longer apply. Indeed the reader is himself invited at Keats's own request not only to accept but to take part in a world where wishing has the force of willing:

These [the revelers] *let us wish away,*
And turn, *sole-thoughted,* to one Lady there.
(41–42)

Thus, as by the magic of a wish, the argent revelry is resolved back into shadows, and we give ourselves up to the charm of Madeline's endeavor, a bit of harmless conjuring that can take on a more sober cast simply through a willingness to take it seriously: "Full of this *whim* was *thoughtful* Madeline" (55). It is as if the poem were subtly arguing the power of the characters, the poet, and even the reader, to shape a kind of reality from the stuff of illusion by an act of will.

The same kind of sophistication underlies the histrionics of Porphyro's arrival on the scene. Filled with "barbarian hordes, / Hyena foemen" (85–86), the castle holds, beyond Madeline herself, no one from whom he can hope mercy, "Save one old beldame, weak in body and in soul" (90). And then immediately, as if in answer to his prayers—

Ah, happy chance! the aged creature came,
Shuffling along with ivory-headed wand.
(91–92)

Here again, Keats is both using and spoofing the conventions of romance—the suspension of all normal standards of probability—as the bumbling crone gropes for Porphyro's hand to greet him as well as to reassure herself of his identity. Indeed it is the variable identity of the characters that now proves so fascinating; for, beyond its obvious melodrama, the deeper interest of the narrative lies in the changing psychological relationships it develops—the way the characters react upon and modify each other. Badly frightened by Porphyro's impulsive threat to reveal himself to his enemies, Angela protests herself "A poor, weak, palsy-stricken, churchyard thing" (155), virtually a ghost already. Yet only a little while earlier, in her amazement at seeing him, she has bid him "flit! / Flit like a ghost away" (104–105) and gone on to liken his appearance to some supernatural visitation:

> Thou must hold water in a witch's sieve,
> And be liege-lord of all the Elves and Fays,
> To venture so.

(120–22)

Though they are all creatures of the romance world of the poem, the characters nevertheless lay claim at various times to different levels of existence or reality that continually play off against, challenge, or modify each other.

There is, for example, the enchanting scene in which Porphyro is led through many a winding corridor into Angela's little chamber, "Pale, lattic'd, chill, and silent as a tomb" (113), where the garrulous dame, as if through a sudden start of recollection, first reveals her mistress's intention:

> St. Agnes' Eve!
> God's help! my lady fair the conjuror plays
> This very night: good angels her deceive!

(123–25)

There follows one of the brilliant "camera stills" the poem makes such effective use of:

> Feebly she laugheth in the languid moon,
> While Porphyro upon her face doth look,
> Like puzzled urchin on an aged crone
> Who keepeth clos'd a wond'rous riddle-book,
> As spectacled she sits in chimney nook.

(127–31)

Dominated by the pallor of the chamber and the old dame's mocking laughter, Porphyro is momentarily transformed, as if before our eyes, into a child held spellbound by the enigma of a nanny's bedtime riddle, the pastime of a winter evening, while Madeline's intention appears nothing more than an empty piece of childish self-deception. Yet it is at this moment that he is moved to tears by his recognition of her adventure's unfulfilled potential, the solution to the puzzle's mystery which lies in his own power to supply. Immediately the pallor of the scene is filled with imagery of color:

> Sudden a *thought* came like a full-blown rose,
> Flushing his brow, and in his pained heart
> Made purple riot.

(136–38)

It is, of course, not the formulated "thought" but the wish that underlies it, or rather the sudden flowering of the one into the fullness of the other, that Keats conveys in the dynamic image of a rose's unfolding. Transformed, Porphyro rises up brilliant-eyed to assume his proper role as lover with his enterprise fully formed in the reality of his imagination. It is at such moments of alternate contraction and expansion, when Keats takes daring freedoms with the whole decorum of romance, that we sense within the shifts of background and convention the maturity of his control over the focus of his narrative and the intimate connection it establishes between technique and meaning.

The impulse toward contraction immediately resumes with Angela's expressions of pious horror on first construing his intent. His enterprise is now a "strategem" (139) and the adoring lover "cruel" and "wicked" (140, 143)—"Thou canst not surely be the same that thou didst seem" (144). Her words, for all their commonplaceness, have a further point; for through its sudden changes in background, mood, convention, the poem continually creates new contexts for visualizing the characters and their actions, among which we find it difficult to decide which are the most probable, believable, "real." Angela's objections now have the effect of forcing Porphyro partly to conceal, partly to disguise his full intention. He must swear "by all saints" (145), disavow all "ruffian passion" (149), and hope for grace "When my weak voice shall whisper its last prayer" (147), even threatening to reveal himself to his foes and so call down upon himself a kind of martyrdom. He must, in short, attempt to sublimate the more questionable aspects of his enterprise by proposing it in terms acceptable to religious or moral orthodoxy. It is somewhat ironical to reflect that the hero's plight was in certain ways similar to Keats's own when he discovered that passages in the completed manuscript of the poem offended the scruples of his publishers and he was forced to revise them, partly unwillingly, to bring them into conformity with the demands of propriety.[10] We miss the point of how details in the history of the poem's publication serve to illuminate one of its major thematic preoccupations when we see the problem in terms of mere prurience, duplicity, hypocrisy, or cynical expedience. The devices of disguise and censorship perform an integral and even aesthetic function throughout the whole formation of the work—well before Woodhouse and Taylor required their particular changes—for they have to do with Keats's larger grasp of human psychology, his mastery of the interplay between the various levels of human intuition, both unconscious and conscious, and the means by which they achieve accommodation.

It is in the portrayal of Madeline and her dream that Keats's treatment of such deeper concerns becomes more difficult and subtle. His famous declaration to Bailey over a year earlier in November 1817 that "the Imagination may be compared to Adam's dream—he awoke and found it truth" (I, 185) has an undeniable yet inconclusive bearing on the meaning of *St. Agnes*. For the relationships within the poem are too complicated to be resolved into the simple terms of the earlier equation. For one thing Madeline never fully awakens from her dream; and if she partly wakes as her "blue affrayed eyes" (296) open, that awakening is not an altogether happy one.

> Her eyes were open, but she still beheld,
>   Now wide awake, the vision of her sleep:
>   There was a painful change, that nigh expell'd
>   The blisses of her dream so pure and deep,
>   At which fair Madeline bgan to weep,
>   And moan forth witless words with many a sigh;
>   While still her gaze on Porphyro would keep;
>   Who knelt, with joined hands and piteous eye,

Fearing to move or speak, she look'd so
    dreamingly.

                  (298–306)

Like the knight-at-arms of Keats's famous ballad written later in the spring, Porphyro is "pallid, chill, and drear" (311), momentarily isolated from the sustaining warmth and vitality of her dream, which, in the fullness of its imagined blisses, has outrun the vision of her human lover. Marked by her tears, there is the same recognition of a gap between desire and appearance, a moment of painful contraction followed immediately by a more intense reintegration of vision and reality in which the lovers are united.

Into her dream he melted, as the rose
Blendeth its odour with the violet,—
Solution sweet.

                  (320–22)

Porphyro's success comes not through any shattering of the dream or diminution of its spell, but through his power, sensed almost from the moment of his first appearance, to suggest and to inform its content, to bring it slowly to the point of consciousness and recognition where, while it still remains a dream, he can become a part of it and find acceptance. In his infinite persistence and resourcefulness, he expresses the power of human desire, of the wish, to create its own fulfillment, to achieve, relative to other things, its own kind of truth.

Yet the inherent relativity of the poem, the shifting use it makes of subtly different conventions and attitudes which continually puzzles us and makes the work impossible to summarize in terms of any single statement, is never clearer than when we look more closely at its treatment of Madeline's dream. Her soul "Flown, like a thought, until the morrow-day" (239), she fades into sleep, into that state of benign unconsciousness where the powers of intelligence recover a measure of their innocence and instinctual vitality—"As though a rose should shut, and be a bud again" (243). Porphyro is free to emerge from his concealment, to proceed to his "complainings dear" (313), the expressions of his desire muted by the tide of unconsciousness. Yet he emerges, in Keats's marvelously suggestive phrase, "Noiseless as fear in a wide wilderness" (250); and the note of anxiety relates not merely to his fear of interrupting her slumber but also to the awe we sense, on peering with him through the bed-curtains, at the profundity of her repose, "where, lo!—how *fast* she slept" (252). For her sleep, and the dream already begun to form within it, which before had seemed so warm and protective, now, by a slight variation in imagery, is made to appear aloof, cold, almost inhuman. There is indeed something frenetic in the way Porphyro, "half anguish'd" (255), proceeds to heap up in abandon the fruits and syrups, and something somber in the way they stand, forlorn and apart, "Filling the chilly room with perfume light" (275). For the charm that holds Madeline, for all Porphyro's attempts to soften it, is now "Impossible to melt as iced stream" (283), seemingly impervious even to the touch of his "warm, unnerved arm" (280) as it sinks into her pillow. She lies "entoil'd in woofed phantasies" (288). Confronted by a situation calling for Prince Charming to awake his sleeping princess with a kiss, we have instead a heroine who appears to have gone over the line where sleep turns into coma and dreaming into endless fantasy.

The continual modulation between such different sets of contexts and conventions keeps us perpetually off balance and prevents our settling into any simple attitude in reading *St. Agnes*. True it is that the brief terror of Madeline's awakening and its moment of schizophrenic anguish is rapidly dissolved within the lovers' rapturous union and flight. Yet in another way the sense of Madeline's dilemma, the momentary rift the poem opens between the Porphyro of her dream and the mortal lover isolated by her human vision, retains its haunting power, so that the sexual culmination the poem proposes, however "sweet," remains a "Solution" (322), a resolving of difficulties that does not so much command as entreat our willing suspension of disbelief. We accept the romance of the poem—in a sense we *will* it—in its triumph over the oppositions that confront it, even while we recognize the way in which the adequacy of such means are called in question. Nor is it possible to ignore the way the poem lets us down from its heights of magic quite deliberately and in a fashion that to some degree anticipates Keats's other great poem of sleep and awakening, the "Ode to a Nightingale." The beating of the sleet upon the panes rouses the lovers:

'Tis dark: quick pattereth the flaw-blown sleet:
"This is no dream, my bride, my Madeline!"
'Tis dark: the iced gusts still rave and beat:
"No dream, alas! alas! and woe is mine!
Porphyro will leafe me here to fade and
    pine.—
Cruel! what traitor could thee hither bring?"
                                    (325–30)

Porphyro's words have a triumphant ring, as though they heralded an emergence from dream into reality. Their immediate effect, however, is an unhappy one, for they momentarily place Madeline in another role familiar to us, although now from popular romance—that of the damsel robbed of her maidenhead by a faithless lover who departs at dawn, the type of the forsaken Gretchen. Porphyro, nevertheless, is "no rude *infidel*" (342). He has already twice called Madeline his "bride" (326, 334) and has a home awaiting her across the southern moors. The poem, in fact, seems virtually on the point of ending on a note of domesticity, with the storm, for all its icy gusts, marking a return to the world of the natural elements and breathing humanity. Such homely expectations, however, are quickly lost amid the onset of some final magic. "Hark! 'tis an elfin-storm from faery land" (343), Porphyro exclaims. The lovers are not destined for a return into the mortal world but for some nebulous transcendence of their own. And while they steal away through the familiar stage-props of the castle, they flee as "phantoms" (361, 362), unfelt, unheard, unseen by all but the wakeful bloodhound, a descendant of Sir Leoline's supernaturally sensitive old mastiff.

And they are gone away: ay, ages long ago
These lovers fled away into the storm.
                                    (370–71)

While Angela, the Beadsman, the Baron and his guests are carried off by death or nightmare, the lovers may, as Arthur Carr has argued, take flight into "a happier and warmer reality." Nevertheless there is something sad about the way they flee away, almost like ghosts, into the storm, just as the immemorial realm they gain is strangely vague, remote, and insubstantial. Nor, as Carr himself has pointed out, are they permitted to escape without the poet's reminder "that we have been listening to a fairy-tale, with its formula of happiness after danger."[11] Thus we remain charmed but also perplexed by the poem and its blend of domesticity, elvishness, gothicism, realism, courtly romance, riddle, fairy tale, and legend, a combination that remains to the last deliberately anachronistic and refuses to relate itself to what we commonly mean by "reality" in any way that can be readily defined. If the poem continually suggests the transforming power of the aroused imagination, the logic of "Adam's dream," it simultaneously exposes, through the heterogeneous devices and conventions it employs, the kinds of stratagem to which poetic magic must resort.

NOTES

1. Leigh Hunt, *Imagination and Fancy,* 2nd ed. (London, 1845), p. 314.

2. The two most influential discussions have been Earl Wasserman's chapter on the poem in *The Finer Tone: Keats' Major Poems* (Baltimore, 1953), pp. 97–137; and Jack Stillinger's essay, "The Hoodwinking of Madeline: Scepticism in The Eve of St. Agnes,' " *Studies in Philology,* LVIII (1961), 533–55. Wasserman broke sharply with earlier interpreters by reading the poem (in a way that would have staggered the Rossettis) as an illustration or enactment of Keats's metaphor of life as a "Mansion of Many Apartments" and of the imagination as "Adam's dream." The poem thus becomes a metaphysical progression culminating, with the lovers' union, in the demonstration of "the truth of Imagination—What the imagination seizes as Beauty must be truth" (I, 184). Stillinger's essay skillfully analyzes the shortcomings of Wasserman's method. Yet he makes his case only to move to the opposite extreme by reading the poem as antiromance, an instance of Keats's later skepticism and disillusionment with the imagination. Thus with a little shift of emphasis Romeo becomes Lothario, romance becomes seduction, and the lovers' passion little more than the culmination of a rake's sordid stratagem. The interpretation seems hardly less one-sided than the one it would correct. Both discussions tend to reduce the poem to the value of a simple thesis, a representation of the imagination as either good or evil, truth or deception.

3. Keats actually applied the adjective to *Isabella,* but the context of his letter makes it clear he thought the objection true also of *St. Agnes,* "only not so glaring."

4. See Marian H. Cusac, "Keats as Enchanter: An Organizing Principle of *The Eve of St. Agnes,*" *Keats-Shelley Journal,* XVII (1968), 113–19, a brief, suggestive study of the role of the narrator.

5. For a different view, see Harold Bloom's discussion of the poem in *The Visionary Company* (New York, 1961), pp. 369–75. While essentially an independent one, my own reading of the poem is most indebted to the essays of R. H. Fogle and Arthur Carr cited below, as well as to C. F. Burgess's admirably rounded discussion of structure and technique in " 'The Eve of St. Agnes': One Way to the Poem," *English Journal,* LIV (1965), 389–94. John Jones's argument, in his recent full discussion of the poetry, *John Keats's Dream of Truth* (London, 1969), that the "dream come true" / "just a dream" ambivalence is the major "axis" of Keats's verse (p. 170) is especially appropriate to the study of *St. Agnes.* Jones's later discussion of the poem as a more

intense redoing of *Isabella* (pp. 232–42), however, curiously ignores virtually all the elements of technique, convention, and narrative focus that separate the two works in skill and maturity of control and consequently in their fundamental meaning.

6. Byron wrote Murray on November 9, 1820: "Mr. Keats, whose poetry you enquire after, appears to me what I have already said: such writing is a sort of mental ****_******** his *Imagination*. I don't mean he is *indecent,* but viciously soliciting his own ideas into a state, which is neither poetry or any thing else but a Bedlam vision produced by raw pork and opium" (*The Works of Lord Byron, Letters and Journals,* ed. Rowland E. Prothero [London, 1901], v, 117 [Byron's italics]; see also 109). In all probability, Byron had not seen *St. Agnes* or the 1820 volume at this time but was basing his comments on Keats's earlier verse.

7. See n.2, above.

8. Hunt, *Imagination and Fancy,* p. 332.

9. "A Reading of Keats's 'Eve of St. Agnes,' " *College English,* vi (1945), 326.

10. See *The Letters of John Keats,* ed. Hyder Edward Rollins (Cambridge, Mass., 1958), ii, 162–64, 182–83, for the reactions of Woodhouse and Taylor. The relation of Keats's revisions to earlier versions of the poem is discussed in Stillinger's "The Text of 'The Eve of St. Agnes,' " *Studies in Bibliography,* xvi (1963), 207–12.

11. Arthur Carr, "John Keats' Other 'Urn,' " *The University of Kansas City Review,* xx (1954), 241. A directly opposite view is expressed by Herbert G. Wright in "Has Keats's 'Eve of St. Agnes' a Tragic Ending?" *Modern Language Review,* xl (1945), 90–94.

Keats and the Canon

Our second selection on Keats pairs intriguingly with Sperry's chapter, because Marjorie Levinson so dramatically develops the idea of wish-fulfillment as a key to Keatsian art. In her exciting *Keats's Life of Allegory: The Origins of a Style* she starts from the often-repeated comments on the "badness" of much of Keats's verse and the suggestion first put forward by Byron that it was masturbatory. Levinson's project is to define the poet's central achievement as the paradoxical constituting of its "goodness" out of its "badness," as she illustrates first with "On First Looking into Chapman's Homer." It takes courage thus to found one's overarching critique of a poet's career on so overt a contradiction, but it is by pursuing such contradictions that contemporary critics reach the peculiar originality of their most characteristic insights.

For a critic like Levinson operating within critical parameters defined some time ago, received opinion becomes a challenge to interpretive daring. An example is her judgment that the much-praised admonition (from the "Ode to Melancholy") to "burst Joy's grape against thy palate fine" is "a terrible one." For

> The pleasure of grapes is, literally, the pleasure of *grapes;* the natural, plural clustered condition of the grape. It is, further, the pleasure of a mouth, a throat, and a stomach full of grapes. . . . The full Keatsian pleasure (revealingly a melancholic pleasure) consists of a single grape not swallowed. The real pleasure of the single grape burst against the palate is the swerve from the imagined sensation of a mouthful and a lifetime of grapes swallowed, their fine juice fermenting one's bodily liquors. (77–78)

The fearlessness of such a commentary surely refutes the charge that contemporary academic criticism is drab or lacking in vitality—as does the conclusion of this selection, which claims that Keats's poetry is, indeed, masturbatory, but no more so than Wordsworth's and Byron's. The courage animating this kind of interpretive analysis seems to us characteristic of the most exciting (and therefore inevitably controversial) recent revaluations, both psychological and sociological, of romantic poetry.

From *Keats's Life of Allegory: The Origins of a Style* (Oxford: Basil Blackwell, 1988), pp. 1–17, 39–41.

There's no need, I think, to defend the statement that our commitment to a canonical Keats runs deep. Anyone who has thought critically about Keats in the past five years must appreciate the difference between the Keats commentary and the kinds of inquiries conducted on the poems of the other Romantics. This business of a canonical Keats is not a matter of explicitly idealizing or redemptive readings.[1] I'm talking about the assumptions that organize our practical understanding of the relations between Keats's life and writing and the social context in which they both materialized.

Keats, like Shakespeare, is a name for the figure of the capable poet. The best Keats criticism (Lionel Trilling, John Bayley, Christopher Ricks), and the smartest (the Harvard Keatsians), mark out the canonical extremes and define a range of problems, many of which are addressed in this study.[2] These greatly disparate critiques, sketched toward the end of this chapter, are both founded on a single premise, one which opposes *tout court* the governing thesis of the contemporary criticism of Keats's poetry. We all agree to know the man and his writing by their eminent authenticity: Bayley's 'Gemeine', Ricks's 'unmisgiving' imagination, Eliot's epistolary *idiot savant,* Vendler's true craftsmanship. In order to produce this knowledge, we put what the contemporary reviews called Keats's 'vulgarity' under the sign of psychic, social, and textual unself-consciousness: roughly, the sign of sensuous sincerity. Further, by the providential tale of intellectual, moral, and artisanal, development we find coded in Keats's letters, we put the vulgarity which cannot be so sublimed in the early verse and show its gradual sea-change into the rich, inclusive seriousness that distinguishes the great poetry. Thus do we rescue Keats's deep meanings from his alluring surfaces, his poetic identity from his poetical identifications. By and large, we read the poetry as a sweet solution to a bitter life: a resolution of the actual contradictions. The writing is not, we say, an escape from the real but a constructive operation performed upon it so as to bring out its Truth, which is also a new and deeply human Beauty. We describe, in short, a transformation of experience by knowledge and by the aesthetic practice which that knowledge promotes. The word that best describes this critical plot is romance: a march from alienation to identity. The governing figure of this narrative is the Coleridgean or Romantic symbol and its rhetorical device the oxymoron: irreducibly syncretic ideas. The hero of our critical history is a profoundly associated sensibility and his gift to us is the exemplary humanism of his life and art.

Trilling, Bayley and Ricks have discriminated a stylistic 'badness' that occurs throughout Keats's poetry: a certain remove whereby Keats signifies his *interest* in his representations and, we might add, in his own expressiveness. In so doing, these critics approximate the response of Keats's contemporaries, analyzed below. However, by emphasizing the psychic investment rather than the social remove which prompts it (and, by focusing mimetic and rhetorical rather than subjective disorders), Bayley and Ricks bring Keats's discursive alienations into the dominant romance.[3] Following these powerful writers, we read Keats's lapses from the good taste of innocent, object-related representation and transparent subjectivity as a determined consent to his own voluptuous inwardness *and* to the self-conscious recoil. By this willed abandon, Keats transcends both enthrallments, thereby releasing the reader into a more generous (in today's parlance, 'intersubjective') relational mode. In other words, those critics who acknowledge the stylistic vulgarity of Keats's writing put it in the redeemable field of creaturely instinct and defense, and not in the really unsettling category of externality, materiality, and ambitious reflexiveness. When Keats nods, we say, it is because he *dares* to nod ('swoon', 'sink', or 'cease'), not because he tries too hard.

The early reviews tell a different story. The most casual survey of this commentary (1817–35) reveals a response so violent and sustained, so promiscuous in its blending of social, sexual, and stylistic critique, and so sharply opposed to mainstream modern commentary as to imply a determinate insight on the part of Keats's contemporaries and a determined oversight on the part of his belated admirers. While we're all familiar with *Blackwood's* Cockney School attack (Lockhart's rebuke of Keats's literary presumption ['so back to the shop Mr. John, back to "plasters, pills, and ointment boxes, . . ." ']), we have not attended very closely to the sexual invective, and not at all to the relation between those two discourses. Time and again, the poetry is labelled 'profligate', 'puerile', 'unclean', 'disgusting', 'recklessly luxuriant and wasteful', 'unhealthy', 'abstracted', and 'insane'.[4] More specifically, it is graphed as a stylistically self-indulgent verse: prolix, repetitive, metrically and lexically licentious, overwrought. The diatribes culminate in the epithet 'nonsense'.

We have always related the savaging of the early poetry to the anomaly of Keats's social position and to the literary blunders which follow from that fact: generally, problems of diction, rhetoric, and subject matter, all of them reducible to the avoidable (and, finally, avoided) misfortune of Keats's coterie. Because we situate these blunders at a certain level and within a very contained biographical field, and because we isolate them from the beauties of the so-called great poetry, we have not understood the deeper insult of Keats's writing, that which explains the intensity and displacements of the early response and the equal but opposite distortions of the twentieth-century view.

From the distance of today, one can detect in those vituperative catalogues a governing discursive and even cognitive model. Keats's poetry was characterized as a species of masturbatory exhibitionism, an offensiveness further associated with the self-fashioning gestures of the petty bourgeoisie.[5] The erotic opprobrium pinpoints the self-consciousness of the verse: its autotelic reflection on its own fine phrases, phrases stylistically objectified as acquired, and therefore *mis*acquired property. The sexual language of the reviews was, of course, an expedient way to isolate Keats, but it is also a telling index to the social and existential project outlined by Keats's style. In his overwrought inscriptions of canonical models, the early readers sensed the violence of Keats's raids upon that empowering system: a violence driven by the strongest desire for an authorial manner and means, and for the social legitimacy felt to go with it. In the alienated reflexiveness of Keats's poetry, the critics read the signature of a certain kind of life, itself the sign of a new social phenomenon. Byron's famous epithet for the style of the Cockney writers, 'shabby genteel', puts the matter plainly.

The grand distinction of the under forms of the new school of poets is their *vulgarity*. By this I do not mean that they are *coarse*, but 'shabby-genteel', as it is termed. A man may be *coarse* and yet not *vulgar,* and the reverse . . . It is in their *finery* that the new under school are *most* vulgar, and they may be known by this at once; as what we called at Harrow 'a Sunday blood' might be easily distinguished from a gentleman . . . In the present case, I speak of writing, not of persons. (Extract from letter to John Murray, 25 March 1821)

If we were not already convinced of Byron's ear for social nuance, we would only have to recall Keats's confession, 'I look upon fine Phrases like a Lover.'

Like our own criticism, the early reviews read in Keats's poetry 'a life of Allegory', but the meaning they develop by that allegory lies in the realm of social production, not aesthetics, metaphysics, or humanistic psychology. To those early readers, 'Keats' was the allegory of a man belonging to a certain class and aspiring, as that entire class was felt to do, to another: a man with particular but typical ambitions and with particular but typical ways of realizing them. A world of difference separates this hermeneutic from the 'poignantly allegorical life', an adventure in soul-making, which has become today's John Keats.[6] By respecting the social-sexual compounding evidenced by those reviews, we recover the sense of danger underlying our formalist and rhetorical readings of Keats's middling states: his adolescence, his literariness, his stylistic suspensions, his pronounced reflexiveness. We focus Keats's position—sandwiched between the Truth of the working class and the Beauty of the leisure class—not as a healthy both / and but as the monstrous neither / nor constructed in the reviews. We see that the problem of Keats's early poetry is not its regressive escapism (its instincts, so to speak), but its stylistic project: a social-ego enterprise. The deep contemporary insult of Keats's poetry, and its deep appeal (and long opacity) for the modern reader, is its idealized enactment of the conflicts and solutions which defined the middle class at a certain point in its development and which still to some extent obtain. We remember that Keats's style can delineate that station so powerfully because of his marginal, longing relation to the legitimate bourgeoisie (and its literary exemplars) of his day. In emulating the condition of the accomplished middle class (the phrase is itself an oxymoron), Keats isolated the constitutive contradictions of that class. The final fetish in Keats's poetry is precisely that stationing tension.

By the stylistic contradictions of his verse, Keats produces a writing which is aggressively *literary* and therefore not just 'not Literature' but, in effect, *anti-*Literature: a parody. We will see that Keats's most successful poems are those most elaborately estranged from their own materials and procedures and thus from both a writerly and readerly subjectivity. The poetic I describe, following the lead of Keats's contemporaries, is the opposite of 'unmisgiving'.[7] The triumph of the great poetry is not its capacious, virile, humane authenticity but its subversion of those authoritarian values, effects which it could not in any case, and for the strongest social reasons, realize. This is the triumph of the double-negative. The awfulness of the early work, by contrast, is explained as an expression of the *single,* or suffered negative: a nondynamic reflection of Keats's multiple estrangements and of the longing they inspired. The accomplished poetry may be considered the negative knowledge of Keats's actual life: the production of his freedom by the figured negation of his given being, natural and social. To say this is not to consecrate Keats a precocious post-modernist, only to take seriously the social facts and meanings embedded in his representations and in the contemporary reception. It is to see in 'the continuous manner in which the whole is elaborated' a parodic reproduction of the social restrictions that marked Keats as *wanting:* unequipped, ineffectual, and deeply fraudulent.[8]

Keats did not accomplish by this greatly overdetermined stratagem the goodness he craved: that plenitude of being he worshipped in the great canonical models and which he images in Autumn's breeding passiveness. What he did produce by what Shelley called 'the bad sort of style' was a truly *negative* capability. I call this power 'virtual' to bring out its parodic relation to authorized forms of power, 'virtuoso' to suggest its professional, technically preoccupied character, and 'virtuous' by reference to its imposed and contrived limitations. (See chapter 2, p. 45 and note 2, and chapter 3, pp. 103–8). To generate this verbal sequence is also, of course, to put as the ruling stylistic and social question the question of Keats's virility: to begin, that is, where the early commentary leaves off. We will take Keats's own phrase, the 'wreathed trellis of a working brain', as a figure for Keats's negative power: his inside-out, thoroughly textualized and autotelic accomplishment. In the celebrated poise of Keats's poetry, we read the effect of the impossible project set him by his interests and circumstances: to become by (mis)acquiring; to become by his writing at once authorized (properly derivative) and authorial (original); to turn his suffered objectivity into a sign of his self-estranged psyche, and to wield that sign as a shield and an ornament.

The project of this book is to read the meaning of a life in the style of a man's writing, and then to read that writing, that style, and that life back into their original social context. What I describe is a self-consciously distanced and totalizing study on the order of Sartre's *Saint Genet*.

THE LIFE

The facts of Keats's life are too familiar to bear recounting here. I refer the reader to Aileen Ward's unsurpassed biography and to the important work of Walter Jackson Bate and Robert Gittings.[9] Below, I elaborate those aspects of the story that bear directly on Keats's stylistic development.

To observe that Keats's circumstances put him at a severe remove from the canon is to remark not only his educational deficits but his lack of those skills prerequisite to a transparent mode of appropriation: guiltless on the one side, imperceptible on the other. He knew some French and Latin, little Italian, no Greek. His Homer was Chapman, his Dante was Cary, his Provençal ballads translations in an edition of Chaucer, his Boccaccio Englished. Keats's art education was largely by engravings and, occasionally, reproductions. His absorption of the accessible English writers was greatly constrained by his ignorance of the originals upon which they drew and by his nonsystematic self-education. To say all this is to observe Keats's literally corrupt relation to the languages of poetry: his means of production.

We might also consider a more mundanely mechanical aspect of Keats's composition. Throughout his life, Keats felt compelled *physically* to escape his hard, London reality in order to write. A great deal of the poetry was conceived or composed at a number of modest, middle-class and, as it were, publicly designated resorts: Margate, Shanklin (the Isle of Wight), Burford Bridge (Surrey). Keats could afford only the leanest accommodations, of course, and often he adjourned to these spots alone and off-season. When even these small excursions were not possible, Keats sought his escape on Hampstead Heath, in the British Institution, or in a friend's well-furnished living room. In short, the graciously conformable bowers and dells enjoyed by Wordsworth and Coleridge were no more available to Keats than were the glory and grandeur of Greece and Rome, Byron's and Shelley's enabling resorts.

'Romantic retirement' gains a whole new dimension with Keats. Imagine the solitude of a young man in a seaside rooming house in April, a borrowed picture of Shakespeare his only companion: a man with nothing to do for a set period of time but write the pastoral epic which would, literally, *make* him. Compare this withdrawal to the seclusion of a writer musing in his garden, deserted by his wife and literary friends of an afternoon; or to the isolation of two English aristocrats, recognized poets both, galloping along the Lido and relishing their escape from the cant of high society and from its official voices. Better yet, imagine a conversation poem, a social verse, or a lyrical ballad by Keats; project from Keats's pen a sublimely inspired ode on the order of Shelley's 'Mont Blanc', or a *Defence of Poetry,* or a pamphlet on the Convention of Cintra. The experiment should point up the problematic nature for Keats of those elementary and, in the period, normative literary effects: authority, authenticity, and ease.

Apropos that last and deeply Romantic effect, ease, we recall that Keats hadn't the luxury for a 'wise passiveness'. His early detection of his disease, Tom's condition, the time constraints imposed by his medical training, his assumption of responsibility for his sister, his haste to make a name so he could marry Fanny; all these familiar facts precluded the meditative quiescence which enabled in the other Romantics a rhetoric of surpassing naturalness.[10] Wordsworth's compositional program was simply not an option for a man who could not wait upon memory's slow digestive processes. Nor could Keats draw upon his everyday life, a monotonous struggle to get by and get ahead, for the interest, surprise, and suggestiveness which Byron and Shelley found in their large circumstances. Keats's necessary writing trips were hasty and purposive; the work of this simulated leisure was the production of pleasure, precondition for the rich, selfless, and suspended literary exercise which was Keats's dream of art. The result of these sad, self-vexing outings is a poetry evincing the paradoxes by which it is made. A poetry too happy by far, too full by half. When Shelley disdainfully rejected Keats's advice, 'load every rift with ore', he knew what he was about. He registered the class implications of Keats's plenitude, and knew that he, for one, did not have to plump his poems to the core.

Before we can begin re-reading Keats, we must really imagine what we know. We must see very clearly, as John Bayley saw, that Keats was a man whose almost complete lack of control over the social code kept him from living his life. He could not write his poetry in the manner he required, marry the woman he loved, claim his inheritance, hold his family together, or assist his friends. He could not, in short, seize any of the appurtenances of manhood. Keats was as helplessly and ignominiously a 'boy' poet as Chatterton, and Byron's 'Mankin' was a viciously knowing insult.

The range of paradoxes which Byron and his contemporaries observed in Keats's poetry is ultimately referrable to the fact that it was not given to Keats, a poet in Shelley's 'general sense', to be a poet in the most pedestrian, professional, 'restricted' sense. Keats had to make for himself a life (the training at Guy's; then, getting by on his allowance; finally, when the money ran out, the projected career of ship's surgeon), while writing a poetry that was, structurally, a denial of that life. At no time did Keats make any money from his writing. (One wonders *how,* exactly, Keats applied the title 'poet' to himself. How did he introduce himself in ordinary social interactions?) The oddly abstract materialism of the poetry—its overinvestment in its signs—takes on a new look when we remember both Keats's remove from his representational manner and means, and also his want of those real things that help people live their lives. Is it any wonder that the poetry produced by this man should be so autotelic, autoerotic, so fetishistic and so stuck? Should it surprise us to find that his dearest fantasy—a picture of somebody reading, a window on the one side, a goldfish bowl on the other—takes the form of a multiply framed, *trompe-l'oeil* still life? 'Find the subject', we might call it; or, what is the same thing, 'Find the frame'.

Keats's poetry was at once a tactical activity, or an escape route from an actual life, and a final construction: the concrete imaginary to that apparitional actual. What was, initially, a substitute *for* a grim life became for Keats a substitute life: a real life of substitute things—simulacra—which, though they do not nourish, neither do they waste. At the very end of his career, Keats began, I believe, to position this parodic solution as part of the problem. 'Lamia' is Keats's attempt to frame the problematic of his life and writing and thus to set it aside.

It is crucial to see, as Bayley saw, that the deep desire in Keats's poetry is not for aesthetic things or languages *per se* (that is, Byron's 'finery'), but for the social code inscribed in them, a code which was, to Keats, a human transformational grammar. Indeed, all Keats's meditations on art and identity (typically, plasticity), should be related to his abiding desire, to live. The real perversion of Keats's poetry is not its display of its cultural fetishes but its preoccupation with the system felt to organize those talismanic properties. Keats could have had all the urns, Psyches, nightingales, Spenserianisms, Miltonisms, Claudes, and Poussins he wanted; he was not, however, permitted possession of the social grammar inscribed in that aesthetic array, and this was just what Keats was after.

We illuminate Keats's legitimacy problem by way of the originality anxiety that seems to have beset most of the Romantic and what used to be called pre-Romantic poets. The past only lies like a weight on the brain of those who inherit it. Or rather, the past imposes a special *kind* of burden on those individual talents who feel themselves disinherited by the Tradition, and, thus, excluded from the dialectic of old and new, identity and difference. Wordsworth's celebrated defense of his poetical innovations—'every author, as far as he is great and at the same time *original,* has had the task of *creating* the taste by which he is to be enjoyed'— must be understood as the statement of a man so assured of his entitlement that he can trust his originality to be received as intelligible and valuable. (That Wordsworth's confidence was not always confirmed is not the issue here.) Keats, by contrast, could not begin to invent an original voice without first and *throughout* establishing his legitimacy: roughly, his derivativeness.

Chatterton, the poet with whom Keats felt the strongest affinities, developed a most economical solution to this problem. By his perfect reproduction of 'the medieval', Chatterton not only established that epochal concept as a normative style, thereby sanctioning his persona, Rowley, and that figure's verse, he produced as well and dialectically, *for the knowing reader,* the originality of the entire *oeuvre* (viz. poems, charts, maps, coins). Theoretically, Rowley's canon at once created the taste, which it represented as already venerable and prestigious, and offered itself as the only artifact capable of satisfying it.

Practically speaking, however, Chatterton couldn't begin to fashion the readership he needed. Indeed, the logic of his enterprise compelled him to do all he might to malform—*misinform*—his audience. The literariness of his poetry was strictly a function of its documentary, antiquarian presentation. The aesthetic dimension of the writing only materialized under the pressure of a fundamentally historical interest, and in that case, of course, the literary credit was Rowley's. Chatterton's successful negotiation of the technical imperatives set him by his social facts required his entire self-effacement, as a man and a writer. A rare intuition of this paradox surfaces in the controversy prompted by the hoax poems. We find considerable puzzlement among Chatterton's detractors, and ingenuity on the part of his defenders, regarding the anomaly of a writer who would seem to have preferred the inferior reputation of translator-editor to the glory of proper poetic genius: that is, originality.[11] To us, of course, Chatterton's perversity indicates how completely overdetermined a choice he faced. His election of the lesser fame, scholarly authority, was in fact an embrace of the bad originality of the counterfeiter. In that vexed ideal, we read the situation of the writer whose mastery consists exclusively in his self-violation.

Keats sidestepped Chatterton's final solution. By the self-signifying *imperfection* of his canonical reproductions (a parodic return upon his own derivativeness), Keats drew upon the licensing primacy of the code even as his *representation* of that total form changed the nature of its authority. The pronounced badness of Keats's writing figures the mythic goodness of the canon and, by figuring, at once exalts and delimits it. Thus did Keats plot for himself a scene of writing. By the double unnaturalness of his style, Keats projects the authority of an *anti*-nature, stable by virtue of its continuous self-revolutionizing and secured by its contradictions. The proof of these claims is the rest of this book, but let me offer as a critical instance a reading of 'Chapman's Homer'.

On First Looking into Chapman's Homer

Much have I trevelled [travell'd] in the realms of gold,
  And *many goodly* states and kingdoms seen;
  Round *many* western islands have I been
Which bards in fealty to Apollo hold.
Oft of one wide expanse had I been told
  That deep-browed [brow'd] Homer ruled as his demesne;
  Yet did I never breathe its pure screne
Till I heard Chapman speak out loud and bold.[:]
Then felt I like some watcher of the skies
  When a new planet swims into his ken;
Or like stout Cortez when with eagle eyes
  He stared [star'd] at the Pacific,—and all his men
Looked [Look'd] at each other with a wild surmise—
  Silent, upon a peak in Darien.

I have accented several words in the first three lines by way of amplifying the tone of Keats's address. Even if we were ignorant of Keats's social disadvantages, this fulsome claim to literary ease would give us pause. The very act of assertion, as well as its histrionically commanding and archly literary style, undermine the premise of natural authority and erudition. The contemporary reader might have observed as well some internal contradictions; not only *is* Homer the Golden Age, but not to 'have' Greek and not to have encountered Homer by the age of twenty-three is to make one's claim to any portion of the literary empire suspect. (Keats's acquaintance with Pope's translation is suppressed by the sonnet.) Keats effectively assumes the role of the literary adventurer (with the commercial nuance of that word) as opposed to the mythic explorer: Odysseus, Cortes, Balboa. More concretely, he advertises his corrupt access to the literary system and to those social institutions which inscribe that system systematically in the hearts and minds of young men. To read Homer in translation and after having read Spenser, Coleridge, Cary, and whoever else is included in Keats's travelogue, is to read Homer badly (in a heterodox and alienated way), and to subvert the system which installs Homer in a particular and originary place. Moreover, to 'look into' Chapman's Homer is to confess—in this case, *profess*—one's fetishistic relation to the great Original. Keats does not *read* even the translation. To 'look into' a book is to absorb it idiosyncratically at best, which is to say, with casual or conscious opportunism. Similarly, the substitution of 'breathe' for the expected 'read' in line 7 marks the rejection of a sanctioned mode of literary acquisition. To 'breathe' a text is to take it in, take from it and let it out, somewhat the worse for wear. It is, more critically, to miscategorize the object and in such a way as to proclaim one's intimacy with it. Both the claim and the title of Keats's sonnet are, in a word, vulgar.

One is reminded of Valéry's appraisal of museum pleasure: 'For anyone who is close to works of art, they are no more objects of delight than his own breathing'.[12] Keats, we observe, rejoices in his respiration and goes so far as to fetishize the very air he admits. I single out the phrase 'pure serene' not only because it is structurally foregrounded but because it reproduces in miniature the method— the working contradiction—of the sonnet. What Keats 'breathes' is, of course, anything but pure and Homeric (since he reads in translation and perversely with respect to canon protocol), and the phrase formally exposes that fact. We cannot help but see that 'pure serene', a primary reification, further calls attention to itself as a fine phrase, that Keats clearly looks upon as a lover. Not only is the phrase a Miltonic construction, but more recent usage would have characterized it as a sort of translator-ese. One thinks of Pope's 'vast profound' and indeed, of Cary's own 'pure serene', a description of Dante's ether (1814). Coleridge uses the phrase in his 'Hymn before Sunrise in the Vale of Chamouni', 1802. Keats's reproduction of the phrase designates both his access to the literary system and his mode of access—that of translator to Original. In effect, he intentionalizes the alienation he suffers by his social deficits. By signifying the restriction, he converts it into restraint: 'might half-slumbering on its own right arm'. Let me note here that the translation of an adjective into a noun, while etymologically justifiable, transforms Homer's pure and therefore insensible atmosphere—his aura—into a palpable particular: a detached literary style and a self-reflexive one at that. What figures in Homer as a natural and epochal expressiveness is in Keats, and first, a represented object. Only by performing that office does the Homeric value assume for Keats an expressive function.

The thing to remark is the way Keats produces the virtues of his alienated access to the canon. The consummate imagery of the poem—that which accounts for its overall effect of 'energetic . . . calmness'—is, obviously, that of Cortes/ Balboa 'star[ing] at the Pacific' while 'all his men / Looked [Look'd] at each other with a wild surmise— / Silent, upon a peak in Darien'. Cortes, we notice, is a 'stout' and staring fellow: a solid citizen. 'Stout' means, of course, 'stout-hearted', but in the context, where Cortes's direct stare at the object of his desire is juxtaposed against the 'surmise' of his men (and the alliteration reinforces these visual connections), one feels the energy of the men and the stuck or frozen state of their leader. By their surmise—a liminal, semi-detached state—the men are 'wild', a word which in the Romantic idiom means 'free'. We clearly see that the relation of the men to that (etymologically) literal 'pure serene', the Pacific, is indirect and perverse. Who in that situation would avert his gaze?

Claude Finney has reminded us that according to Keats's sources, Balboa's men were forbidden the prospect until their leader had had his full gaze.[13] We can see that the social discrepancy vividly sketched by Keats's original gets translated in the sonnet into an existential and self-imposed difference, and one that inverts the given power ratio by rendering the men, not the master, free and vital. One does not, I think, go too far in associating Keats with those capably disenfranchised men.

It is the stillness and strangeness of the men—their peculiar *durée*—which stations Keats's sonnet, all the gregarious exploration metaphors notwithstanding. Homer enters the poem as the Pacific enters the sensibilities of Cortes's men: through Chapman's/Cortes's more direct possession of/by the object of desire. Odysseus's extrovert energy animates Keats's sonnet but, again, perversely. In the Keatsian space, that energy turns self-reflexive, reminding us perhaps of Tennyson's 'Ulysses'. The poem looks at itself as the men look at each other. The virtue of both looks is their impropriety; what they refuse by that gesture is the Gorgon stare, the direct embrace of and by the authorizing Original. Keats's poem 'speak[s] out loud and bold' by not speaking 'out' at all. We finish the sonnet, which seems to be predicated on such a simple *donnée,* and we wonder where we have travelled. What happened to Homer, and to Keats for that matter? Why does Keats interpose between himself and his ostensible subject Chapman, Cary, Coleridge, Gilbert, Robertson, Herschel, Balboa, Cortes, and Cortes's men? Why does Keats leave us with this off-center cameo, an image of turbulent stasis among the extras of the cast when what we expect is a 'yonder lie the Azores' flourish by the principal? What *is* this poem? By the conventions it sets, it should strike us as a graceful display of literary inspiration and gratitude. But it seems other, and otherwise. How do we explain the real power of its slant rhyme?

Let me recall Hunt's comment on the sonnet: 'prematurely masculine'. By emphasizing the adverb for a change, we begin to see that Keats's unnatural (illicit) assumption of power, signified by the 'poetical' octet, does not *qualify* the 'masculinity' of the sestet, it constitutes it. The direct and natural compression of the sestet is the stylistic effect of the displayed disentitlement that is the functional representation of the opening eight lines. The pivot which constructs this before-and-after dynamic (the coordinates for a range of ratios: imitation-genuine, protest-power, struggle-ease) is, of course, the experience of reading Chapman. The experience takes place, significantly, in the breach between the two movements of the sonnet. Rather than imitate Chapman, Keats reproduces Chapman's necessarily parodic (that is, Elizabethan) inscription of Homer. The queerness of Chapman's 'mighty line, loud-and-bold' version is rewritten in Keats's own parodic Elizabethan*ism,* and, through the queerness of the Cortes/Balboa image. It is the self-reflexive, fetishistic inscription of the canon—the display of bad access and misappropriation—that emancipates Keats's words, Keats's sonnet breaks free of Homer and Chapman by mis-giving both. By the English he puts on Homer's serenity (he reifies it) and on Chapman's 'masculine' extrovert energy, Keats produces the perpetual imminence which is the hero of his sonnet. In the

Keatsian idiom, we could call that imminence or suspension a 'stationing', with an ear for the full social resonance of Keats's aesthetic word.[14]

The instance of this poem would suggest that Keats's relation to the Tradition is better conceived as dialogic (Bakhtin) than dialectic (Bloom).[15] The poetry does not clear a space for itself by a phallic agon; it opens itself to the Tradition, defining itself as a theater wherein such contests may be eternally and inconclusively staged.[16] The authority of this poetry consists in its detachment from the styles or voices it entertains. By this detachment, these styles become *signatures;* not audible voices but visible, material *signs* of canonical voices. These signs— like all such marks, inauthentic and incomplete—are *not,* ultimately, mastered by the master-of-ceremonies. And because they remain external to authorial consciousness, theirs is the empowering virtue of the supplement. In these magic supplements, 'Things semi-real', lies the terrific charm of Keats's poetry.

The constrained badness of 'Chapman's Homer' constitutes its goodness, which is to say, its rhetorical force. The paradox hinges, naturally, on the word 'contained'. When Keats is great, it is because he *signifies* his alienation from his *materia poetica,* a fact that modern criticism and textual studies have suppressed.[17] This alienation—inevitable, given Keats's education, class, and opportunities— was highly expedient. By it, Keats could possess the 'stuff of creativity' without becoming possessed by it. By 'stuff', I do not mean Bloom's primary, inspirational matter but the means and techne for exercises in literary production. Keats's poetry, inspired by translations, engravings, reproductions, schoolroom mythologies, and Tassie's gems, delivers itself through these double and triple reproductions as the 'true, the blushful Hippocrene'. That phrase describes, ironically, *precisely* a substitute truth. Again, Byron understood these things; 'You know my opinion of *that second-hand* school of poetry.'

DISCUSSION

The early commentary has more to teach us. Byron's vivid epithets—'a Bedlam vision', a 'sad abortive attempt at all things, "signifying nothing" '—suggest that the masturbation trope was a most economical way of designating the poetry nonsense: not bad Literature but *non*Literature. In practical terms, it would seem that the association of Keats's poetry with masturbation was a way to isolate Keats without agonizing him.

We make sense of this tactic in two ways. First, the commonplace alignment of masturbation with madness suggests that whereas homosexuality was part of the normative heterosexual configuration—either a standard deviation or binary Other—masturbation was outside the curve: the age's ⅒, 'signifying nothing'.[18] This speculation is consistent with the class affronts (revelations of practical and ideological projects) leveled by Keats's poetry and explored below. Second, while 'nonsense' attacks always suppress unwanted sense, this particular noncognition additionally implies a response to the subjective irreality of Keats's self-reflexive poetry. 'Frigging [one's] *Imagination*' is one thing; frigging an imagination tenanted by other minds is another and a double-perversity. ('Frig' means 'to chafe or rub', 'to agitate the limbs' [OED], and most commonly, of course, to copulate. The '*Imagination*' to which Byron refers is, thus, a male and female property; or, Keats was accused of masturbating/fucking a Nothing.) Byron's contempt for

Keats's fetishistic relation to his acquired literary languages—borrowed 'finery'—masks a fearful insight into the subjective vacancy of Keats's writing. The 'Bedlam' association registers Keats's want of a proprietary subject-form: a voice distinct from the entertained canonical echoes and offering itself as a point, however 'bad', of readerly identification and authorial control. In Keats's poetry, the diverse cultural languages which we call the Tradition are both the means and the *manner* of representation, precisely, 'not-self': a fetishized, random collection of canonical signatures. One can see that this bad imitation of that earnest Romantic exercise, self-reflection, was, in effect, a burlesque. Keats's operations objectified the naturalness (originality, autonomy, and candor) of all writerly origins, putting those transparencies at risk. Even Byron, that determinedly mad bad man, was threatened; Byronic irony, no matter how inclusive, is always recuperated by the biographical subject-form coded in all the poems. Keats's poetry is differently, but no *more* masturbatory than Wordsworth's or Byron's, the largest, most virile poets of the age. We could say that Keats offended his generation so deeply by practicing one of its dominant modes of literary production while showing his hand. The sexual slander developed in the reviews registers Keats's relation to the Tradition, understood as a limited-access code with powerful social functions, and the class contradictions which that relation stylistically defined. At the same time, the critique displaces those contradictions to the sphere of private life and pathology: a safety zone. Thus was a serious, or materially designing sensuousness converted into a grave sensual disease.

NOTES

1. Alan Bewell's essay 'The Political Implications of Keats's Classicist Aesthetics' (*Studies in Romanticism,* 25, Summer 1986, pp. 220–9) represents the beginning of a departure from the critical norm for Keats studies. Bewell's sensitivity to the special political discourse of the writer situated by the *polis* on its *under*side or *between* its categorical positions, intimates a criticism beyond the margins of formalist, thematic, biographical, and metaphysical inquiry as these have developed in Romanticist scholarship over the past thirty years, *and also,* beyond the 'new historicism'. This last observation is part of an argument about the new historicism in Romantic studies (see Levinson, 'The New Historicism: What's in a Name', in *Critical Readings of Romantic History: Four Literary Essays,* ed. Levinson, forthcoming Blackwell's, 1988).

2. Walter Jackson Bate, *John Keats* [Cambridge, Mass.: Harvard Univ. Press, 1963); John Bayley, 'Keats and Reality', *Proceedings of the British Academy,* 1962, pp. 91–125; Douglas Bush, *John Keats* (New York, 1966); David Perkins, *The Quest for Permanence* (Cambridge, Mass.: Harvard Univ. Press, 1959); Christopher Ricks, *Keats and Embarrassment* (Oxford: Clarendon Press, 1974); Lionel Trilling, 'The Fate of Pleasure' in *Beyond Culture* (London: Secker and Warburg, 1955); Helen Vendler, *The Odes of John Keats* (Cambridge, Mass.: Harvard Univ. Press, 1983); Earl Wasserman, *The Finer Tone* (Baltimore, Md: Johns Hopkins Univ. Press, 1953).

3. John Bayley shrewdly divines that Keats's badness *is* his goodness. Had Bayley pushed his *aperçu* a little further, he would have come up against the meanings shadowed forth by the contemporary criticism. He would, perhaps, have associated the vulgarity of Keats's poetry with the situation, activities, and interests of the burgeoning middle class. As it is, Bayley's interpretative construct neatly registers this association by negation. 'Das Gemeine'—a postulate of healthy, earthy, Elizabethan (that is,

sociologically and psychically nonstratified) consciousness—is the mirror image of the nineteenth-century Keats, or of a poetry experienced as sick, pretentious, horribly contemporary, and thoroughly mannered. To the early readers, Keats's poetry was the expression of a 'folk' degraded by a bad eminence: the petty bourgeoisie.

4. All excerpts from contemporary notices are drawn from Donald Reiman, *The Romantics Reviewed: Contemporary Reviews of British Romantic Writers* (New York: Garland Publishing, 1972), C, I, 91–3; C, I, 95; C, I, 330–3; C, I, 339; C, I, 344–5; C, I, 385; C, I, 423–4; C, II, 470; C, II, 479; C, II, 531; C, II, 587–90; C, II, 614; C, II, 768–9; C, II, 807–8; C, II, 824–5; C, II, 829–30; and from G. M. Matthews, ed., *Keats, The Critical Heritage* (London: Routledge and Kegan Paul, 1971), pp. 35, 129–31, 150, 208–10, 248, 251. Censored Byron material checked against Leslie Marchand, *Byron's Letters and Journals,* vol. 7, 1820 (Cambridge, Mass.: Belknap Press, 1977), p. 217 (from letter to John Murray, 4 November 1820; Matthews lists it as 4 September).

5. The association of masturbation with the individualism and materialism of the early middle class is something of an established literary theme. Swift's Master Bates, the physician to whom Gulliver is apprenticed, teaches his student more than a middle-class trade, he teaches him the principles of acquisition and display (in Gulliver's case, anthropological), which constitute the middle class an *ideological* phenomenon over and above its economic being.

6. The much-quoted phrase 'poignantly allegorical life' is Bate's allusion to Keats's own observation that Shakespeare led 'a life of Allegory' (*Letters of John Keats,* ed. Robert Gittings, Oxford: Oxford Univ. Press, 1970; 1979, p. 218).

7. 'Unmisgiving' is Ricks's class term, taken from Keats, for the social, psychic, and rhetorical generosity of the poetry.

8. Fredric Jameson, *Sartre: The Origins of a Style* (New York: Columbia Univ. Press, 1961, 1984), p. vii.

In the course of my current research, I've discovered two books, both marvels of textual and theoretical exposition, that coincide closely with my reading of Keats's strategic defenses against, as well as his longing for, social and canonical majority. I refer to Louis Renza's *'A White Heron' and the Question of Minor Literature* (Madison, Wisc.: Univ. of Wisconsin Press, 1984), pp. 11–19; and David Lloyd's *Nationalism and Minor Literature: James Clarence Mangan and the Emergence of Irish Cultural Nationalism* (Berkeley, Calif.: Univ. of California Press, 1987), pp. 19–26. I thank Renza for refreshing my memory of Leslie Brisman's *Romantic Origins* (Ithaca: Cornell Univ. press, 1978): specifically, Brisman's derivation of George Darley's originality from his 'posture of weakness'.

9. Aileen Ward, *John Keats, the Making of a Poet* (New York: Viking, 1963); W. J. Bate, *John Keats,* R. Gittings, *John Keats* (London: Heinemann, 1968). All source information from Claude Finney, *The Evolution of Keats' Poetry,* 2 vols. (New York: Russell & Russell, 1963); Maurice R. Ridley, *Keats's Craftsmanship* (Oxford: Clarendon Press, 1933); Ian Jack, *Keats and the Mirror of Art* (Oxford: Clarendon Press, 1967); Miriam Allott, *The Poems of John Keats* (London and New York: Longman and Norton, 1970; 1972).

10. See Georg Lukács, *History and Class Consciousness,* trans. R. Livingstone (Cambridge, Mass.: MIT Press, 1971), pp. 164–72. See also Fredric Jameson, *Marxism and Form, Twentieth-Century Dialectical Theories of Literature* (Princeton, NJ: Princeton Univ. Press, 1971), on the worker's negative privilege: the lack of that leisure needed to 'intuit [the outside world] in the middle-class sense'. By the adjective 'middle-class' Jameson means the static and contemplative immediacy required by industrial capitalism's productive structures and relations.

11. Marjorie Levinson, *The Romantic Fragment Poem* (Chapel Hill, NC: Univ. of North Carolina Press, 1986), pp. 41–3, 239–40.

12. Quoted in Theodor Adorno, *Prisms,* trans. Weber and Weber (Cambridge, Mass.: MIT Press, 1982). The essay from which that quotation derives, 'Valery Proust Museum', deeply informs my discussion.

13. Finney, *The Evolution of Keats' Poetry,* vol. 1, p. 126: 'When, with infinite toil, they had climbed up the greater part of that steep ascent, Balboa commanded his men to halt, and advanced alone to the summit, that he might be the first who should enjoy a spectacle which he had so long desired'. From Robertson's *History of America.*

14. In his notes on Milton, Keats comments on 'what may be called his stationing or statuary. He is not content with simple description, he must station . . .', quoted in Jack, *Keats and the Mirror of Art,* p. 142.

15. To the extent that the inner voices in Keats's poetry tend to be maintained as signs, and also as signs of otherness, the 'we' experience central to Vološinov's dialogic analysis is missing. Keats's dialogism conforms more to the Bakhtinian model.

16. Allusions to the indeterminancy of Keats's gender (for example, 'Mankin', 'effeminate', 'boyish') should be taken as responses to Keats's mode of literary production or to the androgyny thereby implied. Keats's discourse 'mans' itself by a self-consciously autotelic receptivity, at once 'unmanning' the Tradition and, paradoxically, feminizing itself as well. Indeed, we might illuminate some of the more mysterious female figures in Keats's poetry by identifying them with the code or languages at once feared and desired by Keats: a phallic order. Aileen Ward's compelling defense of Fanny Brawne—her insistence that Keats loved Fanny precisely for the unpoetical distinctness of her character—is not contradicted by Keats's fascination with women like Isabella Jones: protean women who seemed, in addition, capable of transforming others, and, by liberating them from themselves, freeing them from their self-consciousness as well. Keats could love Fanny; he could *use* the Isabella Joneses of his life. What I'm suggesting is a loose association in Keats's poetry binding the phallic fetish-woman and the social code which Keats sought indirectly and defensively to embrace.

17. Jerome McGann, 'Keats and the Historical Method in Literary Criticism', *MLN,* 94 (1979), pp. 988–1032. McGann's discussion of the textual history of 'La Belle Dame' and of the Paolo and Francesca sonnet is an invaluable lesson in the ideological uses of textual scholarship.

18. See Tristram Engelhardt, Jr, 'The Disease of Masturbation: Values and the Concept of Disease', in *Bulletin of the History of Medicine,* 48 (1974), pp. 234–48; Engelhardt, 'Ideology and Etiology', *Journal of Medicine and Philosophy,* I (1976), pp. 256–68; Michel Foucault, *The History of Sexuality, An Introduction,* vol. I, trans. R. Hurley (New York: Pantheon, 1978).

Louis Crompton's fine study, *Byron and Greek Love* (Berkeley: Univ. of California Press, 1985), has opened our eyes to the homophobia of the early nineteenth century. The special ignominy I confer upon 'the masturbator' is not meant to contest or in any way qualify Crompton's representation. I am only elaborating the lesson we first learned from the Romantics. Namely, that Satan is always God's product, structural complement, and support system; that which *threatens* divinity because it reveals the *machina* in the *deus* is either not named, or it is named as a nonphenomenon. Not evil, but monstrous.

THERESA M. KELLEY

Poetics and the Politics of Reception: Keats's "La Belle Dame Sans Merci"

We present as a kind of complementary approach to Levinson's generalizing speculativeness, Theresa M. Kelley's carefully comprehensive analysis not only of "La Belle Dame Sans Merci" but also of the history of the poem's criticism. The ballad has become in recent years perhaps the single most important focus for revaluations of Keats's purposes and special accomplishments (the essay by Jerome McGann from which we have excerpted his commentary on "To Autumn," for example includes an important study of "La Belle Dame Sans Merci" referred to by Kelley). Other important recent studies include Anthony J. Bennett's " 'Alone and Palely Loitering': The Reader in Thrall in Keats's 'La Belle Dame Sans Merci' " (1990) and K. Rosenberg Devine's "Keats and Two Belle Dames Sans Merci" (1989).

The ballad provides interesting textual problems, and has become a rewarding target for feminist investigations, particularly since feminists have usually found Keats the most attractive of the male romantic poets. Kelly, however, in exploring the relation of figuration to fetishization demonstrates a tendency of the best recent literary criticism to make use of the findings in various disciplines, in this case most strikingly those of structuralist anthropology, as a means for reconsidering how early nineteenth-century poets made original use of their intellectual traditions. A primary strength of Kelley's essay—and in this it is representative of some of the most satisfying contemporary criticism—is its use of so wide a range of diverse approaches to articulate Keats's manipulations of his literary heritage. The essay works on and between several methodological axes: new-historicist and rhetorical criticism, reception theory, and to a lesser degree folklore and cultural studies. Its argument critiques new historicist claims that neglect the rhetorical practices of texts and the conditions of their production and revision. "Poetics and Politics of Reception" illustrates elegantly, especially in its articulation of Keats's awareness of the audience he was addressing in publishing his poem in Hunt's *Indicator,* how today's literary criticism exploits a variety of disciplines that less than forty years ago seldom entered into literary discussions.

From *ELH* 54 (1987): 333–362.

Keats's "La Belle Dame sans Merci" illustrates the lesson Keats chose to learn from reviewers who criticized the patently factitious rhyme and figuration of his first published poems. For his early critics, these features betray a Cockney poet's unjustified poetic ambition. For the mature Keats, they register the value of poetic craft and the status of the poet as maker. In "La Belle Dame sans Merci" Keats makes the strongest possible case for this view of his poetic task by presenting the belle dame as a figure whose otherness belongs to allegory, the most factitious of poetic figures. In doing so, he also acknowledges a line of poetic indebtedness and ambition that goes back to Spenser and allegorical romance.

In Keats's poem the knight and male chorus of kings, princes, and warriors claim that the belle dame has them in "thrall," even as her literary antecedents have enthralled their lovers. Although critics have rarely questioned this claim, it masks a prior entrapment.[1] As the object of their dread and fascination, she is a fetish, a figure whose alien status is the product of a collective decision to name her "la belle dame sans merci." Her figurative capture suggests the reciprocal relation between capture and estrangement that exists in poetic figures whose otherness implies an allegorical rather than symbolic structure of meaning. By this I mean that as a figure she resists the instantaneous understanding Coleridge found in Romantic symbols, those figures whose tenor and vehicle are so closely bound (or so represented) that we understand their meaning immediately.[2] As a poem whose central figure is defined by her antithetical relation to the speakers of the poem and to a long tradition of belle dames, Keats's "La Belle Dame sans Merci" explores the value of poetic figures whose meaning is not intuited but learned. As a figure the belle dame dramatizes what readers of traditional allegory assumed: an allegorical structure of meaning (whether or not the figure in question is part of a fully allegorical narrative) takes time to understand.[3]

The allegorical otherness of Keats's belle dame indicates two ways we might understand the historical consciousness of Romantic figures. First, because the poem that bears her name is evidently riddled with signs of its indebtedness to earlier poems, it presents a strong, perhaps deliberately exaggerated, case for the poetic value of figures that acknowledge their history. Second, because her otherness is a provocative if half-evasive reply to Keats's early critics, the belle dame makes this reception history part of her meaning.

Read in these terms, Keats's belle dame suggests how poetic composition may be bound up with the exigencies of publication and critical reception as well as personal circumstance. Clearly the extent to which this mutual binding exists depends on the poet, the occasion for writing, and other circumstances of time, ideology, and place. Until recently, critics have argued that these considerations are marginal, if relevant at all, for reading Keats. Instead, they have often assumed that Keats achieved poetic greatness in part because he transcended the negative criticism that greeted his first published poems.[4] A version of this assessment remains influential among post-structuralist critics. Thus Richard Macksey proposes that as Keats matured he abandoned the "the chatty archaism" of his Cockney style to adopt a simpler, more serene style that renounced much, including the poetic indebtedness of earlier poems.[5]

I suggest instead that as Keats composed then revised "La Belle Dame sans Merci" in 1819 and possibly 1820, he employed provocative elements of his early Cockneyism for specific poetic ends. If, as Jack Stillinger has argued, what distinguishes Keats's mature poetry is not the emergence of new themes but its style, a curious strength of this style is its exploitation of the Cockney "faults" that characterize Keats's early imitations of the language of Spenser and the seventeenth-century Spenserians: participial forms that verbalize nouns or nominalize verbs; metrical pauses and rhymes that loosen or demolish the closed neoclassical couplet; and a mannered blend of sensuous details and abstract figures.[6] These intersections among Keats's poem (both the early draft and the ill-favored *Indicator* version), its poetic tradition, and his early critical reception mark the terrain of Romantic allegory—that poetic space where history and the otherness of poetic figures meet.

In the first section of this essay, I consider the different figurative values assigned to the belle dame in each version of the poem; in the second and third, how both versions respond to a variety of sources and contextual pressures. These include its ambiguous generic identity as ballad and allegorical romance, attacks on Keats's Cockneyism, and other poems and letters that reiterate key figures in "La Belle Dame Sans Merci." The poetic inquiry that holds this matrix of sources and contexts together is Keats's fascination with the allegorical properties of Spenserian figures and emblematic tableaux.[7]

I. KEATS'S BELLE DAMES

Of the two versions of "La Belle Dame sans Merci" that Keats composed, the early draft of April 1819 and the version published in *The Indicator* a little more than a year later, readers have usually preferred the former or, more precisely, one of three later transcripts made of it by Charles Brown and Richard Woodhouse. Claiming that Hunt unduly influenced Keats as he revised the poem for Hunt's periodical, most critics and editors have dismissed the *Indicator* version as aesthetically inferior.[8] In his recent and authoritative edition of Keats's poems, Stillinger prints Brown's 1848 transcript of the early draft and relegates *Indicator* variants to the critical apparatus. His rationale for doing so is textual: Brown's holographs are in general more reliable than early printed texts of poems Keats composed in 1819 and 1820.[9] Jerome McGann argues to the contrary that since the *Indicator* version is the only one Keats chose to publish, it is, or should be, the authoritative text. This assessment assists McGann's larger polemic about the ideological bias that prompted the outcry against the *Indicator* version in the first place. He claims that the "aesthetic" decision in favor of the early draft masks an ideological preference for a Keats untainted by the bad poetic influence of the radical and Cockney Hunt.[10] Though McGann argues persuasively that the *Indicator* version should no longer be suppressed, I am less persuaded that it is the only version Keats authorized and therefore the only one we ought to read. Instead I suggest that Keats composed the early drafts as well as the *Indicator* version with two quite different audiences in mind—the private family audience of George and Georgiana Keats and the more problematic audience of *Indicator* readers. Considered as parallel texts, each offers a slightly different belle dame and anticipates a slightly different reception. Both register Keats's oblique reply to the controversy that dominated reviews of his early poetry.

In the *Indicator* version the "knight-at-arms" of the early draft became a "woeful wight," an archaic and generic term for a human being or, in this case, a man. Along with other revisions, this one makes the poem more emphatically a ballad about a doomed relationship between a faery woman and a mortal lover. In this version the belle dame shows more human fears—or at least more sadness—and the "wight's" response to her is more active, even slightly masterful as he "kisse[s her] to sleep." Unlike the knight, who is lulled to sleep by his faery lover, the wight reports that they both "slumbered on the moss."[11]

Keats suggests the naturalized, human emphasis of this version by using the English spelling of "mercy" in the title and the text. Whereas the early draft and its later transcripts preserve the French spelling, in the *Indicator* text the belle dame is half-Englished, as she is in the translation of Alain Chartier's medieval poem of the same title, which Hunt's *Indicator* preface identifies, somewhat misleadingly, as Keats's source.[12] Keats's substitution of "mercy" also replaces one ambiguity with another. The French *merci* may mean pity, compassion or thanks. In the chivalric context of Chartier's ballad, the "beautiful lady without pity" is she who refuses a lover—in effect, she shows no chivalric *politesse,* or says "no thanks." The English "mercy" of the *Indicator* text abandons the implied chivalric pun. Moreover, its presentation of a belle dame who seems less in control of the love relation encourages us to read her name and the title of the poem as a comment on her woeful predicament as well. Like the wight, she stands in need of the "mercy" neither can expect from a society threatened by her supernatural nature.

McGann contents that the archaism of "wight," already archaic when Spenser used it in *The Faerie Queene,* makes the narrator of Keats's poem more objective by creating a distance between him and the "wight."[13] Yet this apparent objectivity may be little more than a mask for Keats's proximity to the wight as well as the narrator. In July 1819, three months after he drafted the first version, Keats was woeful enough as he wrote poems and letters to Fanny Brawne from the Isle of Wight. As his letters make clear, kisses and honey, what the wight of the poem gets from the belle dame, are what John Keats longed to get from Fanny Brawne (*L,* 2:123, 127). Much as the scene of the poem is an external sign of the wight's inner desolation, so is the Isle of Wight the scene of letters that emphasize Keats's isolation from Fanny Brawne. Even if Keats did not compose the "wight" version at this time, the punning association between the Isle of Wight and the *Indicator* "wight" was certainly available to him after the summer of 1819. Moreover, in both versions the anaphora that links the narrator's "I" at the beginning of stanza three to the knight/wight's "I" in the next stanza undermines the purported narrative distance between the two speakers.[14]

By reversing the order of two stanzas in this version, Keats makes the mutuality of the love relationship take precedence over the wight's eventual enthrallment. In the early draft the knight explains that first he saw the belle dame and made her bands of flowers. Then she "looked at me as she did love, / And made sweet moan." After this he put her on his "pacing steed" and saw nothing else; finally she gave him her wild food. In the early draft the "pacing steed," which waits none too patiently for his owner to cease dallying, signifies the knight's chivalric identity. Thus by putting the belle dame on the horse after she loves him, he implies that her enthrallment has led him to abandon chivalric responsibilities. In the *Indicator* version the wight puts her on his horse before their exchange of love and gifts. This new sequence presents a different view of the protagonist's role in his own enthrallment. Rather than simply succumbing to the belle dame, he now seems to invite her to enthrall him. Keats's reversal of these stanzas also changes the figurative significance of the steed. Now the sexual implications of a horse and female rider overtake the chivalric emphasis of the earlier version.

Yet the different sexual politics of the two versions does not simply make the *Indicator* text a less misogynous narrative about men and women in love. As a poetic figure, the belle dame pays a price for her more sympathetic portrait in the published version: in the figurative economy of Keats's revisions, when she becomes a more sympathetic figure she also becomes a less alien one and for this reason less powerful. In the earlier draft her alien, supernatural identity more clearly sets her apart in the eyes of the narrator, the knight, and the chorus of kings, princes, and warriors who warn that she is fatal to human life and society. Figured in these terms, she is their fetish: an object of worship whose supernatural power over them (which they in fact have assigned to her) inspires dread and fascination.[15] As such, she knows that poetic figures become fetishistic if they are presented as powers that hold our attention precisely because they are extra-human. If the fetishistic power presented in the *Indicator* version illustrates the latent fetishism in human love relationships which Freud describes, the early draft of the poem gives the same power a wider reference.[16] There it shows how some figures belong to an allegorical structure of meaning, in part because they call attention to their separate, alien identity as figures.

The first writer to suggest that fetishism is allied to poetic figuration was Charles de Brosses, whose mid-eighteenth-century treatise on fetish gods in Egyptian and African cults prompted later writers to look for fetishism in modern Western cultures as well. Noting that fetishism reflects a universal human tendency to personify things, de Brosses insisted that "this use of metaphor" (*"cet usage des métaphores"*) is as natural for "civilized peoples" as it is for "savage nations."[17] Although the figurative value of the belle dame in Keats's early draft is not as overtly declared as, for example, that of Spenser's Una or Holiness, it is more apparent there than in the *Indicator* version, which David Simpson prefers because he finds in it an indeterminate play of signs and meaning that is absent in the earlier draft. Simpson's reading ignores the instructive possibility that the figurative status of the belle dame in the early draft dramatizes a necessary, if haunting, risk—the transformation of life and the world into well-wrought urns or, in Mikhail Bakhtin's phrase, the "fetishization" of the art work.[18]

In his study of fetishism and imagination in nineteenth-century literature, Simpson argues that Romantic poets avoided fetishism by engaging in "healthy figurative activity," a continuous process of re-creation by which figures refuse the fixity and alienation that characterize Keats's belle dame.[19] As a poet who repeatedly warns himself and readers about the dangers of figures that are lifeless, Wordsworth is Simpson's exemplary Romantic instance of this refusal. Certainly what Simpson describes is what Romantic poets including Wordsworth, sought to do. Yet even Wordsworth (or especially Wordsworth) created figures that are fixed as objects of his or a speaker's poetic attention—a leech-gatherer, a thorn, a blind beggar. It may be more accurate to say that a healthy recognition of the fetishistic tendency inherent in poetic figures is what helps Romantic poets understand their inclination to confuse natural objects, human beings, and poetic figures. In other words, not all Romantic figures are organic symbols, that is, figures in which the literal and the figurative articulate an organic, indivisible whole. Instead, some Romantic figures are so evidently factitious that their otherness as figures has to be recognized.

In Keats's poem this otherness is a property both of its figures and of their relation to the sources that readers have identified for the poem. For example, in Thomas the Rhymer's medieval ballad about a faery lady who seduces him then tells him prophecies before abandoning him, Thomas spies an "arbour" of fruits which the lady warns him not to eat if he wishes to save his soul.[20] In most versions of Thomas the Rhymer's poem that were published in the eighteenth century, including one reprinted in Sir Walter Scott's *Minstrelsy of the Scottish Border,* the fruits are pears, apples, dates, figs, wineberry, filberts, and damson (a Mediterranean variety of plum)—all cultivated fruits grown in Europe and the Mediterranean. Scott also discusses an ancient manuscript version in which the lady offers Thomas a loaf of bread and wine after she warns him against this rather Blakean "garden of fruits."[21] Keats's version of this story presents a different kind of food. Unlike the cultivated if forbidden fruit of Thomas the Rhymer's poem or the bread and wine offered in the manuscript Scott describes, roots, wild honey, and manna dew are what Keats's lady provides. As foods that are wild and heaven sent, they are manifestly "other," in contrast to the "harvest" mentioned by the narrator as the poem begins.[22]

The belle dame's food is "other" for another reason: in the discourse of the poem, it signifies her alienation from society, represented by the knight, the narrator, and the male chorus. That is to say, her food remains wild, undomesticated, because these speakers insist on this point, not because wild food cannot be domesticated—by ritual or mythic as well as agricultural means—if a society chooses to do so. In *From Honey to Ashes,* the second in the series on structural anthropology that begins with *The Raw and the Cooked,* Claude Lévi-Strauss explains that some South American tribes domesticate honey by converting it into a food that is gathered and distributed according to specific rituals. Among these tribes, several myths tell of a woman who tries to grab honey for herself by defying rituals for gathering and distributing it. (This woman is not authorized to gather honey for the tribe; that job is the woodpecker's, whom she often marries to get honey.)[23]

These myths and the rituals they authorize pit woman's greed for honey against a well-orchestrated social network for food production and consumption. By presenting honey as a sign of the belle dame's alien as well as sexual power, the speakers of Keats's poem specify what such myths imply. Yet this difference masks an intriguing parallel. In both cases, social and linguistic processes define the meaning of honey and woman. In Lévi-Strauss's structuralist analysis such processes domesticate honey and women by assigning them tasks and limits that neutralize or eradicate their "natural" wildness or greediness (or both). In Keats's poem this process places the belle dame and her food outside the society of speakers represented by the narrator, the knight, and the male chorus of kings, princes, and warriors whose warning the knight receives in a dream. Paradoxically, like all fetishes her alien status is a social, linguistic invention.

In Keats's early draft and its later transcripts, then, the belle dame is fixed, even impaled by the narrator, the knight, and the chorus as someone who opposes the social plenty of harvest and granary. She is the reason their lips are "starv'd" of everything except incantatory warnings that the knight will repeat their history. The balladic repetition of the opening and closing stanzas emphasizes the collective understanding the figure of the belle dame reflects. In the first stanza the narrator asks the knight why he is "alone and palely loitering" when "The sedge is withered from the lake, / And no birds sing"; in the last one the knight explains that "this—meaning his union with the belle dame—is why he is "alone and palely loitering." The fact that both narrator and knight use the same phrases to specify the knight's situation suggests that each gives the same interpretation to the story he tells. Although the *Indicator* version has virtually the same opening and closing stanzas, the "this" to which the knight refers in the last stanza is not the same because Keats has altered his story. As a figure with a fixed if different currency in each version, the belle dame makes these mirror exchanges between the narrator and the speaker possible. By presenting the belle dame as a figure whose otherness separates her from the knight despite her evident sympathy for him, Keats makes her figurative enthrallment more apparent and thus more chilling.

II. "LA BELLE DAME SANS MERCI" AND POETIC TRADITION

This enthrallment is all the more compelling because it does not end at the border of Keats's text (or texts). Indeed, insofar as reading "La Belle Dame sans Merci" requires reading its relation to its sources, among them Chartier's medieval poem of the same title, Thomas the Rhymer's ballad, and Spenser's *Faerie Queene*, Keats's poem dramatizes the otherness that prompts its poetic speech.[24] Keats's most obvious acknowledgment that extratextual pressures are part of the meaning of his poem is generic. The poem is at once a ballad and an allegorical romance.

Subtitled "A Ballad" in the Brown and Woodhouse transcripts (but not in Keats's early draft or the *Indicator* version), its ballad meter, rhyme, and stanza make its formal commitment to this genre clear.[25] This commitment appears to serve two purposes. First, as a genre with a less than exalted position in the neoclassical hierarchy of literary genres, the ballad would be an appropriately humble literary vehicle for a Cockney poet. More immediately, the early Romantic rehabilitation of the ballad, accomplished largely by Scott, Wordsworth, and Coleridge, had made the ballad respectable poetic fare for the next generation of young poets. By writing "La Belle Dame sans Merci" as a ballad, then, Keats may play a double game with his audience. For if writing ballads is on the surface less ambitious than writing in the more aristocratic genres of epic, tragedy, or allegorical romance, writing ballads after Scott and Wordsworth is also a bid for a contemporary poetic fame and audience. The Wordsworthian echo of "her eyes were wild" may assist this double appeal for poetic authority and successorship. This appeal may mask an intriguing, perhaps deliberate tension between Keats's political sympathy for the liberal values implied in the early Romantic ballads, particularly the *Lyrical Ballads,* and his rejection of the Tory politics adopted by the older Wordsworth. Although he was by 1819 a political ally of those who had criticized Keats's poetic ambition and his politics, here Wordsworth's early poetic practice legitimates Keats's present poetic ambition. Second, whatever the narrative gaps or lack of narrative progress in traditional as well as lyrical ballads, the ballad meter and rhyme of "La Belle Dame sans Merci" keep the poem going or, more to the point, they keep its readers reading. By choosing the ballad form, then, Keats restrains his youthful fondness for the lingering metrical pauses and syntactic inversions that irritated reviewers of *Endymion*.[26]

The ballad features of "La Belle Dame sans Merci" mask its more problematic relation to Spenser and allegorical romance. As many readers have noted, the union between Keats's belle dame and knight echoes those between Spenser's errant knights and evil enchantresses disguised as virtuous women. Specifically, the garland, bracelets, and "fragrant zone" Keats's knight makes for the belle dame recall the bands two of Spenser's knights make for the False Fidessa and False Florimel, as well as the magic girdle the true (if hapless) Florimel loses as she flees would-be despoilers. Although Keats's belle dame is not, like Spenser's deceitful simulacra, False Fidessa and False Florimel, antitruth, she is a figure for the "erring" of meaning that allegorical truth requires in *The Faerie Queene*.[27]

Not content to make the lady just one band of flowers, Keats's knight makes her three, a garland, bracelet, and fragrant "zone." Considered together, they are a redundant visual sign of Keats's indebtedness to Spenser, an emblematic portrait something like the pictorial tableaux Spenser uses to reveal and conceal allegorical meaning. Keats's knight presents the belle dame as though he were listing details in an emblem or a Spenserian tableau, among them her long hair, light foot, and wild eyes, as well as the gifts she receives and the food she gives. Along with her tears and sighs, there are the signs of who or what she is. Neither the reader nor the knight is privy to her inner thoughts. As a figure known exclusively by her attributes, then, the belle dame is alien to her human observers, and alien in a thoroughly Spenserian manner. For if she is clearly not a full-fledged allegorical figure like Spenser's Fidessas and Florimels, she shares their emblematic separateness.

As a poetic figure borrowed from a long tradition and defined within the discourse of Keats's poem, the belle dame of the early draft directs our attention to the alienation of other figures in the poem, including the landscape, the knight, and the chorus. Of these, the human characters are the most suggestive, since the figures Keats invents to depict them are themselves alienated from their referent—death or its approach. This "language strange," thoroughly Keatsian by way of Spenser, illustrates how figurative meaning tends to "err," half-mistaking itself as it wanders from its referent in ways that dramatize the allegorical potential of figures as factitious *and* referential signs.

Two deletions in the early draft make it clear that the lily and fading rose the narrator "sees" on the knight's countenance are Petrarchan figures of death. Keats first wrote but then crossed out "death's" in the phrases "death's lily" and "death's fading rose." Scholars have suggested several sources for these figures, including Tom Keats's death of tuberculosis in the winter of 1818. In his copy of Burton's *Anatomy of Melancholy,* Keats underlined Drayton's use of the same Petrarchan figures in one of his *Heriocall Epistles*. In Drayton's poem an abandoned female lover uses the terms "Rosie-blush" and "lily-vale" to indicate that she grows "pale" and is about to die. The visual source for the "death's lily" or "lily" in Keats's poem is probably William Hilton's early nineteenth-century painting *The Mermaid*. On exhibit in Sir John Leicester's gallery when Keats visited it in early April, 1819, the painting depicts a knight lying dead in a mermaid's lap with a water-lily on his brow.[28]

Keats's poem alters the way readers construe the visual aspects of its figures. We are not likely to think of them as visual or visualizable in the same way that the water-lily of Hilton's painting is. Instead, we are more likely to assume that the lily and rose on the knight's face are poetic figures because their obvious Petrarchanism invites us to make this assumption. By forcing us to notice what these figures do as figures, Keats emphasizes their mannered, Spenserian relation to their referents. Both the figures that describe the knight's face and the "starv'd lips" of the "death-pale" chorus are death-masks; they have the look a face assumes just before death or in a death-like state of exhaustion.[29] The difference is of course that the chorus is dead and the knight isn't dead yet. Even so, each of these figures emphasizes what is left—remnants of life that is going or gone. As fixed, residual, even disembodied images, they signify death or its approach much as the cheshire cat's smile is a lingering, residual sign of the cheshire cat. None of these is a fetish, yet all are detached, and as such patently objects of poetic attention. The material separateness that is part of the aura of the primitive fetish—whether it is a stone, a carved stick, or something else—is oddly yet appropriately reborn in these figures.

III. "HONEY WILD AND MANNA DEW"

Two revisions in "La Belle Dame sans Merci" register the climate of reception embedded in the figurative project of the poem. The first revision appears in the stanza where the knight presents the belle dame's gifts of food and "language strange" as syntactically parallel. The second reveals Keats's half-playful, half-serious recognition of earlier critical objections to his rhymes. Considered together, these revisions help to define the intersection between Keats's early reception and his mature poetics.

In both versions of the poem, the knight declares:

> She found me roots of relish sweet,
>   And honey wild, and manna dew,
> *And* sure in language strange she said—
>   I love thee true.
> (25–28; my emphasis)

The perplexities of language and truth implied by the knight's conviction that he understands what she tells him recall the Spenserian dilemma of mistaking the false Florimel for the true one and vice versa. A stronger perplexity in Keats's poem concerns the status of its key figures, whose sensuous details contend with their abstract or semi-abstract meaning in ways that make the language of the poem alien poetic food.

Nineteenth-century readers who objected to Keats's poetry often attacked his frequent use of food and eating imagery to represent poetic or sexual longing. Byron repeatedly charged that Keats indulged in "onanism" or "mental masturbation," while Carlyle somewhat less harshly chastized Keats for his insatiable and infantile desire for "treacle." In his more sympathetic account of Keatsian treacle, Christopher Ricks suggests that the risk of this diction is the unsettled middle ground it occupies between primitive sensuality and self-conscious poetic refinement. Ricks astutely observes that nineteenth-century criticism of Keats's frequent use of "honey" as a poetic figure shows just how provocative this poetic strategy was.[30]

Even before he wrote the notorious phrase "honey-feel of bliss" in *Endymion* (1.903), "honey" was for Keats a figure for poetic language. For example, he began an 1817 verse in praise of "The Flour and the Leafe," a poem then attributed to Chaucer, with this simile:

> This pleasant tale is like a copse:
>   The honied lines do freshly interlace
>   To keep the reader in so sweet a place
>   (1–3)

Ricks notes a more personal use of "honied" in an acrostic verse on his name in which Keats composed for his sister-in-law Georgiana Keats in 1818 (*L,* 2:123). A year later "honey" reappers in two letters he wrote to Fanny Brawne from the Isle of Wight. On July 1, 1819, he asks her to kiss the "softest words" she writes in her next letter. A week later, replying to her reply, he writes: "I kiss'd your writing over in the hope you had indulg'd me by leaving a trace of honey" (*L,* 2:127). In his last letter to Fanny Brawne, Keats recalls his earlier use of "honey" as a figure for desire by figuring the barriers to that desire as bitter in taste. He tells her he cannot be happy without her because "everything else tastes like chaff in my Mouth." Rebelling against plans then being made for his departure for Italy, he declares: "the fact is I cannot leave you, and shall never taste one minute's content until it pleases chance to let me live with you for good." Echoing lines from the abandoned *Hyperion,* he complains, "the last two years taste like brass upon my Palate (*L,* 2:311–12).[31]

In "The Eve of St. Agnes" "honey" assists the provocative sensuality that is the crux of the modern critical debate about the poem. For some readers the poem is a quasi-allegorical narrative whose sensuous diction serves a non-sensuous end. For others it is a thoroughly sensual and rakish poem about the deception and seduction of a maid who doesn't quite know what is happening until it has happened. Earl Wasserman defends the first view, arguing that Porphyro's gifts of food and sex are ultimately transmuted into "a finer tone," whereas Jack Stillinger contends that the "solution sweet" of Porphyro and Madeline is preeminently a sexual act that concludes the "hoodwinking of Madeline" which began with her enthrallment by "enchantments cold" (299–318). The last to assist in this hoodwinking is Porphyro, whose seduction of Madeline begins with the exotic foods and spices he heaps beside her bed and ends when he joins her there.[32]

Although the sensuous imagery of "La Belle Dame sans Merci" is less overtly provocative, its echoes of "The Eve of St. Agnes" also explore the unsettled middle ground of Keatsian figuration. Much as Porphyro plays the melody of "La belle dame sans mercy" (292) to assist his seduction of Madeline, so does Keats's version of this "ancient ditty long since mute" seek to persuade readers to accept a mature version of the figurative project that his early critics had dismissed as vulgar Cockneyism. It is not surprising that other textual resonances linking the two poems concern the figure of "honey." According to "The Eve of St. Agnes," legend has it that maidens will receive "soft adorings" from their future lovers "upon the honey'd middle of the night" (49). In his astute analysis of this revision of a line from *Measure for Measure* ("the heavy middle of the night"), Ricks emphasizes the "delighted physicality" of Keats's figure.[33] The noun "honey" figures in a series of revisions that extend from this poem to "La Belle Dame sans Merci," where Keats's successive revisions of the line "And honey wild and manna dew" echo his revisions of a line in "The Eve of St. Agnes." In the final text of the latter poem the line in question reads, "Manna and dates, in argosy transferr'd / From Fez" (268–69). Remarking that this is "the most worked over line in all of Keats's MSS," Stillinger proposes that the sequence of revisions probably began with two different attempts to include "Manna wild" among the foods Porphyro heaps beside Madeline.[34] A few months after he drafted this poem, Keats rehearsed the same textual debate as he composed "La Belle Dame sans Merci." In the phrase that became "honey wild and manna dew" in the final text of the draft version, Keats replaced "honey dew" with "manna dew" and restored the "wild" dropped from the manuscript of "The Eve of St. Agnes."

The textual and figurative implications of these revisions go back to Keats's early critical reception. Among the charges levied against *Endymion* in the 1818 reviews were several pointed criticisms of his frequent use of "honey" as a figure (and an adjective). For example, the anonymous reviewer for the *British Critic* complained that by using phrases like "honey-dew," and "the honey-feel of bliss" the poet of *Endymion* repeated the stylistic excesses of Leigh Hunt's poetry. Reviewing *Endymion* for the *Quarterly Review,* John Croker cited the second phrase to show how Keats "spawns" new nouns to replace those he has transformed into verbs.[35] The implied premise of this objection is syntactic decorum: using the noun "honey" as an adjective or as the adjective portion of an invented compound word violates the legislated boundaries of syntax. The poetic implications of Keats's lawlessness (and Croker's critique), however, extend beyond matters of syntax. By verbalizing nouns, Keats layers his poetic texture much as Spenser's allegorical tableaux layer descriptive and sensuous details. Keats acknowledges this literary debt in his early poem "In Imitation of Spenser," where the noun "oar" is verbalized: the king-fisher "oar'd himself along with majesty" (15). Forty years later, in an otherwise favorable assessment of Keats's poetry, the Victorian editor and critic David Masson cited the by then infamous phrase "honey-feel of bliss" to demonstrate Keats's occasional poetic vulgarity.[36] For Keats's contemporaries and his later critics, syntactic irregularity signals a broader debate about the self-absorbed blend of sensuous details and abstract, or semiabstract, poetic figures to which such irregularities call attention.

When Keats revised the early draft of "La Belle Dame sans Merci," then, he tacitly acknowledged the objection raised by the reviewers for the *British Critic* and the *Quarterly* by substituting "manna" for the second "honey" in the line that originally read: "And honey wild, and honey dew." Yet if this revision removed an obvious invitation for criticism, the final version of the line retains a strong poetic reminder of Keats's desire to participate in the great tradition of English poets— the Miltonic inversion of "honey wild." Moreover, his syntactic error remains even after the removal of the second "honey." For whatever else "manna" is, it too is a noun that here serves as an adjective; moreover, its figurative task is at least as provocatively Keatsian as that of "honey dew." Because "manna" signifies supernatural rather than human food, its appearance in the list of foods the belle dame gives the knight emphatically reiterates the uneasy blend of sensuous and semi-allegorical details that troubled Keats's early critics.

The rhetorical figure suggested by this and similar Keatsian figures is *catachresis*, a "harsh" or "unnatural" figure whose misuse or misapplication of one category for another forces us to acknowledge it as a figure. To borrow Joseph Priestley's example, when trees are called the "*hair of mountains,* or the walls of cities their *cheeks,*" the figure is a catachresis.[37] Although Keats's early critics do not specifically charge him with this "figure of abuse," their critique of his poetic language emphasizes the unnaturalness of its figures, particularly those that appear in an allegorical or quasi-allegorical context. Keats's repeated use of "honey" as a figure thus signals a larger, more troubling, figurative deformation that his early critics called "vulgar Cockneyism," either because that is what they believed it was or because they wanted to dismiss his poetic radicalism by presenting it as the uneducated, pretentious ravings of a lower class versifier. In different ways, both versions of "La Belle Dame sans Merci" anticipate possible critical objections to its figurative argument. The *Indicator* version minimizes the allegorizing tendencies of the early draft, making it less easy to abuse this version for its unnatural figuration. At the same time, this published version flaunts its Cockney sensuousness. The unpublished early draft is more daring insofar as it emphasizes the tension between its sensuous and semi-allegorical referents. When Keats revised this draft in his letter to George and Georgiana Keats, he removed the most obvious markers of its radical poetic argument.

By making the love relationship between the wight and the belle dame the focus of the *Indicator* text, Keats draws attention away from the allegorizing tendency of details like the belle dame's food. For this reason, the association between honey and language receives less notice than the more natural or more sensuous association between honey and desire. Yet Keats also makes this sensuousness more provocative by signing the poem with the pseudonym "Caviare." Taken from a speech in which Hamlet explains that a pay did not succeed because it was "caviare to the general," that is, food too rich or elevated for plebian tastes, the pseudonym ironically presents the poet and the poem as just this kind of poetic food. Keats thus makes it clear that he is still the Cockney poet who dares to offer the public a poetic fare that is supposed to be beyond his and their capabilities—a reminder that is all the more pungent for its appearance in one of Hunt's periodicals. Critics who have supposed that Hunt dictated the *Indicator* revisions usually claim that the pseudonym was also his idea.[38]

This claim is suspect for two reasons. The first concerns the authorship of the *Indicator* revisions. Keats may have written them himself either before Hunt decided to print the poem in *The Indicator* or for the occasion of its publication. As Stillinger and Hyder Rollins note, after Georgiana Keats's death her second husband John Jeffrey sent a list of Keats's verse manuscripts in his possession that included a poem whose first line is "Ah, what can ail thee, wretched wight."[39] If Jeffrey's description is accurate, Keats must have sent the *Indicator* version as well as the early draft to his brother and sister-in-law between the spring of 1819 and the publication of the later version. Even if Keats composed the *Indicator* version just before its publication, he would hardly have sent it to George and Georgiana Keats if he thought it inferior to the early draft. Instead, it seems likely that he sent it along so that his best familial audience could compare it to the draft. Second, the turns and counterturns in Keats's friendship with Hunt after the *Endymion* reviews strongly suggest that by 1820 Keats could no longer be unduly influenced by his early mentor. Keats's sharp-eyed criticisms of Hunt's character and talent in 1817 and 1818 show that the younger poet had become a good deal less suggestible than he had been earlier in their friendship. Perhaps because Hunt's poetic influence had cost Keats much, he had reason enough to learn what he did and did not value in Hunt. Even in the spring and summer of 1820, when an ill Keats was grateful to Hunt for his kindness, their personal relationship was not smooth. Keats angrily left the Hunt household when one of his letters was opened by a servant. Afterward he said he had been a "prisoner" while staying with the Hunts.[40]

I review these matters to suggest another view of the Keats-Hunt collaboration for the two poems Keats published in the *Indicator*. Even if the "Caviare" pseudonym was Hunt's idea, its allusion to *Hamlet* is one Keats himself might have chosen to defend his poetic Cockneyism. Instead of being led by Hunt, he probably recognized that publishing one of his poems in a Hunt periodical would inevitably create an ideologically charged context for its reception. For this reason, Keats may have shaped the poem and its pseudonym to fit the goals and intended audience of this periodical in ways that would invite a more sympathetic reception than his early published poetry had received.[41]

Attached to a poem where honey is a figure for forbidden, probably fatal food, Keats's pseudonym exploits the resonances of the title Hunt chose for *The Indicator*. Commenting on the first of two mottoes that appear at the beginning of the first eight issues, Hunt explains that, like the Indicator (also known as the Bee Cuckoo or Honey Bird), an African bird that instinctively guides bees to honey, his "business is with the honey of the old woods"—stories from antique literature and mythology gathered to entertain readers.[42] The second motto, which Hunt retained throughout the run of *The Indicator,* is taken from Spenser's *The Fate of the Butterfly, or Muiopotmos,* which had earlier supplied Keats with the epigraph for *Sleep and Poetry:*

> There he arriving round about doth flie,
> And takes survey with busie curious eye:
> Now this, now that, he tasteth tenderly.[43]

Although the "he" in these lines refers to the butterfly whose fate Spenser's poem describes, the analogy suggested by these lines works equally well for the bee of Hunt's title.

In the first issue of *The Indicator,* Hunt refers obliquely to the political turmoil in which he had long been embroiled as editor of *The Examiner* to insist that his new periodical will be apolitical: "the Editor has enough to agitate his spirits during the present eventful times, in another periodical work." Yet if *The Indicator* was not intended to be and never became identified with a specific political program, Hunt's assessment of its intended audience invokes the old squabble about Keats and Hunt as charter members of the "Cockney School of Poetry":

> To the unvulgar he [Hunt as Editor] exclusively addresses himself; but he begs it to be particularly understood, that in his description of persons are to be included all those, who without having had a classical education, would have turned it to right account; just as all those are to be excluded, who in spite of that "discipline of humanity," think ill of the nature which they degrade, and vulgarly confound the vulgar with the uneducated.[44]

This appeal to an audience not necessarily trained in the classics offers a new perspective on that debate. Instead of preparing to defend contributors to his new periodical against similar charges, Hunt chooses to imagine and invite an audience less likely to object to him or his contributors. Mindful of the class bias evident in

Lockhart's charge that in *Endymion* Keats used classical materials without benefit of a classical education, Hunt proposes a new distinction between the vulgar and the unvulgar: the vulgar are those who consider people who are uneducated in the classics vulgar. Hunt's intended audience is "the unvulgar," a group that includes, among others, those who lack a classical education but who, had they had one, would have "turned it to right account." By this Hunt presumably means that they would not have used it to bludgeon the reputations of poets who lacked training in classical languages and literature.

Seen from the perspective of the *Indicator* mottoes and Hunt's description of its intended audience, the *Indicator* version of "La Belle Dame sans Merci" plays an intriguing double game with its probable reception. By emphasizing the erotic, sensuous appeal of its story for a plebeian (that is, middle class) palate eager to be offered the rich poetic food that better educated critics would deny them, Keats both allies himself with the audience for which *The Indicator* was intended and taunts his early critics. Yet because the *Indicator* version mutes the figurative argument of the early draft, where the alliance between sensuous details and the fetishistic powers of its key figures is more prominently displayed, this taunt operates on safe ground. In the preface to the *Indicator* version, Hunt assists this strategy by suggesting that, like its medieval source, Keats's poem is a love story. Precisely because the published context and the text of the *Indicator* "La Belle Dame sans Merci" emphasize the love relation between a wight and a faery lady, the differences between this version and the early draft make the figurative risks of the draft more apparent.

Another revision in the draft version of "La Belle Dame sans Merci" marks a second intersection between the critical reception of *Endymion* and Keats's mature poetics. To defuse possible objections to rhymes richer in sound than earlier critics wanted them to be, Keats replaced these lines in the early draft,

> And there she wept and sigh'd full sore
> And there I shut her wild wild eyes
> With kisses four,
>
> (30–32)

with the lines printed in the *Indicator* text:

> And there she gazed and sighéd deep.
> And there I shut her wild sad eyes—
> So kissed to sleep.
>
> (30–32)

In the journal-letter to George and Georgiana Keats, Keats's adroit defense of the original "sore"/"four" rhyme suggests why the rhyme he later chose for the *Indicator* version would be even less likely to invite the kind of criticism leveled at the end-rhymes of *Endymion:*

Why 4 kisses—you will say—why four because I wish to restrain the headlong impetuousity of my Muse—she would have fain said 'score' without hurting the rhyme—but we must temper the Imagination as the Critics say with Judgment. I was obliged to choose an even number that both eyes might have fair play: and to speak truly I think two a piece quite sufficient—Suppose I had said seven; there would have been three and a half a piece—a very awkward affair—and well got out of on my side. (*L*, 2:97)

John Crowe Ransom's examples of single, duple and triple perfect rhyme or *rime riche* make its potential for excess apparent: "Keats-beets"; "Shelley-jelly"; "Tennyson-venison."[45] By substituting the less suggestive rhyme "deep"/"sleep" in the *Indicator* version, Keats retained the perfect rhyme but avoided the patently archaic sensuousness of the original rhyme ("sighed full sore"/"kisses four"). Much as this revisionary strategy declares Keats's apprehensiveness about the reception of the poem, so does the *Indicator* revision suggest that he gave up the sensuousness of the early draft as one too many provocations in a version that makes amorousness its theme.

The apparent defensiveness of Keats's revision may mask a more aggressive stance toward neoclassical (and Tory) values implied and declared in negative reviews of *Endymion*. As William Keach and others have observed, reviewers attacked the Cockney couplets of *Endymion* because they undermined the poetic and political values identified with the neoclassical couplet. Croker in particular singled out Keats's rhymes for special blame, arguing that Keats played the game of *bouts rimés* badly by writing rhymes that were still nonsense at the end of the poem.[46] The point of this complaint is not that Keats should have played the game better, but that he should not have played it at all. The implied neoclassical touchstone for Croker's criticism is an issue of the *Spectator* devoted to a discussion of false wit. Using the game of *bouts rimés* as one example, Joseph Addison chastized the French for inventing the game and then playing it relentlessly.[47] According to Croker, then, Keats's rhymes display both his poetic shortcomings and a penchant for foreign affectation. A year later, in his 1819 letter to his brother and sister-in-law, Keats chose to defend a rhyme in "La Belle Dame sans Merci" by playing *bouts rimés* to show how much more mannered and self-conscious he could have been. Had he written "kisses score," the resulting "sore"/"score" rhyme would have been, if anything, a Keatsian version of *rime très riche*. Moreover, so many kisses would have been a Keatsian excess of another kind.

In this witty and rebellious reply to his early critics, Keats presents himself as someone whose rhymes exemplify poetic restraint, not Cockney license. Yet his playful inventory of possible rhymes also suggests that he could let rhymes dictate to sense if he chose, as Francis Jeffrey later accused Keats of doing in his 1820 review *Endymion*.[48] This notice of the potential lawlessness of rhyme belongs to Keats's larger poetic recognition of the factitious, at times arbitrary, character of poetic figures as well. In his letter to George and Georgiana Keats, Keats implies this alliance between rhyme and figure when he explains his choice of rhyme as though it were a compromise among the half-personified, abstract forces of "Imagination," "Critics," and "Judgment"—all key elements in reviews of *Endymion*. The plural "Critics" pointedly shows how badly Keats and his defenders were outnumbered in that battle. If Keats appears to grant the merit of some of this criticism when he chooses (or says he chooses) to temper his imagination with judgment, the language he uses to make this point shows him as willing as before to create poetic figures that are factitious and semi-abstract and, in doing so, to transform real critics into abstract ones.

The tentative allegory implied by this half-playful, half-serious defense of the rhyme Keats eliminated altogether in the *Indicator* version echoes an allusion to Spenserian allegory in the journal entry that precedes this one in his long letter of February 14 to May 3, 1819. Explaining tht he had agreed to review Reynolds's parody of Wordsworth's *Peter Bell,* which had not yet been published, Keats quotes the first section of his review to show how "politic" it is:

> This false florimel has hurried from the press and obtruded herself into public notice while for ought we know the real one may be still wandering about the woods and mountains. Let us hope she may soon appear and make good her right to the magic girdle—The Pamphleteering Archimage we can perceive has rather a splenetic love than a downright hatred to real florimels. (*L,* 2:93)

By using a Spenserian conceit to make the truth or falseness of an allegorical character a figure for the difference between a real poem and its parody, Keats can be in good "conscience" about reviewing the parody before the real thing. The conceit also suggests a Spenserian antecedent for the syntactic parallel between "language strange" and "honey" in "La Belle Dame sans Merci." Two echoes, or putative echoes, link Keats's poem to this review: Florimel's "girdle" reappears in Keats's poem as one of the knight's gifts and *florimel* is "language strange" for "flower honey" (the same "language strange" used in Chartier's poem). Although Keats does not mention this etymology in his letter, Spenser's blend of allegorical abstraction and sensuous detail in his portraits of Florimel and other ladies, both false and true, suggests why Keats admired "honey'd lines," including his own.

Much as Spenser's allegorical romance makes erring—in the double sense of making mistakes and wandering—the condition of knowing or discerning allegorical truth, so do Keats's sensuous and semi-abstract figures elicit readings that err between sensuous detail and abstract meaning. Wandering and making mistakes about which category is which are what readers do to find out how Keatsian figures work. Thus, for example, the interpretive mistake of thinking the belle dame a deceiving enchantress (like Spenser's false ladies) makes it easier to see that she is neither false nor true, but simply alien. By this I do not mean that Keats's figurative truth is relative or, conversely, that Spenser's is fixed. My point is rather that Keats's poetic figures, like Spenser's allegory, persistently work the terrain between referential truth and its representation, borrowing obliquely from one to characterize the other. Specifically, the materiality of Keats's figures— those "honey-feels" that disgusted his early critics because they consorted with archaic, semi-abstract figures like Spenser's—belong to his signifying practice, much as the *realia* of Spenser's emblematic portraits belong to their referents.

When Keats's early critics attacked the lusciousness of his diction and rhyme, they blundered on the network of poetic concerns and figures that Keats later clarified in "La Belle Dame sans Merci." Both versions of the poem, but especially the early draft, retain the essence of Keats's Cockney style—its odd blend of sensuous and archaic or semi-abstract figures—to represent the belle dame. In the early draft, she dramatizes the consequences, for art and for life, of turning natural objects and human beings into poetic figures or poetic abstractions. As Keats's version of a traditional personification, the enchantress who enthralls human lovers, her sympathetic qualities are subordinated to her fixed, supernatural value in the poem as a semi-abstract figure. So regarded, she is an object animated by the supernatural powers Keats and the speakers of the poem attribute to her. Like a fetish, whose material fixity is one sign of its special status, her identity isolates her. By presenting the belle dame in this way, Keats examines how and why some poetic figures are patently alien objects of a speaker's attention. Like Keats's nightingale and grecian urn, she shows how such figures are alien poetic powers that hold our attention precisely because they are extra-human.

Unlike Romantic symbols, whose figurative meaning is presented as an organic, simultaneous extension of their literal meaning, Romantic figures that tend toward allegory emphasize the fact that their meaning is not organic, not simultaneously understood. Such figures encourage historical awareness among readers. Unlike symbols, whose meaning is supposed to be understood at first glance, allegories require a process of reading and reflection. So understood, Keats's belle dame presents one model for the presence of history and allegory in Romantic figures.

NOTES

I began work on this essay while a fellow of The Society for the Humanities, Cornell University. I am grateful to its director, Jonathan Culler, and staff for their support of the larger study of allegory from which this essay is taken, to audiences at University of Rochester and the 1985 Convention of the Modern Language Association who commented on earlier versions, and to Peter Manning and Susan Wolfson for their responses to the final version.

1. Those who read the poem as a narrative about the knight's enthrallment include: Dorothy Van Ghent, *Keats: The Myth of the Hero,* ed. Jeffrey C. Robinson (Princeton: Princeton Univ. Press, 1983), 63–64, 128; Robert Graves, who identifies the belle dame with various literary enchantresses and concludes that she represents "Love, Death by Consumption . . . and Poetry" (*The White Goddess,* 3rd ed., enlarged [1971; reprinted, London: Faber and Faber, 1972], 128–29); and Richard Macksey, who presents the belle dame as someone who (like Keats's Lamia) "imprison[s]" the knight and "exile[s] him from the human" (" 'To Autumn' and the Music of Mortality: 'Pure Rhetoric of a Language without Words'," in *Romanticism and Language,* ed. Arden Reed [Ithaca: Cornell Univ. Press, 1985) 270n. But in *La Belle Dame sans Merci and the Aesthetics of Romanticism* (Detroit: Wayne State Univ. Press, 1974), Barbara Fass notes that the belle dame is not always presented as a deceitful enchantress (18); and in *Keats the Poet* (Princeton: Princeton Univ. Press, 1973), Stuart Sperry observes that the tradition from which Keats derives his belle dame includes several Januslike figures who are both benevolent and malevolent (237). In a paper delivered at the 1985 Convention of the Modern Language Association, Karen Swann presents a strong feminist reading of the belle dame's enthrallment by the narrator and speakers of the poem.

2. Coleridge, *The Statesman's Manual,* in *Lay Sermons,* ed. R. J. White, in *The Collected Works of Samuel Taylor Coleridge,* 16 vols. Bollingen Series 75 (Princeton: Princeton Univ. Press, 1972), 6:29–31. For fuller accounts of Coleridge's distinctions between symbol and allegory, see John Gatta, Jr., "Coleridge and Allegory," *Modern Language Quarterly* 38 (1977): 62–77; and Jerome C. Christensen, "The Symbol's Errant Allegory: Coleridge and His Critics," *ELH* 45 (1978): 640–59. See in particular Paul de Man's influential essay, "The Rhetoric of Temporality," in *Interpretation: Theory and Practice,* ed. Charles S. Singleton (Baltimore: Johns Hopkins Univ. Press,

1969) 173–209. My analysis differs insofar as it considers how referentiality and history extend de Man's account of the "temporality" of allegory.

3. Gordon Teskey discusses the role of error in allegory in "From Allegory to Dialectic: Imagining Error in Spenser and Milton," *PMLA* 101 (January 1986): 13; for an analysis of allegorical narratives that specifies the reader's task, see Carolynn Van Dyke, *The Fiction of Truth* (Ithaca: Cornell Univ. Press, 1985), esp. 247–87.

4. For example, Lionel Trilling argued in "The Poet as Hero: Keats in His Letters" that one source of Keats's genius is his geniality, which allowed him to discern the larger poetic or philosophical implications of his and others' private concerns. This claim assumes that Keats's poetic achievement derives in part from his ability to transcend personal crises like the hostile reception of his early poetry. See Trilling, *The Opposing Self* (New York: Viking Press, 1955), 11–19. Working against Trilling's biographical emphasis, de Man argued that Keats's poems are "the work of a man whose experience is mainly literary" principally because he kept "his capacity for personal happiness in reserve" for a better future he did not live to see. Like Keats, de Man turns this biographical pathos into metaphors for poetry and a program for reading. See de Man, ed., *John Keats: Selected Poetry* (New York: Signet NAL, 1966). Introduction, xi. Once again, this critical perspective presents Keats's poetry as an achievement wrought outside the fray of personal circumstance and public opinion. In an astute essay on the ideology of genre in "To Autumn," Geoffrey Hartman proposed that the ode surpasses the sublime ode of his predecessors by offering figures of death whose impersonal tranquility rejects the hysteria of earlier odes as well as Keats's mortal fears after the death of his brother Tom. See Hartman, "Poem and Ideology: A Study of Keats's 'To Autumn'," in *The Fate of Reading and Other Essays* (Chicago: Univ. of Chicago Press, 1975), 146. For all these strong readers of Keats, one mark of his poetic greatness is his superiority to circumstances of career and biography. Jerome McGann invited renewed attention to the relation between Keats's politics and his poetics in "Keats and Politics" in *Studies in Romanticism* 25 (Summer 1986), 171–229. Contributors include Susan Wolfson, Morris Dickstein, William Keach, David Bromwich, Paul H. Fry, and Alan J. Bewell.

5. Macksey (note 1), 264.

6. Jack Stillinger, *John Keats: Complete Poems* (Cambridge: Harvard Univ. Press, 1982), xxiv. Bhabatosh Chatterjee lists these and other Cockney traits of Keats's early style in *John Keats: His Mind and Work* (Bombay: Orient Longman,1 971), 211. Cited by Jerome McGann (note 4), 997.

7. Robert Gittings offers a tactful discussion of Spenser and the allied contexts indexed in the long journal-letter in which the early draft of "La Belle Dame sans Merci" appears in *John Keats: The Living Year* (New York: Barnes and Noble, 1954), 113–23.

8. See for example Walter Jackson Bate, *John Keats* (Cambridge: Harvard Univ. Press, 1963), 479n., and Sidney Colvin, *John Keats* (New York: Scribner's Sons, 1917), 468–69. McGann quotes Colvin's categorical dismissal of the *Indicator* text, 1029n–30n.

9. Jack Sillinger, *The Texts of Keats's Poems* (Cambridge: Harvard Univ. Press, 1974) 70 and 232–34.

10. McGann, 1000–1005.

11. The text of the early draft appears in Keats's *Letters,* ed. Hyder Rollins, 2 vols. (Cambridge: Harvard Univ. Press, 1958), 2:97. Further citations of Keats's letters (*L*) will be included parenthetically in the text. The definitive text of the poem is provided in Stillinger's edition, *The Poems of John Keats* (Cambridge: Harvard Univ. Press, 1978), 356–67. Line numbers appearing parenthetically in the text refer to this edition.

Miriam Allott reproduces the *Indicator* text in her carefully annotated edition, *The Poems of John Keats* (Harlow: Longman, 1970), 757–58. See *The Indicator,* No. 31 (May 10, 1820), 248.

12. *The Indicator,* No. 31 (May 10, 1820), 246–47. Keats probably took little more than his title from Chartier's poem, a chivalric love *debat* between the narrator (the hopeful but finally disappointed suitor) and the unwilling lady who, he complains, lacks compassion. Robert Graves rightly emphasizes Keats's stronger debt to Thomas the Rhymer's medieval ballad about an encounter with a faery woman. See Graves, 430.

13. McGann, 1002.

14. Susan Wolfson and David Simpson both comment on the implications of this narrative doubling. See Wolfson, "The Language of Interpretation in Romantic Poetry: A Strong Working of the Mind'," in *Romanticism and Language* (note 1), 38, and Simpson, *Irony and Authority in Romantic Poetry* (Totowa, N.J.: Rowman and Littleheld, 1979), 15–17.

15. S.v. "fetish," *OED*. See too Simpson's analysis of eighteenth and nineteenth-century accounts of fetishism in *Fetishism and Imagination* (Baltimore: Johns Hopkins Univ. Press, 1963), 214–19.

16. Freud, "Fetishism," in *Sexuality and the Psychology of Love* (New York: Colliers Books, 1963), 214–19.

17. Charles de Brosses, *Du Culte des dieux fétiches* (Paris, 1760), 215–16. Quoted by Simpson, *Fetishism and Imagination,* 14–15.

18. Simpson, *Irony and Authority,* 16–18; Bakhtin/Vološinov, "Discourse in Life and Discourse in Art," in *Freudianism: A Marxist Critique,* trans. I. R. Titunik (New York: Academic Press, 1976), 96.

19. Simpson, *Fetishism and Imagination,* 14.

20. Chartier's medieval poem does not include a garden of fatal fruits. This detail appears in several versions of Thomas the Rhymer's ballad. See especially Robert Jamieson's edition, *Popular Ballads and Songs,* 2 vols. (London: John Murray, 1806), 219. Noted by Graves, 430.

21. Scott, *Ministrelsy of the Scottish Border,* ed. T. F. Henderson, 4 vols. (1902; reprint, Detroit: Stinging Tree Press, 1968), 4:85.

22. Kenneth Gross points out that whereas manna is an exilic, Old Testament food for prophets and their peoples, honey is mentioned in post-exilic and New Testament narratives as a food for prophets. By using both in his version of "an ancient ditty," Keats elaborates the range of prophecy granted Thomas the Rhymer by his lady.

23. Lévi-Strauss, *From Honey to Ashes,* trans. John and Doreen Weightman (Chicago: Univ. of Chicago Press, 1983), 39, 47, and 105–23.

24. Allott (note 11) lists these sources in her edition, 500–506. See also Sperry's (note 1) analysis of the significance of Keats's allusion to Spenser, 236–39.

25. See Stillinger, ed., *The Poems of John Keats,* 644.

26. See reviews published in the *Edinburgh Magazine,* the *British Critic,* and the *Quarterly Review.* Excerpted or quoted in full in G. M. Matthews, ed., *Keats: The Critical Heritage* (New York: Barnes and Noble, 1971), 72, 92, 98–109, and 111–14.

27. For the relevant passages in Spenser see *The Faerie Queene,* in *The Works of Edmund Spenser,* eds. Edwin Greenlaw *et al.,* 11 vols. (Baltimore: Johns Hopkins Univ. Press, 1947), 1:26 (1.2.30) and 3:98 (3.7.17). See Teskey (note 3), 9 and 13.

28. Allott (note 11) points out Keats's echoes of Burton's *Melancholy* and mentions his visit to Sir John Leicester's gallery, 501.

29. For a discussion of the allegorical properties of *facies hippocratia,* a death mask

or death's head, see Walter Benjamin, *The Origin of German Tragic Drama*, trans. John Osborne (London: NLB, 1977), 53.

30. Byron's comments appear in letters to John Murray, [Nov. ?] and 9 November 1820, *Byron's Letters and Journals*, ed. Leslie A. Marchand, 16 vols. (Cambridge: Harvard Univ. Press, 1977), 7:217 and 225. Carlyle's complaint is recorded in *William Allingham's Diary*, ed. H. Allingham and D. Radford (1907; reprint, Carbondale: Southern Illinois Univ. Press, 1967), 205; quoted by Matthews (note 26), 35. For Ricks's remarks see Ricks, *Keats and Embarrassment* (Oxford: Clarendon Press, 1974), 120.

31. In his edition of the letters Rollins cites H. Buxton Forman's notice of the *Hyperion* echo: "Instead of sweets, his ample palate took / Savour of poisonous brass and metal sick" (1:188–89).

32. Earl Wasserman, *The Finer Tone: Keats's Major Poems* (Baltimore: Johns Hopkins Univ. Press, 1953), 109–16, 120–21; Stillinger, *The Hoodwinking of Madeline and Other Essays on Keats's Poems* (Urbana: Univ. of Illinois Press, 1971), 67–93.

33. Ricks, 136–37.

34. Stillinger, *Poems of John Keats*, 312n. Noted by Gittings (note 7), 116.

35. Quoted in Matthews (note 26), 92–93 and 114. Keats's frequent use of nominalized verbs as adjectives in "To Autumn" and other poems composed in 1819 may reply to Croker's earlier charge by offering a mirror image of his Cockney tendency to verbalize nouns.

36. Extracts of Masson's 1860 essay appear in Matthews, 371.

37. George Puttenham calls catachresis the "figure of abuse" in *The Arte of English Poesie*, eds. Gladys D. Willcock and Alice Walker (Cambridge: Cambridge Univ. Press, 1936), 180. Joseph Priestly calls it a "harsh" and "unnatural" figure in *A Course of Lectures on Oratory and Criticism*, eds. Vincent Bevilacqua and Richard Murphy (Carbondale: Southern Illinois Univ. Press, 1965), 185.

38. McGann argues that "the *Hamlet* allusion shows us that Keats means to share a mildly insolent attitude toward the literary establishment with his readers in *The Indicator*, who are presumed to represent an undebased literary sensibility" (1002). Ricks reiterates the attribution of the pseudonym to Hunt, 120–21.

39. Stillinger, *The Poems of John Keats*, 644, and Rollins, ed., *The Keats Circle*, 2nd ed., 2 vols. (Cambridge: Harvard Univ. Press, 1948), 2:119.

40. Edmund Blunden suggests that during 1819 "the bitterness [between Keats and Hunt] went away" in *Leigh Hunt: A Biography* (1930; reprint, New York: Archon, 1970), 143. Keats's remarks about Hunt in letters written between 1817 and 1820 suggest instead that their relationship was uneven throughout this period. See *L* 1:170; 1:191; 2:11; 2:301; 2:309; 2:313; 2:351.

41. In the same 1819 letter that included the draft of "The Belle Dame sans Merci," Keats remarks concerning his review of Reynolds's parody of Wordsworth that he wished to "suit" it "to the tune of the examiner" (*L*, 2:95). By 1819, the "tune" (or tone) of this periodical seems to have become more moderate, in part because Hunt probably could not afford to be jailed again for his incendiary articles but also because Charles Lamb's extensive contributions to the *Examiner* during this period are characteristically moderate in tone.

42. *The Indicator*, No. 1 (October 13, 1819), 1.

43. *The Works of Edmund Spenser*, 8:161–73. Stillinger notes Keats's use of lines from *Muiopotmos* as the epigram for "Sleep and Poetry" in *Poems of John Keats*, 736.

44. *The Indicator*, No. 1 (October 13, 1819), 1. In the second issue (October 20, 1819), Hunt rather disingenuously compares the subject matter of the two periodicals:

"as far as the Editor is concerned, the Examiner is to be regarded as the reflection of his public literature, and the Indicator of his private. . . . The Examiner is his tavern room for political pleasantry, for criticism upon the theatres and living writers. The Indicator is his private room, his study, his retreat from public care and criticism, with the reader who chuses to accompany him" (9).

45. Ransom's examples are cited in the *Princeton Encyclopedia of Poetry and Poetics* (Princeton: Princeton Univ. Press, 1974), s.v. "Perfect, True or Full Rhyme." See William Keach's remarks on Shelley's use of *rime riche* in *Shelley's Style* (New York: Methuen, 1984), 192 and 198, and John Hollander's on true *rime très riche* ("total homonymic rhyme") in *Vision and Resonance* (1975: reprint, New Haven: Yale Univ. Press, 1985), 118. Cited by Keats, 257n.

46. Croker's analysis of Keats's rhyme is reprinted in Matthews, 112. For a thoughtful account of Croker, Addison, Jeffrey, and Keats's rhymes, see Keach, "Cockney Couplets: Keats and the Politics of Style," *Studies in Romanticism* 25 (Summer 1986): 191–93.

47. Addison, *The Spectator,* ed. Donald F. Bond, 5 vols. (Oxford: Clarendon Press, 1965), No. 60 (May 9, 1711), 1:253–58. Keach notes that the "self" / "elf" rhyme in "Ode to a Nightingale" may recall Croker's attack on Keats's *bouts rimés* ("Cockney Couplets," 192).

48. Jeffrey's remark is reprinted in Matthews, 203.

GEOFFREY H. HARTMAN

Poem and Ideology:
A Study of Keats's "To Autumn"

Geoffrey H. Hartman's most significant contribution to romantic studies is his monumental *Wordsworth's Poetry, 1787–1814* (1964), which probably sits—spine broken, pages tattered, filled with underlines and exclamation points—within easy reach of every Wordsworthian in the world. Hartman has been for over three decades a primary conduit for the transmission of advanced European thinking about literary art to the American academy. His attention to the faintest shades of poetic nuance, his love of the polysemous nature of language, and his continued insistence on a role for art as art have placed his work in a productive tension with the more unabashedly mythic and deconstructive elements of what has become known as the "Yale School."

Hartman has also become the master of the occasional essay, with which we represent him here. Our final segment, which consists of three essays dealing with Keats's "To Autumn," gives dramatic form to the process of critical argument and assimilation on which we have centered this part of our collection. The occasion of the exchange was Geoffrey Hartman's provocatively titled "Poem and Ideology: A Study of Keats's 'To Autumn.' " Hartman's work is already reflexive, poising its understanding of ideology against the common understanding of the term in Marxist usage. As Hartman puts it, his "uncovering Keats's ideology" remains "as far as possible within terms provided by Keats himself, or furnished by the ongoing history of poetry."

"Most English great poems have little or nothing to say."[1] Few do that nothing so perfectly, one is tempted to add, as Keats's "To Autumn." Our difficulty as interpreters is related to the way consciousness almost disappears into the poem: the mind, for once, is not what is left (a kind of sublime litter) after the show is over. "To Autumn" seems to absorb rather than extrovert that questing imagination whose breeding fancies, feverish overidentifications, and ambitious projects motivate the other odes.

It is not that we lack terms to describe the poem. On the contrary, as W. J. Bate has said, "for no other poem of the last two centuries does the classical critical vocabulary prove so satisfying." We can talk of its decorum, "the parts . . . contributing directly to the whole, with nothing left dangling or independent," of its lack of egotism, "the poet himself . . . completely absent; there is no 'I', no suggestion of the discursive language that we find in the other odes," and finally of a perfect concreteness or adequacy of symbol, the union in the poem of ideal and real, of the "greeting of the Spirit" and its object.[2]

Yet terms like these point to an abstract perfection, to something as pure of content as a certain kind of music. They bespeak a triumph of form that exists but not—or not sufficiently—the nature of that form: its power to illumine experience, to cast a new light, a new shadow maybe, on things. In what follows I suggest, daringly, that "To Autumn" has something to say: that it is an ideological poem whose very form expresses a national idea and a new stage in consciousness, or what Keats himself once called the "gregarious advance" and "grand march of intellect."

There are problems with *ideological,* a word whose meaning is more charged in Marxist than in general usage. Marxism thinks of ideology as a set of ideas that claim universality while serving a materialistic or class interest. "Ideology is untruth, false consciousness, lie. It shows up in failed works of art . . . and is vulnerable to criticism. . . . Art's greatness consists in allowing that to be uttered which ideology covers up."[3] The attack on ideology in Marxism resembles that on "unearned abstractions" in Anglo-American formalistic theory, except that it engages in "depth politics" to uncover these abstractions. Formalistic criticism can worry overt ideas or idealisms. Keats's "Beauty is Truth, Truth Beauty," for example, yet it accepts gladly the disappearance of ideas, or disinterestedness of form in "To Autumn." There is no attempt to demystify this form by discovering behind its decorum a hidden interest. In a low-risk theory of this kind the presence of ideas can be disturbing but not, obviously, their absence.

The great interpretive systems we know of have all been interest-centered, however; they have dug deep, mined, undermined, removed the veils. The Synagogue is blind to what it utters, the Church understands. The patient dreams, the doctor translates the dream. The distant city is really our city; the *unheimlich* the *heim-lich;* strange, uncanny, and exotic are brought home. Like those etymologies older scholars were so fond of, which showed us the fossilized stem of abstract words, so everything is slain, in interest-theories, on the stem of generational or class conflict.

Yet like nature itself, which has so far survived man's use of it, art is not polluted by such appropriations. Some works may be discredited, others deepened—the scandal of form remains. From Kant through Schopenhauer and Nietzsche, the aesthetic element proper is associated with disinterestedness, impersonality, and resistance to utilitarian concepts. Beauty of this undetermined kind becomes an itch: the mind, says Empson, wants to scratch it, to see what is really there, and this scratching we call interpretation. Most men, says Schopenhauer, seek in objects "only some relation to their will, and with everything that has not such a relation there sounds within them, like a ground-bass, the constant, inconsolable lament, 'It is of no use to me.' " Though the link between art and impersonality is often acknowledged—in New Criticism as well as Neoclassic theory—no very successful *interpretive* use of the principle exists. The notion of impersonality is vulnerable because so easily retranslated into unconscious interest or the masked presence of some *force majeure.*

I try to face this problem of the ideology of form by choosing a poem without explicit social context and exploring its involvement in social and historical vision. This would be harder, needless to say, if Keats had not elsewhere explicitly worried the opposition of dreamer and poet or poet and thinker. Even if "To Autumn" were a holiday of the spirit, some workday concerns of the poet would show through. My use of the concept of ideology, at the same time, will seem halfway or uncritical to the Marxist thinker. In uncovering Keats's ideology I remain as far as possible within terms provided by Keats himself, or furnished by the ongoing history of poetry. This is not, I hope, antiquarianism, but also not transvaluation. It should be possible to consider a poem's *geschichtlicher Stundenschlag* (Adorno)—how it tells the time of history—without accepting a historical determinism. Keats's poetry is indeed an event in history: not in world-history, however, but simply in the history of fiction, in our awareness of the power and poverty of fictions.

My argument runs that "To Autumn," an ode that is hardly an ode, is best defined as an English or Hesperian model which overcomes not only the traditional type of sublime poem but the "Eastern" or epiphanic consciousness essential to it. The traditional type was transmitted by both Greek and Hebrew religious poetry, and throughout the late Renaissance and eighteenth century, by debased versions of the Pindaric or cult hymn.[4] Only one thing about epiphanic structure need be said now: it evokes the presence of a god, or vacillates sharply between imagined presence and absence. Its rhetoric is therefore a crisis-rhetoric, with priest or votary, vastation or rapture, precarious nearness or hieratic distance ("Ah Fear! Ah frantic Fear! I see, I see thee near!"). As these verses by William Collins suggest, epiphanic structure proceeds by dramatic turns of mood and its language is ejaculative (Lo, Behold, O come, O see). Keats's "Hesperianism" triumphs, in "To Autumn," over this archaic style with its ingrained, superstitious attitude toward power—power seen as external and epochal. The new sublimity domesticates with the heart; the poet's imagination is neither imp nor incubus. Though recognizably sublime, "To Autumn" is a poem of *our* climate.

Climate is important. It ripens wits as well as fruits, as Milton said in another context.[5] The higher temperature and higher style of the other odes are purged away: we have entered a temperate zone. What is grown here, this "produce of the air," is like its ambience: Hesperian art rather than oriental ecstasy or unnatural flight of the imagination. Autumn is clearly a mood as well as a season, and Stevens would have talked about a weather of the mind. Yet "mood" and "weather" have an aura of changeableness, even of volatility, while the Autumn ode expresses something firmer: not, as so often in Stevens or in the "Beulah" moments of other poets, a note among notes but, as in Spenser, a vast cloud-region or capability. The very shape of the poem—firm and regular without fading edges but also no overdefined contours—suggests a slowly expanding constellation that moves as a whole, if it moves at all.

Its motion is, in fact, part of the magic. Time lapses so gently here; we pass from the fullness of the maturing harvest to the stubble plains without experiencing a cutting edge. If time comes to a point in "To Autumn" it is only at the end of the poem, which verges (more poignant than pointed) on a last "gathering." The scythe of time, the sense of mortality, the cutting of life into distinct, epochal phases is not felt. We do not even stumble into revelation, however softly—there is no moment which divides before and after as in the "Ode to Psyche" with its supersoft epiphany, its Spenserian and bowery moment which makes the poet Psyche's devotee despite her "shadowy thought" nature. The Autumn ode is nevertheless a *poesis*, a shaped segment of life coterminous with that templar "region of the mind" which the other poems seek, though they may honor more insistently the dichotomy of inside and out, fane and profane. Poetry, to change "the whole habit of the mind,"[6] changes also our view of the mind's habitat. To say that "To Autumn" is ideological and that its pressure of form is "English" has to do with that also.

I begin with what is directly observable, rather than with curious knowledge of archaic ode or hymn. In the odes of Keats there is a strong, clearly marked moment of disenchantment, or of illusion followed by disillusion. Fancy, that "Queen of shadows" (Charlotte Smith), becomes a "deceiving elf"—and although the deception remains stylized, and its shock releases pathos rather than starker sentiments, it is as pointed as the traditional turn of the Great Ode. (Compare the turn, for example, from one mode of music to another in Dryden's *Alexander's Feast* or the anastrophe "He is not dead, he lives" in pastoral elegy.) The transition leading from stanzas 7 to 8 in the Nightingale ode is such a turn, which results in calling imagination a "deceiving elf." An imaginative fancy that has sustained itself despite colder thoughts is farewelled.

There is, exceptionally, no such turn in "To Autumn." The poem starts on enchanted ground and never leaves it. This special quality becomes even clearer when we recall that "La Belle Dame sans Merci," with its harvest background and soft ritual progression, ends in desolation of spirit on the cold hillside. But because the final turn of the Nightingale ode, though clear as a bell, is not gross in its effect, not productive of coital sadness, a comparison with Autumn's finale is still possible. In "To Autumn" birds are preparing to fly to a warmer clime, a "visionary south," though we do not see them leave or the cold interrupt. In "To a Nightingale" the poet is allowed a call—adieu, adieu—which is birdlike still and colors the darker "forlorn," while his complete awakening is delayed ("Do I wake or sleep?") and verbal prolongations are felt. There is no complete disenchantment even here.

"To Autumn," moreover, can be said to have something approaching a strophic turn as we enter the last stanza. With "Where are the songs of Spring? Aye, where are they?" a plaintive anthem sounds. It is a case, nevertheless, where a premise is anticipated and absorbed.[7] The premise is that of transience, or the feel of winter, and the rest of the stanza approaches that cold threshold. The premise is absorbed because its reference is back to Spring instead of forward to Winter; by shifting from eye to ear, the music-theme, Keats enriches Autumn with Spring. We remain within a magical circle where things repeat each other in a finer tone, as Autumn turns into a second Spring: "While barred clouds *bloom* the soft-dying day."[8] The music now heard is no dirge of the year but a mingling of lullaby and aubade. For the swallows a second summer is at hand (aubade). For us—if we cannot follow them any more than the elusive nightingale—what comes next is not winter but night (lullaby). We go gently off, in either case, on extended wings.

Thus "To Autumn," like Stevens's "Sunday Morning," becomes oddly an Ode to Evening. The full meaning of this will appear. But in terms of formal analysis we can say that the poem has no epiphany or decisive turn or any absence / presence dialectic. It has, instead, a *westerly drift* like the sun. Each stanza, at the same time, is so equal in its poetical weight, so loaded with its own harvest, that westering is less a natural than a poetic state—it is a mood matured by the poem itself. "To Autumn," in fact does not explicitly evolve from sunrise to sunset but rather from a rich to a clarified dark. Closely read it starts and ends in twilight.

"Season of mists and mellow fruitfulness"—though the mists are of the morning, the line links fertility and semidarkness in a way that might be a syntactical accident were it not for the more highly developed instance of "I cannot see what flowers are at my feet . . . ," that famous stanza from the Nightingale ode where darkened senses also produce a surmise of fruitfulness. The Autumn ode's twilight is something inherent, a condition not simply of growth but of imaginative growth. Westering here is a spiritual movement, one that tempers visionariness into surmise and the lust for epiphany into finer-toned repetitions. We do not find ourselves in a temple but rather in Tempe "twixt sleepe and wake."[9] We can observe the ode unfolding as a self-renewing surmise of fruitfulness: as waking dream or "widening speculation" rather than nature-poem and secularized hymn.

Concerning *surmise:* I have suggested elsewhere its importance for Romantic poetry, how it hovers between factual and fantastic.[10] Its presence is often marked by a "magic casement" effect: as in Wordsworth's "Solitary Reaper," a window opens unexpectedly on a secret or faraway scene.

No nightingale did ever chaunt
More welcome notes to weary bands
Of travellers in some shady haunt,
Among Arabian sands:

Keats has the interesting habit of interpreting pictures (usually imaginary) as scenes beheld from a magic window of this kind. Yet since the frame of the window is also the frame of the picture, he finds himself on an ambiguous threshold, intimately near yet infinitely removed from the desired place. Most of the odes are a feverish quest to enter the life of a pictured scene, to be totally where the imagination is. In the Autumn ode, however, there is no effort to cross a magic threshold: though its three stanzas are like a composite picture from some Book of Hours, we are placed so exactly at the bourn of the invisible picture window that the frame is not felt, nor the desperate haunting of imagination to get in. There is no precipitous "Already with thee" and no stylized dejection.

Something, perhaps, is lost by this: the sense of dangerous transition, of consciousness opening up, of a frozen power unsealing. But the ode remains resolutely meditative. When important images of transition occur they are fully *composed* and no more vibrant than metrical enjambments: "And sometimes like a gleaner thou dost keep / Steady thy laden head." Or, "Sometimes whoever seeks may find / Thee sitting careless." Strictly construed the "sometimes" goes here both with the seeking and with the finding: it is factored out and made prepositional. This is a framing device which further augments the feeling of surmise, of lighthearted questing. What reverberates throughout, and especially in this image of the gleaner, the most pictorial of the poem, is a light but steady pondering. It is not a pondering, of course, devoid of all tension: "keep / Steady," understood as a performative or "cozening imperative,"[11] suggests that the poet is not so much describing as urging the image on, in-feeling it. Let us follow this picture-pondering from verse to verse.

The opening stanza is so strongly descriptive, so loaded with told riches, that there seems to be no space for surmise. A desire to fill every rift with Autumn's gold produces as rich a banquet as Porphyro's heap of delicates in "The Eve of St. Agnes." Thesaurus stanzas of this kind are self-delighting in Keats; but they also have a deeper reason. Porphyro knows that Madeline will find reality poorer than her dream and enhances his value by serving himself up this way. The sumptuous ploy is to help him melt into his lady's waking thought. So Autumn's banquet, perhaps, intends to hold the awakening consciousness and allow the dream to linger. Not only the bees are deceived; the dream "Warm days will never cease" is not in them alone; it is already in Autumn, in her "conspiring." On this phrase all the rich, descriptive details depend; they are infinitives not indicatives, so that we remain in the field of mind. "Conspiring how to load and bless . . . To bend with apples . . . fill all fruit . . . To swell the gourd." As we move through Autumn's thought to the ripening of that thought, we cease to feel her as an external agent.

Thus, the descriptive fullness of the first stanza turns out to be thought-full as well: its pastoral furniture is a golden surmise, imagination in her most deliberate mood. By moving the point of view inward, Keats makes these riches mental riches, imaginative projects. He does not, at the same time, push the mental horizon to infinity: the mood remains infinitive, looking onto "something ever-more about to be."

Once we see that what is being satisfied is empathy or in-feeling,[12] and that to satisfy it Keats (like Autumn) fills outside with more and more inside, the structure of the poem as a progressive surmise becomes clear. In-feeling, in Keats, is always on the point of overidentifying; and even here it demands more than the first stanza's dream of truth. However glowing a prospect Autumn paints, it must still, as it were, come alive. This happens in the second stanza where the drowsy ponderer meets us in person. Now we are in the landscape itself; the harvest is now. The figure of Autumn amid her store is a moving picture, or the dream personified. Yet the two stanzas are perfectly continuous; in-feeling is still being expressed as the filling-up of a space—a figure like Autumn's was needed to plump the poem. Though we approach epiphanic personification in the figure of Autumn, the casualness of "sometimes," together with the easy mood of the opening question, gives us a sense of "widening speculation" and prevents a more than cornucopial view of the goddess.

But the dream is almost shattered at the end of the stanza. The word "oozings" extends itself phonically into "hours by hours," a chime that leads to the idea of transience in "Where are the songs of Spring?" Though immediately reabsorbed, this muted ubi sunt introduces the theme of mutability. Oozings—hours—ubi sunt . . . A single word, or its echoes, might have disenchanted Keats like the turn on "forlorn" in the Nightingale ode. Disenchantment, however, does not occur: there is no reverse epiphany as in "La Belle Dame sans Merci," no waking into emptiness.

We have reached, nevertheless, the airiest of the stanzas. Does a chill wind not brush us, an airiness close to emptiness? Do we not anticipate the "cold hill's side"? Even if the mood of surmise is sustained, it might well be a surmise of death rather than fruitfulness.

Here, at the consummate point of Keats's art, in-feeling achieves its subtlest act. Keats conspires with autumn to fill even the air. Air becomes a granary of sounds, a continuation of the harvest, or *Spätlese*. In this last and softest stanza, the ear of the ear is ripened.

More than a tour de force or finely sustained idea is involved. For at the end of other odes we find an explicit *cry,* which is part of their elegiac envoi. Here that cry is uttered, as it were, by the air itself, and can only be heard by an ear that knows how to glean such sounds. What is heard, to quote the modern poet closest to Keats,

> is not a cry of divine attention,
> Nor the smoke-drift of puffed-out heroes, nor human cry.
> It is the cry of leaves that do not transcend themselves.[13]

In lyric poetry the cry is a sign of subjective feelings breaking through and in the cult-hymn of being possessed by divine power. It signifies in both a transcendence absent from this "final finding of the air." Lyricism, in "To Autumn," frees itself for once of elegy and ecstasy: it is neither a frozen moment of passion nor the inscription that prolongs it.

The Grecian urn's "Beauty is Truth, Truth Beauty" remains an extroverted, lapidary cry. However appropriate its philosophy, its form is barely snatched from a defeat of the imagination. "To Autumn" has no defeat in it. It is the most negative capable of all of Keats's great poems. Even its so-called death-stanza[14] expresses no rush toward death, no clasping of darkness as a bride, or quasi-oriental ecstasy. Its word-consciousness, its mind's weather—all remains Hesperian. As its verses move toward an image of southerly flight (the poem's nearest analogue to transcendence), patterns emerge that delay the poet's "transport to summer." Perception dwells on the border and refuses to overdefine. So "full-grown lambs" rather than "sheep." Add such verbal ponderings or reversing repetitions as "borne aloft . . . hilly bourn," a casual chiastic construction, playing on a mix of semantic and phonetic properties. Or the noun-adjective phrase "treble soft" which becomes an adjective-noun phrase when "treble" is resolved into the northern "triple." And consider the northernisms. The proportion of northern words increases perceptibly as if to pull the poem back from its southerly orientation. There is hardly a romance language phrase: sound-shapes like sallows, swallows, borne, bourn, crickets, croft, predominate.[15] And, finally, the poise of the stanza's ending, on the verge of flight like joy always bidding adieu. How easily, in comparison, Hölderlin turns eastward, and converts wish into visionary transport on the wings of an older rhetoric:

> These my words, when, rapt
> faster than I could have known,
> and far, to where I never
> thought to come, a Genius
> took me from my own house. They glimmered
> in the twilight, as I went,
> the shadowy wood
> and the yearning brooks
> of my country; I knew the fields no more;
> Yet soon, brighter and fresher,
> mysterious
> under the golden smoke
> flowering, rising fast before me
> in the sun's steps
> with a thousand fragrant hills
> Asia dawned
>
> ("Patmos")

Less magnificent, equally magnanimous, "To Autumn" remains a poem "in the northwind sung." Its progress is merely that of repetitions "in a finer tone," of "widening speculation," of "treble soft" surmise. Yet in its Hesperian reach it does not give up but joins a south to itself.

Keats's respect for the sublime poem does not have to be argued. There is his irritation with the "egotistical sublime" of Wordsworth, his admiration for Milton who broke through "the clouds which envelope so deliciously the Elysian field of verse, and committed himself to the Extreme," his anguished attempt to write the *Hyperion,* and the testimony of lesser but affecting verses like those to the "God of the Meridian" in which he foresees madness:

> when the soul is fled
> To high above our head,
> Afrighted do we gaze
> After its airy maze,
> As doth a mother wild,
> When her young infant child
> Is in an eagle's claws—
> And is not this the cause
> Of madness?—God of Song,
> Thou bearest me along
> Through sights I scarce can bear

The "bear . . . bear" pun shows well enough the tension of epic flight. I must now make clear what kind of problem, formal and spiritual, the sublime poem was.

A first difficulty centers on the relation of romance to sublime or epic. The romance mode, for Keats, is now presublime (and so to be "broken through") and now postsublime. Where, as in the first *Hyperion,* Keats wishes to sublimate the sublime he turns with relief to the "golden theme" of Apollo after the Saturnine theme of the first two books. In the *Fall of Hyperion,* however, romance is an Elysium or Pleasure-garden to be transcended. While in "La Belle Dame sans Merci" romance becomes sheer oxymoron, a "golden tongued" nightmare.

It is best to find a view beyond this special dialectic of romance and epic in Keats, all the more so as that is complicated by the dream-truth, or vision-reality split. No formal analysis will disentangle these rich contraries. It can only reduce them to the difference suggested in the *Fall of Hyperion* between "an immortal's sphered words" and the mother-tongue. This is the dichotomy on which Keats's epic voyage foundered: the opposition between Miltonic art-diction and the vernacular. "Life to him [Milton] would be death to me." "English must be kept up." Yet such a distinction is no more satisfying than one in terms of genre. Vernacular romance is perhaps more feasible than vernacular epic—but we get as mixed up as Keats himself when we define each genre in family terms and put romance under mother, epic under father. In the *Fall of Hyperion* Moneta is as patriarchal as she is womanly.

A solution is to consider both romance and epic—or the high-visionary style in general—as belonging to an older, "epiphanic" structuring of consciousness. Against it can be put a nonepiphanic structuring; and if the older type is primarily associated with the East, the modern would be with the West or, at its broadest,

Hesperia.[16] It is possible to treat this distinction formally as one between two types of structuring rather than two types of consciousness. Eventually, however, Keats's charge of superstition or obsolescence against the earlier mode will move us into ideology and beyond formalism. A man who says, like Keats, that life to Milton is death to him is concerned with more than formal options.

Epiphanic structure implies, first of all, the possibility of categorical shifts: of crossing into *allo genere,* and even, I suppose, out of ordinary human consciousness into something else. Apotheosis (as at the end of *Hyperion*), metamorphosis, and transformation scenes are type instances of such a crossing. It is accompanied by a doctrine of states, a philosophy of transcendence, and a formulary for the "translation" of states. Epiphanic structure can bear as much sophistication as an author is capable of. Take the sequence, based on *Paradise Lost,* Book VIII, which haunted Keats: "The Imagination may be compared to Adam's Dream: He awoke and found it truth."[17] This refers chiefly to Adam seeing Eve first in dream and, upon waking, in the flesh. Keats will often use it ironically rather than not use it at all. So in the "Eve of St. Agnes" Madeline wakes into Imagination's truth and finds it—how pale, how diminished! She melts the reality—Porphyro—back into her dream in a moment of, presumably, sexual union.

A more complex instance is the dark epiphany in "La Belle Dame sans Merci" where the enchanted knight wakes, as it were, into the arms of the wrong dream and cannot find his way back to the right one. Whereas, in Milton, one cunning enjambment expresses the intensity of the quest springing from imaginative loss,

> She [Eve] disappear'd, and left me dark, I wak'd
> To find her

a moment Keats repeats faintly in the Autumn ode,

> Sometimes whoever seeks abroad may find
> Thee

in "La Belle Dame" there is nothing—no natural food—can satisfy the knight. He starves for his drug, like Keats so often for the heightened consciousness of epiphanic style.

In *Paradise Lost,* Adam's dream prepares him for the truth he is to meet. Truth is conceived of as a fuller, perhaps more difficult, dream; and God seeks to strengthen Adam's visionary powers by engaging him in these dream-corridors. Instead of a single dramatic or traumatic change there is to be a gradual tempering of the mind. This modification of epiphanic structure may have inspired a favorite speculation of Keats, that happiness on earth would be enjoyed hereafter "repeated in a finer tone and so repeated." Miltonic tenderness, by allowing Adam's consciousness to develop, by giving it time for growth, lightens the all-or-nothing (sometimes, all-and-nothing) character of epiphanic vision.[18] Though the end remains transport and deification, the means are based, at least in part, on a respect for natural process.

The naturalization of epiphanic form is less effective in "La Belle Dame" than in this prototypal sequence from Milton. The reason lies perhaps in the genre as much as in Keats himself. Quest-romance is a particularly resistant example of epiphanic form. Though Spenser helps to detumesce it he also throws its archaic lineaments into relief: his faërie remains a montage, a learned if light superposition. The dominant feature of quest-romance (as of fairy-tale) is the ever-present danger of trespass: of stepping all at once or unconsciously into a daemonic field of force. Often the quest is motivated by redeeming such a prior trespass; but even when it starts unburdened it cannot gain its diviner end without the danger of *allo genere* crossings. Keats's knight steps ritually, if unknowingly, into demonry. So also Coleridge's mariner, whose act of trespass is clear but who before it and after crosses also invisible demarcations. From this perspective the exile of Adam and Eve and the wanderings of Odysseus are both the result of a trespass against the divine, or of stepping willy-nilly into a daemonic sphere.[19]

This is not the place to work out the formal variations of quest-romance. But when a poet does succeed in subduing the form, the result is both remarkable and mistakable. In "Strange Fits of Passion" Wordsworth's rider is a becalmed knight from Romance whose rhythm parodies the chivalric gallop and who is always approaching yet never crossing a fatal border. The moon that drops and deflates the dreaming into a mortal thought is a pale metonymy of itself when considered against the backdrop of epiphanic romance. It alone belongs to the sphere of "strange fits"; and while it still divides before and after and even suggests that an imaginative or unconscious trespass has occurred, it cannot be drawn fully into the lunatic symbolism of romance. Keats, I think, did not manage to humanize this form: he feared too much that leaving Romance behind meant being exiled from great poetry. He was unable to "translate" the inherited code either into the Miltonic Extreme or into Wordsworth's fulfillment of Miltonic tenderness.

And yet: did he not humanize epiphanic form in the special case of the ode? Recent scholarship by Kurt Schlüter and others has established the basic form of the ancient cult-hymn as it impinged on European poetry.[20] The easiest division of the form is, as you might expect, into three: invocation, narrative or mythic portion, and renewed invocation. Sappho's "Ode to Aphrodite" is a clear example, so is Shelley's "Ode to the West Wind." Basically, however, the structure consists simply of a series of apostrophes or turns petitioning an absent god or attesting his presence. To the modern reader it may all seem somewhat hysterical: a succession of cries modulated by narrative or reflective interludes.

The sublime or greater or Pindaric ode flourished in the eighteenth century like a turgid weed, all pseudo-epiphany and point, bloat and prickles, feeding off an obsolescent style. Dr. Johnson vilified Gray's Pindaric experiments as "cucumbers." The best that can be said for the genre is that like contemporary opera it became a refuge for visionary themes: an exotic and irrational entertainment which reminded the indulgent consumer of the polite good sense of his society, and sent him back, all afflatus spent, to trifle with the lesser ode. It is not till Collins that a dialogue begins within the genre between its sublime origins and the English ground to which it is transplanted.

A brief notice of this dialogue in Collins's "Ode to Evening" prepares us for Keats. Collins uses all the features characterizing the sublime ode except one. His extended apostrophe suggests the hieratic distance between votary and the invoked power, anticipates at the same time its presence, and leads into a narrative second half describing in greater detail the coming of the divinity and its effect on the poet. This is followed by a renewed invocation which acts as the poem's coda. The one feature conspicuously absent is the epiphany proper. The invoked personification, evening, is a transitional state, a season of the day, whose advent is its presence. By addressing in epiphanic terms a subject intrinsically non-epiphanic, and adjusting his style subtly to it, Collins opens the way to a new, if still uneasy, nature-poetry.

What adjustments of style are there? The movement of the ode is highly mimetic, as Collins, suiting his numbers to the nature of evening, slows and draws out his musings.

> If aught of oaten stop, or pastoral song,
> May hope, chaste Eve, to soothe thy modest ear,
> Like thy own solemn springs
> Thy springs and dying gales
> O nymph reserved, while now . . .

Instead of hastening some eclipsing power, or leaping into a fuller present, his verse becomes a programmatic accompaniment to the gradual fall of night. The form, in other words, is self-fulfilling: as the processional verse blends with processual nature, and an expanding shadow (a "gradual, dusky veil") is all of relevation there is, the poet's prayer results in what it asks for: "Now teach me, *Maid* compos'd / To breathe some soften'd Strain." This "now" is only in echo that of an ecstatic, annihilative present: it refers to an actual time of day, and perhaps to a belated cultural moment. With this drawn-out "now" nature-poetry is born:

>   and now with treble soft
> The red-breast whistles from the garden-croft;
> And gathering swallows twitter in the skies.

Collins's "soften'd strain," his conversion of epiphanic style, will find its culminating instance in Keats's poetry of process.

That Collins represents Evening as a god is more than a naturalized archaism. Evening, invoked as the source of a new music, stands for Hesperia, the evening-star land; and what the poet asks for, in these prelusive strains, is a genuinely western verse, an *Abendlandpoesie*. Like Keats's Psyche, Evening is a new goddess: the poetic pantheon of the East contained only Sun and Night, but Evening is peculiar to the Western hemisphere. In the courts of the East, as Coleridge noted in his *Ancient Mariner,* "At one stride comes the dark." The East, in its sudden dawn and sudden darkness, is epiphanic country. But the English climate, in weather or weather of the mind, has a more temperate, even, evening effect. Collins embraces the idea that his native country, or the cultural region to which it belonged, has a style and vision of its own.[21] He shows spirit of place as a felt influence, and gothic eeriness as eariness. That is, he uncovers a new sense for nature by uncovering a new sense: the natural ear. What the sublime ode had attempted by overwhelming the eye—or the "descriptive and allegoric style" which dominates the age—Collins achieves through this finer sense. The eye, as in Wordsworth's "Tintern Abbey," and in the last stanza of "To Autumn," is made quiet by "the power of harmony."

In the "Ode to Evening" the concept of a Hesperian poetry conditions even sensory mimesis or impels it into a new region. It is no accident that the last stanza of "To Autumn" contains an evening ode in small. That "Evening Ear," which Collins elsewhere attributes to Milton, is, to use a rare Wordsworthian pun, an *organ of vision:* responsive to a particular climate or "spiritual air" (*Endymion,* IV) in which poets feel themselves part of a belated and burdened cultural yet find their own relation to the life of things. As the landscape darkens gently, the blind and distant ear notices tones—finer tones—that had escaped a dominant and picture-ridden eye: a weak-eyed bat flits by, curious emblem, and the beetle emerges winding its horn, as if even pastoral had its epic notes. There is still, in Collins, this airy faërie which has often dissolved in Keats—who, however, is never very far from it. What matters is that creatures jargon, like "To Autumn" 's parliament of birds; that the sounds are real sounds, a produce of the air; that the heard is not exclusively divine or human; and that within the sheltering dark of the ear other senses emerge: "I cannot see what flowers are at my feet, / Nor what soft incense hangs upon the bough, / But in embalmed darkness guess each sweet." Here absence is presence, though not by way of mystical or epiphanic reversal. In every temperate zone the air is full of noises.

This sensory ideology, if I may call it such,[22] must have affected Keats one early autumn day looking at stubble fields:

> How beautiful the season is now—How fine the Air. A temperate sharpness about it. Really, without joking, chaste weather—Dian skies—I never lik'd stubble fields so much as now—Aye better than the chilly green of the spring. Somehow a stubble plain looks warm—in the same way that some pictures look warm—this struck me so much in my sunday's walk that I composed upon it.

That ideology is in the air is proven by what follows:

> I always somehow associate Chatterton with Autumn. He is the purest writer in the English language. [Chatterton's language is entirely northern.] He has no French idiom, or particles like Chaucer—tis genuine English idiom in English words. I have given up Hyperion. . . . English ought to be kept up.[23]

We have already commented on the northernisms in "To Autumn" 's last stanza: even romance language (let alone romance) is gently shunned. Nothing but "home-bred glory."

Can we see the gods die in "To Autumn," the epiphanic forms dissolve, as it were, before our eyes? Autumn is, by tradition, the right season for this dissolution, or dis-illusion.

> Let Phoebus lie in umber harvest

Stevens writes in "Notes toward a Supreme Fiction,"

> Let Phoebus slumber and die in autumn umber
> Phoebus is dead, ephebe.

But, in tradition also, a new god treads on the heels of the old, and loss figures forth a stronger presence. In Hesperian poetry, from Collins to Keats to Stevens, this entire absence/presence vacillation does no more than manure the ground of the poem, its "sensible ecstasy."

Consider the invocation "Season of mists and mellow fruitfulness." The odic O is hardly felt though the verses immediately fill one's mouth with rich labials extended in a kind of chiastic middle between "Season" and "sun." Nothing remains of the cultic distance between votary and personified power: we have instead two such powers, autumn and sun, whose closeness is emphasized, while the moment of hailing or petitioning is replaced by a presumptive question ("Who hath not seen thee") suggesting availability rather than remoteness. The most interesting dissolve, however, comes with the grammatical shift, in the opening line, from mythic-genealogical to descriptive-partitive "of," which effectively diffuses autumn into its attributes. Compare "Season of mists and mellow fruitfulness" with the following apostrophes:

Thou foster-child of silence and slow time.

Here the poet uses clearly and finely a formula which alludes to the high descent of the apostrophized object. In our next example

Nymph of the downward smile, and side-long glance

the grammatical form is analogous, but the "of" has moved from genealogical toward partitive. The nymph is eminently characterized by these two attributes: they *are* her in this statuesque moment. The opening of "To the Nile":

Son of the old moon-mountains African
Stream of the pyramid and crocodile

actually brings mythic-genealogical and partitive-descriptive together. Against this background we see how beautifully dissolved into the ground of description is the mythical formula of "To Autumn" 's first line.

We do, of course, by what appears to be a regressive technique, meet Autumn personified in the second stanza. If the poem approaches a noon-point of stasis—of arrest or centered revelation—it is here. The emergence of myth serves, however, to ripen the pictorial quality of the poem rather than to evoke astonishment. The emphasis is on self-forgetful relaxation (at most on "forget thyself to marble") not on saturnine fixation. No more than in "To Evening" is nature epiphanic: Keats's autumn is not a specter but a spirit, one who steals over the landscape, or "amid her store" swellingly imbues it.[24] The poet's mind is not rapt or astonished and so forced back on itself by a sublime apparition.

It is essential, in fact, to note what happens to mind. In the cult hymn the invocation merges with, or is followed by, the god's *comos:* an enumeration of his acts and attributes.[25] But Keats's first stanza becomes simply the filling up of a form, a golden chain of infinitives hovering between prospect and fulfillment, until every syntactical space is loaded and the poet's mind, like the bees', loses itself in the richness. The stanza, in fact, though full, and with its eleven lines, more than full, is not a grammatical whole but a drunk sentence. The poet's mind, one is tempted to say, has entered the imagined picture so thoroughly that when the apostrophe proper is sprung at the opening of stanza 2, and the grammatical looseness corrected, it simultaneously opens a new speculative movement. And when the generative figure of Autumn appears in the second stanza, it is self-harvesting like the poet's own thoughts. The last stanza, then, leaves us in a "luxury of twilight" rather than dropping us into a void where "no birds sing."

The demise of epiphanic forms in "To Autumn" raises a last question: is not the sequential movement of the whole poem inspired by a progressive idea with Enlightenment roots? There seems to be, on the level of sensation, something that parallels the first *Hyperion*'s progress from heavier to lighter, from Hyperion to Apollo, and from fixed burdens to a softer oppression. Several key phrases in Keats's letters suggest an "enlightenment" of this kind. The poet talks of "widening speculation," of "the regular stepping of Imagination toward a Truth," and of easing the "Burden of the Mystery." Magical moments like the fourth stanza of "Ode on a Grecian Urn"

> Who are these coming to the sacrifice?
> To what green altar, O mysterious priest

are surely related to this lightening. Mystery survives, but in a purged, airy, speculative form. The "overwrought" questions of the ode's beginning, which sought to penetrate or fix a symbol-essence, are purified into surmise and evoke a scene of "wide quietness" rather than bacchic enthusiasm.

There is a progress then; but is it toward a truth? We know what the conclusion to the Grecian Urn ode suggests. "Beauty is Truth, Truth Beauty" is a chiastic phrase, as self-rounding as the urn. No ultimate turn or final step toward a truth occurs. Though there are turns in the poem, they are more musical than epiphanic, and the very notion of "the turn" merges with that of the art-object: Keats turns the urn in his imagination until the urn is its turnings. The poet's speculation is circular.

Keats's rondure, his counterprogression, subverts without rejecting the received idea of "enlightenment." Poetry clearly has its own progress, its own lights. Formalistic or art-centered terms have, therefore, a certain propriety. But they cannot suffice for Keats any more than for Wordsworth, who also seeks to ease the "burthen of the mystery" ("Tintern Abbey," line 39). Consider the profound difference between these poets, who both believe in a dispersion of older— poetical or religious—superstitions. Such qualities as decorum, impersonality, symbolic adequacy are a function mainly of the concenteredness of "To Autumn": the poem turns around one image like a "leaf-fring'd legend." Though Wordsworth's poems may also have a center of this kind (Lucy's death, a peculiar landscape, a remembered scene), it rarely appears as picturesque symbol or image. Wordsworth's kernels are mysteries: charged spiritual places which confront and confuse a mental traveler who circles their enchanted ground—or who, like a policeman, tries to cordon off the disturbance. This too is an important "enlightenment" form, delimiting a romance apparition or sublime feelings—yet how different from Keats! In Wordsworth the spirit must find its own containment, and never quite finds it; those "spots of time" erupt from their hiding-places like the Hebraic God; the structure of his poems expresses various attempts at containment which accrete with difficulty into a personal history ("Tintern Abbey") or an eschatological and cultural one ("Hart-Leap Well"). But Keats's experience is limited from the outset by Greek or picturesque example. What perplexes his imagination is a mysterious picture rather than a mystery.

Keats's formal a priori takes us back to Greece and where, according to Hegel, modern consciousness began. Formal beauty mediates "between the loss of individuality . . . as in Asia, where spiritual and divine are totally subsumed under a natural form, and infinite subjectivity." Greek character is "individuality conditioned by beauty" and in its respect for divine images modern and free, rather than Asiatic and superstitious. "He [the human being] is the womb that conceived them, he the breast that suckled them, he the spiritual to which their grandeur and purity is owing. Thus he feels himself calm in contemplating them, and not only free in himself, but possessing the consciousness of his freedom."[26]

That Hegel's description can fit Keats makes one cautious about the whole enterprise of dividing consciousness into historically localized phases. All the more so as Hölderlin has his own myth of the Hesperian character, which is said to begin when Homer moderates oriental pathos or "fire from heaven."[27] I make no claim for the historical exactness of either Hegel or Hölderlin. Historical speculation and criticism stand, as Professor Wimsatt has observed, in a highly problematic relationship.[28]

Yet there is something like "Hesperian" freedom in "To Autumn," a poem which becomes—in Hegel's words—the womb for the rebirth of an astral or divine image. Such a divine image is certainly there; we should not exaggerate the absence of poetical superstition in Keats. Though his central figure is picturesque its star quality glimmers through.

Much has been written on Autumn's affinities to Demeter or other harvest deities.[29] The divinity, however, that haunts Keats early and late is Apollo: sun-god, god of song, and "fore-seeing god."[30] The difference between Hyperion and Apollo is, in good part, that the former is now doomed to live under "the burden of the mystery." Hyperion cannot dawn any more; he remains darkling. But Apollo in *Hyperion,* even though that poem breaks off and leaves the young god's metamorphosis incomplete—even though he too must shoulder the mystery—should break forth like the sun to "shape his actions" like "a fore-seeing god."[31] In the Autumn ode the major theme of clairvoyance—at once foreseeing and deep-seeing (deep into the heart or maw of life)—is tempered.[32] Yet it is far from absent.

For Autumn's "conspiring" function is comparable to that of the guardian genius, the *natale comes qui temperat astrum.*[33] An idea of poetic or personal destiny enters, in however veiled a form. The poet who writes this ode stands under the pressure of an omen. As summer passes into autumn (season of the year or human season), his dreaming deepens into foresight:

When I have fears that I may cease to be
Before my pen has glean'd my teeming brain,
Before high-piled books, in charact'ry,
Hold like rich garners the full-ripen'd grain . . .

Herr: es ist Zeit. Der Sommer war sehr gross[34]

In fear of early death, and sensing riches his pen might never glean, Keats evokes a figure of genial harvests. Three times he renews his surmise of fruitfulness, three times he grasps the shadow without self-defeating empathy. Even fruitfulness is not a burden in "To Autumn." This, at last, is true impersonality.

NOTES

1. Jonathan Wordsworth, *Cornell Library Journal* 11 (1970): 22. Compare Allen Tate, *Collected Essays* (Denver, 1959), p. 168: " 'Ode to Autumn' is a very nearly perfect piece of style but it has little to say."

2. *John Keats* (Cambridge, Mass., 1963), pp. 581 ff.

3. Theodor Adorno, "Rede über Lyrik und Gesellschaft," in *Noten zur Literatur* I (Frankfurt, 1958). The debate that took place in the thirties and forties, under the influence of T. S. Eliot, concerned literature and belief—where "belief" referred primarily to religious dogma, or political and moral positions inspired by it.

4. See Kurt Schlüter, *Die Englische Ode* (Bonn, 1964), chap. 2.

5. On "climate" theory in Milton, see Zera Fink, *The Classical Republicans,* 2d ed. (Evanston, 1962), pp. 91–94.

6. Wallace Stevens, "The Westwardness of Everything," in *Wallace Stevens: Collected Poems* (New York, 1954), p. 454.

7. W. J. Bate, *John Keats,* pp. 581 ff.

8. My italics. "Dying" is qualified by "soft" but also perhaps by the pictorial sense of the word continued in "rosy hue."

9. On *templum* and its suggestive context in Renaissance poetry, see Angus Fletcher, *The Prophetic Moment* (Chicago, 1971), pp. 14 ff. See also Northrop Frye on *tenemos* in Keats, in *A Study of English Romanticism* (New York, 1969).

10. *Wordsworth's Poetry* (New Haven, 1964), pp. 9–13.

11. See John Hollander, "The Metrical Emblem," *Kenyon Review* 21 (1959): 290.

12. "Always the goal is his mastery of infelt space." See John Jones, *Keats's Dream of Truth* (London, 1969), p. 11 and passim.

13. Wallace Stevens, "The Course of a Particular."

14. John Jones, *Keats's Dream of Truth,* p. 269. Jones has fine and inward remarks on the ode's "antiphonal whisper," on "gathering" as "the last of the poem's harvesting and perfecting words" and on the poem's objectivity.

15. The presence of nonmigrating robins as well as migrating swallows increases the tension between staying and departure. Some have felt that the swallows are not gathering, at this point, for longer flight; but if the impression is, as I think, that night comes before winter, the precise nature of the gathering is not that important. The word "bourn" (1.30) is from the French only if it means "boundary"; if "stream" it comes from an Anglo-Saxon root.

16. Hesperia belongs to what Vico calls "poetical geography" (*Scienza Nuova,* bk. 2, sec. 11, chap. 1). It referred originally to the western part of Greece, and extended into Italy (Hesperia magna) and Spain (Hesperia ultima). England seems excluded except from a visionary point of view. And although the extension is partly of my own making (a visionary concept of this kind being needed to clarify the geospiritual sense of writers like Milton and Collins), the Tudor myth encouraged it by its linking of James and Elizabeth to the Hesperus-Hesperides-Atlas complex. See, for example, Ben Johnson, *Pleasure Reconciled to Virtue* (1619). Hesperia, as Lemprière also defines it, is basically the region of the setting sun.

17. Letter to Benjamin Bailey, 22 November 1817, in *Selected Poems and Letters of John Keats,* ed. Robert Gittings (London, 1966), pp. 36–38.

18. Wordsworth was highly impressed by Milton's "Union of Tenderness and Imagination." See *Wordsworth's Poetry,* p. 266, and pp. 51–53 (on *Paradise Lost* VIII).

19. See Charles I. Patterson, Jr., *The Daemonic in the Poetry of John Keats* (Urbana, 1970), for an interesting but very different approach. His chap. 7 on "The

Triumph of the Anti-Daemonic" emphasizes the distinctiveness of the Autumn ode in Keats's work, and anticipates the tenor of the interpretation given here.

20. *Die Englische Ode,* chap. 2.

21. On the development of "Hesperianism," see G. H. Hartman, "Romantic Poetry and the Genius Loci" in *Beyond Formalism* (New Haven, 1970). See also pp. 287–89, for remarks on the ideology of temperateness. There is no study of the relation between poetics and politics (or national ethos) centering on the "frame of Temperance," but important indications can be found passim in Angus Fletcher's book on Spenser, *The Prophetic Moment* (Chicago, 1971). Fletcher's interest in the encyclopedic (and cyropedic) qualities of *The Faerie Queene* led him to weigh the interactions of law, culture, national ideals, and poetry. Leo Spitzer's study, *Classical and Christian Ideas of World Harmony* (Baltimore, 1963), contains information and speculation galore on the semantic field of *temperare*.

22. Marx and Engels would doubtless interpret Hesperianism, as I have described it, as the penetration of a mystifying ideology into the poetical domain. "We do not set out from what men say, imagine, conceive, nor from men as narrated, thought of, imagined, conceived, in order to arrive at men in the flesh. We set out from real, active men, and on the basis of their real life-process we demonstrate the development of the ideological reflexes and echos of this life-process. The phantoms formed in the human brain are also, necessarily, sublimates of their material life-process, which is empirically verifiable and bound to material premises. . . . Life is not determined by consciousness, but consciousness by life" (*The German Ideology,* trans. by Roy Pascal [New York, 1947], pp. 14–15). It is important to acknowledge, therefore, that I do indeed set out from "what men say, imagine, conceive . . . from men as narrated"—in short, from literature. The question is whether this starting point is as inauthentic as the authors of *The German Ideology* believe. Is literature, as treated here, the *English* ideology, or is it in its own way a "material premise"?

23. Letter to J. H. Reynolds, 21 September 1819. I have inserted the sentence in brackets, which comes from a journal-letter of the same date to George and Georgiana Keats, and which goes on to the famous statement that "Life to him [Milton] would be death to me."

24. See what W. K. Wimsatt says about latent design in "The Structure of Romantic Nature Imagery," in *The Verbal Icon* (Lexington, Ky., 1954), p. 110. He refers, inter alia, to Keats's ode.

25. See Schlüter, *Die Englische Ode,* chap. 2. His important, specific analysis of the Autumn ode (pp. 218–35) recognizes the muting of epiphanic structure but fails to understand its structural or ideological context.

26. *Philosophy of History,* trans. J. Sibree (New York, 1901), pp. 317–19. This book was compiled posthumously from a series of lectures given by Hegel between 1822 and 1831. Sibree's translation is not always very literal but it catches well enough the spirit of the original. "Individuality conditioned by beauty" renders a conception of the Greek aesthetic character introduced by Winckelmann but which Lessing associated specifically with Classicism's understanding of the limits of the picturesque.

27. See Peter Szondi, "Überwindung des Klassizismus. Der Brief an Böhlendorff vom 4. Dezember 1801," in *Hölderlin-Studien* (Frankfurt, 1967). It is interesting that, as Szondi points out, Hölderlin should use the word "Geschik" to suggest both "destiny" and "(poetic) skill." To be a poet, yet a national poet, is always a complex fate. See also Hölderlin's remarks on Weather, Light, and the natural scenery of his native country in the second letter to Böhlendorff (2 December 1802): "das Licht in seinem Wirken, nationell und als Prinzip und Schicksalsweise bildend . . . das philosophische Licht um mein Fenster."

28. "History and Criticism: A Problematic Relationship," in *The Verbal Icon* (Lexington, Ky., 1954)

29. The best treatment is in Schlüter, *Die Englische Ode,* pp. 223–35.

30. For Keats's "Imitatio Apollinis," see especially Walter H. Evert, *Aesthetic and Myth in the Poetry of Keats* (Princeton, 1965).

31. Letter to B. J. Haydon, 23 January 1818.

32. "Temper my lonely hours / And let me see thy bow'rs / More unalarm'd," Keats wrote in his poem to Apollo ("God of the Meridian") of January 1818. The poem breaks off at that point and in the letter to J. H. Reynolds which quotes it, is followed by "When I have fears that I may cease to be."

To emphasize Apollo is not to discount Demeter but to suggest a transmythologic merging in the poem of "conspiring" (foreseeing) and "maturing" functions. The poem to Apollo breaks off, like *Hyperion,* when "bearing" becomes "overbearing," when maturing, instead of strengthening the prophetic or foreseeing character, leads to an overload destructive of it.

33. Horace, *Epistle* 2.2.187.

34. The first quotation comes from Keats's sonnet of late January 1818; the second is the opening line of Rilke's sonnet "Herbsttag."

JEROME McGANN

Keats and the Historical Method in Literary Criticism

Like Geoffrey H. Hartman, Jerome McGann—the leading scholar and critic of Lord Byron of his generation—appears slightly out of context in this collection. A writer of intimidating productivity, McGann gave the scholarly world in what must be record time the authoritative five-volume collection of *The Poetic Works* of Lord Byron (1980–1991). He has also concentrated in a series of provocative books on issues involved in textual production and textual editing, and he has become—even more visibly—the embodiment in the American academy of new historicist studies of romanticism.

McGann's response to Hartman's essay, "Keats and the Historical Method in Literary Criticism" confirms Hartman's fear that his use of "the concept of the ideology . . . will seem half-way or uncritical to the Marxist thinker." And, indeed, McGann argues that Hartman's essay is "a neo-Romantic reading of an old Romantic poem, and this fact itself tells us much about the judgment upon our own age which is implicit in Hartman's nostalgic commentary."

This picks up an important theme of McGann's recent work, developed in his *Romantic Ideology*. McGann perceives earlier commentators as insufficiently critical, as unconsciously adopting the fundamental views about poetry that the romantic poets held. The issue McGann poses is intellectually fascinating. Hartman quite deliberately and consciously endeavors to recover Keats's position and attitudes as the best ground for critical understanding; McGann's critique of this purpose reasonably enough suggests it therefore will entail a disastrous loss of analytical objectivity.

Conflicts between formal or stylistic analysis and historical scholarship are a traditional problem in literary studies. In the field of hermeneutics, where the lines of disagreement tend to sharpen, the best commentators—Lionel Trilling, for example—have generally aimed for, and achieved, various pragmatic agreements. Few critics would take seriously any suggestion that Byron's poetry could be adequately interpreted without bringing a fair amount of historical and biographical information to bear.[1] On the other hand, a text-only approach has been so vigorously promoted during the last thirty-five years that most historical critics have been driven from the field, and have raised the flag of their surrender by yielding the title "critic" to the victor, and accepting the title "scholar" for themselves.

From *MLN* 94 (1979): 988–989, 1000–1032.

This division of labor has produced a fundamentally unstable situation because it is based upon unresolved and, what is worse, unexamined tensions and conflicts. The problems appear, at first, in a purely practical form: for the student needs to know how he is to decide whether (or in what way) historical and biographical information is needed for interpretation. Confronted with a particular text, we cannot always tell at what points (if any) we ought to press for some particular "extrinsic" material or approach.[2] Textual problems of these sorts are widespread, nor are they a function of a certain sort of poem (like a topical satire) or a certain type of writer (like, say, Byron). They exist because of general critical assumptions about "the mode of existence of a literary work of art."[3] The introductory remarks in Paul deMan's well-known essay on Keats amount to a literary consensus not only about that author, but about the nature of poetry itself:

> In reading Keats, we are . . . reading the work of a man whose experience is mainly literary. . . . In this case, we are on very safe ground when we derive our understanding primarily from the work itself.[4]

DeMan is a brilliant critic, and he knows perfectly well that no reading of a poem—not even a poem by Keats—can take place in a bell jar. This is why he is careful to say that we must "derive our understanding primarily from the work itself," for with that "primarily" he allows himself the option to invoke, when he feels that it is necessary, "extrinsic" material of various sorts. The maneuver is a theoretical blind which sets free the insight of his shrewd practical criticism. But the problems of theory and of method only arise more insistently than ever: how are we to decide—even if we grant deMan's premises about Keats—when to admit "extrinsic" materials and approaches?

Such practical decisions will always remain problematic so long as the critic agrees to accept the great commonplace of 20th century literary criticism: that a poem is fundamentally a word-construct, a special arrangement of linguistic units, or—as we now like to say—a "text."[5] Once that idea is accepted, the originally heuristic categories "extrinsic" and "intrinsic" are instantly reified, and the so-called poem becomes alienated from its social setting. Consequently, the practical problem I initially pointed toward—how does a person decide when to invoke historical materials or methods?—reveals itself as fundamentally a procedural question. A comprehensive theory will show that we need not doubt the relevance of "extrinsic" methods and materials; rather, what the critic must weigh are the problems of how best and most fully to elucidate the poem's (presumed) networks of social relations. . . . [Sections of the original essay not reprinted here worked from Bakhtinian premises to express the need for a comprehensive sociohistorical theory of poetry and to illustrate through detailed readings neglected social implications of Keats's "Cockney" style. We take up the essay at the point at which McGann asserts "how and why poetic analysis requires an historical method if it is to achieve either precision or comprehensiveness."]

"La Belle Dame Sans Merci" is a great and famous poem, and has been much commented upon; yet for all that attention, its physical text has not been much analyzed, nor ever satisfactorily. One is made especially aware of this problem of Jack Stillinger's new edition of Keats, which Harvard Press announces as "Definitive."[6] In the Harvard edition the poem is printed in the physical form all of us, probably, have always read. The interesting thing is that this is not the text which

Keats himself printed. Many questions arise in such a situation, but to an histori-
cal critic the bibliographical question will be the fundamental one; for in that
question we begin to elucidate the poem's critical history. Astonishing as it may
seem, that history remains to this day tangled and even mystified, despite the fact
that the material for unravelling it is largely ready to hand.

Keats wrote his poem in April, 1819. He did nothing with it immediately, but
later published it, in May, 1820, in Leigh Hunt's weekly literary periodical *The
Indicator.* It appeared there signed simply "Caviare," which was an allusion to
the line in *Hamlet* " 'twas caviare to the general" (Act II, Scene 2). This text is
the only one Keats ever published, for he did not choose to print the poem in his
1820 collection, an interesting fact in its own right (the volume was published in
June). The poem first entered Keats's collected works in 1848, in Richard
Monckton Milnes' *Life, Letters, and Literary Remains, of John Keats.* In this
1848 printing, however, the text was taken from a copy of the poem made by
Charles Brown. No one knows the source of Brown's text, though editors have
conjectured, not implausibly, that it was made from a (now lost) holograph fair
copy. This 1848 text, derived from Brown's copy, is the one we all now read, and
it differs greatly from the text printed by Keats himself. The new Harvard
edition also prints the Brown/1848 text.[7]

Under the circumstances, the *prima facie* bibliographic facts would normally,
and without any question, demand that an editor—especially an editor in 1978—
print *The Indicator* text, not the Brown/1848 text, for it is *The Indicator* text
which, so far as we can tell, most closely corresponds to the author's final, active
intentions. The question then naturally arises: why has the postauthorial critical
tradition from 1848 to the present normally printed, read, and studied the poem in
the Brown/1848 text? For a study of that tradition, particularly during its past fifty
years or so, shows that editors and commentators are aware of the problem and
have all along deliberately chosen not to print *The Indicator* text.

Arguments have been made to suggest that the Brown/1848 text more closely
represents Keats's final intentions, but they are all suppositions, and have per-
suaded no one. The history of the criticism further shows that the choice was in
fact made because certain key readers felt that *The Indicator* text was not so good
a poem as the other.[8] An impressionistic argument was set off against a biblio-
graphic one, and the former has prevailed. At this point I am not trying to make a
case for restoring the authority of *The Indicator* text, but merely to understand the
history which descends upon us, in a largely invisible form, whenever we read "La
Belle Dame Sans Merci." In order to elucidate such material we would have to
begin by studying both texts of the poem in relation, primarily, to their respective
initiating contexts on the one hand (the literary and historical contexts circa 1819
and 1848), and to the people most involved in establishing both texts (that is,
Keats, Fanny Brawne, Brown, Hunt, and Milnes).

Without attempting to develop an exhaustive analysis along these lines, let me
merely indicate a few important matters. The first line of *The Indicator* text reads

Ah what can ail thee, wretched wight . . .

rather than, as in Brown/1848:

Oh what can ail thee, knight-at-arms. . . .

The difference is important, in the literary context of the period, for "wretched wight" is a locution which had acquired—in the course of its belated Spenserian history through the late 18th and early 19th century—a distinctly ironic overtone.[9] The phrase is a consciously archaic signifier used by poets, in certain limited contexts, to tell the reader to stand at a critical distance from the signified. When Keats opens his ballad with this phrase, then, he is also introducing a personal note into the poem by letting his reader glimpse the poet in his self-consciousness as an artist. More specifically, Keats show his reader that he, as a poet, stands at a slightly critical distance from his subject.

In this respect, the "wretched wight" usage supports the general tonal approach which characterizes *The Indicator* version of the poem. Unlike Hunt's *Examiner, The Indicator* was a non-political publication which devoted itself to literary and artistic matters.[10] Byron published in *The Examiner* and *The Liberal,* not in *The Indicator.* But if it was not a political publication as such, *The Indicator* decidedly tendentious in its aims. Hunt established the magazine as an alternative to the more traditional periodicals of the day. Thus, when Keats signed his poem "Caviare," he was, once again, adopting a self-conscious pose for the reader, only in this case he was glancing at his ballad in relation to the prevailing literary climate. The *Hamlet* allusion shows us that Keats means to share a mildly insolent attitude toward the literary establishment with his readers in *The Indicator,* who are presumed to represent an undebased literary sensibility.

Everyone would agree that these facts illuminate how the poem would have been originally received, and understood, by readers of *The Indicator.* The more important point, for the present, is that this history continues to affect the way people read the poem today. Our present text is the product of a long historical struggle, carried out in the Lilliputian land of bibliographers and literary critics, to suppress one form of the poem and to elevate another. Understanding this history helps to define the differences betwen the two physical texts, but it likewise helps to explain what the Brown/1848 text presently means by showing what meanings it has forbidden to us.

The Brown/1848 text shows many more variants than the one already mentioned, and their cumulative effect is pronounced. Perhaps the most important result of the Brown/1848 changes was to make the character of the knight more sympathetic to the reader and the character of the elfin lady less so. In *The Indicator* the lady does not have "wild, wild eyes" but "wild sad eyes," and she does not lull the knight to sleep. The "kisses four" with which he shuts her eyes in Brown/1848 are very different in *The Indicator:*

And there I shut her wild sad eyes—
  So kissed to sleep.
And there we slumbered on the moss. . . .
                    (31–33)

Here we see that *The Indicator*'s kisses are given in a mutual exchange, and that both fall asleep together after their lovemaking. This last fact seriously diminishes the demand made upon the reader by the Brown/1848 text to see the lady as a bewitching siren.

After 1848 readers of Keats characteristically saw the elfin lady as a sort of demon lover who had ensnared the unsuspecting knight. This is still an influential way of reading the poem, though with the coming of the ironies of the twentieth century the issue has sometimes been seen as more problematic than that. A persuasive case could be made showing that Brown and Milnes share the immediate responsibility—not merely in fact, but by ideological design—for giving us the idea that the elfin lady is simply demonic, a sort of uncomplicated lamia. (It was a commonplace of Victorian criticism that the lady of Keats's *Lamia* narrative was unambiguously evil.) Brown's attitudes toward women in general, and his crude behavior to Fanny Brawne in particular, are notorious. For his part, Milnes had an enormous library of erotica and pornographic works, and he was the principal figure behind the introduction of Sade's books into English culture. It was Milnes who later specifically introduced the young Swinburne to Sade and other pornographic writers.[11]

Furthermore, Brown was one of a group of Keats's friends who strongly opposed Keats's inclination, which Keats shared with Hunt, of giving no quarter to his establishment enemies (i.e., to those who controlled the publishing world of that day).[12] Both of the poems which Keats published in *The Indicator* were signed "Caviare," and neither was printed in the 1820 volume, whose publication was overseen by Keats's conservative friends. The other poem was Keats's great Paolo and Francesca sonnet, whose bibliographical history is at least as interesting, and very similar to, the history we have been following.

This sonnet, written in mid-April, 1819, comes to us in two holograph copies, the draft (written on a blank leaf of Keats's copy of H. F. Cary's translation of Dante) and the fair copy (which Keats sent in his journal letter of 14 February–3 May 1819). Keats later published the poem in June 1820 in *The Indicator,* but he did not include it in the 1820 volume. The standard editions of Keats from Milnes to the present have always published the text which derives from Keats's early MSS or the copy Brown made from them.

The Indicator has three substantive variants which are unique to it, but these have usually been dismissed by Keats's editors.[13] Stillinger's recent commentary is both lucid and typical:

> The *Indicator* text . . . has "a" in 8, and unique variants that almost surely ought to be disregarded in 7 ("Not unto" for "Not to pure") and 10 (" 'mid" for "in" and "world-wind" for "whirlwind"). . . . Keats presumably supplied copy for the *Indicator* version—he was living at Hunt's at the time the poem was published—and possibly by dictation, since the erroneous "world-wind" sounds much like Keats's "whirlwind." The *Indicator*'s variants in 7 and 10 are almost certainly corruptions (" 'mid" perhaps an editorial change by Hunt).[14]

The argument for refusing *The Indicator* reading in line 7 is a textual one: "Not unto Ida' in 7 looks like a copyist's or printer's mistake based on the similar wording in the next line."[15] Although the point is a good one, Keats's situation at the time of publication makes it something less than conclusive, especially since Keats almost certainly read a proof of the sonnet before it was printed.

In the case of line 10 we really have no good textual or bibliographical grounds for rejecting *The Indicator*'s readings as "erroneous" or "corruptions." Stillinger's arguments against " 'mid" are pure supposition; and even were it true that Hunt suggested the reading " 'mid" we would have to conclude that Keats agreeed to it. As for that most important variant of all, *The Indicator*'s "world-wind," once again Stillinger must resort to supposition. For it is clear that no copyist or printer would be likely to misread "whirlwind" as "world-wind." A copyist or a printer might conceivably read the unusual usage "world-wind" as the more common word "whirlwind," but an error occuring in the reverse order is, to say the least of it, unlikely. Stillinger's extraordinary suggestion that the poem was printed from a dictated copy is advanced because, as a skilled textual critic, Stillinger knows that *The Indicator*'s "world-wind" can hardly be a copyist's error.

Why, then, have editors continued to print "whirlwind" instead of *The Indicator*'s reading? Three reasons suggest themselves immediately. First, Milnes printed the poem in 1848 from the Brown MS copy, and that printing exercised great authority over later editions. Second, *The Indicator*'s text of the sonnet lost some of its attraction when, in the twentieth century, its text of "La Belle Dame Sans Merci" fell out of favor. Third, our knowledge of Keats's debt to Cary's translation of Dante tends to support the "whirlwind" reading. When Keats first wrote his sonnet he certainly borrowed this word, as well as other verbal usages, from Cary.[16] Under the circumstances, one can easily take "world-wind" not for a deliberate change, but as a strange corruption.

I think we have to see, however, that "world-wind" is not a textual error but a purposeful change. The "Not unto Ida" in line 7 *may* be a corruption, but the whole of line 10 has to be presumed to be Keats's deliberate work.

The importance of these bibliographical issues for our understanding of Keats's sonnet appears very clearly when we make a full return to *The Indicator* text and read the poem in its original constitution. There the sonnet is titled "A Dream, after Reading Dante's Episode of Paolo and Francesca," and it is signed "Caviare." Under the ideological circumstances which *The Indicator* localizes, and which I have already discussed, the reading "world-wind" acquires a powerful significance which affects the whole sonnet. The word emphasizes the virtually allegorical meaning which the fate of Paolo and Francesca represented for Keats in 1819. They suffer not in a "whirlwind" but in a "world-wind," that is, in the storm of a "world" antagonistic to everything which the lovers represent (recall, in this context, the end of "The Eve of St. Agnes"). It is unnecessary to re-emphasize here what students of Keats have known and commented upon for a long time: that this theme is pervasive in Keats, and that it grows particularly obsessive after 1818, for reasons that are well known, and that have as much to do with his love for Fanny Brawne as they do with his literary career and his financial problems.[17]

VI

When we look at "La Belle Dame Sans Merci" and the Paolo and Francesca sonnet in the light of the foregoing material, we are likely to feel, first, that the two poems have at least two important texts. In both cases one can show with a fair degree of conclusiveness that *The Indicator* texts represent Keats's last deliberate choices, and that later editors have returned to Keats's earlier versions of both poems. From a bibliographical point of view, this situation indicates that editors have been choosing the less authoritative texts of both poems. On the other hand, since all the texts in question derive pretty directly from Keats himself, the dominant editorial tradition has established its own bibliographical argument. We are not dealing here with textual errors, but with textual options.

But one must see as clearly as possible where these options take their origin, for in that information one begins to see the "meaning" of the later editorial choices, and hence the meaning of the poems as they have been constituted by various readers and critics. Colvin and others believe that "wretched wight" is a poor substitute for "knight-at-arms." It seems to me, however, that the issue is not a neutrally "aesthetic" one, but rather that it involves a choice between a more and a less "romantic" version of the ballad.[18]

As we have already seen, *The Indicator*'s ballad is slightly self-conscious of its romance materials. That self-consciousness arises directly from Keats's decision to *print* his poem, and hence to place it, and himself, in a specific relation to his audience. The Brown/1848 text, on the other hand, represents a poem which Keats gave to a very different audience (that is, to the circle of those close to him). Under those circumstances, Keats (originally) wrote a much less self-conscious ballad; but even then he felt called upon—when he sent the poem to his brother and sister-in-law—to append an ironic commentary:

> Why four kisses—you will say—why four because I wish to restrain the headlong impetuosity of my Muse—she would have fain said 'score' without hurting the rhyme—but we must temper the Imagination as the Critics say with Judgement. I was obliged to choose an even number that both eyes might have fair play: and to speak truly I think two a piece quite sufficient—Suppose I had said seven; there would have been three and a half a piece—a very awkward affair—and well got out of on my side. . . .[19]

This (private) communication shows us the sort of position into which Keats put himself, and his poem, in its early version. These comments are the "private" equivalent of everything which Keats meant to imply when he signed his poem "Caviare" in the version he chose to make "public." It would not be difficult to show that Keats's ironic remarks in his letter helped to support the more complex readings of the poem developed in the twentieth century.[20]

From the outset, then, the ballad was written in such a way, and under such circumstances, that urged its readers to stand at a slightly critical distance from the poem's materials. The best criticism of the poem has always responded to those urgings. When Keats finally printed his poem, he behaved as any good artist does when he comes before the public: he revised the poem so as to define—through those public and conventional devices which readers of poetry at that time would recognize—the "meaning" of the poem which he meant it to carry. That is to say, the poem's appearance in *The Indicator*—the event of it and the physique of it alike—was a determinate character: from that printing of Keats's audience was meant to recognize, and respond to, the poem's self-conscious and slightly critical treatment of its romance subject.

Though later readers of Keats did not usually have access to *The Indicator* version, the "spirit" (as it were) of that version was kept alive in the critical tradition. This occurred partly because Keats's letters have always been of great interest to his readers, and partly because the bibliographic issue has remained a nagging scholarly problem. In the case of the Paolo and Francesca sonnet, however, *The Indicator*'s poem has not been nearly so accessible. As a result, that aspect of the poem which is defined by *The Indicator*'s "world-wind" has not been strongly preserved in the critical tradition. This neglect has weakened the life of the sonnet.

A polemic for the stylistic superiority of "world-wind" over "whirlwind" can and ought to be made. Readers should be asked to consider whether "world-wind" does not noticeably strengthen the sonnet by forcing it to operate in multiple ways even at its surface levels. "World-wind" not only suggests everything contained in "whirlwind," it adds the polemically allegorical dimension I have already noted. In addition, however, this portmanteau word allows the reader to experience Keats forcibly drawing a connection between Dante's "whirlwind" and Keats's "world." This equation results in the startling critical reevaluation which the sonnet contains: that Dante's lovers suffer, not in the misery of their sinful love, but in the cruel assaults of an indifferent and hostile world. Like Byron's fine translation of the Paolo and Francesca episode, this great sonnet represents a Romantic reinterpretation of Dante precisely analogous to the Romantic reinterpretation of Milton carried out by Blake and Shelley.

But the sonnet's power does not come simply from its illustration of a central concept of Romantic Love.[21] Rather, it appears (first) in the poem's ability to tell its audience that only the poetic imagination is able to understand the conflicts between a social existence and personal love. Keats's poem tells us that Dante saw these contradictions. But when Keats emphasizes the distance between his sonnet and the original passage in Dante—when, for example, he writes "world-wind" for "whirlwind" and titles the sonnet "A Dream" based on Dante—then he is telling his audience something Dante does not tell: that Dante understood the pathos of Paolo and Francesca because he was a poet, and that only poetry has the power to reach such insights.

This implicit assertion is, like the poem's idea of Love, deeply Romantic. Yet the poem has something futher to say—a more grim assertion which emerges as a terrible function of the poem's ideas about love, the "world," and poetry. For the sonnet's "melancholy" tone also asserts that the conflicts between the World and Romantic Love cannot be resolved in the terms defined by the poem. Poetry itself is affected by these conflicts. The sonnet tells us—finally, desperately—that poetry's power to see these contradictions carries with it the fate of ineffectuality. Here, at all levels, we see a situation in which everything is to be endured, but nothing is to be done.

VII

The particular cases of "La Belle Dame Sans Merci" and the Paolo and Francesca sonnet show how the general historical method, outlined earlier, might be applied to specific and current problems in criticism. Each part of the general method must be able to be uniformly invoked when any literary work is under study, but particular cases will always be demanding different critical emphases. In the case of the "Ode on a Grecian Urn," for example, we do not have a problematic textual history comparable to the ones I have just been discussing. The ode does have a famous textual crux in the final two lines, as we know from the poem's critical history, and the crux seriously affects the poem's internal syntax. Nevertheless, the textual issues here are quite different because the two possible texts for lines 49–50 of the ode are both traceable directly to Keats. Moreover, careful bibliographical analysis will show, and has already shown, that the two readings are not, finally, incompatible at the level of textual criticism. The textual problems in the ballad and the sonnet, on the other hand, are not yet solvable at such a level—simply because the issues have not been so thoroughly discussed and analyzed as have the comparable issues in the ode.[22]

Yet the ode has its own special problems, one of which appears in the contempt with which many twentieth century critics look upon the great obsession of older Keats critics: I mean the quest for the "original" urn of the poem. Even Walter Jackson Bate, perhaps the most distinguished living critic of Keats's life and work, patronizes the labors of those older scholar-adventurers:

> Attempts continue to be made to determine a particular vase or urn that Keats may have had in mind when he wrote the ode. Especially with a poem so distinguished for its universality, one thinks of Keats's own remark . . . that 'they are very shallow people who take everything literal.'[23]

But the "universality" of the ode is surely no more extensive than the "universality" of any great poem. Moreover, this "universality" is a direct function of certain historical specifics. It makes a difference—a marked difference—that Keats decided to publish the poem first in *The Annals of the Fine Arts.* This small bibliographical point locates a set of contextual facts of the greatest relevance to any interpretation of the ode.

In the same way, it makes a great difference whether or not we see the ode as an attempt to describe a "real" urn. Scholars now tend to agree with Ian Jack on this matter.[24] That the ode's urn is a composite imagining based upon Keats's knowledge of various artifacts (vases, sculptures, and paintings) which he saw either directly or in illustrated books of Greek antiquities. Nevertheless, two points must be insisted upon. First, Jack's widely accepted conclusions could never have been formulated at all had not older scholars spent so much labor searching after that "original" urn. Second, the impetus for that scholarship was supplied by certain characteristics of the poem as Keats originally published it.

The corollary of the first point is that all current interpretations of the ode which treat the urn as an imaginary object are only justified on the basis of certain past historical research. Nor is this merely a point in professional decorum, a request that we pay our dues to our worthy scholarly forebears. The crucial interpretive point is that the urn of the ode is an imaginary object in a very specific, historical sense. The ode's urn is placed before its readers (both past and present) as an ideal example of such vases. Keats's urn—in the context alike of his poem, its place of original publication, and the Romantic Classicism which both represented—aims to be taken as both a real concrete object *and* as an ideal; for it is central to the Romantic understanding of Greek art that such art actually produced, at its finest moments, perfect and complete embodiments of a perfect and complete idea of The Beautiful. *The Annals of the Fine Arts,* which printed Keats's poem was one of that age's chief ideological organs for disseminating such ideas.[25]

Consequently, part of the poem's fiction—and this is why scholars spent so much time trying to find the "original" urn—is that the urn it describes is an actual urn comparable to the Townley, Borghese, or Sosibios vases. Not to grasp this fact about the poem means that we do not see the importance of when the poem was written, and by whom, and where it was published. But the poem itself insists that we react to its historical dimensions, and in so doing it forbids that we understand its "universality" outside of the ode's special historical context. To see this elementary point more clearly all we need to do is imagine that the poem was written fifty years before or after 1819. It would make a difference.

The poem's fiction—that its *ideal* subject is an *actual* urn—asks its readers to try to visualize, in a concrete way, the urn of the poet's imagining. Yielding to the poem's direction in this way will profoundly alter how we read the ode, and may even enrich our grasp of the poem's purely verbal art. Let me give an example.

Only one critic, so far as I am aware, has noticed that the phrase "leaf-fringed legend" involves a pun.[26] Furthermore, no critic has ever remarked on the fact that the urn has given a specific answer, in the poem itself, to the poet's initial question about that legend. When they were conducting their searches for the ode's original urn, those older scholars were attempting to answer many of the same questions which the poet raises in the poem: as if, should they be able to find that original urn, they might then be able to see *in fact* what men or gods Keats was speaking of. In any case, they did not have to search far to answer the question about the "leaf-fringed legend." The urn itself supplies the answer when it says to Keats: "Beauty is truth, truth beauty." A reader can easily fail to see these aspects of the poem if he is concentrating his attention on the verbal surface. But it all leaps to one's awareness as soon as a person looks past the words to the scene being described, and to the objects that occupy that scene; as soon as a person, that is to say, begins to read more in the spirit of those older scholars, with their deep (if excessively empiricist) historical awareness.

After the poet's initial address to the urn in the poem's first two lines, he quickly moves into his series of questions. At the moment my interest is only in the first of them, where the word "legend" is employed in a typically Keatsian fashion: it means both a particular story from ancient myth or history, as well as an inscription. With the phrase "leaf-fringed legend," then, Keats is in part asking the reader to see something typical of certain Greek funerary vases: that they carried inscriptions, or legends, characteristically surrounded by elaborate leaf decorations. Keats apparently asks his question of the urn because (according to the poem's fiction) he cannot clearly see the faded characters of the Greek inscription. Indeed, we are probably meant to take the poem's famous Beauty-Truth apothegm not as the urn's actual inscription (translated, perhaps?) but as Keats's substitute for an inscription which had grown too faded to be read any longer (as, according to the moral of the "Ode to Psyche," all the ancient myths and legends of the Olympian hierarchy had faded). Those characters (in both senses) are illegible, yet Keats's poetic urn can still speak, as if it were some literalized example of the idea of a poem as a speaking picture.

VIII

These discussions of the ballad, the sonnet, and the ode have been chosen because they illustrate some of the critical powers which an historical method of criticism can supply. The examples are also meant to show that the general taxonomic structures of the historical method sketched earlier are not all equally useful or pertinent at different times. Changing circumstances alter the immediate relevance of particular methodological categories.

Furthermore, particular poems are defined in terms of certain relatively fixed structures (e.g., those of form and genre for the works themselves; or those of sex, nation, class, and geographical location for their authors and commentators). Because such forms are historically stable (some of these are more stable than others), they pre-exist the critical discussion and often determine the relative usefulness of different categories within the general taxonomy of the historical method.

For example, the sort of textual discussion which is presently relevant to the ballad and the sonnet and which has been, in the past, equally relevant to the ode, will never be relevant to the poem we now know as "To Fanny" ("What can I do to drive away")—never, that is, unless the bibliography of the poem undergoes, in the future, some drastic alteration (e.g., if a MS of the poem were to be discovered, or if some hard evidence were to turn up which pinpointed the date of composition more specifically). On the other hand, although the poem has no textual problems to be sorted out, the textual history *is* important. Furthermore, "To Fanny" raises all sorts of issues which are peculiarly relevant to it, and which have little relevance (for example) to either the ballad or the ode.

The special problems raised by "To Fanny" begin to define themselves in the poem's early textual history.[27] No MS survives and Keats never printed the poem himself. It was first printed by Milnes in 1848 from a (now lost) transcript which he had from Charles Brown. This transcript Brown made from a holograph MS given by Keats to Fanny Brawne, who allowed Brown to copy it sometime before 1829. The poem seems to have been written late in 1819, probably around October.

When Milnes printed the poem in 1848, his prefatory remarks left no doubt as to the intimate nature of the work.[28] His printing, in other words, established the tradition of biographical criticism which has dominated the later critical commentary on this poem. But Milnes' edition was not forcing its readers to adopt some "subjectively biassed" view of "To Fanny"; on the contrary, Milnes took the most appropriate vantage possible on the poem, and the one most in the spirit of Keats's own purposes and intentions. This poem was written to and for Fanny Brawne, and was even given to her by Keats. It is not, in other words, a "public" poem the way "La Belle Dame Sans Merci" or the ode are, and always were, "public."

On the other hand, the poem is not, nor was it ever, a "private" poem strictly speaking (by "private" I mean a poem written but never deliberately communicated to anyone else: in Keats's case for example, a poem like "This living hand, now warm and capable"). "To Fanny" is, rather, a "personal" poem—by which I mean simply to distinguish it in a position between the other two categories, and to indicate thereby that its most immediate contextual range is defined in biographical terms, rather than in historical or psychological ones. Consequently, if a person were to read this poem without giving paramount attention to its biographical materials, he would be introducing a special bias into the critical act. In such a case, the criticism would be forcing upon the poem an "extrinsic" approach precisely analogous to the sort of "extrinsic" approach we recognize in biographical or Freudian readings of (say) *Lamia*. Special critical studies of these sorts are often important and useful, of course, but in relation to *Lamia* we have to see that they *are* specialized. In the case of "To Fanny," it is the purely formal or stylistic reading which would constitute the specialized approach. Poems like this one are, by virtue of certain pre-emptive definitions created out of their historical circumstances, formally and, as it were "by nature," biographical works.

A reading of "To Fanny" therefore always begins, consciously or otherwise, at the biographical level; if it does not, we cannot understand the simple lexical references to the poem's words. To read the poem—ultimately, to develop a full critical analysis—requires that we be aware of Keats's peculiar financial situation at the time; of the special circumstances of his love for Fanny Brawne (their relationship had just entered a new phase); and of the state of his physical health (the fact, in particular, that he had not yet suffered the haemorrhage of February 1820 which betrayed his fatal illness). It also requires that we be aware of his special feelings for his siblings, and especially for his brother George in America, who was on the verge of financial ruin. Finally, the poem demands our understanding of Keats's utter commitment to the life of imagination and a poetic career, and of the conflicts which these pursuits engendered both in his attitudes toward the quotidian world around him and in his feelings for Fanny Brawne.[29]

All of these details taken by themselves would be properly called "biographical" in nature. But the total set of relations which these details establish when they are considered together constitute a biographical nexus which reveals the forceful presence of larger, socio-historical frames of reference. Keats's highly personal poem about Fanny Brawne localizes a set of tensions and conflicts which can only be adequately understood if we place the poem in a more comprehensive historical context. Why Keats, for example, should establish in his poem a dialectic between his erotic feelings for Fanny Brawne and his sublimated devotion to his (also feminine) "Muse" is partly explainable in biographical terms, but finally requires the more comprehensive context of Romanticism to be understood. And that larger, predominating ideological context only acquires its analytic frame of reference within the still larger context of the history of the early nineteenth century. In short, biographical criticism only receives its complete set of analytic possibilities when it is placed in the controlling framework of a general socio-historical methodology.

IX

Biographical criticism is, taken by itself, a pseudo-historical method, though in our culture it is the critical path which still seems most closely connected with actual human history. Formally oriented critics have been wary of the approach for precisely that reason. But the fundamental problem with a strictly biographical (or psychoanalytic) criticism is not that its method imports "extrinsic" materials into the analysis. On the contrary, biographical analysis falters because it maintains the poem, and the poetic analysis, in the artificially restricted geography of the individual person. Such a criticism is aware that the artist writes in a dialectical relation to the objective world, but it is unaware that this relationship is fundamentally social rather than personal or psychological, and hence that objective history exerts a shaping influence upon the poetry.

Though biographical and psychoanalytic criticism remain in practice, a collateral type of pseudo-historical criticism dominates the field today, especially in the United States. In this case, the historical focus is upon literary history, which becomes the ultimate framing context for studying poems, poetic forms, and patterns of literary transmission. "World" or "epochal" history is deliberately removed from the analysis, or it is subordinated to literary categories, because of the premises of the general approach: that history at large can only enter literature via a system of artistic mediations, and these mediations are the necessary and immediate locus of attention.

The premises of this position—about the mediating function of literary categories—are strong, and they would be assented to by most historical critics. Literary mediations must indeed be the critic's focus of attention. Nevertheless, certain practical conclusions generally flow from this approach, and these conclusions expose a basic theoretical weakness. To hold a literary analysis within a purely poetic space is to ensure the conclusion—rampant in such criticism—that the subject of literature is—literature. Indeed, such conclusions are inevitable in a method which makes no serious attempt to analyze, and thereby explain, the special human significance of artistic mediations. Because the mediations are regarded as ultimate, they become mystified categories-indeed, fetishes.

A particularly apt example of this method is observable in Geoffrey Hartman's famous essay on Keats's "To Autumn."[30] The purpose of his essay, he says, is to examine a special sort of poem, one "without explicit social context," and to explore "its involvement in social and historical vision." Hartman goes on to say that his "use of the concept of ideology [in the essay] will seem half-way or uncritical to the Marxist thinker." Nevertheless, he feels justified in using the term because, in his view, and contrary to more traditional readings of the poem, "To Autumn" is a poem that "has something to say: that it is an ideological poem whose very form expresses a national idea and a new stage of consciousness." Hartman's method, then, will be both historical and non-historical:

> In uncovering Keats's ideology I remain as far as possible within terms provided by Keats himself, or furnished by the ongoing history of poetry. . . . Keats's poem is indeed an event in history; not in world-history, however, but simply in the history of fiction. . . .[31]

One would want to argue with Hartman's essay on more fronts than I have opened up here through these selective quotations. I confine myself to these remarks in order to focus on Hartman's idea that "To Autumn" is a poem "without explicit social context." What Hartman means by this statement is that "To Autumn" does not make the immediate factual context *circa* September 1819 an explicit part of his poem. It differs, in this respect, from the "Ode to Psyche" and the "Ode to a Nightingale," for example, or—even more obviously—from Shelley's "The Mask of Anarchy" (which was written around the same time as "To Autumn").

Hartman's engagement with "To Autumn" is part of the poem's non-explicit social context, and one of the functions of criticism is to analyze the ideology of significant critical engagements like his. But I must pass by that subject here, interesting though it is, and return to Keats's poem. For if the social context of a poem achieves its first *visibility* in the immediate context of the reader of the poem, the poem's explicit social context achieves its first *constitution* at its point of origin. Let us turn now to that social context and examine what Keats has made explicit in his poem.

To understand the "explicit social involvement" of "To Autumn"—or of any literary work for that matter—demands that we constitute the initial stages of the poem's socialization. This means that we ask ourselves the question: when and where and by whom was the poem originally published? Defining these particulars allows us to see once again the initial historical moment of the poem's explicit and continuing social involvement, a moment that has often been removed from immediate consciousness by the passage of time. That initial moment of publication constitutes the first explicit appearance of the poem's meaning (a meaning that arises in the communication-event involving the author's expression and the reader's response). The special importance of this moment lies in its priority: whatever changes may occur in later readings of the poem, all subsequent responses derive in some way from the initial event.

"To Autumn" was first published in *Lamia, Isabella, The Eve of St. Agnes, and Other Poems,* the so-called 1820 volume (published 1 July, 1820). The character of this book—widely and, generally speaking, very favorably reviewed[32]—is intimately related to the "meaning" of "To Autumn." To elucidate the nature of this relationship we have to see the book, and its original context, very clearly.

The publishers of the 1820 volume were Taylor and Hessey, who also published *Endymion* in 1818. It was *Endymion* (not the 1817 volume, published by Ollier) that had been the immediate target of the hostile reviews of Keats, and the poet was not the only person who suffered in that literary world-wind. Consequently, when Keats approached Taylor and Hessey again, in the latter part of 1819, about publishing the new book of poems he had been planning, they were interested but wary. They had no intention of bringing out a volume that would call down again the sort of hostility and ridicule which greeted *Endymion.*[33]

Keats's struggles with his publishers over the 1820 volume are well known. At first it seemed that the poems would not be published at all, but a stroke of luck—the decision (later rescinded) by the Drury Lane Theatre to stage *Otho the Great*—changed Taylor's mind about Keats's new poems. If the play were to be performed, a book of poems might just have a chance of succeeding, despite the apparently hostile predisposition of the periodical establishment.[34]

The key fact in the pre-publication history of the 1820 poems is the insistence by Keats's publishers that the book not contain anything that would provoke the reviewers to attack (they were especially concerned about charges of indecency and political radicalism). Keats struggled with them over these issues, but he was eventually persuaded to follow their line. The two poems published in Leigh Hunt's *Indicator* did not find a place in the 1820 volume, and the reason for this is that Keats and his publishers did not want to give the reviewers any occasion for linking Keats's new work with the politically sensitive name of Leigh Hunt. For his part, Keats was also worried about the book's reception, but his concerns were slightly different. His principal interests were to show (a) the strength of his poetical technique, and (b) that he was not a "sentimental" or "weak-sided" poet.[35]

The 1820 volume, in other words, was constructed with a profoundly self-conscious attitude about that climate of literary opinion which prevailed at the time. It was designed as a book that would not provoke the critics in the ways that *Endymion* had done earlier. Indeed, Keats reacted so explosively to the notorious "Publisher's Advertisement" to the 1820 poems because he felt that the paragraph would call up the whole of that painful history surrounding *Endymion's* public reception, and expose him once again to the same set of charges.[36]

This history is important because it reflects the set of dialectical relations which converge in Keats's book. All of the 1820 poems were written in the post-*Endymion* period and they show very clearly the depth of Keats's response to his earlier treatment at the hands of the reviewers. Many of the new poems were deliberately written with an eye to attracting the favorable attention of the public (this especially apparent in the case of the three narrative poems in the book).[37] In the final event itself we see how successful Keats and his publishers were, for the book was received well, even warmly, in almost every quarter. Keats wrote, in his 1820 poems, what most readers at the time were quite pleased to hear.

The special character of Keats's 1820 volume manifests itself very clearly if we compare it to some other books published around that time. Byron's *Don Juan* volumes—especially Cantos I–II (1819) and Cantos VI–VIII (1823)—were deliberately written to provoke discussion and conflict, and the same is true of all of Shelley's works published in 1819–1820: *Rosalind and Helen,* for example, or *Prometheus Unbound,* or *Oedipus tyrannus* (the last a work of such inflammatory character that its publication had to be suppressed). Keats's 1820 poems, however, were issued not to provoke but to allay conflict. In sharp contrast to a poem like *Prometheus Unbound,* Keats's mythologically oriented works in his new book presented their early readers with ideas about art, myth, and imagination which did not open an explicit ideological attack upon the book's audience. The *Lamia* volume represented Keats's effort to show his readers how they might, by entering his poetic space, step aside from the conflicts and tensions which were so marked an aspect of that period. The whole point of Keats's great and (politically) reactionary book was not to enlist poetry in the service of social and political causes— which is what Byron and Shelley were doing—but to dissolve social and political conflicts in the mediations of art and beauty. (I should note here that although the 1820 poems were politically reactionary at the time of their publication, they were deeply subversive at the time of their rediscovery by the Pre-Raphaelite Circle).[38]

All of these matters constitute an "explicit" part of a poem like "To Autumn," for they were (quite literally) *made* explicit in the event of the poem's publication. Today the explicit character of these subjects only reveals itself to an historical analysis, since analysis alone can overcome the loss of memory which necessarily occurs over a period of time. Yet such an analysis is important not merely for recovering a lapsed memory of the past. It reveals as well the dynamic relations which play themselves out at all points in the history of the poem's transmission. Our present responses to "To Autumn" are closely tied into this entire historical development, whether we are aware of it or not.

Having reconstituted the essential features of the ode's publication history, we are now in a position to move to the next phase of the analysis. In this case— because of the prevailing anti-historical climate of opinion epitomized in Hartman's essay—what is needed is a further exploration of the original circumstance surrounding Keats's poem.

X

Keats has, for example, chosen a slightly yet recognizably archaic style for his poem about autumn. The season, that is to say, is personified, even directly addressed in its personified character. Furthermore, this personified figure is suggestively related to mythic divinities like Ceres and Bacchus, thus reinforcing the poem's self-consciously assumed archaic quality.[39] The poetical machinery is carried very lightly, however, and the second stanza explicitly superimposes images of contemporary peasant laborers on the androgynous figure of the pagan divinity. Finally, the agricultural laborers and the mythic being assume highly stylized poses in the poem. They are picturesque figures, that is to say, and the reason is that they enter the poem via Keats's experience of them in the artistically mediated forms of various 18th century paintings and engravings, and the landscapes of Poussin and Claude.[40] The explicit fiction of the poem, then, is not to present a series of "natural" images of autumn, but rather to deliver autumn over to the reader's experience in a series of framed pictures—in forms, that is to say, which already emphasize the fact that art mediates human experience. Into the context of these poetic materials the ode introduces, with equal explicitness, the subject of the seasonal change from summer to winter with all its traditional thematic associations: living and dying, maturing and decaying, staying and leaving.

The significance of these themes in the poem must, however, remain at an inexplicit level without the application of an historical analysis. Indeed, the meaning of these thematic meanings is poetically defined by the historically specific ideological mediations invoked by the poem—in this case, by the specific materials Keats has drawn from the fine arts.

Let me explain this further. It is clearly important to know that "To Autumn" contains allusions to pictures done in the tradition of Poussin and Claude. But it is equally important to know how Keats himself understood and interpreted this tradition of painting. In fact, Keats's ideas about these matters, as scholars have known for a long time, run parallel to Hazlitt's ideas—are, indeed, drawn from Hazlitt's writings, conversations, and public lectures. Keats's poem alludes at once to the historical tradition in the fine arts and to Hazlitt's Romantically interpretive extension of that tradition. "To Autumn" makes explicit, in its verbal picture, what Hazlitt made explicit in discursive prose in another context. The landscapes of Poussin, he tells us, like those of Claude,

> carry imagination back two or four thousand years at least, and bury it in the remote twilight of history. There is an opaqueness and solemnity in his colouring, assimilating with the tone of long-past events: his buildings are stiff with age; his implements of husbandry are such as would belong to the first rude stages of civilization; his harvests are such . . . as would yield to no modern sickle; his grapes . . . are a load on modern shoulders; there is a simplicity and undistinguishing breadth in the figures; and over all, the hand of time has drawn its veil.[41]

"To Autumn" draws its set of attitudes from the same ideological well which here serves Hazlitt. These attitudes have even been given a name by scholars: Romantic Classicism.

Let me return now to the problem of the meaning of "To Autumn's" thematic meanings. The poem's special effect is to remove the fearful aspects of these themes, to make us receive what might otherwise be threatening ideas in the simpler truth of certain forms which the poet presents as images of The Beautiful. This effect is produced by so manipulating the mythological and artistic mediations that the reader agrees to look at autumn, and to contemplate change and death, under certain precise and explicitly fictional guises. The reader accepts the invitation because these mediations, though recognizably fictional, nevertheless promise a real, human benefit: the beauty of the mediations can transform one's felt response to the ideas of change, death, decay. Keats's poem is itself the proof that such historically generated fictions, self-consciously embraced, can have this consoling power.

Up to this point, the textual analysis has only attempted to bring to light some of the historical specifics latent in the traditional line of criticism which has received its most finished statement in Hartman's essay. But from the vantage of an historical methodology the analysis has only just begun, for what we now have to develop is an explanatory context for the analysis. Thomson's famous poem about autumn, for example, does not concern itself with the consolations of fictional mediations. Why does Keats's poem do so?

In Thomson's poetry, and eighteenth century verse generally, when the theme of human mortality is taken up in the context of natural processes, human values emerge as a part of what have recently been called "the sciences of the artificial."[42] In *Windsor-Forest* and *The Seasons* we observe how human practical arts, including the art of politics, place Nature—including human nature—under control and regulation. But in "To Autumn"—and here the poem is typical of its age—the factor of human control is not found in the practical arts, but in myth and in the illusions of the fine arts (both of which are made to stand for poetic artifice in general). In "To Autumn" Beauty is not only Truth, it is Power. But what is it, we want to know, which drives Keats to place his faith in poetry as the most distinctively human achievement, rather than in the practical and the useful arts?

The most general and explicit answer to this question was formulated by Wordsworth in his "Preface" to the *Lyrical Ballads,* and by Shelley in his great *Defence of Poetry.* Both argued from the current state of affairs, which they saw as destructive of a truly human life. Science, or Natural Philosophy, as well as the allied practical arts, did not seem to be ameliorating the conditions of human life; if anything, these forces only exacerbated suffering and social injustice. The Romantic maneuver—both from the left and from the right wing—was to turn to poetry and the fine arts as the only available instrument of human melioration.

The Romantic program developed along two distinct strategic lines. On the one hand, poetry was employed as a weapon to be used in the context of an explicit, and accepted, audience which the poet aimed to persuade, reinforce, or attack. Though Blake consciously adopted this strategy, only his work between 1790–1795 shows consistently effective practical results. Shelley and Byron use this strategy throughout their careers with repeated success. The other strategy, which dominates the work of Wordsworth, Coleridge, and Keats, received its most important formulation in Wordsworth's "Essay Supplementary" (1815) where he said that poets would now have to create their own audiences.[43] Here Romanticism developed its patterns of "internalization," as they have been so memorably called, because it was unwilling to make contracts with the audiences available to it. Keats, who is especially typical of this Romantic line, showed how poetry could establish "a world elsewhere." In that alternative geography, personal and social tensions could be viewed with greater honesty and intellectual rigor.

"To Autumn" asks us to believe—to willingly suspend our disbelief—that all autumns are the same. We must imagine them to be, universally, the "season of mists and mellow fruitfulness." But Keats asks us to believe this because he knows, as we know, that it is not true. Such an autumn of perfect harvests and luxurious agricultural abundance is an autumn in the mind. City people, industrialized communities, do not know of these autumns except in the memories of art;

and in the country such abundance is rare indeed, particularly in the early nine-teenth century. In fact, 1819 brought in a good harvest in England, and the year was notable for its abundance precisely because of the series of disastrous harvests which characterized many of the years immediately preceding.

Keats encountered his imaginative autumn when he fled his "little coffin of a room at Shanklin"[44] for the ease and tranquil beauty of Winchester, where he wrote "To Autumn" in the middle of September. His letters from 12 August to the beginning of October—the period of his Winchester sojourn—recur to his feel-ings of pleasure and relief. Winchester, and his time there, are repeatedly seen as a respite from the tensions not only of his own personal affairs, but of the contem-porary social scene at large. The massacre at St. Peter's Fields (Peterloo) took place four days after Keats arrived in Winchester, and he was glad to feel removed from the political turmoil which followed in its wake. "We shall have another fall of Siege-arms,"[45] he wrote to Woodhouse, but even as he followed the events of August and September in the *Examiner*'s radical reports, he found Winchester a wonderful refuge: "This Winchester is a place tolerably well suited to me; there is a fine Cathedral, a College, a Roman-Catholic Chapel, a Methodist do, an inde-pendent do,—and there is not one loom or any thing like manufacturing beyond bread & butter in the place. It is a respectable, ancient aristocratical place—and moreover it contains a nunnery."[46] Winchester has for Keats an old world, even a slightly archaic quality about it which he consistently recurs to in his letter. "The abbottine Winchester,"[47] he calls it in a letter to his brother. The city and its environs are magical in their ability to carry him away to a charmed world far removed from the quotidian press of his money affairs and the dangerous political tensions of his society.[48] "The Eve of St. Mark" begins as a tribute to this environ-ment and "To Autumn" is its finished expression:

> How beautiful the season is now—How fine the air. A temperate sharpness about it. Really, without joking, chaste weather—Dian skies—I never lik'd stubble fields so well as now—Aye better than the chilly green of the spring. Somehow a stubble plain looks warm—in the same way that some pictures look warm—this struck me so much in my sunday's walk that I composed upon it.[49]

This well-known passage from the letters locates the ode's point of origin. No one but Ian Jack has remarked on the important reference to painting in the passage, and not even Jack notes what Keats has in fact said here: that the subject of "To Autumn" is explicitly the relationship between natural scenes and their expression in a certain tradition in the fine arts.

All of these biographical details illustrate Keats's special point of engagement with a number of large cultural and political issues which bore upon his age, and which had equally particular effects on everyone else, and which produced equally particular responses. (Shelley, for example, wrote a whole series of poems immedi-ately after Peterloo in which he attacked the terrorist policies of the government forces.) "To Autumn" is only *fictionally* a poem about "any" autumn, or autumn "in general." Such an autumn is, the poet tells us, a myth, or an artistic reconstruc-tion of a myth. Hartman discusses "To Autumn" as a poem about poetic fictions, and in this respect much of the foregoing analysis can be seen as merely supplying greater specificity to his sense of the ode. To study this work's allusive use of the pictorial arts is to see more clearly the exact form of the poem's chief fictionalizing devices. But in the specification of the poem's fictions we also acquire further explanatory powers. For now we can ask yet another question: why does Keats resort to pictorial tradition for his poem's fictionalizing models? Why not depend more exclusively on, for example, literary models?

One way of answering this question is to recall briefly the long critical tradition which has responded to the poem's "impersonal quality."[50] "To Autumn's" words seem aspiring to the condition of pictorial silence, where images present themselves in arranged groupings and sequences. In such a work the poet—as so many critics have said—seems almost to have achieved a state of negative capability: to have removed himself from his poem and to have erased his self-consciousness. Like the Grecian urn, the images in "To Autumn" are "silent forms" which "tease us out of thought."

Although this does seem to me to be the poem's ideological argument, it is not the poem's artistic achievement. For the "impersonality" achieved in the poem is an explicit function of a conscious desire, as one clearly sees in those great and famous lines which open the final stanza:

> Where are the songs of spring? Aye, where are they?
>   Think not of them, thou hast thy music too. . . .
>   (23–24)[51]

Keats's autumn is the emblem of a condition freed from all weariness, fever, and fret, and his effort to describe such an autumn "impersonally" is the sign of his own attempt to achieve such a condition himself. But these lines remind us that the poem has been born in a desire, and that Keats's ideal autumn is not an impersonal or even an abstract autumn, but the dream of a mind that recalls the lost promise of the spring. Keats imagines such an autumn—he writes this ode—because he needs to develop some means for silencing that melancholy question: "Where are the songs of spring?" Instead of the songs of spring—the poems of desire and self-conscious thought—Keats offers the song of autumn—the poem of fruitfulness and picturesque sensation.[52] What is crucial to see, however—and this is what the above passage shows us—is that "To Autumn" dramatizes Keats's self-conscious polemic for an art of sensations rather than an art of thought. The poem is not impersonal, it is tendentious and ideological in quite specific ways. Its message is that the fine arts, and by extension imagination generally, are more humanly productive than any of the other more practical sciences of the artificial. More even than this, "To Autumn" argues for the power of a specific type of imaginative art, that is, for an art that can imagine the sufficiency of the imagination.

The poem tries to persuade its readers that human beings sometimes have need of its imaginings, that the poetic fictions of the fanciful (as opposed to the polemical) imagination can be as objectively real and socially functional as any more work-a-day realities. Criticism, for its part, turns upon such poems and tries to explain how and why poets and readers might be prepared to believe, early in industrialized nineteenth-century England (or at some later point in time and place), that such a myth—that such fantastic and "romanticized" poetry—can be "useful" and full of power.

The explanation necessarily asks us to see, very clearly, that the poem's autumn is an historically specified fiction dialectically called into being by John Keats as an active response to, and alteration of, the events which marked the late summer and early fall of a particular year in a particular place. Keats's poem is an attempt to "escape" the period which provides the poem with its context, and to offer its readers the same opportunity of refreshment. By this I do not mean to derogate from Keats's poem, but to suggest what is involved in so illusive a work as "To Autumn" and in all the so-called escapist poetry which so many readers have found so characteristic of Romanticism.[53] For the preoccupations of the Romantic style came to pass a fearful judgment upon the age which generated its various forms of artistic extremity. Already in Keats we begin to hear whispers of the motto of his great inheritor, D. G. Rossetti: "Fiat ars, pereat mundus." And why not? The viewless wings of poesy will carry one to the heavens of intensity where pleasure and pain, life and even death, all seem to repossess some lost original value. This is the reflexive world of Romantic art, the very negation of the negation itself, wherein all events are far removed from the Terror, King Ludd, Peterloo, the Six Acts, and the recurrent financial crises of the Regency, and where humanity escapes the inconsequence of George IV, the absurd Prince Regent, the contemptible Wellington. Here evil will appear heroic, Satanic, Byronic—not banal, like Castlereagh.

Without historical analysis we can at best—and this is what Hartman has achieved—see Keats's poem as an elaborately structured poetic artifice. The poem is, he says, an "imagined picture . . . self-harvesting like the poet's own thoughts."[54] And this is both a correct, and a traditional, view. But it is a view which agrees to read the poem simply, that is, wholly in terms of Keats's own artificially constructed fantasy. It takes the poem to be true, exclusively true, when in fact such a work—like all human works—is true only in the context of its field of social relations. The Romantic idea of imagination becomes, in Hartman's essay, a universal rather than an historical phenomenon. Hartman's is, then, a neo-Romantic reading of an old Romantic poem, and this fact itself tells us much about the judgment upon our own age which is implicit in Hartman's nostalgic commentary.

XI

I want to conclude with two sets of remarks. First, permit me to re-emphasize what, in my view, this sort of historical method undertakes to perform. Traditionally, literary criticism has been divided into three separate provinces: Analysis, Explanation, Evaluation. In the modern period, historical methods have been allowed to govern the second of these provinces (Explanation); formal (or intrinsic) criticism, on the other hand, is taken to govern the first province (Analysis). The third province, Evaluation, is currently ungoverned, and has been ever since the demolition of the classical science of Evaluation as it was embodied in the theory of decorum.

My argument here is that the historical method—and specifically a sociological poetics—must be recognized not only as relevant to the *analysis* of poetry, but in fact as central to analysis (that is, to the study of the so called "purely poetic" or "intrinsic" aspects of literature). Though I have not argued here the necessary consequence of such a view, it should be evident that to establish the pertinence of historical method to the field of literary analysis is tantamount to establishing the hegemony of historical method to literary studies in general. This is not to say that more specialized literary investigations should be discouraged; quite the contrary. But it is to say that the governing context of all literary investigations must ultimately be an historical one. Literature is a human product, a humane art. It cannot be carried on (created), understood (studied), or appreciated (experienced) outside of its definitive human context. The general science governing that human context is socio-historical.

The second point I want to make is related to the first. I cannot develop here the arguments which would be needed to demonstrate, theoretically, the crucial significance of historical method for the analysis of the aesthetic effect of literature. But I would like to conclude with some directory remarks on that subject.

The *locus classicus* in Marxist aesthetics for a discussion of this matter is in Marx's *Introduction to the Critique of Political Economy.* In a famous passage Marx poses for himself the difficult problem of explaining why the great artistic products of Greece—an admittedly "primitive . . . social order"—should "still constitute with us a source of aesthetic enjoyment and in certain respects prevail as the standard and model beyond attainment." His answer to this question has been something of an embarrassment to Marxist aesthetics ever since.

> A man cannot become a child again unless he becomes childish. But does he not enjoy the artless ways of the child and must he not strive to reproduce its truth on a higher plane? Is not the character of every epoch revived perfectly true to nature in child nature? Why should the social childhood of mankind, where it had obtained its most beautiful development, not exert an eternal charm as an age that will never return? There are ill-bred children and precocious children. Many of the ancient nations belong to the latter class. The Greeks were normal children. The charm their art has for us does not conflict with the primitive character of the social order from which it had sprung. It is rather the product of the latter, and is rather due to the fact that the unripe social conditions under which the art arose and under which alone it could appear can never return.[55]

Although Marx's comments are confused and wholly lacking in analytic rigor, his nostalgia for "the glory that was Greece" is the emotional sign of an important, and characteristically Marxian, insight. This passage shows Marx's profound sense of the pastness of the past, and of the importance which this differential has for all aesthetic experiences.

Neither Marx nor his immediate followers were able to develop the necessary analysis which these insights called for. The next step toward such an analysis was not taken until certain Russian critics gave a name to what Marx naively saw as the charm of a childlike art. The name is "estrangement."[56]

The aesthetic effect of literature is profoundly related—paradoxical though it may seem—to the reader or viewer's sense of history. Aesthetic effect depends upon the distancing of the art work, the estrangement of it, its isolation from our immediacy. We say that it seems to occupy a place outside of time, as it were. But this is merely a way of saying that art works are forever placed *in* history, that is, the vertical and horizontal circumstances which define human events. The apparent immobility of art, Bate's "universality," is a function of the reader's historical sense, which registers the distance between the (past) object and the (present) experience.

This estrangement effect, however, cannot begin to be analyzed without an historical method. Nor will a method that confines itself to *literary* history suffice, for art at all times is a part of a human activity which transcends the limited materials and special history of art itself. Thus it has often, and properly, been said that poetry holds a mirror up to human life. But something more must be said. For poetry does not hold a mirror up to an immobilized "Human Nature"; it reflects— and reflects upon—human nature in its social and historical reality. The celebrated estrangement effect of art is simply the sign of art's own inherent historical dimension vis-à-vis its audience. To analyze, in literature, this deeply felt distance between us and our pasts requires the precise specification of historic details— from the merest facts picked up in a gloss, to the most sharply defined general categories of ideological order.

Literature focusses moments of intense feeling, of deep human sympathy, and these experiences occur because all readers of poems register in their feelings the social and historical gulfs which, even while they separate and define exact differences, ultimately join together by calling out human sympathy—that special feeling of a social union which, in our historical experience to this period, has remained, like Wordsworth's cuckoo, something "longed for, never seen." What remains to be seen is the human limits which history imposes even on those famous words. Their meaning, their power—indeed, their ability to transcend their own historical limits—all depend upon the existence of those specific limits; and our appreciation of such power and transcendence equally depends on our ability to understand the fact of those limits, and to analyze it. Failing such things, I do not see how we can reciprocate the transcendence of Romantic verse, or feel anything but shame when we read such poetry.

NOTES

1. Even an anti-historical critic like Northop Frye recognizes that this demand which Byron makes on criticism is an indication of a more widespread problem in literary studies. See his *Fables of Identity* (New York, 1963). 174. But Frye does not propose a method for coping with the problems he sees.

2. I take the term "extrinsic" from the heuristic distinction between "extrinsic" and "intrinsic" approaches to literature set forth in René Welleck and Austin Warren's widely circulated handbook *Theory of Literature* (New York, 1949).

3. The formulation is Wellek and Warren's, *Theory of Literature*.

4. "Introduction," *John Keats: Selected Poetry* (New York, 1966), xi.

5. This idea is so fundamental to modern English and American critics that one even finds it advanced by commentators who profess an historical, social, even Marxist orientation. See, for example, Evan Watkins, *The Critical Act* (New Haven, 1978), 158–159.

6. *The Poems of John Keats* (Cambridge, Mass., 1978).

7. For a good brief synopsis of the essential bibliographical data see Jack Stillinger, *The Texts of Keats's Poems* (Cambridge, Mass., 1964), 232–234 and Stillinger's edition, 643–644.

8. Sidney Colvin, in his *John Keats* (London, 1920), vehemently denounces *The Indicator* text on aesthetic grounds, and explicitly calls upon "the Oxford University Press" to revise its edition by removing *The Indicator* text. His argument (which is typical of this approach) deserves full quotation because it has been so influential (pp. 469–470):

During those unhappy months at Kentish Town Keats's best work was given to the world. First, in Leigh Hunt's *Indicator* for May 20, *La Belle Dame sans Merci,* signed, obviously in bitterness, 'Caviare' (Hamlet's 'caviare to the general'), and unluckily enfeebled by changes for which we find no warrant either in Keats's autograph or in extant copies made by his friends Woodhouse and Brown. Keats's judgment in revising his own work had evidently by this time become unsure. We have seen how in recasting *Hyperion* the previous autumn he changed some of the finest of his original lines for the worse: and it is conceivable that in the case of *La Belle Dame* he may have done so again of his own motion, but much more likely, I should say, that the changes, which are all in the direction of the slipshod and the commonplace, were made on Hunt's suggestion and that Keats acquiesced from fatigue or indifference, or perhaps even from that very sense of lack of sympathy in most readers which made him sign 'Caviare.' Hunt introduced the piece with some commendatory words, showing that he, at all events, felt nothing amiss with it in its new shape, and added a short account of the old French poem by Alain Chartier form which the title was taken. It is to be deplored that in some recent and what should be standard editions of Keats the poem stands as thus printed in the *Indicator,* instead of in the original form rightly given by Lord Houghton from Brown's transcript, in which it had become a classic of the language.

It is surely a perversion in textual criticism to perpetuate the worse version merely because it happens to be the one printed in Keats's lifetime. No sensitive reader but must feel that 'wretched wight' is a vague and vapid substitute for the clear image of the 'knight-at-arms,' while 'sigh'd full sore' is ill replaced by 'sighed deep,' and 'wild wild eyes' still worse by 'wild sad eyes': that the whimsical particularity of the 'kisses four,' removed in the new version, gives the poem an essential part of its savour (Keats was fond of these fanciful numberings; compare the damsels who stand 'by fives and sevens' in the Induction to Calidore, and the 'four laurell'd spirits' in the Epistle to George Felton Mathew): and again, that the loose, broken construction—'So kissed to sleep' is quite uncharacteristic of the poet: and yet again, that the phrase 'And there we slumbered on the moss,' is what any amateur rimester might write about any pair of afternoon picknickers, while the phrase which was cancelled for it, 'And there she lullèd me asleep,' falls with exactly the mystic cadence and hushing weight upon the spirit which was required.

9. See "wight" in the *OED*, where the word's history of two interlocked meanings is clearly set forth. Essentially, the two meanings are epitomized in Spenser's use of the term in *The Shepheardes Calender* on the one hand, and *The Faerie Queene* on the other. In the latter case the term develops through the literature of heroic romance and carries no ironic overtones. In the former, however, the word signifies a base individual and is used in mild contempt and derision. By the time the word reaches the nineteenth century, its archaic character is established, so that its romance meaning (as used in some of Walter Scott's poems, for example in *Marmion* VI, xx) is continually threatened by an ironic overtone. This situation occurs not simply because "wight" is seen to be an archaic word, but because the word itself carries its own ironic history in its alternative tradition. The entire process emerges quite clearly in the influential opening stanzas of Byron's *Childe Harold*, Canto I, where the ironization of the romance usage is complete. That Keats was aware of these matters is plain enough from his treatment of romance materials in other poems written around the time of the ballad. See especially "On the Character of C. B."

10. On the significance of the "Caviare" signature see Robert Gittings, *John Keats*

(London, 1968), 400, and Colvin, *op. cit.* n. 27. On the matter of *The Indicator*'s ideological function see Leigh Hunt, *Autobiography,* ed. J. E. Morpurgo (London, 1949), 280, 489 n.8.; and Edmund Blunden, *Leigh Hunt and His Circle* (New York, 1930), 146–150.

11. Brown was a misogynist, and his behavior toward Fanny Brawne was especially contemptible: see Aileen Ward, *John Keats: The Making of a Poet* (New York: Viking, 1963), 249–250, and Gittings, *ibid.,* 285, 337, 363, 385. For Milnes and his library see *The Swinburne Letters,* ed. Cecil Y. Lang (New Haven, 1959) I, xlvi.

12. Brown was one of the principal people who encouraged Keats to try to make his way as a hack London journalist and dramatic writer. He also sought to separate Keats from Hunt.

13. See immediately below. But this count does not include the poem's title and signature in *The Indicator,* though both are especially important elements of the poem and ought to be considered as important "variants."

14. Stillinger, *The Texts of Keats's Poems,* 226–227.

15. Stillinger, *The Poems of John Keats,* 636.

16. See Robert Gittings, *The Mask of Keats* (Cambridge, Mass., 1956), esp. 26–33.

17. See Gittings, *John Keats,* chaps. 22–24, and Ward, chaps. 11–12.

18. By "romantic" here I mean simply that the Brown/1848 text does not distance itself from itself the way *The Indicator* text does. The former is a more self-absorbed and self-absorbing text, whereas the latter is more self-conscious and critical.

19. *The Letters of John Keats,* ed. Hyder Rollins (Cambridge, Mass., 1958) II, 97.

20. See Colvin's remarks in the passage quoted in n. 10 above. See also Robert Gittings, *John Keats: The Living Year* (London, 1962), 113–121, and Walter Jackson Bate, *John Keats* (Cambridge, Mass., 1963), 480.

21. See Frederick L. Beaty, *Light From Heaven* (De Kalb, Ill., 1971), chap. 7. Beaty does not, however, emphasize the social reflex of this attitude toward love.

22. See Stillinger, *The Texts of Keats's Poems,* 246–247, and Miriam Allott, ed., *The Poems of John Keats* (London, 1970), 537–538n.

23. Bate, 510–511n.

24. Ian Jack, *Keats and the Mirror of Art* (Oxford, 1967), chap. XIII.

25. See *Ibid.,* chap. III.

26. *Ibid.,* 283 n. 13.

27. Stillinger, *The Texts of Keats's Poems,* 264–265.

28. See The World's Classics reprint of Milnes's work (Oxford, 1931), 229.

29. Allott's notes and commentary (686–689) on the poem bring together many of the pertinent biographical references.

30. "Poem and Ideology: A Study of Keats's 'To Autumn'," in *The Fate of Reading* (Chicago, 1975), 124–146.

31. These quotations are taken from pages 124–126.

32. Cf. John O. Hayden, *The Romantic Reviewers* (Chicago, 1968), 196–204.

33. See Ward, 315–316, 332–333.

34. *Ibid.,* 341.

35. See *The Keats Circle: Letters and Papers 1816–1879,* ed. H. E. Rollins (Cambridge, Mass., 1965) I, 90–97, and Letters II, 174.

36. See Ward, 363, and Allott, 764.

37. See the Letters II, 139, 174; Allott, 326–327, 450–451, 614–615; and Ward, 289, 315, 333.

38. It is, I hope, unnecessary to point out that the "reactionary" and the "subversive" character of Keats's poems is, in this context, a function of particular historical circumstances, and that the fundamentally *critical* aspect of the poetry persists

through these changes. In both cases we see that Keats's poems refuse to be reconciled with the "actual world," though in each case the poems pass their critical judgments on the world from differing points of vantage. For a fuller theoretical discussion of this point see Theodor Adorno, "Reconciliation Under Duress," in *Aesthetics and Politics* (London, 1977); see especially pp. 159–160: "Art and reality can only converge if art crystallizes out its own formal laws, not by passively accepting objects as they come. In art knowledge is aesthetically mediated through and through. . . . In the form of an image the object is absorbed into the subject instead of following the bidding of the alienated world and persisting obdurately in a state of reification. The contradiction between the object reconciled in the subject . . . and the actual unreconciled object in the outside world, confers on the work of art a vantage point from which it can criticize actuality. Art is the negative knowledge of the actual world. . . . Only by virtue of [aesthetic distance] can a work of art become both work of art and valid consciousness."

39. Ian Jack discusses the Ceres allusions in his essay on "To Autumn" in *Keats and the Mirror of Art* (Oxford, 1967), chap. XV. Bacchus he does not discuss, but that divinity's history in art and poetry shows him frequently represented as a handsome youth with fine, long-flowing hair.

40. See Jack's discussion, *ibid.*

41. Quoted in Jack, 69.

42. Herbert A. Simon, *The Sciences of the Artificial* (Cambridge, Mass., 1969).

43. Prof. James Chandler has pointed out to me that this idea was not originally Wordsworth's. He first had it from Coleridge (see Wordsworth's letter to Lady Beaumont of 21 May 1807).

44. *Letters* II, 141.

45. *Letters* II, 175.

46. *Letters* II, 189.

47. *Letters* II, 201.

48. See, e.g., *Letters* II, 209.

49. *Letters* II, 167.

50. Hartman's essay explicitly builds on this tradition. See especially p. 146 of his essay, where he concludes: "Even fruitfulness is not a burden in 'To Autumn.' This, at last, is true impersonality."

51. The self-consciousness of these lines is anticipated in the poem at lines 9–11. There Keats suggests, by pathetic fallacy, a charming mood of querulousness in his poem's bees.

52. One could easily develop here a (useful) biographical analysis by associating the "songs of spring" with the great "spring odes" Keats had written a few months before. In this analysis, "To Autumn" would be seen not merely as an *acceptance* of the idea of "fruitfulness," but also as the *resort* to that idea.

53. That Romanticism is a reactionary and "escapist" art movement is a critical commonplace. One can (and should) assent to this view, but only after one also sees that the "reaction" of Romanticism is also an intense expression of critique. See above n. 38, and Arnold Hauser, *The Social History of Art* (New York, 1951). III, 196, 174–176. Perhaps the most profound expression of this view of Romanticism can be found in the *first* detailed commentary on the subject in Heine's great essay on the Romantic Movement: see "The Romantic School," in *Heinrich Heine: Selected Works*, ed. Helen Mustard (New York, 1973).

54. Hartman, *op. cit.*, p. 143.

55. Quoted in Berel Lang and Forrest Williams, *Marxism and Art* (New York, 1972), p. 38.

56. The concept of estrangement, as developed by the Russian Formalists and subsequent epigones, is used in a much more limited frame of reference than the one I am developing here. See also the Bakhtin School's trenchant critique of the concept in P. N. Medvedev/M. M. Bakhtin, *The Formal Method in Literary Scholarship* (Baltimore, 1978), *passim*, but especially pp. 60–62.

PAUL H. FRY

History, Existence, and "To Autumn"

By location as well as tendency, Paul H. Fry continues and extends Yale school criticism—his first book, *The Poet's Calling in the English Ode* (1980)—having announced the arrival of a critic of range and virtuosity. In Fry's contribution to this collection, Jerome McGann's essay on "To Autumn" becomes the focus of his refutation of what he sees as McGann's overly simplified "political" interpretation of Keats's text. Yet, just as William Keach improves on Frances Ferguson's commentary on *Mont Blanc* by questioning some of his predecessor's assumptions, so Fry's argument is no mere "regression" to Hartman's original position.

Fry, in fact, is sympathetic to McGann's desire for historical contextualizing; his objection is to schematized history. Fry—unlike Hartman—wants to renew our awareness of the "venerable" distinction between "historicality" and "historicity." This desire is characteristic of recent criticism in that it takes for granted (as even a decade ago was not so common) the idea "that nature was invented by culture." Accepting this presupposition, Fry is positioned to argue that McGann's historical understanding is founded on a "misplaced concreteness" that inadvertently mystifies the true historicity of a work of art such as "To Autumn."

Whomever one sides with in this debate, the significance of the controversy to the evolution of romantic criticism lies in the fact that now the ground of dispute has been moved away from formalistic interpretation toward what may or may not be "truly" historical issues. (For still another discussion of these one may consult David O. Haney " 'Viewing 'the Viewless Wings of Poesy': Gadamer, Keats, and Historicity" [1989].) Our final trio of essays, then, defines with unusual clarity the center of disagreement probably most important to a majority of contemporary students of romantic literature.

In his 1979 *Modern Language Notes* article, "Keats and the Historical Method in Literary Criticism," Jerome McGann takes "To Autumn" as his star exhibit quite understandably in order to prove the flexibility of his approach. Whereas other critics follow Keats into his Winchester retreat, McGann proposes to return him to the busier sphere of historical explanation. There had been bad harvests for the last several years, McGann says, but in 1819 there was a good one, and Keats was lulled by its transitory munificence into writing the ahistorical myth of its eternal return.[1] This argument is offered in contrast to the readings of those who have

From *Studies in Romanticism* 25 (1986): 211–219. Courtesy of the Trustees of Boston University.

forgotten to admit that even the countryside is enclosed by the hedges and crofts of history, and that Autumn itself is a leisure-class commodity produced by field hands too worried about the coming cold to notice the pleasures of merely circulating. History on this view is the subtext, pretext, and context even and especially of *poésie pure*.

Yes and no. The issue turns (together with a good many other issues in current critical debate) on the question whether there is any part of culture that is not historical. My supposition, which I cannot pause here to defend, is that indeed, within what I would venture to call the experience of culture, there is a refuge from history: it is the "historicity"—to invoke a venerable distinction—that withstands the purposefulness of "historicality." And not only in poems like "To Autumn": if "To Autumn" were indeed about the harvest, which in the end I think it is not, and if the laborers of the second stanza were brought under an obligation to be studies from the life unmediated by pictorial and literary precedents, the resulting ode to rural toil could still step out of history, although perhaps it would not be appropriate for *that* sort of poem to do so. The question in other words is not whether we all understand that nature was invented by culture—we all do—but whether in interpreting poems like "To Autumn" we can reserve the conviction that within culture the existential register is still sometimes more appropriate to emphasize than the historical one.

Yes, Peterloo happened shortly after Keats arrived at Winchester, and he remarks in a letter that in Winchester there are no looms and no signs of manufacturing;[2] but it scarcely seems pertinent to say that "To Autumn" is therefore an evasion of social violence when it is so clearly an encounter with death itself. To be sure, the scenes of stanzas one and two are *property* in the sense in which Brown's Farm in Emerson is property according to Frank Lentricchia,[3] but the scene of the last stanza designedly belongs to no one and everyone—and is not surprisingly ignored altogether by McGann's reading. Keats was already trying to put down a rebellious sore throat. He went on and on in a letter to his publisher about the importance of avoiding damp climates. These were the important significations of violence and of locale for Keats by the Fall of 1819, and I think it more relevant to say therefore that the "last oozings" of stanza two that take us from the humid stanza one to the dry stanza are there to squeeze moisture out of the air even at the risk of chilling life entirely—I think this more relevant than to say that Keats squeezes society out of the poem.

None of which is to say that "To Autumn" is not a social poem. It is, but what it is not is a politically encoded escape from history, a coerced betrayal—as McGann's interprets it—of its author's radicalism. McGann thinks to rescue Keats from the imputation of political naiveté by saying that he was a radical browbeaten into quietism, if not conservatism, by his reactionary friends and publishers. Now, if I say that on the contrary I find relatively little evidence of radicalism in Keats's life or work, I must of course explain what I mean by "radical." To David Bromwich's characterization of radicalism as the term was applied in Keats's day to persons as various as Orator Hunt and Hazlitt—and even Byron— there can be no objection, and I would agree that at various moments Keats is certainly a radical of that kind. But our understanding of radicalism today is inevitably colored by Marx, and it may as well be said that Keats's "radicalism" was precisely what Marx attacked again and again, in his most spirited invectives, as bourgeois utopian Socialism.

For this reason one feels that George Bernard Shaw should have known better than to juxtapose the "socialist" stanzas of *Isabella* with Marx.[4] "With her two brothers this fair lady dwelt, / Enriched from ancestral merchandize."[5] If this and what follows about the oppression of the Ceylon diver and the seal with its piteous bark were in any way to resemble Marxism, then Keats would have to indict the lady along with her brothers. But in fact he does not shirk the decision not to do so: the syntax of the lines I just quoted leaves no doubt that the lady has her share of commercial wealth. And if Isabella is intrinsically good despite her wealth and rank, it must follow that her brothers are intrinsically bad quite apart from their happening to occupy a social niche that for Marx would necessarily entail oppression. The same implied argument from intrinsic value and vice subverts the appearance of class analysis in the opening lines of *Endymion,* Book Three: "There are those who lord it o'er their fellow-men / With most prevailing tinsel" (III: 1–2; *Poems* 163). Here and in what follows Keats does not object to social hierarchy; on the contrary, he objects to a prevailing weakness, vanity, and selfishness among those who rule, evoking by implied contrast a happy myth of restored Feudal leadership—strong, noble, and generous—by those who do not "lord it" but are lords.

There is certainly a great deal of evidence that what Keats called the "poetical character" is a radically social character, almost dangerously so. It was the insight of Paul de Man, in an essay that McGann handles roughly, that Keats's "snail-horn" personality is caught up so intimately in the social matrix that his very empathy becomes an evasion, an escape from self-confrontation.[6] Keats's "poetical character" in any case "lives in gusto, be it fair or foul," which is to say that it enters into and is penetrated by all the workers and workings-through of society: a quarrel in the streets, an Iago or an Imogen. But the chameleon poet is social without being programmatically political: there is nothing tendentious in him to please the virtuous philosopher. The poet, the "man of genius," suffers the identities of others, even infants in a nursery, to "press upon" him indiscriminately, and remains forever the antipodes of the significantly so-named "man of power."

Or so Keats wants to claim. Nothing is easier to demystify than the petit-bourgeois affectation of aloofness from the political. In fact it is so easy to do that we are tempted to assert that Keats's politics were cleverer and more far-seeing than we find them to be, to permit ourselves what de Man in this context calls "a trace of condescension or defensiveness, as if [we] were forced to look at attenuating circumstances."[7] But the record is not encouraging. Keats would have disdained to vote for Humphrey against Nixon; that is, he preferred Burdett's views to Castlereagh's, but still complained that there was "nothing manly or sterling in any part of the Government" (*Letters* 1: 396). Like Dickens after him, Keats always prefers the individual to the collective, inveighing repeatedly against his friend Dilke's Godwinism and declaring that "the first political duty a Man ought to have a mind to is the happiness of his friends" (*Letters* 2: 213). In April 1819 we find him reading Voltaire's *Siècle de Louis* XIV and Robertson's *America* side by side and concluding in his letter to America—where his brother's wife had been criticizing the social pretensions of frontier life in Louisville—that people make themselves miserable wherever they are, whether they begin in a state of nature or end in a state of despotism: "The whole appears to resolve in this," he goes on, "that man is originally 'a poor forked creature' subject to the same mischances as the beasts of the forest, destined to hardships or disquietude of some kind or other" (*Letters* 2: 101). Although he alludes here to the politics of *King Lear* (and Shakespeare is "on the arbitrary side of the question," he says elsewhere, quoting Hazlitt), what he arrives at is the still less ameliorative politics of Aeschylus in the *Agamemnon:* "Do you not see how necessary a world of pains and troubles is to school an intelligence and make it a soul?" (*Letters* 2: 102). Like the Vale of Tears that is recurrently exposed as reactionary doctrine by the political critique of religion, Keats's Vale of Soul-Making—which comes next in this letter—presupposes suffering, not excluding the sting of political injustice, if it is to succeed in schooling the imagination.

These then are the political views of the poet whom we are tempted to portray, in the current critical climate, as a silenced radical. If there is something not only politically naive but decidedly retrograde about them, we should remember that such views, implicit not promoted, half-conscious and far from systematic, scarcely qualify as political views at all. Just as the Ptolemaic universe makes better poetry than the Copernican, so benevolent Feudalism makes better poetry than progressive social radicalism, as long as (in either case) by "poetry" we mean the lyric or narrative evocation of the heroic individual quest.

Certainly Keats did loathe all forms of despotic authority; he was quick to find reflected in Church and State the tyranny of Richard Abbey over his personal affairs and of Milton over his imagination. There is no doubt that in plain prose he was "on the Liberal side of the question," as he wrote no more than two days after writing "To Autumn," announcing his decision to support himself as a political journalist (*Letters* 2: 180; also see 174, 176, 178, 181). There is no doubt further- more that Keats understood the importance of class conflict, whether or not he learned his lesson from the sneering reviews of *Endymion,* as McGann suggests. "You see what it is to be under six foot and not a lord," writes Keats (*Letters* 2: 61); or again, on his walking tour, the vistas "make one forget the divisions of life: age, youth, poverty and riches" (*Letters* 2: 299). But it is typical of Keats that in both these passages the social causes of quotidian unhappiness are named second, as aggravations of the primary causes for which he evidently believes radicalism has no cure.

Nor can the author of "If thy mistress some rich anger shows, / Emprison her soft hand, and let her rave" ("Ode on Melancholy," *Poems* 374) be saved for feminism. McGann says that if Keats's friend Charles Brown and his editor Monckton Milnes had not authorized the 1848 version of "La Belle Dame Sans Merci" beginning "Oh what can ail thee, knight-at-arms," all of us today would be reading the superior *Indicator* text of 1820 beginning "Ah what can ail thee, wretched wight." He prefers the latter first line because it is wittily archaic and shows Keats's ballad to be critical of the medieval-feudal ballad tradition with its mystification of women. But with the approval of every other modern critic and editor, Brown, who behaved badly to Fanny Brawne, and Milnes, who collected erotica, printed the version which reflects their own unhealthy view of women as lamias. Now, perhaps it is true that Brown and Milnes were consciously or ob- scurely so moved, but what one cannot accept is the implied exoneration of Keats from similar squalid attitudes on the grounds that the 1820 version of "La Belle Dame" was the only one he authorized. We know perfectly well from both the poetry and the life that the combination of prolonged adolescence, fear of rejec- tion, small stature, and the sexual hectic that goes with fevers confused Keats even beyond the Regency norm about women. Near the end of his life, just when his jealous broodings about Fanny Brawne were at their darkest, Keats tried without much success to discuss women dispassionately in a letter to none other than Charles Brown: "The sale of my book is very slow, though it has been very highly rated. One of the causes, I understand from different quarters . . . is the offense the ladies take at me. On thinking that matter over, I am certain I have said nothing to displease any woman I would care to please: but there still is a tendency in my book to class women with roses and sweetmeats,—they never see themselves dominant" (*Letters* 2: 327). Apart from Keats's insecure tendency to coddle and demean women in the same gesture, what remains here is a commonplace insinuation against the Bluestockings that a Brown or a Milnes would find wholly congenial.

It is with much the same effort to lend Keats his own enlightenment that McGann considers the overall character of the 1820 volume of poems that includes "To Autumn." He argues that Keats did not print certain poems in this volume because they were ideologically controversial—the poems in question are "La Belle Dame" and the sonnet about Paolo and Francesca—and that all the poetry he does include was both written and chosen to placate the literary establishment. Here appears the main anomaly of McGann's politization of Keats: at one and the same time he declares that Keats was himself shy of further abuse and thus tailor-made his poems for approval *and* that Keats—quite another Keats— would have continued to write boldly, even radically, if his friends had not persuaded him to lick the boots of the "State Apparatus" reviewers. In the grip of this virtual contradiction it is necessary for McGann to say that "To Autumn" is not simply a co-opted, escapist betrayal of political hope but also a subtle acknowledgement of political realities which takes the form of omitting to mention them— or does mention them, more subtly still, in a kind of code.

Here is what McGann says about "To Autumn" in the course, as he puts it, of "supplying greater specificity" to Geoffrey Hartman's reading, "Poem as Ideology," in *The Fate of Reading*. The way to be specific, McGann says, is to determine "when and where and by whom . . . the poem [was] originally published" and first read ("Historical Method" 1015). Specifically, then, we take it, "To Autumn" was published on the advice of reactionary friends in an ideologically camouflaged state and read with approval by reviewers who did not know that their ruling-class tastes were being truckled to. The publishers Taylor and Hessey certainly were not Leigh Hunt or the Bookseller Carlisle, but can we infer from this that "Keats struggled with them" expressly over the political content of his book (as distinguished from unfavorable commercial omens of other kinds), as McGann puts it without offering any evidence beyond his suspicious interpretations of the poems ("Historical Method" 1016)? Keats wanted the new poems to be better than *Endymion,* which is to say that he wanted them to be less "Cockney" in the senses offered for our consideration by William Keach, but it hardly follows that he specifically wanted them to be more servile to the canons of the ruling class.

McGann periodizes "To Autumn" by contrasting it with Thomson's Enlightenment poem, "Autumn": uniquely in Keats, he argues, "the factor of human control is not found in the practical arts, but in myth and in the illusions of the fine arts" ("Historical Method" 1020). The laborers in the second stanza are in states of arrested productivity, more winnowed than winnowing, and they look more like pictures than peasants. By this means the poet implies—abetted by the success of the 1819 harvest—that nature's spontaneous bounty and not unalienated human labor is the key to happiness. Conforming to the ideology of the idyll, " 'To Autumn' asks us to believe . . . that all Autumns are the same" ("Historical Method" 1021). "Its message," McGann continues, "is that the fine arts, and by extension imagination generally, are more humanly productive than any of the other more practical sciences of the artificial" ("Historical Method" 1023). I think that McGann is right about Keats's laborers, and I think that the inference I have quoted here is interesting and largely valid, with the anti-historical reservation only that never since Linus and Orpheus has there been a lyric poet who did not believe the fine arts to what Imlac in *Rasselas* calls "the highest form of learning." The trouble is that McGann stops at the second stanza, which Keats supersedes with a stanza in which the fine arts and all human projects whatsoever seem suddenly as marginal as the georgic arts of stanza two.

Even if "To Autumn" were about the harvest, it could scarcely be a celebration of plenty. Amid stubble-fields, dried-up cottage gardens, and sounds that are humanly intelligible only insofar as they seem mournful, a requiem for plentitude, the senses complete the eclipse of the season by turning to the high frequencies of the empty sky. This too is escapism, perhaps from the Peterloo Massacre among other things. I would be more willing to bring in Peterloo if I did not suspect that that and a few other events are overdetermined signs of historicality in the current schematization of the Regency past, hence more important to us than they were to Keats. The real challenge for "the historical method" is to resist arranging a few beads like Peterloo, Pentridge, the Holy Alliance, and the arrest of Major Cartwright along the string of class conflict and calling it history. When concreteness is misplaced, when we backpeddle without intellectual hindrance from diverse effects to isolated and specific causes and offer the result as a model of precision, just then we succumb to conceptual vagueness. It is a fallacy of misplaced concreteness, a blindness to what is *there,* to suppose that "To Autumn" is very deeply determined by or concerned with social conflicts or the social arts. Somewhat reluctantly, knowing what angry misunderstandings this sort of vocabulary can inspire, I persist in thinking that "To Autumn" concerns the ontology of the lyric moment.

Appearances notwithstanding, this assertion can itself be couched in historical terms. Geoffrey Hartman has already done so in the great essay that McGann indicts for its alleged Keatsian suppression of the real world. What Hartman says is that "To Autumn" is an English poem in which Keats supposes to be the spirit of Chatterton; its chastened northerly language transumes the materials of the Eastern sublime ode and the Mediterranean georgic poem, both traditionalist genres, in a way that is both patriotic and—if I may—radical.[8] The result, to elaborate on Hartman's thesis, is an English equivalent of the negative litany that is common in American books of the Revolutionary period like Crevecoeur's *Letters from an American Farmer.* Here in America, the refrain goes, there are no Popes, no magistrates, no Kings, no arbitrary authority of any kind. Keats would have heard this still-popular sentiment from his brother and sister-in-law. Of course he could not make such claims for English institutions, but we should remember that even the vilest misdeeds of the Regency at home would seem moderate to one who had witnessed the squalor of Scotland and Ireland and who was willing enough to believe, with most of his countrymen, that with French hopes extinguished the entire European mainland had relapsed into tyranny. What Keats could do, then, necessarily coloring his patriotisim with its politically austere American equivalent, was to suggest that the relative latitude of English life leaves one free to purify the language expressive of that life from the despotism of its encrustations disclosing a clearing in which existence is encountered as such, precisely as a release from the tyranny of history and the language that encodes it.

The third stanza is a ritual of clearing away, intimating the possibility of release from what Shelley finally called Life: release along the sketchy boundaries—the stanza is full of them—where, with no pain, existence and nothingness coincide. Existence grows thin, transparent, while nothingness, the blank of nature, acquires a discernably human outline. The rough-edged cirrus, the stubble, the sallows, the hilly bourn, the hedge, the croft—all demarcate this place and make the landscape seem almost like a faintly breathing thing, "soft-dying," "bourne aloft / Or sinking as the light wind lives or dies" like the lungs in an interval of pain. Like the clouds that bar the first lines of Coleridge's "Dejection" and intensify the jaundice of the world's brow (with its "peculiar tint of yellow-green"), Keats's barred clouds imprison a fevered face here below, blooming rosy through the stubble. But the varied chorus chanting the mortal hours with no tone is cheered a little as it rises by stages above the sallow complexion of the earth. The swallows defy the bars, each swallow a triumph, and gather either for freedom or for rest.

Walking idly in the neutral air, Keats is not likely to have thought about the goodness or badness of the harvest. During the "chaste" September weather under the "Dian skies" of the Winchester countryside, Keats is intent upon austerity, not plenitude. His Albion is not a green and pleasant land, but it is a dry and bracing place nonetheless once he has released it from the burden of being sociohistorical into an ahistorical moment of soft dying—an even sadder burden that is eased, however, by its independence from the teleological oppressions that make history a progressive narrative. What appears most clearly when it is placed in contrast with this or that version of history is the special achievement of Keats in "To Autumn," which is precisely his refusal to sublimate mortality as a social conspiracy. In an article called "Politics as Opposed to What?" Stanley Cavell has spoken of the "intimacy with existence" he finds in Emerson and Thoreau,[9] and if we add that that intimacy is a dangerous one, an *amour fatale,* then it will be Cavell's expression and not any of its negative equivalents, such as "alienation from history," that takes the measure of "To Autumn."

NOTES

1. See McGann, "Keats and the Historical Method in Literary Criticism" *MLN* 94 (1979): 1021. Henceforth cited parenthetically by page as "Historical Method."

2. See *The Letters of John Keats 1814–1921,* 2 vols., ed. Hyder E. Rollins (Cambridge, Mass.: Harvard U P, 1958) 2:189.

3. See Lentricchia, *After the New Criticism* (Chicago: U of Chicago P, 1980) 83–84.

4. See *Bernard Shaw's Nondramatic Literary Criticism,* ed. Stanley Weintraub (Lincoln: U of Nebraska P, 1972) 134–35.

5. *The Poems of John Keats,* ed. Jack Stillinger (Cambridge, Mass.: Harvard U P, 1978) 249. Henceforth cited parenthetically as *Poems* by page.

6. See de Man, "Introduction," *The Selected Poetry of John Keats*, ed. de Man (New York: Signet, 1966) xxiv. See also McGann, "Historical Method" 988–89.

7. De Man, "Introduction" xi.

8. See Hartman, "Poem and Ideology: A Study of Keats's 'To Autumn' " in *The Fate of Reading and Other Essays* (Chicago: U of Chicago P, 1975) 126 ff.

9. Cavell, "Politics as Opposed to What?" *CI* 9 (1982): 161.

Selective Bibliography of Criticism

This bibliography incorporates citations of literary criticism, cultural criticism, and theory in English or English translation from the notes and headnotes of the selections. For reasons of space, we have been unable to include citations of editions and other primary sources. Our thanks to Frances R. Botkin, University of Illinois at Chicago, for her painstaking work in helping to compile and check this bibliography.

Aarslef, Hans. *From Locke to Saussure: Essays on the Study of Language and Intellectual History.* Minneapolis: University of Minnesota Press, 1982.

Abrams, M. H. *The Correspondent Breeze: Essays on English Romanticism.* New York: Norton, 1984.

————. "English Romanticism: The Spirit of the Age." In *Romanticism Reconsidered: Selected Papers from English History,* ed. Northrop Frye. New York: Columbia University Press, 1963.

————, ed. *English Romantic Poets: Essays in Criticism.* New York: Oxford University Press, 1960.

————, ed. *Literature and Belief: English Institute Essays, 1957.* New York: Columbia University Press, 1958.

————. *The Mirror and the Lamp: Romantic Theory and the Critical Tradition.* New York: Oxford University Press, 1953.

————. *Natural Supernaturalism: Tradition and Revolution in Romantic Literature.* New York: Norton, 1971.

————. "On Political Readings of *Lyrical Ballads.* In *Romantic Revolutions,* ed. Kenneth R. Johnston et al. Bloomington: Indiana University Press, 1990.

————. "Rationality and Imagination in Cultural History." *Critical Inquiry* 2 (Spring 1976): 447–464.

Adorno, Theodore. *Prisms.* Trans. Samuel Weber and Shierry Weber. Cambridge: MIT press, 1982.

————. "Reconciliation under Duress." In *Aesthetics and Politics,* ed. Ernest Bloch, et al., trans. Ronald Taylor. London: NLB, 1977.

Aers, David. "William Blake and the Dialectic of Sex." *ELH* 44 (1977): 500–514.

Allott, Miriam. *John Keats.* Harlow: Longman, 1967

Altick, Richard. *The English Common Reader: A Social History of the Mass Reading Public, 1800–1900.* Chicago: University of Chicago Press, 1957.

Anderson, George. *The Legend of the Wandering Jew.* Providence: Brown University Press, 1965.

Arac, Jonathan. "Bounding Lines: *The Prelude* and Critical Revision." *boundary 2* 7 (1979): 31–48.

————. *Critical Genealogies: Historical Situations for Postmodern Literary Studies.* New York: Columbia University Press, 1987.

————"Repetition and Exclusion: Coleridge and New Criticism Reconsidered. *boundary 2* 8 (1979): 261–273.

Arnold, Matthew. "Wordsworth." In *Essays in Criticism, Second Series.* London: Macmillan, 1896.

Baker, John Jay. "Myth, Subjectivity, and the Problem of Historical Time in Shelley's 'Lines Written among the Euganean Hills.' " *ELH 56 (1989): 149–172.*

Bakhtin, M. M. *The Dialogic Imagination: Four Essays.* Ed. Michael Holquist. Trans. Caryl Emerson and Michael Holquist. Austin: University of Texas Press, 1981.

Barrell, John. "The Language Properly So Called." In *English Literature in History, 1730–1780: An Equal, Wide Survey.* New York: St. Martin's Press, 1983.

――――. *Poetry, Language, and Politics.* Manchester: Manchester University Press, 1988.

Barthes, Roland. *Image, Music, Text.* Trans. Stephen Heath. New York: Hill & Wang, 1977.

Bate, Jonathan. *Romantic Ecology.* London: Routledge, 1991.

Bate, Walter Jackson. *The Burden of the Past and the English Poet.* Cambridge: Harvard University Press, 1970.

――――. *From Classic to Romantic: Premises of Taste in Eighteenth-Century England.* Cambridge: Harvard University Press, 1946.

――――. *John Keats.* Cambridge: Harvard University Press, 1963.

Bateson, F. W. *Wordsworth: A Re-Interpretation.* 2d ed. London: Longman, 1956.

Bayley, John. "Keats and Reality." In *Proceedings of the British Academy,* 91–125. London: G. Cumberlege, Oxford University Press, 1962.

Beaty, Frederick L. *Byron the Satirist.* DeKalb: Northern Illinois University Press, 1985.

――――. *Light from Heaven: Love in British Romantic Literature.* DeKalb: Northern Illinois University Press, 1971.

Beer, J. B. *Coleridge The Visionary.* London: Chatto & Windus, 1959.

Behrendt, Stephen C. *Shelley and His Audiences.* Lincoln: University of Nebraska Press, 1989.

Benjamin, Walter. *The Origin of German Tragic Drama.* Trans. John Osborne. London: NLB, 1977.

Bennett, Anthony J. " 'Alone and Palely Loitering': The Reader in Thrall in Keats's 'La Belle Dame Sans Merci.' " *Style* 24 (1990): 73–88.

Bennett, Tony. *Formalism and Marxism.* London: Methuen, 1979.

Bentley, G. E., Jr. "The Great Illustrated-Book Publishers of the 1790's and William Blake." In *Editing Illustrated Books,* ed. William Bissett. New York: Garland Publishing, 1980.

Berlin, Isaiah. *Against the Current: Essays in the History of Ideas.* New York: Viking, 1980.

――――. *The Crooked Timber of Humanity: Chapters in the History of Ideas.* London: John Murray, 1990.

Bewell, Alan. "The Political Implications of Keats's Classicist Aesthetics." *Studies in Romanticism* 25 (1986): 220–229.

――――. *Wordsworth and the Enlightenment: Nature, Man, and Society in the Experimental Poetry.* New Haven: Yale University Press, 1989.

Bialostosky, Don H. "Coleridge's Interpretation of Wordsworth's Preface to *Lyrical Ballads.*" *PMLA* 93 (1978): 912–924.

――――. *Making Tales: The Poetics of Wordsworth's Narrative Experiments.* Chicago: University of Chicago Press, 1984.

――――. *Wordsworth, Dialogics, and the Practice of Criticism.* Cambridge: Cambridge University Press, 1992.

Bindman, David. *Blake as an Artist.* Oxford: Phaidon Press, 1977.

Blackstone, Bernard. *Byron.* Harlow: Longman, 1970.

Blank, G. Kim. *Wordsworth's Influence on Shelley: A Study of Poetic Authority.* London: MacMillan, 1988.

Bloom, Harold. *The Anxiety of Influence: A Theory of Poetry.* New York: Oxford University Press, 1973.

———. *Kabbalah and Criticism.* New York: Seabury Press, 1975.

———. *A Map of Misreading.* New York: Oxford University Press, 1975.

———. *Poetry and Repression: Revisionism from Blake to Stevens.* New Haven: Yale University Press, 1976.

———, ed. *Romanticism and Consciousness: Essays in Criticism.* New York: Norton, 1970.

———. *Shelley's Mythmaking.* Ithaca: Cornell University Press, 1969.

———. *The Visionary Company: A Reading of English Romantic Poetry.* 1961. Rev. ed., Ithaca: Cornell University Press, 1971.

Blunden, Edmund. *Leigh Hunt and His Circle.* New York: Harper & Brothers, 1930.

Boime, Albert. *Art in an Age of Revolution, 1750–1800.* Chicago: University of Chicago Press, 1987.

Bostetter, Edward E. "The Nightmare World of *The Ancient Mariner.*" *Studies in Romanticism* 1 (1962): 241–254.

———, ed. *Twentieth Century Interpretations of Don Juan.* Englewood Cliffs, N.J.: Prentice-Hall, 1969.

Boulger, James. "Imagination and Speculation in Coleridge's Conversation Poems." *Journal of English and Germanic Philology* 64 (1965).

Bové, Paul. *Destructive Poetics: Heidegger and Modern American Poetry.* New York: Columbia University Press, 1980.

Bradley, A. C. "Wordsworth." In *Oxford Lectures on Poetry.* 1909. Rpt., Bloomington: Indiana University Press, 1961.

Brantley, Richard E. *Locke, Wesley, and the Method of English Romanticism.* Gainesville: University of Florida Press, 1984.

Brier, Peter. "Reflections on Tintern Abbey." *The Wordsworth Circle* 5 (1974): 5–6.

Brinkley, Robert. " 'Our Chearful Faith': On Wordsworth, Politics, and Milton." *The Wordsworth Circle* 18 (1987): 57–60.

———. "Vagrant and Hermit: Milton and the Politics of 'Tintern Abbey.' " *The Wordsworth Circle* 16 (1985):126–133.

Brisman, Leslie. *Milton's Poetry of Choice and Its Romantic Heirs.* Ithaca: Cornell University Press, 1973.

———. *Romantic Origins.* Ithaca: Cornell University Press, 1978.

Bromwich, David. "The French Revolution and 'Tinturn Abbey.' " *Raritan* 11 (1991): 1–23

Brooks, Cleanth. "Implications of an Organic Theory of Poetry." In *Literature and Belief,* ed. M. H. Abrams. New York: Columbia University Press, 1958.

Brown, Homer Obed. "The Art of Theology and the Theology of Art: Robert Penn Warren's Reading of Coleridge's *The Rime of the Ancient Mariner.*" *boundary 2* 7 (1979): 201–233.

Brown, Huntington. "The Gloss to *The Rime of the Ancient Mariner.*" *Modern Language Quarterly* 6 (1945): 319–324.

Brown, Marshall. *The Shape of German Romanticism.* Ithaca: Cornell University Press, 1979.

Bruns, Gerald R. "Wordsworth at the Limits of Romantic Hermeneutics." *Centennial Review* 33 (1989): 393–418.

Burgess, C. F. " 'The Eve of St. Agnes': One Way to the Poem." *English Journal* 54 (1965): 389–394.

Bush, Douglas. *John Keats: His Life and Writings.* New York: Macmillan, 1966.

Butler, Marilyn, ed. *Burke, Paine, Godwin and the Revolution Controversy.* Cambridge: Cambridge University Press, 1984.

———. "Literary London." In *London: World City, 1800–1840,* ed. Celina Fox. New Haven: Yale University Press, 1992.

———. *Peacock Displayed: A Satirist in His Context.* London: Routledge & Kegan Paul, 1979.

———. "Romanticism in England." In *Romanticism in National Context,* ed. Ray Park and Mikulas Teich. Cambridge: Cambridge University Press, 1988.

Byrd, Max. *London Transformed: Images of the City in the Eighteenth Century.* New Haven: Yale University Press, 1978.

Campbell, Colin. *The Romantic Ethic and the Spirit of Modern Consumerism.* Oxford: Basil Blackwell, 1987.

Carr, Arthur. "John Keats's Other 'Urn.' " *University of Kansas City Review* 20 (1954): 237–242.

Carr, Steven Leo. "Illuminated Printing: Toward a Logic of Difference." In *Unnam'd Forms: Blake and Textuality,* ed. Nelson Hilton and Thomas A. Vogler, 177–196. Berkeley and Los Angeles: University of California Press, 1986.

Castle, Terry. "The Carnivalization of Eighteenth-Century English Narrative." *PMLA* 99 (1984): 903–916.

———. "Eros and Liberty at the English Masquerade, 1710–1790." *Eighteenth-Century Studies* 17 (1983–84): 156–176.

———. *Masquerade and Civilization: The Carnivalesque in Eighteenth-Century English Culture and Fiction.* Stanford: Stanford University Press, 1986.

Cavell, Stanley. "Politics as Opposed to What?" *Critical Inquiry* 9 (1982): 157–178.

Chambers, Ross. *Story and Stituation: Narrative Seduction and the Power of Fiction.* Minneapolis: University of Minnesota Press, 1984.

Chandler, James K. *Wordsworth's Second Nature: A Study of the Poetry and the Politics.* Chicago: University of Chicago Press, 1984.

Chatterjee, Bhabatosh. *John Keats: His Mind and Work.* Bombay: Orient Longman, 1971.

Chayes, Irene H. "A Coleridgean Reading of 'The Ancient Mariner.' " *Studies in Romanticism* 4 (1965): 81–103.

———. "The Presence of Cupid and Psyche." In *Blake's Visionary Forms Dramatic,* ed. David V. Erdman and John E. Grant. Princeton: Princeton University Press, 1970.

Chernaik, Judith. *The Lyrics of Shelley.* Cleveland: Case Western Reserve University Press, 1972.

Christensen, Jerome. "Byron's Career: The Speculative Stage." *ELH* 52 (1985): 59–84

———. *Coleridge's Blessed Machine of Language.* Ithaca: Cornell University Press, 1981.

———. "Perversion, Parody, and Cultural Hegomony: Lord Byron's Oriental Tales." *South Atlantic Quarterly* 88 (1989): 570–603.

———. "Setting Byron Straight: Class, Sexuality, and the Poet." In *Literature and the Body: Essays on Populations and Persons,* ed. Elaine Scarry. Baltimore: Johns Hopkins University Press, 1988.

———. "The Symbol's Errant Allegory: Coleridge and His Critics." *ELH* 45 (1978): 640–659.

———. "Theorizing Byron's Practice: The Performance of Lordship and the Poet's Career." *Studies in Romanticism* 27 (1988): 477–90.

———. " 'Thoughts That Do Often Lie Too Deep for Tears': Toward a Radical Concept of Lyrical Drama." *Wordsworth Circle* 12 (1981): 52–64.

Clark, David Lee, ed. *Shelley's Prose, or The Trumpet of a Prophecy.* Albuquerque: University of New Mexico Press, 1954.

Clark, J.C.D. *English Society 1688–1832: Ideology, Social Structure and Political Practices During the Ancient Regime.* Cambridge: Cambridge University Press, 1985.

Clark, Timothy. Embodying Revolution: The Figure of the Poet in Shelley. Oxford: Claredon Press, 1989.

Clarke, Colin. *Romantic Paradox: An Essay on the Poetry of Wordsworth.* New York: Barnes & Noble, 1962.

Cohen, Murray. *Sensible Words: Linguistic Practice in England, 1640–1785.* Baltimore: Johns Hopkins University Press, 1977.

Colley, Linda. "Whose Nation? Class and National Consciousness in Britain, 1750–1830." *Past and Present* 113 (1986): 96–117.

Colvin, Sidney. *John Keats: His Life and Poetry, His Friends, Critics and After—Fame.* New York: Scribner's, 1917. Rpt., New York: Octagon Books, 1970.

Cooke, Michael. *The Blind Man Traces the Circle: On the Patterns and Philosophy of Byron's Poetry.* Princeton: Princeton University Press, 1969.

———. *The Romantic Will.* New Haven: Yale University Press, 1976.

Cooper, Andrew M. "Blake and Madness: The World Turned Inside Out." *ELH* 57 (1990): 585–642.

———. "Chains, Pains, and Tentative Gains: The Byronic Prometheus in the Summer of 1816." *Studies in Romanticism* 27 (1988): 529–550.

———. *Doubt and Identity in Romantic Poetry.* New Haven: Yale University Press, 1988.

———. "Shipwreck and Skepticism: *Don Juan* Canto II." *Keats-Shelley Journal* 32 (1983): 63–80.

Crehan, Stuart. *Blake in Context.* Dublin: Gill & Macmillan, 1984.

Crompton, Louis. *Bryon and Greek Love: Homophobia in 19th-Century England.* Berkeley and Los Angeles: University of California Press, 1985.

Cunningham, Hugh. "The Language of Patriotism, 1750–1914." *History Workshop* 12 (1981): 8–33.

Curran, Stuart. "The Political Prometheus." *Studies in Romanticism* 25 (1986): 429–455.

———. "The I Altered." In *Romanticism and Feminism,* ed. Anne K. Mellor. Bloomington: Indiana University Press, 1988.

Curran, Stewart, and Joseph Anthony Wittreich, Jr., eds. *Blake's Sublime Allegory: Essays on The Four Zoas, Milton, and Jerusalem.* Madison: University of Wisconsin Press, 1973.

Curtius, Ernest Robert. *Essays on European Literature.* Trans. Michael Kowal. Princeton: Princeton University Press, 1973.

———. *European Literature and the Latin Middle Ages.* Trans. Willard Trask. 1953. Rpt., New York: Harper, 1963.

Cusac, Marian H. "Keats as Enchanter: An Organizing Principle of *The Eve of St. Agnes.*" *Keats-Shelley Journal* 17 (1968): 113–119.

Daley, Mary. *Beyond God the Father.* (Boston: Beacon Press, 1973.)

de Almeida, Hermione. *Romantic Medicine and John Keats.* New York: Oxford University Press, 1991.

de Man, Paul. "Intentional Structure of the Romantic Image." In *Wordsworth: A Collection of Critical Essays,* ed. M. H. Abrams. Englewood Cliffs, N.J.: Prentice-Hall, 1972.

————. "Introduction." *John Keats: Selected Poetry.* New York: New American Library, 1966.

————. "The Rhetoric of Temporality." In *Interpretation: Theory and Practice,* ed. Charles S. Singleton. Baltimore: Johns Hopkins University Press, 1969.

————. "Shelley Disfigured." In *Deconstruction and Criticism,* ed. Harold Bloom, Paul de Man, et al. New York: Continuum, 1979.

Derrida, Jacques. *Dissemination.* Trans. Barbara Johnson. Chicago: University of Chicago Press, 1981.

————. *Of Grammatology.* Trans. Gayatri Spivak. Baltimore: Johns Hopkins University Press, 1978.

————. *Speech and Phenomena: And other Essays on Husserl's Theory of Signs.* Trans. David B. Allison. Evanston: Northwestern University Press, 1973.

————. "La Loi du Genre/The Law of Genre," trans. Avital Ronell. In *Glyph Textual Studies* 7. Baltimore: Johns Hopkins University Press, 1980.

Devine, K. Rosenberg, "Keats and Two Belle Dames Sans Merci." *Etudes Anglaises* 42 (1989): 188–190.

Dickstein, Morris. "The Price of Experience: Blake's Reading of Freud." In *The Literary Freud: Mechanisms of Defense and the Poetic Will,* ed. Joseph Smith. New Haven: Yale University Press, 1980.

Dodds, E. R. *The Greeks and the Irrational.* Berkeley and Los Angeles: University of California Press, 1951.

Easson, Kay Parkhurst. "Blake and the Art of the Book." In *Blake in His Time,* ed. Robert N. Essick and Donald Pearce, 35–52. Bloomington: Indiana University Press, 1978.

Eaves, Morris. "Blake and the Artistic Machine: An Essay in Decorum and Technology." *PMLA* 92 (1977): 903–927.

————. *William Blake's Theory of Art.* Princeton: Princeton University Press, 1982.

Edmundson, Mark. "Criticism Now: The Example of Wordsworth." *Raritan* 10 (1990): 120–141.

Elledge, W. Paul. "Divorce Italian Style: Byron's *Beppo.*" *Modern Language Quarterly* 46 (1985): 29–47.

————. "Parting Shots: Byron's Ending *Don Juan I.*" *Studies in Romanticism* 27 (1988): 563–577.

Ellison, Julie. *Delicate Subjects: Romanticism, Gender, and the Ethics of Understanding.* Ithaca: Cornell University Press, 1990.

Empson, William, "The Ancient Mariner." *Critical Quarterly* 6 (1964): 298–319.

————. *The Structure of Complex Words.* 1951. Rpt., Ann Arbor: University of Michigan Press, 1967.

Engell, James. *The Creative Imagination: Enlightenment to Romanticism.* Cambridge: Harvard University Press, 1981.

Erdman, David V. *Commerce des Lumières: John Oswald and the British in Paris, 1790–1793.* Columbia: University of Missouri Press, 1986.

————. *William Blake: Prophet Against Empire: A Poet's Interpretation of the History of His Own Times.* Rev. ed. Princeton: Princeton University Press, 1969.

Essick, Robert N. "Blake and the Traditions of Reproductive Engraving." *Blake Studies* 5 (Autumn 1972): 59–103.

————. "How Blake's Body Means." In *Unnam'd Forms: Blake and Textuality,* ed.

Nelson Hilton and Thomas Vogler, 197–217. Berkeley and Los Angeles: University of California Press, 1986.

———. "Teaching the Variations in *Songs.*" In *Approaches to Teaching Blake's Songs of Innocence and Experience,* ed. Robert Gleckner and Mark L. Greenberg, 93–98. New York: Modern Language Association, 1989.

———. "Variation, Accident, and Intention in William Blake's *The Book of Urizen.*" *Studies in Bibliography* 39 (1986): 230–235.

———. *William Blake and the Language of Adam.* Oxford: Clarendon Press, 1989.

———. *William Blake: Printmaker.* Princeton: Princeton University Press, 1980.

———. "William Blake, William Hamilton, and the Materials of Graphic Meaning." *ELH* 52 (Winter 1985): 833–872.

Evert, Walter. *Aesthetic and Myth in the Poetry of Keats.* Princeton: Princeton University Press, 1965.

Fabian, Bernhard. "English Books and Their German Readers." In *The Widening Circle: Essays on the Circulation of Literature in Eighteenth-Century Europe,* ed. Paul J. Korshin. Philadelphia: University of Pennsylvania Press, 1976.

Fass, Barbara. *La Belle Dame sans Merci and the Aesthetics of Romanticism.* Detroit: Wayne State University Press, 1974.

Felman, Shoshana. "Rereading Femininity." *Yale French Studies* 62 (1981): 19–44.

Ferber, Michael. " 'London' and Its Politics." *ELH* 48 (1981): 310–338.

Ferguson, Frances. "Coleridge and the Deluded Reader: *The Rime of the Ancient Mariner.*" *Georgia Review* 31 (1977): 617–635.

———. "Shelley's 'Mont Blanc': What the Mountain Said." In *Romanticism and Language,* ed. Arden Reed. Ithaca: Cornell University Press, 1984.

———. *Wordsworth: Language as Counter-Spirit.* New Haven: Yale University Press, 1977.

Ferry, David. *The Limits of Mortality: An Essay on Wordsworth's Major Poems.* Middletown: Wesleyan University Press, 1959.

Fink, Zera. *The Classical Republicans: An Essay in the Recovery of a Pattern of Thought in Seventeenth-Century England.* 2d ed. Evanston: Northwestern University Press, 1962.

Finney, Claude. *The Evolution of Keats' Poetry.* 2 vols. New York: Russell & Russell, 1963.

Fletcher, Angus. *The Prophetic Moment: An Essay on Spenser.* Chicago: University of Chicago Press, 1971.

Foakes, R. A. *The Romantic Assertion: A Study of the Language of Nineteeth-Century Poetry.* Folcroft, Penn.: Folcroft Press, 1958.

Fogle, R. H. "A Reading of Keats's 'Eve of St. Agnes.' " *College English* 6 (1945): 325–328.

Foucault, Michel. *The History of Sexuality, An Introduction.* Vol. 1, trans. R. Hurley. New York: Pantheon, 1978.

Fox, Celina, ed. *London: World City, 1800–1840.* New Haven: Yale University Press, 1992.

Fox, Susan. "The Female as Metaphor in William Blake's Poetry." *Critical Inquiry* 5 (Spring 1977): 507—520.

Frank, Jospeh. "Spatial Form: An Answer to Critics." *Critical Inquiry* 4 (Winter 1977): 231–252.

Franklin, Caroline. " 'Quiet Cruising over the Ocean Woman': Byron's *Don Juan* and the Woman Question." *Studies in Romanticism* 29 (1990) 603–631.

Fry, Paul H. "History, Existence, and 'To Autumn.' " *Studies in Romanticism* 25 (1986): 211–219.

———. *The Poet's Calling in the English Ode.* New Haven: Yale University Press, 1980.

Frye, Northrop. *Anatomy of Criticism.* Princeton: Princeton University Press, 1957.

———. *Fables of Identity: Studies in Poetic Mythology.* New York: Harcourt, Brace, & World, 1963.

———. *Fearful Symmetry: A Study of William Blake.* Princeton: Princeton University Press, 1947.

———. "Poetry and Design in William Blake." *Blake, A Collection of Critical Essays,* ed. Northrup Frye, 119–126. Englewood Cliffs, N.J.: Prentice-Hall, 1966.

———. *Romanticism Reconsidered: Selected Papers from the English Institute.* New York: Columbia University Press, 1963.

———. *A Study of English Romanticism.* New York: Random House, 1968.

———. "Towards Defining an Age of Sensibility." *ELH* 23 (1956): 144–152.

Gallant, Christine. *Blake and the Assimilation of Chaos.* Princeton: Princeton University Press, 1978.

———. *Shelley's Ambivalence.* New York: St. Martin's, 1989.

Garber, Marjorie. *Vested Interests: Cross-Dressing and Cultural Anxiety.* London: Routledge, 1992.

Gaskill, Howard. "Ossian Macpherson: Toward a Rehabilitation." *Comparative Criticism* 8 (1986): 113–146.

Gatta, John, Jr. "Coleridge and Allegory." *Modern Language Quarterly* 38 (1977): 62–77.

Gaull, Marilyn. *English Romanticism: The Human Context.* New York: Norton, 1988.

George, Diana Hume. *Blake and Freud.* Ithaca: Cornell University Press, 1980.

Giddens, Anthony. *A Contemporary Critique of Historical Materialism.* Berkeley and Los Angeles: University of California Press, 1981.

Gilbert, Sandra M. "Costumes of the Mind: Transvestism as Metaphor in Modern Literature." In *Writing and Sexual Difference,* ed. Elizabeth Abel. Chicago: University of Chicago Press, 1982.

———, and Susan Gubar. *The Madwoman in the Attic: The Woman Writer and the Nineteenth-Century Imagination.* New Haven: Yale University Press, 1979.

Gilboy, Elizabeth. *Wages in Eighteenth-Century England.* New York: Russell & Russell, 1934.

Gill, Stephen. *William Wordsworth: A Life.* Oxford: Clarendon Press, 1989.

Girouard, Mark. *The Return to Camelot: Chivalry and the English Gentleman.* New Haven: Yale University Press, 1981.

Gittings, Robert. *John Keats.* London: Heinemann, 1968.

———. *John Keats: The Living Year, 21 September 1818 to 21 September 1819.* New York: Barnes & Noble, 1954.

———. *The Mask of Keats: A Study of Problems.* Melbourne: Heinemann, 1956.

Glazer, Myra. "Blake's Little Black Boys: On the Dynamics of Blake's Composite Art." *Colby Library Quarterly* 16 (Winter 1980): 220–236.

Glazer, Myra, and Gerda Norvig. "Blake's Book of Changes: On Viewing Three Copies of the *Songs of Innocence and Experience." Blake Studies* 9 (1980): 100–121.

Gleckner, Robert. *Byron and the Ruins of Paradise.* Baltimore: Johns Hopkins University Press, 1967.

Glen, Heather. "Blake's 'London.' " In *Vision and Disenchantment: Blake's "Songs" and Wordsworth's "Lyrical Ballads."* Cambridge: Cambridge University Press, 1983.

Gomme, A. H. "Some Wordsworthian Transparencies." *Modern Language Review* 68 (1973): 507–520.

Goslee, Nancy Moore. "Slavery and Sexual Character: Questioning the Master Trope in Blake's *Visions of the Daughters of Albion.*" *ELH* 57 (1990): 101–128.

Graff, Gerald. "Literature as Assertions." In *American Critics at Work: Examinations of Contemporary Literary Theories,* ed. Victor A. Kramer, 81–110. Troy, N.Y.: Whitstone Publishing, 1984.

———. *Poetic Statement and Critical Dogma.* Evanston: Northwestern University Press, 1970.

Graham, Peter. *Don Juan and Regency England.* Charlottesville: University Press of Virginia, 1990.

Grant, John. "Review Article: Who Shall Bind the Infinite and Arrange It in Libraries? *William Blake's Writings* and *Blake Books.*" *Philological Quarterly* 61 (Summer 1982): 277–304.

Graves, Robert. *The White Goddess: A Historic Grammer of Poetic Myth.* 3d ed. 1971. Rpt., London: Faber & Faber, 1972.

Griffin, Susan. *Women and Nature: The Roaring Inside Her.* New York: Harper & Row, 1978.

Gross, George C. " 'Lamia' and the Cupid-Psyche Myth." *Keats–Shelley Journal* 39 (1990): 151–165.

Hagstrum, Jean H. "Babylon Revisited, or the Story of Luvah and Vala." In *Blake's Sublime Allegory: Essays on the Four Zoas, Milton and Jerusalem,* ed. Stuart Curran and Joseph Anthony Wittreich, Jr. Madison: University of Wisconsin Press, 1973.

———. *The Romantic Body: Love and Sexuality in Keats, Wordsworth, and Blake.* Knoxville: University of Tennessee Press, 1985.

Haney, David P. "Viewing 'the Viewless Wings of Poesy': Gadamer, Keats, and Historicity." *Clio: A Journal of Literature, History, and the Philosophy of History* 18 (1989): 103–122.

Hartman, Geoffrey. *Beyond Formalism: Literary Essays, 1958–1970.* New Haven: Yale University Press, 1970.

———. *The Fate of Reading and Other Essays.* Chicago: University of Chicago Press, 1975.

———. "Poem and Ideology: A Study of Keats's 'To Autumn.' " In *The Fate of Reading and Other Essays.* Chicago: University of Chicago Press, 1975.

———. " 'Timely Utterance' Once More." In *Rhetoric and Form: Deconstruction at Yale,* ed. Robert Con Davis and Ronald Schilefer. Norman: University of Oklahoma Press, 1985.

———. *Wordsworth's Poetry 1787–1814.* New Haven: Yale University Press, 1964.

Hauser, Arnold. *The Social History of Art.* New York: Knopf, 1951.

Haven, Richard. " 'The Ancient Mariner' in the Nineteenth Century." *Studies in Romanticism* 11 (1972): 360–374.

———. *Patterns of Consciousness: An Essay on Coleridge.* Amherst: University of Massachusetts Press, 1967.

Heinzelman, Kurt. "The Cult of Domesticity: Dorothy and William Wordsworth at Grasmere." In *Romanticism and Feminism,* ed. Anne K. Mellor. Bloomington: Indiana University Press, 1988.

———. *The Economics of the Imagination.* Amherst: University of Massachusetts Press, 1980.

Henriques, Fernando. *Prostitution and Society.* 2 vols. London: MacGibbon & Kee, 1962–1968.

Hertz, Neil. *The End of the Line: Essays on Psychoanalysis and the Sublime.* New York: Columbia University Press, 1985.

Hilton, Nelson. *Literal Imagination: Blake's Vision of Words.* Berkeley and Los Angeles: University of California Press, 1983.

Hilton, Nelson, and Thomas A. Vogler. *Unnam'd Forms: Blake and Textuality.* Berkeley and Los Angeles: University of California Press, 1986.

Hirsch, E. D. "Byron and the Terrestrial Paradise." In *From Sensibility to Romanticism,* ed. Frederick W. Hilles and Harold Bloom. New York: Oxford University Press, 1965.

Hobsbawm, Eric, and Terence Ranger, eds. *The Invention of Tradition.* Cambridge: Cambridge University Press, 1983.

Hodgson, John A. *Coleridge, Shelley, and Transcendental Inquiry.* Lincoln: University of Nebraska Press, 1989.

———. *Wordsworth's Philosophical Poetry, 1797–1814.* Lincoln: University of Nebraska Press, 1980.

Hoeveler, Diane. *Romantic Androgyny: The Woman Within.* University Park: Pennsylvania State University Press, 1990.

Hofkosh, Sonia. "The Writer's Ravishment: Women and the Romantic Author—The Example of Byron." In *Romanticism and Feminism,* ed. Anne K. Mellor. Bloomington: University of Indiana Press, 1988.

Hogle, Jerrold E. *Shelley's Process: Radical Transference and the Development of His Major Works.* New York: Oxford University Press, 1988.

Hollander, John. "The Metrical Emblem." *Kenyon Review* 21 (1959): 279–296.

———. *Vision and Resonance: Two Senses of Poetic Form.* New York: Oxford University Press, 1975. Rpt., New Haven: Yale University Press, 1985.

Holmes, Richard. *Shelley: The Pursuit.* New York: E. P. Dutton, 1975.

Homans, Margaret. *Women Writers and Poetic Identity: Dorothy Wordsworth, Emily Brontë, and Emily Dickinson.* Princeton: Princeton University Press, 1980.

Hough, Graham. *The Romantic Poets.* London: Hutchinson University Library, 1967.

Jack, Ian. *Keats and the Mirror of Art.* Oxford: Clarendon Press, 1967.

Jacobus, Mary. "The Law of/and Gender: Genre Theory and *The Prelude.*" Diacritics (Winter 1984): 47–57.

———. *Reading Woman: Essays in Feminist Criticism.* New York: Columbia University Press, 1986.

———. *Romanticism, Writing, and Sexual Difference.* Oxford: Clarendon Press, 1989.

———. " 'Splitting the Race of Man in Twain': Prostitution, Personification, and *The Prelude.*" In *Romanticism, Writing, and Sexual Difference.* Oxford: Clarendon Press, 1989.

Jakobson, Roman. "The Metaphoric and Metonymic Poles." In *Fundamentals of Language.* The Hague: Mouton, 1956.

Jameson, Fredric. *Marxism and Form: Twentieth-Century Dialectical Theories of Literature.* Princeton: Princeton University Press, 1972.

———. *The Political Unconscious: Narrative as a Socially Symbolic Act.* Ithaca: Cornell University Press, 1981.

———. *Sartre: The Origins of a Style.* New York: Columbia University Press, 1984.

Johnston, Kenneth R. "The Politics of 'Tintern Abbey.' " *The Wordsworth Circle* 14 (1983): 6–14.

———. *Wordsworth and "The Recluse."* New Haven: Yale University Press, 1984.

———. "Wordsworth and *The Recluse:* The University of Imagination." *PMLA* 97 (1982): 60–82.

Jones, John. *John Keats's Dream of Truth.* London: Chatto & Windus, 1969.

Jones, Mark. "Interpretation in Wordsworth and the Provocation Theory of Romantic Literature." *Studies in Romanticism* 30 (1991): 565–604.

Jordan, Frank, ed. *The English Romantic Poets: A Review of Research.* New York: Modern Language Association, 1985.

Katz, Marilyn. "Early Dissent Between Wordsworth and Coleridge: Preface Deletion of October, 1800." *The Wordsworth Circle* 9 (1978): 50–56.

Keach, William. "Cockney Couplets: Keats and the Politics of Style." *Studies in Romanticism* 25 (1986): 182–224.

———. "Rhyme and the Arbitrariness of Language." In *Shelley's Style.* London: Methuen, 1984.

———. *Shelley's Style.* New York: Methuen, 1984.

Keen, Maurice. *Chivalry.* New Haven: Yale University Press, 1984.

Kelley, Theresa M. "Poetics and the Politics of Reception: Keats's 'La Belle Dame sans Merci.' " *ELH* 54 (1987): 333–362.

———. *Wordsworth's Revisionary Aesthetics.* Cambridge: Cambridge University Press, 1988.

Kernan, Alvin. *The Plot of Satire.* New Haven: Yale University Press, 1965.

Kernberger, Katherine. "Power and Sex: The Implication of Role Reversal in Catherine's Russia." *The Byron Journal* 8 (1980): 42–49.

Kissane, James. " 'Michael,' 'Christabel' and the *Lyrical Ballads* of 1800." *The Wordsworth Circle* 9 (1978): 57–63.

Klancher, Jon. *The Making of English Reading Audiences, 1790–1832.* Madison: University of Wisconsin Press, 1987.

Knapp, Steven. *Personification and the Sublime: Milton to Coleridge.* Cambridge: Harvard University Press, 1985.

Knight, G. Wilson. *The Starlit Dome: Studies in the Poetry of Vision.* 1941. Rpt., London: Oxford University Press, 1971.

Korshin, Paul J., ed. *The Widening Circle: Essays on the Circulation of Literature in Eighteenth-Century Europe.* Philadelphia: University of Pennsylvania Press, 1976.

Kramer, Lawrence. "Gender and Sexuality in *The Prelude:* The Question of Book Seven." *ELH* 54 (1987): 619–637.

Kroeber, Karl. *British Romantic Art.* Berkeley and Los Angeles: University of California Press, 1986.

———. *Romantic Landscape Vision: Constable and Wordsworth.* Madison: University of Wisconsin Press, 1975.

———. "Shelley's 'Defence of Poetry.' " In *British Romantic Art.* Berkeley and Los Angeles: University of California Press, 1986.

Lacan, Jacques. *Ecrits: A Selection.* Trans. Alan Sheridan. New York: Norton, 1977.

Land, Stephen K. "The Silent Poet: An Aspect of Wordsworth's Semantic Theory." *University of Toronto Quarterly* 42 (1973): 157–169.

Lang, Berel, and Forest Williams, eds. *Marxism and Art: Writings in Aesthetics and Criticism.* New York: McKay, 1972.

Lang, Cecil Y. "Narcissus Jilted: Byron, *Don Juan* and the Biographical Imperative." In *Historical Studies and Literary Criticism,* ed. Jerome J. McGann. Madison: University of Wisconsin Press, 1985.

Leavis, F. R. *Revaluation: Traditional Development in English Poetry.* 1936. Rpt., Harmondsworth: Penguin, 1972.

Lentricchia, Frank. *After the New Criticism.* Chicago: University of Chicago Press, 1980.

———. "Coleridge and Emerson: Prophets of Silence, Prophets of Language." *Journal of Aesthetics and Art Criticism* 32 (1973): 37–46.

————. "Patriarchy against Itself: The Young Manhood of Wallace Stevens." *Critical Inquiry* 13 (1986–87): 742–786.

Levinson, Marjorie. "Keats and the Canon." From *Keats's Life of Allegory: The Origins of a Style.* Oxford: Basil Blackwell, 1988.

————. *Keats's Life of Allegory: The Origins of a Style.* Oxford: Basil Blackwood, 1988.

————. "The New Historicism: Back to the Future." In *Rethinking Historicism: Critical Readings in Romantic Studies,* ed. Marjorie Levinson, Marilyn Butler, Jerome J. McGann, and Paul Hamilton. Oxford: Basil Blackwell, 1989.

————. *The Romantic Fragment Poem: A Critique of Form.* Chapel Hill: University of North Carolina Press, 1986.

————. *Wordsworth's Great Period Poems: Four Essays.* Cambridge: Cambridge University Press, 1986.

Lévi-Strauss, Claude. *From Honey to Ashes.* Trans. John Weightman and Doreen Weightman. New York: Harper & Row, 1973. Rpt., Chicago: University of Chicago Press, 1983.

Lindenberger, Herbert. *On Wordsworth's "Prelude."* Princeton: Princeton University Press, 1963.

Lipking, Lawrence. *The Ordering of the Arts in Eighteenth-Century England.* Princeton: Princeton University Press, 1970.

Little, Geoffrey. " 'Tintern Abbey' and Llsywen Farm." *The Wordsworth Circle* 8 (1977): 80–82.

Liu, Alan. "The Economy of Lyric: *The Ruined Cottage.*" In *Wordsworth: The Sense of History.* Stanford: Stanford University Press, 1989.

Lloyd, David. *Nationalism and Minor Literature: James Clarence Mangan and the Emergence of Irish Cultural Nationalism.* Berkeley and Los Angeles: University of California Press, 1987.

Lovejoy, A. O. *The Reason, the Understanding, and Time.* Baltimore: Johns Hopkins University Press, 1961.

Lukács, Georg. *History and Class Consciousness: Studies in Marxist Dialectics.* Trans. Rodney Livingstone. Cambridge: MIT Press, 1971.

————. *The Ontology of Social Being.* Trans. David Fernbach. London: Merlin, 1978.

McCalman, Iain. *The Radical Underworld: Prophets, Revolutionaries, and Pornographers in London, 1795–1840.* Cambridge: Cambridge University Press, 1988.

McFarland, Thomas. "The Clamour of Absence: Reading and Misreading in Wordsworthian Criticism." In *William Wordsworth: Intensity and Achievement.* Oxford: Clarendon Press, 1992.

————. *Coleridge and the Pantheist Tradition.* Oxford: Clarendon Press, 1969.

————. "Field, Constellation, and Aesthetic Object." *New Literary History* 13 (1982): 421–47.

————. "The Originality Paradox." *New Literary History* 5 (1974): 447–476.

————. "Symbiosis of Coleridge and Wordsworth." *Studies in Romanticism* 11 (1972): 263–303.

McGann, Jerome J. "The Ancient Mariner: The Meaning of Meanings." In *The Beauty of Inflections: Literary Investigations in Historical Method and Theory.* Oxford: Clarendon Press, 1985.

————. *The Beauty of Inflections: Literary Investigations in Historical Method and Theory.* Oxford: Clarendon Press, 1985.

————. "Byron, Mobility and the Poetics of Historical Ventriloquism." *Romanticism, Past and Present* 9 (1985): 66–82.

———. *A Critique of Modern Textual Criticism.* Chicago: University of Chicago Press, 1983.

———. *Don Juan in Context.* Chicago: University of Chicago Press, 1976.

———. *Fiery Dust: Byron's Poetic Development:* Chicago: University of Chicago Press, 1968.

———. "Keats and the Historical Method of Literary Criticism." *Modern Language Notes* 94 (1979): 988–1032.

———. "The Meaning of 'The Ancient Mariner.' *Critical Inquiry* 8 (1981): 35–67.

———. "My Brain Is Feminine: Byron and the Poetry of Deception." In *Byron: Augustan and Romantic,* ed. Andrew Rutherford. London: Macmillan, 1990.

———. *The Romantic Ideology: A Critical Investigation.* Chicago: University of Chicago Press, 1983.

———. "The Text, the Poem, and the Problem of Historical Method." *New Literary History* 12 (1981): 269–288.

McGowan, John. *Postmodernism and Its Critics.* Ithaca: Cornell University Press, 1991.

Macksey, Richard. " 'To Autumn' and the Music of Mortality: 'Pure Rhetoric of Language without Words.' " In *Romanticism and Language,* ed. Arden Reed. Ithaca: Cornell University Press, 1984.

McNulty, John Bard. "Wordsworth's Tour of the Wye: 1798." *Modern Language Notes* 60 (1945): 291–295.

Magnuson, Paul. *Coleridge and Wordsworth: A Lyrical Dialogue.* Princeton: Princeton University Press, 1988.

———. *Coleridge's Nightmare Poetry.* Charlottesville: University of Virginia Press, 1974.

———. " 'The Eolian Harp' in Context." *Studies in Romanticism* 24 (1985): 3–20.

———. "The Politics of 'Frost at Midnight.' " *The Wordsworth Circle* 22 (1991): 3–11.

Manley, Laurence. "Concepts of Conventions and Models of Critical Discourse." *New Literary History* 13 (1982): 31–52.

Mann, Paul. "Apocalypse and Recuperation: Blake and the Maw of Commerce." *English Language History* 52 (Spring 1985): 1–32.

Manning, Peter J. *Byron and His Fictions.* Detroit: Wayne State University Press, 1978.

———. "*Don Juan* and Byron's Imperceptiveness to the English Word." *Studies in Romanticism* 18 (1979): 207–233.

———. "The Nameless Broken Dandy and the Structure of Authorship." In *Reading Romantics.* New York: Oxford University Press, 1990.

———. *Reading Romantics: Text and Context.* New York: Oxford University Press, 1990.

Marchand, Leslie. *Byron: A Biography.* 3 vols. New York: Knopf, 1957.

Marcus, Steven. *The Other Victorians: A Study of Sexuality and Pornography in Mid-Nineteenth-Century England.* 1966. Rpt., New York: Basic Books, 1975.

Marcuse, Herbert. *The Aesthetic Dimension: Toward a Critique of Marxist Aesthetics.* Boston: Beacon Press, 1978.

Marshall, J. D. "Agrarian Wealth and Social Structure in Pre-Industrial Cumbria." *Economic History Review,* 2d series, 33 (1980): 503–521.

———. "The Domestic Economy of the Lakeland Yeoman: 1660–1749." *Transactions of the Cumberland and Westmorland Antiquarian and Archeological Society,* n.s., 75 (1975): 275–282.

———. "Kendal in the Late Seventeenth and Eighteenth Centuries." *Transactions of* the Cumberland and Westmorland Antiquarian and Archeological Society, n.s., 75 (1975): 188–257.

_____. Old *Lakeland: Some Cumbrian Social History*. Newton Abbott, U.K., 1971.

Marshall, William H. *The Structure of Byron's Major Poems*. Philadelphia: University of Pennsylvania Press, 1962.

Mayo, Robert. "The Contemporaneity of the *Lyrical Ballads*." *PMLA* 69 (1954): 486–522.

Medvedev, P. N. / M. M. Bakhtin. *The Formal Method in Literary Scholarship: A Critical Introduction to Sociological Poetics*. Trans. Albert J. Wehrle. Baltimore: Johns Hopkins University Press, 1978.

Mee, Jon. *Dangerous Enthusiasm: William Blake and the Culture of Radicalism in the 1790s*. Oxford: Clarendon Press, 1992.

Mellor, Anne K. *Blake's Human Form Divine*. Berkeley and Los Angeles: University of California Press, 1974.

_____. "Blake's Portrayal of Women." *Blake: An Illustrated Quarterly* 16 (1982–83): 148–155.

_____. *English Romantic Irony*. Cambridge: Harvard University Press, 1980.

_____, ed. *Romanticism and Feminism*. Bloomington: Indiana University Press, 1988.

_____. "Why Women Didn't Like Romanticism: The Views of Jane Austen and Mary Shelley." In *The Romantics and Us: Essays on Literature and Culture*, ed. Gene W. Ruoff. New Brunswick: Rutgers University Press, 1990.

Miller, J. Hillis. "The Fiction of Realism." In *Dickens Centennial Essays*, ed. Ada Nisbet and Blake Nevius. Berkeley and Los Angeles: University of California Press, 1971.

Mitchell, W. J. T. *Blake's Composite Art: A Study of the Illuminated Poetry*. Princeton: Princeton University Press, 1978.

_____. *Iconology: Image, Text, Ideology*. Chicago: University of Chicago Press, 1986.

Modiano, Raimonda. "Word and 'Languageless' Meaning: Limits of Expression in *The Rime of the Ancient Mariner*." *Modern Language Quarterly* 38 (1977): 40–61.

Moore, Doris Langley. *Lord Byron: Accounts Rendered*. London: John Murray, 1974.

Moorman, Mary. *William Wordsworth: A Biography*. 2 vols. Oxford: Clarendon Press, 1957–65, corrected edition.

Newlyn, Lucy. *Coleridge, Wordsworth, and the Language of Allusion*. Oxford: Clarendon Press, 1986.

O'Donnell, Brennen. "Numerous Verse: A Guide to the Stanzas and Metrical Structures of Wordsworth's Poetry." *Studies in Philology* 86, no. 4 (1989).

O'Hara, Daniel. *The Romance of Interpretation: Visionary Criticism from Pater to de Man*. New York: Columbia University Press, 1985.

Ostriker, Alicia. "Desire Gratified and Ungratified: William Blake and Sexuality." *Blake: An Illustrated Quarterly* 16 (1982): 156–165.

_____. "My William Blake." In *The Romantics and Us*, ed. Gene W. Ruoff. New Brunswick: Rutgers University Press, 1990.

Owen, Charles A. "Structure in *The Ancient Mariner*." *College English* 23 (1962): 261–267.

Pafford, Ward. "Coleridge's Wedding-Guest." *Studies in Philology* 60 (1963): 618–626.

Paley, Morton D. *Energy and the Imagination: A Study of the Development of Blake's Thought*. Oxford: Clarendon Press, 1970.

_____. "The Truchessian Gallery Revisited." *Studies in Romanticism* 16 (Spring 1977): 165–177.

Park, Ray, and Mikulas Teich, eds. *Romanticism in National Context*. Cambridge: Cambridge University Press, 1988.

Parker, Patricia. *Inescapable Romance: Studies in the Poetics of a Mode.* Princeton: Princeton University Press, 1979.

Parker, Reeve. " 'O could you hear his voice!': Wordsworth, Coleridge, and Ventriloquism." In *Romanticism and Language,* ed. Arden Reed. Ithaca: Cornell University Press, 1984.

Patterson, Charles I., Jr., *The Daemonic in the Poetry of John Keats.* Urbana: University of Illinois Press, 1970.

Peckham, Morse. *Beyond the Tragic Vision: The Quest for Identity in the Nineteenth Century.* New York: Braziller, 1962.

———. "On Romanticism: Introduction." *Studies in Romanticism* 9 (1970): 217–224.

———. "Toward a Theory of Romanticism: II. Reconsiderations." *Studies in Romanticism* 1 (1961): 1–8.

———. *The Triumph of Romanticism: Collected Essays.* Columbia: University of South Carolina Press, 1970.

Perkins, David. *The Quest for Permanence: The Symbolism of Wordsworth, Shelley, and Keats.* Cambridge: Harvard University Press, 1959.

Phillips, Michael, ed. *Interpreting Blake: Essays.* (Cambridge: Cambridge University Press, 1978.)

———. "Printing Blake's *Songs:* 1789–94." *The Library* 18 (September 1991): 205–229.

———. "William Blake's *Songs of Innocence* and *Songs of Experience* from Manuscript Draft to Illuminated Plate." *The Book Collector* (Spring 1979): 17–59.

Poovey, Mary. *The Proper Lady and the Woman Writer: Ideology as Style in the Works of Mary Wollstonecraft, Mary Shelley, and Jane Austen.* Chicago: University of Chicago Press, 1984.

Praz, Mario. *The Romantic Agony. London: Oxford University Press, 1933. Rpt., Cleveland: World Publishing, 1956.*

Pulos, C. E. *The Deep Truth: A Study of Shelley's Scepticism.* Lincoln: University of Nebraska Press, 1954.

Radner, J. B. "The Youthful Harlot's Curse: The Prostitute as Symbol of the City in 18th-Century English Literature." *Eighteenth Century Life* 2 (1976): 59–64.

Rajan, Tilottama. "The Broken Mirror: The Identity of the Text in Shelley's *Triumph of Life.*" In *The Supplement of Reading: Figures of Understanding in Romantic Theory and Practice.* Ithaca: Cornell University Press, 1990.

———. *Dark Interpreter: The Discourse of Romanticism.* Ithaca: Cornell University Press, 1980.

———. *The Supplement of Reading: Figures of Understanding in Romantic Theory and Practice.* Ithaca: Cornell University Press, 1990.

Reed, Arden. "The Mariner Rimed." In *Romanticism and Language,* ed. Arden Reed. Ithaca: Cornell University Press, 1984.

———, ed. *Romanticism and Language.* Ithaca: Cornell University Press, 1984.

Reed, Mark. *Wordsworth: The Chronology of the Early Years, 1770–1799.* Cambridge: Harvard University Press, 1967.

———. *Wordsworth: The Chronology of the Middle Years, 1800–1815.* Cambridge: Harvard University Press, 1975.

Reiman, Donald H. "The Beauty of Buttermere as Fact and Romantic Symbol." *Criticism* 26 (1984): 139–170.

———. "Shelley as Athanase." In *Shelley and His Circle,* vol. 7, ed. Donald H. Reiman. Cambridge: Harvard University Press, 1986.

Renza, Louis. *"A White Heron" and the Question of Minor Literature.* Madison: University of Wisconsin Press, 1984.

Richards, I. A. *Practical Criticism: A Study of Literary Judgment.* London: Routledge & Kegan Paul, 1929.

Ricks, Christopher. *Keats and Embarrassment.* Oxford: Clarendon Press, 1974.

Ridenour, George. *The Style of Don Juan.* New Haven: Yale University Press, 1960.

Ridley, Maurice R. *Keat's Craftsmanship: A Study in Poetic Development.* Oxford: Clarenden Press, 1933.

Robinson, Jeffrey. *Radical Literary Education: A Classroom Experiment with Wordsworth's "Ode."* Madison: University of Wisconsin Press, 1987.

Roe, Nicholas. *Wordsworth and Coleridge: The Radical Years.* Oxford: Clarendon Press, 1988.

Rogers, Katherine M. *Feminism in Eighteenth-Century England.* Urbana: University of Illinois Press, 1982.

Ross, Marlon B. *The Contours of Masculine Desire: Romanticism and the Rise of Women's Poetry.* New York: Oxford University Press, 1989.

————. "Romantic Quest and Conquest: Troping Masculine Power in the Crisis of Poetic Identity." In *Romanticism and Feminism,* ed. Anne K. Mellor. Bloomington: Indiana University Press, 1988.

Rudé, George. *Hanoverian London.* London: Secker & Warburg, 1973.

Ruoff, Gene W., ed. *Jane Austen and English Romanticism.* Special issue of *The Wordsworth Circle* 7, no. 4 (Autumn 1976).

————. "Romantic Lyric and the Problem of Belief." In *The Romantics and Us: Essays on Literature and Culture,* ed. Gene W. Ruoff. New Brunswick: Rutgers University Press, 1990.

————, ed. *The Romantics and Us.* New Brunswick: Rutgers University Press, 1990.

————. *Wordsworth and Coleridge: The Making of the Major Lyrics, 1802–1804.* New Brunswick: Rutgers University Press, 1989.

————. "Wordsworth on Language: Toward a Radical Poetics for English Romanticism." *The Wordsworth Circle* 3 (1972): 204–211.

Rutherford, Andrew. *Byron: A Critical Study.* Stanford: Stanford University Press, 1961.

————, ed. *Byron: The Critical Heritage.* New York: Barnes & Noble, 1970.

Rzepka, Charles. *The Self as Mind: Vision and Identity in Wordsworth, Coleridge, and Keats.* Cambridge: Harvard University Press, 1986.

St. Clair, William. "The Impact of Byron's Writing: An Evaluative Approach." In *Byron: Augustan and Romantic,* ed. Andrew Rutherford. London: Macmillan, 1990.

Sartre, Jean-Paul. *Search for a Method.* Trans. Hazel Barnes. New York: Knopf, 1968.

Schenk, H. G. *The Mind of the European Romantics: An Essay in Cultural History.* London: Constable, 1966.

Scheuerle, William H. "A Reexamination of Coleridge's 'The Eolian Harp.' " *SEL* 15 (1975): 591–599.

Schulz, Max F. "Coleridge, Wordsworth, and the 1800 Preface to *Lyrical Ballads. Studies in English Literature* 5 (1965): 619–639.

————. *The Poetic Voices of Coleridge: A Study of His Desire for Spontaneity and Passion for Order.* Detroit: Wayne State University Press, 1963.

Sedgwick, Eve Kosofsky. *Between Men: English Literature and Male Homosocial Desire.* New York: Columbia University Press, 1985.

————. "The Character in the Veil: Image and Surface in the Gothic Novel." *PMLA* 96 (1981): 255–270.

Sennett, Richard. *The Fall of the Public Man.* New York, Knopf, 1976.

Shilstone, Frederick W. *Byron and the Myth of Tradition.* Lincoln: University of Nebraska Press, 1988.

Shoaf, R. A. *Dante, Chaucer, and the Currency of the Word: Money, Images, and Reference in Late Medieval Poetry.* Norman: Pilgrim Books, 1983.

Showalter, Elaine. "Critical Cross-Dressing: Male Feminists and the Woman of the Year." *Raritan* 3, no. 2 (Fall 1983): 130–149.

Simon, Herbert A. *The Sciences of the Artificial.* Cambridge: M.I.T. Press, 1969.

Simpson, David. *Fetishism and Imagination: Dickens, Melville, Conrad.* Baltimore: John Hopkins University Press, 1982.

————. "Figuring Class, Sex, and Gender: What Is the Subject of Wordsworth's 'Gipsies' "? *South Atlantic Quarterly* 88 (Summer 1989): 451–567.

————. *Irony and Authority in Romantic Poetry.* Totowa, N.J.: Rowan & Littlefield, 1979.

————. " 'Simon Lee': The Poet as Patron.' " In *Wordsworth's Historical Imagination: The Poetry of Displacement.* New York: Methuen, 1987.

————, ed. *Subject to History: Ideology, Class, Gender.* Ithaca: Cornell University Press, 1991.

————. *Wordsworth and the Figurings of the Real.* Atlantic Highlands, N.J.: Humanities Press, 1982.

————. *Wordsworth's Historical Imagination: The Poetry of Displacement.* London: Methuen, 1987.

Singer, June. *The Unholy Bible: A Psychological Interpretation of William Blake.* New York: Putnam, 1970.

Siskin, Clifford H. *The Historicity of Romantic Discourse.* New York: Oxford University Press, 1988.

Smith, Gayle S. "A Reappraisal of the Moral Stanzas in *The Rime of the Ancient Mariner.*" *Studies in Romanticism* 3 (1963): 42–52.

Smith, Olivia. *The Politics of Language: 1791–1819.* Oxford: Clarendon Press, 1984.

Smith, Stan. "Some Responses to Heather Glen's 'The Poet in Society.' " *Literature and History* 4 (Autumn 1976): 94–98.

Spacks, Patricia Meyer. *Gossip.* Chicago: University of Chicago Press, 1986.

Spanos, W. V. *Repetitions: The Postmodern Occasion in Literature and Culture.* Baton Rouge: Louisiana State University Press, 1987.

Sperry, Stuart M., Jr. *Keats the Poet.* Princeton: Princeton University Press, 1973.

————. "Romance as Wish-Fulfillment: *The Eve of St. Agnes.*" In *Keats the Poet.* Princeton: Princeton University Press, 1973.

Spitzer, Leo. *Classical and Christian Ideas of World Harmony: Prolegomena to an Interpretation of the Word "Stimmung."* Baltimore: Johns Hopkins University Press, 1963.

Spivak, Gayatri. *In Other Worlds: Essays in Cultural Politics.* New York: Methuen, 1987.

————. "Sex and History in *The Prelude* (1805): Books Nine to Thirteen." *Texas Studies in Literature and Language* 23 (1981): 324–360.

Stedman, Jane W. "From Dame to Woman: W. S. Gilbert and Theatrical Transvestism." In *Suffer and Be Still: Women in the Victorian Age,"* ed. Martha Vicinus. Bloomington: Indiana University Press, 1972.

Steffan, Truman Guy. "The Devil a Bit of Our *Beppo.*" *Philological Quarterly* 32 (1953): 154–171.

————. *The Making of a Masterpiece: Byron's "Don Juan."* Vol. 1 of *Byron's "Don Juan": A Variorum Editon,* 4 vols., 2d ed. Austin: University of Texas Press, 1982.

Stevenson, Lionel. " 'The Ancient Mariner' as Dramatic Monologue." *The Personalist* 30 (1949): 39–69.

Stillinger, Jack. "The Hoodwinking of Madeline: Scepticism in 'The Eve of St. Agnes.' " *Studies in Philology* 58 (1961): 533–555. Rptd. in *The Hoodwinking of Madeline and Other Essays on Keats's Poems.* Urbana: University of Illinois Press, 1971.

———. *The Hoodwinking of Madeline and Other Essays on Keats's Poems.* Urbana: University of Illinois Press, 1971.

———. "The Multiple of Versions of Coleridge's Poems: How Many *Mariners* Did Coleridge Write?" *Studies in Romanticism* 31 (1992): 127–146.

———. "The Text of 'The Eve of St. Agnes.' " *Studies in Bibliography* 16(1963): 207–212.

———. *The Texts of Keats's Poems.* Cambridge: Harvard University Press, 1974.

———. "Textual Primitivism and the Editing of Wordsworth." *Studies in Romanticism* 28 (1989): 3–28.

Swann, Karen. "*Christabel:* The Wandering Mother and the Enigma of Form." *Studies in Romanticism* 23 (1984): 533–553.

———. "Harassing the Muse." In *Romanticism and Feminism,* ed. Anne K. Mellor. Bloomington: Indiana University Press, 1988.

———. "Literary Gentlemen and Lovely Ladies: The Debate on the Character of *Christabel.*" *ELH* 52 (1985): 397–418.

Swingle, L. J. "Frankenstein's Monster and Its Romantic Relatives: Problems of Knowledge in English Romanticism." *TSLL* 15 (1973): 51–65.

———. *The Obstinate Questionings of English Romanticism.* Baton Rouge: Louisiana State University Press, 1987.

———. "On Reading Romantic Poetry." *PMLA* 86 (1971): 974–981.

———. "The Romantic Emergence: Multiplication of Alternatives and the Problem of Systematic Entrapment. *Modern Language Quarterly* 39 (1978): 264–283.

Teskey, Gordon. "From Allegory to Dialectic: Imagining Error in Spenser and Milton." *PMLA* 101 (1986): 9–23.

Thompson, E. P. "Disenchantment or Default?" In *Power and Consciousness,* ed. Conor Cruise O'Brien and William Dean Vanech. London: University of London Press, 1969.

———. "London." In *Interpreting Blake: Essays,* ed. Michael Phillips. Cambridge: Cambridge University Press, 1978.

———. *The Making of the English Working Class.* London: Victor Gollancz, 1965. Rpt., Harmondsworth: Penguin Books, 1968.

Timpanaro, Sebastian. *On Materialism.* London: NLB, 1975.

Todd, F. M. *Politics and the Poet: A Study of Wordsworth.* London: Methuen, 1957.

Trilling, Lionel. "The Fate of Pleasure." In *Beyond Culture: Essays on Literature and Learning.* New York: Viking Press, 1965.

———. *The Opposing Self.* New York: Viking Press, 1955.

———. "The Poet as Hero: Keats in His Letters." In *The Opposing Self: Nine Essays in Criticism.* London: Secker & Warburg, 1955.

Turbayne, Colin. *The Myth of Metaphor.* Columbia: University of South Carolina Press, 1970.

Tyson, Gerald P. *Joseph Johnson: A Liberal Publisher.* Iowa City: University of Iowa Press, 1979.

Van Dyke, Carolynn. *The Fiction of Truth: Structures of Meaning in Narrative and Dramatic Allegory.* Ithaca: Cornell University Press, 1985.

Van Ghent, Dorothy. *Keats: The Myth of the Hero.* Ed. Jeffrey C. Robinson. Princeton: Princeton University Press, 1983.

Vassallo, Peter. *Byron: The Italian Literary Influence.* New York: St Martin's, 1984.

Vendler, Helen. "Lionel Trilling and the Immortality Ode." *Salamagundi* 41 (Spring 1978): 66–86.

――――. *The Odes of John Keats.* Cambridge: Harvard University Press, 1983

Viscomi, Joseph. *Blake and the Idea of the Book.* Princeton: Princeton University Press, 1993.

――――. "Recreating Blake: The M.E.W. Blake Facsimiles." *Blake/An Illustrated Quarterly* 19 (Summer 1985): 4–23.

――――. "William Blake, Illuminated Books, and the Concept of Difference."

Vitale, Marina. "The Domesticated Heroine in Byron's *Corsair* and William Hone's Prose Adaptation." *Literature and History* 10 (1984): 72–94.

Vivian, Charles H. "The One 'Mont Blanc.' " *Keats-Shelley Journal* 4 (1955): 55–65.

Vološinov, V. N. *Freudianism: A Marxist Critique.* Trans. I. R. Titunik. Bloomington: Indiana University Press, 1987.

――――. *Marxism and the Philosophy of Language.* Trans. M. Matejka and I. R. Titunik. New York: Seminar Press, 1973.

Ward, Aileen. *John Keats: The Making of a Poet.* New York: Viking, 1963.

Ware, Malcolm. "*The Rime of the Ancient Mariner:* A Discourse on Prayer?" *Review of English Studies* 11 (1960): 303–304.

Warren, Robert Penn. "A Poem of Pure Imagination: An Experiment in Reading." *Kenyon Review* 8 (1946): 391–427.

Wasserman, Earl R. *The Finer Tone: Keats's Major Poems.* Baltimore: Johns Hopkins University Press, 1953.

――――. *Shelley: A Critical Reading.* Baltimore: Johns Hopkins University Press, 1971.

――――. *The Subtler Language: Critical Readings of Neoclassic and Romantic Poems.* Baltimore: Johns Hopkins University Press, 1959.

Watkins, Evan. *The Critical Act: Criticism and Community.* New Haven: Yale University Press, 1978.

Weeks, Jeffrey. *Sex, Politics, and Society: The Regulation of Sexuality since 1800.* London: Longman, 1981.

Weiskel, Thomas. *The Romantic Sublime: Studies in the Structure and Psychology of Transcendence.* Baltimore: Johns Hopkins University Press, 1976.

Wellek, René. "The Concept of Romanticism in Literary History." *Comparative Literature* 1 (1949): 1–23.

――――. *A History of Modern Criticism: 1750–1950.* Vol. 3. New Haven: Yale University Press, 1955.

Wellek, René, and Austin Warren. *Theory of Literature.* New York: Harcourt, Brace & World, 1949.

Whalley, George. "The Mariner and the Albatross." *University of Toronto Quarterly* 16 (1947): 381–398.

Wheeler, Katherine. *The Creative Mind in Coleridge's Poetry.* Cambridge: Harvard University Press, 1981.

Willey, Basil. *Nineteenth-Century Studies.* New York: Columbia University Press, 1949.

Williams, Raymond. *The Country and the City.* New York: Oxford University Press, 1973.

Wilson, Douglas B. "Two Modes of Apprehending Nature: A Gloss on the Coleridgean Symbol." *PMLA* 87 (1972): 42–52.

Wilson, Milton. *Shelley's Later Poetry: A Study of His Prophetic Imagination.* New York: Columbia University Press, 1957.

Wimsatt, W. K. *The Verbal Icon: Studies in the Meaning of Poetry.* Lexington: University of Kentucky Press, 1954.

Wittreich, Joseph. A., Jr. "Milton's 'Destin'd Urn': The Art of *Lycidas.*" *PMLA* 84 (1968): 60–70.

Woodman, Ross. *The Apocalyptic Vision in the Poetry of Shelley.* Toronto: University of Toronto Press, 1964.

Woodring, Carl. R. *Politics in the Poetry of Coleridge.* Madison: University of Wisconsin Press, 1961.

———. "The New Sublimity in 'Tintern Abbey.' " In *The Evidence of the Imagination: Studies of Interactions Between Life and Art in English Romantic Literature,* ed. Donald H. Reiman, Michael Jaye, and Betty Bennett. New York: New York University Press, 1978.

Wolfson, Susan J. "Individual in Community: Dorothy Wordsworth in Conversation with William." In *Romanticism and Feminism,* ed. Anne K. Mellor. Bloomington: Indiana University Press, 1988.

———. "The Language of Interpretation in Romantic Poetry: A Strong Working of the Mind." In *Romanticism and Language,* ed. Arden Reed. Ithaca: Cornell University Press, 1984.

———. " 'Their She Condition': Cross-Dressing and the Politics of Gender in *Don Juan.*" *ELH* 54 (1987): 585–617.

Wordsworth, Jonathan. *The Music of Humanity: A Critical Study of Wordsworth's "Ruined Cottage" Incorporating Texts from a Manuscript of 1799–1800.* New York: Harper & Row, 1969.

Wright, Herbert G. "Has Keats's 'Eve of St. Agnes' a Tragic Ending?" *Modern Language Review* 40 (1945): 90–94.

Young, Robert. "The Eye and Progress of His Song: A Lacanian Reading of *The Prelude.*" *Oxford Literary Review* 3 (1979): 78–98.

Index

Notes on Contributors

JONATHAN ARAC is a professor of Literature at the University of Pittsburgh. He is the author of *Commissioned Spirits: The Shaping of Social Motion in Dickens, Carlyle, Melville, and Hawthorne* (Rutgers University Press, 1979) and *Critical Genealogies: Historical Situations for Postmodern Literary Studies* (Columbia University Press, 1987). In addition, he has edited or coedited *The Yale Critics: Deconstruction in America* (University of Minnesota, 1983), *Postmodernism and Politics* (University of Minnesota Press, 1986), *After Foucault: Humanistic Knowledge, Postmodern Challenges* (Rutgers University Press, 1988), and *Macropolitics of Nineteenth-century Literature: Nationalism, Exoticism, Imperialism* (University of Pennsylvania Press, 1991). He is currently at work on a study entitled " 'Huckleberry Finn' and the Functions of Criticism."

MARILYN BUTLER is the King Edward VII Professor of English Literature and a fellow of King's College, Cambridge University. She is the author of *Maria Edgeworth: A Literary Biography* (Oxford University Press, 1972), *Jane Austen and the War of Ideas* (Oxford University Press, 1975), *Peacock Displayed* (Routledge, 1979), and *Romantics, Rebels and Reactionaries* (Oxford University Press, 1981). Her many edited volumes include novels by Maria Edgeworth and Mary Shelley, an edition of the works of Mary Wollstonecraft, and *Burke, Paine, Godwin and the Revolution Controversy* (Cambridge University Press, 1984).

JEROME CHRISTENSEN, professor of English at Johns Hopkins University, is the author of *Coleridge's Blessed Machine of Language* (Cornell University Press, 1981), *The Practice of Enlightenment: Hume and the Formation of a Literary Career* (University of Wisconsin Press, 1987), and *Lord Byron's Strength: Romantic Writing and Commercial Society* (Johns Hopkins University Press, 1992). He is currently at work on a collection of essays, "The Romantic Movement: Theory and Practice," which will be published in 1994 by Basil Blackwell.

ANDREW M. COOPER is an associate professor of English at the University of Texas at Austin. He is the author of *Doubt and Identity in Romantic Poetry* (Yale University Press, 1988) and, most recently, essays on Keats and Virgil and on George Herbet and Francis Bacon. He is currently writing a book on Blake.

STUART CURRAN is the Andrea Mitchell Professor of English at the University of Pennsylvania. He is the author of *Shelley's "Cenci": Scorpions Ringed with Fire* (Princeton University Press, 1970), *Shelley's Annus Mirabilis: The Maturing of an Epic Vision* (Huntington Library, 1975), and *Poetic Form and English Romanticism* (Oxford University Press, 1986, 1989). His edited or coedited works are *Blake's Sublime Allegory* (University of Wisconsin Press, 1973), *Cambridge Companion to British Romanticism* (1992), and *The Poems of Charlotte Smith* (Oxford University Press, 1992).

FRANCES FERGUSON is a professor of English at Johns Hopkins University. She is the author of *Wordsworth: Language as Counter-Spirit* (Yale University Press, 1977) and

Solitude and the Sublime: Romanticism and the Aesthetics of Individuation (Routledge, 1992), as well as numerous articles on romanticism, modern poetry, and aesthetics. She is coeditor of *Misogyny, Misandry, and Misanthropy* (University of California Press, 1989).

PAUL H. FRY is a professor of English at Yale University. He is the author of *The Poet's Calling in the English Ode* (Yale University Press, 1980), *The Reach of Criticism: Method and Perception in Literary Theory* (Yale University Press, 1984), and *William Empson: Prophet Against Sacrifice* (1991). He is now completing a book on the pre-cognitive occasion of literary expression, tentatively to be called "The Hum of Literature."

HEATHER GLEN is Director of Studies in English at New Hall, Cambridge University, and a university lecturer in English. She is the author of *Vision and Disenchantment* (Cambridge University Press, 1983), from which her contribution to this book is taken. She has edited critical editions of Emily Brontë's *Wuthering Heights* (Routledge, 1988) and Charlotte Brontë's *The Professor* (Penguin, 1989). She is currently working on a critical study of the novels of Charlotte Brontë.

GEOFFREY H. HARTMAN is the Karl Young Professor of English and Comparative Literature at Yale University. One of our most prolific and ranging literary critics, he is still known best among romanticists for *Wordsworth's Poetry, 1787–1814* (Yale University Press, 1964). Important gatherings of his essays include *Beyond Formalism: Literary Essays, 1958–1970* (Yale University Press, 1970), *The Fate of Reading and Other Essays* (University of Chicago Press, 1975), *Criticism in the Wilderness: The Study of Literature Today* (Yale University Press, 1980), *Easy Pieces* (Columbia University Press, 1985), and *Minor Prophecies: The Literary Essay in the Culture Wars* (Harvard University Press, 1991).

MARY JACOBUS is the John Wendell Anderson Professor of English at Cornell University. She is the author of *Tradition and Experiment in Wordsworth's Lyrical Ballads, 1798* (Oxford University Press, 1976), *Reading Woman: Essays in Feminist Criticism* (Columbia University Press, 1986), and *Romanticism, Writing, and Sexual Difference: Essays on The Prelude* (Oxford University Press, 1989). She edited *Women Writing and Writing Women* (Croom Helm, 1979) and coedited *Body/Politics: Women and the Discourses of Science* (Routledge, 1989). She is currently completing a collection of essays on feminism, literature, and psychoanalysis, entitled "The Mother at the Source," for Routledge.

KENNETH R. JOHNSTON, a professor of English at Indiana University, is best known as the author of *Wordsworth and "The Recluse"* (Yale University Press, 1984). He has edited or coedited several books, including *The Age of William Wordsworth: Critical Essays on the Romantic Tradition* (Rutgers University Press, 1987) and *Romantic Revolutions: Theory and Criticism* (Indiana University Press, 1990). He has two book-length studies forthcoming: *Young Wordsworth: Creation of the Poet* (Harper-Collins) and *Wordsworth's Poetry and Prose* (Indiana University Press).

WILLIAM KEACH is a professor of English at Brown University. He is the author of *Elizabethan Erotic Narratives* (1977) and *Shelley's Style* (Methuen, 1984). His recent work includes contributions to the forthcoming *Cambridge Companion to British Romanticism* and to the eighteen-century volume in the *Cambridge History of Literary Criticism*. He is currently writing a book on the politics of language in British Romantic writing and working on an edition of Coleridge's poems for the Penguin English Poets series.

THERESA M. KELLEY, an associate professor of English at the University of Texas at Austin, is the author of *Wordsworth's Revisionary Aesthetics* (Cambridge University Press, 1988), as well as articles on Wordsworth, Keats, Blake, J.M.W. Turner, Enlightenment aesthetics and Kantian philosophy, the sister arts tradition, Robert Browning, and the allegorical tradition. She is currently at work on a book entitled "Reinventing Allegory." a study of allegorical fictions and figures that have survived since the Renaissance, to be published by Cambridge University Press.

KARL KROEBER is the Mellon Professor of the Humanities at Columbia University. Among his books are *Romantic Narrative Art* (University of Wisconsin Press, 1960), *The Artifice of Reality* (University of Wisconsin Press, 1964), *Styles in Fictional Structure* (Princeton University Press, 1971), *Romantic Landscape Vision: Constable and Wordsworth* (University of Wisconsin Press, 1975), *British Romantic Art* (University of California Press, 1986), *Romantic Fantasy and Science Fiction* (Yale University Press, 1988), and *Retelling/Rereading: The Fate of Storytelling in Modern Times* (Rutgers University Press, 1992).

MARJORIE LEVINSON, a professor of English at the University of Pennsylvania and a visiting professor at the University of Michigan, is the author of *The Romantic Fragment Poem: A Critique of a Form* (University of North Carolina Press, 1986), *Wordsworth's Great Period Poems: Four Essays* (Cambridge University Press, 1986), and *Keats's Life of Allegory: The Origins of a Style* (Basil Blackwell, 1990). She is also the editor of an influential collection of new-historicist essays, *Rethinking Romanticism: Critical Readings in Romantic History* (Basil Blackwell, 1990).

ALAN LIU is an associate professor of English at the University of California at Santa Barbara. Best known for his monumental study, *Wordsworth: The Sense of History* (Stanford University Press, 1989), Liu has continued in recent articles in *Representations, ELH,* and the *Yale Journal of Criticism* to explore the powers and pitfalls of cultural criticism and the new historicism. He is currently at work on two large projects, a collection of essays on cultural criticism entitled "Local Transcendence: Cultural Criticism and Postmodernism," and a book on the theory and practice of the new historicism entitled "Flat Literary History: Literary History and Postmodernism."

THOMAS MCFARLAND is Murray Professor of English Literature, emeritus, at Princeton University. In addition to work in Shakespeare, he is the author of *Coleridge and the Pantheist Tradition* (Clarendon Press, 1969), *Romanticism and the Forms of Ruin: Wordsworth, Coleridge, and Modalities of Fragmentation* (Princeton University Press, 1981), *Originality and Imagination* (Johns Hopkins University Press, 1985), *Shapes of Culture* (University of Iowa Press, 1987), *Romantic Cruxes: The English Essayists and the Spirit of the Age* (Clarendon Press, 1987), and *William Wordsworth: Intensity and Achievement* (Clarendon Press, 1992). He is currently at work on an edition of *The Opus Maximum of Samuel Taylor Coleridge,* to appear in Princeton University Press's Bollingen Foundation series.

JEROME MCGANN is the John Stewart Bryan Professor of English at the University of Virginia. Much of his work over the past decade has been as editor of *Lord Byron: The Complete Poetical Works* (1980–), the seventh and final volume of which was published by Oxford University Press in 1993. That same year saw the publication of his *Black Riders: The Visible Language of Modernism* (Princeton University Press) and his edition of *The New Oxford Book of Romantic Period Verse*. He is also the author of *Fiery Dust: Byron's Poetic Development* (University of Chicago Press, 1968), *Don Juan in Context* (University of Chicago Press, 1976), *A Critique of Modern Textual Criticism* (University of Chicago Press, 1983), *The Romantic Ideology* (University of Chicago Press, 1983), *The Beauty of Inflections* (Clarendon Press, 1985), *Social Values and Poetic Acts: A Historical Judgment of Literary Work* (Harvard University Press, 1988), and *The Textual Condition* (Princeton University Press, 1991). Among his current projects is "The Complete Writings and Pictures of Dante Gabriel Rossetti: A Hypermedia Research Archive."

PAUL MAGNUSON is a professor of English at New York University. He is the author of *Coleridge's Nightmare Poetry* (University of Virginia Press, 1974) and *Coleridge and Wordsworth: A Lyrical Dialogue* (Princeton University Press, 1988). He is coeditor with Raimonda Modiano of the forthcoming (and long-awaited) Norton Critical Coleridge. His essay in this volume forms part of a projected book, one of a series of pieces on the social dimensions of "private" poems drawn from his recent talks in the United States and England.

PETER J. MANNING is a professor of English at the University of Southern California. He is the author of *Byron and His Fictions* (Wayne State University Press, 1978), *Reading Romantics: Text and Context* (Oxford University Press, 1990), and numerous essays on the romantics. His current project is a book-length study of the later Wordsworth.

RAIMONDA MODIANO is a professor of English at the University of Washington. She is the author of *Coleridge and the Concept of Nature* (Macmillan, 1985) as well as several articles on various aspects of romanticism. She is co-editor of volumes 2 through 5 of Coleridge's *Marginalia* (Princeton University Press, 1984–) and working on two more editions: the Norton Critical Coleridge with Paul Magnuson and "Coleridge on Nature," under contract to Macmillan. Her book-in-progress is provisionally entitled "Contracts of the Heart: Gift Exchange and Sacrifice in Wordsworth and Coleridge."

ALICIA OSTRIKER, professor of English at Rutgers University, is the author of seven volumes of poetry, the most recent of which are *The Imaginary Lover* (University of Pittsburgh Press, 1986), which won the William Carlos Williams Award of the Poetry Society of America, and *Green Age* (University of Pittsburgh Press, 1989). As a critic she is the author of *Vision and Verse in William Blake* (University of Wisconsin Press, 1965) and editor of Blake's *Complete Poems* (Penguin, 1977). She has written two books on American women's poetry, *Writing Like a Woman* (University of Michigan Press, 1983) and *Stealing the Language: The Emergence of Women's Poetry in America* (Beacon Press, 1986). A forthcoming book of critical essays, "Unwritten Volume: Feminism and the Bible," will be published by Blackwell's, and her current work in progress, "The Nakedness of the Fathers: Biblical Visions and Revisions," is a set of experimental commentaries on the Bible.

TILOTTAMA RAJAN is a professor in the Department of English and the Center for Theory and Criticism at the University of Western Ontario. She is the author of *Dark Interpreter: The Discourse of Romanticism* (Cornell University Press, 1980), and *The Supplement of Reading: Figures of Understanding in Romantic Theory and Practice*

(Cornell University Press, 1990). She is also coeditor of *Intersections: Nineteenth-Century Philosophy and Contemporary Theory* (SUNY Press, 1993). Her current projects are a book entitled "Deconstruction Before and After Post-Structuralism" and a study of romantic narrative exploring the relationship between narrative and "difference" in both poetry and prose.

DONALD H. REIMAN, an adjunct Professor of English at the University of Delaware, is editor of the distinguished series *Shelley and His Circle,* published by Harvard University Press and sponsored by the Carl and Lily Pforzheimer Foundation. Reiman is also editor-in-chief of *The Bodleian Shelley Manuscripts* and *The Manuscripts of the Younger Romantics.* Among his recent books are *Romantic Texts and Contexts* (University of Missouri Press, 1987) and *The Harvard Shelley Poetic Manuscripts* (Garland Publishing, 1991). Forthcoming from Johns Hopkins University Press is *The Study of Modern Manuscripts, Public, Confidential, and Private,* containing the James P. R. Lyell Lectures that he delivered in 1989. With Neil Fraistat, Reiman is coeditor of the projected four-volume *Complete Poetry of Percy Bysshe Shelley,* also to be published by Johns Hopkins University Press.

GENE W. RUOFF is a professor of English and director of the Institute for the Humanities at the University of Illinois at Chicago. He is the author of *Wordsworth and Coleridge: The Making of the Major Lyrics, 1802–1804* (Rutgers University Press, 1989) and *Jane Austen's Sense and Sensibility* (Harvester Wheatsheaf, 1992). In addition, he coedited *The Age of William Wordsworth: Critical Essays on the Romantic Tradition* (Rutgers University Press, 1987) and edited *The Romantics and Us: Essays on Literature and Culture* (Rutgers University Press, 1990). His current project is a book-length study provisionally titled "Romantic Inheritance: Blood, Land, and Culture from Edmund Burke to Emily Brontë."

DAVID SIMPSON is a professor of English at the University of Colorado at Boulder. He is the author of *Irony and Authority in Romantic Poetry* (Rowman and Littlefield, 1979), *Fetishism and Imagination: Dickens, Melville, Conrad* (Johns Hopkins University Press, 1982), *Wordsworth and the Figurings of the Real* (Humanities Press, 1982), *The Politics of American English* (Oxford University Press, 1986), and *Wordsworth's Historical Imagination: The Poetry of Displacement* (Methuen, 1987). In addition he has edited such works as *The Origins of Modern Critical Thought: German Aesthetic and Literary Criticism from Lessing to Hegel* (Oxford University Press, 1988) and *Subject to History: Ideology, Class, Gender* (Cornell University Press, 1991). His most recent work is *Romanticism, Nationalism, and the Revolt against Theory,* forthcoming in 1993 from University of Chicago Press.

STUART M. SPERRY is a professor of English at Indiana University. He is the author of *Keats the Poet* (Princeton University Press, 1973) and *Shelley's Major Verse: The Narrative and Dramatic Poetry* (Harvard University Press, 1988), and essays on Wordsworth, Byron, and romantic irony.

KAREN SWANN, associate professor of English at Williams College, has published numerous articles on Burke, Coleridge, Wordsworth, and Keats. She is currently completing a book titled "Public Transports: Romantic Experiments in Sensationalism," a study of the major romantic poets' relations to the public and popular genres, and beginning a project called "Lives of the Dead Poets," a study of the famously dead English poets of the late eighteenth and early nineteenth centuries.

L. J. SWINGLE is a professor of English at the University of Kentucky. He is the author of *The Obstinate Questionings of English Romanticism* (Louisiana State University Press, 1987) and *Romanticism and Anthony Trollope: A Study in the Continuities of Nineteenth-century Literary Thought* (University of Michigan Press, 1990). He is currently at work on a book-length study entitled "Crusoe's Children."

JOSEPH VISCOMI is an associate professor of English at the University of North Carolina at Chapel Hill. He is the author of *Blake and the Idea of the Book* (Princeton University Press, 1993), from which his contribution to this volume is derived. He has curated numerous exhibitions, including *Prints by William Blake and His Followers,* Herbert F. Johnson Museum of Art (1983), for which he wrote the catalogue. Viscomi also wrote *The Art of William Blake's Illuminated Prints* (Manchester Etching Workshop, 1983) to accompany an edition of facsimiles of *Songs of Innocence and Experience.* He is the coeditor of volumes 3 and 5 of *William Blake's Illuminated Books,* forthcoming from Princeton University Press and Tate Gallery Publications.

SUSAN J. WOLFSON is a professor of English at Princeton University. She is the author of *The Questioning Presence: Wordsworth, Keats, and the Interrogative Mode in Romantic Poetry* (Cornell University Press, 1986), as well as numerous articles on various aspects of English romanticism. She is completing "Formal Changes," a book on the problematic of poetic formalism in English romanticism, and at work on two other studies bearing on questions of gender in romanticism, "Figures on the Margin" and "Figures in Conversation."